BARRON'S
THE TRUSTED NAME IN TEST PREP

ASVAB
Study Guide
Premium

DISCARD

Terry L. Duran, LTC (Ret)

Armed Services Vocational Aptitude Battery (ASVAB) is a test of the U.S. Department of Defense, which neither sponsors nor endorses this product.

© Copyright 2022, 2018, 2015, 2012, 2009, 2006 by Kaplan, Inc., d/b/a Barron's Educational Series

Previous editions © Copyright 2003, 2000, 1997, 1992, 1989, 1986, 1984 under the
title *How to Prepare for the ASVAB Armed Services Vocational Aptitude Battery*
by Kaplan, Inc., d/b/a Barron's Educational Series

Published by Kaplan, Inc., d/b/a Barron's Educational Series
1515 W Cypress Creek Road
Fort Lauderdale, FL 33309
www.barronseduc.com

ISBN: 978-1-5062-8364-7

10 9 8 7 6 5 4 3 2 1

Kaplan, Inc., d/b/a Barron's Educational Series print books are available at special quantity
discounts to use for sales promotions, employee premiums, or educational purposes. For
more information or to purchase books, please call the Simon & Schuster special sales
department at 866-506-1949.

Contents

Dedication

*This book is dedicated to the glory of God
and in honor of my wonderful, loving, supportive family—
my angelic, beautiful, brilliant, talented, wise, witty, and wonderful wife, June;
our awesome children and their spouses; and our delightful grandchildren—
without whom I am nothing,*

and

in memory of fallen brothers:

Cadet Woodrow K. "Woody" Ratliff '82

Specialist Guy W. Walker, U.S. Army

Staff Sergeant Shawn A. Graham, Texas Army National Guard

Colonel Thomas H. Felts, Sr., U.S. Army

Lieutenant Colonel Todd J. Clark '94, U.S. Army

and

*Senior Master Sergeant (Retired) Travis C. Duran, U.S. Air Force
Thanks, Dad*

*Softly call the Muster,
Let comrade answer, "Here!"
Their spirits hover 'round us
As if to bring us cheer.*

*Mark them "present" in our hearts.
We'll meet some other day
There is no death, but life etern
For old friends such as they!*

—from *Roll Call for the Absent*, Dr. John Ashton '06

All About the ASVAB and AFQT

1

HOW TO USE THIS BOOK

Congratulations! You've made a great choice in buying this test preparation book. It has been designed and refined over many years to help you do your best on the Armed Services Vocational Aptitude Battery, or ASVAB, but make no mistake, this book contains the latest updates and information available.

To get the most benefit from this book, follow this approach:

- Read the first two chapters, "All About the ASVAB and AFQT" and "How to Achieve Your Best ASVAB and AFQT Scores."
- Take the Diagnostic Test in Chapter 3. Remember to follow all the instructions, including the time limits. After you finish, check your answers and record your score on the Progress Chart on page 28 in Chapter 2.
- Use the Study Guide on page 29 in Chapter 2 to plan your time. Concentrate your efforts on the areas where you did not do well, but don't neglect reviewing the other areas. Remember, your goal is the highest score possible in each section so that you will qualify for the widest possible number of specialties.

"If we chase perfection we can catch excellence."

—Vince Lombardi

- Reread the section in Chapter 2 on test-taking techniques. Then take Practice Exam One. Remember to pay attention to the time limits for each subtest. Check your answers, review the answer explanations, and fill in the Progress Chart on page 28. Go back over the review sections for any subtest where you scored less than Excellent.
- Take Practice Exam Two. Once more, keep yourself to the time limits for each subtest. Check your answers, review the answer explanations, and fill in the Progress Chart on page 28. Review any subjects where you scored less than Good.
- Take the AFQT Focus Exam. The AFQT is the most important part of the ASVAB, so this is a second look at your top-priority subtests. If you are still not doing well, consider getting someone to help you with your most challenging areas. At a minimum, go back to those areas in the review chapters and go slowly through the relevant information. Make sure you understand every bit of it—think of wringing every drop out of a wet cloth.
- Go to the online tests and, still keeping yourself to the time limits, take the first test. Chart your score on the Progress Chart on page 29. Do you see any trends developing? Go back over the review sections for any subtest where you scored less than Excellent.

"Genius is one percent inspiration and ninety-nine percent perspiration."

—Thomas Edison

- If you have not scored Excellent on every subtest by now, take the other two online practice tests. Don't skimp on areas where you have done well. If you know the material, repetition will make the pattern of knowledge stronger. If you don't know a subject as well as you thought you did, the additional practice will both identify your weaknesses and help you correct them.

- Look at the subtests or composite scores that affect the specialties in the military branch you are interested in. If you are not yet scoring in the Excellent category for those subtests as well, the online tests will give you valuable practice.
- If you have scored either Good or Excellent in every category on the Progress Chart, it is probably time to take the actual test—your championship game. Good luck!

EXTRA WAYS THIS BOOK WILL HELP YOU STUDY

From time to time throughout this book, except for on the practice tests themselves, you will see boxed material to help you focus on key points. Sometimes the information will appear in the middle of the text, such as an explanation of the makeup of living cells. At other times, the information will be found in smaller boxes in the margins. These smaller boxes in the margins contain information that emphasizes specific points or encourages you. In these smaller marginal boxes, you will see the following symbols:

This icon indicates something you need to keep under your helmet—i.e., something you need to remember.

This icon indicates information to give you extra insight or more in-depth understanding of the topic at hand.

This icon indicates information to keep you on target with your studies.

If you want jokes and cartoons—or information about historical scores, sample norms from 1997, and last year's cutoff score for a certain specialty—sorry, you'll have to look elsewhere. This book will help you understand what applies to you and some context regarding the ASVAB and the AFQT, a whole lot about the subtest areas in the ASVAB, and a little bit about the U.S. military. The focus of this book is about helping you do your best on the test, period. Your local recruiter will have the most up-to-date information on what scores you need for what specialty and which ones are available right now based on the needs of that service. The rest of the fluff—well, you won't find it here.

WHAT IS THE ASVAB?

The ASVAB is the most widely used multiple-aptitude test battery in the world. Its purpose is to determine whether you qualify for military service, and if so, for which specific military specialties and programs. It is also used to help high school students identify job-related interests and aptitudes. The ASVAB consists of either 9 or 10 subtests (depending on whether you are taking the computerized or paper-and-pencil version) that measure your ability in specific job-related areas.

ASVAB Background

When the United States decided to enter World War I in April 1917, the military had to expand rapidly. The Army developed the Alpha and Beta Tests to classify volunteers and draftees for appropriate military service. The Alpha Test measured knowledge, verbal and mathematical skills, and the ability to follow directions using 212 multiple-choice and true/false questions. The Beta Test used illustrations for illiterate and non-English-speaking recruits.

By the beginning of World War II, the Army and Navy had both developed their own General Classification Test versions. As military equipment and operations became more complex, the services developed more specialized tests. After the war ended, both branches also developed separate aptitude tests.

By 1950, all the services used the 100-question Armed Forces Qualification Test to determine who was qualified to join. However, the different branches still had their own specialized tests to classify and assign recruits into appropriate jobs. By 1976, all five services started using the first version of the ASVAB to screen potential service members and classify recruits for appropriate assignments.

Since then, the ASVAB has undergone four major revisions. The current version has either 9 or 10 sections, depending on whether the test is taken on a computer or with pencil and paper. The paper version has 9 sections because Automotive and Shop Information is all one subtest. In contrast, the computerized version has 10 sections because it contains separate Automotive and Shop Information subtests. However, the scores are consolidated so that examinees taking both versions are evaluated in the same way.

Today's ASVAB and AFQT

The current version of the ASVAB has subtests for Word Knowledge, Paragraph Comprehension, Mathematics Knowledge, Arithmetic Reasoning, General Science, Electronics Information, Automotive and Shop Information, Mechanical Comprehension, and Assembling Objects. Your scores on the first four subtests are used to calculate your **Armed Forces Qualification Test (AFQT)** score. Your AFQT score determines whether you are qualified to join the military. The other, more specialized subtests are used by the services (Army, Navy, Air Force, Marines, and Coast Guard) to determine the jobs for which you are eligible.

The Department of Defense (DoD) provides a customized version of the ASVAB to high schools, called the ASVAB Career Exploration Program (CEP), to encourage students to learn more about themselves and their interests while exploring potential career options.

ASVAB VERSIONS AND COMPOSITION

There are four versions of today's ASVAB, two computer-administered and two paper-based. Results from all of them can be used for military recruiting purposes.

The paper-based ASVAB is given by Armed Forces recruiters to those who wish to join a military service. It is usually given at a Military Entrance Processing Station (MEPS). However, the ASVAB can be given at a Military Entrance Test (MET) site instead, depending on the candidate's particular location and schedule. MEPS sites administer the computer-administered ASVAB, while MET sites give the paper-and-pencil version. Education centers on active and reserve military installations also administer the paper-based ASVAB to current service members who want to raise their scores to qualify for advancement or particular specialties.

Subtest	CAT-ASVAB		Paper and Pencil		Emphasis
	# Questions	# Minutes	# Questions	# Minutes	
General Science (GS)	16	8	25	11	Knowledge of physical and biological sciences
Arithmetic Reasoning (AR)	16	39	30	36	Ability to solve arithmetic word problems
Word Knowledge (WK)	16	8	35	11	Ability to select correct meaning of words in context and identify best synonyms
Paragraph Comprehension (PC)	11	22	15	13	Ability to interpret and obtain information from written passages
Mathematics Knowledge (MK)	16	18	25	24	Knowledge of high school level mathematics principles
Electronics Information (EI)	16	8	20	9	Knowledge of electricity and electronics
Automotive Information	11	6	N/A	N/A	Knowledge of automobiles
Shop Information	11	5	N/A	N/A	Knowledge of tools and shop terminology and practices
Automotive and Shop Information (AS)	N/A	N/A	25	11	Knowledge of automobiles and of tools and shop terminology and practices
Mechanical Comprehension (MC)	20	19	25	19	Knowledge of mechanical and physical principles and ability to visualize how illustrated objects work
Assembling Objects (AO)	9	16	16	9	How an object will look when its parts are mentally assembled or connected

The computer-administered version of the test is called the **CAT-ASVAB**. On the paper version, all examinees answer the same set of questions. The CAT-ASVAB is adaptive, meaning that it tailors questions to the ability of the test-taker. For example, the first CAT-ASVAB question in a particular subtest is in the middle range of difficulty. It you get it right, the next question is harder. If you did not answer the first question correctly, the next one is easier. The subtest continues in this way until your proficiency in that area is determined. This means you spend more time answering questions that are appropriate to your ability level—which means there are fewer questions overall and less time needed for each subtest.

The advantages of the CAT-ASVAB are that you can finish it in less time, it can be scored immediately, and you don't need to wait to start the next subtest. However, you can't skip around or go back to change an answer, and you can't go back and review your answers at the end of the test. The average CAT-ASVAB test-taker finishes in about an hour and a half.

Unlike the paper ASVAB, CAT-ASVAB subtest raw scores are not equal to the total number of correct answers. CAT-ASVAB subtest scores are computed using formulas that take into account the difficulty of the test item. However, CAT-ASVAB scores are also adjusted to put them on the same basis as paper-and-pencil ASVAB raw scores to be able to report scores from both tests on an equivalent basis.

The Automotive Information and Shop Information tests are two separate tests on the CAT-ASVAB (they're combined on the paper tests). However, your scores for these two tests will be combined when your results are published.

Pre-Screening, Internet-Delivered Computer Adaptive Test (PiCAT)

The Pre-screening, Internet-delivered Computer Adaptive Test (PiCAT) is an unproctored version (i.e., nobody's watching you) of the full ASVAB that lets recruiters determine if an applicant is qualified before sending him or her to a MEPS or MET site.

Recruiters assign prospective enlistees a web address and a unique access code, then applicants have 72 hours to start the test on their own computers. Once an applicant starts the test, he or she has 24 hours to complete it. When the applicant is finished, the recruiter can see the applicant's score immediately.

The PiCAT helps both the applicant and the recruiter. The applicant gains familiarity with the ASVAB, and recruiters can determine whether or not the applicant is likely to achieve a qualifying score on the AFQT segment of the official test. This saves everyone time and saves the recruiters, MEPS, and MET sites money.

Just like the official test at a MEPS or MET site, test-takers are not allowed to use external references (such as books, the Internet, or other people) while they are taking the test. Applicants who are satisfied with their PiCAT score can then take a short verification test at a MEPS or MET site, and (presuming their verification test score is close to their PiCAT score) they get their official ASVAB score of record.

Applicants who don't do well enough on the verification test—plus applicants who want to try to do better than their PiCAT scores—are routed into a full-length, proctored ASVAB at a MEPS or MET site.

Neither the ASVAB nor the PiCAT tests by themselves obligate the test-taker to actually join the military. If an applicant did not do well enough on either test, he or she may take it again after 30 days, and yet again after another 30 days. However, if the applicant wants to retake it a third time, he or she must wait six months.

It's important to remember that the PiCAT is an adaptive test, just like the CAT-ASVAB. You only get to see one question at a time, you can't skip around, and the program chooses how hard your next question will be based on how well you've done up to that point.

The ASVAB Career Exploration Program for High School Students

The ASVAB Career Exploration Program (CEP) is a career exploration and planning program for 10th through 12th graders designed to connect students with potentially satisfying occupations, whether they plan on finding immediate civilian or military employment after high school or pursuing further education.

The CEP—offered at more than 14,000 U.S. high schools and post-secondary schools nationwide—is a paper-based version of the ASVAB that does not include the Assembling Objects subtest, but does include an interest inventory and various career planning tools to help students explore the world of work.

ASVAB SCORING, FORMAT, AND THE AFQT

ASVAB questions and subtests are statistically linked across the different forms and administration modes through a process called "equating," which gives ASVAB scores the same meaning, regardless of which form or administration mode the examinee used.

Some people find they score higher on the CAT-ASVAB than they do on the paper-and-pencil ASVAB. This is probably because the basic nature of the CAT-ASVAB saves them time and effort by offering them questions tailored to their demonstrated ability level. *On the paper-and-pencil versions, unanswered items are counted as incorrect*—so it's to your advantage to try to answer all the questions you can.

On the paper ASVAB, unanswered questions are counted as wrong.

On your overall ASVAB score calculation (not the individual subtest scores, known as "line scores"), the Mathematics Knowledge (MK) and Arithmetic Reasoning (AR) questions on the ASVAB are weighted, with harder questions worth more than easier questions. However, the ASVAB is not an IQ or intelligence test. It was designed specifically to measure an individual's aptitude (probability of success) to be trained for a range of particular jobs.

If you want to enlist in the military, you must achieve a minimum AFQT score—and then you may have to score at a certain level on particular subtests to qualify for certain specialties. The AFQT score is calculated from your scores on the Word Knowledge (WK), Paragraph Comprehension (PC), Arithmetic Reasoning (AR), and Mathematics Knowledge (MK) subtests using the formula AR + MK + (2 × VE). The VE (verbal) score is determined by adding the raw scores (how many questions answered correctly) from the PC and WK tests and then using a table to get the VE score from that combined PC and WK raw score.

AFQT scores are reported as percentiles ranging from 1 to 99. An AFQT percentile score reflects the percentage of examinees in a reference group that scored at or below that particular score. The current reference group is a sample of 12,000 18- to 23-year-olds who took the ASVAB as part of a 1997 national study.

Therefore, an AFQT score of 90 indicates that the examinee scored as well as or better than 90 percent of the national sample. An AFQT score of 50 indicates that the examinee scored as well as or better than 50 percent of the sample.

The AFQT score is often referred to as the "overall" ASVAB score, even though it is based on only four subtests. This is not entirely incorrect, since your AFQT score is the most important score, and determines whether you can get into the military at all. It can also influence what rank and pay grade you start with.

Your AFQT score determines whether or not you can join the military.

The U.S. military divides AFQT scores into five categories—the lower the number of your category, the higher your chance of getting into the military and getting a job you want.

AFQT Category	Percentile Score Range
I	93–99
II	65–92
IIIA	50–64
IIIB	31–49
IVA	21–30
IVB	16–20
IVC	10–15
V	1–9

Almost all new service members are in AFQT Categories I through III, and more than 90 percent have a high school diploma—slightly higher than the national average. Since the early

1990s, new Category IV accessions are limited to no more than 20 percent of enlistees, and all of those recruits have to have a high school diploma (a General Equivalency Diploma, or GED, isn't enough). And no Category V enlistees are allowed at all.

The individual services have tougher standards than the law, and you will need a higher AFQT score to have the same opportunities if you have a GED versus a high school diploma. The services adjust these standards some from time to time based on their needs, but they don't change that much. The military is a respected profession, but it's also an increasingly technical profession—long gone are the days where all you had to have was a pulse and a willing attitude to join the military. Usually, a GED holder who also has at least 15 college semester hours is considered the same as a high school graduate.

AFQT Minimum Standards by Branch of Service

Service Branch	High School Diploma	GED
Army/Army Reserve/Army National Guard	31	50
Navy/Navy Reserve	35	50
Air Force/Air Force Reserve/Air National Guard	36	65
Marine Corps/Marine Corps Reserve	32	50
Coast Guard/Coast Guard Reserve	40	50

The Army currently requires a minimum AFQT of 31 to enlist for high school diploma holders, and 50 for GED recruits. AFQT scores over 50 may qualify the individual for enlistment bonuses—these come and go, so be sure to ask your recruiter.

Navy recruits need a 35 AFQT score to qualify for active duty, but Navy Reserve billets may be available for those who score at least a 31. GED holders, besides needing a 50 on their AFQT, also need at least three references from prominent community members and no drug or illegal activities in their records.

The Air Force is in some respects the most competitive service branch when it comes to AFQT scores: more than 90 percent of Air Force recruits have an AFQT of 50 or more, and only about 0.5% of all Air Force recruits have a GED—and GED holders must score a 65 on the AFQT to qualify. However, in either case, if you have at least 15 semester hours of college, you may be able to start at a higher rank.

The Marine Corps AFQT standard is a minimum of 32 for high school graduates, but like the other services, requires at least a 50 for those with only a GED. Less than five percent of Marine recruits get in without a high school diploma regardless of score, and those who do must have a GED.

The Coast Guard has the highest AFQT standards for high school graduates. However, there may be possibilities for a waiver if a recruit's score on other subtests—such as Electronics or Mechanical Comprehension—qualify them for a specific job.

ASVAB results for non-prior service recruits are valid for two years. After taking an initial ASVAB (an ASVAB test taken in school doesn't count as an "initial test"), you can retake the ASVAB after 30 days. After the second re-test, you must wait at least six months before you can take the test again. The military services use the latest ASVAB scores, not the highest, for service and job qualifications.

If you've taken the ASVAB in high school, those scores (if they aren't over two years old) should be acceptable for enlistment. If you'd like a chance to increase your scores, you may want the recruiter to arrange for you to take the version of the ASVAB given to people who didn't take the high school version.

The ASVAB is offered at many high schools across the country; if your high school isn't one of them, ask your guidance counselor for alternatives. If you are already out of high school, call a local military recruiter.

The information collected when someone takes the ASVAB is used by the DoD for recruiting and research purposes. Scores and personal information obtained during the test are also released to the United States armed forces, the United States Coast Guard, and your local school.

OTHER SUBTEST SCORES AND WHY THEY'RE IMPORTANT

Various combinations of subtest scores are used to determine whether you qualify for particular specialties. For example, to qualify for a cyber or communications specialty, you might have to have sufficiently high scores on the Arithmetic Reasoning, Mathematics Knowledge, Electronics Information, and General Science subtests.

As previously stated, the AFQT score is the most important ASVAB score because it determines if you can enlist in the military at all. However, the different services also convert your ASVAB subtest scores into composite score areas called *line scores* that determine what specialty you qualify for.

The Army and Coast Guard also use some of the ASVAB subtest scores as part of their prerequisites for Officer Candidate School. Both services use the "general technical" (GT) score, which is derived from ASVAB scores on the Word Knowledge, Paragraph Comprehension, and Arithmetic Reasoning subtests. The Army and Marines require a 110 GT score for their Officer Candidate School (OCS), while the Coast Guard requires a 109 GT score. Applicants for the Marine Corps' Officer Candidate Class (OCC) or Platoon Leaders Course (PLC) must earn a minimum GT score of 115 to qualify.

Even though the Automotive and Shop sections are treated as two different subtests on the computerized ASVAB, they are combined to provide the Automotive and Shop Information (AS) line score for specialty qualification purposes. To help you better understand the next few sections, here are the subtests in alphabetical order and the abbreviations used to link them to their respective line scores.

Arithmetic Reasoning	AR
Assembling Objects	AO
Automotive and Shop Information	AS
Electronics Information	EI
General Science	GS
Mathematics Knowledge	MK
Mechanical Comprehension	MC
Paragraph Comprehension	PC
Word Knowledge	WK

Minimum scores for a particular specialty or category may change over time based on that service's needs. However, by paying attention to the subtests that affect not only the AFQT but also the specialty or specialties you are interested in, you can target those knowledge areas for extra attention. Remember, though, that first and foremost you need to concentrate on doing well on the Word Knowledge (WK), Paragraph Comprehension (PC), Arithmetic Reasoning (AR), and Mathematics Knowledge (MK) sections so that your AFQT will be as high as possible.

ACADEMIC COMPOSITES

Composite	Potential ✔	Subtest Composition	Purpose
VERBAL	——— ———	(Word Knowledge + Paragraph Comprehension)* + General Science	Measures capacity for verbal activities
MATH	———	Mathematics Knowledge + Arithmetic Reasoning	Measures capacity for mathematical activities
ACADEMIC ABILITY	——— ———	(Word Knowledge + Paragraph Comprehension)* + Arithmetic Reasoning	Measures potential for further formal education

*Subtests in parentheses are weighted as one unit.

MILITARY SPECIALTIES BY SERVICE

Army

The Army uses the ASVAB individual subtest scores (often called *line scores*) to determine 10 *composite scores*.

- **CLERICAL (CL)**—Determined from Verbal Expression (VE), Arithmetic Reasoning (AR), and Mathematics Knowledge (MK).
- **COMBAT (CO)**—Determined from Verbal Expression (VE), Automotive and Shop Information (AS), and Mechanical Comprehension (MC).
- **ELECTRONICS (EL)**—Determined from General Science (GS), Arithmetic Reasoning (AR), Mathematics Knowledge (MK), and Electronics Information (EI).
- **FIELD ARTILLERY (FA)**—Determined from Arithmetic Reasoning (AR), Mathematics Knowledge (MK), and Mechanical Comprehension (MC).
- **GENERAL MAINTENANCE (GM)**—Determined from General Science (GS), Automotive and Shop Information (AS), Mathematics Knowledge (MK), and Electronics Information (EI).
- **GENERAL TECHNICAL (GT)**—Determined from Verbal Expression (VE) and Arithmetic Reasoning (AR).
- **MECHANICAL MAINTENANCE (MM)**—Determined from Automotive and Shop Information (AS), Mechanical Comprehension (MC), and Electronics Information (EI).
- **OPERATORS AND FOOD (OF)**—Determined from Verbal Expression (VE), Automotive and Shop Information (AS), and Mechanical Comprehension (MC).
- **SURVEILLANCE AND COMMUNICATIONS (SC)**—Determined from Verbal Expression (VE), Arithmetic Reasoning (AR), Automotive and Shop Information (AS), and Mechanical Comprehension (MC).
- **SKILLED TECHNICAL (ST)**—Determined from General Science (GS), Verbal Expression (VE), Mechanical Comprehension (MC), and Mathematics Knowledge (MK).

The Army groups its Military Occupational Specialty (MOS) codes into Career Management Fields (CMFs). Each CMF encompasses a varying number of MOSs. Some MOSs are not entry level and are open only to those above a certain grade.

Although the Army—like all the other branches of service—adjusts what scores are needed for each specialty based on the Army's needs at a particular time, the table below shows which composite scores determine eligibility for which entry-level positions by CMF.

Army Entry-Level Occupational Fields

Career Management Field (CMF)	MOS Title	MOS Designator	Relevant Composite Score(s)
Infantry (11)	Infantryman	11B	CO
	Indirect Fire Infantryman	11C	CO
Engineer (12)	Combat Engineer	12B	CO
	Bridge Crewmember	12C	CO
	Diver	12D	ST, GM, GT
	Quarrying Specialist	12G	GM
	Plumber	12K	GM
	Firefighter	12M	GM
	Horizontal Construction Engineer	12N	GM
	Prime Power Specialist	12P	ST, EL, GT
	Power Distribution Specialist	12Q	EL
	Interior Electrician	12R	EL
	Technical Engineer	12T	ST
	Concrete and Asphalt Equipment Operator	12V	GM
	Carpentry and Masonry Specialist	12W	GM
	Geospatial Engineer	12Y	ST, GT
Field Artillery (13)	Cannon Crewmember	13B	FA
	Field Artillery Automated Tactical Data Systems Specialist	13D	FA
	Fire Support Specialist	13F	FA
	Multiple Launch Rocket System Crewmember	13M	OF
	Multiple Launch Rocket System Operations/Fire Direction Specialist	13P	FA
	Field Artillery Firefinder Radar Operator	13R	SC
	Field Artillery Surveyor/Meteorological Crewmember	13T	EL
Air Defense Artillery (14)	Patriot Fire Control Enhanced Operator/Maintainer	14E	MM
	Air Defense Battle Management System Operator	14G	GT, MM
	Air Defense Early Warning System Operator	14H	GT, MM

Career Management Field (CMF)	MOS Title	MOS Designator	Relevant Composite Score(s)
Air Defense Artillery (14) (continued)	Air and Missile Defense Crewmember	14S	OF
	Patriot Launching Station Enhanced Operator/Maintainer	14T	OF
Aviation (15)	Aircraft Powerplant Repairer	15B	MM
	Aircraft Powertrain Repairer	15D	MM
	Unmanned Aircraft Systems Repairer	15E	EL, MM
	Aircraft Electrician	15F	MM
	Aircraft Structural Repairer	15G	MM
	Aircraft Pneudraulics Repairer	15H	MM
	OH-58D/ARH* Armament/Electrical/ Avionics Systems Repairer	15J	EL, MM
	Utility Helicopter Repairer (Reserve Component only)	15M	MM
	Avionic Mechanic	15N	EL
	Aviation Operations Specialist	15P	ST
	Air Traffic Control Operator	15Q	ST
	AH-64 Attack Helicopter Repairer	15R	MM
	OH-58D Helicopter Repairer	15S	MM
	UH-60 Helicopter Repairer	15T	MM
	CH-47 Helicopter Repairer	15U	MM
	Unmanned Aircraft Systems Operator	15W	SC
	AH-64D Armament/Electrical/Avionic Systems Repairer	15Y	EL, MM
Cyber (17)	Cyber Operations Specialist	17C	GT, ST
Special Forces (18)	Special Forces Enlistment Option**	18X	GT, CO, SC
Armor/Cavalry (19)	Cavalry Scout	19D	CO
	M1 Armor Crewman	19K	CO
Signal (25)	Information Technology Specialist	25B	ST
	Radio Operator/Maintainer	25C	SC, EL
	Cyber Network Defender	25D	GT, ST
	Network Switching Systems Operator/ Maintainer	25F	SC, EL
	Cable Systems Installer/Maintainer	25L	SC, EL
	Multimedia Illustrator	25M	EL, ST
	Microwave Systems Operator/Maintainer	25P	EL
	Multichannel Transmission Systems Operator/Maintainer	25Q	EL, SC
	Visual Information Equipment Operator/ Maintainer	25R	EL
	Satellite Communication Systems Operator/Maintainer	25S	EL
	Signal Support Systems Specialist	25U	SC, EL
	Combat Documentation/Production Specialist	25V	EL, ST

Career Management Field (CMF)	MOS Title	MOS Designator	Relevant Composite Score(s)
Paralegal (27)	Paralegal Specialist	27D	CL
Electronic Warfare (29)	Electronic Warfare Specialist	29E	SC, ST, EL
Military Police (31)	Military Police	31B	ST
	Criminal Investigations Special Agent	31D	GT, ST
	Internment/Resettlement Specialist	31E	ST
Military Intelligence (35)	Intelligence Analyst	35F	ST
	Geospatial Intelligence Imagery Analyst	35G	ST
	Human Intelligence Collector	35M	ST
	Signals Intelligence Analyst	35N	ST
	Cryptologic Linguist	35P	ST
	Cryptologic Cyberspace Intelligence Collector/Analyst	35Q	ST
	Signals Collector/Analyst	35S	ST
	Military Intelligence Systems Maintainer/Integrator	35T	ST
Financial Management (36)	Financial Management Technician	36B	CL
Psychological Operations (37)	Psychological Operations Specialist	37F	GT
Civil Affairs (38)	Civil Affairs Specialist	38B	GT
Human Resources (42)	Human Resources Specialist	42A	GT, CL
	Band Member	42R	N/A
	Special Band Musician	42S	N/A
Public Affairs (46)	Public Affairs Specialist	46Q	GT
	Public Affairs Broadcast Specialist	46R	GT
Chaplain Assistant (56)	Chaplain Assistant	56M	CL
Health Services (68)	Biomedical Equipment Specialist	68A	EL
	Orthopedic Specialist	68B	ST, GT
	Operating Room Specialist	68D	ST
	Dental Specialist	68E	ST
	Patient Administration Specialist	68G	CL
	Optical Laboratory Specialist	68H	GM
	Medical Logistics Specialist	68J	CL
	Medical Laboratory Specialist	68K	ST
	Nutrition Care Specialist	68M	OF
	Cardiovascular Specialist	68N	ST, GT
	Radiology Specialist	68P	ST
	Pharmacy Specialist	68Q	ST
	Veterinary Food Inspection Specialist	68R	ST
	Preventive Medicine Specialist	68S	ST
	Animal Care Specialist	68T	ST

Career Management Field (CMF)	MOS Title	MOS Designator	Relevant Composite Score(s)
Health Services (68) (continued)	Respiratory Specialist	68V	ST
	Healthcare Specialist	68W	ST, GT
	Mental Health Specialist	68X	ST
Chemical, Biological, Radiological, and Nuclear (74)	Chemical, Biological, Radiological, and Nuclear Operations Specialist	74D	ST
Transportation (88)	Cargo Specialist	88H	GM
	Watercraft Operator	88K	MM
	Watercraft Engineer	88L	MM
	Motor Transport Operator	88M	OF
	Transportation Management Coordinator	88N	CL
	Railway Equipment Repairer (Reserve Component only)	88P	MM
	Railway Section Repairer (Reserve Component only)	88T	MM
	Railway Operations Crewmember (Reserve Component only)	88U	MM
Ammunition (89)	Ammunition Stock Control and Accounting Specialist	89A	ST
	Ammunition Specialist	89B	ST
	Explosive Ordnance Disposal (EOD) Specialist	89D	ST
Mechanical Maintenance (91)	M1 Abrams Tank System Maintainer	91A	MM, GT
	Wheeled Vehicle Mechanic	91B	MM, GT
	Utilities Equipment Repairer	91C	GM, GT
	Power Generation Equipment Repairer	91D	GM, GT
	Allied Trade Specialist	91E	GM, GT
	Small Arms/Artillery Repairer	91F	GM, GT
	Fire Control Repairer	91G	EL, GT
	Track Vehicle Repairer	91H	MM, GT
	Quartermaster and Chemical Equipment Repairer	91J	MM, GT
	Construction Equipment Repairer	91L	MM, GT
	Bradley Fighting Vehicle System Maintainer	91M	MM, GT
	Artillery Mechanic	91P	MM, GT
	Stryker Systems Maintainer	91S	MM, GT
Supply and Services (92)	Petroleum Supply Specialist	92F	CL, OF
	Food Service Specialist	92G	OF
	Petroleum Laboratory Specialist	92L	ST
	Mortuary Affairs Specialist	92M	GM

Career Management Field (CMF)	MOS Title	MOS Designator	Relevant Composite Score(s)
Supply and Services (92) (continued)	Parachute Rigger	92R	GM, CO
	Shower/Laundry and Clothing Repair Specialist	92S	GM
	Water Treatment Specialist	92W	GM
	Unit Supply Specialist	92Y	CL
Electronic Maintenance (94)	Land Combat Electronic Missile System Repairer	94A	EL
	Air Traffic Control Equipment Repairer	94D	EL
	Radio and Communications Security Repairer	94E	EL
	Computer/Detection Systems Repairer	94F	EL
	Test Measurement and Diagnostic Equipment Maintenance Support Specialist	94H	EL
	Radar Repairer	94M	EL
	Multiple Launch Rocket System Repairer	94P	EL
	Avionic and Survivability Equipment Repairer	94R	EL
	Patriot System Repairer	94S	EL
	Avenger System Repairer	94T	EL
	Integrated Family of Test Equipment Operator and Maintainer	94Y	EL

*ARH = Armed Reconnaissance Helicopter

**Guarantees only the *opportunity to qualify* through training

Navy

ASVAB SCORE. Navy recruits who do not have prior military service must score at least 35 on the AFQT. A higher score may be required based on local recruiting goals and requirements. Nonprior service (NPS) applicants with AFQT scores less than 50 must have a traditional high school diploma and at least 15 college semester hours.

Applicants with prior Navy service can use their previous ASVAB entry scores regardless of AFQT, provided they are either enlisting in a Navy job equivalent to what they had before or meet line score requirements for the rating they want. Prior service applicants who don't have qualifying line scores must take the ASVAB again. Veterans from the other services with military skills directly convertible to a Navy rating may enlist in that rating, regardless of previous AFQT or line scores.

The Navy uses the term *rating* to describe its individual specialties, which are grouped in Navy Ratings Communities. (Don't confuse *rating* with *rate*. The Navy and Coast Guard use the term *rate* for what the other services call the *rank* of their enlisted personnel.) For instance, Navy Aviation Community ratings include air traffic controller (AC), aviation machinist's mate (AD), aviation electrician's mate (AE), aviation aerographer's mate (AG), aviation ordnanceman (AO), and aviation electronics technician (AT). Some lower-level ratings converge at higher grade levels.

The Navy uses formulas for each rating based on ASVAB line scores. Those scores can change over time based on the needs of the Navy. Since the line scores involved don't change very often, though, the table below shows you how the Navy uses your ASVAB line scores to determine your eligibility. The code VE indicates the sum of the WK and PC scores; ratings with two formulas listed give test-takers two possible ways to achieve the cutoff score.

Navy Entry-Level Occupational Fields

Rating	Abbreviation	ASVAB Line Scores Formula for Eligibility
Aviation Boatswain's Mate—Launching & Recovery	ABE	VE + AR + MK + AS
Aviation Boatswain's Mate—Fuels	ABF	VE + AR + MK + AS
Aviation Boatswain's Mate—Aircraft Handling	ABH	VE + AR + MK + AS
Air Traffic Control	AC	VE + AR + MK + MC
Aviation Machinist's Mate	AD	VE + AR + MK + AS
Aviation Electrician's Mate	AE	AR + MK + EI + GS or VE + AR + MK + MC
Aviation Aerographer's Mate	AG	VE + MK + GS
Aircrew Program	AIRC/AIRR	AR + 2MK + GS
Aviation Structural Mechanic—Equipment	AME	VE + AR + MK + AS or VE + AR + MK + MC
Aviation Structural Mechanic—Hydraulics	AMH	VE + AR + MK + AS or VE + AR + MK + MC
Aviation Structural Mechanic—Structures	AMS	VE + AR + MK + AS or VE + AR + MK + MC
Aviation Ordnanceman	AO	VE + AR + MK + AS or MK + AS + AO
Aviation Support Equipment Technician	AS	VE + AR + MK + AS or VE + AR + MK + MC
Aviation Electronics Technician	AT	AR + MK + EI + GS or VE + AR + MK + MC
Avionics Technician	AV	AR + MK + EI + GS
Aviation Warfare Systems Operator	AW	VE + MK + GS
Aviation Maintenance Administration	AZ	VE + AR
Boatswain's Mate	BM	AFQT
Builder	BU	AR + MC + AS
Construction Electrician	CE	AR + MK + EI + GS
Construction Mechanic	CM	AR + MC + AS
Culinary Specialist	CS	VE + AR
Culinary Specialist (Subsurface)	CS (SS)	AR + MK + EI + GS or VE + AR + MK + MC
Cryptologic Technician—Administration	CTA	VE + MK
Cryptologic Technician—Interpretive	CTI	VE + MK + GS
Cryptologic Technician—Maintenance	CTM	AR + MK + EI + GS
Cryptologic Technician—Communications	CTO	VE + AR
Cryptologic Technician—Collection	CTR	VE + AR

Rating	Abbreviation	ASVAB Line Scores Formula for Eligibility
Cryptologic Technician—Technical	CTT	VE + MK + GS
Damage Controlman	DC	VE + AR + MK + AS or MK + AS + AO
Navy Diver	ND	AR + VE and MC
Engineering Aide	EA	AR + 2MK + GS
Electrician's Mate	EM	VE + AR + MK + MC
Engineman	EN	VE + AR + MK + AS or VE + AR + MK + AO
Equipment Operator	EO	AR + MC + AS
Explosive Ordnance Disposal	EOD	AR + VE and MC or GS + MC + EI
Electronics Technician	ET	AR + MK + EI + GS
Electronics Technician (Subsurface)	ETN	AR + MK + EI + GS or VE + AR + MK + MC
Fire Controlman	FC	AR + MK + EI + GS
Fire Control Technician (Subsurface)	FT	AR + MK + EI + GS
Gunner's Mate	GM	AR + MK + EI + GS
Gas Turbine Systems Technician—Electrical	GSE	VE + AR + MK + MC
Gas Turbine Systems Technician—Mechanical	GSM	VE + AR + MK + AS or VE + AR + MK + AO
Hospital Corpsman	HM	VE + MK + GS
Hull Maintenance Technician	HT	VE + AR + MK + AS or MK + AS + AO
Interior Communication Electrician	IC	VE + AR + MK + MC
Intelligence Specialist	IS	VE + AR
Information System Technician	IT	AR + 2MK + GS or AR + MK + EI + GS
Legalman	LN	VE + MK
Logistics Specialist	LS	VE + AR
Master at Arms	MA	AR + WK
Mass Communication Specialist	MC	VE + AR
Machinist Mate	MM	VE + AR + MK + AS or VE + AR + MK + AO
Machinist Mate (Subsurface)	MMS	VE + AR + MK + MC
Mineman	MN	VE + MC + AS
Machinery Repairman	MR	VE + AR + MK + AS or MK + AS + AO
Missile Technician	MT	AR + MK + EI + GS or VE + AR + MK + MC
Musician	MU	AFQT only
Nuclear Field	NF	Note 1*
Operations Specialist	OS	VE + MK + CS or AR + 2MK + GS

Rating	Abbreviation	ASVAB Line Scores Formula for Eligibility
Personnel Specialist	PS	VE + MK or VE + MK + CS
Aircrew Survival Equipmentman	PR	VE + AR + MK + AS or MK + AS + AO
Quartermaster	QM	VE + AR
Religious Program Specialist	RP	VE + MK or VE + MK + CS
Submarine Electronics	SECF	AR + MK + EI + GS or VE + AR + MK + MC
Ship's Serviceman	SH	VE + AR
Sonar Technician—Surface	STG	AR + MK + EI + GS
Sonar Technician (Subsurface)	STS	AR + MK + EI + GS or VE + AR + MK + MC
Steelworker	SW	AR + MC + AS
Utilitiesman	UT	AR + MK + EI + GS
Yeoman (Surface)	YN	VE + MK or VE + MK + CS
Yeoman (Subsurface)	YNS	AR + MK + EI + GS or VE + AR + MK + MC

*Note 1: The Navy Advanced Programs Test (NAPT) is a two-hour supplementary test for potential Nuclear Field program applicants who don't qualify based on their ASVAB line scores alone. Currently, if your VE + AR + MK + MC or AR + MK + EI + GS scores are 252 or more, you don't have to take the NAPT. However, if your score by either of these two formulas is 235 or greater but less than 252, you must take the NAPT and score at least a 55 to be considered for the Nuclear Field program.

Air Force

The Air Force has four composite scores drawn from individual ASVAB subtests.

- **MECHANICAL APTITUDE SCORE**—Determined from General Science (GS), Mechanical Comprehension (MC), and Automotive and Shop Information (AS).

- **ADMINISTRATIVE APTITUDE SCORE**—Determined directly from the Verbal Expression (VE) score.

- **GENERAL APTITUDE SCORE**—Determined from Arithmetic Reasoning (AR) and Verbal Expression (VE).

- **ELECTRONICS APTITUDE SCORE**—Determined from General Science (GS), Arithmetic Reasoning (AR), Mathematics Knowledge (MK), and Electronics Information (EI).

The Air Force organizes its enlisted Air Force Specialty Codes (AFSCs) into the following overall career fields: Operations, Maintenance and Logistics, Support, Medical and Dental, Legal and Chaplain, Acquisition, and Special Investigations. Within these categories, AFSCs are further assigned to career fields. A career field may have only one AFSC assigned to it, or (more likely) it may have several. AFSCs with similar functions are grouped together in the same career field.

USAF Career Fields

Operations

1A — Aircrew Operations

1B — Cyberspace

1C — Command and Control Systems Operations

1N — Intelligence

1P — Aircrew Flight Equipment

1S — Safety

1T — Aircrew Protection

1U — Unmanned Aerospace Systems

1W — Weather

Maintenance and Logistics

2A — Aerospace Maintenance

2E — Communications—Electronics/Wire Systems Maintenance

2F — Fuels

2G — Logistics Plans

2M — Missile and Space Systems Maintenance

2P — Precision Measurement

2R — Maintenance Management

2S — Materiel Management

2T — Transportation and Vehicle Management

2W — Munitions and Weapons

Support

3A — Administration

3D — Cyberspace Support

3E — Civil Engineering

3H — Historian

3M — Services

3N — Public Affairs

3P — Security Forces

3S — Mission Support

Medical and Dental

4A–V — Medical

4Y — Dental

Legal and Chaplain

5J — Paralegal

5R — Chaplain's Assistant

Acquisition

6C — Contracting

6F — Financial

Special Investigations

7S — Special Investigations

Marine Corps

ASVAB SCORE. Marine Corps recruits currently must have an AFQT score of at least 31. A small handful of exceptions are made (about 1 percent) for some recruits who are otherwise exceptionally qualified but have AFQT scores as low as 25.

EDUCATION. As with the Army and Air Force, those without a high school education or equivalent are ineligible. The Marine Corps limits GED enlistments to no more than 5 percent a year. GED applicants must achieve an AFQT score of at least 50 to even be considered for enlistment.

The Marines use four composite scores derived from ASVAB line scores to determine qualifications for a particular specialty.

- **CLERICAL (CL)**—Word Knowledge (WK) + Paragraph Comprehension (PC) + Math Knowledge (MK). Used to determine eligibility for MOSs dealing with administration, supply, and finance.

- **ELECTRONICS REPAIR (EL)**—Arithmetic Reasoning (AR) + Math Knowledge (MK) + Electronics Information (EI) + General Science (GS). Used to determine eligibility for specialties related to missile repair, electronics, and communications.

- **GENERAL TECHNICAL (GT)**—Arithmetic Reasoning (AR) + Mechanical Comprehension (MC) + Paragraph Comprehension (PC) + Word Knowledge (WK). Used to determine eligibility for special and officer programs.

- **MECHANICAL MAINTENANCE (MM)**—Arithmetic Reasoning (AR) + Electronics Information (EI) + Mechanical Comprehension (MC) + Automotive and Shop Information (AS). Used to determine eligibility for specialties involving mechanics, construction, utility maintenance, and hazardous materials handling.

Four-digit Marine Corps Military Occupational Specialties (MOSs) are grouped into occupational fields. The first two digits of an MOS are the code for the specific field, as shown in the table on page 20. For instance, within the Infantry Occupational Field, the MOS for Infantry Rifleman is 0311, the MOS for Light Amphibious Vehicle Crewman is 0313, the MOS for Machine Gunner is 0331, and so on.

The table on page 20 shows the Marine Occupational Field, its two-digit code, and the composite score(s) that affect eligibility for the MOSs in that category. There are too many MOSs to show the formula for each one—and they differ by MOS within each occupational field. However, the table will give you an idea on which areas of knowledge you should focus your efforts, based on your interests and career goals.

Marine Corps Entry-Level Occupational Fields

Occupational Field	Code	Relevant Composite Score(s)
Personnel and Administration	01	CL
Intelligence	02	GT, EL
Infantry	03	GT
Logistics	04	GT
Marine Air-Ground Task Force (MAGTF) Plans	05	GT
Communications	06	GT, EL
Artillery	08	GT
Utilities	11	EL, MM
Engineer, Construction, Facilities, and Equipment	13	MM, GT
Tank and Amphibious Assault Vehicle	18	GT
Ground Ordnance Maintenance	21	MM
Ammunition and Explosive Ordnance Disposal	23	GT
Signals Intelligence/Ground Electronic Warfare	26	GT
Linguist	27	(dependent on language)
Data/Communications Maintenance	28	EL
Supply Administration and Operations	30	CL
Traffic Management	31	CL
Food Service	33	CL, GT
Financial Management	34	CL
Motor Transport	35	MM
Public Affairs	43	GT
Legal Services	44	CL
Combat Camera	46	GT
Music	55	GT, AFQT of 50
Chemical, Biological, Radiological, and Nuclear (CBRN) Defense	57	GT
Military Police and Corrections	58	GT
Electronics Maintenance	59	EL
Aircraft Maintenance	60/61/62	CL, MM
Avionics	63/64	EL
Aviation Ordnance	65	GT
Aviation Logistics	66	CL
Meteorological and Oceanographic	68	GT
Airfield Services	70	MM, CL
Air Control/Air Support/Anti-air Warfare/Air Traffic Control	72	GT
Enlisted Flight Crews	73	GT

Coast Guard

ASVAB SCORE. The Coast Guard requires a minimum AFQT score of 45 for enlistment. A waiver is possible if a recruit's ASVAB line scores qualify him or her for a specific job and the recruit is willing to enlist in that job.

EDUCATION. For a very few (about 5 percent) who will be allowed to enlist with a GED, the minimum AFQT score is 50.

JOB QUALIFICATION. The Coast Guard uses direct ASVAB line scores for determining job qualification.

Like the Navy, the Coast Guard calls its individual specialties *ratings*. Also like the Navy, the Coast Guard uses formulas for each rating based on ASVAB line scores. However, since the Coast Guard is much smaller than the Navy, it has far fewer ratings. Although qualifying scores may change over time based on the service's needs, the following table shows Coast Guard ratings and the ASVAB line score formulas that affect eligibility for each. The code VE indicates the sum of the WK and PC scores.

Coast Guard Entry-Level Occupational Fields

Coast Guard Rating	Abbreviation	ASVAB Line Scores Formula for Eligibility
Aviation Maintenance Technician	AMT	AR + MC + AS + EI
Aviation Survival Technician	AST	VE + MC + AS
Avionics Electrical Technician	AET	MK + EI + GS
Boatswain's Mate	BM	VE + AR
Culinary Specialist	CS	VE + AR
Damage Controlman	DC	VE + MC + AS
Electrician's Mate	EM	MK + EI + GS
Electronics Technician	ET	MK + EI + GS
Gunner's Mate	GM	AR + MK + EI + GS
Health Services Technician	HS	VE + MK + GS + AR
Intelligence Specialist	IS	VE + AR
Information Systems Technician	IT	MK + EI + GS
Maritime Enforcement Specialist	ME	VE + AR
Machinery Technician	MK	AR + MC + AS
Marine Science Technician	MST	VE + AR
Operations Specialist	OS	VE + AR
Public Affairs Specialist	PA	VE + AR
Storekeeper	SK	VE + AR
Yeoman	YN	VE + AR

Where Can I Take the ASVAB?

The ASVAB is administered year-round at Military Entrance Processing Stations (MEPS) located throughout the United States, as well as by mobile teams and at satellite locations. Officials of the Military Entrance Processing Command proctor (supervise) the tests.

How Do I Apply?

Ask your school guidance counselor to make arrangements for you, or contact the nearest recruiter of the service of your choice. There is no cost for this examination since the Department of Defense wants to tell you about military service opportunities and assist you in career exploration.

Do I Have to Join the Military if I Take the ASVAB?

Absolutely not. Taking the ASVAB does not obligate you to the military in any way. You are free to use your test results in whatever manner you wish. Additionally, ASVAB results will *not* be used to enter your name in any draft registration system.

You will, however, be required to sign a statement authorizing the release of your test scores to representatives of all the military services, and (like the majority of high school students), if you are an upperclassman, you will probably be contacted by a recruiter sometime before you graduate. You should expect this whether or not you ever take the ASVAB.

Nevertheless, it's to your advantage to find out about the many job and career opportunities in the U.S. military services (Air Force, Army, Marine Corps, and Navy), the National Guard, the Reserves, and the U.S. Coast Guard.

Hundreds of thousands of students enter the military services every year. Your ASVAB test scores are good for enlistment purposes for two years after you take the test. Contact a service recruiter to determine whether you qualify to enter that service (assuming that you meet other qualifications such as age, physical requirements, etc.).

Who Sees My Test Scores?

The ASVAB is used by the Armed Services for recruiting purposes and by your counselor for guidance counseling. Your test scores will be provided to your counselor and to the recruiting services.

The personal information you will provide at the time of testing will be maintained in a computer file. After two years, individual test scores, identified by student name and social security number, are retained by the Department of Defense only for research purposes to assist in evaluating and updating test materials.

Your personal identity information and related test information will not be released to any agency outside the Department of Defense and your school system. This information will not be used for any purpose other than recruiting by the Armed Services, counseling in your school, and research on test development and personnel measurement.

How to Achieve Your Best ASVAB and AFQT Scores

2

Lots of people have two false beliefs about test taking.

First, they think that the *amount* of time spent studying is the most important—or maybe even the only—factor in improving their test results.

Likewise, many people believe that last-minute studying (commonly referred to as "cramming") will get the job done.

Both of these ideas are just flat wrong.

Yes, the amount of time you spend studying is a factor. And a last-minute review of facts or formulas can't hurt.

But the proven truth is that *efficient* studying *ahead of time* is by far the best method—*and it's the only really effective way to get significantly better results on whatever test you're preparing for.* While it is true that any time spent studying is better than none, the question you have to ask yourself is this: am I getting the most benefit possible out of the time I am spending studying? And am I doing what is necessary to prepare myself to get the best results possible?

Since time is a limited resource, it's a very good idea to use it as wisely and efficiently as possible. Remember that you have the same number of minutes in an hour and hours in a day as did Aristotle, Leonardo da Vinci, Michelangelo, Benjamin Franklin, Thomas Edison, and the Wright brothers—and you have tremendously more resources available than they ever did. And just look what *they* managed to accomplish.

To make the time you *do* have count for as much as possible, *plan* your studying, and do it as far ahead of time as possible; you've already taken an important step in that direction by buying this book. Wading through the review material and taking the practice tests will make the time you spend studying more effective, instead of just time spent reading—there's a difference!

Spending an hour a day in uninterrupted studying in a quiet, nondistracting place will pay off far more than spending two or three times that amount of time in shorter segments, especially if you are in a place where there are distractions or interruptions. Any distraction takes away from your focus on what you're studying, so it's bad. And, if you can start studying a month or more before your test—or, if not, as far ahead as possible—it will give your brain and memory time to shift the material from your short-term memory (think of a temporary file on your computer) to your long-term memory (think of a file permanently stored on your hard drive), where you will be able to access it more easily.

> "Whether you think you can or you can't, you're right."
> —Henry Ford

"Plan the work, then work the plan."

—A senior NCO

If this book belongs to you, make notes in the margins and use other ways to help emphasize things that you want to remember—underlining, circling, highlighting text, etc.

PREPARING FOR YOUR CHAMPIONSHIP GAME

Since you bought this book (or made the effort to borrow it from a friend or check it out from a library), it is overwhelmingly likely that you want to do your best on the ASVAB. If you are joining the military, this is not just an assessment to see if you are eligible to enter the service. Your ASVAB scores will either open or shut the door to numerous military specialties. Treat the ASVAB like the first-round championship game that it is, and be serious when you prepare for it.

Here are some important guidelines for successful, efficient, *effective* studying.

1. **MAKE A STUDY SCHEDULE AND *STICK TO IT*.** Don't put off studying until it's convenient, or for some time when you have nothing else to do. If the test is important enough for you to take, it's important enough to invest the time to do as well as you can.

    Make studying a priority, at least as important as your social life or watching television or getting on your favorite social media app—how many music stars or actors are going to take your test for you? Even if they did, you probably wouldn't like the results. Schedule your study time and make every effort not to let anything else interfere with that schedule.

2. **CONCENTRATE YOUR STUDY EFFORTS IN YOUR WEAKEST AREAS.** Chances are you already have an idea of the general areas where you are weak, strong, or just average. The first practice test will give you some more focused insight into the kinds of questions you do well on, as well as the ones where you need some work—but don't neglect your stronger areas and let them become your new "need work" categories! Go back and review the information in the specific areas where you realize you need help; if some area is still not clear to you, do further research in a library or on the Internet.

3. **STUDY WITHOUT INTERRUPTION OR STOPPING FOR AT LEAST 30 MINUTES AT A TIME.** Set up your schedule so that you can study for an uninterrupted period of at least 30 minutes, and preferably more. If you have set aside a couple of hours, for instance, take a short break (no more than 10 minutes) after 30–45 minutes—get a drink, go to the restroom, stretch briefly—but don't lose your focus! It's easy to get distracted during this time, so stay away from the TV, don't make any phone calls, don't check Facebook, don't start organizing your closet—don't do anything that's going to keep you from diving right back into your studying. BUT, when you are taking a practice test, do the complete examination in one sitting, just as you will have to do when it comes time to actually take the test.

4. **MAKE SURE YOU UNDERSTAND THE CORRECT MEANING OF EVERY WORD YOU READ OR HEAR.** Your ability to grasp and comprehend what you read is the key to doing well on the test—after all, it is a *written* test, right? If it was a test on making baskets from the free throw line, would you practice more on dribbling and passing—or on what you were going to be tested on? Remember, the ASVAB you're preparing for is not just a test to earn a grade on a report card; it's a test to see if you have what it takes to take advantage of a whole wealth of opportunities . . . or not. So, starting now, every time you see a word for which you aren't completely sure of the meaning, make the effort to look it up. If you can't look it up right then, write it down and look it up when you can. This will require self discipline, but you will get the benefit on the test *and* in your daily life.

5. **KEEP A LIST OF THE WORDS YOU DIDN'T KNOW AND HAD TO LOOK UP.** Then go back and review them periodically. Try to use them in conversation when it's appropriate—not to make yourself look like an egghead, but to be able to express yourself more precisely and concisely. Stretch your mental muscles by doing crossword puzzles.

6. **WRITE THINGS DOWN.** It is a proven fact that you retain things you write down better and longer than those things you just hear, or even if you say them—so take the time and effort to write down the word and its definition. Not on a computer, but *longhand*—print it in block letters if you want, but *write it down*. Then write a sentence using that word as it might be used in a real conversation, or in an imaginary term paper. The mental and physiological effort you expend to write that word or concept down significantly reinforces your memory of it far above just hearing or even saying it. Even if you never see those notes again—and you *should* review them—you will still retain the material better.

7. **SIMULATE TEST CONDITIONS WHEN STUDYING—AND ESPECIALLY WHEN TAKING PRACTICE TESTS.** To the extent that you can, simulate the conditions you will encounter when you are taking the actual test. The more you do this when you are "just" studying—not to mention when you are taking a practice test—the more you will be used to this kind of environment when it comes time for your ASVAB championship game. If you have other people in the household, tell them that you are taking a practice test and ask for their support by not disturbing you. Chances are they will be happy to comply.

8. **FOLLOW THE RECOMMENDED TECHNIQUES FOR ANSWERING MULTIPLE-CHOICE QUESTIONS.** This chapter will provide you with some very valuable techniques for maximizing your chances of getting multiple-choice questions right—and not just making it "multiple guess"!

9. **TIME YOURSELF WHEN TAKING PRACTICE TESTS.** Running out of time on a multiple-choice test is a tragedy you can avoid. Learn through practice how much time is reasonable to spend on any particular question—then stick to that guide.

10. **EXERCISE REGULARLY AND STAY IN GOOD PHYSICAL SHAPE.** It's hard to remember sometimes that life is supposed to be about balance, especially when you have too many things to do and not enough time to do even half of them. However, the bottom line here is that if your body isn't in at least decent shape, you will not do as well on the test as you could. Do at least 20–30 *uninterrupted* minutes of aerobic exercise (something that makes you breathe hard) at least two to three times a week, and preferably more. Strength training (lifting some kind of weights) is good, but balance the amount of weight you can lift with how many repetitions you can do, and don't overdo things to the extent that you risk injury. If nothing else, even a temporary injury is a distraction you don't need.

11. **PRACTICE, PRACTICE, PRACTICE—STAY IN GOOD *MENTAL* SHAPE, TOO.** Even if you do well on the first or second practice test, don't neglect the others—there's always room for improvement. If you think vocabulary is a strong point for you, for instance, don't rest on your laurels; look on the Internet for practice questions for the SAT, ACT, and GRE tests, even if they are older versions available in the library—the meaning of "indubitably" won't change, nor will the formula for the area of a circle or for calculating distance traveled when you know the velocity and the time elapsed. Do crossword and sudoku puzzles. Keep learning, keep practicing, keep your brain nimble and flexible.

TIPS AND TECHNIQUES FOR ANSWERING MULTIPLE-CHOICE QUESTIONS

This section lays out some specific test-taking techniques to help you on this and other multiple-choice tests. Learn these techniques and then practice them so that they are second nature to you when it comes time to take the test.

1. **READ THE DIRECTIONS.** Don't assume you know what the directions are for a specific subtest without reading them. Make sure you read them as thoroughly as if it was the first time you had seen them, and make sure you understand them fully. This is not *spending* time so much as *investing* it—and why take a chance on canceling out all the effort you've made studying and preparing? Besides, the test monitor or proctor won't let you start until everyone has had plenty of time to read the directions—usually they read them aloud, too—so there's no reason *not* to read the directions.

2. **LOOK CLOSELY AT THE ANSWER SHEET.** The answer sheets on your practice exams in this book are typical of what you should see when you take the test, but don't take anything for granted. Read the directions on the answer sheet carefully, all the way through, and make sure you understand the format.

3. **BE CAREFUL WHEN YOU MARK YOUR ANSWER ON PAPER TESTS.** Make sure you mark your answers in accordance with the instructions. Pay special attention to make sure you:

   ☑ **MARK THE NUMBERED ANSWER FOR THE QUESTION YOU THINK YOU ARE ANSWERING.** While this may seem pretty obvious (and it is), lots of test-takers have failed because of this kind of carelessness. All it takes is getting off track on one question—you probably won't notice it right away, so you'll continue being off for even more questions. If you do notice, you'll spend time you might not be able to afford trying to fix your mistake—and if you don't notice, you'll be baffled why you did so poorly on a section that was supposed to be your strong area.

   ☑ **DON'T MAKE ANY EXTRA MARKS ON YOUR ANSWER SHEET.** Your test will be machine-graded, and it's not going to help to confuse the scanner or optical character reader.

   ☑ **COMPLETELY FILL IN THE ALLOTTED SPACE** (circle, oval, rectangle) for the answer you choose.

   ☑ **MARK ONLY ONE ANSWER FOR EACH QUESTION AND ERASE *COMPLETELY* ANY ANSWERS YOU WANT TO CHANGE.** This goes back to your preparation—you need to bring a good, fresh eraser that works; check it before the test to make sure it does the job. The machine grading the test won't know that you realized that Choice B was really the right answer, and not Choice A; it will just note that two choices were marked for Question 22, and grade you as WRONG.

4. **MAKE SURE YOU UNDERSTAND WHAT THE QUESTION IS REALLY ASKING.** Read carefully the root or stem of the question—the part before the answer choices—to make sure you know what the question really is. Don't be in such a galloping hurry that you slam through it and miss a "not" or "except" or some other small but important indicator. Read the question twice—and if none of the choices seems correct after the first time you look at them, read the question again.

5. **READ ALL THE CHOICES BEFORE YOU CHOOSE AN ANSWER.** Don't fall into the trap of thinking that the best distractor (a plausible but still incorrect answer) is it because it's first and oh, boy, it seems right, and let's get on to the next question!

6. **KNOW THE KEY "TIPOFF" WORDS THAT OFTEN SIGNAL A WRONG ANSWER.** Absolute words like *never, nobody, nothing, always, all, only, any, everyone, everybody*, and the like are often clues that this answer is too broad and therefore wrong.

7. **KNOW THE KEY WORDS THAT OFTEN SIGNAL A *POSSIBLY* CORRECT ANSWER.** Limiting words such as *usually, generally, sometimes, possible, many, some, occasionally*, and *often*, often signal a choice that at least *could* be correct—but read it carefully to be sure.

8. **LOOK AT HOW THE MEANING OF THE CHOICES COMPARE TO EACH OTHER.** If two choices have a conflicting or opposite meaning, chances are high that one of them is correct. And if two choices are very close in meaning, chances are pretty good that *neither* of them is correct.

9. ***NEVER* MAKE A CHOICE BASED ON THE FREQUENCY OF LETTERED ANSWER CHOICES.** This is the same thing as rolling dice—the odds are stacked against you. If this is what you think will work, please just go directly to the casino and don't waste time and taxpayer money taking the test.

10. **ELIMINATE CHOICES YOU RECOGNIZE AS BEING INCORRECT.** *This is the most important guideline to success on any multiple-choice test.* As you read through the choices, eliminate any choice you know is wrong. If you can eliminate all the choices except one, there's your answer! Read the choice one more time to make sure you haven't missed anything, then mark that answer on your answer sheet and move on to the next question. If you can only, for example, eliminate one or two of the possible choices, read through the question and the remaining choices once more. Many times the right answer will become apparent; if not—even if you have to flat-out guess between two or three possible choices that you think *could* be right—you will have significantly increased your odds of answering that question correctly.

11. **NEVER RECONSIDER ANSWER CHOICES THAT YOU HAVE ALREADY ELIMINATED.** If you thought it was wrong the first time through, you were probably correct. Focus on the ones that *could* be right.

12. **SKIP QUESTIONS THAT GIVE YOU TOO MUCH TROUBLE (PAPER VERSION ONLY).** Don't dwell on any one question too long on your first trip through that subtest. If you've read the question twice, tried to eliminate any obviously incorrect answers, and still have no clue between three or four choices, it's time to go to the next question and come back when you get to the end of that section. Once you have answered all the questions you are at least reasonably sure of in a section or subtest, check to see how much time you have remaining. If you can, go back to the questions you skipped and re-read the question and the choices. Sometimes a subsequent question will jar something loose in your memory and you will then be able to make a good choice. If you read the question again and you still are having trouble, make the best guess you can, following the guidelines above. If you are allowed to mark in your test booklet, or if you have scratch paper, circle the number of the question you skipped, or else write it down on the scratch paper.

13. **NEVER LEAVE ANY QUESTIONS UNANSWERED.** You can't get credit for an unanswered question. It will be counted as wrong.

14. **BE VERY RELUCTANT TO CHANGE ANSWERS YOU HAVE ALREADY CHOSEN.** Unless you have an *excellent* reason, *don't* change an answer you have already marked in the initial belief that it was correct. Studies have shown again and again that, if you are still unsure, you are far more likely to change a right answer to a wrong one than the other way around.

CHART YOUR PROGRESS

After you take the Diagnostic Test, record your scores on the Progress Chart below. Identify the subjects in which you have the lowest scores and study those topics. Then take Practice Tests One and Two and the AFQT Focus Test and see your progress as your scores rise.

PROGRESS CHART

Subtest	Number of Questions	DIAGNOSTIC TEST	TEST ONE	TEST TWO	AFQT FOCUS TEST	Excellent	Good	Fair	Poor
1. General Science	25					25–23	22–21	20–19	18 or less
2. Arithmetic Reasoning	30					30–28	27–26	25–23	22 or less
3. Word Knowledge	35					35–32	31–29	28–26	25 or less
4. Paragraph Comprehension	15					15	14	13–12	11 or less
5. Mathematics Knowledge	25					25–23	22–21	20–19	18 or less
6. Electronics Information	20					20–19	18–17	16–15	14 or less
7. Automotive and Shop Information	25					25–23	22–21	20–19	18 or less
8. Mechanical Comprehension	25					25–23	22–21	20–19	18 or less
9. Assembling Objects	16					16	15	14–13	12 or less

ONLINE TEST PROGRESS CHART

Subtest	Number of Questions	ONLINE TEST ONE	ONLINE TEST TWO	ONLINE TEST THREE	Excellent	Good	Fair	Poor
1. General Science	25				25–23	22–21	20–19	18 or less
2. Arithmetic Reasoning	30				30–28	27–26	25–23	22 or less
3. Word Knowledge	35				35–32	31–29	28–26	25 or less
4. Paragraph Comprehension	15				15	14	13–12	11 or less
5. Mathematics Knowledge	25				25–23	22–21	20–19	18 or less
6. Electronics Information	20				20–19	18–17	16–15	14 or less
7. Automotive and Shop Information	25				25–23	22–21	20–19	18 or less
8. Mechanical Comprehension	25				25–23	22–21	20–19	18 or less
9. Assembling Objects	16				16	15	14–13	12 or less

STUDY GUIDE

After you finish each test, determine your score, and record it on the Progress Chart. You should plan how and what to study to improve your scores.

- If you need improvement in Subtest 1, concentrate on Chapter 4—General Science Review.
- If you need improvement in Subtests 2 and/or 5, concentrate on Chapter 5—Mathematics Review.
- If you need improvement in Subtests 3 and 4, concentrate on Chapter 6—Word Knowledge and Paragraph Comprehension Review.
- If you need improvement in Subtest 6, concentrate on Chapter 7—Electronics Information Review.
- If you need improvement in Subtest 7, concentrate on Chapter 8—Automotive Information Review and Chapter 9—Shop Information Review.
- If you need improvement in Subtest 8, concentrate on Chapter 10—Mechanical Comprehension Review.
- If you need improvement in Subtest 9, concentrate on Chapter 11—Assembling Objects.

Note: Consider yourself as "needing improvement" in a section if you receive other than an excellent rating in it.

ON THE DAY OF THE TEST

First, *get a good night's sleep* the night before the test. If you've established a plan and followed it, you won't be up until the wee hours cramming. If you haven't—well, good luck. Even better, try to get an adequate amount of sleep for the preceding several days before the test, and don't neglect an appropriate amount of physical exercise during those days. This will help you sleep better at night, and you'll be more relaxed and have better stamina and resistance to stress during the day.

The night before the test, *organize everything you will need* the next day. Lay out your clothes and test-taking materials the night before. Wake up early enough so you can avoid rushing through your morning routine. Eat a good breakfast, but go easy on the carbs—some are okay, but just say "no" to that second stack of pancakes or second helping of hash browns. Your body won't understand that you need that blood to go to your brain, and it will be trying to divert more blood to your digestive system than you can afford during the test. Drink plenty of water early on, but not so much that you are guaranteed to need a restroom break after the first 15 minutes of the test.

If you have a choice, *wear comfortable clothes* to the test. If you are wearing a uniform, make sure that you are wearing a fresh uniform, have a fresh haircut and shave (as appropriate), and generally look as if you are ready to be inspected by the local general or admiral. You will not get extra points for showing up in rumpled clothes and looking haggard because you have been up studying nonstop for days—but you will feel more confident and sharper if you look squared away and you know it. This applies whether you are wearing a uniform or not.

Take a light jacket or sweater that you can put on or take off with a minimum of fuss. It might be cold in the testing area, and why subject yourself to an avoidable distraction?

Get to the test location early. If you think it will take you 15 minutes to get there, allow 30. If you've been there a hundred times before and it's never taken longer than 30 minutes, allow an hour; this is the one day there will be road construction or a traffic jam in your way. If it's somewhere local but you haven't been there before, try to do a reconnaissance of the location, including the room itself, in the week before you take the test. The one time you get bad directions from the "always reliable" map-generating application will be the time you need them to get to the test site on time. If you have to rush into the test site frustrated and out of breath, you are not setting yourself up for success—and, in some circumstances, if you get there late, you'll be out of luck. Put yourself on Lombardi time: if you're not there early, you're late.

Tell yourself that you can do it. And, if you have been putting these principles into practice, chances are you'll be right.

What Should I Expect on the Day of the Test?

You can expect to encounter one of three major scenarios on the day you take your ASVAB.

If you are a high school student, you will take a paper-and-pencil version of the ASVAB CEP, probably in the cafeteria or auditorium.

If you are committed to joining the military right now and your recruiter is taking you to a Military Entrance Processing Station or MEPS, you will take the CAT-ASVAB (computerized version) as an early part of a long day of examinations, forms, and briefings.

If you are researching entrance into the military service, or if you are retaking the ASVAB in an effort to raise one or more of your test scores, you will likely be taking a paper-and-pencil version, probably in a school or government building.

If you are taking the paper version of the ASVAB, you will be given a booklet with nine subtests; if you are taking the ASVAB CEP, your information will also include an interest inventory. The subtests will each consist of practice questions and actual test questions. You will also be given a separate answer sheet on which to mark your answers, a pencil, and some scratch paper for doing any figuring you may want to do.

If you are taking the computerized version of the ASVAB, you will be seated at a computer monitor with a specially modified keyboard (more about this in a minute).

The people administering your test will give you complete instructions about what to do and how much time you have for each test. After you have been given the instructions, you will be allowed to practice by answering some sample questions. Finally, you will be given an opportunity to ask questions before you start, so that you will understand exactly what you are supposed to do on the tests.

How to Take the Test

For each of the ASVAB subtests, there are four possible answers, labeled A, B, C, and D, for each question. Only one answer for each question is correct. Your job is to read each question carefully and decide which of the answers given is the best answer. Then, for paper tests, record your choice on the separate answer sheet by filling in the space with the same number and letter as your choice. For computerized tests, just click on the letter of the answer you choose.

In all cases, you should choose the best answer and mark your answer sheet in the space for it. Don't make any stray or random marks on the answer sheet, because the scoring machine might record those marks as wrong answers. You also should not make any marks in the ASVAB test booklet.

On most of the subtests, you will have enough time to try every question, and you *should* try to answer every one—but be sure to work as quickly and accurately as you can.

Some tests will be easier for you than others, but do the best you can on all of them. All are important. For the paper-and-pencil ASVAB, *unanswered questions will be counted wrong*, so guess if you have to, but don't leave any blank. The CAT-ASVAB will present you with one question at a time, and you will have to answer that question before you go to the next one, but you must still answer as many questions correctly as possible to make sure the test algorithm captures your level on each subtest. Answering too few questions is as bad as answering them incorrectly.

PAPER VS. COMPUTER-ADMINISTERED TESTS

You will be taking the CAT-ASVAB if you are at a Military Entrance Processing Station (MEPS). This computerized version measures the same abilities as the paper-and-pencil ASVAB version, but there are two significant differences in content: the Automotive and Shop Information tests are split into two separate tests, and the test itself is *adaptive*.

Being *adaptive* means the computerized ASVAB customizes questions based on the demonstrated ability level of the test taker. Questions on the CAT-ASVAB are categorized as low, middle, or high difficulty. The first question on a subtest will be in the middle range. If you answer it correctly, the next question will be harder. If you answer the first item incorrectly, the next one will be less difficult. The test continues this way until your proficiency level is solidly determined. You will answer questions that are appropriate for your knowledge and ability level, based on your demonstrated performance. You won't waste time zipping through questions that are too easy for you, and you won't get a lot of questions that are too hard for you. In the end, you will actually have to wade through fewer questions than you would on the paper-and-pencil version.

Although it doesn't change the content, one thing the CAT-ASVAB doesn't let you do is skip a question and then come back to it. You *can* skip a question, but you can't go back to it later—nor can you go back and check your answers as you would be able to on the paper-and-pencil ASVAB. Changing your answers usually isn't a good idea, anyway, and neither is skipping questions.

The raw scores from the CAT-ASVAB are not directly based on the number of correct answers—because of the adaptive nature of the test, your scores are calculated by sophisticated algorithms that have been tested on millions of test takers over the years. These algorithms will calculate equivalent information to the paper-and-pencil ASVAB version results, so you will be able to compare apples to apples, instead of apples to watermelons.

Taking the CAT-ASVAB

When you arrive at the MEPS, the test administrator will give you some directions, check your Social Security number, and seat you at an assigned test administration station at a table with a computer keyboard and monitor.

The computer keyboard you'll use for the CAT-ASVAB is modified so only the keys you need to answer the test questions are labeled—the letters on the rest of the keys have been covered. You will have "A," "B," "C," and "D" keys (different than what you're used to) and the 0–9 numbers on the keypad; the spacebar becomes the ENTER key, and the F1 key will be your HELP key.

The keyboard will look something like this:

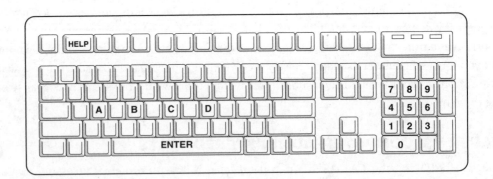

You'll get an on-screen orientation that describes the modified keyboard and explains how to use the keys that are available to answer test questions, change answers if desired, and move from one question to the next.

You will be instructed to press the red HELP key only if a problem comes up that requires the attention of a monitor or test administrator. If you do press the HELP key, the time stops for the test you are on and does not resume until you return to the test questions. Time spent reading instructions won't count against you, either.

You will have the opportunity to practice (if you need it) until you are ready to take the ASVAB on the modified computer keyboard.

ANSWER SHEET
Diagnostic Test

General Science—Subtest 1

1. Ⓐ Ⓑ Ⓒ Ⓓ   6. Ⓐ Ⓑ Ⓒ Ⓓ   11. Ⓐ Ⓑ Ⓒ Ⓓ   16. Ⓐ Ⓑ Ⓒ Ⓓ   21. Ⓐ Ⓑ Ⓒ Ⓓ
2. Ⓐ Ⓑ Ⓒ Ⓓ   7. Ⓐ Ⓑ Ⓒ Ⓓ   12. Ⓐ Ⓑ Ⓒ Ⓓ   17. Ⓐ Ⓑ Ⓒ Ⓓ   22. Ⓐ Ⓑ Ⓒ Ⓓ
3. Ⓐ Ⓑ Ⓒ Ⓓ   8. Ⓐ Ⓑ Ⓒ Ⓓ   13. Ⓐ Ⓑ Ⓒ Ⓓ   18. Ⓐ Ⓑ Ⓒ Ⓓ   23. Ⓐ Ⓑ Ⓒ Ⓓ
4. Ⓐ Ⓑ Ⓒ Ⓓ   9. Ⓐ Ⓑ Ⓒ Ⓓ   14. Ⓐ Ⓑ Ⓒ Ⓓ   19. Ⓐ Ⓑ Ⓒ Ⓓ   24. Ⓐ Ⓑ Ⓒ Ⓓ
5. Ⓐ Ⓑ Ⓒ Ⓓ   10. Ⓐ Ⓑ Ⓒ Ⓓ   15. Ⓐ Ⓑ Ⓒ Ⓓ   20. Ⓐ Ⓑ Ⓒ Ⓓ   25. Ⓐ Ⓑ Ⓒ Ⓓ

Arithmetic Reasoning—Subtest 2

1. Ⓐ Ⓑ Ⓒ Ⓓ   7. Ⓐ Ⓑ Ⓒ Ⓓ   13. Ⓐ Ⓑ Ⓒ Ⓓ   19. Ⓐ Ⓑ Ⓒ Ⓓ   25. Ⓐ Ⓑ Ⓒ Ⓓ
2. Ⓐ Ⓑ Ⓒ Ⓓ   8. Ⓐ Ⓑ Ⓒ Ⓓ   14. Ⓐ Ⓑ Ⓒ Ⓓ   20. Ⓐ Ⓑ Ⓒ Ⓓ   26. Ⓐ Ⓑ Ⓒ Ⓓ
3. Ⓐ Ⓑ Ⓒ Ⓓ   9. Ⓐ Ⓑ Ⓒ Ⓓ   15. Ⓐ Ⓑ Ⓒ Ⓓ   21. Ⓐ Ⓑ Ⓒ Ⓓ   27. Ⓐ Ⓑ Ⓒ Ⓓ
4. Ⓐ Ⓑ Ⓒ Ⓓ   10. Ⓐ Ⓑ Ⓒ Ⓓ   16. Ⓐ Ⓑ Ⓒ Ⓓ   22. Ⓐ Ⓑ Ⓒ Ⓓ   28. Ⓐ Ⓑ Ⓒ Ⓓ
5. Ⓐ Ⓑ Ⓒ Ⓓ   11. Ⓐ Ⓑ Ⓒ Ⓓ   17. Ⓐ Ⓑ Ⓒ Ⓓ   23. Ⓐ Ⓑ Ⓒ Ⓓ   29. Ⓐ Ⓑ Ⓒ Ⓓ
6. Ⓐ Ⓑ Ⓒ Ⓓ   12. Ⓐ Ⓑ Ⓒ Ⓓ   18. Ⓐ Ⓑ Ⓒ Ⓓ   24. Ⓐ Ⓑ Ⓒ Ⓓ   30. Ⓐ Ⓑ Ⓒ Ⓓ

Word Knowledge—Subtest 3

1. Ⓐ Ⓑ Ⓒ Ⓓ   8. Ⓐ Ⓑ Ⓒ Ⓓ   15. Ⓐ Ⓑ Ⓒ Ⓓ   22. Ⓐ Ⓑ Ⓒ Ⓓ   29. Ⓐ Ⓑ Ⓒ Ⓓ
2. Ⓐ Ⓑ Ⓒ Ⓓ   9. Ⓐ Ⓑ Ⓒ Ⓓ   16. Ⓐ Ⓑ Ⓒ Ⓓ   23. Ⓐ Ⓑ Ⓒ Ⓓ   30. Ⓐ Ⓑ Ⓒ Ⓓ
3. Ⓐ Ⓑ Ⓒ Ⓓ   10. Ⓐ Ⓑ Ⓒ Ⓓ   17. Ⓐ Ⓑ Ⓒ Ⓓ   24. Ⓐ Ⓑ Ⓒ Ⓓ   31. Ⓐ Ⓑ Ⓒ Ⓓ
4. Ⓐ Ⓑ Ⓒ Ⓓ   11. Ⓐ Ⓑ Ⓒ Ⓓ   18. Ⓐ Ⓑ Ⓒ Ⓓ   25. Ⓐ Ⓑ Ⓒ Ⓓ   32. Ⓐ Ⓑ Ⓒ Ⓓ
5. Ⓐ Ⓑ Ⓒ Ⓓ   12. Ⓐ Ⓑ Ⓒ Ⓓ   19. Ⓐ Ⓑ Ⓒ Ⓓ   26. Ⓐ Ⓑ Ⓒ Ⓓ   33. Ⓐ Ⓑ Ⓒ Ⓓ
6. Ⓐ Ⓑ Ⓒ Ⓓ   13. Ⓐ Ⓑ Ⓒ Ⓓ   20. Ⓐ Ⓑ Ⓒ Ⓓ   27. Ⓐ Ⓑ Ⓒ Ⓓ   34. Ⓐ Ⓑ Ⓒ Ⓓ
7. Ⓐ Ⓑ Ⓒ Ⓓ   14. Ⓐ Ⓑ Ⓒ Ⓓ   21. Ⓐ Ⓑ Ⓒ Ⓓ   28. Ⓐ Ⓑ Ⓒ Ⓓ   35. Ⓐ Ⓑ Ⓒ Ⓓ

Paragraph Comprehension—Subtest 4

1. Ⓐ Ⓑ Ⓒ Ⓓ   4. Ⓐ Ⓑ Ⓒ Ⓓ   7. Ⓐ Ⓑ Ⓒ Ⓓ   10. Ⓐ Ⓑ Ⓒ Ⓓ   13. Ⓐ Ⓑ Ⓒ Ⓓ
2. Ⓐ Ⓑ Ⓒ Ⓓ   5. Ⓐ Ⓑ Ⓒ Ⓓ   8. Ⓐ Ⓑ Ⓒ Ⓓ   11. Ⓐ Ⓑ Ⓒ Ⓓ   14. Ⓐ Ⓑ Ⓒ Ⓓ
3. Ⓐ Ⓑ Ⓒ Ⓓ   6. Ⓐ Ⓑ Ⓒ Ⓓ   9. Ⓐ Ⓑ Ⓒ Ⓓ   12. Ⓐ Ⓑ Ⓒ Ⓓ   15. Ⓐ Ⓑ Ⓒ Ⓓ

Mathematics Knowledge—Subtest 5

1. Ⓐ Ⓑ Ⓒ Ⓓ   6. Ⓐ Ⓑ Ⓒ Ⓓ   11. Ⓐ Ⓑ Ⓒ Ⓓ   16. Ⓐ Ⓑ Ⓒ Ⓓ   21. Ⓐ Ⓑ Ⓒ Ⓓ
2. Ⓐ Ⓑ Ⓒ Ⓓ   7. Ⓐ Ⓑ Ⓒ Ⓓ   12. Ⓐ Ⓑ Ⓒ Ⓓ   17. Ⓐ Ⓑ Ⓒ Ⓓ   22. Ⓐ Ⓑ Ⓒ Ⓓ
3. Ⓐ Ⓑ Ⓒ Ⓓ   8. Ⓐ Ⓑ Ⓒ Ⓓ   13. Ⓐ Ⓑ Ⓒ Ⓓ   18. Ⓐ Ⓑ Ⓒ Ⓓ   23. Ⓐ Ⓑ Ⓒ Ⓓ
4. Ⓐ Ⓑ Ⓒ Ⓓ   9. Ⓐ Ⓑ Ⓒ Ⓓ   14. Ⓐ Ⓑ Ⓒ Ⓓ   19. Ⓐ Ⓑ Ⓒ Ⓓ   24. Ⓐ Ⓑ Ⓒ Ⓓ
5. Ⓐ Ⓑ Ⓒ Ⓓ   10. Ⓐ Ⓑ Ⓒ Ⓓ   15. Ⓐ Ⓑ Ⓒ Ⓓ   20. Ⓐ Ⓑ Ⓒ Ⓓ   25. Ⓐ Ⓑ Ⓒ Ⓓ

Electronics Information—Subtest 6

1. Ⓐ Ⓑ Ⓒ Ⓓ   5. Ⓐ Ⓑ Ⓒ Ⓓ   9. Ⓐ Ⓑ Ⓒ Ⓓ   13. Ⓐ Ⓑ Ⓒ Ⓓ   17. Ⓐ Ⓑ Ⓒ Ⓓ
2. Ⓐ Ⓑ Ⓒ Ⓓ   6. Ⓐ Ⓑ Ⓒ Ⓓ   10. Ⓐ Ⓑ Ⓒ Ⓓ   14. Ⓐ Ⓑ Ⓒ Ⓓ   18. Ⓐ Ⓑ Ⓒ Ⓓ
3. Ⓐ Ⓑ Ⓒ Ⓓ   7. Ⓐ Ⓑ Ⓒ Ⓓ   11. Ⓐ Ⓑ Ⓒ Ⓓ   15. Ⓐ Ⓑ Ⓒ Ⓓ   19. Ⓐ Ⓑ Ⓒ Ⓓ
4. Ⓐ Ⓑ Ⓒ Ⓓ   8. Ⓐ Ⓑ Ⓒ Ⓓ   12. Ⓐ Ⓑ Ⓒ Ⓓ   16. Ⓐ Ⓑ Ⓒ Ⓓ   20. Ⓐ Ⓑ Ⓒ Ⓓ

Automotive & Shop Information—Subtest 7

1. Ⓐ Ⓑ Ⓒ Ⓓ   6. Ⓐ Ⓑ Ⓒ Ⓓ   11. Ⓐ Ⓑ Ⓒ Ⓓ   16. Ⓐ Ⓑ Ⓒ Ⓓ   21. Ⓐ Ⓑ Ⓒ Ⓓ
2. Ⓐ Ⓑ Ⓒ Ⓓ   7. Ⓐ Ⓑ Ⓒ Ⓓ   12. Ⓐ Ⓑ Ⓒ Ⓓ   17. Ⓐ Ⓑ Ⓒ Ⓓ   22. Ⓐ Ⓑ Ⓒ Ⓓ
3. Ⓐ Ⓑ Ⓒ Ⓓ   8. Ⓐ Ⓑ Ⓒ Ⓓ   13. Ⓐ Ⓑ Ⓒ Ⓓ   18. Ⓐ Ⓑ Ⓒ Ⓓ   23. Ⓐ Ⓑ Ⓒ Ⓓ
4. Ⓐ Ⓑ Ⓒ Ⓓ   9. Ⓐ Ⓑ Ⓒ Ⓓ   14. Ⓐ Ⓑ Ⓒ Ⓓ   19. Ⓐ Ⓑ Ⓒ Ⓓ   24. Ⓐ Ⓑ Ⓒ Ⓓ
5. Ⓐ Ⓑ Ⓒ Ⓓ   10. Ⓐ Ⓑ Ⓒ Ⓓ   15. Ⓐ Ⓑ Ⓒ Ⓓ   20. Ⓐ Ⓑ Ⓒ Ⓓ   25. Ⓐ Ⓑ Ⓒ Ⓓ

Mechanical Comprehension—Subtest 8

1. Ⓐ Ⓑ Ⓒ Ⓓ   6. Ⓐ Ⓑ Ⓒ Ⓓ   11. Ⓐ Ⓑ Ⓒ Ⓓ   16. Ⓐ Ⓑ Ⓒ Ⓓ   21. Ⓐ Ⓑ Ⓒ Ⓓ
2. Ⓐ Ⓑ Ⓒ Ⓓ   7. Ⓐ Ⓑ Ⓒ Ⓓ   12. Ⓐ Ⓑ Ⓒ Ⓓ   17. Ⓐ Ⓑ Ⓒ Ⓓ   22. Ⓐ Ⓑ Ⓒ Ⓓ
3. Ⓐ Ⓑ Ⓒ Ⓓ   8. Ⓐ Ⓑ Ⓒ Ⓓ   13. Ⓐ Ⓑ Ⓒ Ⓓ   18. Ⓐ Ⓑ Ⓒ Ⓓ   23. Ⓐ Ⓑ Ⓒ Ⓓ
4. Ⓐ Ⓑ Ⓒ Ⓓ   9. Ⓐ Ⓑ Ⓒ Ⓓ   14. Ⓐ Ⓑ Ⓒ Ⓓ   19. Ⓐ Ⓑ Ⓒ Ⓓ   24. Ⓐ Ⓑ Ⓒ Ⓓ
5. Ⓐ Ⓑ Ⓒ Ⓓ   10. Ⓐ Ⓑ Ⓒ Ⓓ   15. Ⓐ Ⓑ Ⓒ Ⓓ   20. Ⓐ Ⓑ Ⓒ Ⓓ   25. Ⓐ Ⓑ Ⓒ Ⓓ

Assembling Objects—Subtest 9

1. Ⓐ Ⓑ Ⓒ Ⓓ   5. Ⓐ Ⓑ Ⓒ Ⓓ   9. Ⓐ Ⓑ Ⓒ Ⓓ   13. Ⓐ Ⓑ Ⓒ Ⓓ
2. Ⓐ Ⓑ Ⓒ Ⓓ   6. Ⓐ Ⓑ Ⓒ Ⓓ   10. Ⓐ Ⓑ Ⓒ Ⓓ   14. Ⓐ Ⓑ Ⓒ Ⓓ
3. Ⓐ Ⓑ Ⓒ Ⓓ   7. Ⓐ Ⓑ Ⓒ Ⓓ   11. Ⓐ Ⓑ Ⓒ Ⓓ   15. Ⓐ Ⓑ Ⓒ Ⓓ
4. Ⓐ Ⓑ Ⓒ Ⓓ   8. Ⓐ Ⓑ Ⓒ Ⓓ   12. Ⓐ Ⓑ Ⓒ Ⓓ   16. Ⓐ Ⓑ Ⓒ Ⓓ

Diagnostic Test

GENERAL SCIENCE—SUBTEST 1

TIME: 11 MINUTES
25 QUESTIONS

Directions: This test has questions about science. Pick the best answer for each question, then blacken the space on your separate answer form that has the same number and letter as your choice.

Here is a sample question.

1. An example of a chemical change is

(A) melting ice.
(B) breaking glass.
(C) rusting metal.
(D) making sawdust from wood.

The correct answer is "rusting metal," so you would fill in the space for C on your answer form.

Your score on this subtest will be based on the number of questions you answer correctly. You should try to answer every question. Do not spend too much time on any one question.

When you begin, be sure to start with question number 1 in Part 1, and number 1 in Part 1 on your answer form.

THE ACTUAL TEST WILL SAY:

Do not turn this page until told to do so.

1. A ringing bell, placed in a vacuum under a glass bell jar, will

(A) have the pitch of its sound raised.
(B) crack the thick glass of the bell jar.
(C) undergo no change.
(D) be inaudible.

2. The light-year is used to measure

(A) intensity of light.
(B) distance.
(C) time elapsed.
(D) brightness.

3. If a piece of corundum weighs 4 ounces in the air but appears to weigh only 3 ounces when submerged in water, its specific gravity is

(A) $\frac{1}{4}$.
(B) 1.
(C) 3.
(D) 4.

4. Which kind of time does a sundial keep?

   (A) legal
   (B) standard
   (C) solar
   (D) daylight savings

5. Of the following, the best conductor of heat is

   (A) asbestos.
   (B) copper.
   (C) brass.
   (D) glass.

6. Ecology can best be described as the study of

   (A) different methods of fighting pollution.
   (B) the rate of land erosion.
   (C) changes in plants.
   (D) the relationship between the environment and living things.

7. When a candle burns, the most prevalent products are

   (A) carbon monoxide and nitrogen.
   (B) carbon dioxide and nitrogen.
   (C) carbon monoxide and water.
   (D) carbon dioxide and water.

8. Of the following, the one that yields the most energy per ounce as a result of normal metabolism is

   (A) protein.
   (B) sugar.
   (C) starch.
   (D) fat.

9. The half-life of radium is 1,620 years. What fraction of a radium sample will remain after 3,240 years?

   (A) $\frac{1}{16}$

   (B) $\frac{1}{8}$

   (C) $\frac{1}{4}$

   (D) $\frac{1}{2}$

10. Which is a chemical property of water?

    (A) It freezes.
    (B) It evaporates.
    (C) It condenses.
    (D) It decomposes into gases.

11. Which of the following statements correctly refers to the process of photosynthesis?

    (A) Light is necessary for the process to occur.
    (B) Oxygen is necessary for the process to occur.
    (C) Carbon dioxide is given off during this process.
    (D) The process is carried on by all protozoa.

12. The relative humidity of the air when dew forms is

    (A) 100%.
    (B) 75%.
    (C) 50%.
    (D) 25%.

13. To start a fire with the aid of the sun, one should use a

    (A) concave lens.
    (B) flat mirror.
    (C) magnifying lens.
    (D) concave mirror.

14. The change from daylight to darkness is caused by the

    (A) inclination of the earth's axis.
    (B) force of gravitation.
    (C) rotation of the earth.
    (D) revolution of the earth.

15. A substance that is readily absorbed through the walls of the stomach is

    (A) a starch.
    (B) alcohol.
    (C) an amino acid.
    (D) ascorbic acid.

16. The positively charged particle in the nucleus of an atom is a(n)

    (A) proton.
    (B) isotope.
    (C) neutron.
    (D) electron.

17. Which one is most different from the other three?

    (A) Pluto
    (B) Moon
    (C) Neptune
    (D) Uranus

18. Sulfur is mined chiefly for the production of

    (A) sulfa drugs.
    (B) sulfanilamide.
    (C) sulfuric acid.
    (D) superphosphates.

19. To which organism is the whale most closely related?

    (A) tuna
    (B) turtle
    (C) dinosaur
    (D) horse

20. A beam of parallel rays of light is reflected from a plane (flat) mirror. After reflection, the rays will be

    (A) absorbed.
    (B) converged.
    (C) diffused.
    (D) parallel.

21. How much voltage is needed to produce a current of 0.5 ampere in a circuit that has a resistance of 24 ohms?

    (A) 6 volts
    (B) 12 volts
    (C) 24 volts
    (D) 36 volts

22. Aeration of water will produce

    (A) a loss of oxygen.
    (B) a loss of methane.
    (C) a gain of carbon dioxide.
    (D) a gain of carbon dioxide and a loss of oxygen.

23. What is the correct formula for dry ice?

    (A) HO_2
    (B) H_2O_2
    (C) CO
    (D) CO_2

24. If a person lifts a 50-lb. package to the top of a 25-foot ladder, how many foot-pounds of work are performed?

    (A) 75 foot-pounds
    (B) 500 foot-pounds
    (C) 1,000 foot-pounds
    (D) 1,250 foot-pounds

25. What chemical reaction is represented by the following equation?

$$2H_2S \rightarrow 2H_2 \uparrow + S_2 \uparrow$$

    (A) composition
    (B) decomposition
    (C) replacement
    (D) double replacement

ARITHMETIC REASONING—SUBTEST 2

TIME: 36 MINUTES
30 QUESTIONS

Directions: This test has questions about arithmetic. Each question is followed by four possible answers. Decide which answer is correct. Then, on your answer form, blacken the space that has the same number and letter as your choice. Use scratch paper for any figuring you wish to do.
Here is a sample question.

1. If 1 quart of milk costs $0.80, what is the cost of 2 quarts?

   (A) $2.00
   (B) $1.60
   (C) $1.20
   (D) $1.00

The cost of 2 quarts is $1.60; therefore, answer B is correct.
Your score on this test will be based on the number of questions you answer correctly. You should try to answer every question. Do not spend too much time on any one question.
Notice that Part 2 begins with question number 1. When you begin, be sure to mark your first answer next to number 1 on your answer form.

THE ACTUAL TEST WILL SAY:

Do not turn this page until told to do so.

1. The Hamiltons bought a table that was marked $400. On the installment plan, they made a down payment equal to 25 percent of the marked price, plus 12 monthly payments of $30 each. How much more than the marked price did they pay by buying it this way?

   (A) $25
   (B) $50
   (C) $60
   (D) $460

2. A scientist planted 120 seeds, of which 90 sprouted. What percentage of the seeds failed to sprout?

   (A) 25%
   (B) 24%
   (C) 30%
   (D) 75%

3. An airplane traveled 1,000 miles in 2 hours and 30 minutes. What was the average rate or speed, in miles per hour, for the trip?

   (A) 200 miles per hour
   (B) 300 miles per hour
   (C) 400 miles per hour
   (D) 500 miles per hour

4. What is the value of this expression?

   $$\frac{0.05 \times 4}{0.1}$$

   (A) 20
   (B) 2
   (C) 0.2
   (D) 0.02

5. Mackenzie's bank balance was $2,674. Her next four transactions were as follows:

   −$348, +$765, +$802, −$518

   What was her bank balance after the fourth transaction had posted?

   (A) $5,107
   (B) $4,241
   (C) $3,475
   (D) $3,375

6. A snack bar sold $12\frac{1}{2}$ gallons of milk at 35 cents a pint. How much did the snack bar receive for the milk?

   (A) $33.60
   (B) $34.00
   (C) $35.00
   (D) $32.20

7. A square measures 9 feet on a side. If each side of the square is increased by 3 feet, how many square feet are added to the area?

   (A) 144 square feet
   (B) 81 square feet
   (C) 60 square feet
   (D) 63 square feet

8. What is the average of $\frac{1}{4}$ and $\frac{1}{6}$?

   (A) $\frac{5}{24}$

   (B) $\frac{7}{24}$

   (C) $\frac{5}{12}$

   (D) $\frac{1}{5}$

9. Travis' salary was increased from $260 per week to $290 per week. What was the increase in his salary to the nearest percent?

   (A) 12%
   (B) 11%
   (C) 10%
   (D) 9%

10. If 1 pound, 12 ounces of fish costs $2.24, what is the cost of the fish per pound?

    (A) $1.20
    (B) $1.28
    (C) $1.24
    (D) $1.40

11. A front lawn measures 25 feet in length and 15 feet in width. The back lawn of the same house measures 50 feet in length and 30 feet in width. What is the ratio of the area of the front lawn to the area of the back lawn?

    (A) 1:2
    (B) 2:3
    (C) 3:4
    (D) 1:4

12. The price of a used car was increased from $6,400 to $7,200. What was the percentage increase?

    (A) 10%
    (B) 11.25%
    (C) 12.5%
    (D) 15%

13. What is the next term in this series:

    $3\frac{1}{2}, 2\frac{1}{4}, 13\frac{1}{4}, 12,$ _____?

    (A) $1\frac{1}{4}$

    (B) $10\frac{3}{4}$

    (C) 23

    (D) $14\frac{1}{2}$

14. A movie theater opens at 10:00 A.M. and closes at 11:30 P.M. If a complete showing of a movie takes 2 hours and 15 minutes, how many complete showings are given at the movie theater each day?

   (A) 5
   (B) 6
   (C) 7
   (D) 8

15. At a concert, orchestra seats sell for $20 each, and balcony seats sell for $10 each. If 324 orchestra seats were occupied, and the box office collected $10,000, how many balcony seats were sold?

   (A) 375
   (B) 352
   (C) 330
   (D) 310

16. In a certain city, taxicab fare is $0.80 for the first $\frac{1}{4}$ mile, and $0.20 for each additional $\frac{1}{4}$ mile. How far, in miles, can a passenger travel for $5.00?

   (A) 5 miles
   (B) $4\frac{1}{4}$ miles
   (C) $5\frac{1}{2}$ miles
   (D) $5\frac{3}{4}$ miles

17. A scale blueprint drawing of a building has a scale of 1 inch to 40 feet. How many inches on the drawing represent a distance of 175 feet on the blueprint?

   (A) $4\frac{1}{8}$
   (B) $4\frac{3}{8}$
   (C) $4\frac{1}{2}$
   (D) $4\frac{3}{4}$

18. The wholesale list price of a watch is $50. A dealer bought a shipment of watches at a discount of 20 percent and sold the watches at 10 percent above the wholesale list price. What was the profit on each watch?

   (A) $8
   (B) $10
   (C) $12
   (D) $15

19. The minute hand of a clock is missing, but the hour hand is on the 11-minute mark. What time was it when the clock broke?

   (A) 5 minutes after 11
   (B) 11 minutes after 12
   (C) 12 minutes after 2
   (D) 20 minutes after 1

20. During a season a professional basketball player tried 320 shots and made 272 of them. What percentage of the shots tried were successful?

   (A) 85%
   (B) 80%
   (C) 75%
   (D) 70%

21. A painter and a helper spent 3 days painting a house. The painter received twice as much as the helper. If the two men were paid $375 total for the job, how much did the painter receive?

   (A) $175
   (B) $200
   (C) $225
   (D) $250

22. What is the difference between a 50% discount and a discount of $33\frac{1}{3}$ %?

   (A) 0.17
   (B) $\frac{1}{3}$
   (C) 0.25
   (D) $\frac{1}{6}$

23. What is the value of $3a^2 - 2a + 5$ when $a = 4$?

   (A) 43
   (B) 45
   (C) 61
   (D) 21

24. The following table gives the annual premiums for a life insurance policy based on the age of the holder when the policy is taken out.

Age in Years	Premium per $1,000
22	$18
30	$22
38	$28
46	$38

   Over 20 years, how much is saved by taking out a $1,000 policy at age 30, rather than at age 46?

   (A) $16
   (B) $32
   (C) $320
   (D) $400

25. A chair was marked for sale at $240. This sale price was 25 percent less than the original price. What was the original price?

   (A) $300
   (B) $280
   (C) $320
   (D) $60

26. What is the quotient when 0.675 is divided by 0.9?

   (A) 7.5
   (B) 0.075
   (C) 75
   (D) 0.75

27. On May 15, an electric meter read 5,472 kilowatt-hours. The following month, on June 15, the meter read 5,687 kilowatt-hours. The utility charges the following rates for electric service.

   First 10 kilowatt-hours—$2.48

   Next 45 kilowatt-hours—$0.16 per kilowatt-hour

   Next 55 kilowatt-hours—$0.12 per kilowatt-hour

   More than 110 kilowatt-hours—$0.07 per kilowatt-hour

   What was the total charge for the kilowatt-hours consumed during the month from May 15 to June 15?

   (A) $22.53
   (B) $23.63
   (C) $22.63
   (D) $24.43

28. What is the difference between the square of 49 and the square of 31?

   (A) 18
   (B) 1.4322
   (C) 1,440
   (D) 2,056

29. A rectangular auditorium contains x rows, with y seats in each row. What is the number of seats in the auditorium?

   (A) xy
   (B) $x + y$
   (C) $x - y$
   (D) $y - x$

30. When a certain number is divided by 15, the quotient is 8 and the remainder is 7. What is the number?

   (A) 127
   (B) $8\frac{1}{2}$
   (C) $3\frac{3}{5}$
   (D) 77

Directions: This test has questions about the meanings of words. Each question has an **underlined boldface word**. You are to decide which one of the four words in the choices most nearly means the same as the underlined boldface word; then mark the space on your answer form that has the same number and letter as your choice.

Now look at the sample question below.

1. It was a **small** table.

   (A) sturdy
   (B) round
   (C) cheap
   (D) little

The question asks which of the four words means the same as the boldface word, **small**.

"Little" means the same as **small**. Answer D is the best one.

Your score on this test will be based on the number of questions you answer correctly. You should try to answer every question. Do not spend too much time on any one question.

When you begin, be sure to start with question number 1 in Part 3 of your test booklet and number 1 in Part 3 on your answer form.

THE ACTUAL TEST WILL SAY:

Do not turn this page until told to do so.

---

1. **Subsume** most nearly means

   (A) understate.
   (B) absorb.
   (C) include.
   (D) belong.

2. Our committee reached **consensus**.

   (A) accord
   (B) abridgment
   (C) presumption
   (D) quota

3. **Altercation** most nearly means

   (A) defeat.
   (B) concurrence.
   (C) quarrel.
   (D) vexation.

4. Don't accuse him of being **irresolute**.

   (A) wavering
   (B) insubordinate
   (C) impudent
   (D) unobservant

5. **Laconic** most nearly means

   (A) slothful.
   (B) concise.
   (C) punctual.
   (D) melancholy.

6. **Audition** most nearly means

   (A) reception.
   (B) contest.
   (C) hearing.
   (D) display.

7. The job was filled by a **novice**.

   (A) volunteer
   (B) expert
   (C) beginner
   (D) amateur

8. A **conciliatory** attitude sometimes helps.

   (A) pacific
   (B) contentious
   (C) obligatory
   (D) offensive

9. The drug will **counteract** any effect.

   (A) undermine
   (B) censure
   (C) preserve
   (D) neutralize

10. **Precedent** most nearly means

    (A) example.
    (B) theory.
    (C) law.
    (D) conformity.

11. **Diaphanous** most nearly means

    (A) transparent.
    (B) opaque.
    (C) diaphragmatic.
    (D) diffusive.

12. We **deferred** our judgment.

    (A) reversed
    (B) accelerated
    (C) rejected
    (D) delayed

13. To **accentuate** most nearly means to

    (A) modify.
    (B) hasten.
    (C) sustain.
    (D) intensify.

14. **Authentic** most nearly means

    (A) detailed.
    (B) genuine.
    (C) valuable.
    (D) practical.

15. **Unanimity** most nearly means

    (A) emphasis.
    (B) namelessness.
    (C) disagreement.
    (D) concurrence.

16. Their actions made them **notorious**.

    (A) condemned
    (B) unpleasant
    (C) vexatious
    (D) infamous

17. **Previous** most nearly means

    (A) abandoned.
    (B) former.
    (C) timely.
    (D) younger.

18. Use a **flexible** metal.

    (A) breakable
    (B) flammable
    (C) pliable
    (D) weak

19. **Option** most nearly means

    (A) use.
    (B) choice.
    (C) value.
    (D) preference.

20. You should **verify** the facts.

    (A) examine
    (B) explain
    (C) confirm
    (D) guarantee

21. **Pert** most nearly means

    (A) ill.
    (B) lazy.
    (C) slow.
    (D) saucy.

22. **Aesthetic** most nearly means

    (A) sentient.
    (B) sensitive.
    (C) tasteful.
    (D) inartistic.

23. **Decimation** most nearly means

(A) severe damage or injury.
(B) complete annihilation.
(C) truce.
(D) brawl.

24. She made an **indignant** response.

(A) angry
(B) poor
(C) indigent
(D) lazy

25. **Cliché** most nearly means

(A) commonplace.
(B) banality.
(C) hackney.
(D) platitude.

26. **Harmony** most nearly means

(A) rhythm.
(B) pleasure.
(C) discord.
(D) agreement.

27. **Indolent** most nearly means

(A) moderate.
(B) hopeless.
(C) lazy.
(D) idle.

28. His **respiration** was impaired.

(A) recovery
(B) breathing
(C) pulsation
(D) sweating

29. The job requires a **vigilant** attitude.

(A) sensible
(B) watchful
(C) suspicious
(D) restless

30. **Incidental** most nearly means

(A) independent.
(B) needless.
(C) infrequent.
(D) casual.

31. To **succumb** most nearly means to

(A) aid.
(B) oppose.
(C) yield.
(D) check.

32. That solution is not **feasible**.

(A) capable
(B) harmful
(C) beneficial
(D) practicable

33. **Versatile** most nearly means

(A) well-known.
(B) up-to-date.
(C) many-sided.
(D) ambidextrous.

34. His **imperturbability** helps in a crisis.

(A) obstinacy
(B) calmness
(C) sagacity
(D) confusion

35. **Strident** most nearly means

(A) swaggering.
(B) domineering.
(C) angry.
(D) harsh.

PARAGRAPH COMPREHENSION—SUBTEST 4

TIME: 13 MINUTES
15 QUESTIONS

Directions: This test is a test of your ability to understand what you read. In this section you will find one or more paragraphs of reading material followed by incomplete statements or questions.

You are to read the paragraph and select which of the four lettered choices best completes the statement or answers the question. When you have selected your answer, blacken the correct numbered letter on your answer sheet.

Now look at the sample question below.

In certain areas water is so scarce that every attempt is made to conserve it. For instance, on one oasis in the Sahara Desert the amount of water necessary for each date palm tree has been carefully determined.

1. How much water is each tree given?

   (A) no water at all
   (B) exactly the amount required
   (C) water only if it is healthy
   (D) water on alternate days

The amount of water each tree required has been carefully determined, so answer B is correct.

Your score on this subtest will be based on the number of questions you answer correctly. You should try to answer every question. Do not spend too much time on any one question.

When you begin, be sure to start with question number 1 in Part 4 of your test booklet and number 1 in Part 4 on your answer form.

THE ACTUAL TEST WILL SAY:

Do not turn this page until told to do so.

---

1. Twenty-five percent of all household burglaries can be attributed to unlocked windows or doors. Crime is the result of opportunity plus desire.

   To prevent crime, it is each individual's responsibility to

   (A) provide the opportunity.
   (B) provide the desire.
   (C) prevent the opportunity.
   (D) prevent the desire.

2. From a building designer's standpoint, three things that make a home livable are the client, the building site, and the amount of money the client has to spend.

   According to the passage, to make a home livable

   (A) the prospective piece of land makes little difference.
   (B) it can be built on any piece of land.
   (C) the design must fit the owner's income and the site.
   (D) the design must fit the designer's income.

3. Family camping has been described as the "biggest single growth industry in the booming travel/leisure market." Camping ranges from backpacking to living in motor homes with complete creature comforts. It is both an end in itself and a magic carpet to a wide variety of other forms of outdoor recreation.

It can be inferred from the passage that the LEAST luxurious form of camping is

(A) backpacking.
(B) travel trailers.
(C) truck campers.
(D) motor homes.

4. Most drivers try to drive safely. A major part of safe driving is driving at the right speed. But what is the "right" speed? Is it 20 miles per hour, or 35, or 60? That question may be hard to answer. On some city streets and in heavy traffic, 20 miles per hour could be too fast, even if it's within the posted speed limit. On a superhighway, 35 miles per hour could be too slow. Of course, a good driver must follow the speed limit, but he must also use good judgment. The right speed will vary depending on the number of cars, the road surface and its condition, and the driver's visibility.

The general theme of this passage is that a good driver

(A) drives at 35 miles an hour.
(B) adjusts to different driving conditions.
(C) always drives at the same speed.
(D) always follows the speed limit.

5. Gardening can be an easygoing hobby, a scientific pursuit, an opportunity for exercise and fresh air, a significant source of food to help balance the family budget, a means of expression in art and beauty, an applied experiment in green plant growth, or all of these things together.

All of the following are made possible by gardening according to the passage EXCEPT

(A) relaxation.
(B) exercise.
(C) experimentation.
(D) hard work.

6. About three-fourths of the surface of the earth is water. Of the 336 million cubic miles of water, most (97.2 percent) is found in the oceans and is salty. Glaciers hold another 2 percent of the total. Less than 1 percent (0.8 percent) is available as freshwater for people to use—and much of that is not near people who need it.

The amount of freshwater available for people to use is

(A) 97.2%.
(B) 0.8%.
(C) 2%.
(D) 75%.

7. Early settlers in the United States made the most of the herring fishing season. When spring came, the fish arrived in great numbers in the rivers. No nets or hooks were needed. Men used what was called a *pinfold*, a large circular pen built in shallow water. It was made by driving stakes closely together in the floor of the river.

A pinfold was made with

(A) hooks and nets.
(B) only nets.
(C) stakes driven into the river bottom.
(D) fishing rods.

8. The powers of the United States government are divided. The legislative branch, composed of the two houses of Congress (the House of Representatives and the Senate), makes the laws. The executive branch, made up of the president and the heads of the different departments, puts the laws into effect. The judicial branch, made up of the courts, tries cases when laws are broken. The idea behind this organization is to prevent one part or branch of government from having too much power relative to the other branches.

As a result of the divided powers of government,

(A) Congress rules the United States.
(B) the president rules the United States.
(C) power is shared.
(D) no branch has power.

9. A narcotic is a drug that, in proper doses, relieves pain and induces profound sleep, but which, in poisonous doses, induces stupor, coma, or convulsions. Narcotics tend to be habit-forming and, in many instances, repeated doses lead to addiction.

A proper dose of narcotic induces

(A) coma.
(B) convulsions.
(C) deep sleep.
(D) stupor.

10. Because nitrogen, phosphorus, and potassium are used by plants in large amounts, these nutrients are likely to be deficient in the soil. When you buy a fertilizer, therefore, you generally buy it for its content of these materials.

Unfertilized soil naturally deficient in nitrogen, phosphoric oxide, and potash probably lacks these nutrients because

(A) they are not soluble.
(B) manufacturers do not recommend them to gardeners.
(C) they are rare elements never found in the earth.
(D) plants use them up in large quantities.

11. Where does pollution come from? It comes from a wide variety of sources, including furnaces, smokestacks, incinerators, power-generating stations, industrial plants, dirt and dust caused by tearing down old buildings and putting up new ones, ordinary street dirt, restaurants that emit smoke and odors, cars, buses, trucks, planes, and coal- or diesel-burning motor ships. Sixty percent of pollution is caused by motor vehicle exhausts, while another thirty percent is due to industry.

Most air pollution is caused by

(A) industry and incinerators.
(B) cars, trucks, and buses.
(C) airplanes.
(D) smokestacks of buildings.

12. The use of sunglasses as an aid to vision is important. For the most part, the eye is a daytime instrument: It requires light to work properly. However, too much bright light and glare can create discomfort; as a result the eyes blink, squint, get tears, or have trouble seeing well. Sunglasses help by keeping much of this bright light and glare from reaching the eyes.

The main purpose of sunglasses is to

(A) hide the eyes.
(B) screen out harmful rays of the sun.
(C) remove the need for regular glasses.
(D) protect the eyes from dirt.

13. Would you like to be good at a trade? Would you like to know a skill that pays well? One sure way to skill, good pay, and regular work is to train on the job. This is called *apprentice training*. While it is not the only way to learn, apprentice training has good points. You can earn while you learn. You will know the skill "from the ground up," and you can advance on the job.

Apprentice training is described here by discussing

(A) both sides.
(B) the good side.
(C) the bad side.
(D) a specific trade.

14. When you work at a job covered by Social Security, you and your employer contribute equal amounts. Your portion of the tax is taken from your wages or paycheck before you receive it. This is called a *deduction*.

Which of these statements is true according to the passage?

(A) Total tax rate is retirement rate plus insurance rate.
(B) Insurance rates are higher than retirement rates.
(C) Money taken from your pay is called a deduction.
(D) Only your employer contributes to Social Security.

15. Nucleic acids are found in all living organisms, from viruses to humans. Their name refers to their discovery in the nuclei of white blood cells and fish sperm by Swiss physiologist Johann Miescher in 1869. However, it is now well established that nucleic acids occur outside the cell nucleus as well.

Nucleic acids are found

(A) only in cells of humans.
(B) only in viruses.
(C) in all living cells.
(D) only in white blood cells.

MATHEMATICS KNOWLEDGE—SUBTEST 5

TIME: 24 MINUTES
25 QUESTIONS

Directions: This is a test of your ability to solve general mathematical problems. Each problem is followed by four answer choices. Select the correct response from the choices given, then mark the space on your answer form that has the same number and letter as your choice. Use scratch paper to do any figuring that you wish.

Now look at this sample problem.

1. If $x + 8 = 9$, then x is equal to

(A) 0.

(B) 1.

(C) 3.

(D) $\dfrac{9}{8}$.

The correct answer is 1, so B is the correct response.

Your score on this test will be based on the number of questions you answer correctly. You should try to answer every question. Do not spend too much time on any one question.

Start with question number 1 in Part 5. Mark your answer for this question next to number 1, Part 5, on your answer form.

THE ACTUAL TEST WILL SAY:

Do not turn this page until told to do so.

1. Which of the following is the smallest prime number greater than 200?

   (A) 201
   (B) 205
   (C) 211
   (D) 214

2. If 40 percent is equal to the fraction $\dfrac{x}{30}$, what is the value of x?

   (A) 0.4
   (B) 15
   (C) 1,200
   (D) 12

3. The expression "5 factorial" equals

   (A) 125.
   (B) 120.
   (C) 25.
   (D) 10.

4. What is the result of subtracting $3x^2 - 5x - 1$ from $8x^2 + 2x - 9$?

   (A) $5x^2 - 3x - 10$
   (B) $-5x^2 - 3x - 10$
   (C) $5x^2 + 7x - 8$
   (D) $-5x^2 - 7x + 8$

5. What is the meaning of the statement $-30 < -5$?

   (A) 30 is greater than 5.
   (B) 30 is less than minus 5.
   (C) Negative 30 is less than negative 5.
   (D) Negative 30 is greater than negative 5.

6. Solve for x: $8x - 2 - 5x = 8$

   (A) $x = 1.3$

   (B) $x = 2\frac{1}{2}$

   (C) $x = 3\frac{1}{3}$

   (D) $x = -7$

7. Maddalyn has $500 in a bank account. Every week, she writes out a check for $50. If she doesn't make any new deposits, what will her bank account hold x weeks from now?

   (A) $500 + $50x$

   (B) $500 - $50x$

   (C) $550 - x$

   (D) $500 + $50 + x$

8. When the temperature is 20°C, what is it on the Fahrenheit (F) scale? Use the following formula:

   $$°F = \left(\frac{9}{5} \times °C\right) + 32$$

   (A) $93\frac{3}{5}$ degrees

   (B) 78 degrees

   (C) $62\frac{3}{5}$ degrees

   (D) 68 degrees

9. The perimeter of a rectangle is 38 inches. If the length is 3 inches more than the width, find the width.

   (A) $17\frac{1}{2}$ inches

   (B) 8 inches

   (C) 11 inches

   (D) $14\frac{1}{2}$ inches

10. Find the square root of 85 to the nearest tenth.
    (A) 9.1
    (B) 9.2
    (C) 9.3
    (D) 9.4

11. If $5x = 30$, then x is equal to

    (A) 150
    (B) 25
    (C) 6
    (D) 0.6

12. What is the product of $(a - 5)$ and $(a + 3)$?

    (A) $a^2 - 15$
    (B) $a^2 + 2a - 15$
    (C) $a^2 - 2a - 15$
    (D) $a^2 - 2$

13. Solve for z: $3z - 5 + 2z = 25 - 5z$

    (A) $z = 0$
    (B) $z = 3$
    (C) $z = -3$
    (D) no solution

14. A park commissioner designs a new playground in the shape of a pentagon. If he plans to have a fountain at every corner of the park, how many fountains will there be?

    (A) 4
    (B) 5
    (C) 6
    (D) 7

15. If one of the angles of a right triangle is 30 degrees, what are the other two angles?

    (A) 30 degrees, 120 degrees
    (B) 60 degrees, 45 degrees
    (C) 60 degrees, 90 degrees
    (D) 45 degrees, 90 degrees

16. What is the value of x in the equation $\frac{x}{2} = 7$?

    (A) $x = 14$

    (B) $x = 3\frac{1}{2}$

    (C) $x = 9$

    (D) $x = 5$

17. Divide $15a^3b^2c$ by $5abc$.

(A) $10abc$

(B) $3abc$

(C) $5a^2b^2$

(D) $3a^2b$

18. Two circles have the same center. If their radii are 7 inches and 10 inches, find the area that is part of the larger circle but not the smaller one.

(A) 3 square inches

(B) 17 square inches

(C) 51π square inches

(D) 70π square inches

19. Amanda's average grade on a set of five tests was 88 percent. She can remember only that the first four grades were 78 percent, 86 percent, 96 percent, and 94 percent. What was the grade on her fifth test?

(A) 88

(B) 86

(C) 84

(D) 82

20. How many cubic yards of concrete are needed to make a cement floor that is 9 feet by 12 feet by 6 inches thick?

(A) 2 cubic yards

(B) 18 cubic yards

(C) 54 cubic yards

(D) 648 cubic yards

21. A wildlife preserve is laid out in the shape of a perfect circle whose radius is 14 miles. The lions' territory in this preserve is shaped like a wedge and has a fence around it. Two inner sides of a fence meet at a 90-degree angle in the center of the preserve. How much territory do the lions have?

(A) 140 square miles

(B) $3\frac{1}{2}$ square miles

(C) 210 square miles

(D) 154 square miles

22. Find the value of $(-3)^4 + (-2)^4 + (-1)^4$.

(A) 98

(B) -98

(C) -21

(D) 21

23. A cylindrical can has a radius of 7 inches and a height of 15 inches. How many gallons of milk can it hold? (There are 231 cubic inches in a gallon.)

(A) 15 gallons

(B) 14 gallons

(C) 140 gallons

(D) 10 gallons

24. A 10-foot-high ladder is resting against an 8-foot-high wall surrounding a tennis court. If the top of the ladder is exactly even with the top of the wall, how far is the base of the ladder from the wall?

(A) 18 feet

(B) 6 feet

(C) 12 feet

(D) 9 feet

25. Ten ounces of liquid contain 20 percent fruit juice and 80 percent water. The mixture is diluted by adding 40 additional ounces of water. What is the percentage of fruit juice in the new solution?

(A) 4%

(B) 10%

(C) 20%

(D) 40%

TIME: 9 MINUTES
20 QUESTIONS

Directions: This is a test of your knowledge of electrical, radio, and electronics information. You are to select the correct response from the choices given. Then mark the space on your answer form that has the same number and letter as your choice.

Now look at the sample question below.

1. What does the abbreviation AC stand for?

(A) additional charge
(B) alternating coil
(C) alternating current
(D) ampere current

The correct answer is "alternating current," so C is the correct response.

Your score on this test will be based on the number of questions you answer correctly. You should try to answer every question. Do not spend too much time on any one question.

When you are told to begin, be sure to start with question number 1 in Part 6 of your test booklet and number 1 in Part 6 of your answer form.

THE ACTUAL TEST WILL SAY:

Do not turn this page until told to do so.

1. Flux is placed inside electrical solder in order to

    (A) clean the connections during soldering and prevent oxidation.
    (B) raise the melting point of silver.
    (C) increase the conductivity of the connection.
    (D) act as an insulator within the connection.

2. A cold solder connection is

    (A) clean and shiny in appearance.
    (B) dull and brittle in appearance.
    (C) a connection that is properly soldered.
    (D) a connection achieved with a low-wattage iron.

3. A current reading of 1 mA is equivalent to

    (A) 0.1 ampere.
    (B) 0.001 ampere.
    (C) 1 ampere.
    (D) 10 amperes.

4. An ohmmeter is used to check the condition of a fuse. If the fuse is good, the meter reading should be

    (A) 100K ohms.
    (B) 120 volts.
    (C) zero.
    (D) infinity.

5. Which of the following metals has the highest conductivity?

    (A) silver
    (B) copper
    (C) aluminum
    (D) zinc

6. Stranded wire is used in extension cords primarily because

   (A) it costs less than solid wire.
   (B) it is flexible.
   (C) it is a better conductor than solid wire.
   (D) it is the only type of wire available in that gauge.

7. A toaster is connected to 120 volts and draws 10 amperes when in use. How much power does this appliance consume?

   (A) 12 watts
   (B) 120 watts
   (C) 110 watts
   (D) 1,200 watts

8. How many cells does a 12-volt carbon-zinc car battery contain?

   (A) 12
   (B) 8
   (C) 6
   (D) 1

9. The property of a circuit that opposes any change in current is

   (A) inductance.
   (B) capacitance.
   (C) resistance.
   (D) reactance.

10. Of the choices listed below, which component is an example of a transducer?

   (A) resistor
   (B) switch
   (C) diode
   (D) speaker

11. The period of a sine wave is determined by

   (A) its amplitude.
   (B) the distance between the crests of the wave.
   (C) the number of hertz in 1 second.
   (D) the time it takes to complete 1 hertz.

12. What is the effective value of an AC signal of 141 volts peak value?

   (A) 141 volts
   (B) 100 volts
   (C) 120 volts
   (D) 56.5 volts

13. The frequency response of the human ear is in the range of

   (A) 16 to 16,000 Hz.
   (B) 20,000 to 30,000 Hz.
   (C) 50 KHz to 1 MHz.
   (D) 1 MHz to 1,000 MHz.

14. One kilowatt is equivalent to

   (A) 1 watt.
   (B) 10 watts.
   (C) 1,000 watts.
   (D) 1,000 volts.

15. What is the total resistance in this circuit?

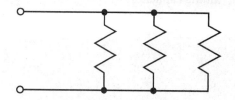

(Each resistor = 900 ohms)

   (A) 100 ohms
   (B) 300 ohms
   (C) 900 ohms
   (D) 1,000 ohms

16.

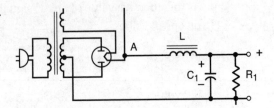

In the above schematic of a DC power supply, an oscilloscope connected at points *A* and *B* would display what type of waveform?

(A) square wave
(B) sine wave
(C) pulsating DC
(D) sawtooth wave

17. Referring to the schematic in 16 above, what is the purpose of C_1?

(A) to bleed R_1
(B) to increase the output voltage
(C) to change the incoming AC to DC
(D) to filter the AC ripple voltage

18. Which is the correct schematic symbol for a tuning capacitor?

(A)

(B)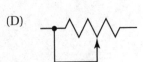

(C)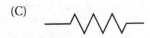

(D)

19.

What is the equivalent solid state component of the vacuum tube drawn above?

(A) semiconductor rectifier
(B) silicon-controlled rectifier
(C) zener diode
(D) transistor

20.

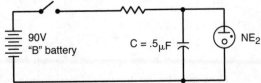

Which choice best describes the operation of the circuit drawn in the above schematic?

(A) The lamp will light constantly when the switch is closed.
(B) The lamp will light only when the switch is open.
(C) The lamp will flash when the switch is closed.
(D) The lamp will not light with the switch open or closed.

AUTOMOTIVE & SHOP INFORMATION—SUBTEST 7

TIME: 11 MINUTES
25 QUESTIONS

Directions: This test has questions about automobiles, as well as tools and common shop terminology and practices. Pick the best answer for each question, then blacken the space on your separate answer form that has the same number and letter as your choice.

Here is a sample question.

1. The most commonly used fuel for running automobile engines is

(A) kerosene.
(B) benzene.
(C) crude oil.
(D) gasoline.

Gasoline is the most commonly used fuel, so D is the correct answer.

Your score on this test will be based on the number of questions you answer correctly. You should try to answer every question. Do not spend too much time on any one question.

When you are told to begin, be sure to start with question number 1 in Part 7 of your test booklet and number 1 in Part 7 on your separate answer form.

THE ACTUAL TEST WILL SAY:

Do not turn this page until told to do so.

---

1. Underinflating a tire will cause excessive wear on

   (A) the center of the tread.
   (B) both outside edges of the tread.
   (C) the bead.
   (D) the sidewalls.

2. A vehicle's "track" is measured from

   (A) bumper to bumper.
   (B) left front wheel to right rear wheel.
   (C) center of left wheel to center of right wheel.
   (D) fender to fender.

3. The resistor used to drop voltage to the ignition coil is called the

   (A) battery resistor.
   (B) ballast resistor.
   (C) ignition resistor.
   (D) dropping resistor.

4. Syncromesh units are used in standard transmissions because they

   (A) are stronger.
   (B) eliminate grinding of the gears.
   (C) cost less.
   (D) give an overdrive effect.

5. The vacuum modulator in an automatic transmission

   (A) allows the transmission only to downshift.
   (B) controls the shifts of the transmission while sensing the engine load.
   (C) creates a vacuum to shift the clutches.
   (D) modulates vacuum for ignition spark advance when overheating.

6. A clutch pedal must have free play so that

(A) the clutch grabs early.
(B) the clutch grabs late.
(C) there is clearance between the disc and the flywheel.
(D) there is clearance between the clutch fingers and the throwout bearing.

7. A limited slip differential is used to

(A) allow a car to climb hills faster.
(B) give better traction on ice.
(C) keep the rear end cooler.
(D) give a softer ride.

8. What are the two main functions of the ignition system?

(A) to provide a primary arc and a secondary spark
(B) to provide a spark and a means to decrease it
(C) to provide a high-voltage spark and the means to time the engine
(D) to provide a path for the wires and the spark plugs

9. In an ignition system using a resistor in the primary circuit, the resistor is located between the

(A) battery and the ignition switch.
(B) ignition switch and the coil.
(C) coil and the distributor points.
(D) distributor points and the condenser.

10. The magnetic field within an alternator is produced by the

(A) rotor.
(B) stator.
(C) diodes.
(D) heat sink.

11. If a horn sounds continuously but the horn relay is good, the most likely cause is

(A) a short in the horn.
(B) a grounded horn.
(C) an open wire at the horn button.
(D) a grounded wire at the horn button.

12. The purpose of the rubber cups in the brake wheel cylinders is to

(A) push out the brake shoes.
(B) prevent brake fluid from leaking out of the cylinder.
(C) maintain the springs in position.
(D) absorb the shock of the brake application.

13. The metering valve in a hydraulic brake system

(A) holds off pressure to the front brakes.
(B) holds off pressure to the rear brakes.
(C) equalizes pressure to all four wheel brakes.
(D) warns the driver of brake system failure.

14. The order in which the events occur in the four-stroke cycle engine are

(A) intake, compression, exhaust, power.
(B) intake, compression, power, exhaust.
(C) intake, power, exhaust, compression.
(D) intake, power, compression, exhaust.

15. If the piston and rod assembly is to be removed from an engine block, any ridge at the top of a cylinder

(A) should be removed using a ridge reamer.
(B) should be drilled out.
(C) should be filed down with a single cut file.
(D) does not interfere with the removal of the assembly.

16. The mitre box is used for cutting

(A) angles from 90 degrees to 45 degrees.
(B) rafters.
(C) joists.
(D) logs.

17. The coping saw is for cutting

(A) wood at any curve or angle desired.
(B) steel at any curve or angle desired.
(C) straight lines along a board.
(D) cross-cutting along a straight line.

18. Another name for the wrecking bar is

(A) lever.
(B) crowbar.
(C) slot maker.
(D) plumb bob.

19. The screwdriver with a cross or "X" on the end is called a

(A) Phillips head screwdriver.
(B) standard screwdriver.
(C) wrench.
(D) plumb bob.

20. A chisel is used to cut wood by striking it with a

(A) screwdriver.
(B) hammer.
(C) fist.
(D) level.

21. A device with glass tubes that have air bubbles in them is used to indicate when a door or window is

(A) nailed in place.
(B) warped.
(C) screwed in place.
(D) level.

22. If you wanted to cut circular holes in wood or metal, which of the following tools would you use?

(A) coping saw
(B) cross-cut saw
(C) hole saw
(D) mitre box

23. The measuring edges of a steel rule are usually graduated in what increments?

(A) $\frac{1}{8}$, $\frac{1}{16}$, $\frac{1}{32}$, and $\frac{1}{64}$ inch

(B) $\frac{1}{8}$, $\frac{1}{4}$, $\frac{1}{2}$, and 1 inch

(C) 1 mm, 10 mm, 100 mm, 1 cm
(D) 0.01 mm, 0.1 mm, 1 mm, 10 mm

24. The back saw has a(n) _____ tooth configuration and is used to cut _____, leaving a _____ piece of work.

(A) open, with the grain, smooth-finished
(B) fine, with the grain, unfinished
(C) fine, cross-grain, smooth-finished
(D) open, cross-grain, rough

25. If a cold chisel starts to "mushroom" at the head, you should remove the splintered ends with a

(A) band saw.
(B) file.
(C) grinder.
(D) pair of bolt cutters.

MECHANICAL COMPREHENSION—SUBTEST 8

TIME: 19 MINUTES
25 QUESTIONS

Directions: This test has questions about general mechanical and physical principles. Pick the best answer for each question, then blacken the space on your separate answer form that has the same number and letter as your choice.

Here is a sample question.

1. The follower is at its highest position between points

   (A) Q and R.
   (B) R and S.
   (C) S and T.
   (D) T and Q.

The correct answer is "between Q and R," so you would blacken the space for A on your answer form.

Your score on this test will be based on the number of questions you answer correctly. You should try to answer every question. Do not spend too much time on any one question.

When you are told to begin, be sure to start with question number 1 in Part 8 of your test booklet and number 1 in Part 8 of your answer form.

THE ACTUAL TEST WILL SAY:

Do not turn this page until told to do so.

---

1. Jolie is sitting in her Velocity Red RX-8 at a stoplight at an intersection. When the light turns green, she steps on the accelerator and moves forward. At the moment that the car starts to accelerate, what is her weight pushing into the seat relative to when the car was stationary?

   (A) less than when stationary
   (B) the same as when stationary
   (C) more than when stationary
   (D) cannot tell from the information given

2. To balance the scale shown, the fulcrum should be moved

   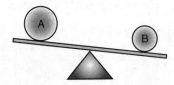

   (A) toward A.
   (B) toward B.
   (C) in either direction.
   (D) The scale cannot be balanced.

3. If the scale in Question 2 above had been balanced before you moved the fulcrum, which ball would be denser?

   (A) ball A
   (B) ball B
   (C) They have the same density.
   (D) cannot determine from the information given

4. If you are trying to cut a branch with pruning shears, where would it be best to hold the handles?

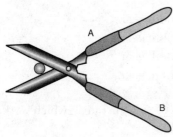

    (A) at point A
    (B) at point B
    (C) halfway between A and B
    (D) depends on the thickness of the branch

5. Which simple machine is in effect when a wrench turns a nut or a bolt?

    (A) pulley
    (B) lever
    (C) wedge
    (D) wheel and axle

6. A symmetrical wooden block balances at its center of gravity (CG). If you cut the block at its CG and weigh each part, which end would weigh more?

    (A) left part
    (B) right part
    (C) Both will weigh the same.
    (D) cannot tell from information given

7. A wrench is used to turn a bolt that has 10 threads per inch. After 12 complete turns of the wrench, the bolt will have moved

    (A) 1.0 inch.
    (B) 1.2 inches.
    (C) 1.5 inches.
    (D) 2.2 inches.

8. If gear #1 (the drive gear) is turning clockwise as indicated, in which direction will gears #2 and #3 turn?

    (A) #2 clockwise, #3 clockwise
    (B) #2 counterclockwise, #3 counter-clockwise
    (C) #2 counterclockwise, #3 clockwise
    (D) #2 clockwise, #3 counterclockwise

9. Two identical rollers have forces applied to them as below (P_1 and P_2), with the objective of getting them over the step from the lower level to the higher level. Which force must be greater to get the roller over the step?

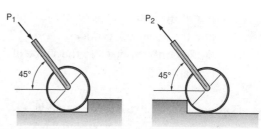

    (A) P_1
    (B) P_2
    (C) $P_1 = P_2$
    (D) cannot tell from the information given

10. Pushing a heavy square stone block up an inclined wooden ramp will be easier if you

    (A) turn the block on its side.
    (B) let the block heat up in the hot sunlight.
    (C) put the block on a wheelbarrow.
    (D) increase the angle of the ramp.

11. A half-full 100-gallon water tank is drained through a valve that has a maximum flow rate of 5 gallons per minute. How many seconds will it take to drain the tank completely?

(A) 50 seconds
(B) 100 seconds
(C) 600 seconds
(D) 1,200 seconds

12. A good example of a first-class lever is

(A) a wheelbarrow.
(B) a see-saw.
(C) a fishing pole.
(D) a wood axe.

13. Pascal's Law states that

(A) an object at rest tends to stay at rest until an outside force acts upon it.
(B) a moving object tends to move in a straight line until an outside force acts upon it.
(C) pressure applied to a completely enclosed fluid is transmitted undiminished to all parts of the fluid and the enclosing surfaces.
(D) liquid conforms itself to the shape of its container.

14. Compressing air in a closed container

(A) increases the volume and lowers the temperature.
(B) lowers the temperature and decreases the volume.
(C) increases both temperature and volume.
(D) decreases the volume and increases the temperature.

15. The greatest amount of mechanical advantage of power is attained when an 11-tooth gear drives a(n)

(A) 29-tooth gear.
(B) 11-tooth gear.
(C) 47-tooth gear.
(D) 15-tooth gear.

16. _____ is the rate at which work is performed.

(A) Torque
(B) Power
(C) Tension
(D) Force

17. Pliers are an example of a

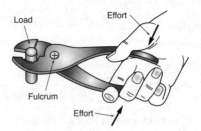

(A) first-class lever.
(B) second-class lever.
(C) third-class lever.
(D) first- and second-class lever.

18. The follower is at its highest position between points

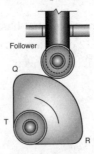

(A) Q and R.
(B) R and S.
(C) S and T.
(D) T and Q.

19. If pulley A is the driver and turns in direction 1, which pulley turns fastest?

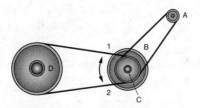

(A) A
(B) B
(C) C
(D) D

20. Which shaft or shafts are turning in the same direction as shaft X?

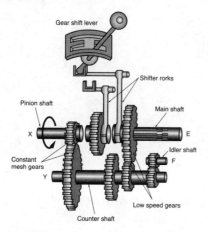

(A) Y
(B) Y and E
(C) F
(D) E and F

21. The human arm is an example of a

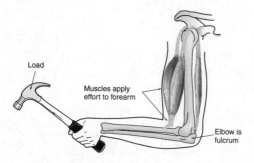

(A) first-class lever.
(B) second-class lever.
(C) third-class lever.
(D) second- and third-class lever.

22. If arm H is held fixed as gear B turns in direction 2, gear

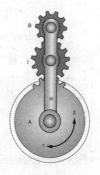

(A) A must turn in direction 1.
(B) A must turn in direction 2.
(C) I must turn in direction 2.
(D) A must be held fixed.

23. Gearset Y is

(A) rack and pinion.
(B) spur.
(C) hypoid bevel.
(D) spiral bevel.

24. If the force on piston X is 10 pounds, then the output force of piston Y will be

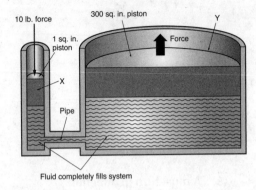

(A) 300 lbs.
(B) 30 lbs.
(C) 10 lbs.
(D) 3,000 lbs.

25. How much effort must be placed at point *A* to lift the weight at point *B*?

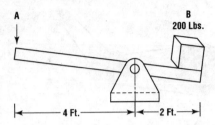

(A) 200 lbs.
(B) 4,000 lbs.
(C) 8,000 lbs.
(D) 100 lbs.

ASSEMBLING OBJECTS—SUBTEST 9

TIME: 9 MINUTES
16 QUESTIONS

Directions: This test measures your ability to picture how an object will look when its parts are mentally put together or connected. There are two types of problems. In the first type of problem, each question will show you several separate shapes, from which you will then pick the choice that best represents how the shapes would look if they were all fitted together correctly, as in the example below. There is only one best answer for each shape. Pick the best answer for each question, then blacken the space on the answer form that has the same number and letter as your choice.

Here is a sample question.

1. Which figure best shows how the objects in the group on the left will appear if they are fitted together?

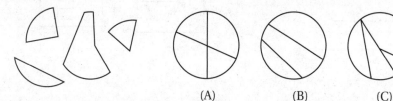

In this example, the correct answer is "D."

In the second type of problem, you will be shown two shapes and a connector line. One point on each of the shapes will be labeled with a letter (for instance, "A" on the first shape and "B" on the second shape). The ends of the connector line will be labeled with the same letters—in this case, one end with "A" and the other end with the letter "B." You will be asked which of the four figures best shows how the two shapes and a connector line in the first group will touch if the letters for each object are matched, as in the example below. There is only one best answer for each shape. Pick the best answer for each question, then blacken the space on the answer form that has the same number and letter as your choice.

Here is a sample question.

2. Which figure best shows how the objects in the group of objects on the left will touch if the letters for each object are matched?

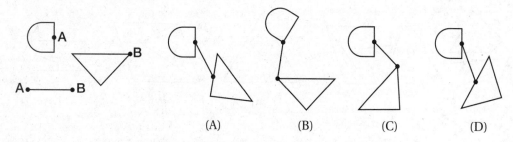

In this example, the correct answer is "C."

Your score on this test will be based on the number of questions you answer correctly. You should try to answer every question. Do not spend too much time on any one question.

When you are told to begin, be sure to start with question number 1 in Part 9 of your test booklet and number 1 in Part 9 on your separate answer form.

THE ACTUAL TEST WILL SAY:

Do not turn this page until told to do so.

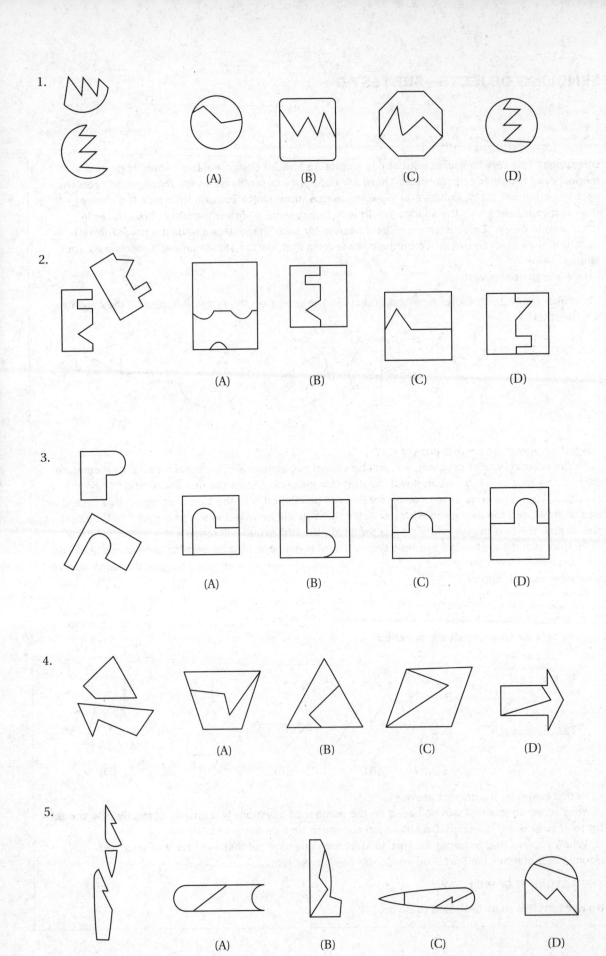

1.

(A)　　(B)　　(C)　　(D)

2.

(A)　　(B)　　(C)　　(D)

3.

(A)　　(B)　　(C)　　(D)

4.

(A)　　(B)　　(C)　　(D)

5.

(A)　　(B)　　(C)　　(D)

6.

 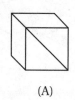 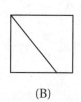 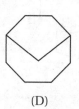 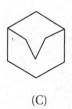

                 (A)   (B)   (C)   (D)

7.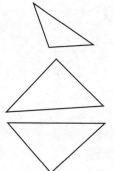

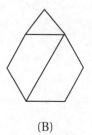 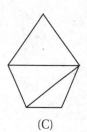 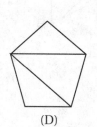

                 (A)   (B)   (C)   (D)

8.

 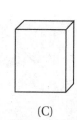 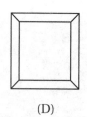

                 (A)   (B)   (C)   (D)

9.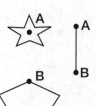

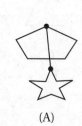   

                 (A)   (B)   (C)   (D)

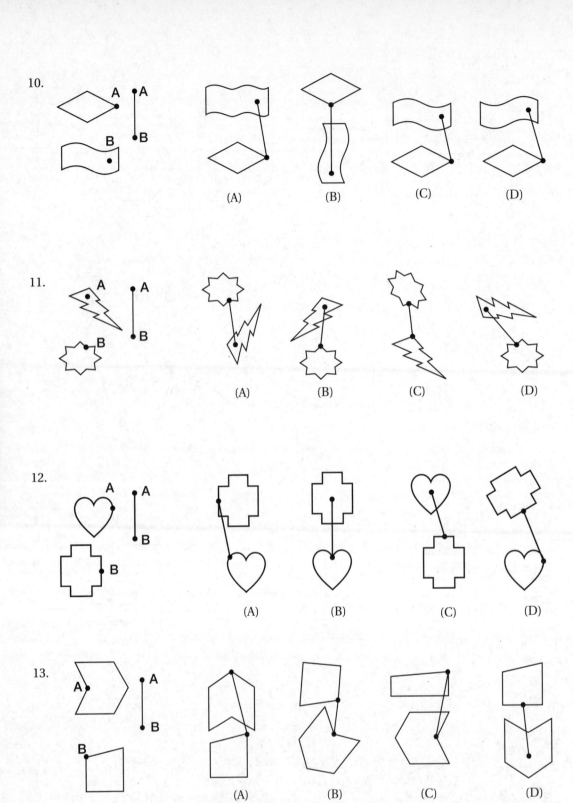

14.

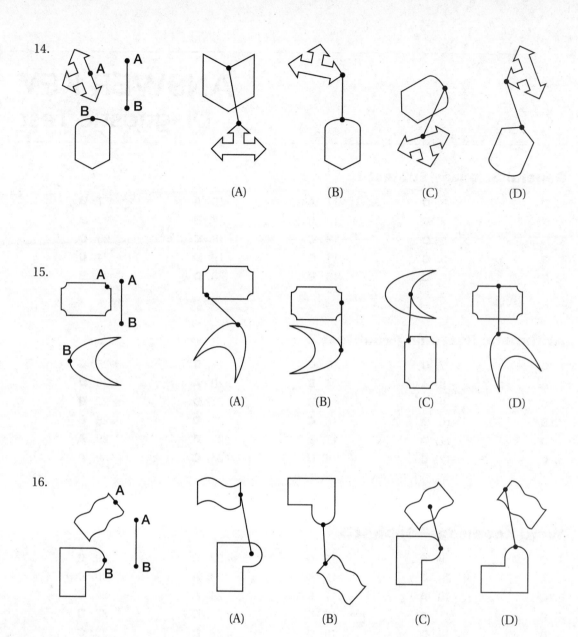

(A)   (B)   (C)   (D)

15.

(A)   (B)   (C)   (D)

16.

(A)   (B)   (C)   (D)

DIAGNOSTIC TEST

General Science—Subtest 1

1. **D**	6. **D**	11. **A**	16. **A**	21. **B**
2. **B**	7. **D**	12. **A**	17. **B**	22. **B**
3. **D**	8. **D**	13. **C**	18. **C**	23. **D**
4. **C**	9. **C**	14. **C**	19. **D**	24. **D**
5. **B**	10. **D**	15. **B**	20. **D**	25. **B**

Arithmetic Reasoning—Subtest 2

1. **C**	7. **D**	13. **C**	19. **C**	25. **C**
2. **A**	8. **A**	14. **B**	20. **A**	26. **D**
3. **C**	9. **A**	15. **B**	21. **D**	27. **B**
4. **B**	10. **B**	16. **C**	22. **D**	28. **C**
5. **D**	11. **D**	17. **B**	23. **B**	29. **A**
6. **C**	12. **C**	18. **D**	24. **C**	30. **A**

Word Knowledge—Subtest 3

1. **C**	8. **A**	15. **D**	22. **C**	29. **B**
2. **A**	9. **D**	16. **D**	23. **A**	30. **D**
3. **C**	10. **A**	17. **B**	24. **A**	31. **C**
4. **A**	11. **A**	18. **C**	25. **D**	32. **D**
5. **B**	12. **D**	19. **B**	26. **D**	33. **C**
6. **C**	13. **D**	20. **C**	27. **C**	34. **B**
7. **C**	14. **B**	21. **D**	28. **B**	35. **D**

Paragraph Comprehension—Subtest 4

1. **C**	4. **B**	7. **C**	10. **D**	13. **B**
2. **C**	5. **D**	8. **C**	11. **B**	14. **C**
3. **A**	6. **B**	9. **C**	12. **B**	15. **C**

Mathematics Knowledge—Subtest 5

1. **C**	6. **C**	11. **C**	16. **A**	21. **D**
2. **D**	7. **B**	12. **C**	17. **D**	22. **A**
3. **B**	8. **D**	13. **B**	18. **C**	23. **D**
4. **C**	9. **B**	14. **B**	19. **B**	24. **B**
5. **C**	10. **B**	15. **C**	20. **A**	25. **A**

Electronics Information—Subtest 6

1. **A**	5. **A**	9. **A**	13. **A**	17. **D**
2. **B**	6. **B**	10. **D**	14. **C**	18. **B**
3. **B**	7. **D**	11. **D**	15. **B**	19. **D**
4. **C**	8. **B**	12. **B**	16. **C**	20. **C**

Automotive & Shop Information—Subtest 7

1. **B**	6. **D**	11. **D**	16. **A**	21. **D**
2. **C**	7. **B**	12. **B**	17. **A**	22. **C**
3. **B**	8. **C**	13. **A**	18. **B**	23. **A**
4. **B**	9. **B**	14. **B**	19. **A**	24. **C**
5. **B**	10. **A**	15. **A**	20. **B**	25. **C**

Mechanical Comprehension—Subtest 8

1. **C**	6. **C**	11. **C**	16. **B**	21. **C**
2. **B**	7. **B**	12. **B**	17. **A**	22. **B**
3. **B**	8. **C**	13. **C**	18. **A**	23. **C**
4. **B**	9. **A**	14. **D**	19. **A**	24. **D**
5. **D**	10. **C**	15. **C**	20. **D**	25. **D**

Assembling Objects—Subtest 9

1. **D**	5. **C**	9. **C**	13. **B**
2. **B**	6. **C**	10. **C**	14. **C**
3. **A**	7. **A**	11. **A**	15. **A**
4. **B**	8. **B**	12. **D**	16. **B**

DIAGNOSTIC TEST

GENERAL SCIENCE—SUBTEST 1

1. **(D)** Sound cannot travel through a vacuum.

2. **(B)** A light-year is a convenient term to measure great distances. Since light travels at the rate of 186,282 miles per second, a light-year is equal to 186,282 miles times 60 seconds per minute times 60 minutes per hour times 24 hours per day times 365 days per year—which equals 5,874,588,800,000, or almost 5.9 trillion miles!

3. **(D)** Specific gravity equals

$$\frac{\text{Weight of substance in air}}{\text{Loss of weight of substance in water}}$$

   Since the weight of the corundum in air is 4 ounces and its weight in water is 3 ounces, the loss of weight in water is 1 ounce. Hence, the specific gravity of corundum is 4 ounces divided by 1 ounce, or 4.

4. **(C)** A sundial consists of a tilted rod that casts a shadow on a clockface. Solar noon is indicated when the rod casts the shortest shadow when the sun is at the highest point in the sky.

5. **(B)** Of the metals listed, copper is the best conductor of heat. Asbestos and glass are very poor conductors of heat, which is why they are used as insulation materials.

6. **(D)** Ecology is the study of the relations of living things with each other and with their environment. The incorrect choices are factors relating to ecology, but they do not describe ecology.

7. **(D)** The paraffin (wax) in the candle contains carbon, hydrogen, and oxygen. The products obtained when the candle burns are, therefore, the oxides of carbon (carbon dioxide) and hydrogen (water).

8. **(D)** Fat has the most carbon molecules in its composition of the substances listed and would therefore yield the most energy per ounce.

9. **(C)** The half-life of a radioactive element is the time it takes for one-half of a given mass of the element to change to something else. In 1,620 years, one-half of the sample radium "disintegrates." In another 1,620 years (making a total of 3,240 years), one-half of the remaining radium disintegrates. This leaves one-half of the remaining one-half in the form of radium.

$$\frac{1}{2} \text{ of } \frac{1}{2} = \frac{1}{4}$$

10. **(D)** When water disintegrates, it becomes molecules of hydrogen and oxygen. It no longer has the properties of water. This is an example of matter undergoing a chemical change. The other changes listed as choices are examples of physical change.

11. **(A)** Light is needed by plants in order to carry on the process of photosynthesis—the manufacture of carbohydrates. During this process green plants absorb carbon dioxide and give off oxygen. Protozoa are one-celled organisms.

12. **(A)** The dew point is the condition when air becomes saturated with moisture.

13. **(C)** To start a fire with the aid of the sun, it is necessary to concentrate, or converge, the rays of sunlight to a focal point. This is done with a convex lens, which is also known as a magnifying glass.

14. **(C)** The rotation of the earth on its axis exposes different parts of the earth to the sun's rays for different parts of each day.

15. **(B)** Alcohol does not have to be digested. The other substances are not broken down, nor are they ready for absorption, until they reach the small intestine.

16. **(A)** An atom contains several types of particles. Its central core, the nucleus, consists of positively charged particles, called protons, and uncharged particles, called neutrons. Surrounding the nucleus and orbiting it are negatively charged particles called electrons. Isotopes are atoms that contain the same number of protons as other atoms of the same element but have different numbers of neutrons.

17. **(B)** The moon is a satellite of a planet, Earth. The others are all planets.

18. **(C)** Sulfuric acid is one of the most important acids used by industry.

19. **(D)** The whale and the horse are mammals. They have a four-chambered heart, mammary glands, and lungs. They bear live offspring, not eggs.

20. **(D)** In a beam of parallel rays, each ray strikes the mirror at a different point. Since the mirror has a plane surface, the rays are all parallel after reflection.

21. **(B)** According to Ohm's law, the voltage (V) needed to produce a current (C) is equal to the current times the resistance (R) that it meets: $V = CR$. In this case, the needed voltage would be

$$24 \text{ (ohms, a measure of resistance)}$$
$$\underline{\times\ 0.5 \text{ (ampere, a measure of current)}}$$
$$12.0 \text{ (volts, a measure of electric potential)}$$

22. **(B)** During aeration of water, methane and carbon dioxide are liberated (eliminated) from the water, and oxygen is absorbed from the air.

23. **(D)** Dry ice is solid carbon dioxide (CO_2) made by cooling this gas to $-80°C$. In this case, CO_2 goes directly from a gaseous state to a solid.

24. **(D)** The scientific measure of work is the foot-pound, which is the force of 1 pound acting through a distance of 1 foot. To measure work (W) in a specific task, multiply the force (F) in pounds by the distance (D) in feet. Thus, in this example,

$$F \times D = W$$

$$50 \times 25 = 1{,}250 \text{ foot-pounds of work}$$

25. **(B)** Chemical reactions can be classified into four main types. In composition (direct combination), two or more elements or compounds combine to form a more complex substance. Decomposition (the reverse of composition) occurs when a complex compound breaks down into simpler compounds of basic elements. Replacement takes place when one substance in a compound is freed and another takes its place. Double (or ionic) replacement occurs when ions in a solution combine to form a new product, which then leaves the solution.

ARITHMETIC REASONING—SUBTEST 2

1. **(C)** The down payment was 25 percent $\left(\text{or } \frac{1}{4}\right)$ of the total payment.

   $\$400 \times \left(\frac{1}{4}\right) = \$100$

   $\$30 \times 12 = \$360$ (sum of monthly payments)
   $\$360 + \$100 = \$460$ (cost on installment plan)
   $\$460 - \$400 = \$60$ (extra cost on installment)

2. **(A)** The number of seeds that failed to sprout was
   $$120 - 90 = 30$$
   The percentage of seeds that failed to sprout was
   $$\frac{30}{120} = \frac{1}{4} = 25\%$$

3. **(C)** To find the average rate of speed, divide the distance covered (1,000 miles) by the time spent traveling $\left(2\frac{1}{2} \text{ or } 2.5 \text{ hours}\right)$.
   Clear the decimal in the divisor.
   $$\frac{1,000}{2.5} = \frac{10,000}{25} = 400 \text{ miles per hour}$$

4. **(B)** Solve by multiplying first and then dividing. Clear the decimal in the divisor.
   $$\frac{0.05 \times 4}{0.1} = \frac{0.20}{0.1} = \frac{0.2}{0.1} = \frac{2}{1} = 2$$

5. **(D)** Find the sum of the deposits and the sum of the withdrawals.

   $\$765 + \$802 = \$1,567$ (deposits)
   $\$348 + \$518 = \$866$ (withdrawals)

   Find the difference between deposits and withdrawals.

   $\$1,567 - \$866 = \$701$ (overall gain)

   Add this gain to the original balance.

   $\$701 + \$2,674 = \$3,375$ (new balance)

6. **(C)** Change $12\frac{1}{2}$ gallons into pints

   (8 pints = 1 gallon).
   $$12\frac{1}{2} \times 8 = \frac{25}{2} \times 8 = 100 \text{ (pints)}$$

   Multiply the cost of 1 pint by 100.
   $\$0.35 \times 100 = \$35$

7. **(D)** Multiply one side of a square by itself to find the area. Thus 9 feet × 9 feet = 81 square feet. By adding 3 feet to each side of the 9-foot square, you produce a 12-foot square. Thus 12 feet × 12 feet = 144 square feet. Find the difference between the areas of the two squares: 144 − 81 = 63 square feet.

8. **(A)** First, change both fractions to a common denominator (12) and add them.

$$\frac{1}{4} = \frac{3}{12} \qquad \frac{1}{6} = \frac{2}{12}$$

$$\frac{3}{12} + \frac{2}{12} = \frac{5}{12}$$

To get the average, divide the sum by 2.

$$\frac{5}{12} \div 2 = \frac{5}{12} \times \frac{1}{2} = \frac{5}{24}$$

9. **(A)** First find the salary increase.

$290 − $260 = $30 (amount of increase)

To find the percentage of increase, use the original salary as the base and carry the division out to three decimal places. Rounded to the nearest hundredth, 0.115 is 0.12.

0.12 = 12 percent

$$\frac{\text{(increase)}}{\text{(original salary)}} = \frac{\$30}{\$260} = \frac{3.000}{26} = 0.115$$

10. **(B)** Express the total weight of the fish in ounces.

1 pound = 16 ounces

16 ounces + 12 ounces = 28 ounces

Find the cost of 1 ounce and multiply it by 16 to find the cost of 1 pound.

$$\$2.24 \div 28 = \$0.08$$

$$\$0.08 \times 16 = \$1.28$$

11. **(D)** Find the area of each lawn.

25 feet × 15 feet = 375 square feet (front lawn)

50 feet × 30 feet = 1,500 square feet (back lawn)

To find the ratio, divide one area by the other.

$$\frac{\text{(front lawn)}}{\text{(back lawn)}} = \frac{375}{1,500} = \frac{1}{4}$$

The ratio of the front lawn to the back lawn is 1:4.

12. **(C)** Find the amount of the price increase. $7,200 − $6,400 = $800

To find the rate of increase, use the original price as your base.

$$\frac{\text{(increase)}}{\text{(original price)}} = \frac{\$800}{\$6,400} = \frac{1}{8}$$

$$\frac{1}{8} = 12\frac{1}{2}\% \text{ (rate of increase)}$$

13. **(C)** Find the relationship between each pair of numbers in the series. Thus

$$\left(3\frac{1}{2}; 2\frac{1}{4}\right) \quad 3\frac{1}{2} - 1\frac{1}{4} = 2\frac{1}{4}$$

$$\left(2\frac{1}{4}; 13\frac{1}{4}\right) \quad 2\frac{1}{4} + 11 = 13\frac{1}{4}$$

$$\left(13\frac{1}{4}; 12\right) \quad 13\frac{1}{4} - 1\frac{1}{4} = 12$$

The pattern so far is $-1\frac{1}{4}$, $+11$, $-1\frac{1}{4}$. To continue the series, add 11 to the fourth number in the series: $12 + 11 = 23$.

14. **(B)** Find the number of hours the movie house is open. From 10:00 A.M. to 10:00 P.M. is 12 hours. From 10:00 P.M. to 11:30 P.M. is $1\frac{1}{2}$ hours.

$12 + 1\frac{1}{2} = 13\frac{1}{2}$ hours

Divide this total by the length of time for a complete showing of the movie $\left(2 \text{ hours and } 15 \text{ minutes, or } 2\frac{1}{4} \text{ hours}\right)$.

$$13\frac{1}{2} \div 2\frac{1}{4} =$$

$$\frac{27}{2} \div \frac{9}{4} =$$

$$\frac{27}{2} \times \frac{4}{9} = 6 \text{ (showings)}$$

15. **(B)** Find the amount taken in for orchestra seats.
$324 \times \$20 = \$6,480$
Out of \$10,000, the remaining amount came from balcony seats.
$\$10,000 - \$6,480 = \$3,520$
Divide this amount by \$10 to find the number of balcony seat tickets that were sold.
$\$3,520 \div \$10 = 352$ balcony seats

16. **(C)** Since the first $\frac{1}{4}$ mile costs \$0.80, this leaves \$4.20 for the balance of the trip. At \$0.20 for each additional $\frac{1}{4}$ mile, find the number of $\frac{1}{4}$ miles that \$4.20 will cover.

(Clear the decimal in the divisor.)

$\$4.20 \div \$0.20 =$
$4.2 \div 0.2 =$
$42 \div 2 = 21$ additional $\frac{1}{4}$ miles

Add the first $\frac{1}{4}$ mile (at \$0.80) to this total.

$21 + 1 = 22 \left(\frac{1}{4} \text{ miles}\right)$

Change the $\frac{1}{4}$ miles to miles.

$22 \div 4 = 5\frac{1}{2}$ (miles for \$5)

17. **(B)** Divide the distance by the number of feet (40) to an inch.

$175 \text{ feet} \div 40 \text{ feet} = 4\frac{15}{40} = 4\frac{3}{8}$ (inches)

18. **(D)** Find the discounted price paid by the dealer.

$50 × 20% =

$50 × 0.2 = $10 (discount)

$50 − $10 = $40 (price paid by dealer)

Then find the dealer's selling price based on an increase over the original wholesale list price.

$50 × 10% =

$50 × 0.1 = $5 (increase over list price)

$50 + $5 = $55 (dealer's selling price)

Finally, find the dealer's profit.

$55 − $40 = $15 (dealer's profit)

19. **(C)** When the hour hand is on the 10-minute mark, it is actually on the number 2 (for 2 o'clock). The hour hand advances to a new minute mark every 12 minutes of actual time. Thus, when the hour hand stopped at the 11-minute mark, it was 12 minutes after 2.

20. **(A)** Divide the number of successful shots by the total number of shots the player tried. Change your answer to percent.

$$\frac{272}{320} = \frac{34}{40} = \frac{17}{20}$$

$$\frac{17}{20} = 0.85 = 85\%$$

21. **(D)** Let x equal the amount the helper receives. Let $2x$ equal the amount the painter receives. Write an equation to show that, together, they receive $375 for painting the house.

$$2x + x = \$375$$

Combine the similar terms, and then divide both sides of the equation by the number with x. (This is to undo the multiplication.)

$3x = \$375$

$x = \$125$ (the helper's wages)

$2x = \$250$ (what the painter receives)

22. **(D)** Find the difference between the two percentages. Divide the answer by 100 percent to change it to a simple fraction.

23. **(B)** To solve, substitute the number value for the letter and do the arithmetic operations.

$$3a^2 - 2a + 5 =$$

$$= (3 \times a^2) - (2 + a) + 5$$

$$= (3 \times 4^2) - (2 + 4) + 5$$

$$= (3 \times 16) - (2 + 4) + 5$$

$$= 48 - 8 + 5$$

$$= 40 + 5 = 45$$

24. **(C)** Find the annual difference between the premium paid by someone who is 30 and the premium paid by someone who is 46.

$38 − $22 = $16

Multiply the answer by 20 to find the total amount saved over 20 years by taking out a policy at an early age.

$16 × 20 = $320 saved

25. **(C)** On sale, the chair is 25% less than the original price. In other words, the sale price is a fraction of the original price.

$100\% - 25\% = 75\% \left(\text{or } \dfrac{3}{4} \right)$ of the original price

If x equals the original price, then the sale price can be written as an equation.

$\left(\dfrac{3}{4} \right) x = \$240$

To solve for x, divide each side of the equation by $\dfrac{3}{4}$. (This is to undo the multiplication.)

$$\frac{3}{4} x \div \frac{3}{4} = \$240 \div \frac{3}{4}$$

$$\frac{3}{4} x \times \frac{4}{3} = \$240 \times \frac{4}{3}$$

$x = \$320$ (original price)

26. **(D)** The quotient is the answer in division. (Clear the decimal in the divisor before doing the arithmetic.)

27. **(B)** For the month between May 15 and June 15, the meter showed that the electric usage was

$5{,}687 - 5{,}472 = 215$ (kilowatt-hours)

The first 10 kilowatt-hours cost	$2.48
The next 45 kilowatt-hours cost $0.16 per kilowatt-hour	$7.20
The next 55 kilowatt-hours cost $0.12 per kilowatt-hour	$6.60
All usage over the first 110 kilowatt-hours was charged at a lower rate. Thus, 215 − 110, or 105 kilowatt-hours cost $0.07 per kilowatt-hour	$ 7.35
TOTAL bill for the month	$23.63

28. **(C)** To square a number, multiply it by itself.

$49^2 = 49 \times 49 = 2{,}401$

$31^2 = 31 \times 31 = \underline{- \ 961}$

$1{,}440$ (difference)

29. **(A)** To find the number of seats in the auditorium, multiply the number of rows (x) by the number of seats in each row (y). This is expressed as xy.

30. **(A)** One way of checking a division example is to multiply the quotient (the answer) by the divisor. After multiplying, add the remainder (if there was one in the division answer). Thus

$$
\begin{array}{ll}
15 & \text{(divisor)} \\
\underline{\times\,8} & \text{(quotient)} \\
120 & \\
\underline{+\,7} & \text{(remainder, after division)} \\
127 & \text{(original number)}
\end{array}
$$

WORD KNOWLEDGE—SUBTEST 3

1. **(C)** To **subsume** means to include within a larger class or order.

2. **(A)** **Consensus**, like *accord*, means agreement.

3. **(C)** **Altercation**, like *quarrel*, means a disagreement.

4. **(A)** **Irresolute**, like *wavering*, means to hesitate between choices.

5. **(B)** **Laconic**, like *concise*, means to express much in a few words.

6. **(C)** **Audition**, like *hearing*, means an opportunity to be heard.

7. **(C)** **Novice** designates one who has no training or experience in a specific field or activity, and hence is a *beginner*.

8. **(A)** *Pacific*, like **conciliatory**, implies trying to preserve or obtain peace.

9. **(D)** To *neutralize*, as to **counteract**, means to render ineffective.

10. **(A)** **Precedent**, like *example*, refers to an individual instance (e.g., act, statement, case) taken as representative of a type.

11. **(A)** **Diaphanous** (*dia-* is a Greek prefix meaning "through, across"), like *transparent*, describes material that light can pass through.

12. **(D)** **Deferred**, like *delayed*, means postponed.

13. **(D)** **Accentuate**, like *intensify*, means to emphasize or increase in degree.

14. **(B)** **Authentic** (from the Greek for "warranted"), like *reliable*, means entitled to acceptance or belief.

15. **(D)** **Unanimity**, like *concurrence*, means complete accord.

16. **(D)** **Notorious**, like *infamous*, means to be known widely but regarded unfavorably.

17. **(B)** *Former* means "preceding in time" and is synonymous with **previous**.

18. **(C)** Both *pliable* and **flexible** mean to be easily bent or yielding, usually without breaking.

19. **(B)** The opportunity to make a *choice* is equivalent to freedom to select or exercise an **option**.

20. **(C)** *Confirm*, like **verify**, means to make certain, to corroborate, or authenticate.

21. **(D)** *Saucy*, like **pert**, means bold or impudent.

22. **(C)** *Tasteful*, similar to **aesthetic** (from the Greek for "perceptive"), means having the ability to appreciate what is beautiful.

23. **(A)** **Decimation** means to remove a large part of a group (literally, a tenth), causing *severe damage or injury*.

24. **(A)** *Angry*, like **indignant** (from the Latin for "deeming unworthy"), implies deep and strong feelings aroused by injury, injustice, or wrong.

25. **(D)** *Platitude*, like **cliché** (originally, to pattern in clay), refers to a remark or an idea that has become trite through overuse and lost its original freshness and force.

26. **(D)** *Agreement* means **harmony** among people, thoughts, or ideas.

27. **(C)** *Lazy*, like **indolent**, applies to one who is not active.

28. **(B)** *Breathing*, like **respiration**, means inhalation and exhalation of air.

29. **(B)** *Watchful*, like **vigilant**, means alert.

30. **(D)** *Casual*, similar to **incidental**, means happening by chance or without definite intention.

31. **(C)** To **succumb** is to cease to resist or contend before a superior force, hence to *yield*.

32. **(D)** **Feasible** describes that which is possible to bring about, and is therefore *practicable*.

33. **(C)** *Many-sided*, like **versatile** (from the Latin for "turning about"), means capable of turning with ease from one task to another.

34. **(B)** **Imperturbability** or *calmness*—the ability to not be bothered by what's going on around you.

35. **(D)** **Strident** (from the Latin for "creaking") means having an irritating or unpleasant—hence *harsh*—sound.

PARAGRAPH COMPREHENSION—SUBTEST 4

1. **(C)** Each individual should prevent the opportunity for crime to occur.

2. **(C)** The design must fit the owner's income and the building site.

3. **(A)** The selection describes a range of camping styles, from backpacking to motor homes with complete creature comforts, so backpacking can be inferred to be the least luxurious.

4. **(B)** According to the selection, the right speed varies depending on the number of cars, the road surface, and the visibility, so a driver should adjust to different driving conditions.

5. **(D)** *Hard work* is the only term in the list not mentioned in the passage.

6. **(B)** The selection states that less than 1 percent (0.8 percent) is available as freshwater for people to use.

7. **(C)** A pinfold is described in the passage as a large circular pen made by driving stakes close together in the floor of the river.

8. **(C)** The division of powers prevents one part or branch of government from having all the power; therefore, power is shared.

9. **(C)** The passage states that a proper dose of narcotic relieves pain and induces profound sleep.

10. **(D)** The passage mentions that nitrogen, phosphorus, and potassium are used by plants in large amounts.

11. **(B)** The passage mentions that 60 percent of pollution is caused by motor vehicle exhausts, so the choice is B—cars, trucks, and buses.

12. **(B)** Since too much bright light can create discomfort for the eyes and create difficulty in seeing well, the main purpose of sunglasses is to screen out harmful rays.

13. **(B)** The selection mentions the good points of apprentice training but none of the negative points.

14. **(C)** The selection does not deal with insurance rates, tax rates, or retirement rates. It defines what a deduction from your paycheck is.

15. **(C)** The first sentence states that nucleic acids are found in all living organisms, from the simplest living things to the most complex.

MATHEMATICS KNOWLEDGE—SUBTEST 5

1. **(C)** A prime number is a number larger than 1 that has only itself and 1 as factors. (It can be evenly divided only by itself and by 1.) 201 is divisible by 3; 205 is divisible by 5; 211, however, is a prime number.

2. **(D)** Change 40 percent to a decimal and write an equation to solve for x.

$$0.4 = \frac{x}{30}$$

Multiply both sides by 30. You are "undoing" the division.

3. **(B)** The product of all integers from 1 to x is called the x *factorial*. The product of all numbers from 1 to 5 is 5 factorial. Thus

$(5)(4)(3)(2)(1) = 20\ (3)(2)(1)$

$\qquad\qquad\quad = 60\ (2)(1)$

$\qquad\qquad\quad = 120\ (1) = 120$

The expression "5 factorial" is equal to 120.

4. **(C)** To subtract one polynomial from another, you change the signs of the terms in the subtrahend. First write the example as a subtraction in arithmetic.
(From) $8x^2 + 2x - 9$
(Take) $3x^2 - 5x - 1$
Then change the signs of the terms in the bottom row (the subtrahend) and combine terms that are alike.

$\quad\ 8x^2 + 2x - 9$
$\underline{-3x^2 + 5x + 1}$
$\quad\ 5x^2 + 7x - 8$

5. **(C)** In deciding whether a number is greater or less than another, it helps to use a number line.

$$-30 \quad -25 \quad -20 \quad -15 \quad -10 \quad -5 \quad 0 \quad 5 \quad 10 \quad 15 \quad 20 \quad 25 \quad 30$$

On the number line above, –5 is to the left of 0 and is, therefore, less than 0. But –30 is to the left of –5. This makes -30 less than –5. The $<$ sign is a symbol of inequality, meaning "less than." The statement $(-30 < -5)$ means "negative 30 is less than negative 5."

6. **(C)** To solve for x, combine all similar terms, and set the equation equal to zero.

$$(8x - 5x) + (-2 - 8) = 0$$

Do the operations inside the parentheses.

$$3x - 10 = 0$$

Next, add 10 to each side. You are undoing the subtraction.

$$3x - 10 + 10 = 0 + 10$$
$$3x = 10$$

Finally, divide each side by 3 to find the value of x. You are undoing the multiplication.

7. **(B)** In x weeks, she will make out checks for x times $50, or $50x$. To find out how much she still has after writing these checks, she would subtract $50x$ from $500. Thus her bank account will hold $500 - $50x$.

8. **(D)** Use the formula

$$F = \left(\frac{9}{5} \times C\right) + 32$$

Substitute 20 degrees for C.

$$F = \left(\frac{9}{5} \times 20\right) + 32$$
$$F = 36 + 32 = 68 \text{ degrees}$$

9. **(B)** The perimeter of a rectangle is the sum of its four sides. If x equals its width, then $x + 3$ equals the length. (The length is 3 inches more than the width.) From this, you can write an equation to find the perimeter. (Use the formula $2w + 2l = P$.)

$$x + x + (x + 3) + (x + 3) = 38$$

To solve for x, combine similar terms.

$$4x + 6 = 38$$
$$4x = 38 - 6$$
$$4x = 32$$
$$x = 8 \text{ (inches)}$$

10. **(B)** One way to solve this is to square each of the suggested answers to see which is close to 85. Thus

9.1	9.2	9.3	9.4
× 9.1	× 9.2	× 9.3	× 9.4
91	184	279	376
819	828	837	846
82.81	84.64	86.49	88.36

The squares of 9.2 and 9.3 are near 85. Find the difference between the square of each of these numbers and 85.

$$(9.2) \quad \begin{array}{r} 85.00 \\ -84.64 \\ \hline 0.36 \end{array} \qquad (9.3) \quad \begin{array}{r} 86.49 \\ -85.00 \\ \hline 1.49 \end{array}$$

The square of 9.2 is closer to 85 than the square of 9.3. Therefore, the square root of 85, to the nearest tenth, is 9.2.

11. **(C)** The statement $5x = 30$ means "5 times a certain number is equal to 30." To find the number, divide each side by 5. This is to undo the multiplication.

$$\frac{5x}{5} = \frac{30}{5}$$
$$x = 6$$

12. **(C)** Set this up as a multiplication example in arithmetic. Remember that when you multiply terms with unlike signs, the product has a minus sign.

$$\begin{array}{r} a - 5 \\ \times\, a + 3 \\ \hline 3a - 15 \\ a^2 - 5a \\ \hline a^2 - 2a - 15 \end{array}$$

13. **(B)** Begin by combining like terms.

$$3z - 5 + 2z = 25 - 5z$$
$$5z - 5 = 25 - 5z$$

Next add $5z$ to each side to eliminate the $-5z$ from the right side.

$$5z - 5 + 5z = 25 - 5z + 5z$$
$$10z - 5 = 25$$

Now add 5 to each side to undo the remaining subtraction.

$$10z - 5 + 5 = 25 + 5$$
$$10z = 30$$
$$z = 3$$

14. **(B)** A pentagon is a five-sided figure. If the park commissioner places a fountain at every corner of the park, there will be five fountains.

15. **(C)** Every right triangle contains an angle of 90 degrees. This particular right triangle also has an angle of 30 degrees. To find the third angle, subtract the sum of these two angles from 180 degrees.

$$180 - (30 + 90) = 180 - 120 = 60 \text{ degrees in the third angle}$$

The other two angles are 60 and 90 degrees.

16. **(A)** To solve for x in this equation, multiply both sides by 2. This is to undo the division.

$$2 \times \frac{x}{2} = 2 \times 7$$
$$x = 14$$

17. **(D)** Divide only similar terms. First divide numbers, then letters. When dividing powers of a letter, just subtract the exponents.

$$\frac{15a^3b^2c}{5abc} = \frac{15}{5} \times \frac{a^3}{a} \times \frac{b^2}{b} \times \frac{c}{c} = 3a^2b$$

18. **(C)** The formula for the area of a circle is $\pi \times r^2$. Find the area of the larger circle first.

$$\pi \times 10^2 = 100\pi \text{ square inches}$$

Then find the area of the smaller circle.

$$\pi \times 7^2 = 49\pi \text{ square inches}$$

To find the part of the larger circle that the smaller one doesn't touch, subtract the two areas.

$$100 - 49 = 51\pi \text{ square inches}$$

19. **(B)** The easiest way to solve this is to form an equation using x as the unknown grade.

$$\frac{78+86+96+94+x}{5} = 88$$

$$\frac{354+x}{5} = 88$$

Multiply both sides by 5. This is to undo the division.

$$5 \times \frac{354+x}{5} = 8 \times 5$$

Simplify both sides of the equation.

$$354 + x = 440$$
$$x = 440 - 354$$
$$x = 86 \text{ (grade)}$$

20. **(A)** First change all measurements to yards.

9 feet = 3 yards; 12 feet = 4 yards;

6 inches = $\frac{1}{6}$ yard

To find the volume of the concrete, multiply the length by the width by the height.

$$3 \times 4 \times \frac{1}{6} = 12 \times \frac{1}{6}$$
$$= 2 \text{ cubic yards}$$

21. **(D)** First find the area of the entire wildlife preserve. Since it is a circle, use the formula for the area of a circle. (Area equals π times the square of the radius.)

$$A = \pi \times r^2$$
$$= \frac{22}{7} \times (14)^2 = \frac{22}{7} \times 196$$
$$= 22 \times 28$$
$$= 616 \text{ square miles}$$

The lions' territory is a wedge formed by a 90-degree angle at the center of the circle. Since a circle has 360 degrees, we can find the part of the preserve inhabited by lions.

$$\frac{90}{360} = \frac{1}{4}$$

Next find what this equals in square miles.

$$\frac{1}{4} \times \frac{616}{1} = 154 \text{ square miles}$$

22. **(A)** Solve by doing each arithmetic operation and combining answers. Remember that the product of two negative or two positive numbers is a positive number. The product of a negative and a positive number is negative.

$(-3)^4 = (-3)(-3)(-3)(-3) = 81$

$(-2)^4 = (-2)(-2)(-2)(-2) = 16$

$(-1)^4 = (-1)(-1)(-1)(-1) = \frac{1}{98}$

23. **(D)** To find the volume (V) of a cylinder, multiply π times the square of the radius (r) times the height (h).

$$V = \pi \times r^2 \times h$$
$$V = \frac{22}{7} \times \frac{7}{1} \times \frac{7}{1} \times \frac{15}{1}$$
$$V = 154 \times 15$$
$$V = 2{,}310 \text{ cubic inches (volume)}$$

To find the number of gallons this cylinder will hold, divide its volume by 231.

$$2{,}310 \div 231 = 10 \text{ gallons}$$

24. **(B)** The wall, the ladder, and the ground in the tennis court form a right triangle. The ladder is on a slant, and is opposite the right angle formed by the wall and the ground. In this position, the ladder is the "hypotenuse" of the right triangle. In geometry, the Pythagorean Theorem states that the square of the hypotenuse (c^2) equals the sum of the squares of the other two sides ($a^2 + b^2$).

Thus, $a^2 + b^2 = c^2$

$\qquad 8^2 + x^2 = 10^2$

Solve by doing the arithmetic operations, and by clearing one side of the equation for x^2.

$$64 + x^2 = 100$$
$$x^2 = 100 - 64$$
$$x^2 = 36$$

Then find the square root of x^2 and of 36.

$$x = 6$$

The base of the ladder is 6 feet from the wall.

25. **(A)** First find how many ounces of the original mixture were fruit juice.

$$10 \times 20\% = 10 \times .2 = 2 \text{ ounces}$$

Next find the total number of ounces in the new mixture.

$$10 + 40 = 50 \text{ ounces}$$

Then find what part of the new mixture is fruit juice, and convert it to a percentage.

$$\frac{2}{50} = \frac{4}{100} = 4\%$$

ELECTRONICS INFORMATION—SUBTEST 6

1. **(A)** Flux is the component in solder that, when liquid, removes the impurities present in the connection and helps prevent oxidation. After it has cooled, the remaining flux present around or between connections acts as an insulator. Tin increases the conductivity of the connection, and it is the combination of tin and lead that results in the combined lower melting point for solder that is desired in electrical work.

2. **(B)** A cold solder connection would appear dull and brittle in appearance and indicate an improperly soldered connection. (A) A connection that is clean and shiny in appearance is an example of a properly soldered connection. (C) A properly soldered connection is clean and shiny. (D) The wattage of the iron used has no effect on the resulting solder connection.

3. **(B)** 1 ampere is equal to 1,000 mA.
   0.1 ampere is equal to 100 mA.
   0.01 ampere is equal to 10 mA.
   0.001 ampere is equal to 1 mA.

4. **(C)** A good fuse will allow current to flow through it, or indicate continuity on a continuity check using an ohmmeter. If there is continuity, or if the fuse is good, the meter will read zero, or very low resistance. Choices A and D indicate a resistance reading that is very high. Choice B is not a reading found on an ohmmeter scale but rather during a voltage check.

5. **(A)** The material with the highest conductivity is silver, followed in order of conductivity by copper, aluminum, and zinc.

6. **(B)** Stranded wire and solid wire of the same gage do not differ in conductivity. Both are available in numerous gages, including the gage used in extension cords. However, solid wire of the gage needed for an extension cord is not nearly as flexible as stranded wire. Because an extension cord is often moved, stranded wire is preferable.

7. **(D)** The formula to calculate power consumption is power = current × voltage, or

   $P = I \times E$. Substituting the values given,
   $P = I \times E$
   $\quad = 10 \text{ amperes} \times 120 \text{ volts}$
   $\quad = 1,200 \text{ watts}$

8. **(B)** A carbon-zinc cell has a voltage of approximately 1.5 volts. In a 12-volt carbon-zinc battery there are 8 cells or 1.5 volts × 8 = 12 volts.

9. **(A)** The circuit property that opposes any change in current is defined as inductance. Capacitance is the circuit property that opposes any change in voltage. Resistance is the opposition to the flow of electrons, and reactance is the opposition to the flow of an alternating current as a result of inductance or capacitance present in a circuit.

10. **(D)** A transducer is a component that converts one form of energy into another form of energy. A speaker converts the electrical energy at audio frequencies in the final stage of a radio receiver into sound energy. A resistor is used in a circuit to limit current flow and drop voltage or consume energy. A diode is used to block energy or rectify an AC signal, and a switch is a mechanical means of turning current on and off.

11. **(D)** The time it takes to complete one sine wave is known as the period of a wave. The distance between the crests of a wave is equal to 1 hertz, and the number of hertz completed in 1 second is known as the frequency. The amplitude of the wave is the distance between the ground line and the highest point of the wave in both the positive and the negative.

12. **(B)** The correct choice is B. To convert from AC peak value to AC effective value the formula is

$$E_{eff} = 0.707 \times E_{peak}$$
$$= 0.707 \times 141 \text{ volts}$$
$$= 100 \text{ volts}$$

13. **(A)** The term *frequency response* is used to denote the range of frequencies that a device, or in this case the human ear, is sensitive to. Sound or audio frequencies fall into the range of 16 to 16,000 Hz.

14. **(C)** The term *kilo* represents a quantity of 1,000. Therefore 1 kilowatt is equal to 1,000 watts. Watts and voltage are not interchangeable terms. A watt is a unit of measurement for power, and a volt is a unit of measurement for voltage.

15. **(B)** The formula for parallel resistors is $R_T = R/n$, where R is equal to the value of one resistor and n is equal to the number of resistors that are of the same value in parallel. Substituting values into the equation:

$$R_T = \frac{900}{3} \text{ ohms}$$
$$R_T = 300 \text{ ohms}$$

16. **(C)** The given schematic is of a full-wave DC power supply. At points A and B before the filter capacitor C_1, the waveform is that of a pulsating direct current. A sine wave could not be displayed because a sine wave indicates a voltage that alternates between positive and negative values. At points A and B the voltage present has been rectified to full-wave direct current by the duo-diode tube. This resultant waveform is known as pulsating direct current. A sawtooth or square wave, although both are examples of pulsating direct current, are waveforms resulting from the introduction of other components after the rectification stage.

17. **(D)** Capacitor C_1 is used to smooth out the AC ripple voltage from the output of the power supply. Choice A is incorrect, as a resistor is used to bleed a capacitor, not vice versa. R_1 is used as an output load resistor. Choice B is incorrect because a capacitor

cannot amplify, and choice C is incorrect because a capacitor cannot rectify a signal; that is the purpose of the duo-diode tube.

18. **(B)** Choices C and D are schematics of resistors. C is a fixed resistor. D is a potentiometer or variable resistor. Choice A is a fixed-capacitor symbol. In choice B the arrow through the fixed capacitor symbol denotes variability. Since a tuning capacitor is a variable capacitor, this is the correct choice.

19. **(D)** The schematic symbol drawn is of a triode tube. Its equivalent solid state component is the transistor. In the triode tube, the elements plate, cathode, and grid correspond to the elements collector, emitter, and base, respectively, in the transistor.

20. **(C)** When the switch is closed, the capacitor will charge through the resistor. When the voltage across the capacitor reaches the voltage necessary for the neon bulb to light, the lamp will glow. As the lamp glows, the capacitor discharges, resulting in a cycle of charge-discharge. This cycle will cause the neon bulb to flash.

AUTOMOTIVE & SHOP INFORMATION—SUBTEST 7

1. **(B)** When a tire is underinflated, the center area of the tread moves upward as the sidewalls flex. This abnormal action places stress on the tire, causing wear to both outside edges.

2. **(C)** The vehicle "track" measurement is taken from the center of the left wheel to the center of the right wheel.

3. **(B)** The resistor inserted in series with the ignition coil is used to drop the 12-volt battery power supply to six volts, for which the coil was designed. This allows for the lower voltage from the battery during cranking operations. The coil can then produce the high voltage needed for the spark plugs.

4. **(B)** A syncromesh unit is designed to bring two gears to the same speed before engagement. A syncromesh unit does not change gear ratios.

5. **(B)** The modulator is a vacuum-operated device connected to a source of manifold vacuum. As vacuum changes in response to engine load, the modulator is actuated and sends a signal to the valve body, resulting in a different shift point. For example, when vacuum is low, as it normally is when the engine is accelerated, the modulator reacts and causes the transmission to shift at a higher vehicle speed. The higher shift point allows the engine to develop more torque, which increases engine power.

6. **(D)** Too much clearance will cause the clutch to grab early. Hard shifting and clashing gears are problems associated with too much free play. Insufficient clearance will cause the clutch to grab late. A slipping clutch usually results from no free play.

7. **(B)** The limited slip differential transmits power to the driving wheel that has traction. In a conventional differential, if one wheel begins to slip, the vehicle will not move. All power remains with the slipping drive wheel.

8. **(C)** The ignition circuit must transform 12 volts to more than 20,000 volts. It must also deliver this high-voltage spark to the spark plugs at the correct time.

9. **(B)** The purpose of the resistor is to lower and control voltage to the ignition coil. Since power for the coil comes through the ignition switch, the resistor is connected between the switch and coil.

10. **(A)** The magnetic field within an alternator is produced by the rotor. Electricity is produced in the stator. Diodes change voltage from AC to DC.

11. **(D)** Under normal operating conditions, whenever the horn button is depressed, a circuit in the relay is grounded and the horn sounds. If the wire to the button becomes permanently grounded due to an insulation breakdown, the horn will blow continuously.

12. **(B)** The rubber cups in the brake wheel cylinders are there to keep brake fluid from leaking out of the cylinder. Wheel cylinder pistons push the brake shoes outward toward the drum when the brakes are applied. Spring tension keeps the springs in place inside the cylinder.

13. **(A)** The metering valve is used on a disc/drum-type brake system. Its purpose is to hold off hydraulic pressure to the front disc brakes until the rear wheel cylinders overcome the tension of the brake shoe return springs. Disc brakes do not use return springs. The pads ride very close to the disc and make contact with the friction surface of the disc as soon as hydraulic pressure is applied.

14. **(B)** The air/fuel mixture is delivered to the cylinder on the intake stroke, compressed on the compression stroke, and ignited on the power stroke. Burned gases are pushed out of the cylinder on the exhaust stroke.

15. **(A)** In normal engine operation a ridge forms at the top of a cylinder bore. To properly remove a piston it is necessary to cut away this ridge. Failure to remove the ridge can result in damage to the piston. The ridge reamer is designed to remove the ridge without damaging the cylinder bore. Filing can ruin a cylinder wall.

16. **(A)** The mitre box is used to cut angles from 45 degrees to 90 degrees in some cases where the angle is adjustable in a metal mitre. In the case of a wooden mitre box there are just two angles, 90 degrees and 45 degrees, cut in the sides of the box to hold the saw.

17. **(A)** The coping saw is used in carpentry to cut moldings to fit at corners. It can also be used to cut wood at any curve or angle desired.

18. **(B)** Other names for the crowbar are *pry bar* and *wrecking bar*. It has many uses and different names in different parts of the country.

19. **(A)** The screwdriver with a straight end is the standard type. The screwdriver with a cross or X shape on the end is referred to as a Phillips screwdriver. It comes in four different end sizes to fit different screw heads.

20. **(B)** In order to use a chisel to cut wood, it is usually necessary to strike it with some type of object to drive the cutting edge along the wood. This is usually done with a hammer.

21. **(D)** The level is made up of at least two glass tubes with air bubbles trapped in the tubes. As the level is moved, the air bubbles move. When the bubbles are aligned in between the two marks on each tube, the level is said to be level.

22. **(C)** The best way to cut circular holes in metal or wood is to use the hole saw. It has the blades shaped to cut the size you need. Just select the diameter you want, place the saw blade in the electric drill, and drill.

23. **(A)** The measuring edges of a steel rule are usually graduated in increments of $\frac{1}{8}$, $\frac{1}{16}$, $\frac{1}{32}$, and $\frac{1}{64}$ inch.

24. **(C)** The back saw has a <u>fine</u> tooth configuration and is used to cut <u>cross-grain</u>, leaving a <u>smooth-finished</u> piece of work.

25. **(C)** If a cold chisel starts to "mushroom" at the head, you should remove the splintered ends with a grinder.

MECHANICAL COMPREHENSION—SUBTEST 8

1. **(C)** Since Jolie is sitting on the seat in the RX-8 and is not rigidly connected to the car as part of its structure, when the car begins to accelerate, inertia tries to keep her in place, but the force of the car moving forward is greater than the force of her weight pressing into the seat. This means that her weight is pressing back more into the seat than it was when the car was stationary.

2. **(B)** To balance the scale, the fulcrum should be moved toward Ball B so that the resulting longer lever arm allows the lighter Ball A to exert more of an influence on the system and level the board.

3. **(B)** When the fulcrum was placed at the centerpoint of the board, Ball B exerted as much force due to gravity (i.e., weight) as Ball A did, even though it was noticeably smaller. Since it is smaller but weighs the same, we can conclude that it is denser than Ball A—the same weight packed into a smaller volume.

4. **(B)** It would be best to hold the handles closer to the end in order to maximize the mechanical advantage of the resulting longer levers that would place more force on the branch for the same amount of effort from the user.

5. **(D)** A wrench uses a wheel and axle effect to turn a nut or a bolt.

6. **(C)** Both parts of the block will weigh the same. If this were not so, there would be a net torque on the block when you try to balance it at its CG.

7. **(B)** If the bolt has 10 threads per inch, the bolt will move $\frac{1}{10}$ (0.1) inch for every complete turn of the wrench. Therefore, if the wrench makes 12 complete turns, the bolt will move $\frac{1}{10} \times 12 = \frac{12}{10} = 1.2$ inches.

8. **(C)** Since meshed gears turn in opposite directions, gear #2 will rotate counterclockwise, causing gear #3 to rotate in a clockwise direction.

9. **(A)** Pushing the roller over the step requires more force than pulling the roller over the step.

10. **(C)** The only one of the options given that will make the job easier is to put the block on a wheelbarrow. Choice A, turning the block on its side, will have no effect because

the block is a cube—none of the parameters of the problem will change, because the size of the block's surface in contact with the ramp will not have changed. Choice B will have no effect, either, and Choice D will make the job harder, not easier.

11. **(C)** A half-full 100-gallon water tank is holding 50 gallons of water. If those 50 gallons are drained out through a valve with a flow rate of 5 gallons per minute, it will take 10 minutes for the water to drain out completely (50 gal/5 gal per min = 10 min). To find the number of seconds in 10 minutes, multiply 10 min × 60 seconds per minute = 600 seconds.

12. **(B)** A good example of a first-class lever is a child's see-saw. A wheelbarrow is an example of a second-class lever, a fishing pole is an example of a third-class lever, and an axe is an example of a wedge.

13. **(C)** Pascal's Law states that pressure applied to a completely enclosed fluid is transmitted undiminished to all parts of the fluid and the enclosing surfaces. Choices A and B are components of Newton's First Law of Motion. Choice D is the second principle of hydraulics.

14. **(D)** The diesel engine is an example of this principle. As a piston moves up on its compression stroke, air in the cylinder is compressed. Ignition takes place when the fuel is injected into the cylinder. The temperature of the compressed air provides the heat for combustion. A diesel engine does not use a spark plug.

15. **(C)** The greater the difference between the teeth of two meshed gears, the greater the torque increases.

16. **(B)** *Power* is the rate at which work is performed.

17. **(A)** The fulcrum is positioned between the effort and the load on a first-class lever.

18. **(A)** The pivot shaft is at T and S. The lobe (high spot) of the cam is between Q and R.

19. **(A)** The smallest pulley will turn the fastest. When a series of pulleys is connected by drive belts, the smallest diameter pulley rotates at the highest speed.

20. **(D)** A pair of meshed gears always turns in opposite directions. X and Y are turning in opposite directions. Since E and F are meshed with Y, both are turning in the direction of X.

21. **(C)** On a third-class lever, the fulcrum is placed at one end, the load is at the other end, and the effect is between the fulcrum and the load.

22. **(B)** Two meshed gears turn in opposite directions. When an idler gear (I is the idler) is placed between the two, both turn in the same direction. The idler gear turns in direction 1.

23. **(C)** The centerline of the small gear or pinion is below the center line of the larger ring gear.

24. **(D)** Pascal's law states that "pressure at any point in a body of fluid is the same in every direction." When a 10-pound force is placed on piston X, which measures 1 square inch, the same force is placed on every square inch of piston Y. Since Y is 300 square inches, then 10 × 300 = 3,000-pound force.

25. **(D)** To calculate the effort needed to lift the load of 200 pounds, use this formula. The effort multiplied by the effort arm equals the load multiplied by the load arm or:

E = effort needed to lift the load

$E \times e = L \times w$

e = length of the effort arm

$E \times 4 = 200 \times 2$

w = load arm

$E \times 4 = 400$; L = load

$$E = \frac{400}{4}$$

$E = 100$ pounds

General Science Review 4

INTRODUCTION

Science can be divided into life, physical, and earth sciences. *Biology* is the general term for the study of life. It covers topics dealing with human health and medicine, and is closely related to the study of *botany* (the study of plants) and *zoology* (the study of animals).

Earth science is a multidisciplinary term that deals with all the sciences relating to the planet Earth. Geophysics, geology, geodesy (the study of the size of the earth), meteorology, planetary magnetism, and oceanography are some of the more prevalent fields in earth sciences.

Chemistry is a physical science that investigates the composition, structure, and properties of matter. It is also concerned with changes in matter and the energy released during those changes. *Physics*, like chemistry, is a physical science that deals with matter and energy. However, in physics, more attention is given to mechanical and electrical forces in areas such as light, sound, heat, motion, and magnetism.

THE SCIENTIFIC METHOD

The *scientific method* is an organized way of solving problems and explaining phenomena. It has evolved over many centuries and includes contributions from many cultures, with some early versions dating back to 1600 B.C. Today's versions differ in detail and labels, but roughly follow the same thought process.

1. **OBSERVATION.** This step requires the accurate sighting and recording of a specific occurrence. The accuracy of an initial observation can be confirmed when a number of independent observers agree that they see the same set of circumstances occurring under the same conditions many times. This step includes collecting information, making observations, and asking questions, as appropriate.

2. **HYPOTHESIS.** A temporary set of conclusions drawn from a set of observations is known as a *hypothesis*. It is usually a very general statement, and suggests the need for a particular experiment to prove or disprove the hypothesis. Often, hypotheses are neither proven completely wrong nor completely right by experiments or repeated observations, so the hypothesis has to be adjusted and tested again.

3. **EXPERIMENT.** To test a specific hypothesis, scientists perform *experiments*. The purpose of the experiments is to answer questions about data truthfully and carefully. Reliable experiments require controlled conditions. This step includes comparing the expected results of the experiment with the actual results and then drawing conclusions.

4. **THEORY.** When a hypothesis is supported by data obtained from experiments, the hypothesis becomes a theory.

5. **LAW OR PRINCIPLE.** When a theory stands up under the test of time and many repeated experiments, it may be called a "law" or principle. It is important to remember, though, that the world around us is not obligated to follow what we think is supposed to happen. The scientific method uses the terms *law* and *principle* as a way of describing what we think happens all the time. As research continues and technology advances in many areas, what were once thought of as laws or principles become obsolete or need modification based on new evidence.

 It's often useful to identify a *mnemonic* (memory aid) to remember the steps in the scientific method:

- Observation
- Hypothesis
- Experiment
- Theory
- Law or principle

One way to help you remember these steps in order is to make up a sentence where each word starts with the same letter as the steps you want to remember. (Interestingly, most people remember odd or silly sentences better.) A popular example is a sentence used to help remember the names and order of the planets in the solar system:

Mnemonic	Planet Name
My	Mercury
Very	Venus
Eager	Earth
Mother	Mars
Just	Jupiter
Served	Saturn
Us	Uranus
Noodles	Neptune

When Pluto was still considered a planet, this used to end with "nine pizzas" instead of "noodles." There are lots of variations—you get the idea.

For the steps in the scientific method, try "<u>O</u>nly <u>H</u>eavy <u>E</u>ggs <u>T</u>aste <u>L</u>ousy." Even better, make up your own version—you will be more likely to remember it.

BASIC CONCEPTS IN BIOLOGY

There are several basic principles, or concepts, that biologists must constantly deal with. *Homeostasis* refers to the balanced, internal environment of a human cell and of the human organism as a whole. To stay alive, cells must regulate their internal and external fluids according to temperature, acid-base balance, and the amount and content of salts and other vital substances.

Unity is shared by all living species insofar as they have certain biological, chemical, and other characteristics in common: there is the unity of the basic living substances (*protoplasm*). All living cells arise from preexisting living cells. All cells synthesize and use *enzymes*. (An enzyme is a substance which speeds up the reaction of chemicals without itself being changed.) The genetic (hereditary) information of all cells is carried by *DNA* molecules. DNA gives cells the ability to *replicate* (make exact copies of themselves).

Metabolism is a term related to all the biochemical activities carried on by cells, tissues, organs, and systems—activities that are necessary for life.

Adaptation refers to a trait that aids the survival of an individual or a species in a given environment.

The basic unit of classification among living things is the *species*. A species is a group of similar organisms that can mate and produce fertile offspring.

LIFE FUNCTIONS

To satisfy all the conditions necessary for life, all living systems must be able to perform certain biochemical and biophysical activities which together are known as *life functions*.

1. **NUTRITION** includes all those activities through which a living organism obtains *nutrients* (food molecules) from the environment and prepares them for use as fuel and for growth. Included in nutrition are the processes of *ingestion, digestion,* and *assimilation.* Ingestion is the process of taking in or procuring food. Digestion refers to the chemical changes that take place in the body so that nutrients can be converted into forms that a cell can use. Assimilation involves changing nutrients into protoplasm.

2. **CIRCULATION** is the movement of fluid and its dissolved materials throughout the body of an organism or within a single cell. In the human body, the circulatory system is made up of three different systems that work together: the heart (cardiovascular), the lungs (pulmonary), and the blood vessels (systemic). The human circulatory system is the way that blood, nutrients, oxygen and other gases, and hormones move to and from cells.

3. **RESPIRATION** consists of *breathing* and *cellular respiration.* Breathing refers to the pumping of air into and out of the lungs of air-breathing animals or the movement of water over the gills of fish. During breathing, oxygen flows into air sacs in the lungs and diffuses into the blood. Carbon dioxide moves out of the blood into the lungs and out of the body through the nose and mouth. Cellular respiration is a combination of processes that release energy from glucose (sugar).

4. **EXCRETION** removes waste products of cellular respiration from the body. The lungs, skin, and kidneys are excretory organs in humans. They remove carbon dioxide, water, and urea from the blood and other body tissues.

5. **SYNTHESIS** involves those biochemical processes in cells by which small molecules are built into larger ones. As a result of synthesis, *amino acids*, the building blocks of proteins, are changed into enzymes, hormones, and protoplasm. A *hormone* is a chemical "messenger" produced by the endocrine glands. It helps to control and coordinate the body's activities.

6. **REGULATION** includes all processes that control and coordinate the many activities of a living thing. Chemical activities inside of cells are controlled by enzymes, vitamins, minerals, and hormones. The *nervous* and *endocrine* systems of higher animals coordinate body activities. The growth and development of plants is regulated by *auxins* and other growth-control substances.

7. **GROWTH** describes the increase of cell size as well as the increase of cell numbers. The increase of cell numbers occurs when cells divide in response to a sequence of events known as *mitosis*.

8. **REPRODUCTION** is the process by which new individuals are produced by parent organisms. There are two major kinds of reproduction: *asexual* and *sexual*. Asexual reproduction involves only one parent. The parent may divide and become two new cells, thus ending the parent generation. Or the new individual may arise from part of the parent cell; in such a case, the parent remains. In either case, replication of the *chromosomes* is involved. (Chromosomes are small rod-shaped bodies in cells. They contain the genes of heredity.) Sexual reproduction requires the participation of two parents, each producing special reproductive cells known as *sex cells*, or *gametes*. The continuation and survival of the species is dependent upon reproduction. Once a species has lost its reproductive potential—its capacity to reproduce—the species no longer survives and becomes extinct.

THE BASIC UNIT OF LIFE: THE CELL

The *cell* is the basic structural and functional unit of virtually all forms of life. It is the basic unit of structure, with its various shapes and sizes giving form to the body of an organism. It is the basic unit of function, acting as a biochemical factory to perform the basic metabolic functions of life.

The cell is also a basic unit of growth, increasing in size and multiplying to form an organism of a specific size and shape. The cell is also a basic unit of heredity, producing cells identical to itself in hereditary makeup and carrying the code for all hereditary information.

Structure of a Cell

A cell is a membrane-enclosed unit containing *cytoplasm* and a *nucleus*. The parts of a cell are known as *organelles*, meaning "little organs." This term is appropriate because parts of the cell have special functions, somewhat like miniature body organs. Although there are some differences between plant and animal cells, all cells have the same basic structure. The major parts of a cell and the function of each follows.

Cell Membrane—Also known as the plasma membrane, the cell membrane holds the cell together and controls the selective passage of certain materials into and out of the cell.

Cytoplasm—The living material of the cell lying within the cell membrane but outside the nucleus, the cytoplasm contains many organelles, or little organs, each with its own specific function.

Nucleus—The control center of the cell, the nucleus contains chromosomes, which carry the genetic, or hereditary, material of the cell.

Endoplasmic Reticulum—A network of membranes extending from the nucleus to the cell membrane, the endoplasmic reticulum allows for the movement of materials within the cytoplasm and to the cell membrane.

Ribosome—A small organelle, a ribosome is a site of protein synthesis within the cell. Ribosomes are very numerous in the cytoplasm.

Golgi Body—A complex of membranes, the Golgi body, or Golgi apparatus, stores and transports materials formed in other parts of the cell.

Mitochondrion—The largest organelle in the cell, the mitochondrion is the powerhouse of the cell, involved in cellular respiration. There are many mitochondria in each cell, and each one has a complex internal structure of folded membranes.

Lysosome—A saclike structure, the lysosome functions in the release of enzymes within the cell.

Differences Between Plant and Animal Cells

Although the basic structure of plant and animal cells is very similar, there are a few differences. Plant cells have a *cell wall* outside the cell membrane. This wall is made up of *cellulose* and other compounds. It gives the plant cell a more rigid outer covering, helps to support it, and keeps it from drying out. Animal cells do not have a structure that can be compared to the cellulose cell wall. Plant cells also contain *chlorophyll*-containing *chloroplasts*, which function in the process of *photosynthesis*, by which green plants convert the energy of the sun into usable foodstuffs. Animal cells do not have chloroplasts and therefore cannot make their own food.

Animal cells sometimes have *flagella* or *cilia*, threadlike structures that function in the movement of simple organisms and the movement of particles in more complex organisms.

The Basic Chemistry of Cells

The cell is like a chemical factory that uses some of the elements present in the nonliving environment. Thus, in the living material of the cell, we find carbon, hydrogen, oxygen, and nitrogen in the greatest amounts, with smaller quantities of sulfur, phosphorus, magnesium, iodine, iron, calcium, sodium, chlorine, and potassium. In the cell, these elements are present in both *organic* and *inorganic compounds*. (A *compound* is a chemical union of two or more substances.)

An inorganic compound is one that does not have the elements carbon and hydrogen in its chemical combination. Inorganic compounds in living cells include water, mineral salts, and inorganic acids.

An organic compound has the elements carbon and hydrogen. Examples are *carbohydrates, lipids, proteins,* and *nucleic acids.*

Carbohydrates are composed of carbon, oxygen, and hydrogen. The hydrogen and oxygen atoms are usually present in the ratio of 2:1. For example, *glucose* (a sugar) has 12 atoms of hydrogen and 6 atoms of oxygen (as well as 6 carbon atoms), $C_6H_{12}O_6$. Carbohydrates are used by cells primarily as sources of energy.

Lipids include fats and fatlike substances. Like carbohydrates, a lipid molecule contains carbon, hydrogen, and oxygen. But the ratio of hydrogen to oxygen is much greater than 2:1. Most lipid molecules provide twice as much energy per gram as do carbohydrate molecules.

Proteins are composed of carbon, hydrogen, oxygen, and nitrogen. Some proteins also contain sulfur. All proteins are built from amino acids, which are essential to life. Some proteins are involved in complex biochemical activities. Others contribute to the structure of cells.

Nucleic acids are essential to the continuance of life. They pass hereditary information from one generation to the next. This makes possible the continuance of life within each species of living things. *Deoxyribonucleic acid* (DNA) molecules are the particular type of nucleic acid out of which genes are made. *Genes* carry hereditary traits from parent to offspring.

Cells are always engaged in chemical activity. The major difference between living things and nonliving matter is that living systems carry out vital chemical activities on a controlled and continuous basis. The control of chemical processes in cells requires the work of enzymes. Enzymes are thus *organic catalysts.* (A catalyst, in this sense, is a molecule that controls the rate of a chemical reaction but is not itself used up in the process.)

Division of Cells

To ensure growth and reproduction, cells must divide. When a normal body cell reaches a certain size, it divides into two cells. These daughter cells are identical to each other and to the parent cell. In the basic cell division process—*mitosis*—the hereditary material in the nucleus replicates, or duplicates itself, and then pulls apart to form two separate nuclei, while the cytoplasmic material doubles and splits. The result is two cells identical to the original single cell.

To ensure that the characteristic species number of chromosomes is maintained generation after generation, sex cells, or *gametes* (egg cells and sperm cells), are produced through a special type of cell division known as *meiosis.* In this process, the number of chromosomes in each gamete is reduced to half, so that upon *fertilization* (the union of sperm and egg), the species chromosome number is maintained.

Cloning

A clone is an individual organism grown from a single body cell of its parent and genetically identical to that parent. Cloning involves stimulating the parent cell to reproduce by asexual (nonsexual) means. Over the past 50 years, tissue culture experiments have been carried out with plants in which single nonembryonic cells have been induced to develop in the same way as a fertilized egg. The results with species such as carrots, African violets, Boston ferns, and Cape sundews show that an entire plant can be reproduced from a single nonreproductive cell.

Among animals (including humans), twinning sometimes occurs naturally, producing two separate organisms with the same genetic makeup. Scientists in the 1950s, 1960s, and 1970s demonstrated that they could clone frog tadpoles from frog embryonic cells by transferring the nucleus of one cell into another. In the 1980s, scientists created clones of mammals by splitting embryos in a process called *artificial twinning*, or by nuclear transfer using embryonic cells.

A major breakthrough in animal cloning occurred in 1997 when Scottish researchers cloned a sheep using genetic material from a nonembryonic cell. Once it was proven possible to clone a new animal from a cell of an adult animal, other groups began to experiment with cloning different species. Cloning from adult cells means that it is possible to be more certain ahead of time what the cloned animal will be like. So far, successfully cloned animals include frogs, mice, rats, sheep, cattle, pigs, goats, cats, rabbits, mules, horses, and deer.

PLANT LIFE

The green *plant kingdom* includes species ranging from single-celled to *multicellular* (many-celled) plants. In multicellular plants, different cells are programmed to carry out special tasks. This is called cell *specialization*, and it goes hand-in-hand with a *division of labor*. According to this division, groups of cells work together to perform some special life function to benefit the entire organism.

Lower plant species, such as the single-celled *algae*, can live in freshwater or saltwater. But most species of plants (the higher forms) are "anchored" in one place. Higher plants are sometimes referred to as *terrestrial* (land-dwelling).

The bodies of these higher plants have parts known as *roots, stems,* and *leaves*. Roots anchor plants in the soil and absorb water and dissolved materials from the ground. Stems have three major functions: (1) they conduct water upward from the roots to the leaves and conduct dissolved food materials downward from the leaves to the roots; (2) they produce and support leaves and flowers; and (3) they provide a means for storing food.

The most important function of green leaves is to carry out *photosynthesis*. This is the food-making process by which inorganic materials are changed into organic nutrients. Green leaves have a pigment called *chlorophyll*. In the presence of that pigment, leaves use the energy of sunlight to make carbohydrates from carbon dioxide (CO_2) and water. These carbohydrates are the food used by plants—and by the animals that eat the plants. During photosynthesis, the oxygen (O_2) needed by animals is released into the atmosphere.

ANIMAL LIFE

All animals are multicellular. One of the simplest forms of animal life is the sponge, which lives in water, attached to rocks. All animals are composed of cells without walls. They *ingest* (take in) food, digest it, and distribute it to cells that make up their body. Most animals can move. Some lower forms of animals reproduce by *budding*. (A new organism grows from cells of the parent, breaks off, and then continues its own existence.) Some forms reproduce through unfertilized eggs, while others reproduce sexually, using sperm and egg. About 90 percent are *invertebrates*—animals without backbones.

Vertebrates are animals with a true backbone made of cartilage or bone. They have a noticeable development of the head, where a brain is enclosed in a *cranium*. Blood is pumped through a closed *circulatory system* by means of a heart with two types of chambers: an *atrium* and a *ventricle*. Most vertebrates (except humans) have a tail. Another characteristic of vertebrates is a mouth that is closed by a movable lower jaw.

CLASSIFICATION

With well over a million different kinds of plants and animals living on earth, some organization is necessary. The science of biological classification is called *taxonomy*. The system currently in use is based on one developed by Swedish botanist Carl Linnaeus in the mid 1700s, based primarily on relationships and similarities in structure. The system currently used most has eight levels. It ranges from the broadest category, the *domain*, to the most specific category, the *species*. The following box explains these taxonomic categories in detail. Specific organisms are referred to by their Latin *genus* and *species* names; this worldwide practice is called *binomial nomenclature*.

You can use many popular mnemonics to help you remember the different taxonomic categories, or you can make up your own.

- Do Kings Play Chess On Fine Glass Sets?
- Dear King Phillip, Come Over For Great Spaghetti
- Dude, Keep Pond Clean Or Froggy Gets Sick

TAXONOMIC CATEGORIES

DOMAIN (ALSO KNOWN AS A SUPERKINGDOM OR EMPIRE): Two of the three domains are made up of single-celled organisms whose cells have no nucleus. The other domain, *Eukarya*, includes all living organisms whose cells have a nucleus and organelles bound by a membrane. This level of classification started gaining acceptance in the 1990s and is still not universally recognized.

KINGDOM: There are five kingdoms, two of which are microscopic. The others are plants, animals, and fungi.

PHYLUM: The phylum is the major taxonomic grouping within a kingdom, categorizing organisms by their main features. Most members of the animal kingdom fall into one of five phyla: vertebrates, invertebrates, arthropods, mollusks, and echinoderms.

CLASS: Phyla are subdivided into classes. Vertebrates, for example, are divided into the classes of mammals, bony fish, cartilaginous fish, birds, amphibians, and reptiles.

ORDER: Classes are divided into *orders*. The class of mammals, for instance, is divided into the orders of carnivores, primates, rodents, and hooved mammals.

FAMILY: Orders are further subdivided into *families*. Members of the same family have similar features. For example, the order of carnivores is divided into families that include cats, dogs, bears, and weasels.

GENUS: As a subdivision of the family, a *genus* is a group of closely related species that usually exhibits similar specific characteristics. The *Felidae* (cat) family includes the genus *Felis* (small and domestic cats), the genus *Panthera* (jaguars, leopards, lions, and tigers), and the genus *Puma* (cougars and panthers).

SPECIES: The members of a *species* are similar to each other and can breed or reproduce together. To continue the feline example, a tiger's binomial nomenclature is *Panthera tigris*, while a lion's is *Panthera leo*, and a jaguar's is *Panthera onca*.

A SPECIAL TYPE OF ANIMAL: HUMANS

Humans belong to a special order of vertebrates called *primates*. What distinguishes primates from other vertebrates? Many scientists believe that at one time all primates lived in trees, and that over a long period of time, some species left the trees and successfully adapted to life on land, but that certain "tree life" characteristics remained. They have (a) hands that can grasp objects; (b) a well-developed sense of sight (primates can see in three dimensions, which enables them to see branches they are going to grasp); and (c) a larger brain with more surface area for nerve cells. Primates also have teeth capable of chewing a variety of foods.

Humans are special primates, set apart from others in their species by special characteristics. They have *bipedalism* (the ability to walk on two legs, instead of four). They can adapt to living in almost any environment. And they have the power of speech, along with the ability to remember and to make associations between ideas. These capabilities give humans the basis to establish a culture and history.

The human organism has several key systems:

- The *skeletal system* (carries the body and supports and protects the organs)
- The *muscular system* (about 40 percent of body weight, it enables the body to move)
- The *nervous system* (permits communication between the organism and its environment)
- The *endocrine system* (includes glands that regulate growth, blood pressure, etc.)
- The *respiratory system* (allows the body to inhale air and exhale carbon dioxide)
- The *circulatory system* (includes the heart and blood vessels)
- The *lymphatic system* (brings oxygen to cells and removes waste products from them)
- The *digestive system* (processes and distributes nutrients)
- The *excretory system* (removes wastes from the body)
- The *reproductive system* (allows humans to reproduce)

The human body has five major *senses*—sight, hearing, taste, smell, and touch—that transmit information about the environment to the nervous system, and eventually to the brain. Two of these senses show the "division of labor" in the body.

1. Human *eyeballs* rest in bony sockets of the skull, and are attached to it by three pairs of small muscles. The colored portion of the front of the eye is the *iris*; in its center is a hole called the *pupil*. Behind the pupil is the *lens*, which flattens or thickens to focus on an object. Light enters the eye through the pupil. It passes through the *cornea* and *lens* (which turns the image upside down and reverses it from left to right), and sets up a barrage of signals in the *retina*. These signals pass through the *optic* nerve to the brain where the image is corrected and "recognized."

2. The *human ear* is made up of three divisions: the *outer ear*, the *middle ear*, and the *inner ear*. The outer ear catches sound waves and transports them to the *eardrum*, causing it to vibrate. Three bones in the middle ear—the *hammer*, *anvil*, and *stirrup*—transmit these vibrations to the *cochlea* in the inner ear. The fluid-filled cochlea is lined with hair cells which transmit the vibrations to the *auditory nerve* and, eventually, to the brain. (The air-filled middle ear is connected by the *Eustachian tube* to the throat. Thus, when you yawn or swallow, you help equalize the air pressure in the middle ear.)

NUTRITION

Nutrition is the sum of all the methods by which an organism satisfies the needs of its body cells for energy, fuel, and regulation. Substances that contribute to the nutritional needs of cells are *nutrients* or (for animals) "food." Nutrients that are needed in large amounts are called *macronutrients*: carbohydrates, proteins, and fats. *Micronutrients*—vitamins and minerals—are needed in smaller amounts. Malnutrition results either from eating too little food or from eating an imbalanced diet. A balanced diet includes an appropriate number of daily choices from the five major food groups: (a) milk and other dairy products, (b) meat and other proteins, (c) vegetables and fruits, (d) breads, cereals, and other grain products, and (e) fats and oils, which occur most often in prepared foods.

Carbohydrates include starches and sugars. Their primary function is to serve as fuel for the body's cells. When cells receive more simple sugar than they can use, some of the excess sugar is stored in the liver and muscles as *glycogen* (animal starch). However, if the quantity of carbohydrates taken in is much too large, the body converts them to fat, which is stored under the skin and around the body's organs. Food sources of carbohydrates include potatoes, fruit, cereal grains, beans, baked goods, etc.

Proteins are the most abundant of the organic compounds in body cells. Hair, nails, and other fibrous structures in the body are composed of proteins. They form part of certain hormones, are vital to the formation of DNA molecules, and help to build the body's resistance to disease. Food sources of proteins include meat, fish, eggs, milk, cheese, beans, nuts, etc.

Fats are also fuel foods. Certain fats are essential to the structure and function of body cells and to the building of cell membranes. Fats also aid in transporting fat-soluble vitamins. Foods rich in fats include butter, bacon, egg yolk, cream, and some cheeses. Fat-rich foods add to the caloric content of the human diet. A *calorie* is the unit of heat necessary to raise 1 liter of water 1 degree Celsius. One gram of fat provides 9 calories. One gram of protein or carbohydrates provides 4 calories.

Vitamins are organic compounds necessary for the proper functioning of the body. The table on the next page summarizes the source and value of some major vitamins.

Minerals are inorganic compounds. *Calcium* regulates muscle activity and, together with *phosphorus*, is used in building bones and teeth. (Both calcium and phosphorus are found in dairy products. Calcium is also found in grains and green leafy vegetables.) *Sodium* functions in the regulation of body temperature: large amounts of the body's salts are excreted by the sweat glands. Nerve cells could not carry impulses, nor could muscles contract, without the assistance of sodium and *potassium*. (Potassium is found in beans, peas, and fruit.)

Other minerals include: *fluorine*, which helps resist tooth decay; *iodine* (found in fish and salts), which aids in metabolism; *magnesium* (found in green leafy vegetables), which is also good for metabolism and for healthy bones and teeth; and *iron* (found in liver, egg yolk, red meats, and grains), which is necessary for *hemoglobin*—a chemical that unites with oxygen in the blood.

Fiber in the human diet comes only from plant sources. Fiber is not a nutrient, but it is important for stimulating the normal action of the intestines in the elimination of wastes. Raw fruits and vegetables, whole cereals and bread, and fruits with seeds (figs, strawberries, and raspberries) are excellent sources of fiber.

Vitamin	Necessary for	Some Food Sources
A	Healthy eyes and skin	Fish liver oil, butter, yellow fruits and vegetables
C (Ascorbic acid)	Healthy teeth, gums, bones; resistance to infection	Citrus fruits, cabbage, green leafy vegetables
D	Strong bones and teeth; regulation of calcium and phosphorus metabolism	Fish liver oil, egg yolk, salmon
E	Prevention of oxidation by red blood cells; good muscle tone	Wheat germ, green leafy vegetables
K	Clotting of blood	Green vegetables, tomatoes
B (Thiamin, Niacin)	Growth; good digestion and appetite; normal nerve functions	Yeast, wheat germ, liver, bread, green vegetables
B (Riboflavin)	Health of skin and mouth; growth; healthy eyes	Same as for thiamin and niacin; meat

Healthy Eating

For decades, the U.S. Department of Agriculture promoted the Food Guide Pyramid and its more recent evolutions, MyPyramid and MyPlate. However, emerging research has developed guidelines better supported by science.

Healthy eating primarily depends on daily exercise and weight control. If you burn as many calories as you take in each day, there's nothing left over for the body to store as fat, and your weight will stay the same. However, if you eat more calories than you burn off, your body will store the excess calories as fat, and you will gain weight. If you eat fewer calories than you burn, your body will use stored fat for energy, and you will lose weight.

The body gets its energy mainly from carbohydrates, which can come from many sources—some healthy (beans, vegetables, fruit, whole grains) and some not so healthy (sweets, sodas, and so on). The healthiest grain-based carbohydrates are whole grains, such as oats, quinoa, and brown rice.

Refined grains (such as white bread, white rice, and white pasta), potatoes, sugary drinks, and sweets can cause explosive increases in blood sugar that can lead to weight gain, diabetes, heart disease, and other chronic disorders. Whole grains generate slower, steadier increases in blood sugar that don't overwhelm the body's ability to handle them.

A healthy diet with plenty of fruits and vegetables has a lot of benefits, such as decreased chances for heart attack or stroke, lower blood pressure, and possibly protection against some types of cancers. Ideally, fruits and veggies should make up at least half of your total intake, and, sadly, most Americans don't get enough of either. How you prepare your fruits and vegetables makes a difference in the benefits you will reap from them. Don't kid yourself by thinking that you will reap much nutritional benefit from fried vegetables or from the strawberries on top of your strawberry shortcake, or the apples in your apple pie. However, if prepared with *healthy* (unsaturated) fats and oils, such as olive oil, you will retain the beneficial vitamins and minerals inherently found in these foods.

Nuts, seeds, and avocados, as well as omega-3-rich fish, such as salmon and tuna, can improve cholesterol levels and protect the heart. Nuts (almonds, walnuts, pecans, peanuts,

Carbohydrates are either *starches* or *sugars*. They give you energy for physical activity, brain function, and organ processes. Excess carbohydrates are stored as fat.

Protein builds muscle, provides energy, and supports tissue repair. It has a role in the production and use of hormones and enzymes, as well as immunity and healing.

hazelnuts, and pistachios) and beans (black beans, navy beans, garbanzos, and lentils), especially when eaten in place of beef, pork, or processed meat, can lower the risk of heart disease and diabetes.

Fish, poultry, and eggs are important sources of protein. Fish rich in heart-healthy omega-3 fatty acids can reduce the risk of heart disease. Chicken and turkey are low in saturated fat and are also good sources of protein. Eggs are another great source of protein and are packed with numerous vitamins, including vitamin A, potassium, and many B vitamins, such as folic acid, choline, and biotin.

Building bone and keeping it strong takes calcium, vitamin D, exercise, and a whole lot more. Milk and dairy products can be beneficial, but not at the levels once thought appropriate. To limit saturated fats and sodium, you should not exceed one or two servings per day. Red meat is high in saturated fat, and processed meats, such as bacon, hot dogs, and deli meats, are very high in sodium. A diet with a lot of red meat and processed meat has been linked to increased risk of heart disease, diabetes, and colon cancer. It's best to avoid processed meat and limit red meat to no more than two serving per week. Switching to fish, chicken, nuts, or beans in place of red or processed meat can improve cholesterol levels and lower chances of heart disease and diabetes.

Calories

Your body needs to have the right amount of calories every day to get the nutrients it needs. How many calories that actually amounts to depends on a variety of factors, including your age, sex, height, weight, and activity level. Caloric needs are also different for people who have a long-term illness and women who are either pregnant or breastfeeding.

The U.S. Department of Agriculture recommends the following daily calorie intake categories:

Age	Sedentary Male	Active Male	Sedentary Female	Active Female
8 or less	<1,400	<1,800	<1,400	<1,800
9–14	1,600–2,200	2,000–2,600	1,400–1,800	1,800–2,200
15–18	2,200–2,400	3,000–3,200	1,800	2,400
19–40	2,400–2,600	2,800–3,000	1,800–2,000	2,200–2,400
41–60	2,000–2,200	2,600–2,800	1,600–1,800	2,200
60+	2,000	2,400–2,600	1,600	2,000

DISEASES

A *disease* is a disorder that prevents the body organs from working as they should. In general, diseases can be classified as *noninfectious* or *infectious*. Among the noninfectious causes of disease are malnutrition, poisoning, radiation, and the malfunctioning of the endocrine system. Infectious diseases can be caused by *germs* (bacteria), fungi, parasitic worms, and *viruses*. Viruses are inorganic, but they grow within living cells. Most infectious diseases are *contagious*—that is, they are spread by body contact or by droplet infection.

The human body has many powerful defenses against disease. The skin itself kills most germs that land on it. So does the saliva in our mouths, the acid in our stomachs, the mucus membrane in our nose and throat. If any germs do get past these defenses, our body releases chemicals to surround and destroy the germs. White blood cells, cells in the lymph vessels, and *antibodies* are also part of this defense. Antibodies are "tailor-made" by the body to fight specific germs.

Our communities can do a great deal to help prevent disease. One strategy is to require that all children be immunized against disease. *Immunization* is the injection of a *vaccine*—a weak or expired agent of the disease—into a person's body. This stimulates the body to produce antibodies that will be ready to fight germs if they invade the body. Successful methods of immunization have been developed against smallpox, polio, measles, typhus, and other contagious diseases that once killed thousands in periodic epidemics.

There are several ways to preserve food—some of them ancient, some relatively recent; drying, salting, smoking, fast-freezing, pickling, and sterilization by heat. Canning sterilizes food and seals it so that no germs can get in. To prevent the spread of disease through milk, dairies *pasteurize* it: They chill milk immediately after collecting it to kill some of the bacteria, and then heat it to a required temperature for a period of time. This kills all the disease-causing germs and not only prevents disease transmission but helps the milk stay fresh longer.

GENETICS

Genetics is the study of the mechanism by which characteristics are passed from parents to offspring. Every human child develops from a fertilized egg that has 23 pairs of chromosomes for a total of 46. The basic principles of heredity were first identified by Gregor Mendel in the late 18th century. Mendel formulated three basic laws of heredity: the *law of segregation,* which stated that individual hereditary traits, or units, separate in the gametes; *the law of independent assortment,* which stated that each trait is inherited independently of other traits; and *the law of dominance,* which stated that when contrasting traits are crossed (e.g., the trait for brown eyes and the trait for blue eyes), one trait is *dominant* over the other, which is *recessive.* Subsequent research corrected and expanded these initial findings. The recognition that the hereditary units are discrete units, now known as genes, on the *chromosomes* opened the way for further studies. We now know that a gene is a unit of a *deoxyribonucleic acid (DNA)* molecule and that it carries a code for the production of a specific protein needed by the organism. A change in a gene (an error in DNA coding or duplication) is a *mutation.* As a rule, mutations occur randomly, and most are harmful to the organism.

In recent years, scientists have been able to identify the genetic basis of many diseases; attempts are being made to find ways of treating genetic disorders. Through a process known as *amniocentesis,* in which a small amount of amniotic fluid surrounding a fetus is removed from a pregnant woman and the fetal cells analyzed, some hereditary defects can now be diagnosed before birth.

ECOLOGY

Ecology is that branch of science that deals with the interaction of organisms and their environment. It is based to a large extent on knowledge of biology and chemistry. The interconnections of plant, animal, and human life are becoming more widely appreciated.

One of the most important concepts in ecology is that of an *ecosystem*, the system by which a particular living community of plant and animal populations interacts with its non-living environment. There is no size requirement for an ecosystem: It may be a forest, a pond, an unused city lot, or a crack in the sidewalk. The structure of an ecosystem is the same, whether its location is on land or underwater. What really defines an ecosystem is a set of interacting forces:

1. The *air* is made up of 21 percent oxygen, 78 percent nitrogen, 0.03 percent carbon dioxide, and other inert gases.

2. The *soil* is the source of minerals that supply plants with compounds of nitrogen, zinc, calcium, phosphorus, and other minerals.

3. The *green plants* in an ecosystem are its *producers*, so-called because they make their own food.

4. The *primary consumers* in an ecosystem are its *herbivores* (plant eaters). These include crickets, grasshoppers, and cattle, for example.

5. *Secondary consumers* (so-called because they feed on the herbivores) are flesh eaters, such as snakes, frogs, and coyotes. These are called *carnivores*.

6. *Tertiary consumers* are those that feed on the herbivores and carnivores.

7. *Scavengers*, such as earthworms and vultures, feed upon dead organic matter.

8. *Decomposers* are those bacteria and other organisms that break down dead organic matter, thus releasing minerals that are returned to the soil. Without the decomposers, valuable minerals would remain trapped in dead organic matter.

The source of all energy in an ecosystem is the sun. Green plants use the sun's light (its energy) to make their own food. This energy is then transferred from plants to the animals that consume them. Animals use energy to do work and, in the process, give off body heat, which radiates into the atmosphere. The cycles of *photosynthesis* (energy trapping) and *respiration* (energy release and use) must continue if the ecosystem is to continue. The flow of energy in the ecosystem can be studied by way of this *food chain* showing the transfer of energy from a producer, lettuce, to a tertiary consumer, the hawk (not all food chains are this simple):

Lettuce → Rabbit → Snake → Hawk

Ecosystems that have become permanent in a broad geographical area are known as *biomes*. The earth is divided into several biomes:

1. The *arctic tundra* includes vast stretches of treeless plains around the Arctic Ocean. Here the temperature is the limiting factor in the ecosystem: It ranges from 60° F in the summer to –130°F in the winter. The ground is permanently frozen a few feet below the surface.

2. In the *taiga*, coniferous (evergreen) forests survive long, severe winters. Canada and Siberia have large taiga biomes.

3. The *deciduous* (leaf-shedding) *forests* of the world are in regions with relatively temperate (mild) climates.

4. *Deserts* form in regions where the annual rainfall is less than 2.5 inches (6.5 cm) or where rain is irregular and the rate of evaporation is very high. The Mojave, Sahara, and Gobi deserts are good examples.

5. *Grasslands* occur where rainfall is low and irregular. The Great Plains in central North America is a grasslands region; the vast, semi-arid grasslands in Siberia, Russia, and Mongolia are called *steppes*.

6. *Tropical rain forests* are characterized by high temperatures and constant rainfall. This type of biome is found in Central and South America, Africa, and Southeast Asia.

7. Oceans and seas form the *marine biome*, the thickest known layer of living things. Here, the depth of water determines where life flourishes.

PRACTICE QUESTIONS

1. Biology is the study of

   (A) plants.
   (B) animals.
   (C) living things.
   (D) minerals.

2. The commonly accepted steps in the scientific method are observation, _____, _____, theory, and law or principle.

   (A) experiment, conclusion
   (B) hypothesis, experiment
   (C) apotheosis, arrogation
   (D) hypothesis, clinical trials

3. Life functions include nutrition, _____, _____, _____, and _____.

   (A) excretion, respiration, stasis, reproduction
   (B) growth, digestion, circulation, mitosis
   (C) mitosis, meiosis, synthesis, excretion
   (D) circulation, respiration, growth, reproduction

4. The parts of a prokaryotic cell include the

   (A) membrane, nucleus, and mitochondrion.
   (B) membrane, nucleus, and neoplasm.
   (C) DNA, cytoplasm, and ribosomes.
   (D) endoplasmic reticulum, mitochondria, and organelles.

5. In animals, the primary purpose of carbohydrates is to

   (A) be converted into fat for later use as energy.
   (B) provide fuel for the body's cells and for brain functions.
   (C) build muscle and support tissue repair.
   (D) facilitate the transportation of hormones and enzymes throughout the body.

6. Botany is the scientific study of

   (A) animals.
   (B) plants.
   (C) botulism.
   (D) matter.

7. All living cells arise from

   (A) living matter.
   (B) dead or deceased matter.
   (C) inert matter.
   (D) enzymes.

8. Animal cells sometimes have flagella, which are threadlike structures that function in the _____ and the movement of _____ .

   (A) division of gamete cells, food particles for simple organisms
   (B) production of chlorophyll, fluid throughout the stem
   (C) movement of simple organisms, particles in more complex organisms
   (D) movement of particles in simple organisms, more complex organisms

9. The _____ is the basic structural and functional unit of virtually all life-forms.

   (A) cell
   (B) organelle
   (C) nucleus
   (D) chromosome

10. Carbohydrates are composed of _____, _____, and _____.

    (A) carbon, hydrogen, glucose
    (B) carbides, hydrates, oxygen
    (C) carbon, hydrogen, oxygen
    (D) carbon, hydrogen, nitrogen

11. _____ carry hereditary traits from parents to their offspring.

    (A) Proteins
    (B) Genes
    (C) Mitochondria
    (D) Ribosomes

12. Vertebrates are animals whose primary defining characteristic is that they

    (A) have no spine or backbone.
    (B) have a spine or backbone.
    (C) walk vertically (upright).
    (D) have an enclosed circulatory system.

13. In humans, the endocrine system

    (A) includes glands that regulate growth and blood pressure.
    (B) brings oxygen to cells and removes wastes from them.
    (C) allows humans to reproduce.
    (D) permits sensory communication between the organism and its environment.

14. Diseases can be divided into two categories,

    (A) helpful and harmful.
    (B) lethal and semilethal.
    (C) viruses and germs.
    (D) infectious and noninfectious.

15. The law of independent assortment, as postulated by Gregor Mendel, says that

    (A) when contrasting traits are independently crossed, one trait is dominant over the other.
    (B) each trait is inherited independently of all other traits.
    (C) individually independent heredity traits, or units, separate in the gametes.
    (D) the distribution of dominant genes is independent of parental gametes.

Answers Explained

1. **(C)** Biology is the study of *living things*. The study of plants is botany. The study of animals is zoology. The study of minerals is minerology, which is a subset of geology.

2. **(B)** The commonly accepted steps in the scientific method are observation, *hypothesis*, *experiment*, theory, and law or principle.

3. **(D)** Life functions include nutrition, *circulation*, *respiration*, *growth*, and *reproduction*. Other life functions are excretion, synthesis, and regulation.

4. **(C)** All organisms with prokaryotic cells (prokaryotes) are single-celled organisms, although there are single-celled eukaryotes, too. The biggest difference between the simpler prokaryotes and more complex eukaryotes is that eukaryotes have a nucleus surrounded by a membrane, while prokaryotes don't have a nucleus or other membrane-bound organelles.

5. **(B)** In animals, the primary purpose of carbohydrates is to *provide fuel for the body's cells and for brain functions.*

6. **(B)** Botany is the scientific study of *plants*. Zoology is the study of animals. Both chemistry and physics study matter but do so from different perspectives. Chemistry investigates the composition, structure, and properties of matter. Physics deals with matter and energy, especially the mechanical and electrical forces such as light, sound, heat, motion, and electromagnetism.

7. **(A)** All living cells arise from *living matter*. Enzymes are synthesized and used by living cells. However, enzymes do not directly give rise to more cells.

8. **(C)** Animal cells sometimes have flagella, which are threadlike structures that function in the *movement of simple organisms* and the movement of *particles in more complex organisms.*

9. **(A)** The *cell* is the basic structural and functional unit of virtually all life-forms.

10. **(C)** Carbohydrates are composed of *carbon*, *hydrogen*, and *oxygen.*

11. **(B)** *Genes* carry hereditary traits from parents to their offspring.

12. **(B)** Vertebrates are animals whose primary defining characteristic is that they *have a spine or backbone.* This spine or backbone is made of bone or cartilage. Invertebrates do not have a spine or backbone. Only a small group of vertebrates walk upright. For example, humans do. However, lizards, whales, and horses—which are all vertebrates—do not walk upright. Having an enclosed circulatory system is not the primary defining characteristic of vertebrates.

13. **(A)** In humans, the endocrine system *includes glands that regulate growth and blood pressure.* The lymphatic system brings oxygen to cells and removes waste products

from them. The reproductive system allows humans to reproduce. The nervous system permits sensory communication between the organism and its environment.

14. **(D)** Diseases can be divided into two categories, *infectious and noninfectious.*

15. **(B)** The law of independent assortment, as postulated by Gregor Mendel, says that *each trait is inherited independently of other traits.*

EARTH SCIENCE

The term *earth science* includes four major related scientific fields that help us understand the world around us: *geology* (the study of the earth); *oceanography* (the study of the seas and oceans); *meteorology* (the study of weather and climate); and *astronomy* (the study of Earth as part of the universe).

GEOLOGY

Geology deals with the formation and composition of the earth. It relates to and borrows from chemistry, physics, and biology. Geologists determine the strength and behavior of rock formations and their reaction to stress. This knowledge is useful for the design and construction of large buildings, dams, bridges, and tunnels; the prediction of earthquakes; and the location and mining of petroleum, coal, and other minerals.

About 4.6 billion years ago, the earth formed from leftovers after the birth of the sun. (The other planets in our solar system were formed in similar ways at about the same time.) About 4.54 billion years ago (that's 4,540,000,000 years), the denser metals sank to the center of the earth and formed the core, while the outside layer cooled and solidified to form the earth's crust. Over the next 100 million years or so, volcanic activity released water vapor into the forming atmosphere. Much of this water vapor came back down as rain, forming the first oceans. Life did not appear on earth until about 3.9 billion years ago.

The geologic history of the earth as we now understand it is divided into *eons*, *eras*, and *periods*, as shown in the following table. Some of these time periods are defined primarily by changes in the earth itself, while others are defined more by changes in life upon the earth. This demonstrates how different scientific fields overlap and tie together in our effort to understand the world around us.

Pre-20th century estimates of the earth's age were based on observed and calculated rates of erosion, rates of ocean salinity, examining sedimentary rock layers, and other methods. These methods led geologists to place the age of the earth between 100,000 and 1.5 billion years old. However, we now know that these methods are not reliable over long periods, because those rates can and do change over time and from place to place.

The most recently developed—and most reliable so far—method of determining the age of extremely old objects uses *radioactivity*. Antoine Henri Becquerel discovered radioactivity in 1896 and won the Nobel Prize for his work. Half of a quantity of a radioactive material will *decay* (lose its radioactivity and transform into a daughter isotope) at a constant rate. By measuring the ratio of the amount of the original radioactive element to the daughter isotopes, geologists can determine how many *half-lives* the element has undergone, thereby determining the age of the sample. By analyzing the decay products of particular elements such as uranium, strontium, and thorium, geologists can determine the age of rock samples. Rocks dated by this method exceeding 3.5 billion years of age have been found on all of earth's continents.

For *fossils* (plant and animal life preserved in rock) that are less than 50,000–60,000 years old, a similar method called *carbon-14 dating* can help establish when a fossil was actually a living plant or animal.

Eon	Era	Period	Significant Events
Hadeon (4.6–3.9 billion years ago)			Formation as a planet; solidification of continental and oceanic crusts
Archean (3.9–2.5 billion years ago)			One-celled life-forms appear in the oceans
Proterozoic (2.5 billion years ago to 540 million years ago)			Continents are merged into the supercontinent of Rodinia; mountain ranges result from tectonic and volcanic activity; multicellular life appears
Phanerozoic (540 million years ago to today)	Paleozoic (540–248 mya*)	Cambrian (540–500 mya*)	Supercontinent Rodinia breaks into smaller continents (not today's continents); marine invertebrates, first vertebrates, and earliest fish appear; period ends in mass extinctions due to glaciation
		Ordovician (500–438 mya*)	High sea levels; global cooling; glaciation; volcanic activity; primitive plants and fish; period ends in huge extinctions due to glaciation
		Silurian (438–408 mya*)	High seas worldwide; first jawed fish plus insects, vascular plants, and corals
		Devonian (408–360 mya*)	Fish and land plants become abundant and diverse; first amphibians, sharks, and bony fish; new insects.
		Mississippian/ Lower Carboniferous (360–325 mya*)	First winged insects, amphibians more common; mass extinction ~345 mya*
		Pennsylvanian/ Upper Carboniferous (325–280 mya*)	First reptiles, cockroaches, mayflies; many ferns
		Permian (280–248 mya*)	Continents merge into supercontinent Pangaea; amphibians and reptiles dominant; increased atmospheric oxygen almost at modern levels; ends with mass extinctions (100% of trilobites, 50% of animals, 95% of marine species) due to glaciation or volcanic activity

Eon	Era	Period	Significant Events
Phanerozoic (540 million years ago to today) (continued)	Mesozoic (248–65 mya*)	Triassic (248–208 mya*)	First dinosaurs and mammals; many reptiles; ends with extinction of 35% of animal families and almost all marine reptiles
		Jurassic (208–146 mya*)	Many dinosaurs; first birds and flowering plants
		Cretaceous (146–65 mya*)	High tectonic and volcanic activity; continents begin to look like current ones; peak of the dinosaurs; first crocodilians, feathered dinosaurs, and butterflies; early snakes, ants, and bees; ends with mass extinctions of dinosaurs and half of marine invertebrates, probably due to asteroid impact or volcanic activity
	Cenozoic (65 mya* to today)	Tertiary (65–1.8 mya*)	Large mammals, primates, rodents, whales, pigs, deer, horses, dogs, modern birds, and hominids
		Quaternary (1.8 mya* to today)	First humans, mammoths, saber-toothed cats; extinction of many large mammals and birds ~10,000 years ago at the end of last ice age; human civilization begins

*mya = million years ago

The Composition of the Earth

The earth is composed of multiple layers:

- Crust
- Mantle
- Liquid outer core
- Solid inner core

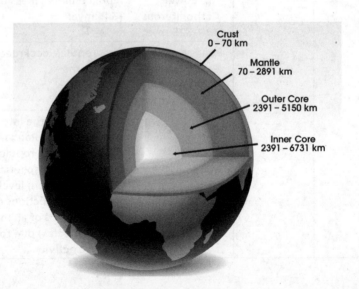

Crust
0 – 70 km

Mantle
70 – 2891 km

Outer Core
2391 – 5150 km

Inner Core
2391 – 6731 km

The continents and ocean basins make up the earth's *crust* or outermost layer (also called the *lithosphere*). It ranges from 3 to 46 miles (5–75 km) thick. The thickest parts of the crust are under the continents, and the thinnest are under the oceans. The crust is divided into huge *tectonic plates* that move slowly over the mantle over hundreds of millions of years. *Plate tectonics* is the theory describing the motion of these plates. Earthquakes happen when one plate grinds against another. Mountains form when tectonic plates collide, and deep trenches are made when one plate slides over another.

The *mantle* under the crust, made up mostly of silicate rocks, is about 1,800 miles (2,890 km) thick. Intense heat from the earth's molten metal core causes these rocks to rise over time. These rocks then cool and sink back down toward the core, where they are heated again. This *convection*—think of a lava lamp in slow motion—is thought to be what causes tectonic plate movement. Material from the mantle pushing through the crust is what causes volcanic eruptions.

Under the mantle is the *core*, which is made up of two parts. The solid, *inner core* is made of iron. It has a radius of about 760 miles (1,220 km) and is surrounded by a molten liquid *outer core* made of a nickel-iron alloy about 1,355 miles (2,180 km) thick. The inner core spins at a different speed than the rest of the planet. This spinning of the inner iron core generates the earth's magnetic field.

Different Types of Rocks

Geologists classify rocks in three groups, according to the major processes that formed them: igneous, sedimentary, and metamorphic.

Igneous rocks form from magma spit out when a volcano erupts; they are also called volcanic rocks. After an eruption, the lava spewed out by the volcano rapidly cools down and solidifies. Crystals formed in this way are usually small. Sometimes magma is trapped underground in pockets of other rocks. In this case, the magma cools more slowly, forming larger crystals and coarse-grained rocks. How the rocks form depends not only on the different cooling temperatures of the magma but also on the magma's chemical composition. Granite, basalt, and obsidian are examples of igneous rocks.

Sedimentary rocks are formed on the earth's surface, either in water or on land. They are sometimes called *secondary rocks* because they often result from an accumulation of small pieces broken off from previously existing rocks and can include mud and organic matter. Most sedimentary rocks become cemented together by minerals and chemicals present when they are formed. Some, however, remain loose, crumbly, and unconsolidated. Sedimentary rocks are divided into three subclasses:

- Clastic: fragmented rock joined together by compaction and cementation.
- Chemical: formed by successive layers of dissolved minerals left behind by evaporating water. Salt and gypsum are characteristic examples.
- Organic: rocks formed from seashells and the bones of animals.

Metamorphic rocks are sedimentary and igneous rocks that have been subjected to intense heat and/or pressure deep within the earth's crust, causing the rocks to undergo a complete change. The process doesn't melt the rocks but, instead, transforms them into other rocks that are denser and more compact. New minerals are formed, either by the rearrangement of the preexisting mineral's components or by reactions with fluids that enter the rocks.

PRACTICE QUESTIONS

1. Geology is the study of

    (A) all the living things on the earth.
    (B) the formation and composition of the earth.
    (C) the earth as part of the universe.
    (D) the history of fossilized deposits.

2. The three major types of rocks are

    (A) igneous, sedimentary, and secondary.
    (B) clastic, chemical, and organic.
    (C) volcanic, secondary, and sedimentary.
    (D) sedimentary, metamorphic, and igneous.

3. The relatively thin outer layer of the earth is called the _____, which rides on the _____, which is heated by the molten metal in the _____.

    (A) crust, mantle, core
    (B) surface, lithosphere, mantle
    (C) tectonic plate, mantle, inner core
    (D) crust, mantle, liquid inner core

4. The earth is about _____ years old as determined by _____.

    (A) 4.54 billion, measuring half-lives of fossils
    (B) 4.54 billion, measuring half-lives of radioactive minerals
    (C) 1.5 billion, erosion studies
    (D) 4.45 billion, measuring half-lives of carbon-based fossils

5. Salt and gypsum are characteristic examples of

    (A) clastic metamorphic rocks.
    (B) organic igneous rocks.
    (C) chemical sedimentary rocks.
    (D) unconsolidated secondary rocks.

Answers Explained

1. **(B)** Geology is the study of *the formation and composition of the earth*. The study of all the living things on the earth is biology. The study of the earth as part of the universe is earth science. The study of fossilized deposits is paleontology.

2. **(D)** The three major types of rocks are *sedimentary, metamorphic, and igneous*.

3. **(A)** The relatively thin outer layer of the earth is called the *crust*, which rides on the *mantle*, which is heated by the molten metal in the *core*.

4. **(B)** The earth is about *4.54 billion* years old as determined by *measuring half-lives of radioactive minerals*. Erosion studies are not reliable over long time periods, because those rates can and do change over the course of time and from place to place. Carbon

dating or carbon-14 dating can be used to determine when a fossil was a living organism, but it is reliable only up to 50,000–60,000 years ago.

5. **(C)** Salt and gypsum are characteristic examples of *chemical sedimentary rocks*.

OCEANOGRAPHY

The earth is unique among the solar system's planets because it has an abundance of water. Other planets—including some moons—have atmospheres, ice, and even oceans, but only our planet has the right combination to support life. Earth's saltwater oceans cover about 71 percent of the planet's surface with an average depth of 2.5 miles (4 km). The oceans hold about 96 percent of all water on the planet.

Using various related sciences, oceanography studies the oceans and seas. Although oceans cover almost three-fourths of earth's surface, only a small portion of this vast area is used by people. Examination of the ocean floor, marine life, and the mineral content of the water in different locations is important for the future development of essential materials, food, and medicines.

There are four major oceans on earth: the Pacific, Atlantic, Indian, and Arctic. In the simplest terms, an ocean may be divided into the *shoreline*, the *water* itself, and the *seabed*, or bottom. However, these classifications need further division into zones (levels), shown in the table below.

Marine Zones

Zone	Average Depth	Average Temperature	Comment
<u>Shore</u> (between high, low tides)	Varies	Varies by season	Wave action, light for photosynthesis
<u>Water</u> (1) shore to continental shelf	600 feet (0–200 meters)	41°–77°F (5°–25°C)	Waves, currents, greatest amount of plant and animal life
(2) downward slope from continental shelf	600–18,250 feet (200–2,500 meters)	41°–59°F (5°–15°C)	Currents, almost dark, fewer marine animals, no plants
(3) deeper plain	8,000–21,250 feet (2,500–6,500 meters)	27°–35°F (3°–4°C)	Dark, limited animal life, no plants
(4) deepest trenches or canyons	21,250–37,350 feet (6,500–11,500 meters)	34°–37°F (1°–3°C)	Dark, very limited animal life, no plants

Oceans and Natural Resources

The oceans represent a vast source of information and natural resources that have not yet been fully tapped because the ocean environment is hostile and not readily accessible. The oceans contain information in the sedentary layers and fossils that line their floors. The core samples that have been retrieved by oceanographic research vessels reveal a lot of information about the Earth's geologic history, and fossils found in these sediments record a history of life in the oceans. The information obtained from ocean sediments about past climates and the ways they have changed helps us understand our present climate. Careful study of ocean bottoms also revealed the mechanism for continental drift, which led to the theory of *plate tectonics.*

The ocean is also an important source of valuable chemical and mineral resources such as bromine, iodine, magnesium, manganese, oil, natural gas, phosphorite, and metal-rich muds. Moreover, as desalination plants are made more efficient, the oceans are becoming a valuable source of freshwater in arid regions. The oceans are also a critical source of food, particularly animal protein. Although aquaculture, or farming the oceans, is still in its infancy, it is becoming an increasingly important source of animals such as clams, oysters, and shrimp, as well as such plants as kelp.

It is difficult to determine the mineral resources of the oceans because they are underwater, and the usual methods of mineral exploration and recovery on land cannot be used. However, the estimated value of the mineral resources of the oceans is staggering.

The most valuable resources we know about are the oil and natural gas found in the sediments of the continental shelf. The value of oil and gas obtained from the oceans yearly is greater than the combined value of all biological resources taken from the ocean.

The rising of magma, or liquified rock material, in the ocean ridges and the movements of magma near subduction zones (a region of the earth's crust where tectonic plates meet) create fluids enriched in minerals, which are then deposited on the ocean floor. The deposits found include such minerals as copper, iron, zinc, manganese, nickel, vanadium, lead, chromium, cobalt, silver, and gold.

Generally, animal life and plant life typical of one zone are not found in a different zone. However, there are exceptions; there are no exact boundaries between zones to prevent a sea creature from moving from one level to another. Knowledge of the deeper levels and the ocean bottom is still incomplete.

An important influence of the ocean on human life comes from tides. Tides are the alternate rising and falling of water levels in the oceans and other large bodies of water, the result of the gravitational pull of the sun and the moon on the freely moving waters of the earth. Since the moon is much closer to the earth than the sun is, the moon has a much greater effect on tides. Tides affect the movement of ships, especially when in port in shallow waters.

PRACTICE QUESTIONS

1. There are _____ major oceans on the earth that together hold about _____ of the planet's water.

   (A) four, 96 percent
   (B) four, three-quarters
   (C) five, 71 percent
   (D) six, two-thirds

2. Subduction zones are

   (A) usually found between the shore and the continental shelf.
   (B) seafloor areas rich in petroleum and mineral resources.
   (C) underwater mountain ranges caused by tectonic activity.
   (D) areas where tectonic plates meet.

3. The deepest marine zones contain a surprising variety of marine animals but no plants.

   (A) True
   (B) False

4. Tides are caused by the

   (A) difference in rotation rates between the inner and outer core.
   (B) gravitational pull of the moon and nearby planets.
   (C) gravitational pull of the moon.
   (D) gravitational pull of the sun and the moon.

5. An ocean can be divided into

   (A) seabed, water, and shoreline.
   (B) seabed, continental shelf, and shoreline.
   (C) shoreline, continental shelf, and underwater canyons.
   (D) populated and unpopulated marine zones.

Answers Explained

1. **(A)** There are *four* major oceans on the earth that together hold about *96 percent* of the planet's water. The four major oceans are the Pacific, Atlantic, Indian, and Arctic.

2. **(D)** Subduction zones are *areas where tectonic plates meet.*

3. **(B)** False. Although it is true that the deepest marine zones have no plants, they contain only a limited variety of animal life, not a surprising variety of marine animals.

4. **(D)** Tides are caused by the *gravitational pull of the sun and the moon* on the freely moving waters of the earth. Since the moon is much closer than the sun, the moon's influence is greater. However, the sun still has an effect on earth's waters.

5. **(A)** An ocean can be divided into *seabed, water, and shoreline.* The continental shelf and underwater canyons are part of the seabed.

ASTRONOMY

Astronomy is related to and interwoven with both physics and the earth sciences. The *rotation* of the earth on its *axis* (an imaginary line running between the North and South Poles) causes day and night, as one side or the other of the planet faces the sun.

The earth's path, or *orbit*, around the sun is not perfectly circular. The earth's axis is tilted 23.5 degrees away from being exactly perpendicular to the plane of its orbit around the sun. This is called the *axial tilt.* (You could say that the earth leans over some, instead of standing straight up.) As the earth orbits the sun, the planet's tilted axis stays pointing in the same direction in relation to its orbit. So throughout the year, different parts of the earth get more or less of the sun's direct rays, causing the seasons.

The earth is part of our *solar system*, which includes the sun and seven other planets (for a total of eight) with their various moons (see table on page 119). Each *revolution* of the earth around the sun takes 365.25 days—which is why we have a leap year every four years. The extra day during leap year balances out those accumulated extra quarter days.

The sun is the largest and most important body in our solar system, containing well over 99 percent of all the mass in the solar system. In fact, the sun's diameter is more than 100 times that of earth. The sun provides the heat, light, and other energy that makes life on earth possible. Electrically charged (and very hot) particles and plasma from the sun's outer layer—the *solar wind*—continually stream into space. These vary in density, temperature, and speed. The solar wind bathes everything in the solar system, sometimes affecting normal magnetic and electromagnetic situations on the planets.

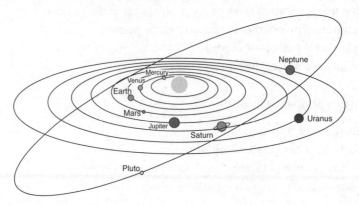

The four inner planets (Mercury, Venus, Earth, and Mars) consist mostly of iron and rock. They are known as *terrestrial* (earthlike) planets because they're somewhat similar to earth in size and composition. The outer planets are huge and have thick, gaseous outer layers, mostly hydrogen and helium. The composition of the outer planets is more like that of the sun than of earth. Beneath their outer layers, the pressure of the outer planets' thick atmospheres turns their insides liquid, though they may have rocky cores. Rings of dust, rock, and ice chunks surround all the giant planets. Saturn's rings are the best known. However, thin rings also encircle Jupiter, Uranus, and Neptune.

A band of *asteroids*—large, irregularly shaped chunks of rock, metals, and other materials—is found between the orbits of Mars and Jupiter. This asteroid belt is more than two and a half times as far away from the Sun as it is from the earth. Most of these asteroids are relatively small, from the size of boulders to a few thousand feet in diameter. Some, though, are much larger. At least 16 of these asteroids are more than 150 miles in diameter. Although there are billions of asteroids in the asteroid belt, scientists believe their total mass is still less than that of our moon.

Pluto was considered the ninth and most distant planet of our solar system from its discovery in 1930 until 2006, when the International Astronomical Union reclassified Pluto as a *dwarf planet*. However, not everyone in the scientific community agrees, and the discussion is still ongoing. You should keep Pluto in mind because the ASVAB questions about the solar system may or may not have been updated to reflect the latest official actions on Pluto's status.

Occasionally, earth's moon goes into *eclipse*. An eclipse occurs when one astronomical body cuts off light from another. A *lunar eclipse* occurs when the earth comes directly between the sun and the moon, thus causing the earth's shadow (*umbra*) to fall directly on the moon. Since the moon shines only in light reflected from the sun, this position of the earth puts the moon into eclipse.

Planet	Average Distance from the Sun (Million Miles)	Rank by Size	Time for Revolution	Number of Moons
Mercury	36.0	8	88 days	0
Venus	67.2	6	225 days	0
Earth	93.0	5	365¼ days	1
Mars	141.6	7	687 days	2
Jupiter	483.8	1	12 years	67
Saturn	890.8	2	29 years	62
Uranus	1,784.8	3	84 years	27
Neptune	2,793.1	4	164 years	14

In a total *solar eclipse*, the moon is directly between the earth and the sun, so that the umbra of the moon's shadow that sweeps across the earth during a solar eclipse is very narrow—only about 170 miles at its maximum. The *penumbra* is a much wider area of partial shadow where the sun's light is only partly cut off.

Two astronomical bodies that interest humans are *comets* and *meteors*. Comets are mostly gaseous bodies that can be seen from earth for periods ranging from a few days to months at a time. The *comet head* contains a small bright nucleus made up of ice, frozen gases, and other particles. When a comet approaches the sun, these gases and particles stream off in the form of a *tail*, sometimes as long as 100 million miles.

A meteor is a small piece of extraterrestrial matter that becomes visible when it enters earth's atmosphere. In the friction that goes along with this entry, a meteor heats up intensely and usually disintegrates before it can reach the ground. Those meteors large enough to reach ground are called *meteorites*. The glow of a meteor's appearance has led it to be called (incorrectly) a "shooting star" or "falling star."

PRACTICE QUESTIONS

1. The earth is part of a solar system that contains the sun and

   (A) seven other planets and an asteroid belt.
   (B) eight other planets and an asteroid belt.
   (C) nine other planets and an asteroid belt.
   (D) moon only.

2. The rotation of the earth on its axis causes

   (A) tides.
   (B) day and night.
   (C) the seasons.
   (D) axial tilt.

3. The earth's axial tilt causes

   (A) tides.
   (B) day and night.
   (C) the seasons.
   (D) the rotation of the earth.

4. The asteroid belt is

   (A) just beyond the orbit of Neptune.
   (B) between Earth and Mars.
   (C) between Mars and Jupiter.
   (D) between Jupiter and Saturn.

5. The smallest planet in the solar system is _____, and the largest body in the solar system is _____.

   (A) Pluto, the sun.
   (B) Mercury, Jupiter
   (C) Pluto, Jupiter
   (D) Mercury, the sun

6. Light travels at an approximate speed of

   (A) 186,000 miles per hour.
   (B) 186,000 miles per second.
   (C) 186,000,000 miles per hour.
   (D) 18,600 miles per minute.

Answers Explained

1. **(A)** The earth is part of a solar system that contains the sun and *seven other planets and an asteroid belt*. Pluto is no longer classified as a planet. So the solar system consists of the sun, the earth, and seven other planets.

2. **(B)** The rotation of the earth on its axis causes *day and night*. Tides are caused by the gravitational pull of the sun and earth's moon. The seasons are caused by the tilt of the earth's axis, which brings parts of the earth closer to the sun at different times of the year. The rotation of the earth around its axis does not cause the tilt of the earth's axis.

3. **(C)** The earth's axial tilt causes *the seasons*.

4. **(C)** The asteroid belt is *between Mars and Jupiter*.

5. **(D)** The smallest planet in the solar system is *Mercury*, and the largest body in the solar system is *the sun*. Jupiter is the largest planet. However, since the sun is about 10 times larger than Jupiter, the sun is the largest body in the solar system. Note that Pluto is no longer classified as a planet. Therefore, it cannot be the smallest planet in the solar system.

6. **(B)** Light travels at an approximate speed of *186,000 miles per second*.

METEOROLOGY

Meteorology is the study of *weather* and *climate*. Weather is the condition of the atmosphere at a particular time and place. Climate is the average of weather conditions in a particular place over a period of time. The services of *meteorologists* in predicting the weather are critical to farmers, travelers, and people in many different kinds of business.

Weather is the description of several atmospheric conditions interacting with one another. These conditions—*temperature, air pressure, winds, humidity*, etc.—are themselves influenced by other factors.

1. The temperature of a place is affected by the angle of the sun's rays, the length of its daylight period, its altitude, and its closeness to bodies of water. Water heats and cools more slowly than land and affects the air above it in the same way. Therefore, breezes blowing off the water tend to moderate the temperature of air over faster-heating and faster-cooling land.

2. The pressure of the air depends on its temperature and humidity. Warm air is lighter than cold air, and moist air is lighter than dry air. Thus moist, warm air has very low pressure. Changes in atmospheric pressure are measured on a *barometer*. When meteorologists at the weather bureau see a "falling" barometer, they predict rain.

3. Wind is the movement of air from one place to another. Winds are caused by differences in air pressure. Winds always move from areas of higher pressure (cold, dry air) to areas of lower pressure (warm, moist air). Sometimes the difference in pressure between two areas is great enough to cause *hurricanes* or *tornadoes*. A hurricane is a wind of 74 miles or more per hour. A tornado is a wind with a funnel-shaped cloud that touches the ground.

4. Humidity refers to the amount of moisture in the air. When the air is warm and dry, moisture on the earth's surface tends to *evaporate* (turn into vapor). When the air is completely filled with moisture (when it is *saturated*), a drop in the temperature will cause the moisture in the air to *condense* (form droplets) and *precipitate* (fall) as rain, snow, sleet, hail, etc.

The Atmosphere

The earth's atmosphere has five layers that perform many functions, including keeping the earth's temperatures within an acceptable range, transmitting sound energy, and protecting us from most of the sun's harmful rays. These five layers are the *troposphere, stratosphere, mesosphere, thermosphere,* and *exosphere*. The *ionosphere* is not considered to be one of the five layers. Instead, it overlaps the *mesosphere* and the *thermosphere*.

TROPOSPHERE

The troposphere is the densest part of the atmosphere; almost all weather occurs in this layer. It starts at the earth's surface and extends to an altitude of 5–9 miles (8–14.5 km) high.

STRATOSPHERE

The stratosphere starts just above the troposphere and extends to 31 miles (50 km) high above the planet. The ozone layer, which absorbs and scatters solar ultraviolet radiation, is in this layer.

MESOSPHERE

The mesosphere starts just above the stratosphere and extends up to 53 miles (85 km) above the surface of the earth. Meteors usually burn up in this layer of the atmosphere.

THERMOSPHERE

The thermosphere starts just above the mesosphere and extends out to about 370 miles (600 km) above the surface of the planet. The northern lights (*aurora borealis*) phenomenon happens here, and most satellites orbit the earth in this layer.

EXOSPHERE

As the upper limit of our atmosphere, the exosphere extends from the top of the thermosphere out to about 6,200 miles (10,000 km) above the planet.

IONOSPHERE

The ionosphere is an abundant layer of electrons and ionized atoms and molecules that stretches from about the top of the stratosphere (30 miles [48 km]) above earth's surface) to the edge of space at about 600 miles (965 km), overlapping the mesosphere and thermosphere. This dynamic region grows and shrinks based on solar conditions. The ionosphere is a critical link in the chain of interactions between the sun and the earth. The ionosphere is also what makes radio communications possible.

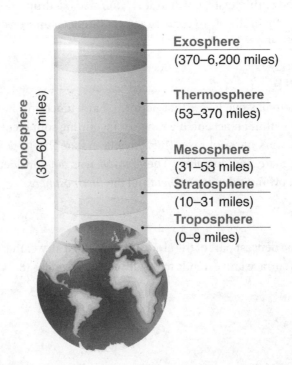

Clouds

Clouds help regulate the earth's temperature and bring vital rain to different areas. Clouds develop out of the process of *convection*, which changes atmospheric moisture from a gas to a liquid.

As solar radiation heats the ground and the air immediately above it, the warmed air becomes lighter and rises upward. As the air rises, the temperature decreases, as does the amount of water vapor the air can hold. This vapor rapidly condenses and forms clouds composed of many billions of tiny water droplets or ice crystals. These droplets are exceedingly small, averaging about 10 microns in diameter. (A micron is one-millionth of a meter. Ice crystals are much larger but less concentrated.) Virtually all types of clouds and precipitation form due to rising air.

On the other hand, as air sinks, its temperature rises again. The air's capacity for holding vapor increases as the temperature increases. Any cloud droplets tend to evaporate. The cloud itself disappears as evaporation changes moisture back from either a liquid or a solid into a gas.

Clouds also form where air masses collide; two different air masses can't mix unless they are very similar in temperature and moisture content. If a cold, dry air mass pushes into a warm, moist air mass, the warmer air is forced upward, rapidly producing clouds that bubble up, perhaps leading to lightning, thunder, and showers. If the cold air retreats instead, warm air pushing over that cold air can bring a much slower process of lowering and thickening clouds. Finally, light precipitation occurs in the form of light rain, mist, or drizzle.

Three major classifications describe the appearance of clouds using Latin terms.

- Cirrus, from the Latin *cirro*, meaning "curly" or "fibrous."
- Stratus, form the Latin *strato*, suggesting sheets or layers.
- Cumulus, from the Latin *cumulo*, indicating "heaped" or "piled."

By combining these with other terms, a number of different clouds can be described. For example, the Latin word for "shower" is *nimbus*, so the technical term for a cloud that produces thunderstorms is *cumulonimbus*.

Clouds are also categorized by how high above the ground they form.

- **High clouds:** *Cirrus, cirrostratus,* and *cirrocumulus* clouds are delicate, wispy clouds at altitudes above 20,000 feet (6,096 mi). These clouds are composed of ice crystals because at such altitudes, temperatures are perpetually below freezing.
- **Middle clouds:** *Altostratus, altocumulus,* and *nimbostratus* clouds are typically found at an altitude between 6,000 and 20,000 feet (1,829–6,096 mi).
- **Low clouds:** *Stratus, cumulus,* and *stratocumulus* clouds occur at altitudes of 6,000 feet (1,829 mi) or lower. Stratus clouds appear as smooth, even sheets from which light rain and drizzle often fall (light snow or freezing drizzle during the winter). Fog is just a stratus cloud reaching to or on the ground. Cumulus clouds can range in size from isolated balls of cotton to big heaps of mashed potatoes in the sky. They are often called *fair weather clouds* because they are not usually associated with precipitation. Occasionally, though, they can grow into clouds that produce thunderstorms (*cumulonimbus*). Low clouds are convective clouds, caused by the sun heating the ground. Stratocumulus clouds, like altocumulus, can appear in a wide variety of shapes and textures.

- **Clouds of great vertical development:** These are the cumulonimbus clouds, often called *thunderhead*s because they can bring torrential rain, vivid lightning, and thunder. The tops of such clouds may reach up to 60,000 feet (18,288 mi) or more. Ice crystals get sheared off and are carried away by strong winds, forming a flattened shield of cirrus clouds that spread out in the shape of an anvil. Sometimes hail—or, more rarely, a tornado—comes from a cumulonimbus cloud.

PRACTICE QUESTIONS

1. The barometric pressure at a particular location directly depends on _____.
   - (A) the air's temperature and humidity
   - (B) solar wind flares and local wind speed
   - (C) local wind speed and temperature
   - (D) the air's humidity and the local prevailing wind speed

2. Climate is the
   - (A) current weather conditions in a certain place.
   - (B) forecast weather conditions in a certain place.
   - (C) seasonally adjusted average rainfall over time.
   - (D) average of the weather conditions in a certain place over time.

3. Humidity refers to
   - (A) the amount of moisture in the air.
   - (B) the distance to the nearest body of water.
   - (C) the temperature of the air at a standstill.
   - (D) the density of the air at the point of measurement.

4. Winds are directly caused by
   - (A) differences in humidity.
   - (B) differences in air pressure.
   - (C) differences in wind speed.
   - (D) differences in temperature.

5. Which one of the following types of clouds is typically found at lower atmospheric levels?
   - (A) Cirrus
   - (B) Altostratus
   - (C) Cirrostratus
   - (D) Cumulus

Answers Explained

1. **(A)** The barometric pressure at a particular location directly depends on *the air's temperature and humidity*. Solar flares and wind speed have nothing to do with barometric pressure.

2. **(D)** Climate is the *average of the weather conditions in a certain place over time*.

3. **(A)** Humidity refers to *the amount of moisture in the air*.

4. **(B)** Winds are directly caused by *differences in air pressure* that seek to equalize themselves.

5. **(D)** *Cumulus* clouds are typically found at lower atmospheric levels. Stratus, cumulus, and stratocumulus clouds occur at altitudes of 6,000 feet (1,829 mi) or less. Cirrus, cirrostratus, and cirrocumulus clouds are delicate, wispy clouds at altitudes above 20,000 feet (6,096 mi). Altostratus, altocumulus, and nimbostratus clouds are typically found between 6,000 and 20,000 feet (1,829–6,096 mi).

CHEMISTRY

Chemistry is a physical science that investigates the composition, structure, and properties of *matter*. Chemistry is also concerned with changes in matter and the *energy* involved during those changes.

MATTER

Matter is anything that occupies space and has mass. *Mass* is the quantity of matter that a substance possesses and, depending on the gravitational force acting on it, has a unit of weight assigned to it. Although the weight can vary, the mass of a body is a constant and can be measured by its resistance to a change of position or motion. For example, an astronaut who weighs 168 lbs. on earth weighs about 28 lbs. on the moon, but still has the same mass. This property of mass to resist a change of position or motion is called *inertia*. Since matter occupies space, we can compare the masses of various substances that occupy a particular unit of volume. This relationship of mass to a volume unit is called the *density* of a substance.

Matter occurs in one of three *states*, or conditions: A substance may be a *solid*, a *liquid*, or a *gas*. A solid has both a definite size and shape (for example, an ice cube before it melts). A liquid has a definite volume, but it takes the shape of the container it's in. For example, an ice cube is a solid with a definite shape. If it melts in a cup, the liquid water then takes the shape of the cup. A gas has neither definite shape nor definite volume. Often, the state of matter that a particular substance is in can be changed by the addition or removal of *heat energy*. For example, water that is cooled sufficiently will freeze; heated sufficiently, it will turn into a gas.

Matter occurs in one of three states: solid, liquid, or gas.

Matter can be categorized in another way: It may be either an *element*, a *compound*, or a *mixture*. An element is a substance that is made up of only one kind of atom. For example, gold, iron, sulfur, oxygen are all elements and each contains only one kind of atom. A compound is a substance composed of two or more kinds of atoms joined together in a definite pattern. For example, water (H_2O) always occurs in the relationship of two atoms of hydrogen to one atom of oxygen. A mixture is an indefinite blending of two or more substances.

Sometimes the substances are very evenly distributed (e.g., food coloring in water). Other times, the mixture is uneven (e.g., raisins in cookie dough).

Matter can undergo two types of change: *physical* and *chemical*. In a physical change, the appearance of a substance may change, but its chemical composition remains the same (for example, broken glass, split wood, melted ice). A chemical change involves a change in the chemical makeup of a substance (for example, burning wood) and is always accompanied by either the release or absorption of energy.

In describing a state of matter and its changes, we speak of the *physical* and *chemical properties* of matter. The physical properties of a substance are those we can observe or measure with our senses: its color, taste, melting point, hardness, etc. The chemical properties of a substance are those that describe its reactions with other substances (for example, iron rusts in the presence of oxygen, gold does not, etc.). The smallest particle of a substance that has all the physical and chemical properties of the substance is called a *molecule.*

PRACTICE QUESTIONS

1. Matter is

    (A) anything that has a definite size and shape.
    (B) anything that occupies space and has mass.
    (C) anything that uses energy to change its state.
    (D) anything that has a definite volume.

2. Inertia is the property of matter to

    (A) resist a change of position or motion.
    (B) resist a change of volume or shape.
    (C) resist a change of composition.
    (D) interact or not interact with other substances.

3. Matter exists in one of three states or conditions: _____, _____, or _____.

    (A) element, compound, mixture
    (B) solid, liquid, gas
    (C) physical, chemical, molecular
    (D) physical, inertial, chemical

4. The density of a substance is

    (A) the relationship of its mass to a unit of volume.
    (B) the relationship of its volume to its chemical state.
    (C) the relationship of its weight to its volume.
    (D) the relationship of its inertia to its volume.

5. A chemical change is always accompanied by

    (A) a physical change.
    (B) the expenditure of energy.
    (C) the release or absorption of energy.
    (D) the appearance of the substance.

Answers Explained

1. **(B)** Matter is *anything that occupies space and has mass*. Matter does not have to maintain a specific size or shape—liquids don't. Matter also does not have to maintain a definite volume—gases don't.

2. **(A)** Inertia is the property of matter to *resist a change of position or motion*. This is addressed by Newton's first law of motion, which states that an object at rest stays at rest and an object in motion stays in motion (at the same speed and in the same direction) unless acted on by an unbalanced force.

3. **(B)** Matter exists in one of three states or conditions: *solid, liquid,* or *gas*. Frequently, a substance's state may be changed by adding or removing heat, such as when heat melts ice into liquid water and then turns that ice into steam. More recent, higher-level texts add a fourth state of matter—plasma—which is different from a gas because plasma is electrically conductive. However, plasma is unlikely to be addressed in an ASVAB question.

4. **(A)** The density of a substance is *the relationship of its mass to a unit of volume*. Density is determined by dividing the substance's mass by its volume. For any particular substance, there's a linear relationship between its mass and its volume: when one increases, so does the other, and vice versa.

5. **(C)** A chemical change is always accompanied by *the release or absorption of energy*. A chemical change involves a change in the substance's chemical makeup. Some examples are burning wood, an egg cooking, iron rusting, and food rotting. In all of these cases, heat is involved. The substance resulting from the process cannot be turned back into the original substance.

ENERGY

Energy is usually defined as the ability to do work. Energy may appear in a variety of forms—as *light, heat, sound, mechanical energy, electrical energy*, and *chemical energy*. Energy can be converted from one form to another. For example: (1) heat from burning fuel is used to vaporize water, changing it to steam; (2) this steam energy is used to turn turbine wheels to produce mechanical energy; (3) the turbine turns a generator to produce electricity; and (4) this electricity is then available in homes for use as light, heat, or in the operation of appliances.

Two general classifications of energy are *potential energy* and *kinetic energy*. Potential energy is due to the position of an object. Kinetic energy is energy of motion. The difference between the two can be illustrated by a boulder on the slope of a mountain. While it remains there, the boulder has high potential energy due to its position above the valley floor. If it falls, however, its potential energy is converted into kinetic energy.

What is the relationship between matter and energy? The *Law of Conservation of Mass and Energy* states that matter and energy are neither created nor lost during chemical reactions. The law also states that matter and energy are interchangeable under special conditions. Albert Einstein's formula for this interchange is

$$E = mc^2$$
$$\text{Energy} = \text{mass} \times (\text{speed of light})^2$$

SYMBOLS AND EQUATIONS IN CHEMISTRY

Chemistry requires the understanding of *symbols* and *equations*. Symbols are short forms for expressing an idea or a term. Symbols in chemistry include the following examples:

$\rightarrow$ means "yields" or "leads" to (arrows are also used in chemical equations, where they perform the same function as the equal sign in mathematics)

$\uparrow$ means "forms a gas"

$\downarrow$ means "forms a *precipitate*" (something that settles to the bottom of a liquid)

An equation resembles a sentence, made up of words. A chemical equation is made up of formulas of molecules. A formula may be of a compound—H_2O or $NaCl$, for example—or an element, Mg, O_2, etc. A *chemical equation* shows what happens when chemical elements or compounds interact. For example, you can read the following as a sentence:

$$2H_2 + O_2 \rightarrow 2H_2O$$

Translated, this chemical equation reads, "Two molecules (or four atoms) of the element hydrogen and one molecule (two atoms) of the element oxygen combine to yield two molecules of a compound called H_2O, which is water." The basic features of a chemical equation are:

- A chemical equation shows a *chemical change*. Either a new chemical compound is formed, or a compound is separated into its elements.
- The equation must *balance*. The total quantities to the left of the arrow ($\rightarrow$) must equal the total quantities to the right of the arrow. In the following equation, you have two hydrogen (H_2) and two chlorine (Cl_2) molecules yielding only one molecule of hydrogen chloride (HCl). This is, therefore, an *imbalanced equation:*

$$H_2 + Cl_2 \rightarrow HCl$$

If you place a "2" before the HCl compound, you make the two hydrogen and two chlorine atoms on the left equal to two hydrogen and two chlorine atoms contained in two hydrogen chloride molecules on the right. Thus, this equation is balanced:

$$H_2 + Cl_2 \rightarrow 2HCl$$

The periodic table of the elements was first used in 1869 by Dmitry I. Mendeleyev as a way of presenting all the elements in a way that shows their similarities and differences. The elements are arranged in increasing order of *atomic number* (Z) as you go from left to right across the table. The horizontal rows are called *periods*, and the vertical columns are known as *groups*.

A *noble gas* is found at the right side of each period. There is a progression from metals to nonmetals across each period. Elements found in groups (e.g., alkali, halogens) have a similar electronic configuration—the number of electrons. The number of electrons in the outer shell is the same as the number of the group (e.g., lithium 2·1).

The block of elements between groups 2 and 13 is called the *transition metals*. Like all metals, they are both *ductile* (can be drawn out into a thin wire) and *malleable* (can be bent or pressed into a new shape without breaking or cracking). Transition metals can conduct heat and electricity. Three noteworthy transition metals are iron, cobalt, and nickel, which are the only elements known to produce a magnetic field.

Periodic Table of the Elements

Legend:
- Atomic Number → 1
- Symbol → H
- Name → Hydrogen
- Atomic Weight → 1.008

Group																	
1 IA	2 IIA	3 IIIB	4 IVB	5 VB	6 VIB	7 VIIB	8 VIIIB	9 VIIIB	10 VIIIB	11 IB	12 IIB	13 IIIA	14 IVA	15 VA	16 VIA	17 VIIA	18 VIIIA

Period 1:
- 1 H Hydrogen 1.008
- 2 He Helium 4.002602

Period 2:
- 3 Li Lithium 6.94
- 4 Be Beryllium 9.0121831
- 5 B Boron 10.81
- 6 C Carbon 12.011
- 7 N Nitrogen 14.007
- 8 O Oxygen 15.999
- 9 F Fluorine 18.998403163
- 10 Ne Neon 20.1797

Period 3:
- 11 Na Sodium 22.98976928
- 12 Mg Magnesium 24.305
- 13 Al Aluminium 26.9815385
- 14 Si Silicon 28.085
- 15 P Phosphorus 30.973761998
- 16 S Sulfur 32.06
- 17 Cl Chlorine 35.45
- 18 Ar Argon 39.948

Period 4:
- 19 K Potassium 39.0983
- 20 Ca Calcium 40.078
- 21 Sc Scandium 44.955908
- 22 Ti Titanium 47.867
- 23 V Vanadium 50.9415
- 24 Cr Chromium 51.9961
- 25 Mn Manganese 54.938044
- 26 Fe Iron 55.845
- 27 Co Cobalt 58.933194
- 28 Ni Nickel 58.6934
- 29 Cu Copper 63.546
- 30 Zn Zinc 65.38
- 31 Ga Gallium 69.723
- 32 Ge Germanium 72.630
- 33 As Arsenic 74.921595
- 34 Se Selenium 78.971
- 35 Br Bromine 79.904
- 36 Kr Krypton 83.798

Period 5:
- 37 Rb Rubidium 85.4678
- 38 Sr Strontium 87.62
- 39 Y Yttrium 88.90584
- 40 Zr Zirconium 91.224
- 41 Nb Niobium 92.90637
- 42 Mo Molybdenum 95.95
- 43 Tc Technetium (98)
- 44 Ru Ruthenium 101.07
- 45 Rh Rhodium 102.90550
- 46 Pd Palladium 106.42
- 47 Ag Silver 107.8682
- 48 Cd Cadmium 112.414
- 49 In Indium 114.818
- 50 Sn Tin 118.710
- 51 Sb Antimony 121.760
- 52 Te Tellurium 127.60
- 53 I Iodine 126.90447
- 54 Xe Xenon 131.293

Period 6:
- 55 Cs Caesium 132.90545196
- 56 Ba Barium 137.327
- 57 - 71 Lanthanoids
- 72 Hf Hafnium 178.49
- 73 Ta Tantalum 180.94788
- 74 W Tungsten 183.84
- 75 Re Rhenium 186.207
- 76 Os Osmium 190.23
- 77 Ir Iridium 192.217
- 78 Pt Platinum 195.084
- 79 Au Gold 196.966569
- 80 Hg Mercury 200.592
- 81 Tl Thallium 204.38
- 82 Pb Lead 207.2
- 83 Bi Bismuth 208.98040
- 84 Po Polonium (209)
- 85 At Astatine (210)
- 86 Rn Radon (222)

Period 7:
- 87 Fr Francium (223)
- 88 Ra Radium (226)
- 89 - 103 Actinoids
- 104 Rf Rutherfordium (267)
- 105 Db Dubnium (268)
- 106 Sg Seaborgium (269)
- 107 Bh Bohrium (270)
- 108 Hs Hassium (269)
- 109 Mt Meitnerium (278)
- 110 Ds Darmstadtium (281)
- 111 Rg Roentgenium (282)
- 112 Cn Copernicium (285)
- 113 Nh Nihonium (286)
- 114 Fl Flerovium (289)
- 115 Mc Moscovium (289)
- 116 Lv Livermorium (293)
- 117 Ts Tennessine (294)
- 118 Og Oganesson (294)

Lanthanoids:
- 57 La Lanthanum 138.90547
- 58 Ce Cerium 140.116
- 59 Pr Praseodymium 140.90766
- 60 Nd Neodymium 144.242
- 61 Pm Promethium (145)
- 62 Sm Samarium 150.36
- 63 Eu Europium 151.964
- 64 Gd Gadolinium 157.25
- 65 Tb Terbium 158.92535
- 66 Dy Dysprosium 162.500
- 67 Ho Holmium 164.93033
- 68 Er Erbium 167.259
- 69 Tm Thulium 168.93422
- 70 Yb Ytterbium 173.045
- 71 Lu Lutetium 174.9668

Actinoids:
- 89 Ac Actinium (227)
- 90 Th Thorium 232.0377
- 91 Pa Protactinium 231.03588
- 92 U Uranium 238.02891
- 93 Np Neptunium (237)
- 94 Pu Plutonium (244)
- 95 Am Americium (243)
- 96 Cm Curium (247)
- 97 Bk Berkelium (247)
- 98 Cf Californium (251)
- 99 Es Einsteinium (252)
- 100 Fm Fermium (257)
- 101 Md Mendelevium (258)
- 102 No Nobelium (259)
- 103 Lr Lawrencium (266)

Atomic Number	Element Symbol	Element Name
1	H	Hydrogen
2	He	Helium
3	Li	Lithium
4	Be	Beryllium
5	B	Boron
6	C	Carbon
7	N	Nitrogen
8	O	Oxygen
9	F	Fluorine
10	Ne	Neon
11	Na	Sodium
12	Mg	Magnesium
13	Al	Aluminum
14	Si	Silicon
15	P	Phosphorus
16	S	Sulfur
17	Cl	Chlorine
18	Ar	Argon
19	K	Potassium
20	Ca	Calcium
21	Sc	Scandium
22	Ti	Titanium
23	V	Vanadium
24	Cr	Chromium
25	Mn	Manganese
26	Fe	Iron
27	Co	Cobalt
28	Ni	Nickel
29	Cu	Copper
30	Zn	Zinc
31	Ga	Gallium
32	Ge	Germanium
33	As	Arsenic
34	Se	Selenium
35	Br	Bromine
36	Kr	Krypton
37	Rb	Rubidium
38	Sr	Strontium
39	Y	Yttrium
40	Zr	Zirconium
41	Nb	Niobium
42	Mo	Molybdenum

Atomic Number	Element Symbol	Element Name
43	Tc	Technetium
44	Ru	Ruthenium
45	Rh	Rhodium
46	Pd	Palladium
47	Ag	Silver
48	Cd	Cadmium
49	In	Indium
50	Sn	Tin
51	Sb	Antimony
52	Te	Tellurium
53	Io	Iodine
54	Xe	Xenon
55	Cs	Cesium
56	Ba	Barium
57	La	Lanthanum
58	Ce	Cerium
59	Pr	Praseodymium
60	Nd	Neodymium
61	Pm	Promethium
62	Sm	Samarium
63	Eu	Europium
64	Gd	Gadolinium
65	Tb	Terbium
66	Dy	Dysprosium
67	Ho	Holmium
68	Er	Erbium
69	Tm	Thulium
70	Yb	Ytterbium
71	Lu	Lutetium
72	Hf	Hafnium
73	Ta	Tantalum
74	W	Tungsten
75	Re	Rhenium
76	Os	Osmium
77	Ir	Iridium
78	Pt	Platinum
79	Au	Gold
80	Hg	Mercury
81	Tl	Thallium
82	Pb	Lead
83	Bi	Bismuth
84	Po	Polonium

Atomic Number	Element Symbol	Element Name
85	At	Astatine
86	Rn	Radon
87	Fr	Francium
88	Ra	Radium
89	Ac	Actinium
90	Th	Thorium
91	Pa	Protactinium
92	U	Uranium
93	Np	Neptunium
94	Pu	Plutonium
95	Am	Americium
96	Cm	Curium
97	Bk	Berkelium
98	Cf	Californium
99	Es	Einsteinium
100	Fm	Fermium
101	Md	Mendelevium
102	No	Nobelium
103	Lr	Lawrencium
104	Rf	Rutherfordium
105	Db	Dubnium
106	Sg	Seaborgium
107	Bh	Bohrium
108	Hs	Hassium
109	Mt	Meitnerium
110	Ds	Darmstadtium
111	Rg	Roentgenium
112	Cn	Copernicium
113	Nh	Nihonium
114	Fl	Flerovium
115	Mc	Moscovium
116	Lv	Livermorium
117	Ts	Tennessine
118	Og	Oganesson

Transition metals are more electronegative than the metals in the *main group* elements in the two columns at the far left of the periodic table and in the six columns on the far right. Where main group metals have just enough electrons to balance the charge of their positive ions, transition metals and the compounds they form have an excess number of negative ions. An *ion* is an electrically charged atom or group of atoms formed by the gain or loss of one or more electrons.

The physical properties of main group and transition metals frequently overlap. For example, the two best conductors of electricity are a main group metal, aluminum (group 13, atomic number 13), and a transition group metal, copper (group 11, atomic number 29).

In the Periodic Table on page 129, you will see two gaps in the first column of the transition metals (group 3), which are tied to the two separate rows at the bottom of the chart. The top row shows the *lanthanides* or *lanthanoids*. The second row shows the *actinides* or *actinoids*. The atomic numbers for these two groups fit into the respective gaps in group 3 in the main table. These groups are shown separately both because of their electron configurations and to make the entire periodic table more easy to read. Because lanthanides and actinides fit in how and where they do, they are sometimes called the *inner transition metals*.

You will notice that the lanthanides have atomic numbers running from 57 to 71. The lanthanides are also known as the *rare earth elements* and are found naturally in only very small amounts. The actinides—atomic numbers 89 through 103—include most of the well-known elements involved in nuclear reactions, such as uranium and plutonium.

The elements with atomic numbers greater than 92, the atomic number of uranium, are called *transuranics*. They generally do not occur naturally. Instead, they have been produced artificially by bombarding other elements with particles in particle accelerators or nuclear reactors. Transuranic elements are all *radioactive* and *unstable*, meaning they decay radioactively into other elements.

MEASUREMENTS IN CHEMISTRY

The *metric system* of measurement is the one used by scientists all over the world, since it is important to use the same units when communicating information. For this reason, scientists use the modernized metric system, designated in 1960 by the General Conference on Weights and Measures as the International System of Units. This is commonly known as the SI system, an abbreviation for the French *Systeme International d'Unites*. It is now the most common system of measurement in the world. The reasons it is so widely accepted are that it uses the decimal system as its base, and in many cases units for various quantities are defined in terms of units for simpler quantities. There are seven basic units that can be used to express the fundamental properties of measurement. These are called the SI base units and are shown in the table below.

SI Base Units

Property	Unit	Abbreviation
mass	kilogram	kg
length	meter	m
time	second	s
electric current	ampere	A
temperature	kelvin	K
amount of substance	mole	mol
luminous intensity	candela	cd

Some basic units and prefixes used with the units of the metric system are as follows:

LENGTH

10 millimeters (mm) = 1 centimeter (cm)
100 cm = 1 meter (m)
1,000 m = 1 kilometer (km)

A unit of length used in expressing the length of light waves is the *angstrom*, abbreviated Å and equal to 10^{-8} cm.

VOLUME

1,000 milliliters (mL) = 1 liter (L)
1,000 cubic centimeters (cm^3) = 1 liter
1 mL = 1 cm^3

MASS

1,000 milligrams (mg) = 1 gram (g)
1,000 g = 1 kilogram (kg)

CONVERSION TABLE

2.54 cm = 1 inch
1 meter = 39.37 inches
(10 percent longer than 1 yard)
28.35 grams = 1 ounce
454 grams = 1 pound
1 kilogram = 2.2 pounds
.946 liter = 1 quart
1 liter (5% larger than a quart) = 1.06 quarts

PRACTICE QUESTIONS

1. A chemical equation shows a(n) _____ and must _____.

   (A) increasing atomic number, balance
   (B) chemical change, balance
   (C) noble gas, progress to a nonmetal
   (D) transition metal influx, be similar

2. The Periodic Table is used to present all the elements in a way that

   (A) shows their similarities and differences.
   (B) shows their similarities only.
   (C) shows their differences only.
   (D) aligns elements in order of decreasing atomic number.

3. The atomic number of the element carbon is

(A) 6
(B) 12.011
(C) 17
(D) 20

4. The block of elements between groups II and III on the Periodic Table are known as

(A) lanthanides.
(B) actinides.
(C) transition metals.
(D) noble gases.

5. The atomic mass of potassium is

(A) 30.97376
(B) 39.098
(C) 195.08
(D) 244

6. The number of _____ in an atom's nucleus determines the element's atomic number.

(A) protons
(B) neutrons
(C) electrons
(D) positrons

7. A _____ is a mixture of one substance completely dissolved in another substance.

(A) suspension
(B) compound
(C) solution
(D) transuranic

Answers Explained

1. **(B)** A chemical equation shows a *chemical change* and must *balance*. A chemical change results in either a new chemical compound or the separation of a compound into its elements. The total quantities to the left of the arrow must equal the total quantities to the right of the arrow.

2. **(A)** The Periodic Table is used to present all the elements in a way that *shows their similarities and differences*. The elements are arranged in order of increasing atomic number.

3. **(A)** The atomic number of the element carbon is 6. The chemical symbol for carbon is C. In the version of the periodic table provided in this book, the atomic number of an element is located just above and to the left of the symbol for the element. Note that

some versions of the Periodic Table arrange the placement of the atomic number and symbol differently within each block.

4. **(C)** The block of elements between groups II and III on the Periodic Table are known as *transition metals*. Lanthanides and actinides, shown in the two separate rows beneath the main part of the Periodic Table, would fit into group 3 and are also considered transition metals. However, the question asked about the entire block of elements between groups II and III.

5. **(B)** The atomic mass of potassium is *39.098*. To find the answer, go to potassium's block in the Periodic Table (symbol K) and look at the number at the bottom of the block.

6. **(A)** The number of *protons* in an atom's nucleus determines the element's atomic number.

7. **(C)** A *solution* is a mixture of one substance completely dissolved in another substance.

Temperature

Temperature is measurable on three different scales—*Celsius* (or *centigrade*), *Fahrenheit*, and *Kelvin* (or *absolute*). Their respective freezing and boiling points are:

	Celsius	Fahrenheit	Kelvin
Boiling point of water	100°	212°	373°
Freezing point of water	0°	32°	273°

There are formulas for converting from one system to another.

EXAMPLE

What is the Fahrenheit value of 30°C?

$$°F = \frac{9}{5}(30°) + 32°$$

$$°F = \frac{9}{\cancel{5}_1}(\cancel{30}^6°) + 32°$$

$$°F = 54° + 32° = 86°F$$

Thus, $\qquad$ 30°C = 86°F

Similarly, the formula for converting from Celsius to Fahrenheit is:

$$°C = \frac{5}{9}(°F - 32)$$

The formula for converting from Kelvin to Celsius is somewhat simpler:

$$°K = °C + 273°$$

Sometimes, when working with very long numbers, you may want to use the *scientific notation system.* This system uses exponents to shorten the form of expressing numbers with many places in them. For example:

1. With very large numbers, such as 3,630,000, move the decimal point to the left; when only one digit remains to the left of the decimal point (3.630000), count the number of places you have moved (in this case, six places). Indicate this number of moves as the exponent of 10 (10^6). Then write the short form of your original number as 3.63×10^6.

2. With very small numbers, such as .000000123, move the decimal point to the right; when the first digit is to the left of the decimal (0000001.23), count the number of places you have moved (in this case, seven places). Indicate this number of moves as a negative exponent of 10 (10^{-7}). Then write the short form of your original number as 1.23×10^{-7}.

Prefix	Multiples	Scientific Notation	Abbreviation
mega-	1,000,000	10^6	m
kilo-	1,000	10^3	k
hecto-	100	10^2	h
....	....	....	....
deci-	.1	10^{21}	d
centi-	.01	10^{22}	c
milli-	.001	10^{23}	m
nano-	.000,000,001	10^{29}	n

ATOMS AND MOLECULES

The idea of small, invisible particles being the building blocks of matter can be traced back more than 2,000 years to the Greek philosophers Democritus and Leucippus. These particles were supposed to be so small and indestructible that they could not be divided into smaller particles. They were called *atoms,* the Greek word for "indivisible." The English word "atom" comes from this Greek word. An *atom,* then, is the smallest unit of an element that retains the general properties of that element.

The core of the atom, the *nucleus,* is very dense and very small by comparison with the rest of the atom. It contains *protons* (positively charged particles) and *neutrons* (particles with no charge). Outside the nucleus are the atom's *electrons* (negatively charged particles). An atom has the same number of electrons as its protons. These electrons are arranged in "shell" layers around the nucleus. It's as though an atom were a marble inside a baseball inside a basketball, etc. Atoms tend to borrow, lend, or share electrons from these outer shells. These are called *valence electrons.*

On the basis of their atomic structure, atoms are considered *metals* if they lend electrons, *nonmetals* if they borrow electrons, and *inert* if they neither borrow nor lend. The *atomic number* of an atom is the number of protons in its nucleus. All atoms of the same element have the same atomic number and each element's atomic number is different from all other elements. The *atomic mass* is the number of protons and neutrons in an atom's nucleus. An atom containing the same number of protons as other atoms of the same element, but having a different number of neutrons, is called an *isotope* of that element.

A *molecule* is the smallest particle of an element or compound that retains the characteristics of the original substance. A molecule of water is a *triatomic* ("three-atom") *molecule* since two hydrogen atoms and one oxygen atom must combine to form water. When atoms do combine to form molecules, there is a *chemical bonding*. When such a bonding takes place, there is an exchange of energy.

PRACTICE QUESTIONS

1. An atom has

   (A) a greater number of electrons than protons.
   (B) a smaller number of electrons than protons.
   (C) the same number of protons and electrons.
   (D) the same number of protons and neutrons.

2. On the basis of their atomic structure, atoms are considered _____ if they lend electrons and _____ if they borrow electrons.

   (A) inert, nonmetals
   (B) metals, inert
   (C) nonmetals, metals
   (D) metals, nonmetals

3. The unit of length called the angstrom (Å) is useful for measuring _____ and equals _____.

   (A) radio waves, 10^8 cm
   (B) the wavelength of light, 10^{-8} cm
   (C) the wavelength of light, 8 nanometers
   (D) the distances between stars, 10^8 m

4. An atom with the same number of protons but a different number of neutrons than other atoms of the same element is a(n)

   (A) isotope of that element.
   (B) precursor atom.
   (C) mutation.
   (D) derivative molecule.

5. Potential energy is due to _____, and kinetic energy is _____.

   (A) the position of an object, the energy of motion
   (B) an object's acceleration, steady movement
   (C) the reaction between certain elements, velocity in a straight line
   (D) how much faster an object could theoretically go, speed plus rate of acceleration

6. A boulder perched precariously at the edge of a long, steep downslope on a mountainside is said to have

(A) potential energy.
(B) kinetic energy.
(C) conserved energy.
(D) mechanical energy.

Answers Explained

1. **(C)** An atom has *the same number of protons and electrons.*

2. **(D)** On the basis of their atomic structure, atoms are considered *metals* if they lend electrons and *nonmetals* if they borrow electrons. The periodic table is organized so that elements with similar chemical and physical properties are aligned in columns or groups. Metals, which are found on the left two-thirds of the periodic table, tend to form compounds by losing or lending electrons.

3. **(B)** The unit of length called the angstrom (Å) is useful for measuring *the wavelength of light* and equals 10^{-8} *cm* (or 0.00000001 cm) or 10^{-10} m (0.0000000001 m).

4. **(A)** An atom with the same number of protons but a different number of neutrons than other atoms of the same element is an *isotope of that element.*

5. **(A)** Potential energy is due to *the position of an object*, and kinetic energy is *the energy of motion.*

6. **(A)** A boulder perched precariously at the edge of a long, steep downslope on a mountainside is said to have *potential energy.* If whatever is propping up the boulder gives way and the boulder rolls down the slope, the boulder will have kinetic energy as it moves downhill.

STATES OF MATTER

Matter exists in basically three states, or forms: gas, liquid, and solid. (A special fourth state of matter, plasma, consists of very hot ionized gases.)

Gases

Of all the gases that occur in the atmosphere, the most important is *oxygen.* Although oxygen makes up only 21 percent of the atmosphere, it is equal in weight to all other elements on earth combined. About 50 percent of the earth's crust (including the seas, oceans, and atmosphere) is oxygen. Most living things require it.

PROPERTIES OF OXYGEN

Physically, oxygen is colorless, tasteless, odorless, and slightly heavier than air. It supports the combustion of other substances but does not burn itself. When oxygen combines slowly with an element (so that no noticeable heat and light are given off), we call the process *slow oxidation.* A common example is rusting iron. (A substance loses electrons in oxidation, and gains them in *reduction.*) When the combination of oxygen with an element is so rapid that the released energy can be seen as light and felt as heat, the process is called *rapid oxidation* or *burning*. Oxygen occurs as molecules containing two oxygen atoms, O_2.

Ozone is a form of oxygen having three atoms in its molecular structure (O_3). Ozone is found in the upper atmosphere and can be formed in the lower atmosphere in the presence of high-voltage electricity.

PROPERTIES OF HYDROGEN

Physically, pure hydrogen is colorless, tasteless, and odorless. It is 1/14 as heavy as air and diffuses (moves from place to place) more rapidly than any other gas. Its chemical properties include burning in air or oxygen, giving off large amounts of heat. Hydrogen molecules also contain two atoms, H_2.

Hydrogen is the lightest of all known elements. The most abundant element in the universe, hydrogen is the major fuel in the sun's fusion reactions. Its ability to burn well makes it an important part of many fuels.

General characteristics of gases. Most gases behave according to these "laws":

1. The particles of a gas move in continuous, random, straight-line motion.

2. As the temperature of a gas increases, its kinetic energy increases, which increases its random motion. As its temperature decreases, the kinetic energy of a gas decreases until it reaches the point where it liquifies.

3. If the pressure on a gas remains the same, its volume will increase with temperature, and vice versa.

4. If the temperature of a gas remains the same, its volume will decrease as pressure on it increases, and vice versa.

5. If the volume of a gas remains the same, its pressure will increase with temperature, and vice versa.

Liquids

A liquid *expands* (grows larger in volume) and *contracts* (grows smaller in volume) very slightly with a temperature change. Nevertheless, the molecules of a liquid are always in motion. If a particular molecule gains enough kinetic energy near the surface of a liquid, it can overcome the attraction of other molecules in the liquid and escape into a gaseous state. When this occurs, the average temperature of the remaining liquid molecules becomes lower than before the "escape."

In an enclosed area (when the temperature of a gas remains the same), opposing changes tend to take place at the same time: Liquid molecules escape into the gaseous stage (*evaporation*), and gas molecules return to the liquid stage (*condensation*). When these opposite changes take place at the same rate, we have what is called *equilibrium*.

When liquid is heated in an open container, equilibrium disappears and liquid molecules begin to pass rapidly into a gaseous stage. When this conversion begins to occur within the liquid as well as its surface, we have reached the liquid's *boiling point*. The temperature at which a gaseous substance cannot return to the liquid phase is called its *critical temperature*.

WATER

Water is so often involved in chemistry that it is important to know how to obtain it chemically and how it is used in science. The method of obtaining pure water in the laboratory is by *distillation:* Water is heated (causing it to evaporate) and then cooled (causing it to condense).

Water has been used in the definition of various standards:

- For weight—1 ml (cm^3) of water at 4°C is 1 gram
- For heat—(a) the heat needed to raise one gram of water one degree on the Celsius scale = 1 Calorie (cal); (b) the heat needed to raise one pound of water one degree on the Fahrenheit scale = 1 British thermal unit (BTU)
- Degree of heat—the freezing point of water = 0°C or 32°F
   —the boiling point of water = 100°C or 212°F

Water forms compounds that are classified as *bases* or *acids*. Metal oxides (compounds of oxygen and a metal) react with water to form bases, which have the following properties:

- Bases can conduct electricity in a water solution. The degree of conduction depends on the ionization of a base—its number of charged particles.
- Bases react with acids to neutralize each other and form a salt and water.
- They react with fats to form soaps.
- They cause litmus paper to change from red to blue. (This is a test for the presence of a base.)

Examples of bases include:

$$2Na + 2H_2O \rightarrow 2NaOH + H_2 \text{ (sodium hydroxide)}$$
$$CaO + H_2O \rightarrow Ca(OH)_2 \text{ (calcium hydroxide)}$$

Nonmetal oxides react with water to form acids, which have the following properties:

- Water solutions of acids conduct electricity. This conduction depends on an acid's ionization.
- Some acids react with some metals and liberate hydrogen.
- Acids react with bases to neutralize each other and form a salt and water.
- Acids react with carbonates to release carbon dioxide.
- They cause litmus paper to change to a pink-red color. (This is a test for the presence of an acid.)
- Acids are corrosive.

Examples of acids include:

$$SO_3 + H_2O \rightarrow H_2SO_4 \text{ (sulfuric acid)}$$
$$P_2O_5 + 3H_2O \rightarrow 2H_3PO_4 \text{ (phosphoric acid)}$$

Water is often referred to as "the universal solvent" because of the number of common substances that dissolve in water. When substances are dissolved in water to the point that no more will dissolve at that temperature, the solution is said to be *saturated*. The substance dissolved is called the *solute*. The medium in which it is dissolved is called the *solvent*. When a small amount of solute is dispersed throughout the solvent, it is called a *dilute solution*. When a large amount of solute is dissolved in the solvent, it is called a *concentrated solution*.

Some substances form geometric (building-block) patterns as they slowly come out of a solution (as they lose water). The process is called *crystallization*.

Solids

Particles at the *solid* stage have the most fixed position and maintain a collective shape. The temperature at which particles of a solid begin to break free from fixed positions and slide over each other is called its *melting point*. At certain pressures, some solids vaporize directly, without passing through the liquid stage. This is called *sublimation*. Solid carbon dioxide and solid iodine have this property.

CHEMICAL REACTIONS

One of the major interests in chemistry is how different substances react with one another. *Chemical reactions* are processes where one or more *reactants* (either chemical elements or compounds) are converted into one or more other substances, the *products*. These chemical reactions rearrange the reactants' atoms to create different substances that are the products.

It is important to understand the difference between chemical and physical changes, such as changes of state. If ice melts to water and the water is then heated and turns into steam, the molecules involved are still water. They still have two molecules of hydrogen and one of oxygen (H_2O). This is a physical change. On the other hand, if that ice, water, or steam encounters sodium metal (Na), the atoms are redistributed for both, yielding molecular hydrogen (H_2) and sodium hydroxide (NaOH). This is a chemical change.

Depending on the classification system, there are either four, five, or six general types of chemical reactions. The following box lists the four most commonly accepted and broadest categories of chemical reactions.

---

1. **(DIRECT) COMBINATION (OR SYNTHESIS)** is the formation of a more complex compound from the union of two elements or molecules. For example, carbon dioxide is formed by a combination reaction:

$$C + O_2 \rightarrow CO_2$$
(carbon and oxygen) $\rightarrow$ (carbon dioxide)

2. **DECOMPOSITION (OR ANALYSIS)** is the breakdown of a compound to release its components as individual elements or simpler compounds. For example, the electrolysis of water into oxygen and hydrogen gas is a decomposition reaction:

$$2H_2O \rightarrow 2H_2 + O_2$$
(water) $\rightarrow$ (hydrogen and oxygen)

3. **SINGLE REPLACEMENT (OR SINGLE DISPLACEMENT)** occurs when one substance replaces another in a compound. For example, in the reaction between iron and copper sulfate, the iron replaces the copper:

$$Fe + CuSO_4 \rightarrow FeSO_4 + Cu$$
(iron and copper sulfate) $\rightarrow$ (iron sulfate and copper)

4. **DOUBLE REPLACEMENT (OR DOUBLE DISPLACEMENT OR METATHESIS)** is when two compounds exchange bonds or ions to form new compounds. For example, in the reaction between silver nitrate and sodium chloride, the silver replaces the sodium and the sodium replaces the silver:

$$AgNO_3 + NaCl \rightarrow AgCl + NaNO_3$$
(silver nitrate and sodium chloride) $\rightarrow$ (silver chloride and sodium nitrate)

In general, the *probability* that a specific chemical reaction will take place depends on the amount of heat needed to produce the reaction. The higher the amount of *heat of formation*, the greater the *stability* ("permanence") of a compound, and vice versa.

How long does it take for a chemical reaction to occur? The measurement of a *reaction rate* is based on the rate of formation of a product or the disappearance of a reactant (reacting substance). There are five important factors that control this rate:

> 1. The nature of the reactants. Some elements and compounds react very rapidly with each other.
>
> 2. The exposed surface areas of the reactants. Most reactions depend on the reactants coming into contact. Thus, the more exposure they have to each other at one time, the faster the reaction.
>
> 3. The concentrations. The reaction rate is usually proportional to the degree of concentration of the reactants.
>
> 4. The temperature. A temperature increase of 10°C above room temperature usually causes a reaction rate to double or triple.
>
> 5. The presence of a catalyst. A catalyst is a substance that speeds up or slows down a reaction, without being (permanently) changed itself.

Some reactions involve products that continuously interact with the original reactants. That is, reactants and their products interact in both directions. This is shown as follows:

$$A + B \leftrightarrows C + D$$

The double arrow indicates that substances C and D can react to form A and B, while A and B react to form C and D. Such a reaction is said to reach an *equilibrium* when the forward reaction rate is equal to the reverse reaction rate. The symbol *Ke*, the *equilibrium constant*, is a symbol for the point at which equilibrium occurs.

In many of the preceding predictions of reactions, we used the concept that reactions will occur when they result in the lowest possible energy state. There is, however, another driving force for reactions that relates to their state of disorder, or of randomness. This state of disorder is called *entropy*. A reaction is also driven, then, by a need for a greater degree of disorder.

KEY ELEMENTS AND THEIR FAMILIES

Sulfur

After oxygen, the most important element is sulfur. Sulfur is found in a free state in volcanic regions of Japan, Mexico, and Sicily. It can also be produced in the laboratory. Sulfur is used in making sprays to control plant disease and harmful insects. It is used in the manufacture of rubber, to *vulcanize* rubber (give it extra hardness). Sulfur is used in the preparation of medicines and gunpowder. It is also used in making *sulfuric acid, hydrogen sulfide*, and *sulfur dioxide*.

Sulfuric acid (H_2SO_4) is called the "king of chemicals" because of its widespread industrial use. Some of these uses include:

- making other acids;
- freeing iron and steel alloys of scale and rust;
- removing objectionable colors from gasoline made by the "cracking" process;
- acting as a dehydrating agent in the manufacture of explosives, dyes, and drugs.

Hydrogen sulfide (H_2S) is used widely in laboratory tests (many sulfides precipitate with distinct colors) and in making paints. Sulfur dioxide (SO_2) is used as a bleach.

Halogens

Fluorine (F_2), the most active nonmetal, is a yellowish, poisonous, highly corrosive element. When it is added at 1 ppm (part per million) to water, it hardens tooth enamel and reduces tooth decay. *Chlorine* (Cl_2) is used to purify water supplies to act as a bleaching agent, and to prepare hydrochloric acid (which is used in the manufacture of other chemicals). *Bromine* (Br_2) is used to keep gasolines free of lead deposits. *Iodine* (I_2) is most widely known for its use as an antiseptic.

Nitrogen

The most common member of this family is *nitrogen* (N_2) itself. It is colorless, odorless, tasteless, rather inactive, and makes up about four-fifths of the air in our atmosphere. Nitrogen-fixing bacteria found in the roots of beans, peas, clover, and similar plants "fix" nitrogen. This means they use nitrogen from the air to form compounds that plants can use. Two important compounds of nitrogen are *nitric acid* and *ammonia*.

Nitric acid (HNO_3) is useful in making dyes, celluloid film, and lacquers for cars. Nitric acid is also used in the manufacture of powerful explosives—for example, TNT and nitroglycerine. Ammonia (NH_3) is one of the oldest known compounds of nitrogen. It is a colorless, pungent gas, extremely soluble in water. A water solution of ammonia is used as a cleanser. Another use of ammonia is as a fertilizer.

Phosphorus

Phosphorus (P), a nonmetallic element, is yellow to white, waxy, and extremely poisonous. Because phosphorus ignites spontaneously when exposed to air, it is stored underwater. The principal use of phosphorus is in compounds that act as fertilizers, detergents, insecticides, soft drinks, and pharmaceuticals. Phosphorus compounds are essential to the diet. (They are important for our bones and teeth.) Phosphorus is a component of *adenosine triphosphate* (ATP), a fundamental energy source in living things.

METALS

Some physical properties of *metals* are: (1) they have a metallic luster or sheen; (2) they can conduct heat and electricity; (3) they can be pounded into sheets (metals are *malleable*) or drawn into wires (metals are *ductile*); and (4) they are not soluble in any ordinary solvent without undergoing a chemical change. A general chemical property of metals is that they are *electropositive* (charged with positive electricity).

Alloys are mixtures of two or more metals. *Bronze* (an alloy of copper and tin) and *brass* (an alloy of copper and zinc) are examples. Certain properties of metals are affected when they are mixed in an alloy. An alloy is usually harder than the metals that compose it, but its melting point is usually lower than that of its components.

The outstanding properties of *aluminum* (Al) are: it is very light, has high strength, can resist oxidation, and can conduct an electric current. Aluminum is prepared from *bauxite ore*.

Magnesium (Mg), the eighth most abundant metal in the earth's crust, is found in plant chlorophyll, and is necessary to the diet of humans and other animals. It is light, rigid, and inexpensive, and is used in the manufacture of aircraft fuselages, cameras, and optical instruments.

Copper (Cu) has been known to humans since the Bronze Age. It is reddish, malleable, ductile, and is an excellent conductor of electricity. It is used in manufacturing wires, utensils, coins, etc. It also is important to the human diet.

Iron (Fe), a malleable, ductile, silver-gray metal, is abundant in the universe. (It is found in many stars, including the sun.) A good conductor of heat and electricity, iron is attracted by a magnet and is easily magnetized. It rusts very easily. Iron is extracted from ores in a blast furnace, after which it can be mixed with other substances to form steel. It is also important in the human diet.

CARBON AND ORGANIC CHEMISTRY

The element *carbon* (C) is present in all living things. It occurs in both crystalline and amorphous (noncrystal) forms.

CRYSTALLINE DIAMONDS, found in South Africa and other regions, are the hardest form of carbon. They are brilliant, both reflecting and refracting light. Diamonds are used as gems and in the making of drills, saws, etc.

GRAPHITE (a crystal) is prepared from hard coal in an electric furnace. It is soft, gray, and greasy, and forms a good electrical conductor. It is used as a lubricant, in making lead pencils, and in the construction of atomic reactors.

CHARCOAL is formed from the destructive distillation of soft coal. It burns with little smoke or flame and is used as a fuel.

COKE is formed from the destructive distillation of soft coal. It burns with little smoke or flame and is used as a fuel.

ANTHRACITE COAL, almost pure carbon, burns with little smoke and is used as a fuel.

Carbon dioxide (CO_2) is a widely distributed gas. The usual laboratory preparation of carbon dioxide consists of reacting calcium carbonate (marble chips) with hydrochloric acid. There are several important uses for carbon dioxide:

1. It is used to make carbonated beverages.

2. Solid carbon dioxide (at –78°C), or "dry ice," is used as a refrigerant.

3. Fire extinguishers make use of carbon dioxide because of its weight and its property of not supporting ordinary combustion.

4. Plants use carbon dioxide in photosynthesis.

Organic chemistry may be defined as the chemistry of the compounds of carbon. Since Friedrich Wöhler synthesized urea in 1828, chemists have synthesized thousands of carbon compounds in the areas of dyes, plastics, textile fibers, medicines, and drugs. The number of organic compounds has been estimated to be in the neighborhood of a million and is constantly increasing.

PRACTICE QUESTIONS

1. About 50 percent of the earth's outer layer—including the seas, oceans, and atmosphere—is made of

   (A) hydrogen.
   (B) oxygen.
   (C) noble gases.
   (D) carbon.

2. When evaporation and condensation take place at the same rate, this is

   (A) equilibrium.
   (B) stasis.
   (C) convection.
   (D) not possible.

3. In chemical reactions, water forms compounds that are classified as

   (A) bases only.
   (B) acids only.
   (C) bases or acids.
   (D) baseless acids.

4. Metal oxides react with water to form _____, and nonmetal oxides react with water to form _____.

   (A) bases, acids
   (B) acids, bases
   (C) carbonates, sodium hydroxide
   (D) dilute solutions, concentrated solutions

5. The four types of chemical reactions are

   (A) combination, sublimation, single replacement, and double replacement.
   (B) combination, decomposition, single replacement, and double replacement.
   (C) catalyzation, decomposition, single replacement, and equilibrium.
   (D) catalyzation, sublimation, double replacement, and saturation.

Answers Explained

1. **(B)** About 50 percent of the earth's outer layer—including the seas, oceans, and atmosphere—is made of *oxygen*. Oxygen is the most abundant element in the universe to our knowledge. Most of the oxygen in the earth's crust is in the form of silicates. These are minerals composed of oxygen, silicon (which is the second most abundant element in the earth's crust), and other elements. Some examples of silicates are mica, feldspar, and quartz.

2. **(A)** When evaporation and condensation take place at the same rate, this is *equilibrium*. Equilibrium is a balanced state.

3. **(C)** In chemical reactions, water forms compounds that are classified as *bases or acids.* Pure water is considered neutral, with a pH of 7. Water acts as an acid (i.e., donates hydrogen atoms) when it reacts with a stronger base, such as sodium hydroxide. Water acts as a base (i.e., accepts hydrogen atoms) when it reacts with a stronger acid, such as hydrochloric acid.

4. **(A)** Metal oxides react with water to form *bases,* and nonmetal oxides react with water to form *acids.*

5. **(B)** The four types of chemical reactions are *combination, decomposition, single replacement, and double replacement.*

PHYSICS

Physics includes many topics, such as *light, heat, mechanics, sound, electricity,* and *magnetism.* Most of these topics have subdivisions. For example, mechanics includes the study of *motion, forces,* and *statics* (objects at rest). *Thermodynamics* deals with relationship of heat and energy. *Nuclear physics,* the study of the actions of particles within the nucleus of an atom, has become especially important.

MEASURING FORCE

A *force* is a "push" or a "pull." If you hold a 5-lb. bag of sugar in your hand, you are exerting a 5-lb. force (a pull) on the bag to keep it from falling. In physics, it is possible to draw this effort symbolically—but not by showing a hand with a bag of sugar. Instead, you draw a diagram of two things: (1) the amount of pull, and (2) the direction of the pull.

To represent the amount of pull, make up a *scale* for one unit of the pull (in this case, one pound). Then draw five connected units (for the five pounds) in the direction of the pull (toward the bottom of the paper, representing the ground). When we deal with both the *magnitude* (size) of the pull and its *direction,* we are working with a *vector quantity.*

Sometimes, two or more forces work on an object. These are called *concurrent forces.* Scientists are interested in finding the combined effect (the *resultant*) of these forces. There are several ways to do this:

The *newton* is a unit of force. It is named after Sir Isaac Newton (1642-1726), an English mathematician, astronomer, and physicist. By definition, one newton is the force needed to accelerate one kilogram (kg) of mass at the rate of one meter per second squared in the direction of the applied force.

1. If both forces are exerted in exactly the same direction, add the forces. For example, if a 3-newton force and a 4-newton force act on an object in the same direction, the resultant force is 7 newtons. A *newton* (N) is a unit of measure in physics.

2. If the two forces act in opposite directions (at an angle of 180 degrees), subtract them. With a 3-newton force and a 4-newton force pulling in opposite directions, the resultant is a 1-newton force, exerted in the direction of the larger force (the 4-newton force).

3. If the two forces are pulling at an angle to one another, the solution requires several steps. Suppose that a 3-newton force and a 4-newton force with a 60-degree angle between them are acting on an object: What is the resultant?

   ■ Select a scale for one unit of the force. (Let 1/4 inch equal 1 newton.)
   ■ Draw the vector AB for the 3-newton force (3/4 inch).

- Using the same scale, draw the vector AC for the 4-newton force (1 inch). Start it from the same point as the first vector. Keep an angle of 60 degrees between both vectors.
- Using AB and AC as the first two sides, draw the parallelogram ACDB.
- Draw the diagonal AD and mark off 1/4-inch units on it. In this example, the diagonal will be a little more than 6 of these units. Since each unit equals 1 newton, we can estimate that the resultant for a 3-newton force and a 4-newton force at a 60 degree angle to each other is about 6.1 newtons.

Sometimes the direction of a vector is given in terms of "north," "south," "east," or "west." In other examples, the direction of one vector is given by relating it to another vector (for example, "85 degrees apart"). If you find two vectors forming a right angle (90 degrees), you can treat the example as one involving a right triangle, and solve it by using the Pythagorean Theorem (*see Mathematics Review*). In such a case, the resultant you are looking for would be the hypotenuse of the right triangle.

If two equal and opposite parallel forces are applied to an object, their resultant force is zero. (Try pressing one hand against an open door while you press the other hand against the opposite side of the door. So long as you exert an equal force through both hands, the door won't move.)

If an object can rotate, we call the force that produces this rotation the *torque*, or the *moment of a force*. The magnitude of the moment of a force is equal to the product of the force and what is called the *length of the moment arm*. The length of the moment arm is the perpendicular distance from the *fulcrum* to the direction of the force. A fulcrum is a stationary point about which an object rotates. For example, the earth's axis is its fulcrum, and a door hinge is the fulcrum of a door.

SPEED AND VELOCITY

Speed is the distance covered per unit of time. Speed is a *scalar quantity*, meaning it describes magnitude only, e.g., miles per hour. The *velocity* (v) of an object is its speed in a given direction. Therefore, velocity is a *vector quantity*—it has magnitude and direction. Velocity changes if either the speed, or the direction of motion, or both, change.

Sometimes we can think of the motion of an object as a combination of velocities. For example, if you walk four miles per hour from the last car of the train toward the front while the train is going 60 miles per hour, your velocity is 64 miles per hour in the direction of the train's motion.

Uniform motion is motion in which the velocity is constant. If the velocity changes, the motion is said to be accelerated. *Acceleration* (a) is the rate of change of velocity. Acceleration is a vector quantity. The formula for finding acceleration is

$$\text{acceleration} = \frac{\text{change in velocity}}{\text{time required for change}}$$

An example of how acceleration is expressed would be "four feet per second per second" or "four feet per second squared," and can be written as 4 ft/sec^2.

Uniformly accelerated motion is motion with constant acceleration. If an object is allowed to *fall freely* near the surface of the earth (to fall with its initial velocity at zero and with no forces other than gravity acting on it), the acceleration of the object remains constant and is independent of the mass of the object. The letter g is used universally for this acceleration. On earth, $g = 32$ ft/sec^2.

For all types of motion, the general formula is

$$\text{average speed} = \frac{\text{distance covered}}{\text{time required}}$$

NEWTON'S LAWS

NEWTON'S FIRST LAW OF MOTION

> Every object persists in its state of rest or of uniform motion in a straight line unless it is compelled to change that state by forces impressed on it.

This law states that if the net force acting on an object is zero, the velocity of the object does not change—that is, its speed and direction of motion remain constant. The term *net force* means the same as resultant force. This law can be stated in other ways: When a body is at rest, or moving with constant speed in a straight line, the resultant of all the forces acting on the body is zero.

An object at rest tends to remain at rest. An object in motion tends to remain in motion unless acted on by an unbalanced force. For example, passengers in a car lurch forward when the driver suddenly applies the brakes.

NEWTON'S SECOND LAW (F = MA)

> Force is equal to the change in momentum per change in time. For a constant mass, force equals mass times acceleration.
>
> $$F = MA$$

According to this law, if the net force acting on an object is not zero, the object will be accelerated in the direction of the force. Its acceleration will be proportional to the net force and inversely proportional to the mass of the object. For example, a push that is enough to give a 3,000-pound car an acceleration of 4 ft/sec^2 will be able to give a 6,000-pound van an acceleration of 2 ft/sec^2.

Think of net force as being used to overcome the *inertia* of an object. The greater the *mass* of an object, the greater the force needed to produce a given acceleration. Mass is the measure of an object's inertia. Inertia is the property by which an object resists being accelerated.

NEWTON'S THIRD LAW

> For every action, there is an equal and opposite reaction.

This law states that when one object exerts a force on a second object, the second object exerts an equal and opposite force on the first object. (This is sometimes stated: Action equals reaction.) This law is the principle underlying the operation of rockets and jet aircraft. As the hot gases are pushed out from the rear, they exert a forward push on the object from which they escape.

When an object moves with constant speed around a circle, the object's velocity is constantly changing, because its direction is constantly changing. Because the velocity is changing, the object is accelerated. This acceleration is produced by the *centripetal force*—the force which keeps an object moving around a circle in a circular path.

NEWTON'S LAW OF UNIVERSAL GRAVITATION

According to this law, two objects attract each other with a force that is proportional to the product of their masses and inversely proportional to the square of the distance between them. The earth's attraction for objects is known as *gravity*. Gravity accounts for the *weight* of an object on earth—the earth's pull on an object. It is an attracting (force) that acts on every part of an object—a tree, for example. The attraction of the earth for a tree is actually a set of parallel forces. The resultant goes through a point in the tree known as its *center of gravity*. (We can increase the *stability* of objects by building them with a low center of gravity and with as big a base as possible.)

WORK

The International System of Units (abbreviated as SI, from the French *Système International (d'Unités)*) is the modern form of the metric system and is the most widely used system of measurement worldwide.

In physics we talk about *work* done on an object, or work done by an object or by a force. When a force moves an object, the force does work on the object. If a 20-lb. force is used to pull an object three feet along a flat surface, we say 60 ft-lb of work was done on the object. Thus, work is equal to the product of the force (in this case, a 20-lb. force) and the distance the object moves in the direction of the force (in this case, three feet). The *units of work* obtained by multiplying a unit of force by a unit of distance may be expressed in terms of the *foot-pound* (ft-lb), the *joule (newton-meter),* or the *erg*.

> The SI unit of work is the *joule*, which is defined as the work expended by a force of 1 newton through a displacement of 1 meter.
>
> The *erg* is a unit of energy and of work equal to 10^{-7} joules, or 0.0000001 joules.
>
> The *foot-pound* (ft-lb) is a unit of work in both the U.S. customary system and the imperial system. A foot-pound is defined as the energy transferred when you apply a force of 1 pound through a linear displacement of 1 foot.

ENERGY

In elementary physics, *energy* is defined as the ability to do work. *Potential energy* is defined as the energy possessed by an object because of its position or condition (for example, a ripe apple at the end of a tree branch). *Kinetic energy* is the energy possessed by an object in motion (for example, a bicycle in motion). When an object does work, it has less energy left after the work. In mechanics, work is done on an object for various reasons:

1. to give it potential energy;

2. to give it kinetic energy;

3. to overcome friction (friction is a force that opposes motion or a tendency to motion);

4. to accomplish some combination of those three reasons.

Principle of *conservation of energy*. Energy cannot be created or destroyed but may be changed from one form into another. As a consequence of Einstein's theory of relativity, mass can be considered a form of energy. When mass is converted to forms of energy such as heat, the following formula applies (m is the mass converted, and c is the speed of light):

$$\text{energy produced} = mc^2$$

Units of energy are the same as units of work. When m is expressed in grams and c is expressed in meters per second (3×10^{10} cm/sec) the energy will be expressed in ergs. When m is expressed in kilograms and c is expressed in meters per second (3×10^8 m/sec), the energy is expressed in joules.

Power is the rate of doing work. Since work is calculated by multiplying the force by the distance that the force moves, we have the following formula:

$$\text{power} = \frac{\text{force} \times \text{distance}}{\text{time}}$$

Units of power are expressed as *foot-pounds per second, horsepower* (hp), or *watts*:

$$
\begin{aligned}
1 \text{ hp} &= 550 \text{ ft-lb/sec} \\
1 \text{ hp} &= 746 \text{ watts} \\
1 \text{ watt} &= 1 \text{ joule/sec}
\end{aligned}
$$

SIMPLE MACHINES

Probably the most direct way of doing useful work on an object is to take hold of it and lift or move it. When this is difficult, we turn to *simple machines* to help us. A machine is a device that will transfer a force from one point of application to another for a practical advantage. There are six simple machines: *lever, pulley, wheel* and *axle, inclined plane, screw,* and *wedge.* The force that we apply to a machine in order to do the work is known as the *effort* (F_E). The force we have to overcome is known as the *resistance* (F_R).

LEVER

A *lever* is a rigid bar that is free to turn on or around a fixed point known as the *fulcrum* or *pivot*. Crowbars, bottle openers, and oars on a boat are examples of levers. So is a seesaw.

What is the principle on which a lever operates? When a lever is perfectly balanced on its fulcrum, the force (effort) on one arm matches the force on the other. If a box (or other form of load) is placed on one end of such a lever, but not the other, the balance is upset. To restore the balance (actually, to lift the load) we exert a compensating force on the end without the box (the effort arm). To calculate this compensating force, we determine the length of each arm from the fulcrum to the end, and apply this equation:

$$\text{effort} \times \text{effort arm} = \text{load} \times \text{load arm}$$

EXAMPLE

Assume that a lever 10 feet long has a carton (load) weighing 35 lbs. on one end (the load arm). If the fulcrum is three feet from the end of the load arm, how much effort is needed on the effort arm to raise the carton?

$$E \text{ (effort)} \times EA \text{ (effort arm)} = L \text{ (load)} \times LA \text{ (load arm)}$$
$$E \times 7 = 35 \times 3$$
$$7E = 105$$
$$E = 15 \text{ pounds of effort}$$

PULLEY

A *pulley* is useful for lifting heavy objects a considerable vertical distance. It consists of a wheel mounted in a frame so that the wheel can turn readily on its axis. The wheel rim is usually grooved to guide the rope (or wire, or string) used with it.

WHEEL AND AXLE

In a *wheel and axle,* the wheel is rigidly attached to an axle, which turns with it. Applications of the wheel-and-axle machine include the steering wheel of an automobile and a doorknob.

INCLINED PLANE

An *inclined plane* is a flat surface, one end of which is kept higher than the other. When heavy objects have to be raised to a platform or put into a truck, it is often convenient to slide these objects up along a board. The board in this case is an inclined plane. The effort to pull or push the object "up" along the plane is usually applied parallel to the plane.

SCREW

A *screw* may be defined as a cylinder around which a narrow inclined plane (the "thread") winds in a spiral manner. A screw can be used to connect one object to another. It is a machine that converts rotational motion (i.e., movement in a circular direction) into linear motion (movement in a straight-line direction).

WEDGE

A *wedge* may be thought of as a double inclined plane. It is used in devices like an axe to split wood. It is easy to use when its length is large compared to its thickness.

PRACTICE QUESTIONS

1. A pulley is used to move heavy objects in a _____ direction.

    (A) horizontal
    (B) vertical
    (C) sideways
    (D) tangential

2. A seesaw is an example of

    (A) an inclined plane.
    (B) the pulley principle.
    (C) a wedge.
    (D) a lever.

3. A cylinder with a narrow inclined plane wrapped around it is a description of

    (A) a screw.
    (B) a double inclined plane.
    (C) a pivot point.
    (D) a wheel and axle.

4. When a lever is balanced on its fulcrum, the force on one arm

    (A) is greater than the force on the other.
    (B) matches the force on the other.
    (C) is less than the force on the other.
    (D) depends on the placement of the fulcrum.

5. A doorknob is an example of

    (A) a pulley.
    (B) a wheel and axle.
    (C) a screw.
    (D) a cylindrical effort arm.

6. If a 5-newton force (Force 1) is directly opposed to a 7-newton force (Force 2), what will be the resultant force?

    (A) A 12-newton force in the direction of Force 1
    (B) A 12-newton force in the direction of Force 2
    (C) A 2-newton force in the direction of Force 1
    (D) A 2-newton force in the direction of Force 2

Answers Explained

1. **(B)** A pulley is used to move heavy objects in a *vertical* direction.

2. **(D)** A seesaw is an example of *a lever*. Specifically, a seesaw is an example of a first-class lever, where the fulcrum is placed between the applied force and the load. Which end has the load and which end has the applied force changes as each person alternates using his or her legs to push off from the ground.

3. **(A)** A cylinder with a narrow inclined plane wrapped around it is a description of *a screw*.

4. **(B)** When a lever is balanced on its fulcrum, the force on one arm *matches the force on the other*. This system is in equilibrium. If a load is placed onto one end of such a lever but not onto the other end, the balance is upset. The lever will tilt to the side with the load on it (think of one person on a seesaw). If we lift the load (the person gets off the seesaw) or apply a similar load to the other end of the lever (think of the second person getting onto the seesaw), the system becomes balanced again.

5. **(B)** A doorknob is an example of *a wheel and axle*. This is a wheel rigidly attached to an axle; the axle turns when the wheel is turned.

6. **(D)** If a 5-newton force (Force 1) is directly opposed to a 7-newton force (Force 2), the resultant force will be *a 2-newton force in the direction of Force 2*. In this problem, you should subtract the smaller force from the larger force since the forces are diametrically opposed.

FLUID PRESSURE AND THE ATMOSPHERE

The term *fluid* refers to both gases and liquids. A liquid has definite volume, but takes the shape of its container, with its top surface tending to be horizontal. A gas has neither definite shape nor volume, and expands to fill any container into which it is put.

Fluids push against the container in which they are placed. *Pressure* (*p*) is the force per unit area. Liquid pressure is independent of the size or shape of the container. It depends only on the depth (or "height," *h*) and the *density* (*d*) of the liquid. (The density of a substance is the mass per unit of volume.) The formula for finding water pressure in a container is

$$p = hd$$

There are several principles that derive from the nature of water pressure:

1. **PASCAL'S PRINCIPLE** states two ideas about pressure applied to a confined fluid (a fluid enclosed on all sides):

   (a) such pressure is transferred throughout the liquid without any loss; and
   (b) this pressure acts perpendicularly on all the surfaces of the liquid's container, regardless of their size.

   Imagine a water-filled, U-shaped container, one of whose arms is wider than the other. Each arm of the "U" is sealed by a *piston*. (A piston is a cylinder that slides inside another cylinder—something like a cork that moves easily in and out of the neck of a bottle.) If you exert a small force against the piston in the smaller arm of the "U," the resulting pressure travels through the water in both arms and acts on the underside of the larger piston. The resulting force in this second piston is then larger than the force applied to the first one.

2. **ARCHIMEDES' PRINCIPLE** states that the apparent loss in weight of an object immersed in a fluid equals the weight of the displaced fluid. For example, an object weighing 50 grams is placed in water, where it weighs 30 grams. Since the apparent loss of weight is 20 grams, we know that the weight of the displaced water is 20 grams.

3. **BERNOULLI'S PRINCIPLE** states that if the speed of a fluid is increased, its pressure is decreased. This principle is made use of in the design of airplane wings to give the plane *lift*. The wing is designed so that the air will move faster over the top of the wing than across the bottom. As a result, the pressure of the air on the top of the wing is less than on the bottom. This makes the upward push on the wing greater than the downward push, and keeps the plane aloft.

HEAT ENERGY

One way of defining *temperature* is to say it is the degree of hotness or coldness of an object. If we think of *kinetic energy*, however, we get a different definition.

The molecules of a substance are in constant random motion. If we heat a gas, its molecules move faster—that is, when the temperature of a gas goes up, the average speed of its molecules increases. When the speed of the motion of a molecule increases, its kinetic energy increases too. This leads to thinking of temperature as a measure of the average kinetic energy per molecule of a substance. Thus, a substance has *internal energy* as a result of its kinetic energy.

When a hot substance is brought into contact with a cold substance, the hot piece gets colder and the cold piece gets hotter. Thus we define *heat* as the form of energy which flows between two substances because they are at different temperatures.

Expansion and Contraction

When heated, most solids, liquids, and gases *expand* (increase in volume); when cooled, most solids, liquids, and gases *contract* (decrease in volume). Solids differ among themselves in their degree of expansion. For example, brass expands more than iron. And different liquids expand by different amounts when subjected to the same temperature change. Gases are more uniform in their expansion and contraction.

Water behaves strangely in this respect. As water is cooled from 100°C, it contracts until the temperature reaches 4°C. If it is cooled further the water will expand—until it freezes at 0°C. Thus, water is densest at 4°C.

Heat Engines

Heat engines are used to convert heat into *mechanical energy*. Examples of heat engines include the *gasoline engine, diesel engine, steam engine,* and the *steam turbine*. In these engines, hot gases are allowed to expand; as they expand they do work.

If the fuel is burned inside the cylinder of the engine itself, the engine is known as an *internal combustion engine*. The gasoline engine and the diesel engine are internal combustion engines. If the fuel is burned in a separate chamber outside the engine proper, the engine is known as an *external combustion engine*. Steam engines and steam turbines are examples of external combustion engines. In these, the fuel—which may be coal—is burned in a separate furnace and is used to heat water in a boiler. Steam from this process is then directed into the engine.

Methods of Heat Transfer

The three methods of heat transfer are *conduction, convection,* and *radiation.* Heat conduction is the process of transferring heat by the flow of "free" electrons through a medium. (Conduction also involves the bombardment of cool molecules by heated molecules.) For example, if we heat one end of a copper rod, the other end gets hot, too. Metals are good conductors of heat (and also good conductors of electricity). Silver is the best. Copper and aluminum are also very good. Liquids, gases, and nonmetallic solids are poor conductors of heat. Poor conductors are known as *insulators.*

Heat convection is the process of transferring heat in a fluid, which involves the motion of the heated portion toward the cooler portion of the fluid. The heated portion expands, rises, and is replaced by cooler fluid, thus giving rise to so-called *convection currents.* Radiators heat rooms chiefly by convection.

Heat radiation is a process of transferring heat by a *wave motion* similar to light. Radiation can occur through space and through a material medium. The higher the temperature of an object, the greater the amount of heat it radiates.

The *vacuum bottle* (also known as a *thermos bottle*) is designed with the three methods of heat transfer in mind. The bottle is made of glass, a good insulator. The stopper is made of cork or plastic—also good insulators. The air is removed from the space between the two walls of the bottle minimizing heat transfer by conduction or convection. The inside surfaces (facing the vacuum in between) are shiny, reflecting radiation that might come from either side. This minimizes heat transfer by radiation.

PRACTICE QUESTIONS

1. Bernoulli's principle states that

    (A) a decrease in the speed of a fluid over an object is caused by a decrease in the fluid's pressure on that object.
    (B) a decrease in the speed of a fluid over an object leads to a decrease in the fluid's pressure on that object.
    (C) an increase in the speed of a fluid over an object occurs simultaneously with a decrease in the fluid's pressure on that object.
    (D) an increase in the speed of a fluid over an object occurs simultaneously with an increase in the fluid's pressure on that object.

2. When they are heated, most solids, liquids, and gases

    (A) contract (increase in volume).
    (B) expand (increase in volume).
    (C) contract (decrease in volume).
    (D) expand (decrease in volume).

3. The three methods of heat transfer are

    (A) mechanical energy, heat energy, and steam power.
    (B) combustion, convection, and radiation.
    (C) insulation, convection, and wave motion.
    (D) radiation, conduction, and convection.

4. A diesel engine is an example of

    (A) an internal combustion engine.
    (B) an external combustion engine.
    (C) heat transfer.
    (D) expansion and contraction.

5. A liquid has _____ and _____.

    (A) definite volume, takes the shape of its container
    (B) no definite volume, expands to fill its container
    (C) no definite shape, exerts pressure on its container based on the container's shape
    (D) a definite shape, exerts constant pressure on its container

Answers Explained

1. **(C)** Bernoulli's principle states that *an increase in the speed of a fluid over an object occurs simultaneously with a decrease in the fluid's pressure on that object.*

2. **(B)** When they are heated, most solids, liquids, and gases *expand* (*increase in volume*). Increased heat causes the substance's atoms to vibrate faster, thereby increasing the space between them and increasing the volume of the substance.

3. **(D)** The three methods of heat transfer are *radiation, conduction, and convection.* The first method, radiation, occurs when electromagnetic waves emitting from a source carry heat energy away from that source to a distant object. (Note that this radiation has nothing to do with nuclear energy.) The second method, conduction, is the transfer of heat between atoms as they collide within a substance. Conduction is usually the most efficient method for heat transfer in solids. The third method, convection, involves a fluid (such as a liquid or air) being heated. That fluid then expands and travels away from the heat source, typically displacing other parts of the fluid. Those other parts of the fluid then move toward the source and get heated. This process continues as the fluid continues to circulate.

4. **(A)** A diesel engine is an example of *an internal combustion engine.* A diesel engine gets its energy from the combustion of a fuel and an oxidizer (air) in a combustion chamber. The expansion of the high-pressure, high-temperature gases produced by this combustion applies direct force to the appropriate engine component to fulfill the engine's purpose.

5. **(A)** A liquid has *definite volume* and *takes the shape of its container.*

ENERGY SOURCES

For heating buildings and operating machines, humans have historically depended largely on *fossil fuels*, such as coal and oil. Waterfalls can be used in the regions where they are located (waterfalls and fossil fuels ultimately owe their energy to the sun). Water wheels have been used since at least the third century BC to do man's mechanical bidding, often utilizing the power of water flowing in a river or over a dam. Since the late 1800s, they have also been used to generate electricity (*hydroelectric power*).

In some areas, solar reflectors trap the sun's radiant energy for conversion to electricity. *Wind energy*, used by mankind since the first sail was put on a ship, has been used for two millennia for mechanical power to grind grain and pump water. Since the late 1800s, it has also been harnessed to generate electricity. Today, *wind farms* consisting of many individual tall turbines turned by the wind contribute power to electric power transmission networks worldwide.

Some people think the hope of the future lies in *nuclear energy*—energy released when certain changes take place in the nucleus of an atom. We have already learned to obtain nuclear energy resulting from the splitting or *fission* of the nuclei of heavy elements, such as uranium. Only small quantities of such fissionable materials are available. Nuclear energy can also be obtained by the combining or *fusion* of the nuclei of light atoms, such as hydrogen. If this can be done in a controllable manner, a practically endless supply of energy will be available, because *hydrogen*, the necessary "fuel," is obtainable from the oceans in almost unlimited quantity.

WAVE MOTION AND SOUND

Wave motion in a medium is a method of transferring energy through a medium by means of a *distortion* (disturbance) of the medium; the distortion travels away from the place where it was produced. The medium itself moves only a little bit. For example, a pebble dropped into still water disturbs it. The water near the pebble does not move far, but the disturbance travels away from that spot. Energy lost by the pebble is carried by the wave, so that if there is a cork floating on the water in the path of the wave, the cork will be lifted by the wave. The cork gets some of the energy that the pebble lost. We can set up a succession of waves in the water by pushing a finger rhythmically through the surface of the water. Similarly, a vibrating tuning fork produces waves in air.

Two basic waves are the *longitudinal wave* and the *transverse wave*. A longitudinal wave is a wave in which the particles of the medium vibrate in the same direction as the path which the wave travels. The waves produced by a tuning fork are examples of longitudinal waves; so are sound waves. A transverse wave is a wave in which the vibrations of the medium are at right angles to the direction in which the wave is traveling. A water wave is approximately transverse.

There are several important measurements related to wave motion. A *wavelength* can be measured as the distance between any two successive peaks of the wave. As we watch a wave moving past a given spot of the medium, we see peak after peak of the wave. The time required for two successive waves to pass a spot is known as the *period* of the wave. The *frequency* of the wave is the number of complete waves (periods) per second. Out of all these measurements comes a key equation:

speed of wave = frequency of wave × wavelength

Sound

In physics, when we talk about *sound,* we usually mean a *sound wave.* Sound waves are longitudinal waves in gases, liquids, or solids. Sound cannot be transmitted through a vacuum. If a sound wave begins in the air and then hits a solid, the frequency of the wave will be the same in the new medium (the solid) as in the air, but the new speed—and therefore the new wavelength—will be different. The *speed of sound* in air is approximately 1,090 feet per second or 331 meters per second at 0°C. In general, sound travels faster in liquids and solids than in air.

MUSICAL SOUNDS

Sounds produced by regular vibration of the air are said to be *musical.* (Irregular vibrations of the air are classified as unpleasant sounds, or "noise.") The *range of frequencies* in musical sounds is 20 to 20,000 cycles per second (Hertz). Longitudinal waves that are higher than those which people can hear are called *ultrasonic* frequencies. (Ultrasonic frequencies are used in *sonar* for such purposes as submarine detection.) The term *supersonic* refers to speed greater than the speed of sound. *Mach* 1 means a speed equal to that of sound. *Mach* 2 is twice the speed of sound. Some airplanes travel at *supersonic* speed.

Musical sounds have three basic characteristics: *pitch, loudness,* and *quality* (timbre). Pitch refers to frequency: the higher the frequency of a sound wave, the higher the pitch. Loudness depends on the amplitude of the wave reaching the ear. The quality of sound depends on the number of different overtones reaching the ear at the same moment.

When a sound wave reaches another medium, part of the wave is usually reflected. Where there is reflected sound, a distant *echo* is heard if the reflected sound reaches the ear at least 1/10 second after the sound traveling directly from the vibrating source to the ear. The *Doppler effect* refers to the way we perceive pitch when the source of a sound is traveling toward or away from us. (This is something a jogger might notice as a car approaches on an otherwise empty road.) As the source of the sound approaches us, the pitch we hear grows higher than the actual frequency produced by the source of the sound. As the source of the sound moves away, the pitch appears to get lower than it actually is.

Light and Illumination

In many ways, *light* coming from the sun behaves like a wave. How can we explain a wave traveling through a vacuum? Electric fields and magnetic fields can exist in a vacuum. Light is one type of *electromagnetic wave,* along with X-rays and radio waves. The wavelength of light is rather short—about 5×10^{-5} cm. The exact wavelength depends on the color of the light. (The *quantum theory of light,* however, says that light is emitted and absorbed in little lumps or bundles of energy called *photons.*)

A *luminous body* is one that emits light because it has been heated (for example, the filament in our electric light bulb) or due to an internal reaction, chemical or otherwise. An *illuminated object* is one that is visible by the light that it reflects (for example, the moon).

REFLECTION

In discussing illumination, the term *ray* is used to represent the direction in which the light is traveling. (Light is considered to travel in a straight line.) When light hits a surface, some of it is reflected. We call the light that travels toward the surface the *incident light,* and the light that is reflected the *reflected light*. The angle of the incident light equals the angle of the reflected light. When parallel light rays strike a smooth surface, they are reflected as parallel rays.

In a *plane mirror* (a perfectly flat mirror), a ray of light striking the mirror is reflected without being changed. In a *convex mirror* (one in which the center bulges outward), the light rays are spread apart by reflection and the reflected image seems smaller than the object. In a *concave mirror* (one in which the center "caves in"), the light rays are focused by reflection and—at a close distance—the reflected image seems larger than the object.

REFRACTION

Refraction is the bending of a wave as it passes from one medium into another. Refraction occurs because of the different speeds at which the wave travels through the two denser media. The medium in which a light wave travels more slowly is known as the optically denser medium. The medium in which light travels faster is known as the optically rarer medium. Light travels faster in air than in liquids and solids. Light travels faster in water than in glass. A ray of light passing obliquely into a denser medium is bent toward the *"normal"* (that is, toward a perpendicular with the surface of the medium). A ray of light entering a rarer medium obliquely is bent away from the normal.

LENSES

A *lens* is a device shaped to *converge* (focus) or *diverge* (spread) a beam of light through it. Lenses are fashioned to be thin, spherical, transparent, and are usually glass. A *convex lens* is thicker at the middle than at the edge; it is a converging lens. A *concave* lens is thinner in the middle than at the edge; it is a diverging lens. Convex lenses form images similar to concave mirrors; concave lenses form images similar to convex mirrors. There is another important difference. Lenses let light through and refract it; mirrors reflect light.

OPTICAL INSTRUMENTS

The *camera* and the human eye have many points of similarity. The camera has a *shutter* to admit the light, corresponding to the eyelid. Light goes through a camera's *convex lens* to the sensitive *film*. In the eye, light goes through the pupil and lens, falling on the retina where the image is formed. The image on both the film and the retina is real, reduced in size, and inverted.

The *astronomical telescope* is used by scientists who want to see very distant objects that are invisible to the naked eye. The *microscope* is used for examining small things close at hand. Both the microscope and the astronomical telescope employ a *magnifying eyepiece*. A *projector* is used to throw an enlarged picture on a screen.

COLOR AND LIGHT

If light goes through a three-dimensional glass *prism*, the emerging rays are bent away considerably from the original direction. If we use so-called *white light* (such as from an incandescent tungsten filament bulb), the light is dispersed (broken) into its component colors. The order of colors, from the one bent the least to the one bent the most is red, orange, yellow, green, blue, indigo, violet. We call this array of colors the *spectrum of visible light*. *Infrared light* has a greater wavelength than red; *ultraviolet light* has a shorter wavelength than violet. Both of these are invisible to the human eye.

The color of an opaque object is determined by the color of the light that it reflects. A red object, for example, reflects mostly red; it absorbs the rest. If an object reflects no light it is said to be black. If an object reflects all the light, we perceive the color to be white.

PRACTICE QUESTIONS

1. The speed of a wave is

   (A) equal to or less than the frequency of the wave multiplied by the wavelength.
   (B) equal to the frequency of the wave divided by the wavelength.
   (C) equal to the frequency of the wave multiplied by the wavelength.
   (D) equal to or greater than the wavelength multiplied by the frequency of the wave.

2. Sound waves are

   (A) longitudinal waves in solids, liquids, or gases.
   (B) transverse waves in solids, liquids, or gases.
   (C) longitudinal waves in a partial or complete vacuum.
   (D) frictionless waves in solids, liquids, or gases.

3. _____ is a method of transferring energy by means of a distortion.

   (A) Wind energy
   (B) Wave motion
   (C) Transverse conduction
   (D) Longitudinal transmission

4. Light traveling toward a reflective surface is called

   (A) reflected light.
   (B) incident light.
   (C) parallel light.
   (D) refracted light.

5. A convex lens

   (A) converges light.
   (B) diverges light.
   (C) reflects light.
   (D) is of uniform thickness throughout.

6. Refraction happens when

   (A) light moves in a straight line.
   (B) light rays strike a flat mirrored surface and bounce off.
   (C) light waves pass straight from one material into another.
   (D) light waves are bent passing from one material into another.

Answers Explained

1. **(C)** The speed of a wave is *equal to the frequency of the wave multiplied by the wavelength*. This equation, known as the *wave equation*, shows the mathematical relationship between the speed of a wave (v), and its wavelength (λ), and frequency (*f*). Using the symbols v, λ and *f*, the equation can be rewritten as

$$v = f \cdot \lambda$$

2. **(A)** Sound waves are *longitudinal waves in solids, liquids, or gases*. Sound waves in solids can also be transverse waves (waves that oscillate perpendicularly to the direction of propagation).

3. **(B)** *Wave motion* is a method of transferring energy by means of a distortion. In wave motion, the distortion travels away from the place where it was produced in the medium.

4. **(B)** Light traveling toward a reflective surface is called *incident light*.

5. **(A)** A convex lens *converges light*. On the other hand, a concave lens diverges the refracted rays so that they appear to come from one point, called the principal focus.

6. **(D)** Refraction happens when *light waves are bent passing from one material into another*.

ELECTRICITY

Nearly all the *mass* of an *atom* is concentrated in the *nucleus*, which ordinarily contains *protons* and (except for the hydrogen atom) *neutrons*. The atom's *electrons* form "shells" around the nucleus. A proton has a positive charge equal to the negative charge of an electron, but its mass is approximately 1,836 times as much as the mass of the electron. A neutron is electrically neutral; its mass is slightly greater than that of the proton. An *ion* is a charged atom or group of atoms.

Charging an object usually results in a gain or loss of electrons. In a solid, the positive charges do not move readily. A gain of electrons results in making an object more negative; a loss of electrons results in making it more positive. A neutral object usually acquires the same kind of *charge* as that of the charged object it touches.

An *electric field* is said to exist wherever an electric force acts on an electric charge. If a positive charge is released in an electric field, the positive charge will move in the direction of the electric field. A negative charge released in an electric field will move in the direction opposite to that of the field. The *potential difference* between two points in an electric field is the work-per-unit charge required to move a charge between the points. The unit of potential difference is the volt. The common flashlight cell supplies 1.5 volts. An American home outlet usually supplies 110–115 volts.

Electric Current

Current is the rate of flow of electric charge. Generally, we speak of *direct current* (DC) and *alternating current* (AC).

Direct current is a flow of current in one direction at a constant rate. To create a circuit for such flow, batteries, dynamos, and generators have two terminals—one, positive; the other, negative. The positive terminal has a deficiency of electrons; the negative terminal has an excess of electrons. Work has to be done to push electrons onto the negative terminal against the repulsion of electrons already there. (According to *Coulomb's law*, particles with the same charge repel one another; unlike particles are attracted to one another.) In this case, the potential difference is the work-per-unit charge that was done to get the terminals charged. This charge is now potentially available for doing work outside the battery (for example, operating a desk lamp).

Resistance of a device is its opposition to the flow of electric charges. Electric energy is converted to heat because of this opposition. *Conductance* is the reciprocal of resistance. The higher the conductance of a device (as with something made of copper or silver), the lower the resistance. According to *Ohm's law*, the current in a circuit is directly proportional to the potential difference that is applied to the circuit and inversely proportional to the resistance of the circuit.

As its name suggests, *alternating current* is a current that goes through a cycle: (a) it increases from zero to a certain maximum in one direction; (b) it decreases to zero; (c) it increases to a maximum in the opposite direction; (d) it decreases to zero.

The number of repetitions of this cycle per second is the *frequency of* the current; in the United States this frequency is 60 cycles per second, but in many European countries it is 50 cycles per second. AC current can do some things better than DC current. It can be transmitted more easily over long distances, and its voltage can be changed more easily. Only DC current can be used for charging batteries, for electroplating, and for operating some electronic circuits.

In today's computer-dominated times, *semiconductors* are very important. A semiconductor is a material whose conductivity is very low by comparison with conductors like copper, but greater than that of insulators like glass. Common semiconductors are germanium and silicon. In practice, a small, precise amount of an impurity is sometimes added to the pure semiconductor to give it desired characteristics (for example, the ability to precisely control the flow of electrons).

MAGNETS

A *magnet* attracts iron and steel. A *magnetic substance* is one that can be attracted by a magnet. Magnetic materials include iron and alloys of iron. Examples of nonmagnetic substances are glass and wood. A *magnetized substance* is a magnetic substance which has been made into a magnet. A *magnetic pole* is the region of a magnet where its strength is concentrated. Every magnet has at least two poles, North and South. The *north pole* (N-pole) of a suspended magnet points toward the earth's magnetic pole in the northern hemisphere. (Magnetic poles do not coincide with the earth's geographic poles.) The *law of magnets* states that like poles repel; unlike poles attract. The *magnetic field* is the region around the magnet where its influence can be detected as a force on another substance. The direction of the field at any point is the direction in which the N-pole of a *compass* would point. A magnetic field can be used to produce an electric current.

CHEMICAL ENERGY

Another important source of electrical energy is *chemical energy*. A *voltaic cell* converts chemical energy into electrical energy. It consists of two dissimilar *electrodes* immersed in an *electrolyte* which acts on at least one of them. An electrolyte may be a liquid that conducts electricity by the motion of ions (such as would occur in a solution of salt in water). The electrodes are conductors. The electrode that is positively charged is called the *anode*. The electrode that is negatively charged is called the *cathode.*

A *primary cell* is a voltaic cell whose electrodes are consumed in an irreversible way when the cell is used. The *dry cell* used in a flashlight is a primary cell. A *secondary cell* is a voltaic cell whose electrodes can be used over and over again, with periodic recharging. The automobile battery is an example of a secondary cell.

PRACTICE QUESTIONS

1. Almost all the mass of an atom is concentrated in the

    (A) nucleus.
    (B) neutrons.
    (C) protons.
    (D) electrons.

2. Direct current (DC) is

    (A) opposition to the flow of electric charges.
    (B) current that increases from zero to a maximum and then reverses.
    (C) used for operating all electric circuits.
    (D) a flow of electric charge in one direction at a constant rate.

3. When a neutral object is charged, it usually

    (A) gains electrons from the charged object it touches.
    (B) acquires the same kind of charge as that of the charged object it touches.
    (C) loses neutrons to the charged object it touches.
    (D) gains protons from the charged object it touches.

4. According to Coulomb's law,

    (A) particles with the same charge attract each other.
    (B) particles with the same charge repel each other.
    (C) particles with opposite charges repel each other.
    (D) the negative terminal of a battery has an excess of protons.

5. A primary cell is a voltaic cell

    (A) whose electrodes can be used over and over again.
    (B) whose electrodes are temporarily out of electrolyte.
    (C) with a positively charged electrode called the cathode.
    (D) whose electrodes are irreversibly consumed when the cell is used.

Answers Explained

1. **(A)** Almost all the mass of an atom is concentrated in the *nucleus*. Protons and neutrons are found in the nucleus of an atom. Of the three types of subatomic particles, protons and neutrons are significantly heavier than electrons.

2. **(D)** Direct current (DC) is *a flow of electric charge in one direction at a constant rate*. In systems using alternating current (AC), the electric charge's direction of movement periodically reverses direction.

3. **(B)** When a neutral object is charged, it usually *acquires the same kind of charge as that of the charged object it touches*. Negatively charged objects have an excess of electrons, which seek to disperse themselves by hopping to the neutral object. As a result, the formerly neutral object is now negatively charged. Positively charged objects have an excess of protons and thereby attract electrons from the neutral object. This results in the formerly neutral object now having an overabundance of protons and being positively charged.

4. **(B)** According to Coulomb's law, *particles with the same charge repel each other*. Also known as Coulomb's inverse-square law, it was discovered by French physicist Charles-Augustin de Coulomb and was first published in 1784. Subsequent extensive tests have invariably found the law to be true.

5. **(D)** A primary cell is a voltaic cell *whose electrodes are irreversibly consumed when the cell is used*. On the other hand, a secondary (rechargeable) cell forms an insoluble product that sticks to the electrodes. A secondary cell can be recharged by applying an electrical potential in the reverse direction, temporarily converting the cell from a galvanic cell to an electrolytic cell.

Mathematics Review

5

TIPS FOR STUDYING ASVAB MATH

The material in this section is a review of basic terms and problem-solving methods taught in high school mathematics courses. There are samples of the types of math problems most often asked on the ASVAB exam, with an explanation of how to solve each. You may also find that you know one or more other ways for working out a problem. Before you study the topics in this section, look over the following suggestions for how to do good work in mathematics.

☑ Develop the habit of careful reading. As you read a problem, look for answers to these questions:

   1. What is given? (the facts in the problem)

   2. What is unknown? (the answer to be found)

   3. What do I use? (the best method or steps for solving the problem)

☑ Pay careful attention to each word, number, and symbol. In mathematics, directions and problems are compressed into very few words. Sometimes, the main directions are expressed as a symbol.

Example
What is the value of 6 – 3? (The minus sign tells you to subtract.)

☑ The reading of mathematics also requires close attention to relationships. How does one fact or idea lead to another? Which facts or ideas are connected? Take the following example:

   Mr. Brown and his partner worked for 5 hours on Monday. For his wages, Mr. Brown received $10 an hour. How much did he earn on Monday?

To solve this problem, you can ignore the day of the week and the fact that there was a partner present. Just multiply the number of hours Mr. Brown worked (5) by the amount he received each hour ($10).

$$5 \times \$10 = \$50 \text{ (Mr. Brown's earnings)}$$

LAWS AND OPERATIONS

The numbers 5 and 10 are *whole numbers*. So are 0, 1, 2, 3, 4, and so on. (By contrast, $\frac{3}{4}$ is a fraction, and $6\frac{3}{4}$ is a mixed number—a whole number plus a fraction.) In mathematics, when we combine two or more whole numbers, we perform an *operation* on them. There are two such basic operations: *addition* and *multiplication*. In addition, we combine individual numbers

(23 + 4) to find an answer called the *sum*. In multiplication, we combine groups of numbers for an answer called the *product*. For example, three times four (3 × 4) means three groups of four; their product is 12.

Basic Operations	Inverse Operations
Addition	Subtraction
23 – 4 = 27 (sum)	27 – 4 = 23 (remainder)
Multiplication	Division
4 × 3 = 12 (product)	12 ÷ 4 = 3 (quotient)

Subtraction and *division* are really *opposite*, or *inverse*, operations of addition and multiplication. Subtraction is performed to undo addition, and division is performed to undo multiplication. The answer in subtraction is called the *remainder*; in division, it is called the *quotient*. Consider these examples.

USE OF PARENTHESES: ORDER OF OPERATIONS

Sometimes, parentheses are used in a math problem to indicate which operation must be done first. For example, in the problem 3 + (5 × 2), you would first multiply 5 × 2, then add 3. Look at the different results you get when you work with the parentheses that are in different places in the same problem.

$$(3 + 5) \times 2 = \qquad 3 + (5 \times 2) =$$
$$8 \times 2 = 16 \qquad 3 + 10 \quad = 13$$

Even though we read a problem from left to right, there is an order in which we must perform arithmetic operations:

Order of Operations

- **Parentheses**
- **Exponents**
- **Multiplication**
- **Division**
- **Addition**
- **Subtraction**

(STEP 1) First, do all work within parentheses.

(STEP 2) Next, do all multiplications and divisions. Do these in left-to-right order.

(STEP 3) Finally, do additions and subtractions.

In the following example, notice the order in which arithmetic operations are carried out.

$$(10 - 6) \times 5 - (15 \div 5) = \qquad \text{(first do operations inside the parentheses)}$$
$$4 \times 5 - 3 = \qquad \text{(next do multiplication)}$$
$$20 - 3 = 17 \qquad \text{(then do subtraction)}$$

ROUNDING OFF NUMBERS

Occasionally, you are asked to *round off* answers to the nearest ten, hundred, thousand, etc. We do this in everyday speech when we say that a pair of shoes priced at $38.50 costs "about $40." Rounding off, estimating, and approximating all mean the same thing. You make a guess as to the approximate value. There is a rule for rounding off numbers. First, look at these labels and the way that the number 195,426,874 is written below them.

millions	thousands	hundreds
1 9 5,	4 2 6,	8 7 4

If you are asked to round off 195,426,874 to the nearest hundred, you would first find the number in the highest hundred place (8), and then look at the number to its right (7). If the number to the right is 5, 6, 7, 8, or 9, you round off the hundreds to the next higher number—(9) and replace the 74 with 00. It's the same as saying that 874 is about 900. Your answer would be 195,426,900.

Suppose your original amount was 195,426,834. In that case, when you check the number to the right of 8, you would find 3. Since 3 is below 5, you would leave the 8 and replace the 34 with 00. Your answer would be 195,426,800.

PRIME AND COMPOSITE NUMBERS

Whole numbers are sometimes classified as either *prime* or *composite numbers*. A prime number is one that can be divided evenly by itself and 1—but not by any other whole number.

Examples of prime numbers are 2, 3, 5, 7, 11, 13.

A composite number is one that can be divided evenly by itself, by 1, and by at least one other whole number.

Examples of composite numbers are 4, 6, 8, 10, 15, 27.

Factors

When a whole number has other divisors besides 1 and itself, we call these other divisors *factors*. In other words, factors are numbers that we multiply to form a composite (whole) number.

Sometimes you will be asked to "factor" a number—for example, 6. The factors of 6 are the numbers that you multiply to produce 6. Since 3 times 2 equals 6, the factors of 6 are 3 and 2.

Exponents

There is a short way of writing *repeated factors* in multiplication. For example we may write 5×5 as 5^2. The small 2 written to the right and slightly above the 5 is called an *exponent*. It tells us that 5 is used twice as a factor. You can read 5^2 as either "5 to the second power," or more briefly, "5 squared." Note that 5^2 does not represent "5×2." The expression 2^3 means "2 to the third power," or "2 cubed," and represents $2 \times 2 \times 2$.

n Factorial

Don't confuse these expressions of repeated factors with the term *factorial*. When you see "6 factorial," for example, it means "find the product of every number between 1 and 6." Thus, 6 factorial means $6 \times 5 \times 4 \times 3 \times 2 \times 1$. The symbol for 6 factorial is "6!"

RECIPROCALS

You may also be asked to find the *reciprocal* of a number. To find the reciprocal of 5, look for the number that you multiply by 5 to get 1. The easiest way to work this out is to divide 1 by 5. You can express the answer either as $\frac{1}{5}$ or as 0.2 (see the following sections on fractions and decimals). Remember that the product of a number and its reciprocal is always 1: the reciprocal of $\frac{1}{4}$ is 4; the reciprocal of $\frac{2}{4}$ is 2.

SERIES AND SEQUENCES

There is a popular type of question involving a *series* or *sequence* of numbers. You are given several numbers arranged in a pattern, and are asked to find the number that comes next. The way to solve this is to figure out the pattern. Try the following two examples:

A.   2, 4, 6, 8, ?

B.   3, 9, 4, 8, ?

Each number in sequence A is 2 higher than the number to its left. Thus, the missing term is 10. By testing the relationships between numbers in series B, you find the following pattern:

3 (+ 6) = 9	The first step is "add 6."
9 (− 5) = 4	The next step is "subtract 5."
4 (+ 4) = 8	The next step is "add 4."

To continue the pattern, the next step will have to be "subtract 3." Thus, the missing number is 5.

FRACTIONS

Many problems in arithmetic have to do with fractions. (Decimals and percents are other ways of writing fractions.) There are at least four ways to think about fractions.

1. A fraction is a part of a whole. The fraction $\frac{2}{3}$ means that something has been divided into 3 parts, and we are working with 2 of them. The number written above the fraction line (2) is the numerator, and the number below it (3) is called the denominator.

2. A fraction is the result of a multiplication. The fraction $\frac{3}{4}$ means 3 times $\frac{1}{4}$.

3. A fraction is an expression of division. Thus $\frac{2}{5}$ is the quotient (result) when 2 is divided by 5. This can also be written as $2 \div 5$.

4. A fraction is an expression of a ratio. A ratio is a comparison between two quantities. For example, the ratio of 6 inches to 1 foot is $\frac{6}{12}$, since there are 12 inches in a foot.

USING ARITHMETIC OPERATIONS WITH FRACTIONS

There are special rules and some shortcuts, too, for multiplying, dividing, adding, and subtracting fractions and mixed numbers. (A *mixed number* is one that is made up of a whole number and a fraction—for example, $3\frac{2}{7}$.)

Multiplying Fractions

The general rule for multiplying two or more fractions is to multiply the numerators by one another, and then multiply the denominators by one another.

EXAMPLE

$$\frac{1}{2} \times \frac{3}{4} \times \frac{5}{8} = \frac{15}{64} \frac{\text{(numerators)}}{\text{(denominators)}}$$

Explanation: $1 \times 3 \times 5 = 15$; $2 \times 4 \times 8 = 64$

Sometimes, the product you get when you multiply two fractions can be expressed in simpler terms. When you express a fraction in its *lowest terms,* you put it in a form in which the numerator and denominator no longer have a common factor.

EXAMPLE

Reduce $\frac{24}{36}$ to lowest terms.

STEP 1 Find a number which is a factor of both 24 and 36. Both numbers can be divided by 4.

STEP 2 Divide 24 and then 36 by 4.

$24 \div 4 = 6$

$36 \div 4 = 9$

Thus, $\frac{24}{36} = \frac{6}{9}$

STEP 3 Check again. Is there a number which is a factor of both 6 and 9? Yes, both numbers can be divided by 3. Divide 6 and then 9 by 3.

$6 \div 3 = 2$

$9 \div 3 = 3$

Thus, $\frac{6}{9} = \frac{2}{3}$

Answer: $\frac{24}{36}$ can be reduced to its lowest terms, $\frac{2}{3}$.

Changing Improper Fractions to Mixed Numbers

When the numerator of a fraction is larger than its denominator, it is called an *improper fraction.* An improper fraction can be changed to a mixed number.

EXAMPLE

Change $\frac{37}{5}$ to a mixed number.

Since a fraction is also an expression of division, $\frac{37}{5}$ means $37 \div 5$. If 37 is

divided by 5, the quotient is 7, and the remainder is 2. Thus, $\frac{37}{5} = 7\frac{2}{5}$.

Changing Mixed Numbers to Improper Fractions

In order to multiply or divide mixed numbers, it is necessary to change them into improper fractions.

EXAMPLE

Change $8\frac{3}{5}$ to an improper fraction.

Convert the whole number, 8, to fifths: $8 = \frac{40}{5}$. $\frac{40}{5}$ and $\frac{3}{5}$ is $\frac{43}{5}$, an improper fraction.

A shortcut for achieving the change from a mixed number to an improper fraction is to multiply the whole part of the mixed number by the fraction's denominator, and then add the result to the original numerator. Thus

$$8\frac{3}{5} = \frac{8 \times 5 + 3}{5} = \frac{43}{5}.$$

Multiplying Mixed Numbers

When multiplying or dividing with a mixed number, change the mixed number to an improper fraction before working out the problem.

EXAMPLE

$$2\frac{2}{3} \times \frac{5}{7} =$$
$$\frac{8}{3} \times \frac{5}{7} = \frac{40}{21} = 1\frac{19}{21}$$

Cancellation

Cancellation is a shortcut you can use when multiplying (or dividing) fractions. Suppose you want to multiply $\frac{8}{9}$ times $\frac{3}{16}$. If you immediately multiply the numerators by each other, and the denominators by each other, you get an answer you have to reduce to lowest terms.

$$\frac{8}{9} \times \frac{3}{16} = \frac{24}{144} = \frac{1}{6}$$

An easier way to handle the problem is to see if there is any number you can divide evenly into both a numerator and a denominator of the original example. In this case, there is. You can divide 8 into both itself and 16.

STEP 1 $\quad \dfrac{\overset{1}{\cancel{8}}}{9} \times \dfrac{3}{\underset{2}{\cancel{16}}} =$

You can also divide 3 into the numerator 3 and the denominator 9. Solve the problem by multiplying the new numerators, and then the new denominators.

STEP 2 $\quad \dfrac{\overset{1}{\cancel{8}}}{\underset{3}{\cancel{9}}} \times \dfrac{\overset{1}{\cancel{3}}}{\underset{2}{\cancel{16}}} = \dfrac{1}{6}$

Dividing Fractions

Division of fractions looks similar to their multiplication, but there is an important extra step. Dividing something by 3 is the same as multiplying it by $\frac{1}{3}$. Therefore we can convert the division example $\frac{1}{2} \div \frac{3}{1}$ into the multiplication example $\frac{1}{2} \times \frac{1}{3}$.

To divide with fractions, *invert* the second term, and change the division sign to a times sign. In other words, write the second term upside down and then treat the problem as a multiplication of fractions. This is also called multiplying the first fraction by the reciprocal of the second fraction. Note that in the example below, 3 can be written as $\frac{3}{1}$.

$$\frac{1}{2} \div 3 = \frac{1}{2} \div \frac{3}{1} = \frac{1}{2} \times \frac{1}{3} = \frac{1}{6}$$

Adding and Subtracting Fractions

To add or subtract fractions, follow two basic rules:

(a) Add or subtract only those fractions which have the same denominator.

(b) Add or subtract only the numerators of the fractions. Keep the same denominator.

If two fractions you want to add or subtract do not have a *common denominator*, find a way to change them so that both denominators are the same. This is easy if one of the denominators divides evenly into the other. To add $\frac{5}{6}$ and $\frac{1}{12}$, you can work with the fact that 6 goes into 12 evenly. You can change the $\frac{5}{6}$ to $\frac{10}{12}$, a fraction with the same value.

STEP 1 Write the fraction you have to change. Next to it, write the new denominator you want to use.

$$\frac{5}{6} = \frac{?}{12}$$

STEP 2 To find the missing numerator: (a) divide the original denominator into the new denominator (6 into 12 = 2), then (b) multiply your answer by the original numerator ($2 \times 5 = 10$). Your new fraction is $\frac{10}{12}$. By changing $\frac{5}{6}$ to $\frac{10}{12}$, you can now add it to $\frac{1}{12}$.

$$\frac{10}{12} + \frac{1}{12} = \frac{11}{12}$$

If you cannot divide one of the denominators into the other, then you have to find a number that both will go into. If you are working with three fractions, you have to find a number that all three denominators can divide evenly.

Suppose you are asked to add $\frac{1}{4}$, $\frac{1}{5}$, and $\frac{1}{6}$. One rule for finding a common denominator for several fractions is to take the largest denominator and start multiplying it by 2, 3, etc., until you find a number that the other denominators will also divide into evenly. In this case, 6 is the largest denominator. If you multiply 6 times 2, you get 12—a number that 5 does not divide into evenly. You have to keep trying until you reach 60—the first product that all three denominators divide evenly. Thus,

$$\frac{1}{4} = \frac{15}{60}$$

$$\frac{1}{5} = \frac{12}{60}$$

$$+\ \frac{1}{6} = \frac{10}{60}$$

By adding the converted fractions, you find that $\frac{1}{4} + \frac{1}{5} + \frac{1}{6} = \frac{37}{60}$.

To add mixed numbers, follow these three steps:

(STEP 1) Add the whole numbers.

(STEP 2) Add the fractions. If the sum of these is an improper fraction, change the sum to a mixed number.

(STEP 3) Add the sum of the whole numbers to the sum of the fractions.

EXAMPLE

$$3\frac{2}{3} + 12\frac{2}{3}$$

(STEP 1) $3 + 12 = 15$

(STEP 2) $\frac{2}{3} + \frac{2}{3} = \frac{4}{3} = 1\frac{1}{3}$

(STEP 3) $15 + 1\frac{1}{3} = 16\frac{1}{3}$

In subtracting mixed numbers, you may have to "borrow" as you do in subtracting whole numbers. For example, if you want to subtract $6\frac{3}{4}$ from $9\frac{1}{4}$, you realize you cannot take $\frac{3}{4}$ from $\frac{1}{4}$. (Try to get \$.75 out of a quarter!) Thus, you borrow 1 from 9, and rewrite the example.

$$9\frac{1}{4} = 8\frac{4}{4} + \frac{1}{4} = \quad 8\frac{5}{4}$$

$$-6\frac{3}{4} = \qquad\qquad -6\frac{3}{4}$$

$$\overline{\phantom{-6\frac{3}{4}}} \qquad\qquad \overline{2\frac{2}{4} = 2\frac{1}{2}}$$

DECIMAL FRACTIONS

Decimal fractions are special fractions whose denominators are always powers of ten. *Powers of ten* are easy to remember. The exponent tells you how many zeros there are in the power of ten. Thus,

$$10^1 = 10 \qquad = 10 \times 1$$
$$10^2 = 100 \qquad = 10 \times 10$$
$$10^3 = 1{,}000 \qquad = 10 \times 10 \times 10$$

You can tell the denominator of a decimal fraction by counting the places in the number to the right of its decimal point. When it is written as a fraction, the denominator has the same number of zeros as this number of places. That is, it has the same power of ten. Thus,

$$0.7 = \frac{7}{10^1} \text{ or } \frac{7}{10} \qquad \text{(seven tenths)}$$

$$0.07 = \frac{7}{10^2} \text{ or } \frac{7}{100} \qquad \text{(seven hundredths)}$$

$$0.007 = \frac{7}{10^3} \text{ or } \frac{7}{1{,}000} \qquad \text{(seven thousandths)}$$

$$0.0007 = \frac{7}{10^4} \text{ or } \frac{7}{10{,}000} \qquad \text{(seven ten-thousandths)}$$

Changing Fractions to Decimals

To change a fraction to a decimal, divide the numerator by the denominator. Place a decimal point to the right of the numerator, and add a zero for each decimal place you want in your answer.

EXAMPLE

$$\frac{2}{5} = 5 \overline{)\begin{array}{c} 0.4 \\ 2.0 \\ \underline{2.0} \end{array}} \qquad \text{so } \frac{2}{5} = 0.4$$

Here's a short list of common fractions, converted to decimals.

$$\frac{1}{2} = 0.50 \qquad \frac{1}{3} = 0.33\frac{1}{3}$$

$$\frac{1}{4} = 0.25 \qquad \frac{3}{4} = 0.75$$

$$\frac{1}{5} = 0.20 \qquad \frac{3}{5} = 0.60$$

$$\frac{4}{5} = 0.80 \qquad \frac{1}{8} = 0.12\frac{1}{2} \text{ (or 0.125)}$$

Changing Decimals to Fractions

Every decimal is really a fraction whose denominator is a power of ten. For example,

$$0.0231 \text{ is } \frac{231}{10,000} \text{ ; 0.25 is } \frac{25}{100} \text{ or } \frac{1}{4} \text{ ; and 3.4 is } \frac{34}{10}$$

MULTIPLYING DECIMALS BY POWERS OF 10

Here is a shortcut for multiplying a decimal by a power of ten. Suppose you want to multiply 0.16 by 10^3.

STEP 1 Count the number of zeros in the power of ten.

$$10^3 = 1,000 \quad \text{(3 zeros)}$$

STEP 2 Move the decimal in 0.16 to the right. Move it as many places as this number of zeros.

Sometimes, you have to add one or more zeros so that you can move the correct number of places.

$$10^3 \times 0.16 = 10^3 \times 0.160 = 160$$

Other examples: $10^2 \times 2.1 = 10^2 \times 2.10 = 210$
$$10^4 \times 0.43 = 10^4 \times 0.4300 = 4,300$$

DIVIDING DECIMALS BY POWERS OF 10

To divide a decimal by a power of ten, count the number of zeros in the power of ten, and move that many places to the left of the decimal.

EXAMPLES

$$158.7 \div 10^1 = 158.7 \div 10 = 15.87$$
$$0.32 \div 10^2 = 00.32 \div 100 = 0.0032$$

ADDING AND SUBTRACTING DECIMALS

To add or subtract decimals, line up the numbers so that the decimal points are directly under one another. Then add or subtract as you would with whole numbers. Write zeros at the end of decimals if you find it easier to work with place holders.

> **EXAMPLE**
>
> Add 3.12 + 14.3 + 205.6 + 0.0324, and subtract their sum from 1,000.55. Remember to put the decimal point in the answers.
>
> | | |
> |---|---|
> | 3.1200 | 1,000.5500 |
> | 14.3000 | −223.0524 |
> | 205.6000 | 777.4976 (remainder) |
> | + 0.0324 | |
> | 223.0524 (sum) | |

MULTIPLYING DECIMALS

Multiply two decimals as though they were whole numbers. Then use these steps to find out where to put the decimal point in your answer.

STEP 1 Add the decimal places in both numbers, counting from the decimal point to the right.

STEP 2 Count off this same number of places from right to left in the answer.

STEP 3 Insert a decimal point where you finish counting off. Add extra zeros, if you need them, to fill out the correct number of places.

> **EXAMPLES**
>
> $0.02 \times 0.12 = 0.0024$
>
> $30 \times 1.5 = 45.0$

DIVIDING DECIMALS

To divide a decimal by a whole number, divide the numbers as though they were both whole numbers. Then place a decimal point in the answer directly above the decimal in the problem.

> **EXAMPLE**
>
> $5.117 \div 17$
>
> $$
> \begin{array}{r}
> 0.301 \\
> 17\overline{)5.117} \\
> \underline{51} \\
> 17 \\
> \underline{17}
> \end{array}
> $$

To divide one decimal by another, begin by making the divisor a whole number. Do this by moving the decimal in the divisor all the way to the right. Count the number of places you move it. Then move the decimal in the other number (the dividend) the same number of places.

$$\frac{1.8}{0.2} = \frac{18}{2} = 9$$

ROUNDING OFF DECIMALS

Many math problems require a rounding-off process to reach an answer. Think about 3.7 yards. Is this closer to 3 yards or to 4 yards? $3.7 = 3\frac{7}{10}$, which is closer to 4 yards. How about 3.5 yards? This is exactly midway between 3 and 4 yards. We must make an agreement on rounding off a number of this type: We agree that 3.5 yards will be rounded off to 4 yards. Now round off 3.346 to the nearest tenth. This lies between 3.3 and 3.4, but is closer to 3.3. A common mistake in rounding off is to start from the right; in this case the 6 in the thousandths place will round the 3.346 off to 3.35. This causes our rounded off number to become 3.4 instead of 3.3. To round off a decimal to the nearest tenth, look at the number in the hundredths place (just to the right of the tenths). If it is 5 or more, round off upward. If it is less than 5, drop it and all numbers following it.

PERCENTAGES

A *percentage* is a way to express a fraction. It simply means hundredths. To use a percentage in solving a problem, change it to a fraction or a decimal.

To change a percentage to a fraction, drop the percent sign and multiply by $\frac{1}{100}$.

EXAMPLES

5 percent means	$5 \times \frac{1}{100}$
20 percent means	$20 \times \frac{1}{100}$
100 percent means	$100 \times \frac{1}{100}$

CHANGING A PERCENTAGE TO A DECIMAL

To change a percentage to a decimal, drop the percent sign and move the decimal point two places to the left. Add extra zeros, if you need them, to fill out the correct number of places. If the percent is given as a fraction, first change the fraction to a decimal.

EXAMPLES

3% = 0.03	1.2% = 0.012
75% = 0.75	$\frac{1}{4}$ % = 0.25% = 0.0025
15% = 0.15	100% = 1.00 (or 1)

CHANGING A DECIMAL TO A PERCENTAGE

To change a decimal to a percentage, move the decimal point two places to the right and add the percent sign.

EXAMPLES

$0.23 = 23\%$ $0.05 = 5\%$

$0.5 = 50\%$ $0.66\frac{2}{3} = 66\frac{2}{3}\%$

ARITHMETIC PROBLEMS USING PERCENTAGES

An arithmetic problem using percent usually falls into one of three categories:

1. Find a number when you are told it is a certain percent of another number. This involves multiplication.

Example:

What is the amount of the discount on a hat marked $49.95 and discounted at 20 percent?

STEP 1   Change the rate of discount to a fraction or decimal. $20\% = 0.2$

STEP 2   Multiply the marked price by the rate of discount.

$$\$49.95 \times 0.2 = \$9.99 \text{ (discount)}$$

2. Find what percent one number is of another. This involves division.

Example:

A baseball team played 20 games and won 17 of them. What percent of its games did it win?

STEP 1   Express the games won by the team as a part of the total games they played. In other words, state the relationship between the two numbers by writing a fraction (a ratio).

$$\frac{17}{20}$$

STEP 2   Convert this fraction to a percent. Divide the numerator by the denominator. (Add a decimal point and zeros to carry the answer out two places.)

$$\frac{17.00}{20} = 0.85$$

STEP 3   Multiply the quotient by 100 to convert to percent.

$$0.85 \times 100 = 85\% \text{ (games won)}$$

3. Find a whole number when you know only a part of it and the percent that the part represents. This involves division.

Example:

A family pays $5,000 a year in premiums for home insurance. If the rate of insurance is $12\frac{1}{2}$ percent, how much is the insurance policy worth?

STEP 1 Change the percent to a decimal.

$$12\frac{1}{2} \text{ percent} = 0.125 \text{ (rate of insurance)}$$

STEP 2 Divide the premium by the rate of insurance.

$$\$5,000 \div 0.125 = 125\overline{)\begin{array}{c} \$40,000 \\ \$5,000,000 \\ \underline{500} \end{array}}$$

The home insurance policy is worth $40,000.

CALCULATING INTEREST

A percentage problem you frequently see has to do with interest earned on a sum of money, the *principal*. A formula for finding interest is: principal (*p*) × rate of interest (*r*) × the period of time (*t*) = interest (*i*). *Time* is always time in years.

$$i = p \times r \times t$$

EXAMPLE

How much interest will there be on $5,000 for 6 months at 5 percent?

STEP 1 Change the rate of interest to a fraction: 5% = $\frac{5}{100}$ (or $\frac{1}{20}$)

STEP 2 Express the time in terms of years. There are 12 months in a year, so 6 months is $\frac{6}{12}$, or $\frac{1}{2}$, of a year.

STEP 3 Apply the formula for finding interest.

$$i \times p \times r \times t$$

$$i \times \frac{\$5,000}{1} \times \frac{1}{20} \times \frac{1}{2}$$

$$i \times \frac{\overset{\$2,500}{\cancel{\$5,000}}}{1} \times \frac{1}{20} \times \frac{1}{\underset{1}{\cancel{2}}}$$

$$i \times \frac{\overset{\$125}{\cancel{\overset{\$2,500}{\cancel{\$5,000}}}}}{1} \times \frac{1}{\underset{1}{\cancel{20}}} \times \frac{1}{\underset{1}{\cancel{2}}} = \$125$$

The interest on $5,000 for 6 months will be $125.

SQUARE ROOTS

The square root of a number is one of the two equal factors (numbers) that, when multiplied together, give that number. For example, the square root of 9 is 3 since $3 \times 3 = 9$, and the square root of 49 is 7 since $7 \times 7 = 49$.

The square root of a number may be indicated by using a radical sign. For example, $\sqrt{81}$ means the square root of 81, that is, $\sqrt{81} = 9$. Similarly, $\sqrt{25} = 5$.

Only numbers that are perfect squares have exact square roots. Some perfect squares are 1, 4, 9, 16, 25, 36, 49, 64, 81, and 100.

FINDING THE SQUARE ROOT OF A NUMBER

You may be asked to find the square root of a number that is not a perfect square, giving your answer correct to the nearest tenth, for example. A trial-and-error procedure can be used to find a square root to the nearest decimal place. For example, suppose you are asked to find $\sqrt{29}$ to the nearest tenth: $\sqrt{29}$ is between $\sqrt{25}$, which we know is 5, and $\sqrt{36}$, which we know is 6. And $\sqrt{29}$ is nearer to $\sqrt{25}$ than it is to $\sqrt{36}$. Guess 5.3 as $\sqrt{29}$ to the nearest tenth. Divide 5.3 into 29:

$$
\begin{array}{r}
5.4 \\
53. \overline{)29\,0.0} \\
26\,5 \\
\hline
2\,50 \\
2\,12 \\
\hline
\end{array}
$$

This was a good guess. We now know that $\sqrt{29}$ is between 5.3 and 5.4. The results of multiplying 5.3×5.3 and 5.4×5.4 show that $\sqrt{29}$ is nearer to 5.4 than to 5.3:

$$
\begin{array}{r}
5.3 \\
\times\ 5.3 \\
\hline
1\,59 \\
26\,5 \\
\hline
28.09 \\
\end{array}
\qquad
\begin{array}{r}
5.4 \\
\times\ 5.4 \\
\hline
2\,16 \\
27\,0 \\
\hline
29.16 \\
\end{array}
$$

ALGEBRA

Algebra is a way to reduce a problem to a small set of symbols. When we can state a problem with a few symbols, letters, and numbers, it seems easier to solve. The solution we are looking for is often an *"unknown"* quantity, and we speak of "finding the unknowns."

Take an example. We know that if a sweater is priced at $20, we have to pay $20 to buy one. If we want three sweaters, we pay three times that amount, or $60. How do we find the answer, $60? We multiply two numbers to find a third number. Using the style of algebra, we can express this operation briefly. Let p equal the price of one sweater, and let c (the "unknown") equal the cost of three sweaters. Here's an algebraic expression for how we find c.

$$c = 3 \times p \text{ (or) } c = 3p$$

In this expression, the letters c and p are called *variables,* meaning that the numbers they stand for can change. (If the price of the sweater is discounted to $18, then p will equal $18, and c will equal $54.)

ARITHMETIC OPERATIONS IN ALGEBRA

All four arithmetic operations are possible in algebra: both basic operations (addition and multiplication), and inverse operations (subtraction and division). We can express these operations algebraically:

> **1.** The sum of two numbers, x and y, is $x + y$
>
> **2.** The difference between two numbers, x and y, is $x - y$
>
> **3.** The product of two numbers, x and y, is $(x) \times (y)$ (or) $x \cdot y$ (or) xy
>
> **4.** The quotient of two numbers, x and y, is $x \div y$ (or) $\dfrac{x}{y}$

EQUATIONS

An *equation* is a statement that two quantities are equal. This is clear when the quantities are expressed in numbers. Thus,

$$3 + 7 = 10 \qquad\qquad 7 \cdot 8 = 56$$
$$5 - 3 = 2 \qquad\qquad 18 \div 2 = 9$$

But in algebra, equations always include variables, or unknowns. Usually, you will be asked to "solve the equation" by finding the unknown number value. In this sense, the *solution* to an equation is the number that proves that the equation is true. (You show that it is true by substituting the number for the variable.) But how do you find the number?

Suppose you heard someone say, "I can afford to buy that car for $8,000, but that will leave me with only $5,000 in my bank account." How would we express his (or her) statement in algebra? (Remember, the "unknown" is the unstated amount, x, now in the bank account.) Here's one way of writing the expression:

$$x - \$8{,}000 = \$5{,}000$$

How do we solve for x?

STEP 1 Think about what the expression now means: A certain number, minus $8,000, equals $5,000.

STEP 2 Think of how you want to express the solution: $x =$ the amount in the bank

STEP 3 Think of how the statement of your solution will differ from the equation you begin with: $8,000 will no longer be on the same side of the equal sign as x.

STEP 4 Now think about how to "get rid of" or "clear" the $8,000 from the side that shows x. Notice that the sign with $8,000 is a minus sign. If you add $8,000 to the left side of the equation, the two 8,000s will cancel each other. But remember that in a true equation, everything on the left side of the equal sign must have the same value as everything on the right side. If you add $8,000 to the left, you have to add it to the right. Thus,

$$x - \$8{,}000 = \$5{,}000$$
$$x - \$8{,}000 + \$8{,}000 = \$5{,}000 + \$8{,}000$$
$$x = \$13{,}000 \text{ (amount in bank)}$$

How is the equation solved? By performing an inverse operation on both sides of the equation. Thus, to solve for x, we go through three steps:

STEP 1   We decide to "solve for x" by removing all other operations from the side of the equation where x is found.

STEP 2   We remove an operation from one side of the equal sign by performing its inverse (opposite) operation on the same side.

STEP 3   We then perform the same operation on the other side of the equal sign. (That is, if we subtract 3 from one side, we subtract 3 from the other side.)

Examples of Using Inverse Operations to Solve Equations

1. The inverse of addition is subtraction.

$$\text{Solve: } x + 7 = 50$$
$$x + 7 - 7 = 50 - 7$$
$$x = 43 \text{ (solution of equation)}$$

2. The inverse of subtraction is addition.

$$\text{Solve: } x - 3 = 4$$
$$x - 3 + 3 = 4 + 3$$
$$x = 7 \text{ (solution)}$$

3. The inverse of multiplication is division.

$$\text{Solve: } 0.05x = 4$$
$$\frac{0.05x}{0.05} = \frac{4}{0.05}$$
$$x = 80 \text{ (solution)}$$

($0.05 \div 0.05 = 1$. When you divide 4 by 0.05, you have to clear the decimal from the divisor first. Thus, 0.05 becomes 5, and 4 becomes 400.)

4. The inverse of division is multiplication.

$$\text{Solve: } \frac{x}{2} = 7$$
$$2\left(\frac{x}{2}\right) = 7 \times 2$$
$$x = 14 \text{ (solution)}$$

Inverse Operations with More Complex Equations

Sometimes, an equation shows x as part of more than one operation. There may also be negative terms (terms with a minus sign). The same basic steps are involved in finding the solution, but may have to be repeated. Remember, the goal is always to isolate x on one side of the equation.

Remember that
in multiplication
and division,
if the signs of
both terms are
plus or minus,
the answer is
signed by a
plus sign. If the
two terms are
different, the
answer is signed
by a minus sign.

EXAMPLE

Solve: $3x + 7 = -11$

STEP 1   Perform the inverse operation of $+ 7$.

$$3x + 7 - 7 = -11 - 7$$
$$3x = -18$$

STEP 2   Perform the inverse operation of $3x$ (which is the same as $3 \cdot x$).

$$\frac{3x}{3} = \frac{-18}{3}$$

$$x = -6 \text{ (solution)}$$

Sometimes, x appears on both sides of the original equation. In that case, the first step is to remove x from one side (or "collect all x's on one side") of the equal sign.

EXAMPLE

Solve: $-7x = 24 - x$

STEP 1   Perform the inverse operation of $- x$.

$$-7x + x = 24 - x + x$$
$$-6x = 24$$

STEP 2   Perform the inverse operation of $(-6)x$.

$$\frac{-6x}{-6} = \frac{24}{-6}$$

$$x = -4 \text{ (solution)}$$

ALGEBRAIC EXPRESSIONS

An *algebraic expression* is any collection of numbers and variables. This collection may have more than one variable. For example, $3x + 4y$ is an algebraic expression meaning "3 times one unknown number (x), plus 4 times another unknown number (y)."

Arithmetic Operations with Algebraic Expressions

ADDITION AND SUBTRACTION

To add or subtract algebraic expressions, remember that only *similar*, or *"like"* terms can be combined. (Terms are similar if they have the same variable, raised to the same power.) Thus, we can subtract $3x$ from $5x$ to get $2x$, but we cannot get x^3 by adding x and x^2, or get $9zh$ out of $4z$ and $5h$.

Example:

Add: $3x + 2y - 4z + 2x - 5y$

$3x + 2x = 5x$ (partial sum)
$2y - 5y = -3y$ (partial sum)
Therefore, $5x - 3y - 4z$ is the sum.

MULTIPLICATION

To multiply algebraic expressions, follow these steps.

(STEP 1)   Multiply the numbers of similar terms.

(STEP 2)   Multiply the letters of similar terms. When multiplying one power of x by another power of x, just add the exponents.

Example:

$(2x^2)(3x^5)$

(STEP 1) $2 \times 3 = 6$ (partial product)

(STEP 2) $x^2 \times x^5 = x^7$ (partial product)

Thus, the product is $6x^7$.

Sometimes, you are asked to multiply more complex algebraic expressions. The rules are basically the same.

Example:

In $x^2y(3x - 5y)$, the parentheses tell you that x^2y is the multiplier for both $3x$ and $-5y$.

(STEP 1) $x^2y \times 3x = 3x^3y$ (partial product)

(STEP 2) $x^2y \times -5y = -5x^2y^2$ (partial product)

The product is $3x^3y - 5x^2y^2$.

Example:

In $(a + 2)(2a - 3)$, think of $(a + 2)$ as a two-place multiplier. An easy way to do this example is to set it up as an ordinary multiplication in arithmetic.

$$
\begin{array}{ll}
\begin{aligned}
2a - 3 \\
\underline{\times\ a + 2} \\
4a - 6 \\
2a^2 - 3a \\
\overline{2a^2 + a - 6}
\end{aligned}
&
\begin{aligned}
\\
\\
\text{Multiply } (2a - 3) \text{ by } 2 \\
\text{Multiply } (2a - 3) \text{ by } a \\
\text{Product}
\end{aligned}
\end{array}
$$

DIVISION

To divide algebraic expressions, follow these steps:

(STEP 1)   Divide the number of similar terms.

(STEP 2)   Divide the letters of similar terms. When dividing one power of x by another power of x, subtract the exponents.

Example:

$x^5 \div x^3 = x^2$

Example:

$$\frac{8x^3}{4x} = \frac{\overset{2}{\cancel{8}}}{\underset{1}{\cancel{4}}} \times \frac{\overset{x^2}{\cancel{x^3}}}{\underset{1}{\cancel{x}}} = 2 \times x^2 = 2x^2$$

Sometimes, a divisor goes into several terms.

Example:

$$\frac{\overset{3x^2}{\cancel{24x^3}} - \overset{1}{\cancel{8x}}}{\underset{1}{\cancel{8x}}} = 3x^2 - 1$$

Evaluating Algebraic Expressions

To evaluate an algebraic expression means to replace the letters with numbers, and then simplify (add, multiply, etc.).

Example:

Evaluate the expression $(a + 2b)$ if $a = 3$ and $b = 2$.

$$a + 2b$$
$$= 3 + 2(2)$$
$$= 3 + 4$$
$$= 7$$

FACTORING IN ALGEBRA

Sometimes, you are given the answer to a multiplication example in algebra, and are asked to find the original multipliers. This is called *factoring*.

FACTOR THE HIGHEST COMMON FACTOR

The highest common factor of an algebraic expression is the highest expression that will divide into every one of the terms of the expression.

Example:

$6x^2 + 3xy$

(STEP 1) The highest number that will divide into the numerical coefficients, 6 and 3, is 3.

(STEP 2) The highest literal factor that will divide into x^2 and xy is x. Note that y is not contained in the first term at all.

(STEP 3) Divide the highest common factor, $3x$, into $6x^2 + 3xy$ to find the remaining factor: The factors are $3x(2x + y)$.

Example:

$2a^2b^3 - 4ab^2 + 6a$

The highest common factor of the three terms is $2a$, so the factors are $2a(ab^3 - 2b^2 + 3)$.

FACTORING THE DIFFERENCE OF TWO SQUARES

In this case, your example contains the square of one number, minus the square of another number. (The square of another is the product you get when you multiply a number by itself. The *square root* of a number is the number that was multiplied by itself to produce the square.)

Example:

$x^2 - 9$

STEP 1 Find the square root of x^2 and place it to the left, within each of two "empty" parentheses. The square root of x^2 is x.

$$(x\quad)(x\quad)$$

STEP 2 Find the square root of 9 and place it to the right, within each of these parentheses. The square root of 9 is 3.

$$(x\quad 3)(x\quad 3)$$

STEP 3 Place a plus sign between one pair of terms, and a minus sign between the other pair of terms.

$$(x + 3)(x - 3)$$

The factors of $x^2 - 9$ are $(x + 3)$, $(x - 3)$.

FACTORING A QUADRATIC TRINOMIAL

A quadratic trinomial is an algebraic expression of the form $ax^2 + bx + c$, where a, b, and c are numbers and a does not equal 0. Its factors are always two pairs of terms. The terms in each pair are separated by a plus or minus sign.

Example:

Factor $x^2 - 11x + 30$.

STEP 1 Find the factors of the first term in the trinomial. The factors of x^2 are x and x.

$$(x\quad)(x\quad)$$

STEP 2 Look at the last term in the trinomial. It has a plus sign. This means that both factors of the trinomial are either plus or minus. Which one? Since the middle term ($-11x$) has a minus sign, both factors must have minus signs.

$$(x-\quad)(x-\quad)$$

STEP 3 Find the factors of 30. There are several numbers you can multiply to get 30: 30×1, 10×3, etc. But the two multipliers you use must also combine somehow to give you 11, the middle term. When 5 and 6 are multiplied, they give you 30. When they are added, they give you 11. We know the factors have minus signs. So the factors of 30 are actually –6 and –5.

$$(x - 6)(x - 5)$$

The factors of $(x^2 - 11x + 30)$ are: $(x - 6)$, $(x - 5)$.

SOLVING QUADRATIC EQUATIONS

A *quadratic equation* is an equation that contains a term with the square of the unknown quantity and has no term with a higher power of the unknown. In a quadratic equation, the exponent is never higher than 2 (x^2, b^2, c^2, etc.). Examples of quadratic equations include:

$$x^2 + x - 6 = 0$$
$$3x^2 = 5x - 7$$
$$x^2 - 4 = 0$$
$$64 = x^2$$

How do we solve equations like this? Basically, we factor them, and then set each factor equal to zero. After that, it's easy to solve for x. Let's take it step by step.

EXAMPLE

Solve: $x^2 = 3x + 10$

Step 1. Place all terms on one side of the equal sign, leaving the equation equal to 0. (Remember inverse operations.)

$$x^2 - 3x - 10 = 0$$

Step 2. Factor this equation.

$$(x - 5)(x + 2) = 0$$

Step 3. Set each factor equal to zero, and solve the equations.

$$x - 5 = 0 \qquad\qquad x + 2 = 0$$
$$x = +5 \qquad\qquad\quad x = -2$$

Step 4. To check its accuracy, substitute each answer in the original equation.

$x^2 = 3x + 10$	$x^2 = 3x + 10$
$(5)^2 = 3(5) + 10$	$(-2)^2 = 3(-2) + 10$
$25 = 15 + 10$	$4 = -6 + 10$
$25 = 25$ (proof)	$4 = 4$ (proof)

The solution of the quadratic equation is $x = 5, -2$.

INEQUALITIES

Not everything in algebra is an equation! An *inequality* is a statement that two quantities are not equal to each other. With an inequality, one of these two things must be true:

1. The first quantity is greater than the second.

OR

2. The first quantity is less than the second.

A number line helps to show how this is true.

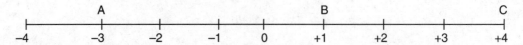

On the number line, A is to the left of B, and B is to the left of C. Whenever one variable is to the left of another on a number line, it is less than the other. Thus, −3 is less than +1, and +1 is less than +4. We can make a few general statements.

1. Any negative number is less than zero.
2. Zero is less than any positive number.
3. Any negative number is less than any positive number.

There are symbols for statements of inequality.

Symbols	Meanings
$6 \neq 7$	6 does not equal 7
$7 > 6$	7 is greater than 6
$6 < 7$	6 is less than 7
$x \geq 8$	x is greater than or equal to 8
$x \leq 8$	x is less than or equal to 8

Solving Inequalities

The rules for solving inequalities are similar to those used for solving equations with one important difference, which is illustrated in the second of the two examples below. The difference is that when both sides of an inequality are multiplied or divided by a *negative* number, the direction of the inequality sign must be reversed. To illustrate, if $8 > 5$ has each side multiplied by −2, then $−16 < −10$.

EXAMPLES

Solve: $x - 3 < 8$

"Clear" for x by transferring −3 to the other side of the inequality symbol. Do this by performing an inverse operation.

$$x - 3 + 3 < 8 + 3$$
$$x < 11 \text{ (solution)}$$

The solution means that any number less than 11 will make the original statement of inequality true. You can prove that by substituting numbers less than 11 for x. Try letting $x = 10$.

$$x - 3 < 8$$
$$10 - 3 < 8$$
$$7 < 8 \quad \text{This is certainly true!}$$

Solve: $13 - 2x < 7$

"Clear" the x term by subtracting 13 from both sides of the inequality.

$$13 - 13 - 2x < 7 - 13$$
$$-2x < -6$$

To obtain x alone, divide both sides of the inequality by −2. Since division is by a *negative* number, the direction of the inequality sign must be reversed.

$$x > 3$$

The solution means that any number greater than 3 will make the original inequality true. To prove this, substitute any number greater than 3 for *x*. Try letting *x* = 5.

$$13 - 2x < 7$$
$$13 - 2(5) < 7$$
$$13 - 10 < 7$$
$$3 < 7$$

This is certainly true!

GEOMETRY

Geometry has to do with the world around us. Some knowledge of geometry is necessary for everyone. Both arithmetic and algebra are used in solving geometry problems. Many geometry problems involve measurement, and use familiar words, such as line or point. An important term in geometry is *angle*.

ANGLES

An angle is formed by two lines meeting at a point. The point is called the *vertex* of the angle. You can name an angle in three ways.

1. By the point at the vertex (for example, angle B).

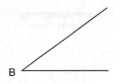

2. By the letter names of the lines that meet to form the angle, with the vertex in the middle (for example, angle ABC).

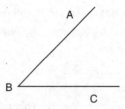

3. By a number inside the angle on a diagram (for example, angle #2).

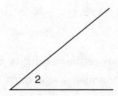

PROTRACTOR

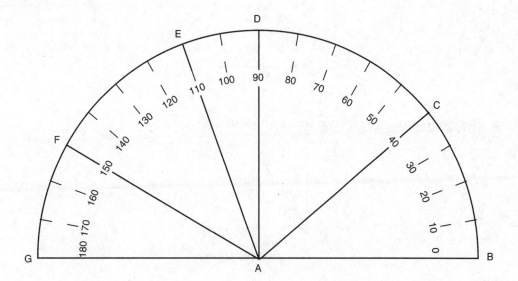

To measure an angle, we use an instrument called a *protractor*. Angles are measured in *degrees* (°). Just as a foot is divided into 12 inches, a degree is divided into minutes (′) and seconds (″). Don't confuse these with time!

1. A *straight line* can also be considered an angle of 180 degrees.

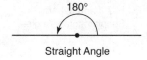

Straight Angle

2. A *right angle* is an angle of 90 degrees.

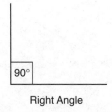

Right Angle

3. An *obtuse angle* is an angle of more than 90 degrees, but less than 180 degrees.

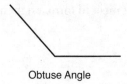

Obtuse Angle

4. An *acute angle* is an angle of more than 0 degrees but less than 90 degrees.

Acute Angle

5. *Complementary angles* are two angles whose sum is 90 degrees.

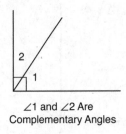

∠1 and ∠2 Are
Complementary Angles

6. *Supplementary angles* are two angles whose sum is 180 degrees.

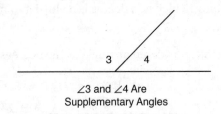

∠3 and ∠4 Are
Supplementary Angles

LINES

Parallel lines are two lines that are equally distant from one another at every point along the lines.

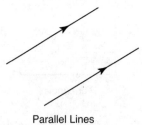

Parallel Lines

Perpendicular lines are two lines that meet to form a right angle.

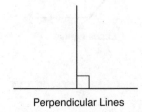

Perpendicular Lines

Parallel Lines and Pairs of Angles

Lines in the same plane that do not touch or meet are called *parallel lines*. The notation for $\overline{AB} \parallel \overline{CD}$ is read as: "Line *AB* is parallel to line *CD*."

When these two parallel lines are cut by a *transversal*, any two angles will be either equal or supplementary (add up to 180 degrees).

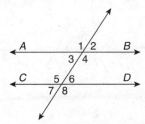

Supplementary angles: 1 and 2, 3 and 4, 5 and 6, 7 and 8

Equal angles: 1 and 4, 2 and 3, 5 and 8, 6 and 7

Pairs of angles that are "inside" the parallel lines and on opposite sides of the transversal are called *alternate interior angles* and are equal in measure (3 and 6, 4 and 5).

Pairs of angles that are "outside" the parallel lines and on opposite sides of the transversal are called *alternate exterior angles* and are equal in measure (1 and 8, 2 and 7).

Pairs of angles that are on the same side of the transversal, but where one is interior and the other exterior, are called *corresponding angles* and are equal in measure (1 and 5, 2 and 6, 3 and 7, 4 and 8).

POLYGONS

A *polygon* is composed of three or more lines, connected so that an area is closed in. There are several types of polygons.

> **1.** A *triangle* has three sides.
>
> **2.** A *quadrilateral* has four sides.
>
> **3.** A *pentagon* has five sides.
>
> **4.** A *hexagon* has six sides.
>
> **5.** An *octagon* has eight sides.
>
> **6.** A *decagon* has ten sides.

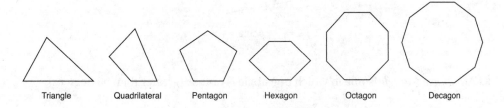

Triangle   Quadrilateral   Pentagon   Hexagon   Octagon   Decagon

Triangles

A triangle is a geometric figure with three straight lines. There are several ways to classify a triangle, but all triangles contain 180 degrees.

1. An *equilateral* triangle is one in which all three sides are equal, and all three angles are equal—60 degrees each.

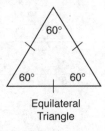

Equilateral
Triangle

2. An *isosceles* triangle is one in which two sides are equal. (The angles opposite these sides are also equal.)

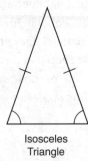

Isosceles
Triangle

3. A *scalene* triangle is one in which all the sides and all the angles are unequal.

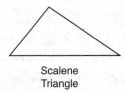

Scalene
Triangle

4. An *acute triangle* is one in which all three angles are acute (less than a right angle).

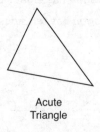

Acute
Triangle

5. An *obtuse triangle* is one in which one angle is obtuse (greater than 90 degrees).

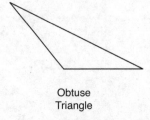

Obtuse
Triangle

6. A *right triangle* is one which includes a right angle (90 degrees). The longest side of a right triangle is called the *hypotenuse*. It is always the side opposite the right angle (side c). The other two sides are called *legs*.

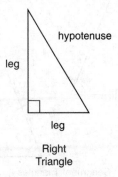

leg

hypotenuse

leg

Right
Triangle

There is a very important idea connected with right triangles called the *Pythagorean Theorem*. It says that in a right triangle, the square of the hypotenuse is equal to the sum of the square of the legs. As an equation, the Pythagorean Theorem would be expressed as follows:

$$c^2 = a^2 + b^2$$

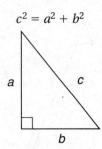

a

c

b

EXAMPLE

A gardener placed a 5-foot ladder against a 4-foot wall. If the top of the ladder touched the top of the wall, how far away from the base of the wall was the bottom of the ladder?

Solution: The angle formed by the base of the wall and the ground is a right angle. Therefore, we can use the Pythagorean Theorem. Since the ladder was opposite the right angle, let c = 5.

$$c^2 = a^2 + b^2$$
$$5^2 = 4^2 + x^2 \text{ (Clear for } x.)$$
$$5^2 - 4^2 = 4^2 - 4^2 + x^2$$
$$25 - 16 = x^2$$
$$9 = x^2 \text{ (Find the square roots.)}$$
$$3 = x$$

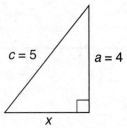

c = 5   a = 4

x

7. *Congruent triangles* are alike in every respect. All three sides and all three angles of one triangle are exactly the same as those of the other.

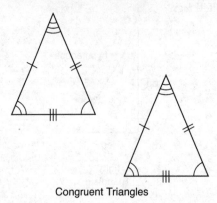

Congruent Triangles

8. *Similar triangles* are triangles with exactly the same shape, but not necessarily the same size. The angles of two similar triangles are the same.

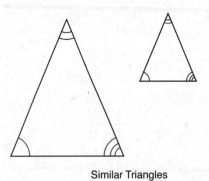

Similar Triangles

9. *Special lines in a triangle* include altitudes, medians, and angle bisectors.

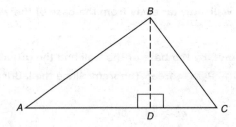

BD is an *altitude.*

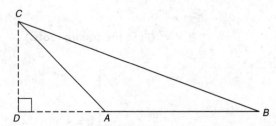

CD is an *altitude*. Notice that *AB* must be extended for the perpendicular to meet it at right angles.

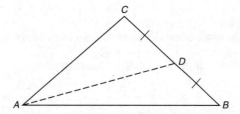

AD is a *median* if *CD* = *BD*.

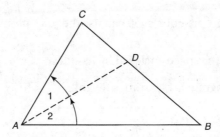

AD is an *angle bisector* of ∠*A* if ∠1 = ∠2.

Quadrilaterals

There are several types of quadrilaterals, but the measure of all angles of all quadrilaterals add up to 360 degrees.

> 1. A *parallelogram* is a quadrilateral with its opposite sides parallel. In a parallelogram the opposite sides and angles are also equal.
>
> 2. A *rectangle* is a parallelogram in which all angles are right angles.
>
> 3. A *square* is a rectangle all of whose sides are equal.
>
> 4. A *rhombus* is a parallelogram in which all four sides are equal.
>
> 5. A *trapezoid* is a quadrilateral with two sides parallel, and two sides not parallel.

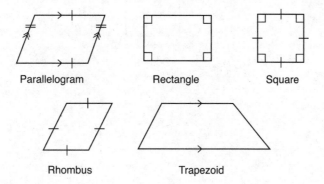

Parallelogram   Rectangle   Square

Rhombus   Trapezoid

PERIMETER AND AREA

The *perimeter* of a polygon is the sum of all its sides.

Example:
Find the perimeter of a triangle whose sides measure 3 feet, 4 feet, and 5 feet.

$$3' + 4' + 5' = 12' \text{ (perimeter)}$$

Example:
Find the perimeter of a square whose side is 9 yards.

$$9 + 9 + 9 + 9 = 36 \text{ yards (perimeter)}$$

Since all four sides of a square are equal, you can use the rule "perimeter (P) of a square equals four times a side (s)": $P = 4s$.

The *area* of a polygon is the space enclosed by its sides.

1. The area of a parallelogram is base times height.

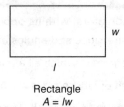

Parallelogram
$A = bh$

2. The area of a rectangle is length times width.

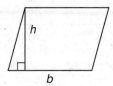

Rectangle
$A = lw$

3. The area of a square is one side "squared."

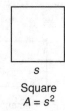

Square
$A = s^2$

4. The area of a triangle is one-half the base times the height.

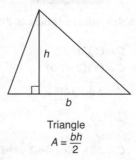

Triangle
$$A = \frac{bh}{2}$$

Example:

Find the area of a room whose length is 20 feet and whose width is 18 feet.

$$A = lw$$
$$x = 20' \times 18'$$
$$x = 360 \text{ square feet (area)}$$

CIRCLES

A *circle* is a closed curved line, all of whose points are equally distant from the center. A circle contains 360 degrees. There are several special "parts" to a circle.

The *circumference* of a circle is its "length"—once around the rim.
The *radius* of a circle is a line drawn from the center to any point on the circumference.
The *diameter* is a line passing through the center of a circle, and is equal to twice the radius.

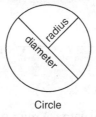

Circle

Perimeter and Area of a Circle

To find the circumference (perimeter) of a circle, we use a new number, pi (π). Pi is actually a Greek letter. In geometry it expresses an unchanging relationship between the circumference of a circle and its diameter. In other words, the circumference is always π times the diameter. Since the diameter is twice the radius, we can also say that the circumference of a circle is π times twice the radius. Thus,

$$C = (\pi)d \ \text{ OR } \ C = (\pi)2r$$

When we do arithmetic operations with π, we use either 3.14 or $3\frac{1}{7}$ for π.

Find the circumference of an ice rink whose radius is 70 yards.

$$C = (\pi)2r$$
$$C = (\pi)(2 \times 70)$$
$$C = 3\frac{1}{7} \times 140$$
$$C = \frac{22}{1\cancel{7}} \times \cancel{140}^{\,20}$$
$$C = 22 \times 20 = 440 \text{ yards}$$

The area of a circle also has a fixed relationship to π. The area equals π times the square of the radius. Thus,

$$A = (\pi)r^2$$

_____

Find the area of a circular tract of land whose diameter is 20 miles.

STEP 1   Find the radius (one-half of the diameter).

20 ÷ 2 = 10 miles (radius)

STEP 2   Apply the formula for the area of a circle.

$$A = (\pi)r^2$$
$$A = 3.14 \times 10^2$$
$$A = 3.14 \times 100$$
$$A = 314 \text{ square miles (area)}$$

VOLUME

Volume is the space occupied by a solid figure. A *solid*, or three-dimensional object, has a base, height, and depth. Volume is measured in cubic units.

A *rectangular solid* has length, width, and height. The formula for finding its cubic measure is length times width times height. Thus,

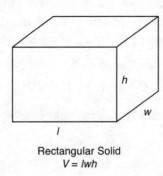

Rectangular Solid
$V = lwh$

A *cube* is a solid whose length, width, and height are the same. The volume of a cube is one side "cubed"—or one side raised to the third power. Thus,

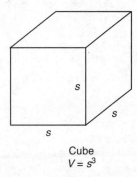

Cube
$V = s^3$

A solid in which both bases are circles in parallel planes is called a *cylinder*. The volume of a cylinder is the area of its base (a circle) times its height. Thus,

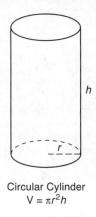

Circular Cylinder
$V = \pi r^2 h$

EXAMPLE

Find the difference between the capacity of a rectangular solid measuring 3 feet by 5 feet by 10 feet and a cylinder with a radius of 7 feet and a height of 3 feet.

STEP 1   Find the volume of the rectangular solid.
$V = lwh$
$V = 3' \times 5' \times 10'$
$V = 150$ cubic feet

STEP 2   Find the volume of the cylinder.
$V = (\pi)r^2h$
$V = 3\frac{1}{7} \times 7^2 \times 3$
$V = \frac{22}{7} \times \overset{7}{\cancel{49}} \times 3$
$V = 22 \times 7 \times 3$
$V = 462$ cubic feet

STEP 3   Find the difference between both volumes.
$462 - 150 = 312$ cubic feet

Word Knowledge and Paragraph Comprehension Review

6

HOW TO BUILD YOUR VOCABULARY

WHY A GOOD VOCABULARY IS IMPORTANT

Why is a good vocabulary important?

Here's the answer to the question: *It's important for you to have a good vocabulary because it will help you better understand the world around you, and help the world see you as more useful.*

The words in your vocabulary are important because they are the foundation of communication between people. *Words represent ideas.* They are the building blocks of how we form thoughts—of how we transform ideas and concepts into reality. So the more words you know and understand, the more tools you have to understand the world around you and to communicate that understanding to others.

Since nearly everything people do involves communication, it makes sense to conclude that *those who communicate better will often be rewarded more.* And since almost all of the communicating (and thinking) that people do is based in some way on language—which is made up of words—the more words you know, the better your communication will be . . . and the more you will be rewarded, both professionally and personally.

If you *know* a word, that means you *understand* it—what it means and the concepts it represents. Very often, single words (*faith, hope, love,* and *honor,* as some examples) represent complex concepts that literally take books or even whole libraries to examine, much less explain. But even if you don't understand *everything* about the full range of concepts that one word represents, if you are familiar with the word, you at least know *something* about it.

But if you don't know the word at all—if your vocabulary is not that big—then you know *nothing* about it . . . and you are worse off because of that. Ultimately, you will be rewarded less, whether it's in the workplace or in your personal life.

And for every new word you learn and understand, you also get an added benefit: it will help you better understand the words you already know.

A good vocabulary is one of the characteristics most common to successful people all over the world, in all walks of life. This doesn't mean you will automatically be successful if you have a good vocabulary—*but it sure can help.* The bigger your vocabulary, the more ideas you can express accurately . . . and the more you will be rewarded for your value to the world!

The Word Knowledge subtest of the ASVAB will test you directly on your knowledge of what certain words mean. Your score on this part of the ASVAB is one of four scores that factor into your Armed Forces Qualification Test (AFQT) score, which is the primary score that

> "The limits of my language are the limits of my mind. All I know is what I have words for."
> —Ludwig Wittgenstein (1889–1951), Austrian philosopher

determines the level of your eligibility for military service. *The higher your AFQT score, the more choices you will have when it comes to picking your military specialty.* The first part of this chapter will help you refine and expand your vocabulary.

The second part of this chapter will help you with paragraph comprehension. The Paragraph Comprehension subtest of the ASVAB tests your ability to understand what you read using multiple-choice questions based on passages between one and five paragraphs long, with each paragraph running around 30–120 words. Each passage is used for one to five questions.

Vocabulary is pretty important here, too. If you can't understand the individual words, there's no way you can understand the sentences and paragraphs those words make up.

So let's get started making sure you have that "good vocabulary" that will be important to you all throughout your entire life. We're going to do that by looking at

- ☑ How to add a word to your vocabulary
- ☑ The parts of a word: prefixes, roots, and suffixes
- ☑ Synonyms and antonyms
- ☑ Associating words by topics or ideas
- ☑ Abbreviations

Then we're going to work through the basic vocabulary that you *should* have—the one that will help you do well on the ASVAB. These words are grouped into nouns, verbs, and adjectives. For each word, you'll find today's most common or widely used definition; however, you need to know that today's meaning may be a long way from the word's original or literal meaning.

Some words have an alternate meaning that will be useful for you to know. It's a good idea to learn these alternate meanings, as well as to practice using them in sentences; this will help you remember the words and be able to use them correctly when you need them.

One last note: you may look at these words and think that you already know them, but take the time to go through them carefully and make *sure*—many times the meaning you've deduced from seeing the word in context may not be quite right, or it may even be quite wrong.

Remember what Mark Twain said: "It's not what we don't know; it's what we do know that ain't so."

HOW TO ADD A WORD TO YOUR VOCABULARY

The best way to improve your vocabulary is to *read.* Read the newspaper, read online articles, read magazines, read books—read about things you're interested in, read about things you realize that you need to know about, read the sports section, but *read!*

You also need to *write.* No one said you have to write for publication. No one's demanding that you win the Pulitzer Prize. But in order for you to be able to apply what you're learning by reading, you need to write—then go through it yourself after it's cooled off and revise it . . . and then have someone who is skilled and experienced in writing look at it and give you some pointers. It's the only way you will learn what you need to know, and it's the best way to significantly improve your vocabulary.

Let's look at a couple of examples of how reading can help you add words to your vocabulary.

Let's say that you don't know the meaning of the word *waning*. There's a classic American short story that starts with this sentence:

"It was late in the afternoon, and the light was *waning*."

The sentence itself provides a clue to the meaning of the word "waning." "Late in the afternoon" the light gets less, grows dim. Referring to the dictionary confirms this guess at the meaning from the clues provided in the sentence. One definition reads: "to grow dim, as a light." It will help you retain the meaning of the word if you jot it down in a vocabulary notebook. The notation for *wane* or *waning* should include the following:

Word (correctly spelled)	Meaning	Example of use
wane	grow dim, get less	The light began to wane.

Now, to lock in your understanding and retention of the word, make up your own sentence using the new word in a different context. One possibility here might be: "As he reached the end of his term, his influence began to wane."

In this example, we used five steps to master a new vocabulary word:

STEP 1 Find the word as it is used in the sentence or paragraph you're reading.

STEP 2 Make a tentative conclusion (a first guess) about the meaning of the word from the clues contained in the sentence where you found it—this is the *context*.

STEP 3 Check your tentative conclusion (guess) regarding its meaning by checking a dictionary the first chance you get.

STEP 4 If possible, add the word to a continuing list you develop in a small pocket-size notebook. Include the meaning and a typical context, such as the sentence where you found it.

STEP 5 Use the new word in a new sentence, preferably in a new context.

Now try your hand at the next example. This is taken from another fine American short story.

"It was a *desolate* country in those days; geographers still described it as The Great American Desert, and in looks it deserved the title."

How would you master the word "desolate"?

You could make a tentative conclusion about its meaning based on the clue in the sentence that it was similar to a desert. But what quality or characteristic of a desert is the one the author meant? You can find out by checking *desolate* in the dictionary. The dictionary gives four meanings and you start with the first: "lonely; solitary." That is the original meaning and the most precise. It's often best to choose the first definition if it fits the sentence. In this case, the others are all possible extensions of the main meaning, "lonely": uninhabited; laid waste; forlorn. Your notebook list might read something like this:

Word (correctly spelled)	Meaning	Example of use
desolate	lonely	The station was in a desolate part of the city.

There's one more important clue in the dictionary entry for *desolate*. The origin of the word is given: [>L. *de-* intens. + *solus,* alone]. The word comes to us from Latin—*de* is an intensifier, meaning *very*, but the important clue is the Latin word *solus*, meaning *alone*. Other English words use forms of the Latin word *solus*. These are some that might occur to you: *sole, solitaire, solitary, solitude, solo.*

Many English words have Latin and Greek roots, and many come from other languages. One of our most frequently used words is an example of this: the word *television* came to English from the French *télévision*. But *télévision* was not originally a French word. In fact, its journey through history includes both Latin and Greek.

> *tele* from the Greek tele, meaning "at a distance," or "far off"
> *vision* from the Latin visio, meaning "see"

Put the two parts together and you have a good definition of television: pictures that let you see what's going on at a distance.

STUDY THE PARTS OF A WORD

This method of vocabulary building requires you to work with three elements of a word: *roots, prefixes,* and *suffixes.*

The most essential part of any word is the root. It may be a word in itself (for example, *flex*) or a word element from which other words are formed (for example, *aud*). Knowing many word roots is one way of multiplying your vocabulary, for each root can lead you to the understanding of several words.

A prefix is a syllable or group of syllables added to the beginning of a word that changes its meaning. Let's return to the example *flex*. By itself, it means to bend or contract. If we pick a context of the human body, you can flex an arm or you can flex a muscle. If you add the prefix *re* to the beginning of the root, *flex*, you get a new word, *reflex*, with a new meaning. *Reflex* describes an action that you can't control, such as a sneeze.

We can further change the meaning of the root *flex* by adding a suffix. A suffix is a word part (a syllable or group of syllables) added to the end of a word that changes its meaning. If you add the suffix *ible*, you get another new word, *flexible*, with a new meaning. *Flexible* means *able to bend without breaking* or, in a broader meaning, *able to adjust to change.*

It is also possible to add both a prefix and a suffix to a root and get still another word. If you add both the prefix *in* (meaning *not*) and the suffix *ible* (meaning *able*), you get a new word, *inflexible*. *Inflexible* means *unbending* or, in a broader meaning, *stubborn* and *unable to adjust to change.*

To give you some idea of the *flex* family of words, here are a number of other words (*flect* is another form of *flex*).

flexibility	reflection
deflect	circumflex
inflection	genuflect

Here is a list of widely used prefixes in English. Make up at least one word using each prefix and check your accuracy in the dictionary.

Prefix	Meaning	Word
a-	no, not	
ab-	away, from	
ad-	to	
amphi-	both	
ante-	before	
anti-	against	
arch-	highest, supreme	
be-	completely, covered with	
circum-	around	
co-	with	
contra-	against	
de-	from, away, reverse action	
dia-	across	
dis-	not opposite of; reverse action, get rid of	
en/em-	make into, put into	
eu-	well	
ex-	out of, former	
extra-	beyond	
hind-	after	
fore-	before	
hyper-	above	
hypo-	below, under	
in-	into	
in -	not	
inter-	between	
intra-	within	
mal-	bad, badly	
mid-	middle	
mini-	small	
mis-	wrong, wrongly	
ob-	against	
out-	from, beyond	
over-	above, too much	
para-	beside	
peri-	around	
poly-	many	
post-	after, behind	
pre-	before	
pro-	forward; in favor of	
re-	back, again	

Make sure you work through the words, roots, prefixes, and suffixes on these tables! Just reading through the tables won't necessarily make the information stick. Study a page or two at a time, but don't blow them off. Having a good vocabulary will help you do better on eight of the nine ASVAB subtests.

Prefix	Meaning	Word
retro-	back	
se-	apart	
sub-	under	
super-	above, beyond	
syn-	together, with	
tele-	far off, far away, at a distance	
trans-	across	
twi-	two	
ultra-	beyond	
un-	not; against, opposite of	
under-	below	
up-	greater, higher, better	
with-	against, back	

Here is a list of prefixes from both Greek and Latin that indicate a number. Find one word for each prefix and add it to your vocabulary.

Meaning	Latin		Greek	
half	semi	....	hemi	....
one	uni	....	mono	....
two	bi	....	di	....
three	tri	....	tri	....
four	quadr	....	tetra	....
five	quint	....	penta	....
six	sex	....	hexa	....
seven	sept	....	hepta	....
eight	oct	....	octa	....
nine	nona	....	(rarely used)	....
ten	dec	....	deca	....
hundred	cent	....	(rarely used)	....
thousand	mill	....	kilo	....

Here is a list of widely used word roots. Think of at least one word using each root and check your word in the dictionary. Try to combine the root with one of the prefixes previously listed.

Root	Meaning	Word
act	do	
anim	spirit, life	
anthro	man	
ann(u)	year	
aqua	water	
ast/aster	star	
aud	hear	

Root	Meaning	Word
auto	self	
bene	well, good	
cas	fall	
chrom	color	
chron/chrono	time	
ced(e)	go	
cid(e)	kill	
clud(e)	close	
cor	heart	
corp	body	
cred	believe	
curr	run	
dem	people	
dic(t)	say	
do(n)	give	
duc(t)	lead, make	
fac(t)	make	
fer	carry	
fin	end	
flect	bend	
flu(x)	flow	
fract	break	
frater	brother	
gen	give birth, start	
graph	write	
gress	walk	
hetero	different	
homo	same	
hydro(o)	water	
ject	throw	
jur/jus	law	
litera	letter	
lith	stone	
luc	light	
magn	large, great	
mal	evil	
mand	order	
man(u)	hand	
mar	sea	
mater	mother	
ment	mind	
met(er)	measure	

Root	Meaning	Word
micro	small	
mit	send	
mono	one	
mort	death	
mot	move	
multi	many	
nom(y)	science of	
norm	rule	
nov	new	
omni	all	
ortho	right	
pan	all	
pater	father	
path	suffer, feel	
ped	foot	
pend	hang	
phil	love	
phon	sound	
photo	light	
port	carry	
psych	mind	
pugn	fight	
rupt	break	
sci	know	
scrib	write	
sect	cut	
sol	alone	
soph	wise	
spect	look	
struct	build	
tele	far	
temp	time	
terr	earth	
tract	draw	
vac	empty	
vad	go	
ven(t)	come	
vert	turn	
vis, visio	see	
vict	conquer	
voc, voke	call	
volv	turn	

Here is a list of common suffixes. Think of at least one word using each root and check your word in the dictionary. Try to combine the root with one of the prefixes listed previously.

Suffix	Meaning	New Word
-able, -ible	capable of, can do	
-ade	derivative or result	
-age	act of, collection of, state of	
-al	relating to	
-ance, -ancy	action, state	
-ant	one who performs an act	
-archy	rule, government	
-ate	cause, make	
-biosis	life	
-chrome	color	
-cidal, -cide	kill	
-cracy, -crat	rule, government	
-derm	skin	
-ful	full of	
-fy, -ify	to make a certain way	
-gamy	marriage	
-gnosis	knowledge	
-gram, -graph, -graphy	writing	
-hedral, -hedron	sided	
-iatrics, -iatry	medical treatment	
-ish	resembling, somewhat	
-ism	in a state of, in an act of	
-ist	one who deals with	
-itis	inflammation	
-ize	transform or change into	
-lith	stone	
-log, -logue	speech, recording	
-logy	study of	
-machy	battle, fight	
-mania, -maniac	craving, strong desire	
-ment	in a state of	
-meter, -metry	measure	
-morphic, -morphous	shape	
-nomy	science of, law of	
-oid	similar to, resembling	
-pathy	suffering, disease	
-phobe, -phobia	fear	
-phone, -phony	sound	
-plasm	matter	

Suffix	Meaning	New Word
-saur	lizard	
-scope, -scopy	observation	
-ty, -ity	a state of being	
-vorous	eating	

LEARN THE SYNONYMS AND ANTONYMS OF WORDS

A *synonym* is a word that has the same or nearly the same meaning as another word in the language. An *antonym* is a word that has the opposite or nearly the opposite meaning from another word. How or where do you find these synonyms and antonyms? The best answer is again: "In the dictionary." The average pocket-size paperback dictionary, however, because of its size, won't give you much help in this particular technique. You need to use a full or unabridged dictionary.

Let's take *Webster's New World Dictionary of the American Language*, College Edition's listing of synonyms for the word *happy*.

SYN.—happy generally suggests a feeling of great pleasure, contentment, etc. (a *happy* marriage); glad implies more strongly an exultant feeling of joy (your letter made her so *glad*), but both glad and happy are commonly used in merely polite formulas expressing gratification (I'm *glad*, or *happy*, that you could come); cheerful implies a steady display of bright spirits, optimism, etc. (He's always *cheerful* in the morning); joyful and joyous both imply great elation and rejoicing, the former generally because of a particular event, and the latter as a matter of usual temperament (the *joyful* throngs, a *joyous* family). See also *lucky*.—*ANT.* sad.

In addition to giving you four synonyms for *happy*, the entry distinguishes among them. It also gives you a context (a group of words in which the synonym appears) for each synonym. And it refers you to *lucky*, under which you find two more synonyms—*fortunate* and *providential*. Finally, it gives you one antonym, *sad*, which itself becomes a clue to five other antonyms—*sorrowful, melancholy, dejected, depressed,* and *doleful*. From the one word, *happy*, the dictionary has led us to seven synonyms and five antonyms, an additional dozen words.

In the same way, the word *large* will lead you to synonyms *big* and *great* and to antonyms *small, little, diminutive, minute, tiny, miniature,* and *petite*.

It is easier to learn related words and remember them than to learn single words in isolation. Surprisingly, it is often the case that one sign you're learning the meaning of a word is when you make a mistake in using its antonym or opposite. You may be associating the word incorrectly or incompletely, but the point is you *are* making an association.

LEARN HOMONYMS

English seems to have so many words that sound the same but are spelled differently and have different meanings. These are homonyms.

EXAMPLES

1. A full moon *shone* brightly last night.
   The film was *shown* on TV last night.

2. Once we nail up this *board*, the tool shed will be finished.
   I was very *bored* during the speech.

3. The *pain* in my right shoulder gets worse in the cold.
   I have to replace the broken *pane* of glass.

LEARN TO ASSOCIATE WORDS BY TOPIC OR IDEA

One of the most helpful aids to vocabulary building is a book based on this principle called *Roget's International Thesaurus*. Peter Mark Roget first thought out the organization of words into one thousand related groups. Roget's *Thesaurus* can't be used by itself. It must be used together with a dictionary, since the thesaurus merely lists the words by idea. For example, under the idea of GREATNESS, the word *consummate* is listed as one of the adjectives. The word *consummate* fits into the general idea of greatness, but it refers to great mastery of a skill, either to be admired or to be disapproved of, as in "with consummate artistry" or "a consummate liar." That is why the thesaurus *must* be used together with a dictionary.

While we're on the subject of association as a way of learning new words, there is another kind of association you can make: associate words that deal with a specific topic or subject. A good place to start is your own interests. Let's try foods and food preparation. Words such as the following might come to mind: *aspic, baste, sauté, truss, buffet, entrée, ragout, simmer, braise, compote, cuisine, curried, garnish, soufflé, meringue, hors d'oeuvres*.

Now for a subject that concerns all of us—health. The following words are the stock in trade of the medical doctor: *abscess, allergy, anemia, cataract, cyst, eczema, embolism, gangrene, hemorrhage, hepatitis, metabolism, neuralgia, pleurisy, sciatica, stroke, tumor*.

And anyone with an interest in motors and tools should be familiar with the terms *compression, gear ratio, ignition, piston, socket wrench, dynamometer, emission, vacuum, value*.

Many books have glossaries, lists of difficult or technical words with definitions. When you read a book on a particular subject, see if it has a glossary, and if it does, study the new words and their definitions.

LEARN TO USE THESE ABBREVIATIONS CORRECTLY

Many people either misuse or don't correctly understand the most common abbreviations. Besides helping you on the ASVAB, being able to use the most common abbreviations correctly will help you in everyday, official, and academic communication.

A.D. (often seen in small capitals as A.D. or AD) is an abbreviation for the Latin phrase *anno Domini*, "in the year of our Lord"; measures time after the birth of Christ (as it was established in the Middle Ages).

ASAP: As Soon As Possible.

B.C. (often seen in small capitals as B.C. or BC), "before Christ."

B.C.E. (often seen in small capitals as B.C.E. or BCE), "before Christian era" or "before common era"; equivalent to B.C.

e.g. is short for the Latin phrase *exempli gratia*, which means "for example." This is used when you want to specify an example of a general statement, as in, "Not all birds can fly, e.g., the ostrich can't fly but can run very fast."

et al. means "and others"; this is the English translation of the Latin *et alia*.

etc. is an abbreviation for the Latin phrase, *et cetera*, which means "and so on"—or, literally, "and other things." You should only use "etc." after a series of at least two or three things, as in, "We unpacked the Christmas tree lights, ornaments, tinsel, etc."

ibid. is short for the Latin term *ibidem*, meaning "in the same place." Used in ciations to refer to a previously listed document or publication.

i.e. is an abbreviation for the Latin phrase *id est*, "that is." Can be thought of as, "in other words."

op. cit. is short for the Latin phrase *opere citato*, "in the work cited."

qv. is short for the Latin *quod vide*, meaning "which to see"; written after a term or phrase that should be looked up elsewhere in the current document.

LEARN ACTION AND DESCRIPTIVE WORDS

If you would like to build your vocabulary and work at improving your writing skills, try increasing the number of action (verbs) and descriptive words (adjectives) you use. You can start by using the word *get* less frequently and using more precise verbs.

Less Interesting	Less Precise
We should **get** a new computer for the office.	We should (**buy, rent, lease**) a new computer for the office.
Milton tried to **get** me to take his side in the debate.	Milton tried to **persuade** me to take his side in the debate.
The first baseman **got** hit by the pitcher's fast ball.	The pitcher's fast ball **struck** the first baseman.

A BASIC ADULT WORD VOCABULARY

To help you build your vocabulary, here are over 1,250 words that every high school graduate should know. They are grouped into lists of nouns, verbs, and adjectives. You should use these lists and definitions together with a good dictionary. Each word has its most widely used definition. It is a good idea to study alternate meanings of each word so that you won't be confused when the context changes. The list also provides words, sentences, and phrases to show you how the particular word should be used.

USEFUL NOUNS

A

Abdication failure to fulfill a responsibility or duty

Aberration a deviation from the standard

Abeyance a temporary postponement

Access (means of) approach or admittance (e.g., to records)

Accord agreement

Adage wise proverb or saying (as "Better late than never")

Adversary enemy, opponent

Advocate one who speaks on behalf of another

Affluence abundance; wealth (e.g., age of ____)

Agenda list of things to be done or discussed (e.g., at a meeting)

Alacrity brisk willingness (e.g., agreed with ____)

Alias assumed name (e.g., Steve Smith, John Doe)

Allusion indirect reference to something else

Ambivalence uncertainty or mixed emotions

Analogy a comparison between two things, usually for the purpose of explanation

Anarchy lawlessness, complete disorder

Anecdote a short and amusing or interesting story about a real situation

Animosity great hatred (e.g., toward strangers)

Anomaly abnormality or irregularity

Anthology collection of stories, poems, or other creative work such as songs

Apathy indifference (e.g., toward poverty)

Apex the highest point (e.g., ____ of a triangle)

Aspersion an attack on the reputation or value of someone or something

Atlas book of maps

Audacity boldness

Autonomy condition of self-government; also, independence

Avarice deep-seated greed or desire for wealth

Awe feeling of respect and wonder (e.g., in ____ of someone's power)

B

Bastion stronghold, fortress

Beacon literally, a "guiding light"; also, a great example (e.g., of knowledge)

Benediction blessing

Bigotry bias or prejudice based on differences from one's self

Blasphemy an insult to something held sacred or holy

Blemish defect (e.g., on one's record)

Bondage slavery

Boon benefit (e.g., a ____ to business)

Brawl noisy fight

Brevity shortness

Brochure pamphlet (e.g., a travel ____)

Bulwark strong protection (e.g., a ____ against corruption)

C

Caliber literally, the size of a bullet at the base in hundredths of an inch; also, a measure of quality

Camouflage disguise that makes something harder to see

Cartographer mapmaker

Caste social class, group, or position

Catastrophe sudden disaster (e.g., an earthquake)

Chagrin feeling of deep disappointment or embarrassment

Chronicle historical record

Clamor uproar

Clemency mercy (e.g., toward a prisoner)

Condolence expression of sympathy (e.g., extended ____ to a bereaved person)

Connoisseur expert judge of quality (e.g., of paintings or food)

Consensus general agreement

Context the words or ideas around a given word or idea

Criterion standard of judgment (e.g., good or poor by this ____)

Crux the essential point (e.g., the ____ of the matter)

Cynic one who doubts the good intentions of others

D

Data known facts (e.g., ____ found through research)

Dearth scarcity (e.g., of talent)

Debacle general defeat (e.g., in a battle)

Debut first appearance before an audience (e.g., actor, pianist)

Deference respect or courtesy

Deluge great flood (e.g., rain, fan mail)

Depot warehouse

Destiny predetermined fate

Detriment damage or loss (e.g., it was to his ____)

Diagnosis determining the nature of a disease or a situation

Diction manner in which words are used or pronounced in speech

Dictum a formal pronouncement from an authoritative source

Dilation becoming or being made more open

Dilemma situation requiring a choice between two unpleasant courses of action (e.g., He was in a ____.)

Din loud continuing noise

Directive a general order (e.g., from an executive or military commander)

Discord disagreement

Discrepancy inconsistency (e.g., in accounts, in testimony)

Discretion freedom of choice; also, the ability to keep a secret

Disposition a person's overall attitude or character; also, the way in which something is placed or arranged

Dissent difference of opinion (e.g., from a decision by a higher authority)

Drought long spell of dry weather

E

Egotist one who judges everything only as it affects his own interest; a self-centered person

Elite choice or higher (quality) part (e.g., of society, an elite unit)

Enigma mystery

Enterprise an important or wide-ranging project

Environment surrounding influences or conditions

Epitome typical representation (e.g., She was the ____ of beauty.)

Epoch period of time identified by an important event or situation

Era period of time marked by an important person or event (e.g., the Napoleonic ____)

Essence basic nature (e.g., ____ of the matter)

Etiquette rules of social behavior or customs which are generally accepted

Excerpt passage from a book or a document

Exodus departure, usually of large numbers

F

Fabrication a lie or made-up story; also, the act of making or manufacturing something

Facet side or aspect (e.g., of a problem)

Facsimile exact copy

Faction one side in a dispute or disagreement; also, a group with common interests

Fallacy mistaken idea; reasoning which contains an error

Fantasy imagination; a made-up situation (e.g., He indulged in ____.)

Feud continued deadly hatred (e.g., between two families)

Fiasco complete, humiliating failure

Fiend inhumanly cruel person

Finale last part of a performance or event

Flair natural talent (e.g., for sports)

Flaw defect

Focus central point (e.g., of attention)

Foe enemy

Format physical appearance or arrangement (e.g., of a book)

Forte one's strong point (e.g., math, sports)

Fortitude steady courage (e.g., when in trouble)

Forum a gathering for the discussion of issues, often public ones

Foyer entrance hall (e.g., to a building or dwelling)

Fraud deliberate deception

Friction rubbing of the surface of one thing against the surface of another

Function purpose served by a person, object, or organization

Furor an outburst of excitement (e.g., over a discovery)

G

Gamut the whole range (e.g., of experiences)

Genesis origin (e.g., of a plan)

Genre a class or category, especially referring to the arts or entertainment

Ghetto city area inhabited by members of a group that others look down on (formerly religious, now usually racial or economic)

Gist essential content (e.g., of a speech or an article)

Glutton one who overeats or who indulges in anything to excess

Grievance complaint made against those responsible for an unjust situation

Guile cunning, deceit

H

Havoc great damage and destruction (e.g., wreak ____ on)

Hazard danger

Heritage inheritance, either of real wealth or of a tradition

Hindrance obstacle; something that delays reaching a goal

Hoax deliberate attempt to trick someone, either seriously or as a joke

Horde crowd, multitude

Horizon limit (of vision, knowledge, experience, or ambition)

Hue shade of color

Hysteria wild emotional outburst

I

Idiom expression peculiar to a language which has a different meaning from the literal meaning of the words which make it up (e.g., "hit the road")

Illusion idea or impression different from reality

Image likeness or reflected impression of a person or object

Impetus moving force

Incentive spur or motive to do something (e.g., profit ____)

Incumbent present holder of an office

Indigence extreme poverty

Inference conclusion reached by analysis or reasoning

Infirmity physical defect

Influx a flowing in (e.g., of money into banks, tourists into a country)

Infraction violation of a rule or a law

Initiative desire or ability to take the first step in carrying out some action

Innovation introduction of a new idea or method

Integrity moral and intellectual honesty and uprightness

Interim meantime (e.g., in the ____)

Interlude period of time between two events (e.g., ____ between the acts of a play)

Intrigue secret plot

Intuition knowledge gained or conclusion reached through instinct rather than thought

Iota very small amount

Irony a significant—and often unexpected—difference between what might be or might have been expected and what actually happens; also, the intentional use of words to convey the opposite of their literal meaning

Itinerary the schedule of stops or route followed on a trip, actual or planned

J

Jeopardy risk of harm (e.g., put into ____)

Jubilation celebration, rejoicing

Junket pleasure trip or excursion

K

Keynote main theme (e.g., he gave the ____ speech of the convention)

Kleptomania a compulsion to steal

Knave a tricky, deceitful person

Knoll small, rounded hill

L

Larceny theft (e.g., they couldn't decide whether it was grand or petty ____)

Layman one who is not a member of a particular profession (e.g., from the point of view of a ____, please explain this technical idea)

Legacy material or spiritual inheritance (e.g., ____ from a parent)

Legend story or stories passed on from generation to generation and often considered to be true

Legion large number

Lethargy sluggishness, drowsiness

Levee a raised, usually earthen, embankment meant to prevent flooding caused by a river or other body of water

Levity lightness of mood, frivolity

Liaison contact between two or more groups (e.g., ____ between headquarters and field units)

Litigation legal proceedings

Lore body of traditional knowledge (e.g., the mythical ____ handed down from prehistoric times)

M

Malady disease (e.g., incurable ____)

Maneuver skillful move (e.g., a clever ____)

Mania abnormal intense focus on one thing or area (e.g., She had a ____ for clothes.)

Marathon a foot race lasting 26 miles, 385 yards; also, any contest requiring endurance; named in commemoration of the messenger who ran that distance to bring news to Athens of the Greek victory over the Persians in 490 B.C. at Marathon

Maverick one who acts independently rather than according to an organizational pattern

Maxim a saying that gives a rule of conduct (e.g., Look before you leap.)

Medium means of communication (e.g., the ____ of radio)

Memento object which serves as a reminder (e.g., a ____ of our trip)

Metropolis a very large city

Milieu surroundings or environment

Morale state of mind as it affects possible future action (e.g., The troops had good ____.)

Morés well-established customs (e.g., the ____ of a society)

Multitude a large number

Myriad a large number of varied people or things

Myth a story or traditional explanation of some occurrence, usually in nature (e.g., the ____ of Atlas holding up the heavens on his back)

N

Negligence carelessness

Neophyte beginner

Niche a suitable and desirable place (e.g., He found his ____ in the business organization.)

Nomad wanderer

Nostalgia desire to return to past experiences or associations

O

Oasis a place which provides relief from difficult conditions (e.g., an ____ of peace in a troubled world)

Objective goal

Oblivion a condition of complete ignorance, forgetfulness, or unawareness

Odyssey long journey

Omen something believed to predict a future event (e.g., an evil ____)

Optimum best possible quantity or quality (e.g., the ____ balance of factors)

Ovation enthusiastic reception, usually accompanied by generous applause (e.g., He received a tumultuous ____.)

Oversight failure to include something through carelessness (e.g., His name was omitted because of an ____.); also, general supervisory responsibility

Overture first step, which is intended to lead to others in either action or discussion (e.g., He made a peace ____.); also, the introduction to an opera or other extended musical piece

P

Pageant public spectacle in the form of a stage performance or a parade (e.g., a historical ____)

Panacea something supposed to cure all diseases or problems

Panorama a clear view of a very broad area

Paradox statement which appears to contradict itself (e.g., a 20-year-old who had only five birthdays because he was born on February 29).

Pastime way of spending leisure time (e.g., He took up golf as a ____.)

Partisan one who supports (usually strongly) a particular cause, person, or idea; in a country occupied by an enemy, one who opposed the occupying enemy by acts of defiance or sabotage

Paucity scarcity or shortage (e.g., a ____ of nuclear scientists)

Pauper very poor person

Pedestrian person who is walking

Peer an equal in age, social standing, ability, or some other quality

Phenomenon a natural occurrence such as the tides

Phobia unreasonably intense fear of something (e.g., a ____ of heights)

Physique build (of the human body)

Pilgrimage long trip to someplace worthy of respect or devotion

Pinnacle highest point (e.g., the ____ of a mountain or of power)

Pitfall trap, disadvantage

Pittance very small amount or sum of money (e.g., He lived on a ____.)

Plateau area of level land, usually located at a height

Plight condition, usually unfavorable (e.g., the sorry ____ of the refugees)

Poise calm and controlled manner of behavior (e.g., He showed ____ in difficult situations.)

Populace the residents of an area; also, used to refer to the masses not in power

Posterity future generations (e.g., leave a peaceful world for our ____)

Precedent event or regulation which serves as an example or provides the basis for approval of a later action (e.g., set a ____)

Predecessor someone or something that came or occurred before another

Predicament unpleasant situation from which it is difficult to free oneself (e.g., He found himself in a ____.)

Preface introductory statement to a book or speech

Prelude something preliminary to some act or work which is more important

Premise statement from which a conclusion is logically drawn (e.g., Granted the ____ that . . . , we may conclude. . . .)

Premium amount added to the usual payment or charge (e.g., He paid a ____ for the seats.)

Prestige respect achieved through rank, achievement, or reputation

Pretext reason given as a cover-up for the true purpose of an action (e.g., He gave as a ____ for stealing it his sentimental attachment to the ring.)

Priority something which comes before others in importance (e.g., He gave ____ to his studies.)

Process step-by-step system for accomplishing some purpose (e.g., the ____ of crafting legislation)

Prodigy an extremely talented or gifted child

Prospect possibility for the future (e.g., the ____ of peace)

Proviso requirement that something be done, usually made in writing

Prowess superior ability (e.g., ____ in athletics)

Proximity nearness

Pseudonym assumed name, usually by an author (e.g., Mark Twain, the ____ of Samuel Clemens)

Pun play on words depending on two different meanings or sounds of the same word (e.g., Whether life is worth living depends on the *liver*.)

Purveyor a person who sells or deals in a particular type of goods; also, a person or group that advocates an idea or perspective

Q

Quagmire literally, a bog or swamp that hinders movement or in which people or vehicles could be badly stuck; figuratively, a challenging situation from which it is very difficult to escape

Qualm uneasy doubt about some action (e.g., He had no ____ about running for office.)

Quandary deep uncertainty about a choice between two courses of action (e.g., He was in a ____ about whether to choose law or medicine.)

Query question

Quest search (e.g., ____ for knowledge)

R

Rapport harmonious relationship that includes good two-way communication (e.g., ____ between teacher and pupil)

Rarity something not commonly found (e.g., A talent like his is a ____.)

Refuge place to which one can go for protection (e.g., He found ____ in the church.)

Remnant remaining part (e.g., ____ of the troops)

Remorse deep feeling of guilt for some bad act (e.g., He felt ____ at having insulted his friend.)

Rendezvous a meeting or a place for meeting

Renown fame (e.g., an actor of great ____)

Repast meal, usually of good quality; sometimes used sarcastically to indicate the opposite

Replica an exact copy (e.g., ____ of a painting)

Reprimand severe criticism or rebuke (e.g., He received a ____ from his boss.)

Reprisal bad action taken in return for something else negative (e.g., ____ for an injury—"An eye for an eye")

Residue remainder, what is left over

Resources assets, either material or spiritual, which are available for use

Respite temporary break which brings relief (e.g., ____ from work)

Resumé summary of work experience and education

Reverence feeling of great respect (e.g., ____ for life)

Robot one who acts mechanically or like a mechanical person; a self-directed mechanical person

Roster list of names (e.g., ____ of guests)

S

Sabotage deliberate damage to vital services of production and supply, usually to those of an enemy in wartime

Saga long tale, usually of heroic deeds

Salutation greeting, written or spoken (e.g., The ____ of a letter may be "Dear Sir.")

Sanction approval, usually by proper authority; can also mean punishment for incorrect behavior

Sarcasm cutting remarks

Satire attack on someone's behavior by making it appear to be ridiculous

Scapegoat someone who is blamed for the bad deeds of others

Scent distinctive smell

Scope entire area of action or thought (e.g., the ____ of the plan)

Scroll roll of paper or parchment containing writing

Sect group of people having the same beliefs, usually religious; often used with negative connotations indicating divergent or radically different beliefs from the mainstream

Segment part or section of a whole (e.g., ____ of a population)

Semblance outward appearance (e.g., He gave the ____ of a scholar.)

Sequel something that follows from what happened or was written before (e.g., ____ to a novel)

Sham false imitation (e.g., His devotion was a ____ of true love.)

Sheaf bundle either of grain or of papers

Sheen luster (e.g., of polished furniture)

Silhouette outline drawing in black

Site location of an object or an action (e.g., original ____ of a building)

Slander negative spoken information about someone which damages his reputation

Slogan motto which is associated with an action or a cause (e.g., Pike's Peak or Bust!)

Slope slant (e.g., ____ of a line); measured from 0 degrees to 90 degrees

Snare trap

Solace comfort (e.g., She found ____ in work.)

Sponsor one who endorses and supports a person or an activity

Spur something which moves one to act (e.g., a ____ to try harder)

Stagnation near or complete lack of movement, usually where movement would be an advantage

Stamina ability to fight off physical difficulties such as fatigue

Stature height reached physically or morally (e.g., a man of great ____)

Status standing, social or professional

Stigma mark of disgrace

Stimulus an encouragement to act or react

Strategy overall plan of maneuver or course of action (e.g., the ____ of the battle)

Strife conflict

Summit the highest point (e.g., the ____ of his career)

Supplement amount added to complete something (e.g., ____ to a budget)

Survey broad study of a topic (e.g., a ____ of employment practices)

Suspense tension brought about by uncertainty about what will happen

Sycophant one who flatters a superior in hope of receiving favor

Symbol something used to stand for something else (e.g., Uncle Sam is a ____ of the United States.)

Symptom indication of something (e.g., ____ of disease)

Synopsis brief summary

Synthesis the combining of parts to form a whole, usually referring to ideas

T

Tact ability to say what is meant without causing undue offense

Tactics specific actions to achieve some purpose (e.g., The ____ he used to win were unfair.)

Tally record of a score or an account (e.g., the ____ of the receipts)

Tang strong taste or flavor

Technique method or skill in doing work (e.g., the ____ of an artist)

Temerity boldness verging on foolhardiness

Temperament natural disposition to act in a certain manner (e.g., He displayed a changeable ____.)

Tempo pace of activity (e.g., The ____ of life is increasing.)

Tension mental or emotional strain (e.g., He was under great ____.)

Theme topic of a written work or a talk

Threshold the starting point (e.g., the ____ of a career)

Thrift ability to save money or spend wisely (e.g., He became wealthy because of his ____.)

Tint a particular shade of a color

Token object or action that represents some object or feeling (e.g., a ____ of esteem)

Tonic something which is a source of energy or vigor

Tradition customs and beliefs that are transmitted from one generation to another

Trait distinguishing feature (e.g., ____ of character)

Transition movement from one situation to another (e.g., ____ from dictatorship to democracy)

Trepidation fear, apprehension

Tribunal place of judgment, such as a court

Tribute showing of respect or gratitude (e.g., He paid a ____ to his parents.)

Turmoil disturbance (e.g., great ____ at the meeting)

Tutor a private teacher

Tycoon wealthy and powerful businessman

U

Ultimatum a final condition or demand ("Take it or leave it!")

Unrest restless dissatisfaction

Upheaval sudden overthrow, often violent

Usage established practice or custom

Utensil implement, tool (e.g., a spatula is a common kitchen ____)

Utopia ideal place or society

V

Valor courage

Venture something involving risk or doing something new

Vicinity neighborhood or surrounding area

Victor winner

Vigor vitality, energy

Vim energy

Volition will or conscious choice

Vow solemn pledge

W

Wager bet

Whim sudden notion or desire

Whit very small amount (e.g., not one ____)

Woe great sorrow (e.g., He brought ____ to his friends.)

Wrath intense anger (e.g., He poured his ____ on his enemies.)

Z

Zeal eager desire

Zenith the highest point

Zest keen enthusiasm (e.g., ____ for competition)

USEFUL VERBS

A

Abhor hate

Abscond escape quickly and secretly

Absolve to free from guilt (e.g., for a crime)

Accede agree to (e.g., a request)

Accelerate speed up

Accost confront and speak to

Acquiesce to give in; to agree to a request or demand

Adhere give support to (e.g., a cause)

Adjourn put off to a later time (e.g., a meeting)

Advocate act in support of (e.g., revolution)

Allay calm (e.g., fears)

Allege claim

Alleviate to lessen or relieve discomfort or pain

Allot assign (e.g., a share)

Allude refer to (e.g., a book)

Alter change

Amass accumulate

Ameliorate make better or more tolerable

Appease to pacify or soothe by giving in to demands

Assent agree

Assuage to lessen the pain of

Atone make up for (e.g., a sin)

Atrophy waste away from lack of use

Augment add to

Avert prevent

B

Baffle puzzle

Ban forbid, ban from an area or consideration

Bar exclude

Befall happen to

Belittle insult or degrade

Berate scold

Beseech plead

Bestow grant, from a superior to an inferior (used with on or upon)

C

Cede give up (e.g., territory)

Censor limit communication to prevent the loss of secrets

Censure blame

Char scorch

Chastise punish

Chide scold

Cite mention in order to prove something

Coalesce come together as one

Coerce force

Collaborate work with someone

Commend praise

Comply act in answer to (e.g., a request)

Concede admit that something is true (e.g., an argument)

Concur agree

Condescend patronize; talk down to someone in an insulting way

Condone approve of

Constrict squeeze

Cull pick out

Curtail cut short or reduce

D

Deduce come to a conclusion from given facts

Deem consider

Defer postpone

Defray pay at least part of

Delete remove or erase (e.g., a word)

Delve investigate

Denounce to speak out against or loudly criticize

Deplete use up

Deplore be sorry about

Deprive keep someone from having or getting something

Deride ridicule or laugh at contemptuously

Desecrate defile a holy place

Despise scorn

Detain delay someone, usually temporarily

Detect uncover something that is not obvious

Deter keep someone from doing something

Detest hate

Detract take away from

Devour eat up greedily

Digress depart from the subject under consideration

Dilute weaken by adding something less strong (e.g., a mixture)

Disburse pay out

Discern make out clearly (e.g., a pattern)

Discriminate to differentiate or make a distinction based on some quality; usually has the modern connotation of unfair racial, ethnic, or gender bias

Disdain look down on with scorn

Disintegrate fall apart

Dismay dishearten

Disparage belittle, say negative things about

Dispel drive away

Disperse scatter

Disrupt break up or disturb

Distort present incorrectly (e.g., facts)

Diverge go in different directions

Divert turn from a course (e.g., a stream)

Divulge reveal

Don put on (e.g., clothing)

Drone talk on and on in a dull, boring way (verb); also, an unmanned aircraft (noun)

E

Efface blot out

Effect bring about (verb); result (noun)

Eject throw out

Elate make happy

Emit give forth (e.g., sounds)

Emulate imitate as a role model

Encounter meet

Encroach intrude on (e.g., property)

Endeavor try

Endorse support officially

Endow provide with (e.g., a desirable quality)

Enhance increase the value of

Ensue follow as a result

Enthrall captivate or charm completely, as if under a spell

Entreat plead

Err make a mistake

Erupt break out

Esteem value

Evade avoid or escape from someone or something

Evict expel

Exalt raise to greater heights

Exceed surpass

Exemplify serve as a representative example of

Expedite speed up the handling of

Exploit take advantage of a situation or a person

Extol praise highly

F

Facilitate make easier

Falter stumble

Famish starve

Feign pretend

Flaunt show off

Flourish thrive

Flout defy openly or mockingly

Foil prevent

Forgo do without

Forsake abandon

Frustrate prevent someone from achieving something

G

Gauge estimate; measure

H

Harass disturb constantly

Heave lift and throw

Heed pay attention to (e.g., advice)

Hinder keep back

Hover hang in the air above a certain spot

Hurl throw with force

I

Ignite set fire to

Immerse plunge completely into a liquid

Impair damage

Impede stand in the way of

Imply suggest

Incite arouse

Incur bring upon oneself (e.g., criticism)

Induce persuade

Indulge satisfy (e.g., a desire)

Infer come to a conclusion based on something known

Inhibit restrain

Innovate find or create a new or better way of doing something

Instigate spur to action

Instill put a feeling into someone (e.g., fear)

Intercept interrupt something (or someone) which is on its (his/her) way

Interrogate question

Intimidate frighten by making threats

Invoke call upon

Irk annoy

J

Jar shake up (e.g., as in a collision)

Jeer poke fun at (e.g., as by sarcastic remarks)

L

Lament feel sorrow for

Languish become hopeless or depressed

Launch set in motion

Loom appear in a threatening manner

Lop cut off

Lure tempt

Lurk remain hidden

M

Magnify make larger

Maim cripple

Meander wander slowly or seemingly aimlessly

Mimic imitate

Mitigate make less severe

Mock ridicule

Molest bother

N

Narrate tell (e.g., a story)

Navigate steer (e.g., a ship)

Negate deny or cancel out

Nullify cancel out or make unimportant, as if nonexistent

O

Obscure unclear, clouded, partially hidden

Orient adjust oneself or someone to a location or situation

Oust expel

P

Parch make dry

Peer look closely

Pend remain undecided; hang

Perfect to complete; make flawless

Perplex puzzle

Persevere continue on a course of action despite difficulties

Pertain have reference to

Perturb upset to a great extent

Peruse read carefully

Pine long for

Placate make calm

Ponder think through thoroughly

Preclude prevent something from happening

Prescribe order (e.g., for use or as a course of action)

Presume take for granted

Prevail win out over

Probe investigate thoroughly

Procure obtain

Profess claim

Prosper be successful

Protrude project

Provoke arouse to action out of irritation

Pry look closely into, be nosy; also, to open a closed object (door, lid) by mechanical force

Q

Quell subdue

R

Ravage ruin

Rebate give back, usually part of an amount paid

Rebuff repulse

Rebuke disapprove sharply

Recede move backward

Recompense repay

Reconcile bring together by settling differences

Recoup make up for (e.g., something lost)

Rectify correct

Recur happen again

Redeem buy back; make good a promise; regain honor or reputation

Refrain keep from

Refute prove false

Reimburse pay back

Reiterate repeat

Reject refuse to take or accept

Rejunevate give new energy or strength, as if made young again

Relinquish give up

Reminisce recall past happenings, usually fondly

Remit send (e.g., money)

Remunerate pay for work done

Renounce give up (e.g., a claim)

Renovate restore (e.g., a house)

Repent feel regret for (e.g., a sin)

Replenish make full again

Repose rest

Repress hold back or keep hidden (e.g., a feeling)

Reproach blame

Repudiate reject the validity of

Repulse drive back

Rescind cancel or officially take back (e.g., a rule or regulation)

Respire breathe

Restrain hold back

Retain keep

Retaliate return in kind (e.g., a blow for a blow)

Retard delay

Retort answer sharply

Retract take back (e.g., something said)

Retrieve get back

Revere have deep respect for or worship

Revert go back to a former condition

Revoke withdraw or cancel a law or rule

Rupture break

S

Salvage save something out of a disaster such as fire

Scald burn painfully with steam or hot liquid

Scan look at closely; also sometimes used to mean to look at briefly

Scoff mock

Scorn treat with contempt

Scour clean thoroughly; move about widely in a search

Scowl make an angry look

Scrutinize examine closely

Seclude keep away from other people

Seep ooze

Seethe boil

Sever divide

Shear cut with a sharp instrument such as scissors

Shed throw off (e.g., clothing)

Shirk seek to avoid (e.g., duty or work)

Shrivel contract and wrinkle

Shun avoid

Shunt turn aside

Sift sort out through careful examination, (e.g., evidence)

Signify mean, symbolize

Singe burn slightly or around the edges

Skim read over quickly

Smite hit hard

Smolder give off smoke after the fire is out (also "smoulder")

Snarl tangle

Soar fly high in the air

Sojourn live temporarily in a place

Solicit ask for (e.g., help)

Spurn reject scornfully

Squander waste

Startle surprise

Stifle suppress (e.g., feelings)

Strew scatter

Strive try hard

Stun daze

Subside lessen in activity

Subsist continue to live with difficulty

Succumb yield to

Suffice be enough

Suppress put down (e.g., a revolt)

Surge increase suddenly

Surmount overcome (e.g., an obstacle)

Sustain support

Swarm move in great numbers

Sway move back and forth

T

Tamper meddle with

Tarnish discolor

Taunt reproach mockingly

Thaw melt

Thrash defeat thoroughly; also, to physically beat severely

Thrive prosper

Throb beat or pulse insistently

Throttle choke

Thrust push forcefully and suddenly

Thwart prevent someone from achieving something

Tinge color slightly

Torment afflict with pain

Transcend go beyond a limit

Transform change the appearance of

Transmit send from one person or facility to another, usually used in the electronic sense

Transpire come about; occur

Traverse cross over

Trudge walk heavily or with difficulty

U

Undergo experience

Undo return to the condition before something was done

Usurp seize power illegally

Utilize use, make use of

Utter speak

V

Vacate leave, make empty

Vacillate to be indecisive; to waver between alternatives

Vanquish conquer

Vary change

Veer turn or swerve sharply

Vend sell

Venerate treat something as holy

Verge be on the point of; almost starting

Verify prove the truth of

Vex annoy

Vibrate move back and forth very rapidly

Vilify to cast as a villain

Violate break (e.g., a law)

Vouch guarantee

W

Waive give up (e.g., a right or privilege)

Wane decrease in strength

Warp twist out of shape

Waver sway back and forth; also, to be indecisive

Whet sharpen or accentuate

Wield put to use (e.g., power or a tool such as a club)

Wilt become limp

Wither dry up or lose vitality (e.g., a flower)

Withstand hold out against (e.g., pressure)

Wrest pull violently

Wring force out by squeezing

Writhe twist and turn about

Y

Yearn long for

Yield give up

USEFUL ADJECTIVES

A

Abstract theoretical, lacking substance; also, a brief summary of a scholarly article or paper

Acrid sharp to the taste or smell (e.g., an odor)

Acute sharp, shrewd; also, an angle of less than 90 degrees

Adamant unyielding

Adept skilled

Adroit skillful

Aesthetic having to do with beauty

Agile nimble

Ambidextrous equally skilled at using both hands

Ambiguous unclear in meaning, confusing

Ambivalent undecided

Amenable disposed to follow (e.g., advice)

Amiable friendly

Animated alive, lively; can also refer to TV/movie cartoons

Apprehensive worried, anxious

Apt suitable

Aquatic living in water; an event or activity performed in or on the water

Ardent passionate

Arrogant overly proud

Articulate able to express oneself clearly

Ascetic austere, self-denying

Astute shrewd

Auspicious favorable (e.g., circumstances)

Austere harsh

Authentic genuine

Authoritarian ruling by force or higher position

Auxiliary helping

B

Banal unoriginal, boring

Barren unfruitful

Belligerent quarrelsome, combative

Benevolent kind, generous

Benign gentle, not harmful

Bizarre strange, extremely unusual

Bland without or almost without taste or defining characteristics

Blatant obvious or flagrant (e.g., a ____ violation of the law)

Blithe carefree, cheerful

Boisterous rambunctious

Brusque rudely brief or short-spoken

C

Callous unfeeling

Candid honest, frank

Casual offhand, not formal

Caustic like acid, corrosive; also, a sharp or hurtful remark

Chic stylish

Chronic continuing over a long period of time

Civic municipal, having to do with the community

Civil courteous, polite

Cogent convincing (e.g., her ____ argument was persuasive)

Coherent clearly holding together

Colloquial conversational, informal

Colossal huge

Compatible capable of getting along together

Complacent satisfied with oneself

Compliant yielding, submissive

Conciliatory peacemaking

Concise brief but complete

Congenial agreeably pleasant

Conspicuous obvious, very noticeable

Contrite genuinely apologetic or remorseful

Copious plentiful

Crafty sly

Credible believable

Credulous given to believing anything too easily

Cryptic mysterious, hard to understand

Cumbersome bulky

Cursory done quickly but only on the surface (e.g., an examination)

Curt rudely brief

D

Deft skillful

Defunct dead; broken, no longer working

Demure overly modest

Derogatory belittling

Desolate lonely

Despondent depressed

Destitute poverty-stricken

Detergent cleansing

Devious indirect

Devoid completely free of (e.g., feeling)

Devout very religious

Didactic instructive

Diffident shy

Diligent hardworking

Diminutive tiny

Dire dreadful

Discreet careful

Discrete distinctly separate; able to be identified or defined

Disinterested impartial

Dismal gloomy

Disparate different, varied

Dispassionate neutral, without emotion

Distraught driven to distraction; unable to think clearly due to being upset

Diverse varied

Docile easily led

Dogmatic stubbornly positive (e.g., opinion)

Domestic having to do with the home or one's home area (city, state, country)

Dominant ruling or stronger

Dormant sleeping; inactive

Drastic extreme (e.g., changes)

Dreary gloomy

Dubious doubtful, uncertain

Durable lasting

Dynamic energetic

E

Earnest intensely serious; sincere

Ebony dark black

Eccentric peculiar or unpredictable (e.g., behavior)

Edible fit to be eaten

Eerie weird or spooky

Elaborate intricate, a result of great effort and attention to detail

Elegant tastefully fine

Eloquent powerfully fluent in writing or speech

Elusive hard to capture or pin down

Eminent distinguished (e.g., author)

Epic heroic in size or actions

Erratic not regular

Esoteric hard to understand, cryptic

Eternal everlasting

Ethnic having to do with race

Exemplary setting a superior example

Exhaustive very thorough and complete

Exorbitant unreasonably high (e.g., price)

Exotic foreign

Expedient suitable in a given situation but not necessarily correct

Explicit clearly indicated

Exquisite extremely beautiful

Extemporaneous spoken or accomplished with little preparation

Extensive broad

Extinct no longer existing, especially a species that no longer exists

Extraneous having nothing to do with the subject at hand

F

Fallacious false

Fanatic extremely and emotionally enthusiastic

Fastidious meticulous, very neat

Feasible possible to carry out (e.g., a plan)

Feeble weak

Fertile productive

Fervent warmly felt

Festive in the spirit of a holiday (e.g., celebration)

Fickle changeable

Flagrant noticeably bad (e.g., violation)

Fleet swift

Flimsy not strong (e.g., a shaky, hastily-built platform)

Fluent smooth (e.g., speech)

Forlorn hopeless

Formidable fear-inspiring because of size or strength (e.g., enemy)

Fortuitous luckily coincidental

Fragile easily broken

Frail delicate

Frank outspoken

Fraternal brotherly

Frigid extremely cold

Frivolous not serious, inconsequential

Frugal thrifty

Furtive secretive, trying to remain hidden

Futile useless

G

Gala festive

Gallant courteously brave (e.g., conduct)

Gaudy tastelessly showy

Gaunt overly thin and weary-looking

Genial kindly

Germane pertinent

Ghastly frightful (e.g., appearance)

Gigantic huge

Glib fluent but insincere

Glum gloomy

Gory bloody

Graphic vividly realistic

Gratis free

Grievous causing sorrow

Grim sternly forbidding

Gross glaringly bad (e.g., injustice); unrefined

Grotesque distorted in appearance

Gruesome horrifying

Gullible easily fooled

Guttural throaty (e.g., sound)

H

Hackneyed overused, trite

Haggard worn-looking

Hale healthy

Haphazard random; disorganized

Hardy having endurance

Harsh disagreeably rough

Haughty overly proud

Hearty friendly (e.g., welcome)

Hectic feverish

Hedonistic pleasure-seeking, overly indulgent

Heinous outrageous (e.g., crime)

Hideous extremely ugly

Hilarious very funny

Homogeneous of like kind (e.g., group)

Horrendous horrible

Hostile unfriendly, antagonistic

Humane merciful, considerate of others

Humble modest, not arrogant

Humid damp

Hypothetical unproven

I

Illicit illegal

Immaculate spotlessly clean

Immense very large

Imminent about to happen (e.g., storm)

Immutable unchangeable

Impartial unbiased, fair

Imperative necessary

Impertinent rude

Impetuous acting on impulse

Implicit implied

Impromptu without any preparation (e.g., remarks)

Impudent rudely bold

Inadvertent accidental

Inane silly

Incendiary causing fire (e.g., bomb); something that starts a conflict

Incessant continuous, uninterrupted

Inclement rough (e.g., weather)

Incognito with real identity hidden

Incoherent not clearly connected or understandable

Incongruous out of place, inappropriate

Indelible unable to be erased

Indifferent showing no interest

Indigent poor

Indignant very angry

Indispensable absolutely necessary

Indulgent lenient, giving in to momentary desires or whims

Industrious hard-working

Inept clumsy, ineffective

Inevitable unavoidable, bound to happen

Infallible unable to make a mistake

Infamous notorious, having a bad reputation

Infinite endless

Infinitesimal very, very small

Inflexible unbending

Ingenious clever

Ingenuous naturally simple

Inherent existing in someone or something

Innate inborn or integral

Innocuous harmless

Insipid uninteresting (e.g., conversation)

Insolent boldly rude

Integral essential to the whole

Intensive concentrated

Intermittent starting and stopping (e.g., rain)

Intolerant unwilling or unable to respect others or their beliefs

Intricate complicated

Invincible unable to be conquered

Irate angry

Ironic marked by an unexpected difference between what might be expected and what acutally happens; using words to convey the opposite of their literal meaning

Irrational unreasonable

J

Jovial good-humored

Jubilant joyous

Judicious showing good judgment

L

Laborious demanding a lot of work

Lank tall and thin

Latent hidden (e.g., talent)

Laudable worthy of praise

Lavish extremely fancy or generous (e.g., praise)

Lax loose, not enforcing standards (e.g., discipline)

Legible easily read (e.g., print)

Legitimate lawful (e.g., claim)

Lethal fatal

Listless lacking in spirit

Literal following the exact words or intended meaning of the original (e.g., translation)

Literate being able to read and write (e.g., a ____ person)

Livid discolored by a bruise (e.g., flesh); so angry one's face is flushed

Loath reluctant

Lofty very high

Loquacious talkative

Lucid clear

Lucrative profitable (e.g., business)

Ludicrous ridiculous

Lurid shockingly sensational (e.g., story)

Lusty vigorous

M

Majestic grand (e.g., building)

Malicious spiteful

Malignant harmful

Mammoth gigantic

Mandatory required

Manifest evident

Manual done with the hands (e.g., labor)

Marine of or pertaining to the sea (e.g., life)

Marred damaged or scarred

Martial warlike

Massive bulky and heavy

Meager scanty

Menial lowly (e.g., task)

Mercenary working only for financial gain

Meticulous extremely careful

Militant aggressive

Mobile movable (e.g., home)

Moot unresolved; made irrelevant by events; of only academic importance (e.g., a ____ point)

Morbid unhealthily gloomy

Mutual reciprocal (e.g., admiration)

N

Naive innocently simple

Nauseous disgusting

Nautical having to do with ships and sailing

Negligent neglectful

Neurotic describing the behavior of one suffering from an emotional disorder

Nimble moving quickly and easily

Nocturnal of the night (e.g., animal)

Nominal small in comparison with service or value received (e.g., fee)

Nonchalant casual and unexcited

Notable important (e.g., person)

Notorious well-known in an unfavorable way (e.g., criminal)

Novel new or original

Null zero; having no effect

O

Obese overly fat

Objective fair, impartial; free from prejudice (e.g., ____ analysis)

Oblique literally, at an angle; figuratively, indirectly indicated (e.g., an ____ suggestion)

Obnoxious extremely unpleasant (e.g., behavior)

Obsolete out-of-date, no longer useful

Obscure unclear, clouded, partially hidden

Obstinate stubborn

Ominous threatening (e.g., clouds)

Onerous burdensome (e.g., task)

Opportune timely

Opulent wealthy

Ornate elaborately decorated

Orthodox usually approved; conventional (e.g., religious beliefs)

Ostensible apparent

Outright complete; also, direct and to the point

Overt open, obvious

P

Paltry insignificant (e.g., sum of money)

Paramount of highest importance

Passive not active (e.g., participation)

Patent obvious

Pathetic pitiful, weak

Pedestrian unimaginative, common (e.g., ideas)

Peevish irritable

Penitent repentant

Pensive thoughtful

Perennial lasting for a long time; recurring

Peripheral literally, "along the edge"; unimportant, of little consequence

Perilous dangerous

Pertinent relevant

Pervasive present throughout, permeating

Petty relatively unimportant

Picayune petty

Pious devoutly religious

Pivotal crucial, result-changing

Placid calm (e.g., waters)

Plausible apparently true; believable (e.g., argument)

Pliable flexible

Poignant keenly painful to the emotions; intensely significant

Pompous self-important (e.g., person)

Portable capable of being carried (e.g., radio)

Posthumous taking place after a person's death (e.g., a ____ award)

Potent powerful (e.g., drug)

Potential possible (e.g., greatness)

Practicable capable of being done

Pragmatic practical

Precarious risky

Precise exact

Precocious advanced to a level earlier than normally expected (e.g., child)

Predominant prevailing

Preposterous ridiculous

Pretentious pompous and self-important

Prevalent widespread

Primary fundamental (e.g., reason)

Prime first in importance or quality

Primitive crude (e.g., tools)

Prior previous (e.g., appointment)

Prodigal extravagant, wasteful, rebellious

Prodigious extraordinary in size or amount (e.g., effort)

Proficient skilled

Profuse abundantly given (e.g., praise)

Prolific producing large amounts (e.g., author)

Prone disposed to (e.g., accidents)

Prosaic ordinary

Prostrate laid low (e.g., by grief)

Provincial narrow (e.g., view of a matter)

Provocative exciting, attracting attention; also, sparking controversy or conflict

Prudent cautious; showing good judgment; discreet (e.g., advice)

Pugnacious quarrelsome (e.g., person)

Pungent sharp to the taste or smell (e.g., odor)

Punitive inflicting punishment (e.g., action)

Puny small in size or strength (e.g., effort)

Putrid rotten

Q

Quaint pleasantly odd or old-fashioned (e.g., custom)

R

Radiant brightly shining

Rampant spreading unchecked (e.g., violence)

Rancid having the taste or smell of food that has gone bad (e.g., butter)

Random decided by chance (e.g., choice)

Rank complete (e.g., incompetency); also, having a strong, bad odor

Rash reckless

Raucous harsh (e.g., sound)

Ravenous extremely hungry

Recalcitrant stubbornly defiant of authority

Redundant repetitive, unnecessary

Reflex involuntary response (e.g., action)

Regal royal

Relentless persistent (e.g., chase)

Relevant pertinent

Remiss careless (e.g., in one's duty)

Remote far distant (e.g., time or place)

Replete filled (e.g., with thrills)

Reprehensible disgraceful, worthy of blame or reproach

Repugnant extremely distasteful

Repulsive disgusting

Reputable respectable, having a good reputation

Resigned submitting passively to (e.g., to one's fate)

Resolute firmly determined

Resonant resounding (e.g., sound)

Restive restless (e.g., pupils)

Reticent speaking little

Rigorous strict, harsh, unyielding

Rigid stiff

Robust strong and healthy

Rowdy rough and disorderly (e.g., mob)

Rugged strong enough to endure hard conditions

Rustic rural; also, simple but worn or aged from long use

Ruthless pitiless (e.g., dictator)

S

Sage wise (e.g., advice)

Salient prominent (e.g., points)

Salutary healthful (e.g., climate)

Sane mentally sound

Sanguinary bloody

Sanguine cheerfully hopeful

Scanty meager

Scholastic having to do with schooling and education (e.g., record)

Scrawny unhealthily thin

Scrupulous careful and honest (e.g., accounting)

Secretive prone to secrecy; purposely not made public

Secular not religious (e.g., education)

Sedate dignified

Serene calm

Servile submissive, subservient

Sheer very thin (e.g., stockings); utter (e.g., nonsense)

Shiftless lazy

Shifty tricky

Shoddy inferior in quality (e.g., material)

Shrewd clever in one's dealings (e.g., businessman)

Simultaneous happening at the same time (e.g., events)

Singular remarkable; strange (e.g., behavior)

Sinister threatening evil

Skeptical showing doubt (e.g., attitude)

Slack not busy (e.g., business season); also, loose or not taut (e.g., rope)

Sleek smooth and glossy (e.g., appearance)

Slender small in size or amount (e.g., contribution)

Slovenly untidy

Sluggish slow-moving

Smug self-satisfied

Snug comfortable

Sober serious

Solemn grave; serious (e.g., occasion)

Solitary lone; just one

Somber dark and gloomy (e.g., outlook)

Sophisticated wise in the ways of the world

Sordid wretched (e.g., condition)

Sparse thinly scattered

Spirited lively

Spiritual of the spirit or soul

Spontaneous happening as a result of natural impulse (e.g., reaction)

Sporadic happening at irregular times (e.g., shooting)

Spry nimble

Staccato with breaks between successive sharp sounds

Stagnant not moving or circulating (e.g., water)

Stalwart robust, strong

Stark bleak (e.g., outlook) or in sharp relief

Stately dignified

Static stationary; unmoving

Stationary not moving

Staunch firm (e.g., friend)

Steadfast firm; well-founded

Stern severe (e.g., look)

Stocky short and heavily built

Stodgy uninteresting

Stoic, Stoical unmoved emotionally

Stout fat; firm (e.g., resistance)

Straightforward honest (e.g., answer)

Strenuous demanding great energy (e.g., exercise)

Stupendous amazing (e.g., effort)

Sturdy strongly built

Suave smoothly polite

Sublime inspiring admiration because of noble quality (e.g., music)

Subsidiary of less importance (e.g., rank)

Substantial of considerable numbers or size

Subtle suggested delicately (e.g., hint)

Sullen resentful

Sultry extremely hot and humid (e.g., weather)

Sumptuous costly, lavish (e.g., meal)

Sundry various

Superb of a high degree of excellence

Supercilious insultingly patronizing

Superficial not going beyond the obvious; only on the suface (e.g., a _____ examination)

Superfluous extra; beyond what is needed

Superlative superior to all others (e.g., performance)

Supple limber, flexible

Surly offensively rude

Susceptible easily affected by (e.g., to colds)

Swarthy dark-skinned

T

Tacit not openly said but implied (e.g., approval)

Taciturn untalkative by nature or temperament

Tangible capable of being touched; actual (e.g., results)

Tardy late (e.g., student)

Tart having a sharp or slightly sour taste

Taut tightly stretched (e.g., rope)

Tedious long and tiresome (e.g., study)

Temperate moderate (e.g., climate)

Tenacious holding fast, doggedly determined

Tentative uncertain or for a temporary period of trial (e.g., an agreement)

Tepid lukewarm (e.g., water)

Terminal concluding

Terse brief but expressing a good deal (e.g., comment)

Thankless unappreciated

Tidy neat (e.g., appearance)

Timeless eternal (e.g., beauty)

Timely happening at a desirable or appropriate time (e.g., arrival)

Timid shy

Tiresome making one weary; boring

Titanic of enormous size or strength

Torrid intensely hot; also, intensely passionate

Tranquil calm (e.g., waters)

Transient passing away after a brief time; temporary

Trifling insignificant; of little importance

Trite ordinary (e.g., remark)

Trivial insignificant

Turbulent agitated

U

Ultimate final (e.g., conclusion)

Unanimous all involved sharing complete agreement (e.g., decision)

Unassuming modest

Uncanny unnatural (e.g., accuracy)

Unconditional absolute (e.g., surrender)

Uncouth crude and clumsy

Undaunted not discouraged

Underhanded sly

Unduly overly (e.g., concerned)

Uneasy disturbed

Ungainly awkward

Uniform consistent throughout

Unique only one of its kind (e.g., specimen)

Unkempt messy; not well taken care of

Unprecedented never seen before

Unruly disorderly, unkempt

Unscathed uninjured, unmarked

Unwieldy clumsy to use, usually because of size or shape (e.g., implement)

Upright honest (e.g., citizen)

Utmost most extreme (e.g., in distance, height, or size)

Utter complete (e.g., failure)

V

Vain futile (e.g., attempt); conceited (e.g., person)

Valiant brave

Valid (legally) sound (e.g., argument)

Vast very large in extent or size (e.g., distances)

Vehement violent in feeling (e.g., protest)

Verbatim word for word, an exact quote (e.g., report)

Verbose overly talkative

Versatile able to perform many tasks well (e.g., athlete)

Vigilant watchful (e.g., sentry)

Vile highly disgusting (e.g., conduct)

Virulent malicious, full of hate

Visible able to be seen (e.g., object)

Vital essential (e.g., contribution)

Vivacious lively

Vivid bright (e.g., color)

Void not binding legally (e.g., contract); empty

Volatile explosive, highly unstable

Voluminous very great in size (e.g., writings)

Voracious greedy for food (e.g., appetite)

Vulnerable open to attack (e.g., position)

W

Wary cautious

Weary tired

Wee very small

Weighty important (e.g., decision)

Wholesome causing a feeling of well-being; not crude or dirty

Willful deliberate; also, obstinate or head-strong

Wily cunning, sly

Wishful showing desire that something be so (e.g., thinking)

Witty amusingly clever (e.g., remark)

Wordy using too many words (e.g., reply)

Worldly enjoying pleasures of this world (versus the afterlife)

Worthy deserving, of good intentions (e.g., choice)

Wretched miserable

Z

Zealous enthusiastically devoted to an idea or cause

The paragraph comprehension part of the ASVAB tests your ability to understand what you read. It does this by asking multiple-choice questions based on passages that vary in length from one to five paragraphs of about 30 to 120 words. Each passage is used for one to five questions.

Reading comprehension involves several abilities:

- ☑ the ability to recognize main ideas;

- ☑ the ability to recall details;

- ☑ the ability to make conclusions (inferences) about the material in a passage;

- ☑ the ability to apply the information in the passage to other material;

- ☑ the ability to recognize and understand sequential, cause-and-effect, and comparative relationships;

- ☑ the ability to paraphrase or summarize a passage.

FINDING THE MAIN IDEA

The main idea is the most important point the author wants the reader to understand. Sometimes the main idea is stated directly by the author, and sometimes it is implied rather than stated.

Whenever you are asked to determine a passage's main idea, look first at the opening and closing sentences of each paragraph. Writers often provide readers with a *topic sentence* that expresses a paragraph's main idea succinctly. Although a topic sentence may appear anywhere in the paragraph, it is very often the first or last sentence.

EXAMPLE

The world faces a serious problem of overpopulation. Right now many people starve from lack of adequate food. Efforts are being made to increase the rate of food production, but the number of people to be fed increases at an even faster rate.

In this paragraph, the main idea is stated directly in the opening sentence. You know that the passage will be about "a serious problem of overpopulation." Like a heading or caption, the topic sentence sets the stage, getting your mind ready for what follows in the paragraph.

EXAMPLE

During the later years of the American Revolution, a government under the Articles of Confederation was formed. This government suffered severely from a lack of power. Each state distrusted the others and gave little authority to the central, or federal, government. The Articles of Confederation produced a government that could not raise money from taxes, prevent Indian raids, or force the British out of the United States.

What is the topic sentence in the preceding paragraph? Certainly, the paragraph is about the Articles of Confederation. However, is the key idea in the first sentence or in the second sentence? In this instance, the *second* sentence does a better job of giving you the key to this paragraph—the lack of centralized power that characterized the Articles of Confederation.

The sentences that complete the paragraph relate more to the idea of "lack of power" than to the time when the government was formed.

Don't assume that the topic sentence is always the first sentence of a paragraph.

EXAMPLE

They had fewer men available as soldiers. Less than one third of the railroads and only a small portion of the nation's industrial production was theirs. For most of the war their coastline was blockaded by Northern ships. It is a tribute to Southern leadership and the courage of the people that they were not defeated for four years.

In this case you will note that the passage builds up to its main point. The topic sentence is the last one.

As we mentioned previously, you may also find that the main idea is not expressed directly at all, but can only be inferred from the selection as a whole.

EXAMPLE

The plane landed at 4 P.M. As the door opened, the crowd burst into a long, noisy outpouring of welcome. The waiting mob surged against the police guard lines. Women were screaming. Teenagers were yelling for autographs or souvenirs. The visitor smiled and waved at his fans.

The main idea of the paragraph is not expressed, but it is clear that some popular hero or famous personality is being welcomed enthusiastically at the airport.

To help find the main idea in a reading passage on the test, ask yourself these questions:

1. Who or what is this paragraph about?
2. What aspect of this subject is the author talking about?
3. What is the author trying to get across about this aspect of the subject?

In addition, look for signal words in the passage—words like *again, also, as well as, furthermore, moreover,* and *significantly.* These signal words may point you toward the main idea.

FINDING DETAILS

In developing the main idea of a passage, a writer will make statements to support his or her point. The writer may give examples to illustrate the idea, or facts and statistics to support it. They may give reasons why the statement is true, or arguments for or against a position stated as the main idea. The writer may also define a complex term, or give a number of qualities of a complicated concept (such as democracy). They may also classify a number of objects within a larger category, or use descriptive details to develop an idea and help the reader envision the situation. Finally, the writer may *compare* two ideas or objects (show how they are similar) or *contrast* them (show how they are different).

Note how the author of the following paragraph uses supporting details.

Episodic memories relate to our individual lives, recalling what we have done and the kinds of experiences we have had. When you recall your first date, the time you fell off your bicycle, or what you felt like when you graduated from high school, you are recalling episodic memories. The information in episodic memory is connected with specific times and places.

To help you understand the term "episodic memory," the author gives three examples in the second sentence. These examples are supporting details.

To answer questions about supporting details, you *must* find a word or group of words in the passage that supports your choice of answer. The following techniques should help:

1. Look for key words (nouns and verbs) in the question stem and the answer choices.
2. Run your eye down the passage, looking for those key words or their synonyms.
3. Reread the part of the paragraph or passage that contains the key word or its synonym.

MAKING INFERENCES

You make inferences by putting together ideas that are specifically stated by the author in order to help you understand other ideas that the author does *not* state. In other words, you draw conclusions from the information the author presents. You do this by locating relevant details and determining their relationships—time sequence, place sequence, cause and effect, and so on.

In inference questions you must put two and two together and see what you get; the passage never tells you directly what the answer is. Inference questions require you to use your own judgment.

Don't take anything directly stated by the author as an inference. Instead, look for clues in the passage that you can use in coming up with your own conclusion. You should choose as your answer a statement that is a logical development of the information the author has provided. Remember that in answering inference questions you must go beyond the obvious—beyond what the author explicitly states—to look for logical implications of what the author says.

Let's try to apply these skills to representative passages you will encounter in the paragraph comprehension part of the test.

> Family camping has been described as the "biggest single growth industry in the booming travel and leisure market." Camping ranges from backpacking to living in motor homes with complete creature comforts. It is both an end in itself and a magic carpet to a wide variety of other forms of outdoor recreation.
>
> It can be inferred from the passage that the LEAST luxurious form of camping is
>
> (A) backpacking.
> (B) travel trailers.
> (C) camping trailers.
> (D) motor homes.

The answer is A. This question requires you to make an inference from the information in the passage. The second sentence in the paragraph refers to the range of camping—from backpacking to the "creature comforts" of rolling homes. From this it can be *inferred* that backpacking is the least luxurious form of camping.

UNDERSTANDING THE ORGANIZATION OF THE MATERIAL

Questions on a reading passage may also test your understanding of the organization of the ideas presented and their relationship to one another. Authors generally organize material in predictable and logical ways to make it easier for the reader to understand. Recognizing common patterns of organization increases understanding, recall, and speed.

Ideas may be organized in a sequential or spatial pattern, or they may be expressed in a cause-and-effect relationship. Ideas may also be compared (looking for similarities) or contrasted (looking for differences) with one another, perhaps in an argumentative or opposing position. A reading passage may also present a solution to a problem or problems mentioned, or a conclusion may be drawn from ideas stated or implied.

Sequential Organization

A sequence is a series of steps or events in which order is important. If the sequence is chronological (time-based), the events are described or mentioned in the order in which they occurred. Clues to sequential organization of ideas include cardinal numbers (*1, 2, 3,* etc.), ordinal numbers (*first, second, third,* etc.), transition words (*next, later, then, finally*), and dates or other words referring to time (*next year, the following winter, in 2002, ten weeks later,* etc.).

> **EXAMPLE**
>
> If you are stung by a bee, first remove the stinger. Next, apply a paste of baking soda and water. Then, apply ice or cold water to help reduce the pain. If the pain is severe or you are allergic to the insect, seek medical help immediately.

Spatial Organization

When the organization is spatial, it means that the passage deals with the physical arrangement of a place or object. Clue words include *above, below, next to, in front of, in back of, to the right of, to the left of.*

> **EXAMPLE**
>
> Taste buds are distributed across the tongue, but the distribution is uneven, and certain areas of the tongue are more sensitive to certain fundamental tastes than other areas. The tip of the tongue is most sensitive to sweetness, but the portion just behind the tip is most sensitive to salty tastes. Only the sides of the tongue are very sensitive to sour tastes, and the rear specializes in bitter tastes.

Cause and Effect

A reading passage may include reasons why something happened and the results that occurred. For example, a history passage may present the events leading up to a war or a science passage may list causes of the greenhouse effect and its effect, in turn, on global climate. Often, the relationship is presented as a *chain of events,* with one or more events leading to or resulting in another. Clue words include *for this reason, resulted in, because, consequently, since, thus.*

Understand How the Material Is Organized:

- By sequence
- By arrangement or placement
- By cause and effect
- By opposing or similar ideas
- By presenting a problem and its solution
- By leading you to a conclusion

> **EXAMPLE**
>
> By the year 2020, there will be approximately one retired American for every two working Americans. In these large numbers, older Americans will become an increasingly powerful political force, and political issues of concern to the elderly—such as special housing, medical benefits, and reduced levels of employment—will become issues taken more seriously by elected officials.

Opposing or Similar Ideas

A reading passage may present the similarities or differences between ideas, people, places, or other things. The presentation may focus on similarities in a *comparison*; clue words may include *like, similarly, likewise, in like manner, also*. Or, the presentation may focus on differences, in presenting a *contrast*; clue words include *however, unlike, in contrast, on the other hand, versus, nevertheless*.

> **EXAMPLE**
>
> One problem in the American farm situation often centers on supply exceeding demand and farm policies that foster surplus production. This is not true in most other parts of the world, where countries cannot produce enough food to support their own population and must import food or face famine.

Solution to a Problem

In this organization pattern, the author presents a problem or describes a situation that is causing difficulty and presents or suggests solutions or remedies. Clue words include *problem, cause, effects, answers, remedies*.

> **EXAMPLE**
>
> In one study, students who lived in dormitories near an area in which earthquakes occurred frequently simply denied the seriousness of the situation and the possible danger they were in.

(In this case, the solution—an unrealistic one—was simply to ignore the problem.)

DRAWING A CONCLUSION

A conclusion is a logical inference based on information presented or implied. If you read a passage critically, you follow the author's train of thought and arrive at logical conclusions. An author may expect a reader to draw the conclusion, or he or she may state it, often using clue words such as *thus, therefore, in conclusion,* or *hence*.

> **EXAMPLE**
>
> A major goal for the disabled is easier access to the mainstream of society. The 1973 Rehabilitation Act has moved them toward this goal. So has the Education for All Handicapped Children Act of 1975, which mandates that all children, however severe their disability, receive a free, appropriate education. Before the legislation, one million handicapped children were receiving no education and another three million were receiving an inappropriate one (as in the case of a blind child who is not taught Braille or is not provided with instructional materials in Braille). In 1987, Congress enacted the Employment Opportunities for Disabled Americans Act, which allows disabled individuals to earn a moderate income without losing their Medicaid health coverage.

This sample passage is about disabled Americans. The reader can conclude that legislation has made progress in moving the disabled into society's mainstream, although the author does not say so directly. Incidentally, you should note the sequence pattern in this passage.

Electronics Information Review

7

ATOMIC STRUCTURE AND ELECTRICITY

Electrical and electromagnetic interactions involve particles with a property called *electric* or *electrical charge*—a characteristic as basic as mass. Just as objects with mass are moved or accelerated by gravitational forces, electrically charged objects are accelerated by electrical forces. Even the forces that hold atoms together to form "solid" matter are fundamentally composed of electrical interactions between the charged particles within those atoms.

Electricity is defined as the flow of electrons along a conductor. A *conductor* is an object that allows electrons to pass easily. That means electrons must be organized and pushed toward a goal. This is done in a number of ways, but we must first know what electrons are before we can start working with them.

Elements are the most basic materials in the universe. There are more than 120 elements, including some that have only been made (as far as we know) in the laboratory. Elements such as iron, copper, gold, lead, and silver have been found in nature. Every known substance— solid, liquid, or gas—is composed of one or more elements.

An *atom* is the smallest particle of an element that retains all the properties of that element. Each element has its own kind of atom—for instance, hydrogen atoms are alike, and they are different from the atoms of all other elements. However, all atoms have certain things in common. They all have an inner part, the *nucleus*, which is composed of very small particles called *protons* and *neutrons*. An atom also has an outer part, consisting of other small particles called *electrons*, which orbit around the nucleus. (See Figure 7.1.)

- **Protons have a positive charge**
- **Electrons have a negative charge**
- **Neutrons have no charge**

Protons have a positive charge, electrons have a negative charge, and neutrons have no charge. Because of their charges, protons and electrons are particles of energy. That is, these charges form an electric field of force within the atom. These charges are always pulling and pushing one another; this action produces energy in the form of movement.

The atoms of each element have a specific number of electrons, and they have the same number of protons (see the Periodic Table on page 129). A hydrogen atom has one electron and one proton (Figure 7.2). The aluminum atom has 13 of each (Figure 7.3). Opposite charges—negative electrons and positive protons—attract each other and tend to hold electrons in orbit. As long as this arrangement is not changed, an atom is electrically balanced.

When electrons leave their orbits, they move from atom to atom at random, drifting in no particular direction. Electrons that move this way are called *free electrons*.

Different kinds of forces can be used to cause electrons to move in a certain direction. Heat is only one type of energy that can cause electrons to be forced from their orbits. A magnetic field can also be used to cause electrons to move in a given direction. Light energy and pressure on a crystal are also used to generate electricity by forcing electrons to flow along a given path. That is how electricity (the flow of electrons along a conductor) is generated. A *conductor* is any material that has many free electrons because of its physical composition.

A positive charge will repel (push away) another positive charge, but it will attract its opposite, the negative charge. Likewise, a negative charge will repel a negative charge but attract a positive charge.

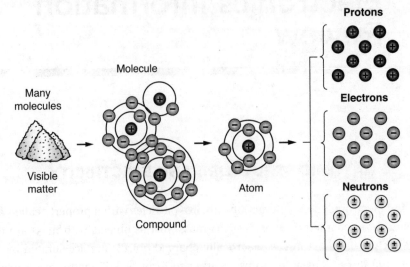

Figure 7.1.

ELECTRICITY

ELECTRIC ENERGY

So far you have read about electrons being very small. The diameter of an electron is about 0.00000000000022 inch or 22 trillionths of an inch. You may wonder how anything so small can be a source of energy. Much of the answer lies in the fact that electrons move at almost the speed of light, which is 186,282 miles per second (299,792 kilometers per second). Due to their size, billions of them can move at one time through a wire. The combination of speed and concentration together produces great energy.

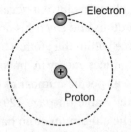

Figure 7.2. The hydrogen atom has one electron and one proton.

When a flow of electrons along a conductor occurs, this is called *current flow*. The movement of electrons is related to electrical current.

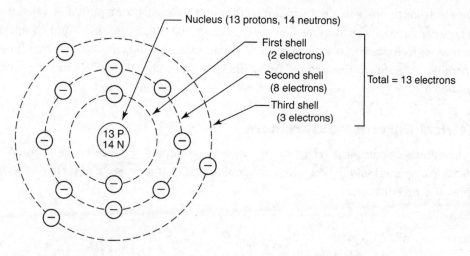

Figure 7.3. The aluminum atom has 13 electrons and 13 protons.

MAGNETISM AND ELECTRICITY

As mentioned before, magnetism and electricity are closely related. Magnetism is used to generate electricity, and electricity produces a magnetic field.

Magnetism is a force that acts between certain objects. The area around a magnet where the force is felt is called a *magnetic field*. Electricity flowing through a wire causes a magnetic field around the wire. A coil of current-carrying wire becomes an *electromagnet* with the magnetic field strongest at the two ends of the coil, the "north" and "south" *poles*. The electromagnet remains magnetic only as long as the electricity flows through it. A magnetic field can also produce electricity. If you pass a wire across a magnetic field, electricity will be generated in the wire. Electric generators are based on this principle. The relationship between electricity and magnetism is also used in transformers, relays, solenoids, and motors.

ELECTRIC CURRENT

In the early years of the study of electricity, electric current was erroneously thought to be a movement of positive charges from positive to negative. This assumption, termed *conventional current flow*, was a concept that became entrenched in the minds of many scientists. Consequently, "conventional current flow" is still found in many textbooks, and the theory's existence should be taken into account.

However, since it has been proven that electrons (negative charges) are what actually move through a wire, the term *electron current* will be used throughout the remainder of this text. Electron current is defined as the directed flow of electrons. The direction of electron movement is from a region of negative potential to a region of less negative potential or more positive potential. Therefore, electric current can be said to flow from a negative potential to a positive potential. The direction is determined by the polarity of the voltage source.

Electric current is classified into two general types. A *direct current* flows continuously in the same direction, whereas an *alternating current* periodically reverses direction.

A *circuit* is a pathway for the movement of electrons. An external force exerted on electrons to make them flow through a conductor is known as *electromotive force*, or *emf*. It is measured in volts. "Electric pressure," "potential difference," and "emf" mean the same thing. The terms *voltage drop* and *potential drop* can be interchanged.

For electrons to move in a particular direction, it is necessary for a potential difference to exist between two points of the emf source. If 6,250,000,000,000,000,000 (6.25 quintillion) electrons pass a given point in one second, there is said to be one *ampere* (A) of current flowing. The same number of electrons stored on an object (a static charge) and not moving is called a *coulomb* (C).

Electrical Current Measurement

The magnitude of current is measured in *amperes* (commonly shortened to *amps*). A current of one ampere is said to flow when one coulomb of charge passes a point in one second. Expressed as an equation:

$$I = \frac{Q}{T}$$

I = current in amperes
Q = charge in coulombs
T = time in seconds

Frequently, the ampere is much too large a unit. Therefore the *milliampere* (mA), one thousandth of an ampere, or the *microampere* (μA), one millionth (0.000001) of an ampere, are used.

Current flow is assumed to be from negative (−) to positive (+) in our explanations here. Electron flow is negative (−) to positive (+), and we assume that current flow and electron flow are one and the same. It makes explanations simpler as we progress into electronics. The *conventional* current flow concept is the opposite, or positive (+) to negative (−).

An *ammeter* is used to measure current flow in a circuit. A *milliammeter* is used to measure smaller amounts, while the *microammeter* is used to measure very small amounts of current.

A *voltmeter* is used to measure voltage. In some instances it is possible to obtain a meter that will measure both voltage and current plus resistance. This is called a *multimeter*, or *volt-ohm-milliammeter* (VM).

PRACTICE QUESTIONS

1. Electricity is defined as

   (A) the acceleration of electrons toward protons.
   (B) the flow of electrons along a conductor.
   (C) the movement of charged metallic atoms to a lower-density area.
   (D) the flow of protons along a conductor.

2. Free electrons

   (A) have left their original orbits and move from atom to atom at random.
   (B) do not exist.
   (C) are captured by atoms with the same kind of charge.
   (D) help balance atoms that are short of protons.

3. The atoms of each element have a specific number of _____ and _____ number of _____.

    (A) neutrons, a higher, protons

    (B) electrons, a lower, protons

    (C) protons, the same, neutrons

    (D) electrons, the same, protons

4. Conventional current flow is

    (A) the theory that positive charges move from positive to negative.

    (B) an outmoded scientific concept.

    (C) still found in many textbooks.

    (D) all of the above.

5. The magnitude of electrical current is measured in

    (A) volts.

    (B) ohms.

    (C) coulombs.

    (D) amperes (amps).

6. What is 1 coulomb per second equal to?

    (A) 1 megawatt

    (B) 1 volt

    (C) 1 joule

    (D) 1 ampere (1 amp)

Answers Explained

1. **(B)** Electricity is defined as *the flow of electrons along a conductor.* Electricity usually flows around a circuit from a negative terminal to a positive terminal.

2. **(A)** Free electrons *have left their original orbits and move from atom to atom at random.* Free electrons are usually influenced by an applied electric or magnetic field.

3. **(D)** The atoms of each element have a specific number of *electrons* and *the same* number of *protons.* The atomic number for an element (listed in the Periodic Table on page 129 at the top of an element's block) is the number of protons in one atom of that element. If the number of protons in an atom changes, the atom becomes a different element. However, when an atom loses or gains electrons, it becomes an *ion*, an atom with an electrical charge.

4. **(D)** Conventional current flow is all *of the above.* The theory states that positive charges move from positive to negative. Conventional current flow is an outmoded scientific concept but is still found in many textbooks.

5. **(D)** The magnitude of electrical current is measured in *amperes* (*amps*). Volts measure voltage; ohms measure electrical resistance in a circuit; and coulombs measure electrical charge.

6. **(D)** 1 coulomb per second is equal to *1 ampere* (*1 amp*). A coulomb is 6.25×10^{18} electrons. Current is the flow of electrons, and an ampere (usually shortened to "amp") is a specific unit of current flow.

CONDUCTORS

A material through which electricity can easily pass is called a *conductor* because it has free electrons. In other words, a conductor offers very little resistance to the flow of electrons.

All metals are conductors of electricity to some extent, but some are much better than others. Silver, copper, and aluminum let electricity pass easily. Silver is a better conductor than copper. However, copper is used more frequently because it is cheaper. Aluminum is used as a conductor where light weight is important.

Why are some materials good conductors? One of the most important reasons is the presence of free electrons. If a material has many electrons that are free to move away from their atoms, that material will be a good conductor of electricity.

Although free electrons usually move in a haphazard way, their movement can be controlled. The electrons can be made to move in the same direction, and this flow is called *electric current*.

Conductors may be in the form of bars, tubes, or sheets. The most familiar conductors are wire. Many sizes of wire are available. Some are only the thickness of a hair. Other wire may be as thick as your arm. To prevent conductors from touching at the wrong place they are usually coated with plastic, rubber, or cloth material, called an *insulator* or insulation.

WIRE GAUGE

Various electrical applications require different conductor sizes. Electrical wire is designed by definite gauge sizes that designate wire of a specific diameter. As the diameter of the wire decreases, the gauge number increases. The following table, which refers to standard annealed solid copper wire, illustrates some various wire sizes, their comparative areas, and resistance per 1,000 ft. These resistance values apply only to copper conductors.

Gauge Number	Diameter (mils)	Cross Section Circular (mils)	Ohms per 1,000 ft 25°C (= 77°F)
0000	460.0	212,000.0	.0500
2	258.0	66,400.0	.159
6	162.0	26,300.0	.403
10	102.0	10,400.0	1.02
14	64.0	4,110.0	2.58
18	40.0	1,620.0	6.51
22	25.3	642.0	16.51
26	15.9	254.0	41.6
30	10.0	101.0	105.0
36	5.0	25.0	423.0
38	4.0	15.7	673.0
40	3.1	9.9	1,070.0

STRANDED WIRE

Copper wire is often stranded because stranded wire is easily bent without breaking. To bend or flex wire constantly, it is necessary to make many smaller strands into a cable or bundle. This allows for flexing of the cable or wire without breaking. The lamp cord in your home is made of many fine strands of copper wire. This allows it to be flexible and bend where you want it on the way from the plug to the lamp.

Larger wires used for wiring commercial or industrial buildings are also stranded. Any number of smaller wires are grouped in a cable to carry the same amount of current as a solid conductor wire. The larger cables have to be stranded or it would be next to impossible to bend them or work with them.

The physical size of flexible wire is greater than the same size, electrically, of solid wire. A solid No. 18 wire is easily bent, but is not as flexible as a multiple-strand cable made up of smaller gage wire to equal the No. 18 wire used in a lamp cord.

INSULATORS

An insulator is a material with very few, if any, free electrons. No known material is a perfect insulator. However, there are materials that are such poor conductors that they are classified as insulators. Glass, dry wood, rubber, mica, and certain plastics are insulating materials.

SEMICONDUCTORS (PART I)

So far, we've looked at both insulators and conductors and their respective properties. In between these two extremes are semiconductors—materials that have conductivity properties about halfway between good conductors and good resistors.

You've probably heard the term *semiconductor* many times and not given it much thought. Semiconductor materials are the foundation of the vast array of electronic devices that surround us, including computers, telephones, radios, televisions, refrigerators, microwave ovens, automobiles, airplanes, traffic lights, light-emitting diodes (LEDs) . . . you get the picture.

The properties of common semiconductor materials such as silicon and germanium are useful in electronic devices like integrated circuits, chips, transistors, diodes, solar cells, and so on. Semiconductor solar photovoltaic panels directly convert light energy into electrical energy. The electronic properties and conductivity of a "pure" or *intrinsic* semiconductor material can be changed in a controlled way to make them limited and predictable conductors by adding very small (0.0000001 percent) quantities of other elements such as boron or phosphorus to the melted semiconductor and then letting them melt to solidify back into a crystal form.

Resistors are the opposite of (good) conductors. Used to give a measured amount of opposition or resistance to the electron flow, their resistance is measured in *ohms* (abbreviated by the Greek letter omega, Ω), which indicates the amount of resistance a piece of this material offers to the flow of electrons. Look at Figure 7.4 to see how these materials are placed between good and poor conductors.

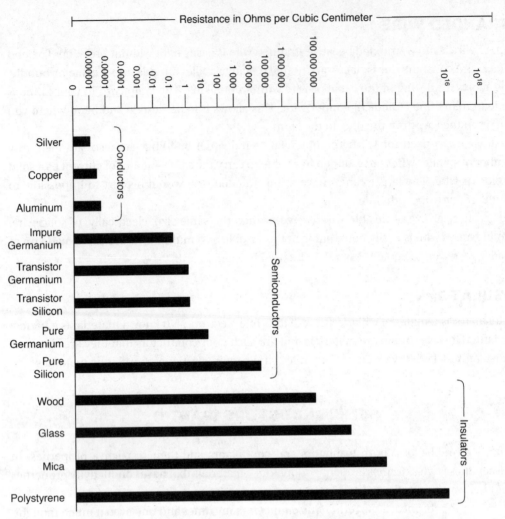

Figure 7.4. Location of insulators, semiconductors, and conductors relative to one another in terms of inherent resistance.

PRACTICE QUESTIONS

1. A conductor of electricity has _____ and _____.

   (A) free electrons, offers little resistance to electron flow
   (B) free protons, offers little resistance to proton flow
   (C) no free electrons, helps move positive charges toward negative charges
   (D) free electrons, helps move positive charges toward negative charges

2. As the diameter of electrical wire _____, the gauge number _____.

   (A) increases, increases
   (B) decreases, decreases
   (C) increases, stays the same
   (D) decreases, increases

3. If a material has _____, it will be a good conductor of electricity.

    (A) few free electrons
    (B) many free electrons
    (C) many free protons
    (D) few free protons

4. Materials such as _____, _____, _____, and _____ are such poor electrical conductors that they are classified as insulators.

    (A) glass, wet wood, rubber, some plastics
    (B) rubber, glass, lead, paper
    (C) rubber, glass, gold, some plastics
    (D) glass, dry wood, rubber, some plastics

5. Resistors are the opposite of

    (A) bad conductors.
    (B) good conductors.
    (C) insulators.
    (D) semiconductors.

Answers Explained

1. **(A)** A conductor of electricity has *free electrons* and *offers little resistance to electron flow*. Copper and silver are good examples of conductors. In fact, many conductors are metals.

2. **(D)** As the diameter of electrical wire *decreases*, the gauge number *increases*. This is similar to many other nonmetric gauging systems but is unlike the metric wire size standard used in most parts of the world. The American Wire Gauge (AWG) system, used since 1857, originally referred to the number of passes through drawing dies that a certain diameter wire required; finer wires required more passes.

3. **(B)** If a material has *many free electrons*, it will be a good conductor of electricity.

4. **(D)** Materials such as *glass, dry wood, rubber*, and *some plastics* are such poor electrical conductors that they are classified as insulators. In these types of materials, the atoms' electrons are tightly bound, as compared to good conductors. In insulators, therefore, the electrons do not move between atoms very easily, virtually stopping the flow of electrons.

5. **(B)** Resistors are the opposite of *good conductors*. Resistors are materials through which electricity can flow but only with some difficulty. The difference among conductors, resistors, and insulators is only a matter of degree—even good conductors have some resistance.

POWER

Power is defined as the *rate* at which work is done. It is expressed in metric measurement terms of watts (W) for power and joules (J) for energy work. A *watt* is the power that gives rise to the production of energy at the rate of one joule per second (W = J/s). A *joule* is the work done when the point of application of force of one newton is displaced a distance of one meter in the direction of the force (J = N • m).

It has long been the practice in this country to measure work in terms of *horsepower* (hp). Electric motors are still rated in horsepower and probably will continue to be for some time.

Power can be electrical or mechanical. When a mechanical force is used to lift a weight, *work* is done. The rate at which the weight is moved is called *power. Horsepower* is defined in terms of moving a certain weight over a certain distance in one minute (e.g., 33,000 lbs. lifted 1 foot in 1 minute equals 1 hp). Energy is consumed in moving a weight or when work is done. The findings in this field have been equated with the same amount of work done by electric energy. It takes 746 W of electric power to equal 1 hp.

The horsepower rating of electric motors is calculated by taking the voltage and multiplying it by the current drawn under full load. This power is measured in watts. In other words, one volt times one ampere equals one watt. When put into a formula it reads:

$$\text{Power} = \text{volts} \times \text{amperes or } P = E \times I$$

where E = voltage, or emf

$\quad I$ = current, or intensity of electron flow

KILOWATTS

The kilowatt is used to express the amount of electric energy used or available. The term *kilo* (k) means "one thousand," so a kilowatt (kW) is one thousand watts.

Milliwatt is a term you will encounter when working with electronics. The milliwatt (mW) means one-thousandth (0.001) of a watt. The milliwatt is used in terms of some very small amplifiers and other electronic devices. Transistor circuits are designed in milliwatts, but power line electric power is measured in kilowatts.

Keep in mind that *kilo* means 1,000 and *milli* means 0.001 (one-thousandth).

RESISTANCE

Any time there is movement, there is some amount of resistance. As mentioned previously, this resistance is useful in electric and electronic circuits. Resistance makes it possible to generate heat, control electron flow, and supply the correct voltage to a device.

Resistance in a conductor depends on four factors: material, length, cross-sectional area, and temperature.

Some materials offer more resistance than others, depending on the number of free electrons present in the material.

The longer the wire or conductor, the more resistance it has. Resistance varies *directly* with the length of the wire.

Resistance varies inversely with the size of the conductor in cross section. In other words, the larger the wire, the smaller the resistance per foot of length.

For most materials, the higher the temperature, the higher the resistance. However, there are some exceptions to this in devices known as *thermistors*. Thermistors change resistance with temperature. They *decrease* in resistance with an increase in temperature. Thermistors are used in certain types of meters to measure temperature.

RESISTORS

Resistors provide measured amounts of resistance. They are valuable when it comes to making sure the proper amount of voltage is present in a circuit, and when generating heat.

Resistors are classified as either *wirewound* or *carbon-composition*. The symbol for a resistor of either type is ‑\/\/\/‑ .

Wirewound resistors are made of wire that has controlled resistance per unit length. Wirewound resistors are used to provide sufficient opposition to current flow to dissipate power of 5 W or more. Remember, a watt is a unit of electric power equal to one volt times one ampere.

Resistance causes a voltage drop across a resistor when current flows through it. The voltage is dropped or dissipated as heat and must be eliminated into the air.

Some variable resistors can be varied but can also be adjusted for a particular setting. Resistors are available in various sizes, shapes, and wattage ratings.

Carbon-composition resistors are usually found in electronic devices. They are of low wattage. They are made in $\frac{1}{8}$-W, $\frac{1}{4}$-W, $\frac{1}{2}$-W, 1-W, and 2-W sizes. The physical size determines the wattage rating or their ability to dissipate heat.

Carbon-composition resistors are usually marked according to their ohmic value with a color code. The colors are placed on the resistors in rings (Figure 7.6).

The table on page 254 shows the values for reading the color code of carbon-composition resistors.

Take a close look at a carbon-composition resistor. The bands should be to your left. Read from left to right. The band closest to one end is placed to the left so you can read it from left to right. The first band gives the first number according to the color code. In this case it is red, or 2. The second band gives the next number, which is violet, or 7. The third band represents the multiplier or divisor.

If the third band is a color in the 0 to 9 range in the color code, it states the number of zeros to be added to the first two numbers. Orange is 3; so the resistor in Figure 7.5 has a value of 27,000 Ω of resistance.

The 27,000 Ω is usually written as 27 kΩ. The k stands for thousand; it takes the place of three zeros. In some cases, resistors are referred to as 27 MΩ (which means 27,000,000, or 27 million Ω), because the M stands for *mega*, and that is the unit for million.

If there is no fourth band, the resistor has a tolerance rating of ± 20 percent (± means plus or minus). If the fourth band is silver, the resistor has a tolerance of ± 10 percent. If the fourth band is gold, the resistor has a tolerance of ± 5 percent.

Silver and gold may also be used for the *third* band. In this case, according to the color code, the first two numbers (obtained from the first two color bands) must be divided by 10 or 100. Silver means divide the first two numbers by 100. Gold means divide the first two numbers by 10. For example, if the bands of the resistor are red, yellow, and gold, then the value is 24 divided by 10, or 2.4 Ω. If the third band is silver and the two colors are yellow and orange, then the 43 is divided by 100 to produce the answer of 0.43 Ω. Keep in mind, though, that the fourth band will still be either gold or silver to indicate the tolerance.

Resistors marked with the color code are available in hundreds of size and wattage rating combinations. Wattage rating refers to the wattage or power consumed by the resistor.

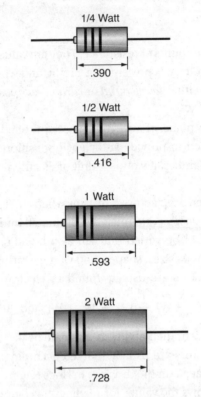

Figure 7.5. Wattage ratings of carbon-composition resistors. All measurements shown here are in inches.

Resistor Color Code	
0 Black	5 Green
1 Brown	6 Blue
2 Red	7 Violet
3 Orange	8 Gray
4 Yellow	9 White

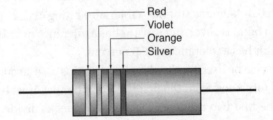

Figure 7.6. A 27,000-ohm (Ω) resistor.

CONDUCTANCE

Electronics is frequently explained in terms of opposites. The opposite of resistance is *conductance*. Conductance is the ability of a material to pass electrons. The factors that affect the magnitude of resistance are exactly the same for conductance, but they affect conductance in the opposite manner. Therefore, conductance is directly proportional to area, and inversely proportional to the length and specific resistance of the material. The temperature of a material is definitely a factor, but assuming a constant temperature, the conductance of a material can be calculated if its specific resistance is known.

The formula for conductance is:

$$G = \frac{A}{pL}$$

where:

> G = conductance measured in siemens (S)
> A = cross-sectional area in cir mils
> L = length measured in feet
> P = specific resistance

The unit of conductance is the *siemen* (formerly the mho, which is ohm spelled backwards). Whereas the symbol used to represent the magnitude of resistance is the Greek letter omega (Ω), the symbol used to represent conductance is S. The relationship that exists between resistance and conductance is a reciprocal one. A reciprocal of a number is one divided by that number. In terms of resistance and conductance:

$$R = \frac{1}{G}$$

$$G = \frac{1}{R}$$

If the resistance of a material is known, dividing its value into one will give its conductance. Also, if the conductance is known, dividing its value into 1 will give its resistance.

OHM'S LAW

In 1827, German physicist Georg Ohm found that in any circuit where the only opposition to the flow of electrons is resistance, there is a relationship between the values of voltage, current, and resistance. The strength or intensity of the current is directly proportional to the voltage and inversely proportional to the resistance.

It is easier to work with Ohm's law when it is expressed in a formula. In the formula, E represents emf, or voltage; I is the current, or the intensity of electron flow; R stands for resistance. The formula is $E = I \times R$. It is used to find the emf (voltage) when the current and the resistance are known.

To find the current, when the voltage and resistance are known, use

$$I = \frac{E}{R}$$

To find the resistance, when the voltage and current are known, use

$$R = \frac{E}{I}$$

Ohm's law is very useful in electrical and electronics work. You will need it often to determine the missing value. In order to make it easy to remember the formula, take a look at Figure 7.7. Here the formulas are arrived at by placing your finger on the unknown and the other two will have their relationship displayed.

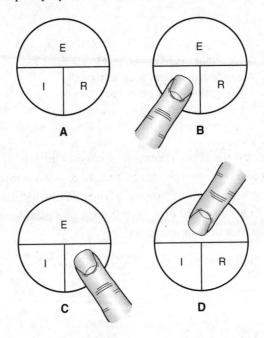

Figure 7.7. Ohm's law. Place your finger on the unknown value and the remaining two letters will give the formula to use for finding the unknown value.

The best way to become accustomed to solving problems is to start with something simple, such as:

1. If the voltage is given as 100 V and the resistance is 25 Ω, it is a simple problem and a practical application of Ohm's law to find the current in the circuit. Use

$$I = \frac{E}{R}$$

Substituting the values in the formula,

$$I = \frac{100}{25}$$

means 100 is divided by 25 to produce 4 A for the current.

2. If the current is given as 2 A (you may read it on an ammeter in the circuit), and the voltage (read from the voltmeter) is 100 V, it is easy to find the resistance. Use

$$R = \frac{E}{I}$$

Substituting the values in the formula,

$$R = \frac{100}{2}$$

means 100 divided by 2 equals 50 Ω for the circuit.

3. If the current is known to be 10 A, and the resistance is found to be 50 Ω (measured before the circuit is energized), it is then possible to determine how much voltage is needed to cause the circuit to function properly. Use

$$E = I \times R$$

Substituting the values in the formula,

$$E = 10 \times 50$$

means 10 times 50 produces 500, or that it would take 500 V to push 10 A through 50 Ω of resistance.

PRACTICE QUESTIONS

1. Power is defined as

    (A) the amount of effort needed to move 1 kilogram a distance of 1 foot in 1 minute.
    (B) the rate at which work is done or weight is moved.
    (C) only an electrical measurement.
    (D) only a mechanical measurement.

2. —\/\/\/\— is the symbol for

    (A) a conductor.
    (B) an open switch.
    (C) a resistor.
    (D) a power source.

3. Resistance

    (A) varies directly with the length of the wire.
    (B) increases proportionately with the cross section of the wire.
    (C) depends on only the material and the temperature of the conductor.
    (D) remains the same for a certain conductor material regardless of size.

4. The opposite of resistance is

   (A) dissipation.
   (B) wattage.
   (C) energy storage.
   (D) conductance.

5. The strength of an electrical current is _____ to the voltage and _____ to the resistance.

   (A) directly proportional, inversely proportional
   (B) inversely proportional, directly proportional
   (C) unrelated, directly proportional
   (D) directly proportional, unrelated

6. Resistance, which is the tendency for a substance to oppose the flow of electrons, is measured in

   (A) amps.
   (B) watts.
   (C) ohms.
   (D) volts.

7. The symbol for a resistor is

   (A) —⧑⧑⧑—

   (B) Ⓡ

   (C) Ω

   (D) |ı|ı

Answers Explained

1. **(B)** Power is defined as *the rate at which work is done or weight is moved.*

2. **(C)** —⧑⧑⧑— is the symbol for *a resistor.* The symbol for a wire that conducts electricity is a simple line ——— . The symbol for an open switch is ___⟍___. There are several symbols for a power source, depending on whether it is AC, DC, or a battery.

3. **(A)** Resistance *varies directly with the length of the wire.* Resistance also varies inversely with the square of the wire's diameter.

4. **(D)** The opposite of resistance is *conductance.*

5. **(A)** The strength of an electrical current is *directly proportional* to the voltage and *inversely proportional* to the resistance.

6. **(C)** Resistance, which is the tendency for a substance to oppose the flow of electrons, is measured in *ohms.* This measurement is named in honor of German physicist Georg Ohm, who discovered the relationship between current, voltage, and resistance in 1827.

7. **(A)** The symbol for a resistor is —⧑⧑⧑— .

There are a number of different types of circuits. Circuits are the pathways along which electrons move to produce various effects.

A *complete* circuit is necessary for the controlled flow or movement of electrons along a conductor (Figure 7.8). A complete circuit is made up of a source of electricity, a conductor, and a consuming device. This is the simplest of circuits. The flow of electrons through the consuming device produces heat, light, or work.

In order to form a complete circuit, these rules must be followed:

1. Connect one side of the power source to one side of the consuming device: A to B (see Figure 7.8).

2. Connect the other side of the power source to one side of the control device, usually a switch: C to D (see Figure 7.8).

3. Connect the other side of the switch to the consuming device it is supposed to control: E to F (see Figure 7.8). When the switch is closed, the circuit is complete.

However, when the switch is open, or not closed, there is no path for electrons to flow, and there is an o*pen circuit* condition where no current flows.

This method is used to make a complete path for electrons to flow from that side of the battery with an excess of electrons to the other side that has a deficiency of electrons. The battery has a negative (−) charge where there is an excess of electrons and a positive (+) charge where there is a deficiency of electrons. Yes, you read it right; the − means excess and + means deficiency. This is due to the fact that we are using the current flow and electron flow as both the same and from − to + in the circuit.

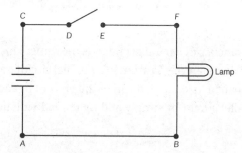

Figure 7.8. A simple circuit with a switch.

A single path for electrons to flow is called a *closed*, or *complete*, circuit. However, in some instances the circuit may have more than one consuming device. In this situation we have what is called a *series circuit* if the two or more resistors or consuming devices are placed one after the other as shown in Figure 7.9.

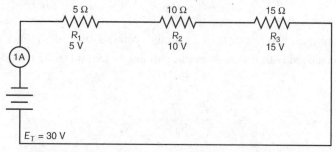

Figure 7.9. A series circuit with three resistors.

SERIES CIRCUITS

Figure 7.9 shows a series circuit. The three resistors are connected in series, or one after the other, to complete the path from one terminal of the battery to the other. The current flows through each of them before returning to the positive terminal of the battery.

There is a law concerning the voltages in a series circuit. *Kirchhoff's voltage law* states that the sum of all voltages across resistors or loads is equal to the applied voltage. Voltage drop is considered across the resistor. Figure 7.9 shows the current flow through three resistors. The voltage drop across R_1 is 5 V. Across R_2 the voltage drop is 10 V. And across R_3 the voltage drop is 15 V. The sum of the individual voltage drops is equal to the total or applied voltage of 30 V. E_T means total voltage. It may also be written as E_A for applied voltage or E_S for source voltage.

To find the total resistance in a series circuit, just add the individual resistances, or $R_T = R_1 + R_2 + R_3$. In this instance (Figure 7.9), the total resistance is 5 + 10 + 15, or 30 Ω.

PARALLEL CIRCUITS

In a parallel circuit each resistance is connected directly across the voltage source or line. There are as many separate paths for current flow as there are branches (Figure 7.10).

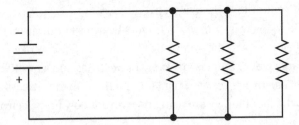

Figure 7.10. A parallel circuit.

The voltage across all branches of a parallel circuit is the same. This is because all branches are connected across the voltage source. Current in a parallel circuit depends on the resistance of the branch. Ohm's law can be used to determine the current in each branch. You can find the total current for a parallel circuit by simply adding the individual currents. When written as a formula it reads

$$I_T = I_1 + I_2 + I_3 + \dots$$

The total resistance of a parallel circuit cannot be found by adding the resistor values. Two formulas are used for finding the total resistance (R_T). If there are *only* two resistors in parallel, a simple formula can be used:

$$R_T = \frac{R_1 \times R_2}{R_1 + R_2}$$

If there are more than two resistors in a parallel, you can use the following formula. This formula may also be used with two resistors in parallel. In fact it can be used for *any* number of resistors.

$$\frac{1}{R_T} = \frac{1}{R_1} + \frac{1}{R_2} + \frac{1}{R_3} + \frac{1}{R_4} + \dots$$

One thing should be kept in mind in parallel resistances: The total resistance is *always* less than the smallest resistance. However, this is not true if one of the resistances is negative. The condition occurs only in active circuits, so for most applications the statement is true enough to be used for quick checks of your math.

SERIES-PARALLEL CIRCUITS

The series-parallel circuit is a combination of the series and the parallel arrangement. Figure 7.11 shows an example of the series-parallel circuit. It takes a minimum of three resistances to make a series-parallel circuit. This type has to be reduced to a series equivalent before it can be solved in terms of resistance. The parallel portions are reduced to the total for the part of the circuit, and then the equivalent resistance is added to the series part to obtain the total resistance.

Total current flows through the first series resistor but divides according to the branch resistances after that. There are definite relationships that must be explored here before that type of circuit can be fully understood.

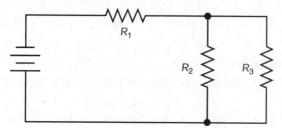

Figure 7.11. A series-parallel circuit.

OPEN CIRCUITS

An open circuit is an incomplete circuit. Figure 7.12 shows an open circuit that will become a closed circuit once the switch is closed. A circuit can also become open when one of the leads is cut or when one of the terminals has the wire removed. A loose connection can cause an open circuit.

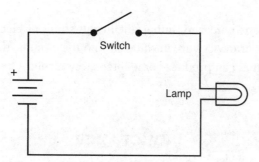

Figure 7.12. An open circuit produced by an open switch.

SHORT CIRCUITS

The short circuit is something to be avoided because it can cause a fire or overheating. A short circuit means that there is a path of low or lower resistance to electron flow that is frequently unintended or accidental. This is usually created when a low-resistance wire is placed across the consuming device (see Figure 7.13). The greater number of electrons will flow through the path of least resistance instead of through the consuming device. A short usually generates an excess current flow, which can result in damage to a number of parts of the circuit. If you want to prevent the damage caused by short circuits, use a fuse.

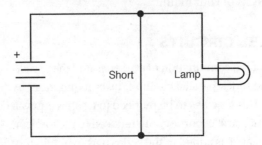

Figure 7.13. A short circuit. The wire has less resistance than the lamp.

FUSES

Fuses are available in a number of sizes and shapes. They are used to prevent the damage done by excess current flowing in a circuit. They are placed in series with the consuming devices. Once too much current flows, it causes the fuse wire inside the fuse case to melt. This opens the circuit and stops the flow of current and prevents the overheating that occurs when too much current is present in a circuit.

The symbol for a fuse is ⁀‿. It fits into a circuit as shown in Figure 7.14.

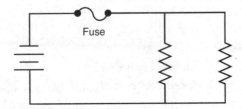

Figure 7.14. The location of the fuse in a circuit.

Resistors and resistance are very important in the study of electricity and electronics. However, when two other devices are introduced into the circuits, there is the possibility of various combinations that can produce some interesting results. One of these devices is the inductor, which produces inductance.

INDUCTANCE

Inductance is the ability of a *coil*, or *choke*, or *inductor* (all three mean the same thing and are interchangeable) to oppose any change in circuit current. This is not so important in a direct current (DC) circuit because the current flows in only one direction, from negative to positive, when it is first turned on, and then it stops when it is turned off. The collapsing magnetic field that was produced by the coil of wire with a current through it produces an emf in the coil when it decays or collapses. This emf is in the opposite polarity to that which caused it to be produced. The emf is called a *counter emf*, abbreviated as *cemf*.

Michael Faraday was an Englishman who performed early experiments with coils of wire and electric current. Faraday started to experiment with electricity about 1805, but it was not until 1831 that he performed experiments on magnetically coupled coils. A voltage was induced in one of the coils by means of a magnetic field created by current flow in the other coil. From this experiment came the induction coil. Faraday's experiment and discovery made possible such devices as the automobile, doorbell, car radio, and television.

Faraday also invented the first *transformer*. A transformer changes electricity into a higher or lower voltage. At that time it had very few practical uses. At the time Faraday was working in England, Joseph Henry was making almost the same discoveries in the United States. Henry worked in New York and discovered the property of self-inductance before Faraday. The unit of measurement for inductance is the henry (H). The symbol for inductance is *L*.

An inductor has an inductance of one *henry* if an emf of one volt is induced in the inductor when the current through the coil is changing at the rate of one ampere per second. Keep in mind that the one-volt, one-ampere, and one-henry relationship deals with the basic units of measurement of voltage, current, and inductance.

Inductors come in many sizes and shapes. Air-core inductors are coils that are wound without a core. They are used in circuits where the frequencies cannot be heard, such as radio frequencies, which are above the human hearing range. The symbol for a radio frequency coil is ‑⁀⁀⁀‑ . Note how the radio frequency air-core inductor is very small and resembles a resistor. The size of the color band to the left is larger than the others. This indicates that it is an inductor of a resistor. The color code tells the size in microhenrys (μH).

Inductors are also called *chokes* because of the way they hold back current or choke it. They are also called *coils* for the simple construction technique used to make them. They are nothing more than a coil of wire.

Inductors with iron cores are used in circuits where the frequencies can be heard. These are called *audio frequencies* and they are referred to as audio chokes or audio inductors. The iron core is usually laminated sheets of specially made silicon steel, used because it can change its magnetic orientation rapidly without causing too much opposition to the changing field or polarity reversals. The symbol for an iron core choke is ‑⁀⁀⁀⁀‑ .

Moisture Resistant

Iron core RF chokes are designed to meet demand for high-reliability ultraminiature components. Suited to network and filter design, delays lines, and computer applications. Coils are impregnated with moisture-resistant lacquer.

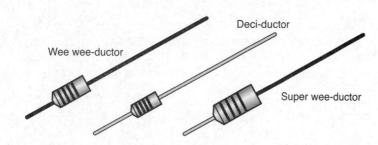

Deci-ductor

Wee wee-ductor

Super wee-ductor

The smallest shielded inductor for high density circuits 0.10 to 1000μH, this grade 2 class B inductor is designed to solve density circuit application problems.

Figure 7.15. Radio frequency chokes.

When two coils are placed near one another, *mutual induction* occurs. A change in the flux or magnetic field in one coil will cause an emf to be induced in the other coil. The two coils have mutual inductance. The amount of mutual inductance depends on the distance between the two coils. If the coils are separated a considerable distance, the amount of flux common to both coils is small and the mutual inductance is low. If the coils are close together nearly all the flux on one coil will link the turns of the other. The mutual inductance can be increased greatly by mounting both coils on the same iron core.

Mutual inductance of two adjacent coils depends on the physical size of the two coils, the number of turns in each coil, the distance between the two coils, the distance between the axes of the two coils, and the permeability of the cores. *Permeability* is the ease with which magnetic lines of force distribute themselves throughout a material.

PRACTICE QUESTIONS

1. A(n) _____ circuit is required for the controlled movement of electrons along a conductor.

    (A) open
    (B) complete
    (C) series
    (D) parallel

2. In a series circuit, the sum of all voltages across resistors is

    (A) greater than the applied voltage.
    (B) equal to the applied voltage.
    (C) less than the applied voltage.
    (D) inversely proportionate to the applied voltage.

3. A short circuit is

    (A) two coils placed near one another.
    (B) a combination of a series and a parallel arrangement.
    (C) a path of lower resistance to electron flow that is usually unintentional.
    (D) a path of higher resistance to electron flow that is usually intentional.

4. The symbol for a fuse is

    (A)
    (B)
    (C)
    (D)

5. The symbol for an inductor with a magnetic core is

(A)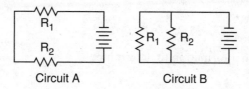

(B) ─○─

(C) ┤├┤├

(D) ─▱─

6. If two resistors and a battery are arranged as shown in each circuit, which circuit arrangement has a greater resistance?

Circuit A   Circuit B

(A) Circuit A
(B) Circuit B
(C) Both circuits have the same resistance.
(D) There's not enough information to answer.

7. What is a "short"?

(A) An inductor that uses no power
(B) An interrupted circuit
(C) An undesired conductive path in a circuit
(D) A bare conductor

8. Which of the following is represented by the symbol X_L?

(A) source output level
(B) coil reactance
(C) load impedance
(D) lowest threshold for filter excitation

9. What is the voltage drop across R_1?

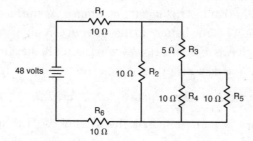

(A) 4.8 V
(B) 9.6 V
(C) 19.2 V
(D) 28.8 V

10. The total applied voltage for the circuit shown below is 30 V. What is the voltage drop across R_1, R_2, and R_3 in order?

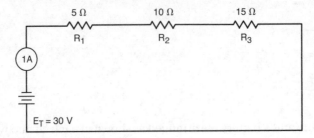

(A) 15 V, 10 V, 5 V
(B) 5 V, 10 V, 15 V
(C) 10 V, 10 V, 10 V
(D) Not enough information to determine

Answers Explained

1. **(B)** A *complete* circuit is required for the controlled movement of electrons along a conductor. You can illustrate this with a string of lightbulbs. If one is burned out, or if the wire is broken somewhere along the line, all of the lightbulbs stop working.

2. **(B)** In a series circuit, the sum of all voltages across resistors is *equal to the applied voltage*. In other words, the total resistance of a series circuit is equal to the sum of the individual resistors.

3. **(C)** A short circuit is *a path of lower resistance to electron flow that is usually unintentional*. It is an accidental extra path for current to flow through and that has little to no resistance when compared with the intended circuit flow.

4. **(C)** The symbol for a fuse is ‿‿. The symbol for a resistor is –⋀⋀⋀– ; the symbol for an AC voltage source is ⊘; and the symbol for a thermistor is –⊘–.

5. **(A)** The symbol for an inductor with a magnetic core is –⌒⌒⌒–. The symbol for a lamp or lightbulb is –⊘–; the symbol for a battery is ⊣|ı⊢; and the symbol for a thermistor is –⊘–.

6. **(A)** If two resistors and a battery are arranged as shown in each circuit, *Circuit A* is the circuit arrangement that has the greater resistance. As the electrical current makes its trip from one polarity of the battery to the other in Circuit A, the current has no choice but to pass through two resistors. However in Circuit B, the current will follow the path of least resistance and take a shortcut that passes through only one resistor.

7. **(C)** A "short" is *an undesired conductive path in a circuit*.

8. **(B)** *Coil reactance* is represented by the symbol X_L. The letter X combined with a subscript is the symbol for reactance. X_L represents the reactance of inductive components, commonly called "coils." X_C represents the reactance of capacitive components.

9. **(C)** The voltage drop across R_1 is *19.2 V*. To find the voltage drop across R_1, first find the total resistance by simplifying the circuit.

The circuit shown consists of a combination of series and parallel paths. The goal of simplifying the circuit is to combine the series and parallel branches into a single resistance value. This is done in several steps until only one value is left.

To combine resistors in series, just add them together. To combine resistors that have the same value but are in parallel branches, divide the value of one branch by the number of branches. To simplify the circuit shown:

1. Combine parallel branches R_4 and R_5: $10\,\Omega/2 = 5\,\Omega$.
2. Combine the result from Step 1 in series with R_3: $5\,\Omega + 5\,\Omega = 10\,\Omega$.
3. Combine the result from Step 2 in parallel with R_2: $10\,\Omega/2 = 5\,\Omega$.
4. Combine the result from Step 3 in series with R_1 and R_6: $5\,\Omega + 10\,\Omega + 10\,\Omega = 25\,\Omega$.

Now use Ohm's law to solve for I, which will give the total current flowing through the circuit. Since the resistors are in series after the simplification, the same amount of current flows through each resistor. Then solve for E (voltage) across R_1 using Ohm's law ($I = E/R$):

$$I = E/R = 48/25 = 1.92\,\text{A}$$

$$E = IR = 1.92 \times 10 = 19.2\,\text{V}$$

10. **(B)** The voltage drop across R_1, R_2, and R_3 in order is *5 V, 10 V, 15 V*. Kirchhoff's voltage law states that the sum of all voltages across resistors or loads is equal to the applied voltage. The circuit drawing shows that the total applied voltage for the circuit is 30 V. In this setup, the voltage drop for each resistor is the same as that resistor's resistance.

ALTERNATING CURRENT

Most of us have grown up with alternating current (AC). We are used to the 60-hertz (Hz) line current that is furnished to houses in the United States, which is much better than direct current (DC) when it comes to transporting power over long distances without huge losses. North and Central American countries, along with a few North African countries and the northernmost South American countries, use primarily 60-Hz electricity at 100–120 volts. Most other countries worldwide, however, use primarily 50-Hz electricity at 200–240 volts, although Japan uses both. There is no technical reason to prefer one system over the other, and large historical investments in equipment at one frequency have discouraged global standardization. Unless specified by the manufacturer to operate at both 50 and 60 Hz, however, appliances may not function correctly or even safely if used on anything other than the intended frequency.

Alternating current is also important because electronics devices rely so heavily on it. The radio frequencies that bring us radio and television are also AC.

Alternating current has a distinct advantage over direct current: it can be stepped up to obtain higher voltages and lower currents but still produce the same amount of power at the other end of the line. It can be transported over long distances through small wires because of the higher voltages and lower currents. Current determines the size of the wire. Then it is stepped down for local distribution. Since transformers are very efficient machines, very low losses are experienced with AC.

Usually, alternating current is generated at 13,800 volts (V). This is then stepped up to at least 138,000 V for distribution. Once the power reaches its destination, it is reduced to as low as 240 V for home use. This is further split for home circuits of 120 V.

AC GENERATOR

Alternating current is produced in an AC generator, or *alternator*, through the interaction of magnetic fields and electric conductors. Basically, the voltage and current that result from this *electromagnetic induction* is called AC electricity. (When necessary, it can be converted to DC.)

Alternating current can be produced by simply rotating one or more turns of wire in a magnetic field. The arrangement shown in Figure 7.16A demonstrates the principle involved in the generation of alternating current. The flux density is a constant that depends on the strength of the permanent magnet or electromagnet. The length of the conductor in the magnetic field is also constant. The loop is revolved at a constant speed by some external mechanical force, such as an internal combustion engine, steam engine, water turbine, or electric motor. It is important to keep in mind that one factor that does change as the coil is rotated is the angle at which the conductor moves in relation to the magnetic lines of force. The angle changes 360 degrees as the coil is rotated.

Figure 7.16A shows the single turn of wire rotated in the magnetic field. This will generate only a small amount of electrical energy. Nonetheless, such a loop or turn becomes part of a complete electrical circuit whenever a load is connected across the terminals of the loop. In Figure 7.16A, the ends of the loop are connected to a pair of slip rings. Power from the loop is then conducted to the load through a pair of brushes. The current in the load is the same as the current induced in the rotating loop.

Figure 7.16B shows the loop in the vertical position at 0 degrees: the rotating conductors are shown moving parallel to the lines of magnetic force. For a brief period the conductors are not cutting any lines of force, so no current is induced.

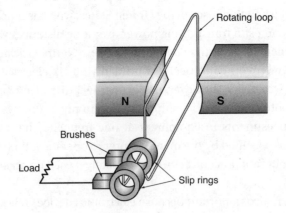

Figure 7.16A. A simple AC generator.

Power from the loop is conducted to the load through a pair of brushes.
The current in the load is the same as the current induced in the rotating loop.

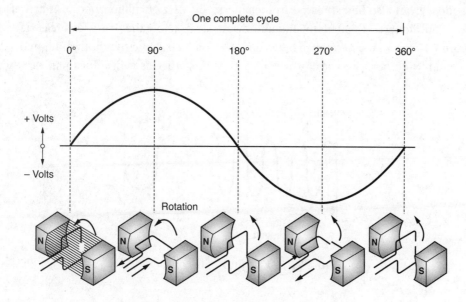

Figure 7.16B. A simple AC generator.
The position of the conductor while rotating in a magnetic field
determines the magnitude and direction of the induced current.

As long as the loop is rotated in the magnetic field, electricity is produced. The amplitude and direction of the current produced changes with time, forming a characteristic *waveform*, or pattern, known as a *sine wave*. The sine wave is the basic waveform of alternating current or voltage (Figure 7.17). As the generator loop continues to turn in a 360° circle, the output of the generator resembles the sine wave shown. Note how the various points on the circuit are shown in relationship to the sine wave.

One complete cycle of the generator is one *hertz*. A hertz (Hz) is a measurement of *frequency*, or the number of times the alternating current changes direction in one second. 60 Hz means the generator makes 60 complete cycles in 1 second. The word hertz means "frequency (cycles) per second" so the words "1 second" are not used with it.

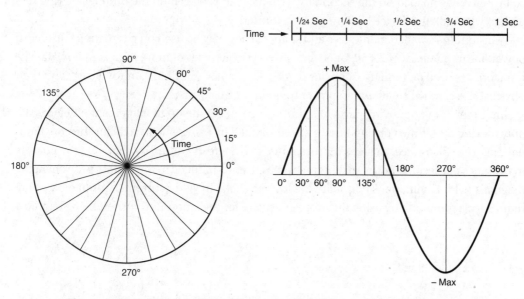

Figure 7.17. A 360° rotation of the loop will produce a sine wave output.

Frequency can also be expressed in megahertz, or MHz (1 million hertz). It can also be expressed in kilohertz (1,000 hertz) and abbreviated kHz. (Note that k is a lowercase letter.)

Figure 7.18 shows the difference between 4 Hz and 1 Hz. Note that both of them occur in one second. Note how the waveform comes closer together as it becomes part of a higher frequency.

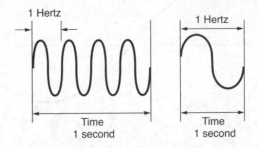

Figure 7.18. 4 Hz and 1 Hz compared.

TRANSFORMERS

A transformer is used to step up or step down alternating current voltages. It is not used with direct current.

A transformer is a device consisting of two coils that can change voltages. The voltage put into a transformer is either stepped up or stepped down. (In some instances, however, isolation transformers are used so that they have the same output as input voltage. They are used to eliminate the ground convention line current. That way you must come across both terminals to receive a shock instead of any ground and the hot side of the line.)

Transformers are used to distribute electric power from the generator to the consumer. Note that the symbols used for the transformer are two coils of wire with straight lines in between to designate the iron core.

A transformer has a primary winding and a secondary winding. A transformer is simply a coil when it has no load on the secondary. When a load is placed on the output side (the secondary winding), the device becomes a transformer.

Transformers come in many sizes and shapes. They may be used on alternating currents at power line frequencies of 25, 50, or 60 and also on frequencies of more than 1 million Hz. The transformers used on radio frequencies do not have cores. They have air for a core, and their physical size is much smaller than power frequency transformers.

Since there are no moving parts in a transformer, it can be up to 99 percent efficient. The only moving part is the current. Losses are eliminated by using silicon steel for the core laminations. The silicon steel reduces the losses due to hysteresis caused by changing the polarity many times per second. Eddy currents are small currents induced in the metal by the changing magnetic field. Laminations eliminate the losses caused by eddy currents. Copper losses are reduced to a minimum by using the proper size wire for the amount of current being handled.

POWER TRANSFORMERS

A power transformer can be both a step-up and a step-down unit (Figure 7.19). The secondary windings can furnish a number of different voltages. These voltages may be either higher or lower than the primary voltage. This type of transformer is used in electronics equipment where a number of different voltages are needed.

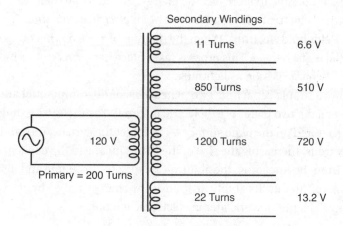

Figure 7.19. Power transformer schematic.

INDUCTIVE REACTANCE

Inductive reactance is the opposition put up to alternating current by a coil. The coil has a definite time or delay built in due to the ratio of inductance to resistance. This built-in delay of current comes in conflict with the AC since the current is constantly changing and not necessarily at the same rate as the natural tendency of the coil. Therefore, the reaction or reactance is in the form of an opposition. Since it is an opposition, it is measured in ohms. Reactance is represented by the symbol X. Inductance is represented by its symbol L. When the inductive reactance is represented, it is written as X_L. It is measured in ohms.

A number of factors determine X_L. One is the frequency of AC, which affects reactance. Another is the size of the inductor. The formula used to calculate X_L is

$$X_L = 2\pi fL$$

In this equation, f is the frequency, measured in Hz. L is inductance, measured in henrys (H). Pi (π) is a standard mathematical term with a value of 3.141592654. Thus, 2π equals 6.28 when rounded off for quick answers.

The major use of inductance is to provide a minimum reactance for low frequencies. Inductors produce high opposition to higher frequencies.

One specific use of inductance is in filters. Filters are used when certain frequencies are desired and others are to be avoided. An inductor is used that has an X_L that passes certain frequencies and opposes others.

Capacitors play an important role in building circuits. A capacitor is a device that opposes any change in circuit voltage. That property of a capacitor that opposes voltage change is called *capacitance.*

Capacitors make it possible to store electric energy. Electrons are held within a capacitor. This, in effect, is stored electricity. It is also known as an *electrical potential*, or an *electrostatic field.* Electrostatic fields hold electrons. When the buildup of electrons becomes great enough, the electric potential is discharged. This process takes place in nature: clouds build up electrostatic fields. Their discharge is seen as lightning.

Figure 7.20 shows a simple capacitor. Two plates of a conductor material are isolated from one another. Between the two plates is a dielectric material. The dielectric conducts electrons easily. Electrons are stored on the plate surfaces. The larger the surface, the more area is available for stored electrons. Increasing the size of the plates increases the capacitance.

As you can see from the foregoing, the ability of a capacitor to charge and discharge can be useful in many types of circuits. Its ability to oppose any change in the circuit voltage can also be helpful. All this will be put to work later in electronic circuits.

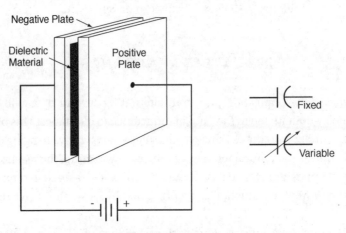

Figure 7.20. Design of a capacitor.

CAPACITY OF A CAPACITOR

The two plates of the capacitor may be made of almost any material. The only criterion is that the material will allow electrons to collect on it. The dielectric may be air, vacuum, plastics, wood, or mica.

Three factors determine the capacity of a capacitor: the area of the plates, the distance between the plates, and the material used as a dielectric. The larger plate area, the greater the capacity, or capacitance.

The distance between the plates of a capacitor determines the effect that electrons have upon one another. That is because electrons possess a charge, or field, around them that can react with those close by. Capacitance increases when the plates are brought close together.

One of the effects of the dielectric materials is determined by its thickness. The thinner the dielectric, the closer the plates will be. A thin dielectric can thus increase capacitance. Some dielectrics have better insulating qualities than others and will allow greater voltages to be applied between the plates before breaking down.

MEASURING CAPACITANCE

Capacitance is measured in farads (F). The *farad* is defined as having the ability to store enough electrons to produce a voltage difference of one volt across the terminals while producing one ampere of current for one second.

The farad is a very large unit of capacitance. The capacitors we use in electricity and in electronics are much, much smaller. They are measured in *microfarads* (0.000001 F) and in micromicrofarads, now called *picofarads* (0.000000000001 F).

CAPACITIVE REACTANCE

Capacitive reactance is that opposition that a capacitor presents to alternating current (AC). A capacitor has a definite time period for charging: $T = R \times C$. The time T in seconds (s) is equal to the resistance (Ω) times the capacitance (F). This produces a time constant which is 63.2 percent of the maximum voltage presented to the capacitor. It takes five time constants for a capacitor to charge to its full, or 99.3 percent, level. It also takes the same amount of time to discharge when presented with a resistance across its terminals.

When AC is present across the terminals of a capacitor, it changes faster than the capacitor can charge and discharge. This reaction or reactance is determined by the frequency of the AC and the capacity of the capacitor. A formula used to express capacitive reactance is

$$X_c = \frac{1}{2\pi fC}$$

where f = frequency, expressed in hertz

C = capacitance, expressed in farads

X_c = capacitive reactance, expressed in ohms since it is opposition to current flow

The following are conditions that occur when a capacitor is introduced into an AC circuit.

1. If the capacitance decreases, the capacitive reactance will increase for the same frequency.

2. If the capacitance increases, the capacitive reactance will decrease as long as the same frequency is presented to the capacitor.

3. If the frequency is decreased and the capacitor is the same, then the capacitive reactance will increase.

4. If the frequency is increased, then the capacitive reactance will decrease provided the capacitance stays the same.

As you can see from these statements and observations, the increase or decrease of the frequency or capacitance will cause the reverse reaction with the X_c.

CHANGING ALTERNATING CURRENT TO DIRECT CURRENT

Since alternating current (AC) is inexpensive, it is used in thousands of devices. It can be stepped up or stepped down by using a transformer. It is a versatile type of power that can easily be changed to fit the voltage or current needs of particular circuits. However, direct current (DC) is also useful for many devices. Electronics depend upon DC for many of its circuit components. This dependence upon DC requires a source of inexpensive direct current for a variety of voltages and currents.

PRACTICE QUESTIONS

1. Alternating current's major advantage over direct current is that alternating current can be

   (A) stepped down to lower voltages and higher currents but still maintain the same power.
   (B) transported over long distances through small wires due to higher voltages and lower currents.
   (C) stepped up to higher voltages and currents for transmission over long distances through small wires.
   (D) used in more areas around the world than direct current.

2. Alternating current is produced

   (A) through the interaction of magnetic fields and electric conductors.
   (B) by the variable flux density coming from a stable magnetic field.
   (C) by flipping a length of wire 180 degrees within a magnetic field.
   (D) by an uninterrupted connection to the positive and negative poles of a power source.

3. One complete cycle of a generator is called one

   (A) ohm.
   (B) hertz.
   (C) amplitude.
   (D) sine wave.

4. A transformer is used to

   (A) step up or step down alternating current wattages.
   (B) step up or step down direct current voltages.
   (C) step up or step down alternating current voltages.
   (D) step up or step down direct current wattages.

5. _____ make it possible to store electric energy, as opposed to an electric charge, in an electric field.

   (A) Filters
   (B) Capacitors
   (C) Transformers
   (D) Inductors

6. Static electricity is

   (A) a theoretical concept used to balance equations.
   (B) direct currect (DC).
   (C) alternating current (AC).
   (D) none of the above.

7. A 120 V electrical power supply produces $\frac{1}{2}$ A to the load. The power that is delivered is

   (A) 60 ohms.
   (B) 60 watts.
   (C) 240 ohms.
   (D) 240 watts.

8. A hertz (Hz) is a measurement of

   (A) the number of times an AC current changes direction in 1 second.
   (B) the number of times an AC current changes direction in 1 minute.
   (C) the number of times a DC current changes direction in 1 second.
   (D) the number of times a DC current changes direction in 1 minute.

9. A capacitor is a device that

   (A) has no impact on circuit voltage.
   (B) facilitates changes in circuit voltage.
   (C) opposes any change in circuit voltage and continuously bleeds off electricity.
   (D) opposes any change in circuit voltage and therefore stores electricity.

10. The symbol for a fixed capacitor is

   (A) ─┤├─
   (B) ─┤⟨─
   (C) ─∿─
   (D) ─⋀⋀⋀─

Answers Explained

1. **(C)** Alternating current's major advantage over direct current is that alternating current can be *stepped up to higher voltages and currents for transmission over long distances through small wires.*

2. **(A)** Alternating current is produced *through the interaction of magnetic fields and electric conductors.*

3. **(B)** One complete cycle of the generator is called one *hertz.* An ohm is a unit of electrical resistance. Amplitude refers to the greatest difference of an alternating electrical current or potential from the average value. A sine wave is a curve that shows periodic oscillations of constant amplitude.

4. **(C)** A transformer is used to *step up or step down alternating current voltages.*

5. **(B)** *Capacitors* make it possible to store electric energy, as opposed to an electric charge, in an electric field.

6. **(D)** Static electricity is *none of the above*. It is definitely not a theoretical concept used to balance equations. It is also neither AC nor DC, which are both currents—hence its accurately descriptive name, *static* electricity.

7. **(B)** A 120 V electrical power supply produces $\frac{1}{2}$ A to the load. The power that is delivered is *60 watts*. This is calculated using the formula $P = EI$, where P equals power in watts, E is the electricity in volts, and I is the intensity in amperes.

$$P = EI$$
$$P = 120\,\text{V} \times 0.5\,\text{A}$$
$$P = 60\,\text{W}$$

8. **(A)** A hertz (Hz) is a measurement of *the number of times an AC current changes direction in 1 second.*

9. **(D)** A capacitor is a device that *opposes any change in circuit voltage and therefore stores electricity.*

10. **(A)** The symbol for a fixed capacitor is ──┤(──.

METALLIC RECTIFIERS

Large copper oxide rectifiers were originally designed to change the AC to DC. One side of the rectifier disk was copper, and the other was copper oxide. The copper allowed the current to flow easily, but the copper oxide side put up a great opposition to the flow of current in the other direction. This meant the AC could be rectified since the copper oxide rectifier allowed the current to flow in only one direction. This produced pulsating DC which was useful for a number of chemical processes and for driving motors which were being developed at the time.

Metallic rectifiers may be used in battery chargers, instrument rectifiers, and many other applications including welding and electroplating. Commercial radios and television sets have been designed to utilize the selenium type of metallic rectifier.

SOLID STATE RECTIFIERS

Semiconductor materials are used to make a *diode*, a device which allows current to flow in one direction but not the other. Germanium and silicon are used as the materials for semiconductor diodes.

Crystals of silicon or germanium are grown from a *melt* that includes small quantities of impure substances such as phosphorus, indium, boron, and other *impurity* or *dopant* atoms. The crystal structure of the resulting metallic chips or wafers permits current flow in one direction only.

The first use of the crystal semiconductor as a rectifier (detector) was in the early days of radio.

The development of the point contact transistor was announced in 1948. The physical construction of the point contact transistor is similar to that of the point contact diode except that a third lead with a metallic point contact is placed near the other metallic point contact on the semiconductor.

The junction diode was first announced in 1949. The junction diode consists of a junction between two dissimilar sections of semiconductor material. One section, because of its characteristics, is called a P semiconductor. The connections to the junction diode consist of a lead to the P semiconductor material and a lead to the N semiconductor. The P material has a deficiency of one electron for every covalent bond of the material. The N material has an extra electron [therefore the (–) or N designation] for every covalent bond of the material. *Covalent* means that the atoms share electron orbits with adjacent atoms.

The junction diode handles larger power than the point contact diode, but the junction diode has a larger shunt capacitance.

Many types of semiconductor diodes are available. They vary in size from those so small that they are hard to see to those as large as two inches in diameter. They can withstand high voltages and carry large currents. The improvement of the semiconductor material creates better-quality diodes.

FILTERS

Up to this point we have discussed the making of pulsating DC from AC. This is fine for some uses, but for most electronic circuits it is not pure enough DC for proper operation of the circuits. Too much pulsating will make a high level of hum, and in some applications—computer circuits, for instance—it will give unreliable results. That, then, calls for something a little purer in the way of making the DC usable and of the proper form to do the work. Filter circuits are the answer to smoothing out the ripple and pulsations of full-wave and half-wave rectifiers.

The unfiltered output of a full-wave rectifier is shown in Figure 7.21. The polarity of the output voltage does not reverse, but its magnitude fluctuates about an average value as the successive pulses of energy are delivered to the load. The average voltage is shown as the line that divides the waveform so that area *A* equals area *B*. The fluctuations of voltage above and below this average value is called the *ripple*. The output of any rectifier is composed of a direct voltage and an alternating or ripple voltage. For most uses, the ripple voltage must be reduced to a very low amplitude. The amount of a ripple that can be tolerated varies with different uses of electron tubes and semiconductors. A circuit that eliminates the ripple voltage from the rectifier output is called a *filter*. Filter systems in general are composed of a combination of capacitors, inductors, and in some cases, resistors.

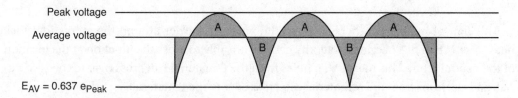

Figure 7.21. Unfiltered output voltage of a full-wave rectifier.

VOLTAGE MULTIPLIERS

High voltage is needed in many circuits and devices. For instance, cathode ray tubes used in oscilloscopes, radar displays, and video displays call for a typical voltage of 5 kV up to 20 kV. They need only a few milliamperes of current and a regulation of ±1 percent.

As you will remember from earlier in this chapter, the term *semiconductor* is applied to both diodes and transistors, as well as to certain special types of electronic devices. The word is based on the fact that germanium and silicon perform somewhere between the level of a conductor and an insulator in terms of opposition to current flow. The amount of opposition is programmed into or manufactured into the device by controlling the impurities introduced into pure germanium or pure silicon. Germanium and silicon can be purified to better than 99.999999 percent. Therefore, any other element introduced is called an *impurity* or *doping agent.* By controlling the amount of doping agent introduced into each crystalline structure, manufacturers can control the amount of opposition to current flow.

SEMICONDUCTOR DIODES

A semiconductor diode is made by joining a piece of P material with a piece of N material. The place where the two materials are joined is referred to as the *junction.* This junction is very thin, and each end has a piece of wire attached for connecting the diode, thus making a circuit. Figure 7.22 shows how the two pieces of material form a diode junction.

Both holes and electrons are involved in conduction in the PN junction diode. There are minority carriers in both regions: holes in the N material and electrons in the P material. The holes produced in the N material near the junction are attracted by the negative ions on the P side of the junction and pass across the junction. These holes tend to neutralize the negative ions on the P side of the junction. Similarly, free electrons produced on the P side of the junction pass across the junction and neutralize positive ions on the N side. This action is an example of intrinsic conduction, which is undesirable.

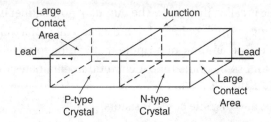

Figure 7.22. Pictorial representation of a PN junction diode.

This flow of minority carriers weakens the potential barrier around the atoms that they neutralize. When this happens, majority carriers are able to cross the junction at the location of the neutral atom. This means that holes from the P material can cross over to the N material, and electrons from the N material can cross over to the P material.

This action results in both holes and electrons crossing the junction in both directions. These motions cancel each other, and the net movement contributes nothing toward the net charge or current flow through the junction. Because of intrinsic conduction, the junction is no longer a rectifier when an external voltage is applied across it. It is analogous to an electron tube diode in which not only the cathode emits electrons, but the plate is heated to the point where it also emits enough electrons to break down the rectifying properties of the diode.

THE POINT CONTACT DIODE

There are a number of diodes (Figure 7.23). They are designed for special applications in some cases. The point contact diode is a very small (physically speaking) unit that is used for rectifying signals. The junction diode is used for rectifying power-line frequencies and higher currents.

Figure 7.23. Symbol for a diode. The + end is the cathode.

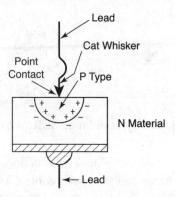

Figure 7.24. A point contact diode.

Unlike the junction diode, the point contact type (Figure 7.24) depends on the pressure or contact between a point and a semiconductor crystal for its operation. One section consists of a small, rectangular crystal of N material (either germanium or silicon) and a fine beryllium-copper, phosphor-bronze, or tungsten wire called the *cat whisker.* The cat whisker presses against the semiconductor material and forms the other part of the diode. The reason for using a fine-pointed wire instead of a flat metal plate is to produce a high-density electric field at the point of contact without using too large an external voltage source. The opposite end of the cat whisker is used as the diode terminal for connection purposes.

This very small contact area has a reduced capacitance effect (over the junction type with two pieces of material actually touching along a wide surface) that can be used for rectifying higher frequencies than the junction diode. However, since the size of the cat whisker is limited, the amount of current the diode can handle is also limited.

TUNNEL DIODES

Tunnel diodes can be used in extremely small spaces, such as part of an integrated circuit (IC) or chip. They can switch at very high rates [2 to 10 gigahertz (GHz)]. A gigahertz is 1,000 megahertz (MHz). A *megahertz* is 1 million times per second, and a *gigahertz* is 1,000 times faster than that, or 1 billion times per second.

Tunnel diodes are doped by using gallium arsenide, gallium antimonide, and indium antimonide.

THE SILICON-CONTROLLED RECTIFIER

Another type of specialized rectifier or diode is the silicon-controlled rectifier (SCR).

The SCR is a specialized four-layer type of device used for the control of current on its cathode-to-anode path. A gate is used to control the resistance between the cathode and the anode. By applying a small voltage between the gate and the cathode, it is possible to control this resistance and, as a result, the amount of current flow through the device. An SCR conducts current in the *forward* direction only. The symbol for the device is shown in Figure 7.25.

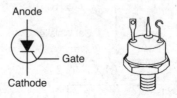

Figure 7.25. Symbol for an SCR, or thyrister.

Figure 7.26 shows a circuit with an SCR. The function of an SCR is current control. Examples of this are a light dimmer and the speed control for an electrically powered small hand drill or other hand tool. The resistor is a rheostat. This adjustable resistor is used to control the amount of voltage delivered to the gate of the SCR. The greater the voltage, the less the anode-to-cathode resistance and the greater the amount of current allowed to flow through the cathode-anode connection. By adjusting the rheostat, it is possible to control the amount of current flow through the device. As the current increases, the load—the device that is being powered—gets brighter if it is a lamp or increases speed if it is a drill or electric motor. Thus, the SCR can be used to control either type of circuit. Other control circuits also use the SCR as their main operating device.

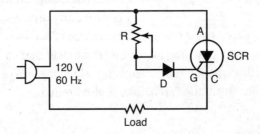

Figure 7.26. A circuit with the SCR as a control device.

TRANSISTORS

The word *transistor* comes from two other words: *transfer* and *resistor*. Thus, it is a transfer resistor or a device that has more impedance (resistance) in the input than in the output, or the other way around depending on its use. By having a difference in impedance between the input and the output, it is able to amplify.

There are two ways in which transistors are used. One is in switching, and the other is in amplifying a signal. The switching ability of a semiconductor has previously been discussed in the section on diodes in this chapter. However, we will mention it briefly here in the study of transistors. The main emphasis will be on the ability of the transistor to amplify and thereby to serve as a replacement for the vacuum tube.

Transistors are made from N and P materials, such as the semiconductor diode. Once they are joined, they resemble two diodes back to back (Figure 7.27).

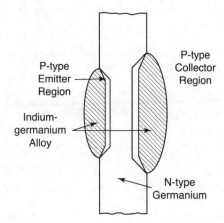

Figure 7.27. PNP transistor junction formation.

INTEGRATED CIRCUITS

The integrated circuit (IC) is a single one-piece chip made of semiconductor material. Transistors, diodes, resistors, and capacitors can all be deposited on a chip instead of having to be wired separately, as was the case when these transistors were relatively new. Diodes can be produced in many groups to do different things. Photolithography, a combination of photographic and printing techniques, has been used to make the complete circuit. This type of printing has made it possible to produce some very sophisticated ICs with very high reliability.

PRACTICE QUESTIONS

1. A diode is a device

    (A) that allows current to flow in one direction but not the other.
    (B) that allows current to flow in either direction through the use of a switch.
    (C) used to generate semiconductor minerals such as silicon and germanium.
    (D) used to control the voltage of current flow in one direction only.

2. Filter circuits

    (A) purify the inputs to direct current circuits.
    (B) reverse the polarity of output voltage.
    (C) induce necessary pulsations into half-wave rectifier output.
    (D) smooth out the pulsations of full-wave rectifiers.

3. The symbol for a light-emitting diode (LED) is

   (A) ─○─

   (B) Anode ─▷|─ Cathode

   (C) Anode ─▷|─ Cathode

   (D) ─[ ]─

4. The silicon-controlled rectifier (SCR) is used to

   (A) divert current on its cathode-to-anode pathway.
   (B) control current on its anode-to-cathode pathway.
   (C) prevent short circuits.
   (D) replace thyristers.

5. Which electrical component acts like a gate for electronic signals by regulating current and voltage?

   (A) Transistor
   (B) Battery
   (C) Circuit breaker
   (D) Resistor

Answers Explained

1. **(A)** A diode is a device *that allows current to flow in one direction but not the other.*

2. **(D)** Filter circuits *smooth out the pulsations of full-wave rectifiers.*

3. **(B)** The symbol for a light-emitting diode (LED) is Anode ─▷|─ Cathode. The symbol for a lamp or lightbulb is ─○─; the symbol for a non-LED diode is Anode ─▷|─ Cathode; and the symbol for a fuse is ─[ ]─.

4. **(B)** The silicon-controlled rectifier (SCR) is used to *control current on its anode-to-cathode pathway.*

5. **(A)** A *transistor* acts like a gate for electronic signals by regulating current and voltage. Many electrical circuits contain transistors.

BATTERIES

A *battery* is a device in which chemical energy is converted to electrical energy. Batteries can also be defined as one or more galvanic cells connected in series or in parallel; a *galvanic cell* is simply one in which chemical energy is converted to electrical energy. Batteries are used in many products, from cars and boats to radios, clocks, computers, toys, and many household items.

A battery usually consists of two or more galvanic cells. Each cell provides from 1.2 to 2.2 volts of electricity. The number and type of cells determine the voltage of the battery.

A simple cell consists of two *electrodes* in a solution called an *electrolyte* or *electrolytic solution* (Figure 7.28). The two electrodes are made of unlike metallic materials, and the electrolyte is nonmetallic, usually an acid or a salt dissolved in water. In the solution, the acid or salt *dissociates*, or separates, into positive and negative ions. The chemical reaction between the electrodes and the solution causes a movement of ions, and the *terminals* (electrodes) of the cell are positive or negative because of this chemical activity. There is an excess of electrons at the negative terminal and a lack of electrons at the positive terminal.

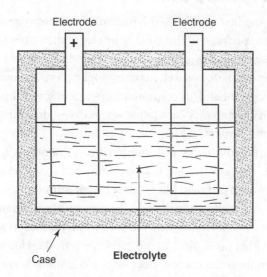

Figure 7.28. Two electrodes and an electrolyte make up a cell, or battery.

When an external circuit is connected between the two terminals, the excess electrons at the negative electrode flow through the external circuit to the positive electrode. This flow of electrons is an *electric current*.

Continuing chemical activity in the cell provides a supply of electrons, and the cell is said to be *discharging*. Because of the chemical activity, however, one or both of the electrodes is eventually consumed or chemically changed. When the available chemical energy is gone, no more electrical power can be drawn from the cell, and the cell is said to be *discharged* (dead).

There are two general types of electrical cells: primary and secondary. In a *primary cell*, chemical energy is converted to electrical energy and the process cannot be reversed. Once the cell is discharged, it is no longer usable and cannot be regenerated as a source of electrical power.

A *secondary cell*, also known as a storage battery, is rechargeable; it is usually designed to have a lifetime of between 100 and 1,000 recharge cycles, depending on the composite materials used. The chemical action in the cell is reversible, and the electrodes and electrolyte can be restored to the same makeup that existed before the discharge; this is done by using an outside source of electricity. Although primary batteries are often made from the same basic materials as secondary (rechargeable) batteries, the design and manufacturing processes are different. Secondary cells are often more cost-effective over a long period of time than primary batteries since the battery can be recharged and reused. A single discharge cycle of a primary battery, however, provides more current for a longer period of time than a single discharge cycle of an equivalent secondary battery—a regular household alkaline battery provides about 50 percent more energy density than the best equivalent secondary or rechargeable version.

A PRIMARY CELL—THE DRY CELL

There are several types of primary cells, including wet cells, reserve cells, and fuel cells. However, the most common type of primary cell, which has now largely replaced all others, is the *dry cell.* A dry cell is unspillable and nonrefillable. The electrolyte is dry or pasty. There are many types of dry cells, differing mainly in the types of electrodes and electrolyte.

The Carbon-Zinc Primary Cell

Carbon-zinc cells were the first widely used household batteries (Figure 7.29). There are still lots of these around—the package in the grocery or electronics store may be labeled "heavy duty" or "transistor power." This is the type of cell found in most flashlights. It is the least expensive type of cell, and it performs well in many applications. However, it does have some limitations. When high current and/or continuous operation is required, it often costs less in the long run to use a higher-capacity—and more expensive—dry cell; the carbon-zinc cell is also of limited use in cold climates.

In the standard round carbon-zinc cell, the positive electrode is a carbon rod mounted in the center of the cell. The negative electrode is a zinc can that also serves as the container for the cell. The electrolyte is a moist, black paste of salt ammoniac (ammonium chloride), chlorine, zinc chloride, and manganese dioxide. To prevent short circuits, all but the positive electrode and the bottom of the zinc can are covered by an insulation jacket.

The chemical activity that takes place at the carbon electrode releases hydrogen gas. If the hydrogen gas collects around the carbon electrode, a condition known as *polarization* can develop, in which the output voltage is reduced because the hydrogen partially insulates the carbon rod from the electrolyte. However, the presence of a *depolarizer*—manganese dioxide—contributes oxygen, which combines with the hydrogen gas to form water. The water not only prevents polarization but also serves to keep the electrolyte moist.

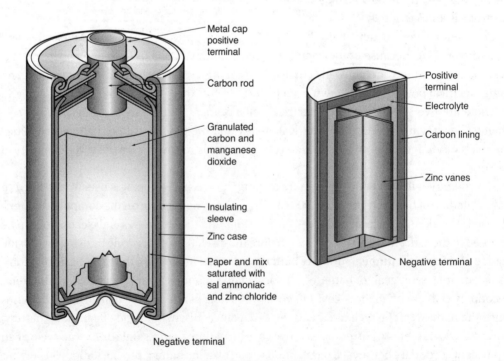

Figure 7.29. Two views of the construction of a carbon-zinc cell.

The chemical action during discharge decomposes the zinc electrode. Therefore, the cell has a definite life, which depends on the discharge current and the rate at which the zinc electrode is decomposed. As the zinc container is being consumed, the electrolyte often leaks into the surrounding area, causing corrosion damage. Thus, it is important to remove this type of cell from the circuit or device as soon as possible after its useful life has ended.

Carbon-zinc cells produce 1.5 volts. The materials in the cell and the chemicals, not the size of the cell, determine the voltage. A small cell has the same voltage as a large one made of the same materials. However, the larger cell has more materials and therefore produces more electrical energy. A large cell can supply more current than a smaller cell during the same period of time.

Popular sizes of dry cells are shown in Figure 7.30. The n-type cell has about 0.02 ampere, and the D cell has about 0.15 ampere. Other batteries are available in various shapes and sizes.

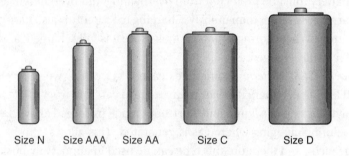

Size N   Size AAA   Size AA   Size C   Size D

Figure 7.30. Standard dry cell sizes.

Other Types of Primary Cells

Probably the most common type of dry cell now is the alkaline cell, which has a lower internal resistance and can deliver a much higher current on a continuous basis than a carbon-zinc cell. Alkaline cells deliver about four times the energy of carbon-zinc cells. In "high-drain" applications such as toys, cameras, and CD players, the difference is even greater—carbon-zinc batteries in these cases can deliver only about one-tenth (10 percent) of that available from an alkaline cell.

Another type of dry cell used in electronic equipment is the mercury or mercuric oxide cell. The mercury cell can be made very small, which is an advantage for use in hearing aids and other miniature electronic devices. These cells are also available in the standard cylindrical shapes, providing high current capacity and long life. The unit cost for the mercury cell is the highest of the three types of dry cells discussed here, but the mercury cell has a higher efficiency than the other two types. The output voltage remains almost constant until the end of the useful life of the cell. Also, mercuric oxide batteries have a long shelf life, sometimes up to 10 years.

Silver oxide cells are commonly found as "button" cells that power small electronic devices such as watches, calculators, hearing aids, and other small specialty devices. Rated at 1.55 volts per cell, their advantages are small size, high energy density, and a long shelf life.

Lithium primary batteries are also available in a variety of chemistries combining lithium with sulfur dioxide, thionyl chloride, manganese dioxide, copper oxide, and iodine. Some of these styles are also rechargeable.

SECONDARY CELLS

There are several types of secondary cells, also known as "storage" or "rechargeable" batteries.

The *lead-acid battery* is the type of battery used in internal combustion cars, small boats, and other vehicles. They are also known as "flooded" batteries because the electrolyte is liquid and, because of this, the battery usually needs to be maintained in a more-or-less upright position. This is the oldest type of secondary battery, developed in the mid-1800s. It has a positive electrode of lead oxide, a negative electrode of porous metallic lead, and sulfuric acid as the electrolyte. Although a separate storage battery is sometimes used to power the electronic equipment in a car, most often the battery that is part of the car's electrical system is also used to supply power for the radio, CD player, and other electronic equipment. To charge the battery, a direct current of the opposite direction is passed through the cell, and this reverses the chemical activity.

A lead-acid battery must be protected from overheating and overcharging. Be sure to discharge the battery slowly rather than quickly. Charging too rapidly is also harmful and reduces the life of the battery. When storing a battery, make sure it is fully charged; a battery lasts longer in storage if it is fully charged.

Sealed lead-acid (SLA) batteries (sometimes called "gel cells") were developed from the familiar flooded lead-acid battery used for many years in cars and trucks. The SLA form uses a gel-type electrolyte instead of a liquid and electrodes made from lead alloys designed to never reach the stage during charging where gas is generated. This allows it to be sealed (i.e., no safety valve is needed), and therefore this type can be used in almost any position or orientation. Since water is not lost, the SLA also requires little maintenance, but, on the other hand, since it's never (theoretically) fully charged, it tends to have a poor energy density—the lowest for all the sealed rechargeables. But, since SLAs are also the cheapest rechargeables, they're best suited for applications where low-cost power storage is the main consideration and bulk and weight are not issues.

Nickel–cadmium cells (commonly called "NiCads") are available in standard household sizes and shapes. It uses nickel hydroxide as the positive electrode and cadmium metal-cadmium hydroxide as the negative electrode, with potassium hydroxide as the electrolyte. The voltage of a nickel-cadmium cell is 1.25 volts, and its output is constant. It can be recharged often, and it can have a long, active life. Like SLAs, sealed NiCads can be used in just about any position, and they have up to double the energy density. However, they have a higher self-discharge rate than SLAs—about 10 percent in the first 24 hours after charging and about 10 percent per month thereafter—and the rate gets even higher in warmer conditions. However, this type of cell can also be discharged completely without being damaged.

Lithium is the lightest metal and has the highest electrochemical potential, which gives it the potential for extremely high energy density. However, the metal itself is highly reactive, and while this isn't a problem with primary cells, it poses an explosion risk with rechargeable types. In order to be safe, lithium ions from chemicals such as lithium-cobalt dioxide are used instead of the metal itself. Typical Li-ion batteries have a negative electrode of aluminum coated with a lithium compound such as lithium-cobalt dioxide, lithium-nickel dioxide, or lithium-manganese dioxide. The positive electrode is generally copper coated with carbon (usually either graphite or coke), while the electrolyte is a lithium salt. Li-ion batteries have about twice the energy density of NiCads and have a relatively low self-discharge rate. However, they can't be charged as quickly as NiCads, and they cost more than either NiCads or NiMH batteries, making them the most expensive rechargeables of all. Part of the reason for this is that they must be provided with built-in protection against both excessive discharging and overcharging—both of which pose a safety risk. Most Li-ion batteries thus come in self-contained battery packs complete with "smart" protective circuitry.

Most current electronics (such as laptops) and electric cars use some type of lithium battery.

ELECTRIC MOTORS

An electric motor changes electrical energy into mechanical energy to do work. It allows electric power to be used to run machinery. Basically, a motor connected to a source of electric power develops a twisting effort, or *torque*, that usually rotates the shaft of the motor. When this shaft is connected, belted, or geared to a machine, it drives the machine to do work.

An electric motor illustrates basic principles of electricity and magnetism. When an electric current is passed through a conductor (coil of wire), the conductor becomes an electromagnet, inducing a magnetic field around it. The direction of the current determines the poles of the magnet. When the current-carrying coil is placed between magnets, it rotates based on the principle that opposite poles attract and like poles repel each other.

There are two basic types of electric motors: direct current motors and alternating current motors.

DC MOTORS

A direct current (DC) motor is powered by direct current. It includes a stationary magnet, known as a *field magnet*; a current-carrying coil, known as an *armature*, that rotates between the poles of the stationary magnet; a device called a *commutator* that changes the direction of current in the armature; and brushes that form a sliding contact between the commutator and the direct current power supply. The armature is usually mounted on a drive shaft that can be used to transmit power to other machines.

Current passes through the armature, making it an electromagnet. The armature rotates so that its poles are next to opposite poles on the stationary magnet. Then the commutator reverses the direction of the current, and the armature rotates so that its poles are again next to the opposite poles of the magnet. When the armature turns, it turns a shaft that runs a machine. There are three basic types of direct current motors: shunt, series, and compound.

AC MOTORS

Alternating current (AC) *motors* are more commonly used than direct current motors because almost all electric supply systems are alternating current systems. In the United States and Canada, electrical power—alternating current—is produced as three-phase (3 Ø). It is used in commercial and industrial applications as it is generated. Three-phase power has many advantages, but it is expensive to distribute to every home and business. Therefore, it is distributed from the generating source to substations where it is converted to single-phase (1 Ø) for local use in homes and small power consumption locations.

AC motors are three-phase and single-phase. *Three-phase motors* have good overall characteristics. They are ideal for driving machines in industrial applications. They can be reversed while running. Reversing any two of the three connections to the power line causes the motor to be reversed.

The performance of electrical circuits must be monitored. The monitoring of circuit operation may require a voltage check, current check, or power check. *Voltmeters* are used to check voltage; *ammeters* are used to check current; and *watt-hour meters* are used to monitor performance in terms of power consumed. *Ohmmeters* are designed to check resistance.

AMMETERS

The term *ammeter* refers to any current-indicating meter that can be used to measure amperes, milliamperes, or microamperes (Figure 7.31). In most ammeters, the coil is designed for about 100 milliamperes or less. The wire in the moving coil is very small and cannot handle large amounts of current. When the current to be measured is greater than the capacity of the meter coil, a special circuit called a *shunt* is used. The shunt bypasses part of the current around the meter. The resistance of the meter and the resistance of the shunt path are selected to give the desired division of current so that the meter movement is not overloaded and burned out.

Figure 7.31. 0–1 milliampere panel meter.

VOLTMETERS

A *voltmeter* is a high resistance current meter that is calibrated in volts (Figure 7.32). Remember Ohm's law: If the current and the resistance of a circuit are known, the voltage can be determined. The voltmeter thus solves the Ohm's law problem. The resistance of the voltmeter is a known value, and the current in this resistance is indicated by the needle deflection. To find the voltage, simply mark the meter scale in volts and read it directly. The voltmeter is connected directly across the voltage source or across the circuit component and should draw as little current as possible. For this reason it should contain a sensitive meter movement and a high resistance.

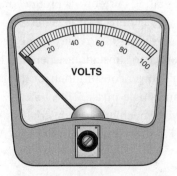

Figure 7.32. Milliammeter with a voltage calibration.

OHMMETERS

It is possible to use resistors with a battery and a meter movement to make a circuit for measuring resistance, or ohms. The meter for measuring ohms is called an *ohmmeter*.

The principle of the ohmmeter is another application of Ohm's law: If the voltage and the current are known, the resistance can be found. In the ohmmeter, the voltage of the battery and the current needed to produce full-scale deflection are known. The meter scale can be calibrated in ohms, and the value can be read directly (Figure 7.33).

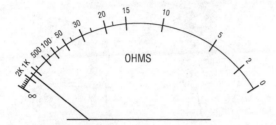

Figure 7.33. Ohmmeter scale.

WATT-HOUR METERS

Watt-hour or *kilowatt-hour meters* are used primarily by power companies to record the total amount of energy used by a customer during a one-month period. *Kilo* means "thousand," so a kilowatt-hour meter measures total energy consumed in thousands of units. A *wattmeter* is used to measure power as energy is being used on a per second basis.

DIGITAL MULTIMETERS

Digital multimeters have replaced many types of mechanical meter movements. A digital meter makes it possible to measure the circuit workings more accurately since it utilizes electronic circuits that require very small amounts of current to indicate the presence of voltage or current. Figure 7.34 shows one of the many types of digital meters available. The digital readouts are easy to read, not like trying to guess what the value is when reading "between the lines" on an analog-type meter.

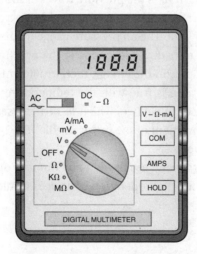

Figure 7.34. Digital multimeter.

CLAMP-ON METERS

Clamp-on ammeters are used to check the current flowing through a wire without having to cut the wire and insert an ammeter. They use the transformer principle to detect the presence of the current, and their sensitive meter movement is calibrated to indicate the correct amount (Figure 7.35). This type of meter is also available in digital readout.

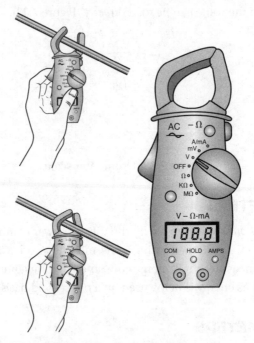

Figure 7.35. Clamp-on meter.

TRANSDUCERS

Transducers are devices that convert pressure, light, heat, and sound to electrical energy. A microphone is a good example. It uses the pressure waves of sound to produce a varying electrical current. This varying current is then amplified and fed to a speaker so it can be heard, or it is recorded on tape, disc, or wire. The oil pressure gauge in an automobile has a transducer that allows it to operate. The transducer responds to the pressure of the oil on a diaphragm that causes a change in resistance in the circuit, thereby allowing the meter or gauge to read the pressure of the oil. The same is true with the temperature gauge in a car. Heat causes the resistance of the transducer to change, which in turn causes a change in current in the circuit as indicated by the movement of the meter needle. The meter is calibrated in degrees Fahrenheit instead of milliamperes.

Transducers take many forms and are used in any number of electronic devices. Without transducers, the electrical control and operation of devices would be extremely limited.

The most common technique for joining wires, lugs, and terminals in electrical and electronics circuits is soldering.

Solder is an alloy metal made from tin and lead. There are three standard alloy mixtures for solder, which are given as percentages; the tin percentage is always stated first. Thus, a 40/60 solder contains 40 percent tin and 60 percent lead. There are also 50/50 and 60/40 solders. In general, the more tin contained in solder, the higher the quality. In industry, 60/40 solder is used by quality manufacturers.

Soldering is the technique of joining electrical or electronic connections where solder is melted to form a coating over the connection point, forming a joint. Standard solders melt at between 450°F and 600°F (232.2°C and 315.5°C).

Most solder contains a chemical, which is called *flux*. The purpose of the flux is to clean the area of the connection. This allows the melted solder to flow easily and also prevents oxidation. Two types of flux are available. One is an acid core flux used primarily in sheet metal soldering. Never use acid core flux when soldering copper. For electrical and electronics work, only rosin flux is used. Rosin flux can be purchased as a paste. However, the most common form is as part of the solder. Flux is built into soldering wire, which is then known as rosin-core solder.

There are three methods of applying solder: contact, dip, and wave.

CONTACT SOLDERING

Contact soldering uses a soldering iron or soldering pencil. A complete soldering station includes a soldering iron, a power supply that controls the current used to heat the iron, and a wet sponge used to clean the tip of the iron.

Other types of equipment are also available for contact soldering. A soldering iron (Figure 7.36) is a self-contained unit that simply plugs into an outlet for use. Soldering irons come in a variety of power ratings. For work on electronics, a low-wattage iron with a rating between 20 and 30 watts is recommended. The wattage may be higher for heavy-duty electrical devices—up to 500 watts. A soldering pencil (Figure 7.37) is similar to a soldering iron but is smaller and is used for finer work. A portable soldering pencil (Figure 7.38) is convenient and easy to use; it has no electric cord but is powered by a rechargeable cell in the handle.

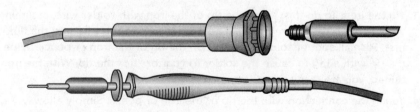

Figure 7.36. Soldering pencil.

Three types of tips are commonly used for soldering irons and pencils: spade, chisel, and needle (Figure 7.39). Any of these can be used for any soldering job.

Soldering guns are popular with many hobbyists. The trigger of the gun activates a transformer within the unit, and heat is generated through induction.

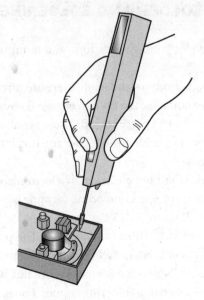

Figure 7.37. Portable soldering pencil.

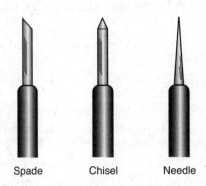

Spade   Chisel   Needle

Figure 7.38. Tips commonly used for soldering irons and pencils.

To form a solder connection, follow these steps:

1. Clean the soldering iron or pencil.

2. Make sure the connection to be soldered is clean.

3. Tin the iron. To do this, touch the tip of the iron with solder wire, assuming you are using rosin-core solder. If not, dip the tip of the wire into the flux first. A small spot of solder will form on the tip of the iron or pencil. Wipe the tip with a rag to cause the solder to coat or "tin" the tip. With the iron tinned, you are ready to solder.

4. Touch the connection with the tip of the iron or pencil. Simply allow the solder to flow into the connection. The flowing solder makes the connection.

5. Check the quality of your work. A good solder connection should be clean and shiny. There should be no cracks. If the solder is cracked or dull, this indicates a cold solder connection. A cold solder connection is unsatisfactory and should be reheated. Also, be careful that the solder does not bridge. Bridging occurs when solder runs across copper strips along a printed circuit board. This can cause a short circuit.

PRACTICE QUESTIONS

1. A galvanic cell

   (A) converts mechanical energy to chemical energy.
   (B) converts chemical energy to potential energy.
   (C) converts electrical energy to chemical energy.
   (D) converts chemical energy to electrical energy.

2. Once a _____ cell is discharged, _____.

   (A) secondary, one or both electrodes are consumed so the cell is no longer usable.
   (B) primary, one or both electrodes are consumed so the cell is no longer usable.
   (C) polarized, electron flow can be reversed and the cell can be used again.
   (D) thyristor, electron flow can be reversed and the cell can be used again.

3. An electric motor

   (A) changes chemical energy into electrical energy for storage.
   (B) changes electrical energy into mechanical energy to do work.
   (C) changes electromechanical energy into torque to do work.
   (D) changes potential energy into chemical energy to produce torque.

4. _____ check voltage, _____ check current, and _____ check resistance.

   (A) Voltmeters, watt-hour meters, ohmmeters
   (B) Voltmeters, ohmmeters, ammeters
   (C) Voltmeters, ammeters, ohmmeters
   (D) Voltmeters, ohmmeters, multimeters

5. Transducers convert _____ to electrical energy.

   (A) sound, light, heat, or pressure
   (B) chemical energy or pressure
   (C) light, heat, or magnetism
   (D) sine waves, pressure, or sound

6. A battery is a device that

   (A) converts mechanical energy to chemical energy.
   (B) converts chemical energy to electrical energy.
   (C) converts mechanical energy to electrical energy.
   (D) releases input-stored mechanical energy to an electrical plate.

7. The higher resolution of high-definition television (HDTV) as compared to a standard TV results from

   (A) bigger scan lines.
   (B) smaller gaps between scan lines.
   (C) higher operating cycles.
   (D) the use of greater amounts of bandwidth.

Answers Explained

1. **(D)** A galvanic cell *converts chemical energy to electrical energy*. A galvanic cell (also known as a *voltaic cell*) is an electrochemical cell that uses the transfer of electrons in oxidation-reduction reactions to supply an electric current. It generally consists of two different metals connected by a salt bridge. A galvanic cell can instead be individual half-cells separated by a porous membrane.

2. **(B)** Once a *primary* cell is discharged, *one or both electrodes are consumed so the cell is no longer usable*. In other words, a primary cell cannot be recharged.

3. **(B)** An electric motor *changes electrical energy into mechanical energy to do work.*

4. **(C)** *Voltmeters* check voltage, *ammeters* check current, and *ohmmeters* check resistance.

5. **(A)** Transducers convert *sound, light, heat, or pressure* to electrical energy. Some common examples of transducers are microphones, loudspeakers, digital thermometers, and pressure sensors.

6. **(B)** A battery is a device that *converts chemical energy to electrical energy.*

7. **(B)** The higher resolution of high-definition television (HDTV) as compared to a standard TV results from *smaller gaps between scan lines.* These smaller gaps therefore allow more scan lines to be on the screen at one time (1,080 in an HDTV vs. 525 in a standard TV).

Automotive Information Review

8

The CAT-ASVAB separates Automotive and Shop Information into two subtests, but they are combined on the paper-and-pencil version. Regardless of which version you take, though, the automotive-related questions the ASVAB asks you will be fairly basic. So, it's time to close the book and go see a movie, right?

And besides, *everybody* knows about cars, right?

Maybe. Maybe not.

This chapter will review some information that you probably already know. But, unless you're already a school-trained auto mechanic, it's just as likely that you will learn some things in this chapter. This chapter goes over the basic parts of an automobile and how they operate, discusses some basic mechanical principles as they apply to the internal combustion engine, and, finally, provides you with a guide to recognizing common problems that may occur with a car or truck.

Now, if you're extremely weak in math, or you can't spell your way out of a wet paper bag, you may honestly be better off focusing the time you have available on those sections, instead of this one. Those will affect your AFQT score, which determine whether you get into the military at all.

But, if you believe you're doing OK in those areas, get in and buckle up.

Fundamentally, an automobile is a compartment mounted on wheels with a self-contained means for propelling it over the ground. "Left" and "right" are determined by your perspective as you are sitting in the driver's seat.

The very least we need to make an automobile go is an engine and some means of connecting the engine—and the power it provides—to the wheels. Generally speaking, the engine turns a shaft that connects to the front or rear pair of wheels, or both. The shaft has a gear on the end that meshes with a gear on the axle connecting the drive wheels together. As the first shaft turns, it rotates the axle and the wheels propel the car. If there were no hills around, and we didn't want to go very fast or turn any corners, this arrangement might work. But in an actual automobile, we have some more parts between the engine and the wheels.

THE ENGINE

The power of an automobile engine comes from the burning of a mixture of gasoline and air in a small, confined space. When this mixture burns, it expands greatly and pushes out in all directions very rapidly—so rapidly that when it happens in an uncontrolled or open environment, this rapid burning is more usually known as an explosion. This push or pressure can be used to move a part of the engine, and the movement of this part is eventually transmitted to the wheels to move the car.

Almost all engines operate on the same basic principles and with the same kinds of basic parts. The biggest difference between the different types of automobiles today is whether the vehicle's power is sent to the front wheels (front-wheel drive), the rear wheels (rear-wheel drive), or both (all-wheel or four-wheel drive). Most of today's cars are either front-wheel or all-wheel drive, but not all. Most of the parts—especially when it comes to the engine itself—are otherwise pretty much the same.

Now, all this is not to say that there is only one kind of internal combustion engine. Most of today's cars use a four-stroke gasoline engine, but there are diesel engines and gas turbine engines, which take fuels that are different from gasoline and function differently than a gasoline engine. Also, there are rotary engines and two-stroke engines that take gasoline like a four-stroke engine, but do different things with that fuel.

Most of these variations, however, have more similarities than differences—and they all have their own particular advantages and disadvantages. That said, we're going to concentrate primarily on four-stroke gas engines because they are the most common—and because they are most likely what the ASVAB is going to ask you about.

First, let's go over some terminology. To start with, an *engine* is any machine that uses energy to develop mechanical power, while a *motor* is a machine that converts electrical energy into mechanical energy. This means that a car or truck uses an engine, rather than a motor, to move the wheels and make the car go. However, lots of people use the terms interchangeably (but you know better now, right?).

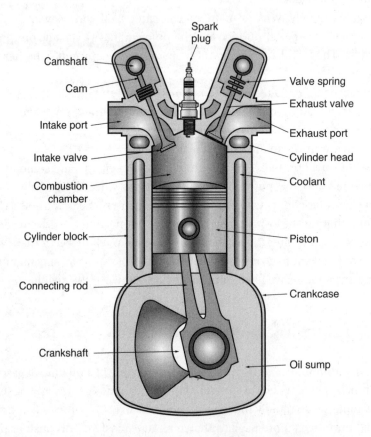

Cutaway view of internal combustion engine.

Most cars use what is called a *four-stroke combustion cycle* to convert gasoline into motion. This four-stroke approach is known as the Otto Cycle after Nikolaus Otto, who invented the first practical four-stroke engine in 1876. The four strokes are the *intake* stroke, the *compression* stroke, the *combustion* stroke, and the *exhaust* stroke.

But, first things first. Going from the inside out, we have a *cylinder* where the controlled explosion, known as *combustion*, takes place; that's why the cylinder is also known as the *combustion chamber*.

Inside the cylinder there is a *piston*, which is a close-fitting plug that can slide up and down easily in the cylinder—think of the top of the piston as the movable floor in the combustion chamber. The piston is connected to the *crankshaft* by a *connecting rod*. Look at the cutaway, and picture the crankshaft turning in a clockwise direction. When it turns, it either pulls down or pushes up the piston in the cylinder, depending on where in its circular cycle the crankshaft is.

When the piston is as high within the cylinder as it can go, the intake valve opens and the piston moves down, which allows the engine to take in a full cylinder's worth of fuel and air (remember, air is an essential component for things to burn, including gasoline). Fuel sprays into the chamber through a valve that functions as an automatic "door" in the top of the cylinder. The fuel/air mixture is mostly air and only a little fuel; this is called the *intake stroke*.

As the crankshaft comes around its circle again, it moves the piston (the "movable floor") back up in the cylinder, which compresses the fuel/air mixture to about 600 or 700 psi. This is the *compression* stroke. When you hear or read something about "compression ratio," it has to do with how much the piston squeezes the mixture in the cylinder before igniting it. The more the mixture is compressed, the more power results. If the cylinder holds 100 cubic inches when the piston is all the way down in its lowest position, and 10 cubic inches when the piston is up as far as it can go, we say the compression ratio is 10 to 1—the mixture has been compressed into a space 10 times as small as it originally occupied. Fifty years ago 4 to 1 was a common compression ratio for automobile engines, but today's typical compression ratios range upward of eight to one (8:1).

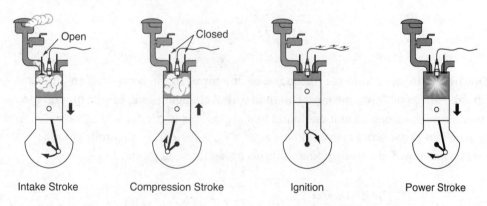

Intake Stroke   Compression Stroke   Ignition   Power Stroke

When the piston reaches the top of its stroke—when the fuel/air mixture is as compressed as it's going to get—the spark plug emits a spark to ignite the mixture, which causes a controlled explosion. This explosion causes outward pressure in all directions inside the chamber, but only the bottom "floor" of the cylinder—the piston—can move, so it gets pushed downward, making the *combustion* stroke.

Once the piston hits the bottom of its stroke, the exhaust valve opens, letting the exhaust leave the cylinder and eventually exit the engine via the tailpipe. There are also intake and exhaust valves in the top of the cylinder. Metal disks fit tightly over the holes to close them, but when pushed down, they open the holes to allow passage of the gases through them. This lets out the burned gases and lets fresh air in to begin the combustion cycle all over again. This, then, is the *exhaust* stroke.

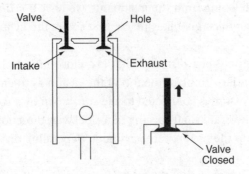

Now the engine is ready for its next cycle, so it takes in another cylinder-full of air and fuel. To change the up-and-down motion of the pistons to rotary motion to move the car, there is a connecting rod and a crankshaft. The *crankshaft*, below the pistons, looks like a straight rod with a series of bends—called throws—in it, one for each cylinder. A *connecting rod* connects the bottom of the piston to one of the throws in the crankshaft. The top end of the connecting rod is fastened to the piston, so it goes up and down in a straight line. The bottom end is fastened to the crank, so that end has to go around in a circle as the piston moves up and down.

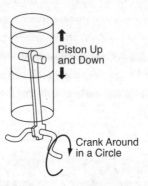

Downward pressure from the piston rotates the throw in the crankshaft and thus rotates the crankshaft itself. This is the most common way of changing straight-line motion to rotary motion. Familiar examples of it are found in a kitchen meat grinder and in a bicycle. In the latter, the foot pedal is the crank, and the rider's leg is the connecting rod. The rider's knee moves up and down in a straight line while his or her foot goes around in a circle.

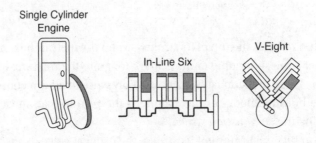

On one end of the crankshaft is a heavy wheel called the *flywheel*. If we turn a grindstone rapidly by hand and then let go, the wheel will keep on rotating. This is the same action as that of the flywheel. Its momentum keeps the engine turning between power impulses from the combustion in each cylinder.

These are the basic parts of an engine. However, these parts would make only a single-cylinder engine. All automobile engines today have at least three, and usually four or more, cylinders; motorcycles and other smaller engines often have just two. They can be arranged in one straight row, which we call an *in-line engine*, or in two rows set at an angle, described as a *V-type engine* (so a V-8 engine is one with eight cylinders: four cylinders set in two rows at an angle to each other). In either case there is only one crankshaft, but it has a number of cranks instead of only one. With more cylinders, the flywheel does not have such a big job to do because the power impulses occur more often and thus keep the crankshaft turning. By simply timing the controlled explosions (combustion) in each cylinder and placing the crankshaft throws at the appropriate angles, the crankshaft's rotation can be controlled so that it isn't fighting itself and all the cylinders are firing in the proper sequence—making a smooth, continuous cycle.

The valves in the top of each cylinder mentioned earlier are controlled by rocker arms and rods, which are moved by a camshaft. This is a shaft with *cams* or bumps on it—one for each valve—that push up on the rods to open the valves. The camshaft is driven by the crankshaft at one-half speed. The cams are accurately shaped and located, and the shaft rotates at just the proper speed, so that the valves open and close at exactly the right time and in the right sequence.

ENGINE IGNITION

To start the fuel/air mixture burning in the cylinder, we need a spark. The two main functions of the *ignition system* are to provide a high-voltage spark for combustion and to furnish the means to time the engine. A *spark plug* is inserted in the top of each cylinder, and a spark is created by electricity jumping across the gap between the two electrodes of the plug. The *battery*, using a 60 percent to 40 percent water-sulfuric acid mixture, furnishes the electricity, but several additional pieces of equipment are necessary for a complete ignition system.

The *coil* and the *breaker* cooperate to develop a very high voltage, and the *distributor* is responsible for getting the high-voltage electricity to the right spark plug at the right time. On a conventional ignition coil, the two small studs at the top of the coil are the primary or low-voltage terminals; the center tower is the secondary or high-voltage terminal. The ignition circuit has to transform 12 volts from the battery into more than 20,000 volts. It also has to deliver this high-voltage spark to the spark plugs at just the right time. The spark plug leads must be installed in the correct tower of the distributor cap to ensure the proper firing order. The firing order is the order in which the spark plugs ignite the fuel/air mixture in the cylinder or combustion chamber. A typical firing order for a six-cylinder engine is 1-5-3-6-2-4.

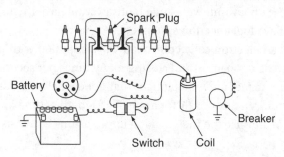

However, to lower and control voltage to the ignition coil, the ignition system has a resistor located between the ignition switch and the coil. This prevents the coil from burning out.

All of this must take place very rapidly. In an eight-cylinder engine driving a car 55 miles an hour, the ignition system has to furnish about 7,350 sparks per minute, or 123 sparks each second. And it must do this at exactly the right time and without a miss.

The valve mechanism and ignition system must perform their duties at just the right time because the engine operates with a certain definite cycle of events—over and over again, at a high rate of speed.

CARBURETORS AND FUEL PUMPS

In order to produce power, the engine needs a supply of gasoline and air mixed in the proper proportions. Up until the early 1980s, a mechanism known as a *carburetor* did the mixing job. Gasoline was pumped from the tank to the carburetor by the fuel pump, working in much the same way as an old-fashioned water pump—each stroke pushing a little fuel onto the carburetor, where it went first to the float chamber. Air entered the carburetor through the air cleaner, being pulled in by the pumping action of the pistons working in the cylinders.

The air flowed through a *venturi* (a reduced-width passage in the carburetor that made the flow speed up) at high speed, then past the end of a tube leading from the float chamber. This sucked the fuel out into the airstream, breaking the liquid up into a fine mist and mixing it thoroughly with the air (an atomizer or garden sprayer works in a similar way). Then the fuel/air mixture went on into the engine, controlled by a throttle valve at the base of the carburetor, which was opened or closed by the movement of the accelerator pedal.

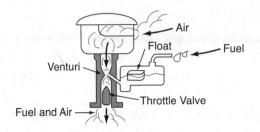

Although carburetors are rare on today's cars, many ASVAB questions have been around for a while. So you should be familiar with this information—and therefore be better prepared for the exam.

In the 1980s, automakers developed electronically controlled carburetors that integrated the sophisticated electronics used in electronic fuel injection with the basic carburetor. The primary difference between a basic carburetor and an electronic carburetor is the addition of an electrically operated device called a *fuel solenoid*, an electronically controlled valve used to regulate the amount of fuel delivered to the engine through the main metering circuit.

FUEL INJECTION SYSTEMS

1990 was the last year that a new car sold in the United States had a carburetor. Smaller engines such as those on lawnmowers and chainsaws still have them, but all cars sold in the United States now have fuel injection systems.

A fuel injector is an electronically controlled valve supplied with pressurized fuel by the fuel pump. It is capable of opening and closing many times per second. When the injector is energized, an electromagnet moves a plunger that opens the valve, allowing the pressurized fuel to squirt out through a tiny nozzle for a specified length of time, called a *pulse width*. The nozzle is designed to atomize the fuel, making it into as fine a mist as possible so that it can burn efficiently.

The environmental awareness trends in the 1960s and 1970s led to stricter exhaust emission requirements, which ushered in the catalytic converter, a device that reduces the carbon monoxide, unburned hydrocarbons, and other pollutants in the car's exhaust.

One result of reducing the car's exhaust byproducts, though, was an increased interest in improving fuel efficiency. This eventually led to today's hand-in-hand system of electronic fuel injection working with the catalytic converter and an oxygen sensor between it and the engine to keep the fuel/air ratio as close to ideal as possible—meaning that, theoretically, all the fuel in the mixture burns using all the oxygen in the mixture. For gasoline, this ideal ratio—called the *stoichiometric point*—is about 14.7:1, meaning that for each pound of gasoline, 14.7 pounds of air is burned during the combustion process.

The types of fuel injection used in today's cars include *single-point* or *throttle body injection* (TBI); *port* or *multi-point fuel injection* (MPFI); *sequential fuel injection* (SFI); and *direct injection*.

Throttle body injection is the oldest and simplest type of fuel injection. It replaces the carburetor with one or two fuel-injector nozzles in the throttle body, which is the throat of the engine's air intake manifold. Although TBI is not as precise as the systems that have followed, it regulates fuel better than a carburetor and is less expensive and easier to service.

Multi-point fuel injection devotes a separate injector nozzle to each cylinder, right outside its intake port, which is why the system is sometimes called port injection. MPFI measures fuel more precisely than TBI designs, improving the air/fuel ratio and fuel economy. Also, it virtually eliminates the possibility that fuel will condense or collect in the intake manifold, which was an issue with TBI and carburetor design.

Sequential fuel injection, also called sequential port fuel injection (SPFI) or timed injection, is a type of multi-port injection. Although basic MPFI uses multiple injectors, they all spray their fuel at the same time or in groups. As a result, the fuel may "hang around" a port for as long as 150 milliseconds when the engine is idling—this may not seem like a big deal, but it's enough to be improved upon. Sequential fuel injection triggers each injector nozzle independently. Timed like spark plugs, they spray fuel just before or just as their intake valve opens, increasing efficiency and decreasing emissions by another small step.

The direct injection method injects fuel directly into the combustion chambers, past the valves. More common in diesel engines, direct injection is starting to be seen in gasoline engine designs. Fuel regulation here is even more precise than in the other injection methods, and the direct injection gives engineers yet another variable to influence precisely how combustion occurs in the cylinders.

Fuel is delivered to the injectors by *fuel rails*, which are attached to the tops of the valve bodies and in which fuel is kept at a constant, predetermined pressure. Generally with V-type engines, the fuel rail is divided into two parts, each of which serves half the total number of valves. The two parts are usually assembled so that one pressure regulator that is integral to the complete assembly serves both halves.

FUEL PUMPS AND REGULATORS

Most cars have two electric *fuel pumps*. The first, located in the fuel tank, is generally a diaphragm-type booster pump that is integral with the fuel gauge and a simple, replaceable-element filter. The second, located in the fuel line ahead of the pressure regulator, is usually a roller-vane pump driven by a motor and designed to produce a constant displacement. This second pump has a check valve (one-way pressure-opened) at the output side that prevents backflow to maintain pressure in the line when the pump is not operating. The pump is usually generally contained within a compact housing mounted inside the engine compartment and connected by an electrical harness to the other components of the system. It is a nonserviceable unit that must be replaced if it becomes faulty.

Because the second fuel pump operates continuously at maximum output, regardless of engine speed or load, the engine seldom requires all the fuel the pump makes available. The pressure regulator returns excess fuel through a bypass line back to the tank to maintain a constant pressure in the fuel rail.

ELECTRONIC CONTROL UNIT

In order to provide the correct amount of fuel for every operating condition, the engine control unit (ECU) has to monitor a wide variety of input sensors, including:

- **MASS AIRFLOW SENSOR:** Tells the ECU the mass of the air entering the engine.
- **OXYGEN SENSOR(S):** Monitors the amount of oxygen in the exhaust so the ECU can determine how rich or lean (compared to the ideal) the fuel mixture is and make adjustments accordingly.
- **THROTTLE POSITION SENSOR:** Monitors the throttle valve position (which determines how much air goes into the engine) so the ECU can respond quickly to changes, increasing or decreasing the fuel flow as needed.
- **COOLANT TEMPERATURE SENSOR:** Allows the ECU to determine when the engine has reached its proper operating temperature.
- **VOLTAGE SENSOR:** Monitors the car's system voltage so the ECU can raise the idle speed if voltage drops, indicating a high electrical load.
- **MANIFOLD ABSOLUTE PRESSURE SENSOR:** Monitors air pressure in the intake manifold, which allows the ECU to calculate how much power is being produced because the amount of air being drawn into the engine is a good indication of how much power it is producing.
- **ENGINE SPEED SENSOR:** Monitors engine speed, one of the factors used to calculate the pulse width for the fuel injectors.

COOLING THE ENGINE

When the fuel and air mix and burn in the cylinder of an engine, it creates a temperature of 4,000–4,500°F. This is almost twice the temperature at which iron melts. Without a cooling system, no engine would last very long.

The usual way of cooling an engine is to put water jackets around the hottest parts. Water is constantly circulated through these jackets by a small pump. The heat of the cylinder makes the water hot, which then goes to the radiator where it is cooled by the outside air passing through. Then it starts back to the engine again to do more cooling.

Using antifreeze in the radiator both makes the cooling more efficient and makes it harder for the liquid to freeze up in cold weather when the engine's not running. Since water expands when it becomes ice, it's desirable to avoid having your radiator coolant freeze.

LUBRICATING THE ENGINE

The engine also needs a lubrication system. If all the rotating and reciprocating parts were running metal against metal with no film of oil between them to reduce friction, they would soon heat up and stick, or "seize." The friction would also make it harder for the parts to turn. Therefore, there is a reservoir of oil in the crankcase; a pump forces it from the crankcase to the bearings and other critical points in the engine. Some of it flows through tubes, and some through passages drilled in the crankshaft and connecting rods. The lubrication system might be compared to the water system in a house. The liquid is forced from one central place through pipes to many different locations where it is needed.

STARTING THE ENGINE

All of what we've talked about so far has taken the perspective that the engine is already running. Now let's look at how to get it started in the first place.

The engine has to be turning over before it can run under its own power, and it gets this initial start from an electric motor called the starter. The starter is an electric motor that engages, spins, and disengages the engine's flywheel in order to start the engine.

Another important piece of electrical equipment is the alternator. It looks something like the starter motor, but its job is just the opposite. Instead of taking electricity from the battery to start the engine, the alternator is driven by the engine and generates electric current that feeds back into the battery to keep it charged for starting. The alternator also supplies power for the ignition system, lights, radio, and other electrical units. There are two slip rings mounted on the alternator's rotor shaft. Two brushes ride on the slip rings and deliver electrical energy to the rotor windings. Therefore, the magnetic field within an alternator is produced by the rotor.

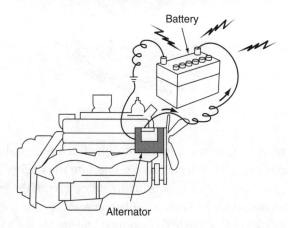

Battery

Alternator

There is a resistor known as a *ballast resistor* that is inserted in series with the ignition coil; its purpose is to drop the 12-volt battery power supply to 6 volts, which is the voltage for which the coil was designed. This allows for the lower voltage from the battery when you crank up the vehicle; the coil can then produce the high voltage it needs for the spark plugs.

CONTROLLING ENGINE EMISSIONS

So far, we have put together a complete automobile engine—at least enough parts of one so that it will start and keep on running. But before we talk about how power from the engine is sent to the wheels to drive the car, let's look briefly at the systems used to control the emission of pollutants into the atmosphere.

Three major pollutants are emitted from automobiles into the atmosphere—hydrocarbons, carbon monoxide, and oxides of nitrogen. Hydrocarbons, which we can think of as essentially unburned gasoline, come from the exhaust pipe and the engine's crankcase as a result of the combustion process. They also enter the atmosphere from the fuel system through an evaporation process. Carbon monoxide (CO) results from partially burned fuel when rich fuel/air mixtures do not allow complete combustion all the way to carbon dioxide (CO_2). Oxides of nitrogen, on the other hand, are gases formed during combustion due to the high temperatures.

Modern autos have built-in systems designed to reduce the three major types of pollutants. The systems may vary somewhat among different makes of cars, but they all work to perform the same job—reducing emissions of hydrocarbons, carbon monoxide, and oxides of nitrogen.

The first emission control applied to automobile engines was called the *positive crankcase ventilation* (PCV) system. This system, introduced in the early 1960s, is still in use today. During the compression strokes of the pistons, small amounts of gasoline vapor are forced past the piston rings out of the combustion chamber and into the engine crankcase. These infinitesimal amounts of vapor expelled during each engine cycle would add up to significant quantities of hydrocarbon (HC) emissions if they were allowed to enter the atmosphere. They aren't, however, because the PCV system directs these vapors back into the intake system so that they are burned in the combustion chambers. The system also increases gas mileage since the fuel vapors are not lost but are burned in the engine.

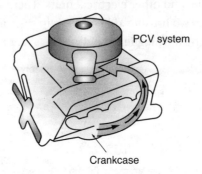

PCV system

Crankcase

Another system—*air injection*—helps control hydrocarbon and carbon monoxide (CO) emissions in the exhaust. Air is injected by a pump into the engine's exhaust ports to cause further burning of the hot gasoline vapors before they pass out the exhaust pipe.

As government emission standards have become more strict, engineers and scientists have had to find new ways to achieve the required control. At the same time, they have had to come up with systems that would provide good fuel economy and not affect a vehicle's smooth operation.

The result was the development of a device called a *catalytic converter*, which was first introduced on most 1975-model cars made in the United States. This emission control system oxidizes hydrocarbons and carbon monoxide into harmless water vapor and carbon dioxide as the exhaust gases pass through a canister containing pellets coated with a catalyst material. A *catalyst* promotes chemical reactions, allowing them to take place at much lower than normal temperatures and more rapidly than a chemical reaction ordinarily would proceed. In the case of the catalytic converter emission control system, this means that catalysts allow more nearly complete oxidation of hydrocarbons and carbon monoxide at a much lower temperature than ordinary burning.

The catalytic converter has played a major role in reducing the emission of hydrocarbons and carbon monoxide from vehicle exhausts into the atmosphere. It has also promoted improved fuel economy and has helped engineers tune the engine for a more pleasant, better-performing car to drive. However, it reaches high temperatures while it's doing its job and has to be shielded from the car body by a heat deflector. An air pump on most cars adds to the combustion that takes place inside the converter and helps to reduce the amount of nitrogen oxides coming from the exhaust pipe.

Although the present catalytic converter, an oxidizing converter, does an excellent job in controlling hydrocarbon and carbon monoxide emissions, it isn't effective in controlling oxides of nitrogen (NO_x), the third type of pollutant in exhaust gases. Oxides of nitrogen are different from hydrocarbons and carbon monoxide because they will not burn to harmless combustion products. Instead, controlling oxides of nitrogen in the engine exhaust usually requires doing something to prevent their formation. One way to do this is to dilute the air/fuel mixture as it enters the combustion chamber.

Oxides of nitrogen are formed any time there are very high temperatures in the oxidation process (usually above 3,000°F or 1,090°C) when air is used to provide the oxygen. Air contains 79 percent nitrogen and 21 percent oxygen, so you could say that air burns.

The formation of oxides of nitrogen in an engine is minimized by diluting the fuel/air mixture entering the combustion chamber. This helps reduce the peak combustion temperature. One system being used is called *exhaust gas recirculation* (EGR). With this system, small quantities of exhaust gases are recirculated back into the intake system of the engine to dilute the fuel/air mixture. Some other systems use a single catalytic converter to remove the majority of all three types of pollutants.

To reduce hydrocarbons that evaporate from the fuel system when the engine is not running, there's a system that vents gasoline vapors into a canister filled with carbon granules. These granules act like a sponge and soak up the fumes and store them while the car is parked. When the engine starts up, the fumes are fed back to the engine and burned.

Further control of exhaust emissions has been brought about within the engine by changing the shape of the combustion chambers, using a leaner air-to-fuel ratio (more air in the mixture that goes to the cylinders for combustion), regulating the temperature of the air entering the carburetor, increasing the speed at which the engine idles, and modifying spark timing for stop-and-go driving. These changes to the engine all combine to help achieve more complete combustion and decrease exhaust emissions.

PRACTICE QUESTIONS

1. What is a carburetor's main function?

    (A) To control the timing of the pistons
    (B) To provide the right mix of fuel and air to the engine
    (C) To keep the engine turning between power impulses from combustion in each cylinder
    (D) To control voltage to the ignition coil

2. What are the four strokes in the combustion cycle, in order?

   (A) Intake, ignition, compression, exhaust
   (B) Intake, compression, combustion, exhaust
   (C) Compression, combustion, intake, exhaust
   (D) Ignition, intake, compression, exhaust

3. The _____ change the up-and-down motion of the pistons into rotary motion.

   (A) rocker arms and rods
   (B) camshaft and valve heads
   (C) connecting rod and crankshaft
   (D) flywheel and crankshaft

4. An automobile's radiator is involved in

   (A) lubricating the engine.
   (B) atomizing fuel flow in the correct ratio.
   (C) pumping fuel from the tank to the engine.
   (D) cooling the engine.

5. The *primary* function of the alternator is to

   (A) generate electric current to feed back to the battery.
   (B) engage, spin, and disengage the flywheel.
   (C) control engine emissions by regulating combustion.
   (D) power the headlights and radio.

6. A starter armature is being tested on a growler. If you hold a hacksaw blade or other similar strip of metal (not aluminum or stainless steel) lengthwise against the armature and then rotate the armature, the blade vibrates. What does this indicate?

   (A) The field coils are grounded.
   (B) The solenoid disk is burned.
   (C) The armature is open.
   (D) The armature is shorted.

7. An ohmmeter test of an electronic ignition pickup coil indicates an infinite reading.

   What does this reading indicate?

   (A) A normal circuit
   (B) A short circuit
   (C) An open circuit
   (D) A grounded circuit

Answers Explained

1. **(B)** A carburetor's main function is *to provide the right mix of fuel and air to the engine.*

2. **(B)** The four strokes in the combustion cycle, in order, are *intake, compression, combustion,* and *exhaust.*

3. **(C)** The *connecting rod and crankshaft* change the up-and-down motion of the pistons into rotary motion.

4. **(D)** An automobile's radiator is involved in *cooling the engine.* The oil pump is involved in lubricating the engine. Either the carburetor or the fuel injection system atomize the fuel flow in the correct ratio for combustion. The fuel pump gets fuel from the tank to the engine.

5. **(A)** The *primary* function of the alternator is to *generate electric current to feed back to the battery.* The clutch, which is connected to the crankshaft, engages, spins, and disengages the flywheel. The emission control system controls engine emissions by regulating combustion. The battery powers the headlights and radio.

6. **(D)** When a hacksaw blade or other similar strip of metal is held lengthwise against a starter armature, is rotated, and then vibrates, *the armature is shorted.* Any started windings will create a magnetic field that attracts the metal strip to the slot where the started winding is. When this happens, the strip of metal vibrates, causing a growling noise. "Opens" in the armature are found by using the meter on the growler.

7. **(C)** An infinite reading on an ohmmeter test of an electronic ignition pickup coil indicates *an open circuit.* (An open circuit is also called an incomplete circuit.) A short circuit would be indicated by a lower than normal reading.

AXLES AND WHEELS

The *axles* are relatively slender steel shafts. They have a flange at the outer end to which the wheel and brake drum are bolted. Around the axle is the axle housing. This holds the parts of the brake that do not turn with the wheel and supports the bearing in which the outer end of the axle shaft runs.

The wheel itself is essentially a metal disk with a rim around the outside into which the tire fits. It is the outside surface of the tire that pushes on the ground and really makes a car move. But the engine furnishes the force, and all the other things just mentioned have a certain part of the job to do in getting that force from one place to the other.

Tracking, in terms of wheel alignment, means that the rear wheels follow the front wheels correctly. Tracking is correct when both rear wheels are parallel to, and the same distance from, the vehicle centerline (an imaginary line drawn down the center of the vehicle). A bent frame or twisted body structure can cause improper tracking.

However—and this can be just a little confusing—a vehicle's *track* is measured from the center of the left wheel to the center of the right wheel.

Tires are rated in several areas, and it's important to have the right kind of tires for your car and the conditions you drive in. The rating is listed on the tire's sidewall. For instance, if your sidewall reads, "P 185/70 R 14," this is what it all means:

P designates a passenger car tire, as opposed to a tire made for a truck or other vehicle. P-metric is the U.S. version of a metric tire-sizing system.

185 is the section width. This is the width of the tire in millimeters from sidewall to sidewall. This measurement varies depending on the width of the rim to which a tire is fitted—larger on a wide rim, smaller on a narrow rim. The number on the tire shows the width measured when the tire is fitted to the recommended rim width.

70 is the aspect ratio, the ratio of height to width. This tire's height is 70 percent of its width.

R refers to construction, how the plies are constructed in the body of the tire. R indicates a radial; B means the tire has belted bias construction; D means diagonal bias construction.

14 is the rim diameter—the diameter of the wheel in inches.

It's important to keep your tires inflated to the proper pounds per square inch (psi). When a tire is underinflated, the center area of the tread moves upward as the sidewalls flex. This abnormal action places undue and unnecessary stress on the tire, causing excess wear to both outside edges. It also decreases the traction and worsens the gas mileage.

Shock absorbers are cylinders connected to each wheel that use hydraulic fluid to lessen the up-and-down movement of the wheel (and therefore the vehicle) caused by traveling over uneven road surfaces. A car with worn-out shock absorbers will bounce a lot on a rough road.

THE BRAKING SYSTEM

We've shown how to get the car to move, but an equally important point is to be able to stop it. This is done by the *brakes*—one in each of the four wheels—which are simply a method of applying friction to the rotating wheels to stop them. It's like rubbing a stick against the rim of the wheels on a kid's wagon.

There are two types of brake systems—drum brake and disc brake. In the *drum brake system,* two stationary brake shoes covered with a special friction material (called the brake lining) are forced outward by hydraulic pressure against the inside of a metal drum that rotates with the wheel. A system of steel tubes filled with hydraulic fluid (brake fluid) runs from a master cylinder to each brake. When the driver steps on the brake pedal, pressure is built up in the master cylinder and this pressure is transmitted through the tubes, called brake lines, to pistons located inside a hydraulic cylinder in each wheel. The pistons move outward and push the shoes against the brake drum. As a safety feature, most cars have a dual master cylinder that provides two independent hydraulic systems, one for the front wheels and one for the rear wheels.

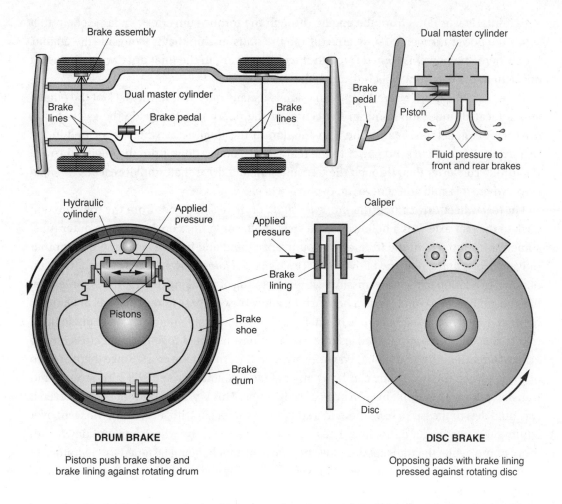

DRUM BRAKE

Pistons push brake shoe and
brake lining against rotating drum

DISC BRAKE

Opposing pads with brake lining
pressed against rotating disc

In the *disc brake system*, the brake lining is bonded to brake shoes positioned on each side of a rotating disc located in the wheel. When the brake pedal is applied, hydraulic pressure transmitted from the dual master cylinder causes a caliper to clamp the opposing shoes against the disc—it's like taking your thumb and forefinger and squeezing them together against a rotating plate. However, if air gets into the hydraulic brake system, the brake pedal action will be spongy or soft because air is much more compressible than hydraulic fluid.

Brakes are friction devices that convert work into heat, and the amount of heat created by the brakes during a fast stop from a high speed is very significant. Because of this, proper cooling of the brakes is an important consideration during their design.

SHAFTS AND UNIVERSAL JOINTS

Most of today's cars are front-wheel drive, whereas 30 or more years ago it was the other way around. Unsurprisingly, this affects a number of systems, including how the engine power is transformed and transmitted to the wheels.

On a front-wheel-drive car, what would be called the "transmission" in a rear-wheel drive vehicle is usually combined with the final drive to form what is called a *transaxle*. The engine on a front-wheel-drive car is usually mounted sideways, with the transaxle tucked under it on the side of the engine facing the rear of the car. The front axles are connected directly to the transaxle and provide power to the front wheels via driveshafts linked by *constant velocity*

(CV) joints. Power flows from the engine through the torque converter to a large chain that sends the power through a 180-degree turn to the transmission that is alongside the engine. From there, the power is routed through the transmission to the final drive where it is split and sent to the two front wheels through the drive axles.

On a rear-wheel-drive car, the transmission is usually mounted to the back of the engine and is located under the hump in the center of the floorboard alongside the gas pedal. A driveshaft connects the rear of the transmission to the *final drive*, which is located in the rear axle and is used to send power to the rear wheels. Power flows from the engine through the torque converter then through the transmission and drive shaft until it reaches the final drive, where it is split and sent to the two rear wheels.

For rear-wheel-drive autos, the *propeller shaft*, or drive shaft, goes from the transmission back to the rear axle. It is a hollow or solid steel shaft, sometimes enclosed in an outer tube, sometimes left open. At the front end is a universal joint, and in many cars there is another universal joint at the rear end of the shaft. The *universal joint* allows the rear axle to move up or down in relation to the transmission without bending or breaking the shaft. It is something like the gimbals of a compass on a boat, which allow the compass to remain level at all times no matter how much the boat rolls or pitches. These universal joints are usually made up of two U-shaped pieces at right angles to each other and fastened together by a cross having arms of equal lengths. The U-shaped yokes pivot on the arms of the cross. Since there are two of these pivots, the two shafts can be at an angle to one another and still turn around and transmit power. They don't have to be in a straight line. This is very important because even if we could design the car to have them in a straight line to begin with, every time we went over a bump they would get out of line. The rear axle moves with the wheels, up and down with every bump, while the transmission does not move as much, being fastened to the frame. So the universal joint lets the propeller shaft keep on turning even though its two ends are moving around relative to each other.

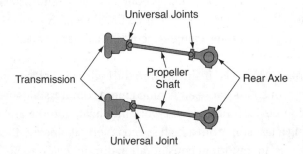

Fastened at the rear end of the propeller shaft is a short shaft carrying a gear on the end. This is a bevel gear and is called the *pinion*. It meshes with the *ring gear*, which is mounted on the rear axle. The job of the pinion and ring gear combination, or *final drive* as it often is called, is to take the torque provided by the propeller shaft, increase it, and turn it at right angles so that it can twist the wheels and drive the car.

For many years these rear axle gears were of the spiral bevel type. But now most cars use what are called *hypoid gears*. These are about the same as spiral bevel gears, except that the pinion does not meet the ring gear at its centerline. It meets it at a lower point, which means that the shape of the teeth must be different. This allows the propeller shaft to be lowered and, in turn, the overall car height.

Since the pinion is much smaller than the ring gear, we know immediately that there is a speed reduction here, and an increase in torque. In today's passenger cars the rear axle ratios generally average about 3 to 1. The axles and wheels turn only about one-third as fast as the propeller shaft. It should be noted that this speed reduction and torque increase are always there and always stay the same. Even when we say that we are in direct drive, we are referring only to the transmission, and its rear axle ratio is still effective. And if the transmission is in low gear, say a ratio of 3 to 1 (it is actually less than this in most of today's cars), the overall ratio between the engine and rear wheels will be 3×3 (or 9), to 1.

THE DRIVE SYSTEM

The first thing needed in the *drive system* is a device that will completely disconnect the engine from the drive wheels and the rest of the power transmission system. This allows the engine to run when the car is standing still, instead of having to turn the engine completely off whenever we stop. And it would be a problem to start the engine while it is connected to the drive system. Also, with manual shift transmissions, we have to disconnect it from the engine to shift gears easily.

There are various ways in which we could take care of these problems, but we need something else. We need something that will take hold gradually, that will not jump abruptly from no connection at all to a direct, solid connection. When we want to start a car, we have to speed the engine up to get enough power to move it. At the same time the wheels are standing still. We cannot, in one moment, bring the speed of the wheels up to the speed of the engine; there would be a terrible jerk. And when we shift gears after the car is moving, we have almost the same situation—the wheels and propeller shaft are not turning at the same speed as the engine. So we want something that will slip a little, that will take hold gently at first and gradually grab harder and harder. Thus the rear wheels can start to move slowly and gradually pick up speed until finally everything is turning at the same rate and the clutch is solidly engaged. From then on, of course, we do not want any slipping because that just wastes power and heats things up.

The kind of clutch we are talking about depends on friction for transmitting power. In fact, its full name is *friction clutch*, as there are other types of devices commonly called clutches.

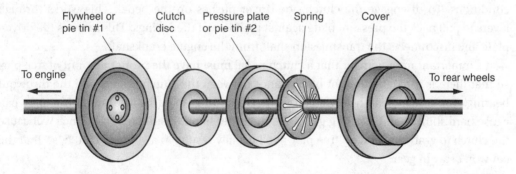

Suppose we mount two ordinary pie plates or tins, each on a shaft, as shown. As long as they are not touching each other, we can spin one as fast as we want to without affecting the other at all. But if we move them together when one of them is spinning, the other will begin to turn and almost immediately both shafts will start turning together as one unit. This is the general operating principle of the disc, or friction, clutch used in automobiles with manual transmissions. The discs are forced together by strong springs and are separated by pushing down on the clutch pedal in the driver's compartment. It is sometimes said that a good clutch must slip while being engaged and must not slip when it is engaged.

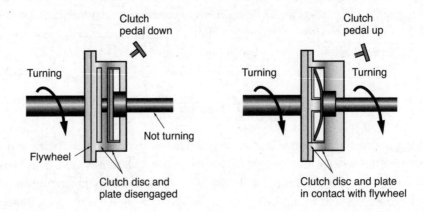

In most automobiles the clutch consists of one plate squeezed tightly between two other plates. The one in the middle is the driven member; it is connected to a shaft leading back into the transmission. The other two are the driving members; they are connected directly to the engine. A strong spring, or springs, forces the two driving members together. This tightens their grip on the middle plate until they are all turning together as one unit.

The *engine flywheel* is used for the first driving member. Its surface is made very smooth where the driven plate pushes up against it. The other driving member is called the *pressure plate*. It is a fairly heavy ring of cast iron that is smooth on one side. It is fastened to the cover, which is bolted to the flywheel, so they all turn together. It is fastened in such a way that it can slide back and forth. The driven plate is a flat disc of steel with friction facing fastened on each side. The plate is fastened by splines to a shaft going to the transmission. This means it fits into grooves on the shaft so that they must turn together, but the plate can slide forward and backward on the shaft. A series of coil springs, or sometimes one large, flat spring, are present between the clutch cover and the pressure plate. They push the pressure plate toward the flywheel, squeezing the driven plate between the two. The springs are always trying to engage the clutch, and they are strong enough to keep it from slipping under ordinary conditions. To disengage the clutch, the driver pushes on the pedal. This works through levers to pull back the pressure plate against the force of the springs. This loosens the driven plate and disconnects the transmission shaft from the engine crankshaft.

It's important to remember that a clutch pedal must have the proper amount of free play so that there is the right amount of clearance between the clutch fingers and the throwout bearing. Too much clearance will cause the clutch to grab early. Too much free play can cause hard shifting and clashing gears. On the other hand, insufficient clearance will cause the clutch to grab late, and no free play at all usually results in a slipping clutch, so that the car won't stay in gear.

There have been many different designs of clutches in the past, and the present ones don't all look just like what we have shown. Sometimes more than one driven plate is used, with a corresponding increase in the number of driving plates—and there may be other differences. But they all work on the same principle.

Cars equipped with automatic transmissions do not have a friction clutch or clutch pedal. We will discuss those shortly, but first we will cover the manual shift type transmission and drive system.

MANUAL TRANSMISSIONS

A *transmission* is used in automobiles to enable us to change the speed of the engine in relation to the speed of the drive wheels. When a car is starting up or in heavy going at low speed, we need more twisting force on the drive wheels to make it go than we need if we're cruising along a good highway at constant speed. The transmission gives us this increased twisting force (torque) and also allows the engine to run faster. The latter is important because an internal combustion engine does not develop very much power at low speed. When the car picks up speed, the transmission is shifted to change the speed ratio between the engine and the wheels, and eventually is shifted into its highest gear.

The transmission is a system of gears. Suppose we have a small gear with 12 teeth driving a larger gear with 24 teeth. When the first gear has made one complete revolution, we might say that it has gone around a distance equivalent to 12 teeth. The second one has gone around the same distance—12 teeth—but this means only one-half a revolution for the larger gear. So this second gear, and the shaft it is fastened to, always turn at one-half the speed of the first gear and its shaft.

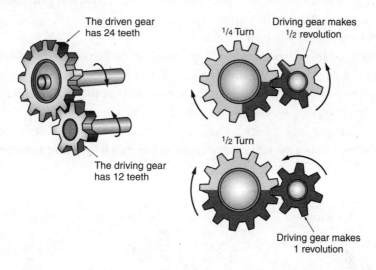

The driven gear has 24 teeth
The driving gear has 12 teeth
1/4 Turn
Driving gear makes 1/2 revolution
1/2 Turn
Driving gear makes 1 revolution

A familiar household example of gears is a hand-operated eggbeater. We can turn the large gear fairly slowly and the small gears meshing with it turn rapidly to drive the beaters at high speed.

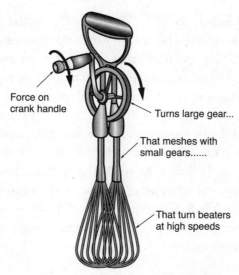

Force on crank handle
Turns large gear...
That meshes with small gears......
That turn beaters at high speeds

The transmission is a case full of gears located behind the clutch. The case is usually fastened to the clutch housing, so the whole unit looks like an extension of the engine. The purpose of the transmission, as mentioned, is to vary the speed and torque of the drive axle in relation to the speed and torque of the engine.

In a manual shift automobile transmission we have several combinations of gears arranged so that we can select the one we want to use at any moment. For *low or first gear*, a small gear on the engine shaft drives a large gear on another shaft. This reduces the speed and increases the twisting force; this is used for starting and for steep hills or heavy going in sand or mud. It lets the engine run fast while the car moves slowly. Then a small gear on the second shaft drives a large gear on the drive shaft, which goes to the drive axle. This reduces the speed and increases the torque still more, giving a ratio of about 3 to 1 for starting up or heavy pulling.

Second or *intermediate gear* works about the same way. The first two gears are the same as in low gear. The next pair are different, however. They are almost the same size, and sometimes the countershaft gear may be the larger. Thus the countershaft runs at the same speed as before, but there is little if any additional reduction from that to the third shaft. So the wheels run faster for the same engine speed than they did in low gear. The usual ratio in second gear is about $1\frac{2}{3}$ to 1. This means that the propeller shaft will run at 1,000 rpm when the engine is running at 1,670 rpm.

The highest gear speed (what number depending on the vehicle) is direct drive. The transmission does not do anything. We simply connect the first and final shafts together, and they turn as one. The propeller shaft turns at the same speed as the engine and delivers engine torque. Sticking to figures, we can say the ratio is 1 to 1.

Most manual transmission vehicles have four or more speeds these days—the other intermediate gears (i.e., all but the highest one) work pretty much the same as second gear above. It's a matter of degree.

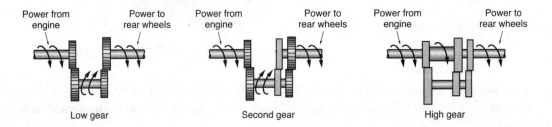

Low gear   Second gear   High gear

Besides the three (and usually more) forward speeds, there are two other possible combinations in a transmission. There is *neutral*, in which the transmission shaft is entirely disconnected from the clutch shaft and the engine cannot drive the propeller shaft or anything beyond the transmission. It has about the same effect as disengaging the clutch. And there is *reverse*. It is a complicated matter to make an internal combustion engine run backward, so we run it in one direction all the time and use gears to reverse the direction of rotation. We put an extra gear between the countershaft and the final drive shaft called the *reverse idler*. We drive the countershaft in the same way as before; it drives the reverse idler, which in turn drives the low speed gear on the final drive shaft. The system is just like low gear except for this extra gear. This changes the direction of rotation, and we can see that the final shaft is turning opposite what it was in all the previous cases. The ratio of reverse is about the same as for low gear, or even lower. This is logical because we may want to pull hard in reverse but we never want to back up very fast.

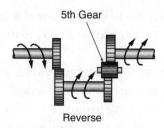

5th Gear

Reverse

The gears are mounted in a metal case filled with oil to lubricate the gears and bearings. The various speeds are selected by moving a gearshift in the driver's compartment—don't forget to put in the clutch first, though.

Most manual transmissions today have five speeds (some have six); the higher gears—if they are differentiated from the first three—are sometimes called *overdrive*, because at these higher gear ratios the engine is actually turning slower than the drive shaft and rear axle. With higher gear ratios and lower engine speeds, fuel economy can be significantly improved—this is why you get the best mileage cruising at a reasonable speed down a highway, not in stop-and-go city driving.

All manual shift transmissions are not exactly like those we have discussed. Some, particularly those in trucks, have a larger number of forward speeds, and the gears may be arranged in a different order on the shafts. Most manual transmissions, however, operate on the principles discussed. There are a number of gears that can be connected together in different ways to give us the different ratios we want. Except in direct drive, a certain amount of torque comes in at the front end from the clutch shaft, and a different amount goes out the back end to the propeller shaft.

Most standard (manual) transmissions have what is known as a *synchromesh* unit that helps eliminate grinding the gears when shifting. It's designed to bring two gears to the same speed before engagement, but it does *not* change gear ratios.

We have described to some extent the main parts of the power path in a car with a manual shift transmission—the clutch and transmission gearing. We covered the propeller shaft, universal joints, axles, differential, and wheels and tires earlier. We will soon discuss automatic transmissions and how they make the power path different from those in cars with manual shift transmissions. Before we do that, however, it would be best to spend a little time talking about planetary gears since they play such an important role in the operation of an automatic transmission.

PLANETARY GEARS

Planetary gears are used in a variety of arrangements in the automobile. Probably the main reason for this is that we can make them do a number of different things, depending on how we connect them into the power system. This is what makes a planetary gear set so interesting. But first, let's look at one and see what it is.

In its simplest form, a planetary gear set is comprised of three gears. There is a sun gear, or pinion, in the center. Then there is a small planet gear meshing with it. On the outside is the ring gear, an internal gear meshing with the planet gears. The planet gears are fastened together by the planet carrier, which holds them in place but lets them rotate. Just how these gears and carriers are fastened to the shafts depends on what we want the mechanism to do.

Suppose we connect the sun gear to the input, or driving shaft, and the planet carrier to the output, or driven shaft. We put a brake band around the outside of the ring gear and hold it tight so it cannot move.

If the engine drives the sun gear, the planet gears must turn around. But they cannot stand still and rotate on their shafts because that would mean the ring gear must move, and we are holding that with the brake. So they have to move around the ring gear, and the planet carrier moves with them. It is something like the differential we described. There are two motions in the planet gears. Each one is rotating about its own shaft, and at the same time they are all moving around in a circle on the teeth of the ring gear. This is where this type of gearing gets its name. The motion is much the same as that of Earth and the other planets about the sun. Each one rotates on its own axis, but they also continually circle around the sun.

The planet carrier, and thus the driven shaft, turns much more slowly than the sun gear and drive shaft and in the same direction. Just what the ratio is depends on the size of the gears, and we will not go into the details of how it is figured. As an example, however, with the smallest practical planets, the ratio cannot be less than 2½ to 1. When the planet and the sun gears are the same size, the ratio is 4 to 1. This of course means that speed is reduced to ¼ and the torque is increased 4 times.

To shift into direct drive, we release the brake on the ring gear and engage a clutch connecting the drive shaft directly to the driven shaft. This can be done by clutching the planet carrier to either the sun gear or the ring gear. In either case, none of the gears can turn on each other, so the whole mechanism is locked and rotates all together without affecting the drive. We mentioned that we can get various results with a planetary transmission by connecting it up in different ways. If we drive the ring gear and hold the sun gear still, we will still increase the torque as we did in the case just described, but it will not be increased as much. Other arrangements will increase the speed and reduce the torque, and by still other means we can get reverse. There are three units, any one of which we can hold stationary and either of the other two can be the driving member. So there are six possible combinations. Practically all of them are used in transmissions in one way or another.

There are various modifications of this simple planetary gear. There are some with double planets of different sizes, and there are compound planetary gears, which consist of two planetary gear sets with certain gears of one connected to certain gears of the other. These act in fundamentally the same way as the simple planetary gear, but following the power flow through them is rather complicated and figuring the gear ratio is not worth the trouble unless we are in the business of designing transmissions.

AUTOMATIC TRANSMISSIONS

Most cars built today have some form of automatic transmission that eliminates the clutch and the need to shift gears manually to obtain the right gear ratios. There are various types, but most of them are similar in the way they affect the driving of the car. They usually have a hydraulic drive of some sort. The type that is in wide use today is the three-element *torque converter*. Imagine taking a doughnut, slicing it in two, and putting blades on the inside of each half. Both halves represent two elements of the torque converter—the *pump*, or driving element, and the *turbine*, or driven element.

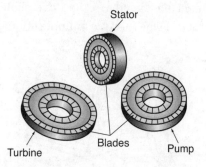

Stator

Turbine   Blades   Pump

Now, between these two halves place a plate that also has blades. This is the third element of the converter and is called the *stator*. All three elements are in a casing filled with oil, which is circulated by means of the blades.

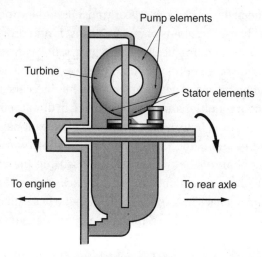

Pump elements

Turbine

Stator elements

To engine   To rear axle

The park (or P) position on an automatic transmission gear selector represents the position that locks up the transmission (without damaging it) and stops the wheels from rolling. The car can be started only when it is in park or neutral (N).

Let's see what happens when we place the automatic transmission selector in the drive position. The pump is mechanically connected to the engine's crankshaft, so it always rotates when the engine runs. When the engine is started, the pump begins rotating and sends oil, spinning in a clockwise direction, against the blades of the turbine to start it turning. The spinning oil has energy that the turbine absorbs and converts into torque, or twisting force, which is then sent to the drive wheels. When the oil leaves the turbine, it spins in a counterclockwise direction, and if it went back to the pump spinning in this direction it would slow it down—we would lose any torque that had been gained. To make sure this doesn't happen, we use the blades of the stator, which does not rotate (not just yet, anyway), to change the direction of the oil flow so that it again spins in a clockwise direction. When the oil enters the pump, it adds to the torque the pump receives from the engine, the pump starts to turn faster, and we start to obtain torque multiplication. The cycle of oil going from the pump to the turbine, through the stator, and then back to the pump is repeated over and over until the car reaches a speed where torque multiplication is no longer needed. When this happens, the stator starts to turn freely (it's fixed to rotate only clockwise). The pump and the turbine then rotate at nearly the same speed and act like a fluid coupling, or clutch. We now have a situation similar to high gear in a manual shift transmission where the crankshaft is connected directly to the drive shaft and both revolve at nearly the same speed. The stator rotates when torque multiplication is needed again.

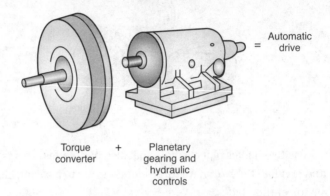

Torque converter + Planetary gearing and hydraulic controls = Automatic drive

The turbine is connected by a shaft to a gear transmission location behind the converter. The transmission usually used contains planetary gear sets and provides the desired number of forward speed gear ratios automatically. These gear ratios can also be selected manually for greater engine braking or exceptionally hard pulling. A reverse gear and neutral gear are also provided. The planetary type of gear transmission has its gears in mesh at all times. Gear ratios for different driving conditions are obtained using hydraulic controls that cause friction bands and clutches to grab and hold certain gears of the set stationary while the others rotate.

An interesting item in automatic transmissions is the *vacuum modulator*, which helps to control the shifting point of the transmission by sensing the engine load at any given moment. The modulator is a vacuum-operated device connected to a source manifold vacuum. As the vacuum changes in response to the engine load, this actuates the modulator, which sends a signal to the valve body, resulting in a different shift point. For instance, when vacuum is low—as it usually is when the engine is accelerated—the modulator reacts and causes the transmission to shift at a higher vehicle speed. The higher shift point allows the engine to develop more torque, which increases engine power.

Hydraulic torque converters can have variations in the design of their basic components. Some elements may have their blades set at a fixed angle to the flow of oil. Others may have blades that are hydraulically operated to provide varying blade angles automatically. For example, a stator could have a low angle for maximum efficiency during the average operating range of the transmission and a high angle for increased acceleration and performance (when more torque is needed at the drive wheels). There are also variations in the way the components are arranged in hydraulic torque converters. Some have two stators, while others have multiple sets of pump and turbine blades. Differences can exist, too, in the way the planetary gears are combined with the pump, turbine, and stator elements.

Under ordinary circumstances, however, these variations do not make a great deal of difference to the driver of the car. He still will find no clutch pedal and will have no shifting to do except when he wants to back up. And for forward driving, all he has to do is step on the accelerator to go and on the brake pedal to stop.

FRONT-WHEEL DRIVE

As mentioned before, most cars today use front-wheel drive. The same basic components are used as for the rear wheel drive system, but all the components are arranged up in front of the driver and the constant velocity (CV) joint transmits power to the drive (front) wheels while allowing the wheels to be steered and the suspension to respond to bumps in the road—taking the place of a universal joint, of which it is a more complex version. The power flow from the engine is to the front-wheel axle shafts. Instead of the rear wheels pushing the car forward, the front wheels pull the car along. The CV joint is housed in a rubber boot (an all-around rubber covering with bellows that allows flexibility while still protecting the joint).

THE REAR AXLE (REAR-WHEEL DRIVE)

In the rear axle we have two sets of gears. The first—a ring gear and a pinion—is simply to transmit the power around a corner. It enables the propeller shaft to drive the axle shafts that are at right angles to it. An old-fashioned ice cream freezer has a set of gears that do the same thing.

If we didn't ever have to turn a corner, that is all the gearing we would need in the rear axle. But when we turn a corner, the outside wheel has to travel farther than the inside wheel, and so it has to go faster during that time. It's like a squad of soldiers making a turn: The outside person has to march much faster than the one on the inside just to stay lined up and even. We have a set of gears called the differential to take care of this.

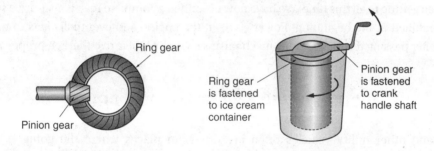

The *differential* consists of two small bevel gears on the ends of the axle shafts meshed with two bevel gears (for simplicity we show only one) mounted in the differential frame. This frame is fastened solidly to the ring gear.

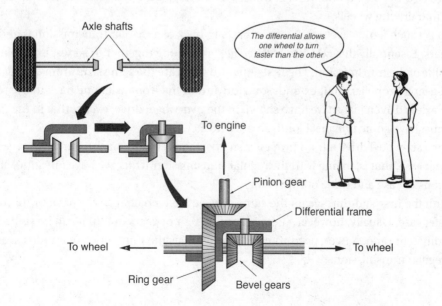

When a car is going straight ahead, the frame and the gears all rotate as a unit, with no motion between one another. But when the car is turning, one wheel must go faster than the other, so the gears on the axle shafts rotate relative to the other small gear. If the ring gear were stationary, one axle would turn frontward and the other one backward. But since the ring gear is turning the whole unit, it means that one axle is turning faster than the ring gear and the other is turning slower by the same amount. This can be carried to the point where one wheel is stationary and the other one is turning at twice ring gear speed, which is the situation we sometimes get when one wheel is on a slippery spot and the other isn't. Some cars, however, can be equipped with a limited slip differential, a type of differential that allows the major driving force to go to the wheel having greater traction.

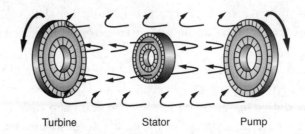

Turbine   Stator   Pump

The axle shafts, of course, drive the wheels and make the car move, which is the point we have been getting to all this time. We have now described a complete rear-wheel-drive system, just as outlined at the beginning. Power starts at the engine and eventually gets to the rear wheels after passing through various mechanisms so that it will arrive there in proper form.

FOUR-WHEEL AND SIX-WHEEL DRIVE

Trucks and other utility vehicles often are driven in places where the going is rough. Sometimes better traction than usual is needed. For example, two wheels might get stuck in a mud hole and not be able to pull out of it. So instead of having the engine drive just two wheels, it drives four wheels or six wheels. A four-wheel vehicle driving on all four wheels is known as a 4 × 4, and one with six wheels, all driving, is a 6 × 6. A 4 × 6 is a six-wheel truck with four driving wheels.

To get such a drive we use a transfer case. In back of a regular transmission is another set of gears. Essentially this consists of three gears meshing together in series, extending out to one side of the transmission. The first and third gears are the same size. From each side of the third gear a propeller shaft extends, one forward to the front axle, one back to the rear axle. Each axle is driven just as we have shown in the two-wheel drive, except that in the front axle we must have some universal joints in order to steer.

For a six-wheel drive a third propeller shaft extends straight back from the first gear in the transfer case, that is, in line with the regular transmission. Thus, we have one input shaft into the transfer case and three output shafts.

With the first and third gears the same size we have no change of speed or torque in the transfer case. Usually, however, there is another pair of gears in it that can be shifted to give us a different ratio. A two-speed transfer case doubles the number of gear ratios available in the regular transmission.

Brake lights are usually controlled by spring-loaded electrical switches. Most cars have mechanically operated switches operated by contact with the brake pedal or with a bracket attached to the pedal. When the brake is applied, the circuit through the switch closes and the brake lights come on. When the brakes are released, the electrical circuit through the brake light is open—broken—and the light goes off. A loose or corroded headlight connection can cause a dim light. If the switch itself is faulty, all the lights will be affected.

The hydraulic type of brake light switch operates on the same principle; its operation depends on hydraulic pressure in the master cylinder of the brake.

PRACTICE QUESTIONS

1. The device used to check the rotor thickness and variation of a disc brake rotor is a

    (A) torque wrench.
    (B) dial indicator.
    (C) micrometer.
    (D) feeler gauge.

2. Which gauge is used to check engine crankshaft endplay?

    (A) Depth gauge
    (B) Plastigauge
    (C) Feeler gauge
    (D) Micrometer

3. A transmission

    (A) controls the speed of the engine.
    (B) trades speed for power.
    (C) transmits torque at an angle.
    (D) trades power for speed.

4. If a rear axle ratio is 4 to 1,

    (A) the pinion gear has four times the number of teeth as the ring gear.
    (B) the ring gear has four times the number of teeth as the pinion gear.
    (C) the rear tire is four times larger than the brake drum.
    (D) the side gear has four times the number of teeth as the spider gear.

5. The motive power of the automotive cranking motor is created by the

    (A) field poles attracting the laminated iron core of the armature.
    (B) repelling force of like poles being formed in the armature opposite the field poles.
    (C) starter neutral safety switch.
    (D) starter drive.

6. If the transmission ratio is 3.29 to 1 and the differential ratio is 3.85 to 1, what is the final ratio?

(A) 7.05 to 1
(B) 0.56 to 1
(C) 12.67 to 1
(D) None of the above

7. If air gets into the hydraulic brake system,

(A) brake application will be hard.
(B) it will have no effect.
(C) the brake pedal action will be spongy.
(D) the brake pedal will stick.

8. The proportioning valve in a hydraulic brake system

(A) reduces pressure to the front brakes.
(B) controls the brake warning switch.
(C) is used only on a drum-type brake system.
(D) reduces pressure to the rear brakes.

9. Helical gears have

(A) slanted teeth.
(B) straight teeth.
(C) curved teeth.
(D) beveled teeth.

10. A gear train that uses a sun gear, internal gear, and three pinion gears is known as

(A) bevel spiral pinion.
(B) worm and sector.
(C) planetary gears.
(D) differential gears.

Answers Explained

1. **(C)** The device used to check the rotor thickness and variation of a disc brake rotor is a *micrometer.*

2. **(C)** A *feeler gauge* is used to check engine crankshaft endplay. It measures the clearance between the crankshaft and the main thrust bearing. This clearance determines the endplay of the crankshaft. A depth gauge is used to measure tire tread. A plastigauge is used to measure crankshaft bearing oil clearance. A micrometer is used to measure crankshaft journal diameter.

3. **(B)** A transmission *trades speed for power.* It uses gear reduction to increase engine torque or turning force. During the time torque is increasing, speed decreases.

4. **(B)** If a rear axle ratio is 4 to 1, *the ring gear has four times the number of teeth as the pinion gear.* The pinion, which connects to the driveshaft, is the driving gear. The ring, which drives axles, is the driven gear. To calculate the gear ratio, divide the drive into the driven gear.

5. **(B)** The motive power of the automotive cranking motor is created by the *repelling force of like poles being formed in the armature opposite the field poles.* When a starter is energized, the magnetic fields created in the armature and field coils produce the turning effect on the armature shaft. The starter drive engages the flywheel ring gear and cranks over the engine when the starter is energized.

6. **(C)** If the transmission ratio is 3.29 to 1 and the differential ratio is 3.85 to 1, the final ratio is *12.67 to 1.* To calculate the final ratio of a transmission and differential, multiply the ratio of the transmission by the ratio of the differential: $3.29 \times 3.85 = 12.67$.

7. **(C)** If air gets into the hydraulic brake system, *the brake pedal action will be spongy.* Air is compressible and will cause a spongy or soft brake pedal action.

8. **(D)** The proportioning valve in a hydraulic brake system *reduces pressure to the rear brakes.* A proportioning valve is commonly used on a vehicle equipped with front disc and rear drum-type brakes. The valve reduces hydraulic pressure to the rear drum brakes to prevent rear wheel lockup and skidding during heavy brake pedal application.

9. **(A)** Helical gears have *slanted teeth.* Spur gears have straight teeth. Hypoid and spiral gears have curved or beveled teeth.

10. **(C)** A gear train that uses a sun gear, internal gear, and three pinion gears is known as *planetary gears.* Planetary gears are used in an automatic transmission. The three members are in constant mesh. They provide gear reduction and reverse without shifting. To obtain a gear reduction or reverse, one member must be held stationary by a band or clutch assembly. Worm and sector gears are used in some types of steering gear assemblies. Differential or spider gears are used in a rear-end assembly.

Shop Information Review

9

A person interested in making or repairing things is lost without tools. Tools make the difference between a person who works efficiently and one who struggles laboriously. There are some tools that are basic to any home shop and are generally used for simple carpentry work. Others are used for more specialized purposes. General shop knowledge also involves knowing basic facts about commonly used materials and about how design and layout are transferred from an idea to a finished product.

TOOLS

Common hand tools may be grouped under several headings: measuring and layout tools, cutting and shaping tools, drilling or boring tools, fasteners and fastening tools, clamping tools, pliers and wrenches, digging tools, grinding and sanding tools, and specialized tools like plumbers' or electricians' tools.

MEASURING AND LAYOUT TOOLS

Some of the most important tools, regardless of trade area, are measuring devices. They may take the form of *folding rules* and *tape measures* (Figure 9.1) or steel rules and precision measuring instruments.

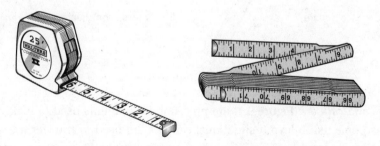

Figure 9.1. Tape measure and folding rule.

When using a folding, or zigzag, rule, place it flat on the work. The "0" end of the rule should be exactly even with the end of the space or board to be measured. The correct distance is indicated by the reading on the rule.

A very accurate reading may be obtained by turning the edge of the rule toward the work. In this position, the marked graduations of the face of the rule touch the surface of the board. With a sharp pencil, mark the exact distance desired. Start the mark with the point of the pencil in contact with the mark on the rule. Move the pencil directly away from the rule while making the mark.

You may notice a problem with a folding rule: if it gets twisted, it breaks. This happens commonly when folding or unfolding the rule and may not be noticed at the time. You should keep the joints oiled lightly so that the rule operates more easily.

Beginners may find a pocket tape the most useful measuring tool for all types of work. It extends smoothly to full length. It returns quickly to its compact case when the return button is pressed. Steel tapes are available in a variety of lengths. For most work, a tape 6, 8, 10, 12, or 25 feet long is suggested.

A *steel rule* (Figure 9.2) is a very accurate version of a common ruler. The measuring edges are usually graduated in 1/8, 1/16, 1/32, and 1/64 of an inch. In addition to being an accurate measuring device, a steel rule can also be used as a *straight edge* to draw or scribe a straight line. This tool is available in lengths ranging from 6 to 48 inches.

Figure 9.2. Steel rule.

Squares are used to set or check 90° angles. The two most common types are the *steel square*, also referred to as a *framing square*, and the *combination square* (Figure 9.3). Because of its size, the steel square is used to check the squareness of large frames. It is also used by carpenters to lay out rafters and staircases. The combination square is used to lay out 90° and 45° angles and is equipped with a sliding steel rule, usually 12 inches in length.

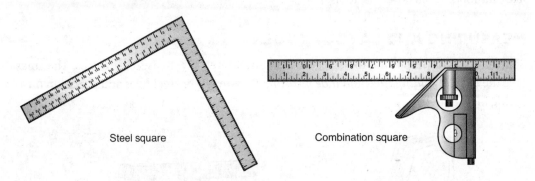

Steel square   Combination square

Figure 9.3. Squares.

Micrometers and *calipers* (Figure 9.4) are precision instruments used to make very close tolerance measurements. In layout situations, calipers are used to transfer measurements from one location to another. These tools can be used to make measurements to one-thousandth of an inch. They are commonly used in precision metal machining and auto engine rebuilding.

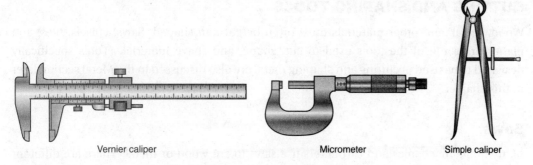

Vernier caliper   Micrometer   Simple caliper

Figure 9.4. Micrometer and calipers.

Levels are used for a number of purposes. The most important one is to make sure that things are properly oriented so that mechanisms will work correctly. A refrigerator, for example, usually has to be level for it to operate correctly; doors and windows have to be level to move up and down or open and shut smoothly—and, of course, things look better when they are level. A level has a vertical indicator and a horizontal indicator (Figure 9.5). The bubbles in the glass tubes in the level tell you if the level is obtained. If the vertical and horizontal bubbles are lined up between the lines, then the window or door is plumb. Being plumb means that the sides of the window are vertical and the top and bottom are at right angles to the sides.

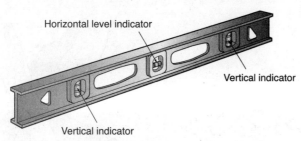

Horizontal level indicator

Vertical indicator

Vertical indicator

Figure 9.5. Level.

A *plumb bob* is a small, pointed weight (Figure 9.6). It is attached to a string and dropped from a height. If the bob is just above the ground, it will indicate the vertical direction by its string. Keeping windows and doors and frames square and level makes a difference in fitting. It is much easier to fit prehung doors into a frame that is square.

A *scratch awl* is a handy tool for a carpenter. It can be used to mark wood with a scratch mark. It can also be used to produce pilot holes for screws. Once it is in your tool box, you can think of a hundred uses for it. Since it has a very sharp point, it is best treated with respect. Figure 9.7 shows the point.

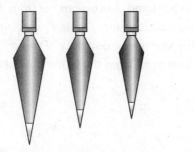

Figure 9.6. Plumb bobs.

Figure 9.7. Scratch awl.

CUTTING AND SHAPING TOOLS

Wood, metal, and other materials must often be cut and shaped. Saws, chisels, files, and planes are some of the tools used to cut, shape, and shave material. (Tools specifically designed to be used in cutting and shaping metal are also discussed in the Metal section later in this chapter.)

Saws

Many home mechanics and carpenters use saws to cut wood or metal. There are different types made for wood or metal and different types designed for specific types of work. The blade determines the use of the saw.

The *back saw* (Figure 9.8) gets its name from the piece of heavy metal that makes up the top edge of the cutting part of the saw. It has a fine tooth configuration. This means it can be used to cut cross-grain—cut wood across the grain—and it leaves a smooth finished piece of work. This type of saw is used by finishing carpenters who want to cut trim or molding.

The standard *skew-back saw* (Figure 9.9) has a wooden handle. It has a 22-inch length. A 10-point saw (with 10 teeth per inch) is suggested for *crosscutting*. The 26-inch length, 5½ point saw is suggested for *ripping*—cutting with the wood grain. This saw is used in places where an electric saw cannot be used. The sharpness of the blade makes a difference in the quality of the cut and the ease with which the saw can be used.

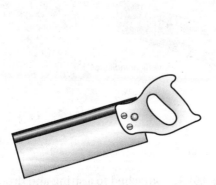

Figure 9.8. Back saw.

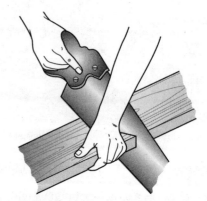

Figure 9.9. Standard skew-back saw.

The *mitre box* (Figure 9.10) has a back saw mounted in it. This box can be adjusted for cuts from 90° to 45° using the lever under the saw handle. The mitre box is used for finishing cuts on moldings and trim materials. The angle of the cut is determined by the location of the saw in reference to the bed of the box. You can adjust the clamp on the bottom of the saw support to adjust the saw to any degree desired. The wood is held with one hand against the fence of the box and the bed. Then the saw is used by the other hand. As you can see from the setup, the cutting should take place when the saw is pushed forward. The backward movement of the saw should be made with the pressure on the saw released slightly. If you try to cut on the backward movement, you will just pull the wood away from the fence and decrease the quality of the cut.

The *coping saw* (Figure 9.11) comes in handy to make cuts that are not straight. The coping saw can cut small thicknesses of wood at any curve or angle desired. It can be used to make a piece of paneling fit properly or a piece of molding fit another piece in the corner. The blade is placed in the frame with the teeth pointing toward the handle. This means it cuts only on the downward stroke. Make sure you properly support the piece of wood being cut. A number of blades can be obtained for this type of saw. The number of teeth in the blade determines the smoothness of the cut.

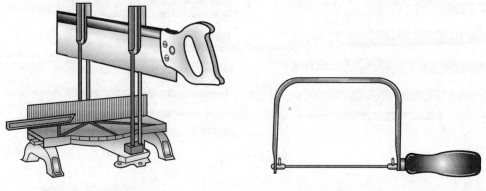

Figure 9.10. Mitre box.   **Figure 9.11.** Coping saw.

A *compass saw* (Figure 9.12) is used to cut holes, such as those needed for electrical outlets.

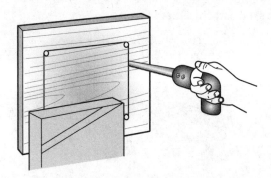

Figure 9.12. Compass saw.

Hacksaws (Figure 9.13) are primarily used for cutting metal. The teeth on a hacksaw blade are much smaller than those on a wood-cutting saw. The blade is made of hardened steel and is either 10 or 12 inches in length. The hacksaw frame can be adjusted to accommodate both sizes. Blades are classified by the number of teeth per inch and are always positioned in the frame so that they are pointed away from the handle.

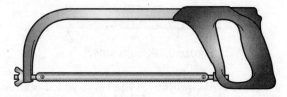

Figure 9.13. Hacksaw.

Files

Files are used to produce finished or semifinished surfaces. A number of different types of files are available (Figure 9.14), each designed for a specific purpose. Machinist's files and curved tooth files are widely used in machine shops and industrial facilities for a variety of repair work. Some files are used for sharpening saws and touching up cutting edges. One type of wood file, known as a *rasp*, is coarse and designed for rough work, while other wood files are used to produce smooth and fine surfaces.

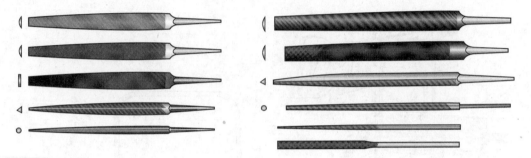

Figure 9.14. Files.

Chisels

Chisels are used to cut wood. They are sharpened on one end. When the other end is struck with a hammer, the cutting end will do its job—that is, of course, if you have kept it sharpened. Figure 9.15 shows a wood chisel.

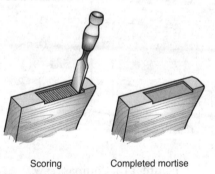

Scoring   Completed mortise

Figure 9.15. Wood chisel.

The *cold chisel* (Figure 9.16) is made with a very sharp edge that can cut metal. This means it can be used to remove a nail. The nail head may have been broken off and the nail must be removed. The chisel can cut the nail and permit separation of the wood pieces. Cold chisels are used for many operations involving the removal of small amounts of metal.

Figure 9.16. Cold chisel.

If a chisel of this type starts to "mushroom" at the head, you should remove the splintered ends with a 3 grinder. Hammering on the end can produce a mushrooming effect. These pieces should be taken off since they can easily fly off when hit with a hammer. This is just one reason for wearing eye protection when using tools.

Planes

Planes are used in carpentry work to shave off material of different thicknesses. They are used to smooth and straighten wood, to bevel it, and to make moldings and special shapes. A *jack plane* is an all-purpose plane, about 12 to 15 inches long, that smoothes boards and other wood pieces. A *block plane* (Figure 9.17) is similar to a jack plane but smaller, about 6 inches long. Block planes are used for small smoothing and fitting jobs because of their small size and because they can be operated with one hand.

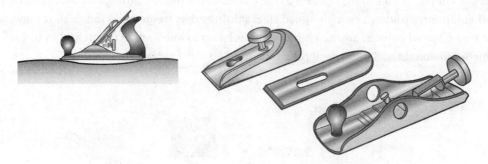

Figure 9.17. Block plane.

BORING AND DRILLING TOOLS

A number of different types of tools are used to bore holes in material. A common type of drilling tool is a *bit brace*, basically a type of hand drill, equipped with different types of tips, or *bits*.

Drill bits are made to cut or bore accurate round holes. Bits made to drill holes in metal are different in design from those used to bore holes in wood. Metals are much tougher to drill; therefore, metal cutting drill bits are made of hardened steel. These bits are commonly referred to as *twist drills* (Figure 9.18) and are sized by diameter.

Figure 9.18. Twist drill.

Wood bits come in a variety of shapes (Figure 9.19). The speed bore, forstner, and brad point bits are used in power drilling equipment, such as electric hand drills or drill presses. The *auger bit* is made to be used with a brace (Figure 9.20) and turned by hand.

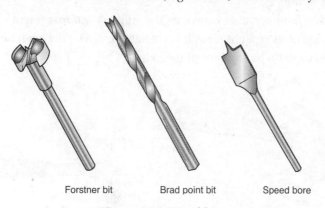

Forstner bit   Brad point bit   Speed bore

Figure 9.19. Wood bits.

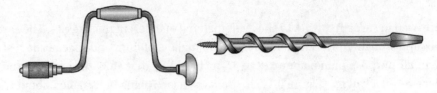

Figure 9.20. Brace and auger bit.

Hole cutters, or *hole saws* (Figure 9.21), are used in the metal-cutting, electrical, plumbing, and automotive trades. The high-speed steel-cutting edge, welded to a tough alloy back, will cut clean, round holes in any machinable material up to one inch in depth and from 9/16 to 6 inches in diameter. Similar designs can be used for cutting holes in wood.

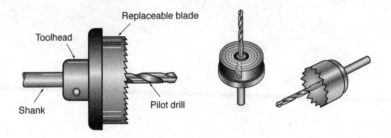

Figure 9.21. Hole saw.

FASTENERS AND FASTENING TOOLS

Many different types of tools and devices are used to fasten objects together or to drive or push one object into another.

Hammers

Hammers are used to drive nails into objects, to strike other tools such as chisels, and to form or shape metal and other materials. Hammers come in many sizes and shapes, each made for specific jobs. The basic parts of a hammer are shown in Figure 9.22.

A *curved claw hammer* (Figure 9.22) is commonly used by carpenters. It can be used to pull and extract nails that have been put in the wrong way or are bent. These hammers come in 20-ounce, 24-ounce, 28-ounce, and 32-ounce weights for carpentry use; the usual carpenter's choice is the 20-ounce.

The *straight claw hammer*, also known as the *ripping hammer* (Figure 9.23), is used for rough work. Because of its straight claw, it can easily be driven between boards and used to separate them and can also be used to split wood.

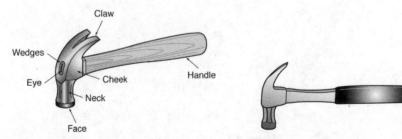

Figure 9.22. Curved claw hammer.   **Figure 9.23.** Straight claw hammer.

The *ball-peen hammer* (Figure 9.24), also known as a *machinist's hammer*, is used in metal working and in mechanical work. It is used to drive punches and chisels and to shape metal parts. It can also be used to set and peen rivets.

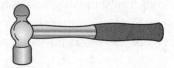

Figure 9.24. Ball-peen hammer.

Other types of hammers include the *mallet*, often made with a wood, plastic, or rubber head, used to drive chisels and shape metal without marring the work surface, and the *sledge-hammer*, used to break concrete and do other heavy, rough work.

Nails

Nails (Figure 9.25) are driven by hammers. Note the relationship between gauge, penny (*d*), and inches. The *d* after the number means penny. This is a measuring unit inherited from the English in the colonial days. There is little or no relationship between penny and inches. If you want to be able to talk about it intelligently, you'll have to learn both inches and penny. The gauge is nothing more than the American Wire Gauge number for the wire that the nails are made from originally. Finish nails have the same measuring unit (the penny) but do not have the large flat heads.

Nail Sets

Nail sets are used to drive finish nails below the surface of the wood. The nail set is placed on the head of the nail. The large end of the nail set is struck by the hammer. This causes the nail to go below the surface of the wood. Then the hole left by the countersunk nail is filled with wood filler and finished off with a smooth coat of varnish or paint.

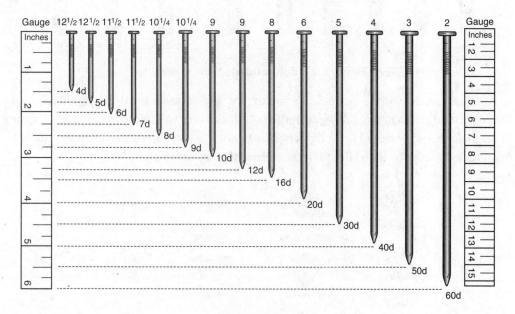

Figure 9.25. Nails.

Screwdrivers

This is one tool that shouldn't be left out of a tool box for a mechanic, carpenter, or anyone doing work around the house. It can be used for many things other than turning screws. There are two types of screwdrivers. The standard, most common type has a straight, slot-fitting blade at its end. The Phillips-head screwdriver has a cross or X on the end; this fits a screw head of the same design. Figure 9.26 shows the two types of screwdrivers.

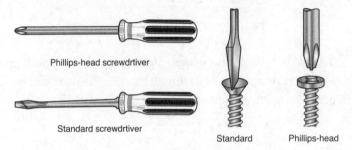

Phillips-head screwdrtiver

Standard screwdrtiver

Standard   Phillips-head

Figure 9.26. Screwdrivers, standard and Phillips-head.

Other Fasteners

The most common forms of threaded fasteners used are bolts, nuts, and machine screws.

Bolts and *machine screws* are available in a variety of shapes and sizes (Figure 9.27) and are classified by head shape, diameter, and length. Most bolts have a hexagonal head. Coarse threads are cut deeper and are fewer in number per inch than are fine threads. Coarse thread nuts and bolts are used when the connection must be extremely tight. A fine thread is used for parts that must withstand a great deal of vibration, such as aircraft parts.

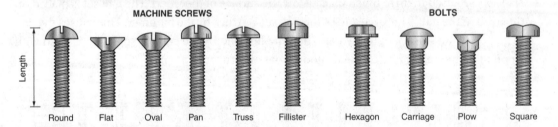

MACHINE SCREWS   BOLTS

Length

Round   Flat   Oval   Pan   Truss   Fillister   Hexagon   Carriage   Plow   Square

Figure 9.27. Bolts and machine screws.

Nuts are made with a hexagonal, square, or self-locking head (Figure 9.28). *Self-locking nuts* are designed to jam against the bolt thread and will not vibrate loose. The *wing nut* is the only nut designed to be tightened by hand. It is used on connections that must be frequently disassembled and do not require excessive tightening.

Hexagon   Hexagon washer faced   Square (chamfer)   Plain

Self locking nut   Wheel nut   Wing nut   Hexagon cap

Figure 9.28. Nuts.

Washers are available as either flat or locking (Figure 9.29). *Flat washers* are used to evenly distribute the compressive load of a bolted connection over a wider area or to compensate for an oversized hole. *Lock washers* are designed to exert force between the bolted connection and the workpiece, preventing the bolt and nut from loosening.

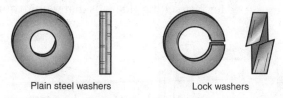

Plain steel washers   Lock washers

Figure 9.29. Washers.

Self-tapping screws, also called *sheet metal screws*, are used to connect thin gauge sheet metal parts (Figure 9.30). The hardened steel screw actually cuts its own thread as it is inserted. These screws have either a hexagonal or slotted head.

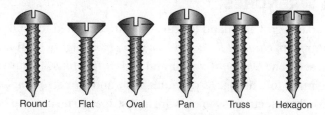

Round   Flat   Oval   Pan   Truss   Hexagon

Figure 9.30. Self-tapping screws.

Rivets (Figure 9.31) are used in sheet metal and aircraft manufacturing to make solid, high strength connections on parts that cannot be welded or bolted. They are classified and sized by head shape, diameter, and length. Rivets are placed in a drilled hole and the shank is peened or hammered over to produce a tight connection.

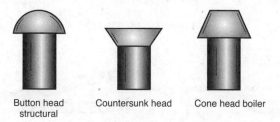

Button head   Countersunk head   Cone head boiler
structural

Figure 9.31. Rivets.

Wood screws (Figure 9.32) are used in place of nails when a much tighter and stronger connection is needed. Screws are much more time-consuming to install and are mainly used in furniture construction or on connections that must be taken apart and reassembled. Wood screws are classified by the shape of the screw head, shank diameter, and length.

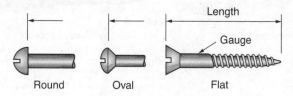

Round   Oval   Flat

Figure 9.32. Wood screws.

Clamps are used to hold parts together. They are most frequently used to hold glued pieces together while they are drying. There are several types of clamps (Figure 9.33). A *C-clamp* is versatile, with many different sized jaw openings available. This type of clamp can also be used as a vise to hold an object to a work surface. A *spring clamp* has a pincer action. Small, this type of clamp is best suited for fast-setting glue jobs that require quick action.

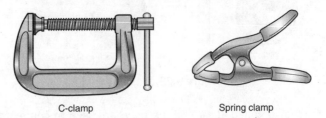

C-clamp   Spring clamp

Figure 9.33. Clamps.

PLIERS AND WRENCHES

Pliers extend a worker's grip and hand length. They are designed to do one of two things—grip or cut. The *slip joint, channel lock,* and *vise grip pliers* (Figure 9.34) have serrated teeth and can grip parts securely. *Diagonal cutting* and *end cutting pliers* (Figure 9.35) have sharpened jaws and are made for cutting. *Electrician's pliers* and *wire stripping pliers* (Figure 9.36) are special tools used by electricians to cut wire and strip wire insulation; both are equipped with insulated handles.

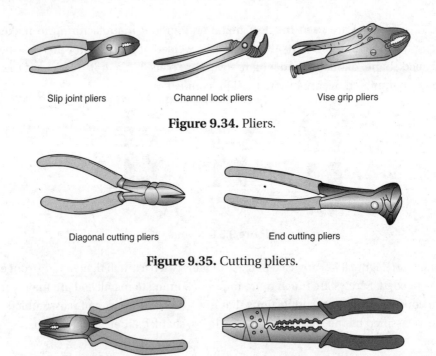

Slip joint pliers   Channel lock pliers   Vise grip pliers

Figure 9.34. Pliers.

Diagonal cutting pliers   End cutting pliers

Figure 9.35. Cutting pliers.

Electrician's pliers   Wire stripping pliers

Figure 9.36. Electrician's pliers and wire stripping pliers.

Wrenches are used to tighten or loosen nuts and bolts. They are classified as open end, box end, combination, or adjustable (Figure 9.37). The *open end wrench* holds the bolt head or nut on two sides only; therefore, it is generally used only for snugging up bolted connections. If secure tightening is attempted, the open end wrench may slip and round off the bolt head or nut. The *box wrench* grips the nut on all six sides, allowing the user to tighten the connection securely without having the wrench slip. The *combination wrench* has an open end on one side and a box end on the other. *Adjustable wrenches* can be adjusted to fit a variety of nut and bolt sizes.

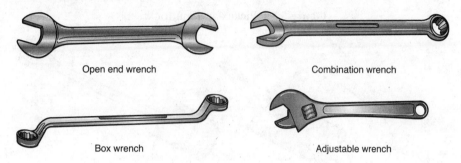

Open end wrench

Combination wrench

Box wrench

Adjustable wrench

Figure 9.37. Wrenches.

Ratchet and *socket wrenches* (Figure 9.38) are designed to do the same job as the box end wrench, but they can turn the bolt and nut continuously without repeated removal, which significantly speeds up the tightening process. Socket wrenches are generally classified as six or twelve point and are available in metric or standard sizes to fit all hexagonal head nuts and bolts. The most common ratchet sizes are 1/4, 3/8, and 1/2 inch drive. The drive size refers to the diameter of the square drive shank on the ratchet head.

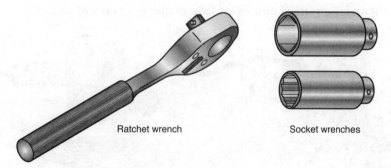

Ratchet wrench

Socket wrenches

Figure 9.38. Ratchet and socket wrenches.

DIGGING TOOLS

Common digging tools are classified as either picks or shovels. The pickax and mattock (Figure 9.39) have sharp edges and are used for breaking up tightly compacted soil. The pickax also has a pointed tip at one end that can be used for breaking up thin concrete slabs. Square and tapered mouth *shovels* (Figure 9.40) are generally used for digging in loose soil or mixing and shoveling wet cement. The *digging spade* has a flat shoulder along the back of the blade so that it can be easily pushed into the soil by foot.

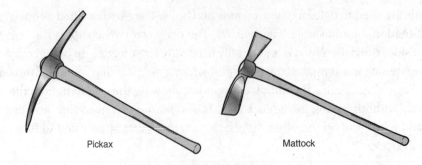

Pickax

Mattock

Figure 9.39. Pickax and mattock.

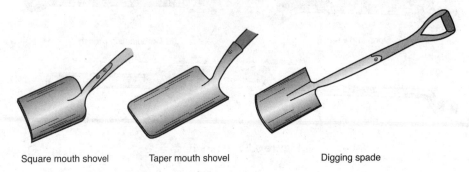

Square mouth shovel

Taper mouth shovel

Digging spade

Figure 9.40. Shovels.

GRINDING AND SANDING TOOLS

Grinders and *sanding machines* are used to remove excess material or smooth rough edges. The machines are abrasive disks or pads similar in texture to sandpaper. *Angle grinders* and *sanders* (Figure 9.41) are primarily used on hard materials such as metals. The *orbital vibrating sander* (Figure 9.42) is most often used for smoothing wood surfaces.

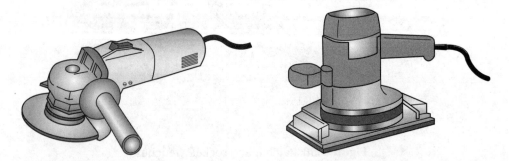

Figure 9.41. Angle grinder / sander.

Figure 9.42. Orbital vibrating sander.

The *bench grinder* (Figure 9.43) is a more precise machine. It is equipped with two grinding wheels and is mainly used for sharpening cutting tools and drill bits.

Abrasives are used to wear down or smooth the surface of another part. The most common of these are sandpaper, emery cloth, and rubbing compound. Abrasives are also used to machine very hard materials such as glass, ceramics, and hardened steel.

Aluminum oxide is the abrasive material used on most *sandpaper*. It is made by fusing bauxite, coke, and iron filings. Aluminum oxide paper can be used for sanding wood or metal. This type of sandpaper is very durable and ideal for use on electric sanders.

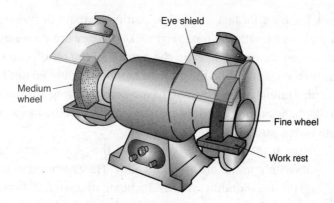

Figure 9.43. Bench grinder.

Emery cloth is similar to sandpaper except it has a cloth backing and is only used for smoothing or polishing metal parts. Emery is a very hard natural material. The advantage of the cloth backing is that it will not tear when used on curved or irregular surfaces. Emery cloth is often lubricated with water or oil for polishing operations.

Rubbing compounds have a pumice base. Pumice is made from granulated volcanic rock or ash. These compounds are primarily used for smoothing the finish on automobile paint and hand-rubbed furniture.

All abrasives are classified by texture or grit. A number 10 grit is the most coarse and a number 600 is the finest.

SPECIALIZED TOOLS

In addition to the commonly used shop tools, each trade has tools specifically designed for its particular type of work.

Plumbing Tools

Many common hand tools have been adapted to fit the requirements of fitting, measuring, cutting, and working with pipes and plumbing fixtures.

Pipe wrenches (Figure 9.44) are made to firmly grip pipe and pipe fittings so that they may be tightened or loosened. The pipe wrench, also commonly known as a *stilson wrench*, has serrated teeth and a pivoting jaw that grips the pipe more securely as pressure is applied to the handle. The *chain wrench* is used primarily for gripping and turning very large diameter pipes.

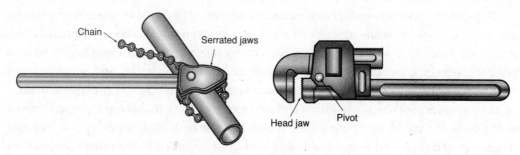

Figure 9.44. Pipe wrenches.

Pipe cutting tools are used for fast, clean pipe cutting by hand or power. Two rollers are adjusted to come in contact with the pipe (Figure 9.45). They are then pushed against the pipe until the cutting tool (a small wheel on the outside of the tool) comes in contact with the pipe. As the cutter is turned around the pipe the handle is tightened until the cutting edge has penetrated the pipe lining and caused it to have a complete ring around it. When enough pressure is applied and the cutting edge has penetrated through the metal body of the pipe, the pieces separate with a smooth edge.

Tubing cutters (Figure 9.46) are smaller versions of the pipe cutters. They are about 5 inches long with a lightweight frame of aluminum alloy. They are used to cut brass, copper, aluminum tubing, and thinwall conduit up to 2½ inches in diameter. Rollers smooth the tubing and make it ready for soldering. A reamer folds in when the cutter is in use. They are also designed to cut stainless steel tubing.

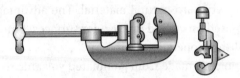

Figure 9.45. Pipe cutter.

Figure 9.46. Tubing cutter.

Electrical Tools

Many of the tools used by electricians are designed to draw and position cable and wire and to attach electrical boxes. Others are measuring devices, designed to measure the output of an electrical circuit. Commonly used electrical measuring devices, or meters, such as the voltmeter, ammeter, and ohmmeter, are discussed in Chapter 7, "Electronics Information Review."

MATERIALS

Various materials are used in general shop and construction work. Among the materials most often used are concrete, wood, metal, glass, plastics, and adhesives.

CONCRETE

Concrete is a mixture of cement, sand, and water. The cement and water form a paste that binds the other materials together as the concrete hardens. Hardened concrete is very strong, and it is both waterproof and fireproof. It also lasts a long time and is easy to maintain. There are special types of concrete, including *precast concrete*, which is cast and hardened into beams, girders, or other units before being used as a building material, and *reinforced concrete*, which is made by casting concrete around steel bars or rods to add strength to them.

You can order concrete ready-mixed and delivered by a truck that keeps it properly mixed until needed; or you can prepare it from a concrete mix by adding water; or you may mix cement, gravel, sand, and water. The ingredients must be added in the proper proportions and mixed to form the correct consistency.

In most instances you will want to place the concrete in a *form* that has previously been prepared for it. You first have to excavate the site. This calls for outlining with stakes the area to be covered with concrete. The area should extend at least 1 foot beyond the edge of a planned site—a patio, for instance. This helps prevent undercutting, which can occur when a base has eroded or fallen away, leaving the slab without sufficient base. Tie a string tautly between all stakes. To make the pattern for digging, simply sprinkle sand or lime over the string onto the ground, thus outlining the pattern for digging.

Then you must prepare the base. This means you should remove all grass, roots, and other organic matter from the surface. Dig to a depth of 6 to 8 inches, sloping gently away from the nearest building. Use sand, gravel, or other fill with a minimum of four inches to bring the site to a uniform grade. Compact the fill with a tamper or similar device, such as a concrete block or 4″ × 4″ piece of wood. Dampen the fill to aid in packing. The base should be uniform, hard, and free from foreign matter.

Make the form to fit the pattern needed. Dampen the forms and base thoroughly, but leave no puddles. Shovel or place the mix into the form. Fill to the full depth of the forms. Start at a corner and do not drag or flow the concrete unnecessarily. After the concrete has been spread, completely filling the forms, strike off and float immediately (Figure 9.47).

To "strike off" means to use a 2″ × 4″ × 6′ board, moving the edge back and forth with a sawlike motion, smoothing the surface. Then use a "darby" (made from a smooth, flat board approximately 3½ inches wide and 3½ feet long with a handle on top) to float the surface. This helps level any ridges and fills voids left by the straight edge. These two procedures help embed all particles of coarse stone or gravel slightly below the surface. Do not "overwork" the concrete. This can cause separation and create a less durable surface.

Before finishing the concrete, allow it to stiffen slightly. This allows all water to evaporate from the surface before troweling. When the surface has turned dull, smooth and compact the concrete with a trowel. For best results keep the trowel pressed firmly and flat. Sweep it back and forth, each pass overlapping half of the previous pass. Good results can be attained by using a trowel measuring 4″ × 14″ (Figure 9.48). Use an edging tool to round the edges along all forms. An edger with a half-inch radius is recommended. To produce a textured, non-skid surface, use a wood float for final troweling. Then use a wet broom to place the marks in the surface that are needed for your purposes.

Figure 9.47. Striking off concrete.

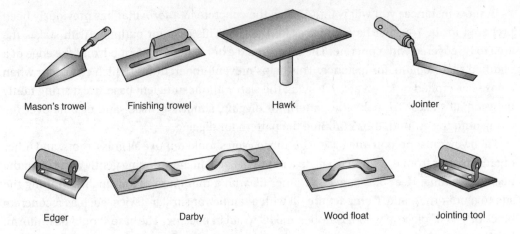

Mason's trowel Finishing trowel Hawk Jointer

Edger Darby Wood float Jointing tool

Figure 9.48. Concrete finishing tools.

Other tools used by persons working with concrete and masonry are the *mason's trowel,* which is used to "butter" a block or brick (Figure 9.49). The *jointer* is used to finish up the joints between the blocks (Figure 9.50). When a wall needs to be covered with mortar, the *hawk* can be used to keep enough near at hand so it can be spread on the surface of the blocks (Figure 9.51).

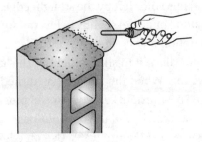

Figure 9.49. Buttering a concrete block.

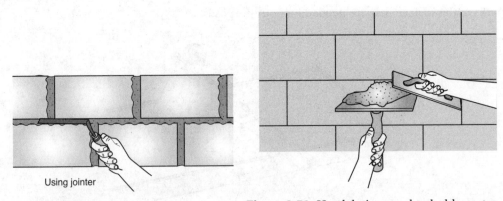

Using jointer

Figure 9.50. Using a jointer. **Figure 9.51.** Hawk being used to hold mortar.

In order to cure concrete properly you should keep it damp for a period of five to seven days after it has been poured. This helps the hardening (hydrating) process, thus producing a more durable surface. Proper curing of all cement mixes is necessary for maximum strength. Concrete that has been moisture cured will be approximately 50 percent stronger than that exposed to dry air. Concrete reaches 98 percent of its strength in 28 days.

WOOD

Wood is the basic substance of trees, and there are many types of wood used for different purposes—furniture making, home building, and many other uses. Wood is easy to work with. It is made up of long cells that grow closely together, forming a compact, yet porous, material. It is elastic, plastic, and honeycomb. The relatively light weight of wood is explained by the fact that approximately half of its volume is made up of hollow cells. If wood is dried and crushed into solid material, it weighs approximately 1.5 times as much as an equal volume of water and consequently sinks in water. It is because of its hollow cell structure that most woods are buoyant, can take finishing materials, and can hold nails, screws, glue, and other fasteners.

Wood is named and classified as hard or soft according to the species of tree from which it is cut. Hardwood comes from the deciduous or broad-leaved trees and softwood comes from the coniferous or needle-bearing trees. This classification does not, however, indicate the degree of hardness of the wood. Some woods classified as hardwoods are actually soft. The pines, firs, and other evergreens are softwoods, and the maples, oaks, elms, poplars, and other shade and fruit trees are the hardwoods.

Trees are cut into logs, usually eight or more feet long. The individual logs are squared by slabbing, or the log is first split through the center and squared into a *cant*. In most cases, the cant is then sawed into timbers, planks, and boards. Sometimes logs are selected for special purposes and cut accordingly.

New lumber contains an excess of moisture. This may run as high as 200 percent when a freshly cut log is sawed. The evaporation of this moisture must be controlled if good lumber is to be obtained for building or furniture making. Rapid drying causes checking and cracks (Figure 9.52). To help prevent rapid drying, freshly cut logs are often submerged in water until they are to be cut into lumber.

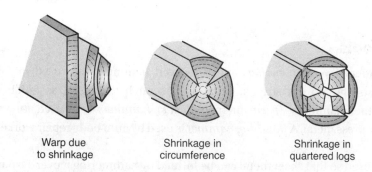

Warp due to shrinkage   Shrinkage in circumference   Shrinkage in quartered logs

Figure 9.52. Warpage and shrinkage of wood.

Controlled drying conditions reduce the intensity of the forces acting on the logs. Drying must be done by air seasoning or by the modern, faster method of kiln drying. Air-dried lumber is better for use outside and kiln-dried lumber is better for use inside. Kiln drying is done by using forced air or fans. It reduces the moisture content to five to eight percent within two to three weeks for one-inch lumber.

Recent developments have produced lumber that will not rot quickly when left outside. Dipping the wood in polyethylene glycol or other chemicals has been found to stabilize the wood over a wide range of relative humidity conditions. The solution replaces most of the water in the wood and causes a reduction of shrinkage.

Wood has often been called nature's most versatile building material. Throughout history, it has been used to construct everything from buildings, ships, and machinery to furniture and airplanes. Because so many types of wood are available, construction applications are almost limitless. Wood can be pressure treated with a preservative to withstand rotting in damp soil for up to 30 years. By-products such as plywood and particle board are commonly used in house construction. Wood, however, does not have the load-carrying capacity or fire resistance of reinforced concrete and structural steel, nor the strength-to-weight ratio of modern plastics. Therefore, applications for wood in modern office buildings are restricted to interior trim and it is not used at all in automobile or airplane construction.

METAL

Metal is the most common material used in manufacturing. There are many different types of metals, ranging from heavy-weight iron to lightweight aluminum and titanium. Since some metals are too soft, rust too easily, or have other characteristics that make them hard to work with, they are combined into *alloys* with specific characteristics. Steel, for example, is an alloy of iron (made with carbon and magnesium) that does not rust and that has added strength.

Cast iron, steel, steel alloys, magnesium, and aluminum are some of the metals commonly used in industry. Cast aluminum and cast iron are used by automobile manufacturers to make engine blocks. Steel beams are used to construct the framework of buildings and bridges. Steel plate is used in shipbuilding, and lightweight metals like aluminum and magnesium are used in many aircraft and aerospace components.

Sheet metal is the most widely used form of metal. It is used to make the bodies of automobiles and aircraft, as well as in duct work for heating and ventilation systems. Special tools have been developed for use on sheet metal. Many of these tools are now also used in other trades to work with metals of different thicknesses and forms.

Special Tools

Special hammers—wooden *mallets* and soft-faced hammers—are used in forming sheet metal because they do not stretch, expand, or scratch the metal as much as do metal hammers. Other hammers—*peen* (or machinist's) *hammers*—are used for riveting or to indent or compress metal. A *bumping hammer* is used by auto body repair workers to smooth out dents.

Stakes are used so that sheet metal can be formed by hammering it over T-shaped anvils of steel (Figure 9.53). *Punches* are used to make holes in sheet metal. It is safer to punch a hole in sheet metal than to drill it. A *groover* is used to lock seams together. You use one that fits the seam and tap it with a mallet as you slide it along the seam. Lay the seam over an anvil while tapping (Figure 9.54).

Tin snips, another sheet metal tool, are similar to scissors. They shear sheet metal just as scissors cut paper or cloth. To cut sheet metal, lay the sheet on a bench and slide snip jaws over the sheet at the side of the cutting mark. Press down on the top handle and let the bench push against the bottom (Figure 9.55).

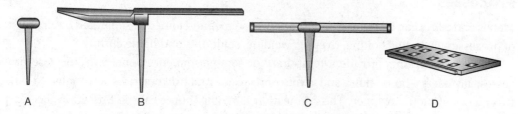

Figure 9.53. Stakes (A) Square stake (B) Beakhorn stake
(C) Double-seaming stake (D) Stake holder.

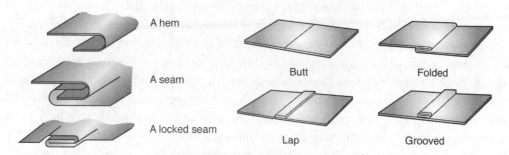

A hem

A seam

A locked seam

Butt

Folded

Lap

Grooved

Figure 9.54. Sheet metal seams.

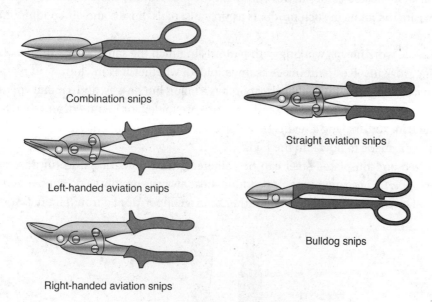

Combination snips

Straight aviation snips

Left-handed aviation snips

Bulldog snips

Right-handed aviation snips

Figure 9.55. Tin snips.

Sheet metal is also processed by hand-driven and automatic machines. A *squaring shear* cuts off sheet metal in a straight line. Edges are turned and hems formed on *bar folders* and *brakes.* Sheet metal can also be formed into round cylinders on a *slip roll.* Turned and wired edges are made on a *rotary machine,* and sheet is pressed into form on *presses* and cut to shape on *punch presses.*

Processes

Metals and alloys can be formed into a variety of shapes and joined or separated by a number of processes, including bolting, riveting, welding, soldering, and flame cutting.

Bolting and *riveting* provide a temporary or semipermanent connection. In these processes, fasteners—bolts, nuts, and rivets—are used, much like screws and nails, to hold two pieces of metal together. The connection is strong, but it can be broken if necessary by removing the bolt or by breaking the head of the rivet and pushing the rivet through the metal. Riveting is less commonly used today, now that welding has been improved.

Welding produces a permanent connection between two metals. The metal parts are melted and fused to form one piece that is very difficult to take apart. In *arc welding*, the intense heat of an electric arc melts the surface of the metalwork pieces and fuses them. This process is commonly used in heavy sheet fabrication and building and bridge construction. In *gas welding*, an oxygen and acetylene mixture in a welding torch produces a flame hot enough to melt and fuse metals. Thinner metals, such as sheet metal, are usually gas-welded.

Soldering is another way of joining metals; it is commonly used to bond sheet metal, wires, and metal pipes. Solder is an alloy made from tin and lead. It is available in different mixtures, each with its own characteristics. In soldering, first the metals to be joined must be cleaned thoroughly, usually with *flux*. Then, using a *soldering gun, soldering iron,* or *soldering pencil,* allow heated solder to flow between the joints of the metals to join them. Hems and seams are the joints in such products as tin cans, pails, boxes, and air conditioning and heating ducts.

Sheet metal work means working with patterns in much the same way as dressmaking or box folding work involves patterns. A seam is folded, whether it is in cloth or in metal. You may not have thought of the medieval armorer as a tailor, but he was, and a metalworker, too. A hem in cloth is sewn in place. In metal, the ends are folded, or hemmed, and then hooked together and locked, making a seam. To stiffen the joint even more and to make sure it holds water, solder is made to flow into the folds.

Galvanized and tin-plated steel can be soldered with a soldering iron (in this case the *soldering copper*). These metals do not conduct heat away as rapidly as do copper and brass. Brass usually requires a flame to solder rather than a copper-tipped iron (Figure 9.56).

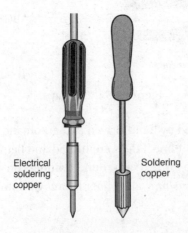

Electrical soldering copper

Soldering copper

Figure 9.56. Soldering copper.

When using the soldering copper to solder sheet metal, first heat the copper until it will melt solder. This is at about 450°F. Then wipe the tip clean with a damp cloth, and dip the hot tip into flux and rub on a small amount of solder. If the tip does not take the solder all over, rub it on a block of wood until it does. This is called *tinning*. A well-tinned copper holds solder better and transfers more heat to the metal than does a dirty one. You are now ready to solder with the tinned end of the soldering copper.

Clean the surfaces of the metal to be soldered. Do not use steel wool on galvanized metal or tin plate. Apply flux to the joint. Hold the tip of the copper against the joint until the metal is hot enough to melt the solder. Then add as much solder as needed to cover the area to be joined.

Flame cutting is a process used to cut heavy steel pieces apart. A high-pressure stream of oxygen in a cutting torch is designed to melt and blow away the molten metal. This process can be used to cut the bolts on a rusty car muffler or steel plate several inches thick.

GLASS

Glass is one of the least expensive and most abundant of all materials. It is made from the fusion of silica, which is found in sand. Glass has almost limitless uses. Glass products make up the windows in our homes, drinking glasses, optical lenses, automobile windshields, mirrors, television screens, and electrical insulators. Glass blocks, similar in shape to concrete blocks, are used in building construction to make a wall transparent to light.

The major disadvantage of glass is its brittleness. Glass can chip, crack, or break very easily if dropped or subjected to sudden impact. Glass, however, can be treated to improve its toughness. The process is called *tempering*, and it is used to make safety eyeglass lenses and tempered glass door panels.

Glassworking tools are specialty items. The *glass cutter* (Figure 9.57) has a hardened steel wheel mounted on a handle. When this tool is drawn across a piece of glass, a line is scored on the surface of the glass, which can be snapped to produce a clean cut. *Glazier's pliers* (Figure 9.58) have broad flat jaws designed to grasp a piece of glass on the cut line for the purpose of snapping a cut on very small or narrow pieces. Holes can be drilled through glass by using a *carbide tip spear point drill bit* (Figure 9.59). During the drilling operation, the bit must be lubricated with water or kerosene.

Figure 9.57. Glass cutter.

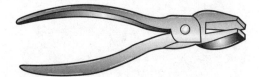

Figure 9.58. Glazier's pliers.

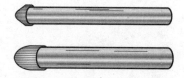

Figure 9.59. Carbide tip spear point drill bits.

PLASTICS

Plastics in one form or another are used in just about every type of manufacturing. They are lightweight and fairly impact resistant, and they can be easily and inexpensively formed into almost any shape. Hand tools, auto parts, machinery covers, and electronic components are just a few examples of the uses of plastics in modern industry.

Plastics have a very high corrosion resistance and excellent electrical insulating qualities. The corrosion resistance of plastic has made this material a popular choice in the manufacture of pipe. It is now used extensively in plumbing applications, particularly in underground systems. Plastic pipe can be quickly and easily glued together with special adhesives. Plastics do not, however, have the strength characteristic of many metals and cannot be used for structures that must withstand heavy loads.

GLUES AND ADHESIVES

Glues and adhesives are now used to join virtually any material or combination of materials. Most are very easy to apply and have the advantage of joining very thin materials or materials so different that they could not be joined any other way (e.g., steel to glass, wood to rubber, plastic to metal). A disadvantage of most adhesives is the inability to maintain strength at high temperatures, although some special types have overcome this problem.

There are several general types of adhesives, each with its own characteristics and uses. *Contact cement* is used when a strong bond is needed, as in bonding laminates to countertops or metal to wood. It is extremely flammable and must be used in a well-ventilated area.

Epoxy adhesives create a strong, moisture-resistant bond between almost any kind of material. They do not set instantly, which is an advantage when parts must be movable until a final fit is made. Epoxy adhesives are used when strong holding power is necessary.

Silicone sealants are used to keep moisture away from a structure, such as where a sink meets a wall or around a bathtub. These sealants usually come in tubes and are easy to apply.

Mastic adhesives are pasty adhesives applied with a *caulking gun* or trowel to glue such things as ceiling tiles, wallboards, and panels.

Polyvinyl resin glues, the typical white glue in a squeeze bottle, can be used to glue everything from paper to wood joints. They dry clear and form a strong bond.

The construction and maintenance of all buildings, bridges, and other structures, as well as of all machines and machine parts, must be carefully designed and planned in detail. Blueprints, layouts, templates, and patterns are some of the means used in design and layout work.

BLUEPRINTS

Blueprints are drawings that graphically describe the construction, installation, maintenance, or repair of structures and machines. Blueprints may be done from different views and angles. However, virtually all are done according to established drawing conventions and use standardized symbols. Lines of various thicknesses and characteristics and specific symbols specify the size, shape, and other features of an object. There are special symbols for various architectural materials (e.g., wood or marble), for electrical configurations, for plumbing fixtures, for appliances, and for heating and ventilation systems.

There are different types of blueprints. Architectural drawings may be site, foundation, or construction plans. Other blueprints may be floor plans or plans that detail the electrical or plumbing systems. HVAC plans describe the heating, ventilation, and air conditioning system.

A basic blueprint is shown in Figure 9.60. Blueprint reading is a skill that requires intensive training.

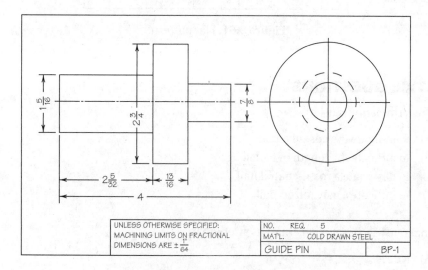

Figure 9.60. Blueprint.

LAYOUT

A *layout* is the transfer of dimensions and lines specified on a blueprint to the material being worked on. For example, if the blueprint specifies that a piece of wood be cut to a length of four feet, you must measure the desired length and draw a line on the spot where the cut must be made and also perhaps on the spot where the piece of wood is to be placed.

PATTERNS AND TEMPLATES

Patterns and templates are models by which parts are made. Figure 9.61 is an example of a *flat pattern*. Commonly used in the fabrication of sheet metal parts, flat patterns represent the shape of the part before it is rolled or bent into final form. *Templates* are a gauge or guide used to check the size and shape of parts so that each will be exactly the same. For example, when a carpenter is building a house, the roof rafters require careful layout and cutting. Each must be cut at the same angle and length to ensure that the roof line will be straight. After the first rafter is cut and checked for accuracy, it is used as the template or pattern for every other rafter.

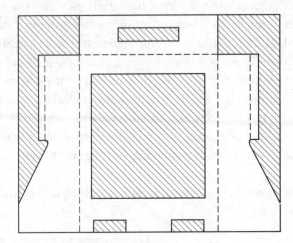

Figure 9.61. Flat pattern.

PRACTICE QUESTIONS

1. The term *penny* is used

   (A) to indicate the cost of a nail.
   (B) to indicate the length of a nail.
   (C) to designate a rosin-coated nail.
   (D) to indicate a galvanized nail.

2. Concrete reaches 98 percent of its strength in

   (A) 3 days.
   (B) 50 days.
   (C) 28 days.
   (D) 10 days.

3. A coping saw blade is placed in the saw

   (A) with the teeth pointing upward.
   (B) with the teeth pointing toward the handle.
   (C) so it cuts with the wood grain.
   (D) so it cuts across the wood grain.

4. Carpenters use

   (A) ball-peen hammers.
   (B) chisel point hammers.
   (C) claw hammers.
   (D) planishing hammers.

5. A welding torch can also be used as

   (A) a light source.
   (B) an etching tool.
   (C) a cutting torch.
   (D) a pipe wrench.

6. Self-locking nuts are designed to

   (A) be tightened by hand.
   (B) be frequently disassembled.
   (C) require periodic tightening.
   (D) jam against the bolt thread and not vibrate loose.

7. Wood floats in water because

   (A) of its hollow cell structure.
   (B) it weighs 1.5 times as much as an equal volume of water.
   (C) its cells are nonporous.
   (D) it has short, compact cells with air between them.

8. Flat washers can be used to

   (A) prevent the bolt and nut from loosening.
   (B) exert force between the bolted connection and the piece being worked on.
   (C) compensate for an oversized hole.
   (D) connect thin-gauge metal parts.

9. The tool used to tighten a cylinder head bolt is a

   (A) box wrench.
   (B) breaker bar.
   (C) ratchet.
   (D) torque wrench.

Answers Explained

1. **(B)** The term *penny* is used *to indicate the length of a nail.* It is an old English term that has no definite relationship to today's measuring units. You can, however, keep in mind that the larger the number is, the longer the nail is.

2. **(C)** Concrete reaches 98 percent of its strength in *28 days.*

3. **(B)** A coping saw blade is placed in the saw *with the teeth pointing toward the handle.* That means you cut with a coping saw on the downward stroke. That also means that you need to use a special type of vise to hold the object you are cutting.

4. **(C)** Carpenters use *claw hammers.* These allow carpenters to remove nails that don't go where they belong or are bent on the way into the wood. Machinists use ball-peen hammers. There is no such thing as a chisel point hammer. Planishing hammers are used by people who are flattening or shaping sheet metal.

5. **(C)** A welding torch can be used as *a cutting torch.* This can be done when the proper amount of oxygen is used. Please note that under no circumstances should a welding torch be used as a light source. That light can cause extreme injury to the eye.

6. **(D)** Self-locking nuts are designed to *jam against the bolt thread and not vibrate loose.* The wing nut is the only nut designed to be tightened by hand. It is used on connections that must be disassembled frequently and that do not require extreme tightening.

7. **(A)** Wood floats in water because *of its hollow cell structure.*

8. **(C)** Flat washers are used to *compensate for an oversized hole.* They can also be used to distribute evenly the compressive load of a bolted connection over a wider area. Lock washers are designed to exert force between the bolted connection and the piece being worked on, preventing the bolt and nut from loosening.

9. **(D)** The tool used to tighten a cylinder head bolt is a *torque wrench.* Failure to tighten the head properly can result in a blown head gasket. So the cylinder head must be tightened in a specific sequence using a torque wrench.

Mechanical Comprehension Review 10

The ASVAB Mechanical Comprehension subtest measures knowledge of basic mechanical and physical principles and the ability to visualize how illustrated objects and simple machines work. Basic mechanical and physical principles are largely governed by the laws of physics—the science of matter and energy and their interactions. This chapter reviews some basic principles of physics and how some simple machines make work easier.

FORCE

One of the basic concepts of physics is the concept of force. *Force* is something that can change the velocity of an object by making it start, stop, speed up, slow down, or change direction. Let's think for a minute of a car. When you take your foot off the gas pedal, your car does not suddenly come to a stop. It coasts on, only gradually losing its velocity. If you want the car to stop, you have to do something to it. That is what your brakes are for: to exert a force that decreases the car's velocity.

When a deep space probe coasts through first the solar system and then the space beyond, nothing is pushing it and nothing is stopping it (unless it comes too close to a star or planet, when their gravity changes the picture). However, if we want it to speed up, slow down, or change direction, we send it signals to fire control rockets—i.e., we exert a force on it to change its velocity.

The Voyager 1 and 2 probes are prime examples. They were launched in 1977 on missions to explore the outer planets. Both were accelerated to their initial escape velocity by main booster rockets that were jettisoned before leaving the neighborhood of Earth. They coasted through the solar system for years from that initial "push" with only small adjustments from onboard thrusters, and very little friction, since there is no atmosphere in space—there was basically nothing to stop them. (Just as a note, the Voyager story doesn't end there. Scientists were able to use the gravitational attraction of the outer planets to "slingshot" both spacecraft further in what has now become an interstellar—no longer just interplanetary—mission. Voyager 1 left the solar system in 1981, and is now about 10 billion miles from Earth. Voyager 2's slower trajectory gave it more time exploring the outer planets, but it still left the solar system in 1989, and is now more than eight billion miles from Earth.)

KINDS OF FORCE

Friction

Your car has two controls whose functions are to change the car's velocity: the gas pedal and the brake pedal. The brakes make use of the same force that stops your car if you just let it coast: friction.

Sliding friction is a force that is generated whenever two objects are in contact and there is relative motion between them. When something is moving, friction *always* acts in such a direction as to retard (slow down or decrease) the relative motion. Therefore, the direction of the force of friction on a moving object is always directly opposite the direction of the velocity. The brake shoes slow down the rotation of the wheels, and the tires slow the car until it comes to rest.

In the simplest case, the force of friction can be easily measured by using a *spring scale* (Figure 10.1). (A spring scale can be used to measure all kinds of forces. Basically, it measures the force pulling on its shackle.) A spring scale is calibrated in force units—*pounds* or (in the SI) *newtons*. A newton (abbreviated N) is a fairly small unit of force; it takes 4.45 newtons to equal 1 pound.

Figure 10.1. Spring scale.

Figure 10.2 shows a spring scale being used to measure the force of sliding friction between a brick and the horizontal surface on which it is resting. The scale is pulling the brick along at constant speed. In this condition, the brick is said to be in *equilibrium*. Since its velocity is not changing, we can conclude that the net force acting on it is zero.

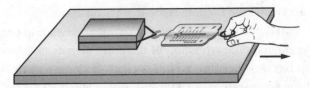

Figure 10.2. Spring scale being used to measure force of sliding friction.

However, the spring scale *is* exerting a force, which is shown on its face; this force is pulling the brick to the right. The brick can remain in equilibrium only if there is an equal force pulling it to the left, so that the net force (the sum of forces acting on it in all directions) acting on it is zero. In the situation shown, the only force pulling the brick to the left is the frictional force between the brick and the surface. Therefore, the reading on the spring scale is equal to the force of friction.

Anyone who has ever moved furniture around, or slid a box across the floor, knows that the frictional force is greater when the furniture or the box is heavier. The force of friction does not change much as the object speeds up, but it depends very strongly on how hard the two surfaces are pressed together.

When a solid moves through a liquid, such as a boat moving through the water, there is a frictionlike force retarding the motion of the solid. It is called *viscous drag*. Like friction, it always acts opposite velocity. Unlike friction, however, it increases greatly with speed, and it depends more on the shape of the object and on the nature of the liquid than on the object's weight. Gases also produce viscous drag; the example of this you are probably most familiar with is the air resistance that acts on a car at high speed.

To summarize, friction and viscous drag are forces that act to retard motion.

Gravity

Probably the first law of physics that everyone learns is this: If you drop something, it falls. Since its velocity keeps on changing as it falls, there must be a force acting on it all the while. That is the force we call *gravity*.

You can measure gravity by balancing it off with a spring scale. When you hang something on a spring scale and read the scale in pounds or newtons, you usually call the force of gravity acting on the object by a special name—you call it the *weight* of the object.

Weight is not a fixed property of an object; it varies with location. A person who weighs 160 pounds at the North Pole will check in at 159.2 pounds at the equator. If he should step on a scale on the moon, it would read only 27 pounds. Everything weighs less where the acceleration due to gravity is smaller. In fact, *weight is directly proportional to the acceleration of an object due to gravity.*

Obviously, weight also depends on something else, since things have different weights even if they are all at the same place. Weight depends on how much "stuff" there is in the object. When you buy 10 pounds of sugar, you expect to get twice as much as if you buy five pounds. And if you take both sacks to the moon, one will still weigh twice as much as the other. The amount of sugar, the *mass* of the sugar, did not change when it was taken somewhere else. And the more sugar you have, the more it weighs—regardless of where you are.

Weight, then, is proportional both to mass and to the acceleration due to gravity. This equation works nicely, without introducing any constants, if the units are carefully defined. Mass is measured in kilograms; the kilogram is one of the basic units of the SI. By definition, when you multiply the mass in kilograms by the acceleration in meters per second squared, the weight comes out in newtons.

To summarize: Weight—the force of gravity—is the product of an object's mass and its acceleration due to gravity.

Lift

Airfoils—wings, in everyday language—generate *lift* so that aircraft can get off the ground. (Yes, they need some kind of propulsion, too, but without the wings they would only be a ground-based accident trying to happen.)

Airfoil shapes are found on wings, fans, and propellers—any application where air needs to be moved. The airfoil shape provides lift when it splits the airstream through which it is moving. An airfoil has a thicker, rounded front or leading edge, and a thinner trailing edge. In between the leading and trailing edge, an airfoil is curved; the top surface usually has a greater curve than the bottom surface. When a surface is curved we say it has *camber*.

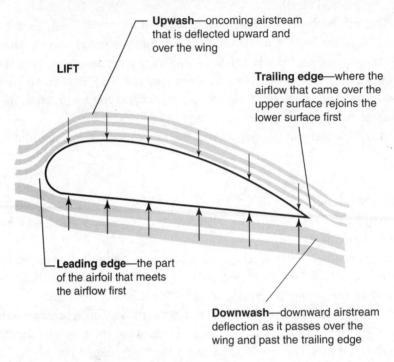

Upwash—oncoming airstream that is deflected upward and over the wing

LIFT

Trailing edge—where the airflow that came over the upper surface rejoins the lower surface first

Leading edge—the part of the airfoil that meets the airflow first

Downwash—downward airstream deflection as it passes over the wing and past the trailing edge

Figure 10.3. Airfoil produces lift.

An airfoil uses the aerodynamics identified by Bernoulli's Principle to provide lift to the aircraft. Since the top surface of the wing has more camber than the bottom surface, the air flows faster over the top of the wing than it does underneath. This means that there is less air pressure above the wing than there is underneath; the difference in air pressure above and below the wing causes lift.

There are four forces that act upon an aircraft in flight: *lift*, *weight* (or gravity), *thrust*, and *drag*. Lift pushes the aircraft up (away from Earth); weight pulls the aircraft down toward Earth (or, more precisely, toward Earth's center); thrust pushes the aircraft forward; and drag tends to slow the aircraft, pushing back on it as it moves forward.

Elastic Recoil

The basic feature of a solid, as opposed to a liquid or a gas, is that it has a definite shape. It resists changes in its shape and, in so doing, exerts a force against whatever force is applied to it.

For example, look at the meter bar supported at its ends shown in Figure 10.4. If you push down on it, you bend it, and you can feel it pushing back on you. The harder you push, the more the bar bends and the harder it pushes back. It bends just enough to push on you with the same force that you exert on it. The force it exerts is called *elastic recoil*.

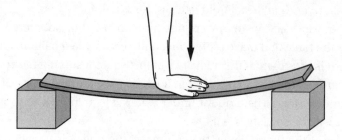

Figure 10.4. Supported meter bar.

The same thing happens when you stand on the floor or on the ground. You can't see the floor bend, but it bends just the same, although not very much. Even a feather resting on the floor bends it a little. The elastic recoil force needed to support the feather is very small, so the amount of bending is too small to detect.

A rope does not resist bending, but it certainly does resist stretching. When a rope is stretched, it is said to be in a state of *tension*. The tension can be measured by cutting the rope and inserting a spring scale into it, as shown in Figure 10.5. The spring scale reads the tension in the rope in pounds or newtons. If you pull with a force of 30 N, for example, the tension in the rope is 30 N, and that is what the scale will indicate. Something, such as the elastic recoil of the wall to which the scale is attached, must be pulling on the other end with a force of 30 N. The tension in the rope is the same throughout and is equal to the elastic recoil force that the rope exerts at its ends.

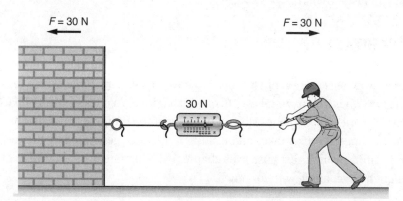

Figure 10.5.

To summarize: A force applied to a solid distorts the shape of the solid, causing it to exert a force back on the force that distorted it.

Buoyancy

If you take a deep breath and dive into a pool, you will have a lot of trouble keeping yourself submerged. Something keeps pushing you up. That force is called *buoyancy*.

When an object is submerged in a fluid, a buoyancy force is created. It acts in an upward direction, equal to the weight of the fluid displaced by the volume of the object. If the weight of the object is less than the weight of the fluid it displaces, the object will tend to rise to the surface of the fluid. If the weight of the object is greater than the weight of the fluid it displaces, the result is *negative buoyancy*—i.e., the object sinks until it reaches a level where increased pressure reverses the situation, or until it reaches the bottom of the fluid.

And remember, a *fluid* can be a liquid *or* a gas. Air is a fluid.

The force of buoyancy acts in an upward direction on anything submerged in a liquid or a gas. Buoyancy is the force that makes ships float and helium-filled balloons rise. A rock sinks because its weight is greater than the buoyancy of the water. A submerged cork rises because the buoyancy is greater than its weight. When it reaches the surface, some of it emerges, but the rest is still under water. The amount under water is just enough to produce a buoyant force equal to its weight, so it stays put.

As an example, in the figure below the volume of the object is concentrated in the two spherical parts. If we submerge this object in water, it will head for the surface.

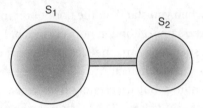

Figure 10.6. Buoyancy.

Since the size of the two spheres is unequal, there will be two unequal forces acting on the object overall. Since the weight of the water displaced by S_1 is greater than that for S_2, S_1 will rise to the surface more quickly than S_2 because the water is pushing S_1 up with a greater amount of force than S_2. In other words, the object will rise to the surface at a slanted angle— S_1 will come up faster than S_2.

Other Forces

There are some other familiar forces, and some not so familiar. You know about magnetism, which attracts iron nails to a red horseshoe. You have met electric force, which makes a nylon shirt cling to you when you try to take it off, or which refuses to release the dust particles from your favorite CD or DVD. Airplanes stay up because of the lift force generated by the flow of air across their wings. A rocket takes off because of the force generated by the gases expanding in it and coming from its exhaust. This chapter will illustrate other examples of force, but we have enough to get along with for now.

ACTION AND REACTION

A batter steps up to the plate and takes a healthy swing, sending the ball into left field. The bat (directed by the batter) has exerted a large force on the ball, changing both the magnitude and the direction of its velocity. But the ball has also exerted a force on the bat, slowing it down. The batter feels this when the bat hits the ball.

Next time up, he strikes out. He has taken exactly the same swing but exerts no force on anything. (Air in this example is small enough not to count.) The batter has discovered that it is impossible to exert a force unless there is something there to push back. *Forces exist only in pairs.* When object A exerts a force on object B, then B must exert a force on A. The two forces are sometimes called *action* and *reaction*, although which is often somewhat arbitrary. The two parts of the interaction are equal in magnitude, are opposite in direction, and act on different objects.

The law of action and reaction leads to an apparent paradox if you are not careful how it is applied. A horse pulls on a wagon. If the force of the wagon pulling the horse the other way is the same, as the law insists, how can the horse and wagon get started?

The error in the reasoning is this: If you want to know whether the horse starts to move, you have to consider the forces acting *on the horse*. The force acting on the wagon has nothing to do with the question. The horse starts up because the force he exerts with his hooves is larger than the force of the wagon pulling him back. And the wagon starts up because the force of the horse pulling it forward is larger than the frictional forces holding it back. To know whether something moves, consider the forces acting *on it*. Action and reaction forces *never* act on the same object.

Again, to summarize, forces exist only in pairs, equal in magnitude and opposite in direction, acting on different objects.

BALANCED FORCES

If a single force acts on an object, the velocity of the object must change. If two or more forces act, however, their effects may eliminate each other. This is the condition of equilibrium in which there is no net force and the velocity does not change. We saw such a condition in the case in which gravity is pulling an object down and a spring scale, used for weighing it, is pulling it upward.

An object in equilibrium may or may not be at rest. A parachutist descending at a constant speed is in equilibrium. Her weight is just balanced by the viscous drag on the parachute, which is why she put it on in the first place. A heavier parachutist falls a little faster; his speed increases until the viscous drag just balances his weight.

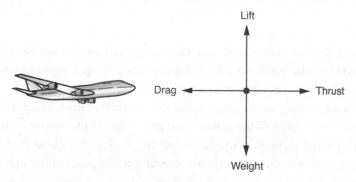

Figure 10.7.

Balancing the vertical forces is not enough to produce equilibrium. An airplane traveling at a constant speed is in equilibrium under the influence of four forces, two vertical and two horizontal. Vertical: gravity (down) is just balanced by the lift produced by the flow of air across the wing. Horizontal: viscous drag is just balanced by the thrust of the engines. Both the vertical and the horizontal velocities are constant.

The brick in Figure 10.2, resting on a tabletop and being pulled along at a constant speed, is another example. Vertical: The downward force of gravity is balanced by the upward force of the elastic recoil of the tabletop. Horizontal: The tension in the spring scale, pulling to the right, is balanced by the friction pulling it to the left, opposite the direction of motion.

If an object is in equilibrium—at rest or moving at a constant speed in a straight line—the total force acting on it in any direction is exactly equal in magnitude to the force in the opposite direction.

COMPONENTS OF FORCE

The crate in Figure 10.8 is being dragged along the floor by means of a rope that is not horizontal. The rope makes an angle θ with the floor.

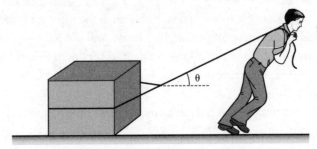

Figure 10.8.

The tension in the rope, acting on the crate, does two things to it. First, it drags the crate across the floor. Second, it tends to lift the crate off the floor. The smaller the angle θ, the larger the effective force dragging the crate, and the smaller the effective force lifting it. When θ = 0, the entire force is dragging and there is no lifting at all. Conversely, when θ = 90°, the entire force is lifting the crate.

THE INCLINED PLANE

A wagon rolls downhill, propelled only by its own weight. But gravity pulls straight down, not at an angle downhill. What makes the wagon go is a *component* of its weight, a part of its weight acting downhill, parallel to the surface the wagon rests on.

A component of a force can act in any direction, not just vertically or horizontally. On an inclined plane, the weight of the wagon has two different effects: it acts *parallel* to the surface of the hill, pushing the wagon downhill; and it acts perpendicular (or *normal*) to the surface, pushing the wagon into the surface. As the hill gets steeper, the parallel component becomes larger and the perpendicular component decreases.

When the wagon is resting on the surface, the elastic recoil of the surface is just enough to cancel the normal component of the wagon's weight. If the wagon is to stay in equilibrium, you have to pull on it, uphill, to prevent it from running away. If there is no friction, the uphill force needed is the same whether the wagon is standing still or going either uphill or downhill at constant speed.

The situation is different if the wagon is moving and there is friction. If the wagon is going uphill, you have to pull harder because the friction is working against you, holding it back. The total force you need to keep the wagon going is then equal to the parallel component of the weight plus the friction. On the other hand, if you are lowering the wagon down the hill, holding the rope to keep it from running away from you, friction is acting uphill, helping you to hold the wagon back. Then the force you must exert is the parallel component of the weight *minus* the friction.

PRACTICE QUESTIONS

1. Weight _____, and mass _____.

    (A) is constant, depends on acceleration due to local gravity
    (B) depends on acceleration due to local gravity, is constant
    (C) is more at the equator than at the north pole, is directly proportional
    (D) is constant regardless of location, depends on acceleration due to local gravity

2. Viscous drag is _____ and _____.

    (A) a constant regardless of weight, can be easily calculated
    (B) similar to gravity, increases with speed
    (C) similar to friction, acts opposite to an object's direction of movement
    (D) dependent on the shape of the object, decreases with speed

3. The four forces acting on a wing in flight are

    (A) lift, gravity, drag, and thrust.
    (B) lift, gravity, parasitic drag, and forward momentum.
    (C) lift, downwash, drag, and thrust.
    (D) buoyancy, drag, thrust, and weight.

4. If a single force begins to act on an object,

    (A) the velocity of the object will not change.
    (B) the velocity of the object may change.
    (C) the object has achieved equilibrium.
    (D) the velocity of the object must change.

5. Which principle of mechanical motion is used in the design of a roller coaster?

    (A) Acceleration
    (B) Momentum
    (C) Friction
    (D) All of the above

6. In the drawing below, a force of 50 pounds is needed to stretch the spring 1 inch. How much force must be applied to the block in order to move the box 4 inches to the right?

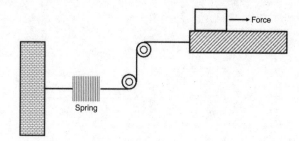

    (A) 50 pounds
    (B) 200 pounds
    (C) 400 pounds
    (D) 800 pounds

7. A block of solid aluminum has a density of 0.098 pounds per cubic inch. If the block has dimensions of 1 inch by 1 inch by 4 inches, what is its weight?

   (A) 0.290 pounds
   (B) 0.392 pounds
   (C) 3.92 pounds
   (D) 30.92 pounds

8. A spring is a flexible device that can resume its original shape and strength after bending or stretching. It would be best made out of

   (A) very thin tin wire.
   (B) thick steel wire.
   (C) wood.
   (D) ceramic pottery.

9. If you add water to a tank, the water pressure on the bottom of the tank will

   (A) decrease.
   (B) stay the same.
   (C) increase.
   (D) depend on the altitude.

10. The condition in which there is no net force on an object and its velocity does not change is called

   (A) stasis.
   (B) equilibrium.
   (C) balanced inertia.
   (D) inertia-less static condition.

11. When a gas is compressed, it

   (A) gains thermal and potential energy.
   (B) gains thermal energy but loses potential energy.
   (C) loses thermal energy but gains potential energy.
   (D) loses both thermal and potential energy.

Answers Explained

1. **(B)** Weight *depends on acceleration due to local gravity*, and mass *is constant*. The terms "mass" and "weight" are often used to mean the same thing. Although they are related, the two are significantly different. Mass is an expression of how much material is in an object, whereas weight is a measurement of the gravitational force exerted on that material in a particular gravitational field. Mass and weight are therefore proportional to each other, with the acceleration due to gravity as the proportional constant.

2. **(C)** Viscous drag is *similar to friction* and *acts opposite to an object's direction of movement*.

3. **(A)** The four forces acting on a wing in flight are *lift, gravity, drag, and thrust*.

4. **(D)** If a single force begins to act on an object, *the velocity of the object must change*. According to Newton's First Law of Motion, an object in motion will stay in motion (in a straight line) and an object at rest will stay at rest unless acted upon by an outside force.

5. **(D)** *All of the principles* of mechanical motion are used in the design of a roller coaster. Acceleration must be considered in designing the maximum rise of the first hill. Momentum must be considered to ensure the train gets back to the starting point since the train has no motor or engine of its own. Friction must be considered when designing the braking system.

6. **(B)** A force of *200 pounds* must be applied to the block in order to move the box 4 inches to the right since a force of 50 pounds is needed to stretch the spring 1 inch. To find the answer, simply multiply 4 inches of movement by 50 pounds per inch to find the 200 pounds of force.

7. **(B)** A block of solid aluminum has a density of 0.098 pounds per cubic inch. If the block has dimensions of 1 inch by 1 inch by 4 inches, its weight is *0.392 pounds*. First calculate the block's volume by multiplying length by width by height: 1 inch × 1 inch × 4 inches = 4 cubic inches. The weight is the density multiplied by the block's volume: 4 cubic inches × 0.098 pounds per cubic inch = 0.392 pounds.

8. **(B)** A spring is a flexible device that can resume its original shape and strength after bending or stretching. It would be best made out of *thick steel wire*. Since a spring is flexible enough to resume its original shape and strength after bending or stretching, the only material listed that would be both flexible enough and strong enough would be thick steel wire. Although you could make a spring out of very thin tin wire, it would break very easily.

9. **(C)** If you add water to a tank, the water pressure on the bottom of the tank will *increase*. Since water pressure on the bottom of the tank depends on the depth of the water, when you add water to the tank, the pressure will increase.

10. **(B)** The condition in which there is no net force on an object and its velocity does not change is called *equilibrium*.

11. **(A)** When a gas is compressed, it *gains thermal and potential energy*. The gain in potential energy is why compressed air can be used to drive nail guns and pneumatic hammers.

There are devices that make work easier. These devices are known as *simple machines.* Without thinking about it, everybody uses a hundred simple machines every day—a light switch, a doorknob, a pencil sharpener, to name just a few.

A pulley illustrates how machines make work easier. After discussing the pulley principle and learning some basic work terms, we will go on to discuss briefly some other simple machines—levers, hydraulic jacks, loading ramps, vises, and machines that spin (for example, winches and gears).

THE PULLEY PRINCIPLE

A piano mover, unable to fit the instrument into a staircase, decides to raise it outside the building to a window. He attaches it to a set of ropes and wheels that somehow make it possible for him to lift it with a force considerably smaller than the weight of the piano. How does it work?

Consider first the heavy block in Figure 10.9 suspended from two ropes. The upward force on the block is the tension (T) in the ropes, and the sum of the two tensions must equal the weight of the block. If the whole system is symmetrical, each rope is under tension equal to half the weight of the block.

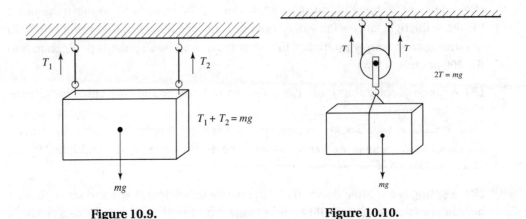

Figure 10.9.   **Figure 10.10.**

Now look at Figure 10.10 where the block has been attached to a wheel. There is now only one rope, which passes over the wheel. The tension in the rope is the same throughout; if it were different on one side than on the other, the wheel would turn until the tension on the two sides equalized. The tension in the rope is still only half the weight of the block since it exerts *two* upward forces on the block. Now you have a system that helps in lifting things. Just fasten one end of the rope to a fixed support and pull on the other end (Figure 10.11). Now you can raise the block with a force equal to only half its weight.

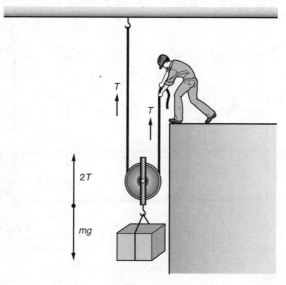

Figure 10.11.

Are you getting something for nothing? Well, yes and no. True, you can now lift the weight with less force, but you have to pull the rope farther than you would if you lifted the block directly. Every time you pull 10 feet of rope through your hands, the block rises five feet. You might look at it this way: If the block rises five feet, *both* sides of the supporting rope have to shorten five feet, and the only way to accomplish this is to pull 10 feet of rope through. You raise the block with only half the force, but you have to exert the force through twice the distance.

You might prefer to pull in a downward direction rather than upward, and you can manage this by attaching a fixed wheel to the support and passing the rope around it as in Figure 10.12. The tension in the rope is still only half the weight of the block; the fixed pulley does nothing but change the direction of the force you exert.

Let's adopt some vocabulary. The weight of the object being lifted we will call the *load*, and the distance it rises is the *load distance*. The force you exert on the rope is the *effort*, and the distance through which you exert that effort is the *effort distance*. With a single movable pulley in use, the effort is half the load and the effort distance is twice the load distance.

There are ways to string up a system of pulleys that will reduce the effort still further. Figure 10.13 shows how the same two pulleys can be connected to a rope in such a way as to divide the load among three strands instead of two. This is done by fastening one end of the rope to the load instead of to the fixed support. Unfortunately, when you do this, you have to shorten all three strands when you raise the object, and the effort distance becomes three times the load distance. By using more pulleys you can reduce the effort still further. Unfortunately, there is a limit to how much you can reduce the effort. The analysis we have done so far neglects a few things, such as friction and the weight of the movable pulleys themselves. Every time you add a pulley, you increase the friction in the system; if it is a movable pulley—the only kind that produces a reduction in force—you have to lift it along with the load. The effort in any real system is always larger than the ideal effort we calculated by dividing up the load. If there are a lot of pulleys, it may be considerably larger. And friction, while it increases the force you must exert, has no effect on the distance you have to pull the rope.

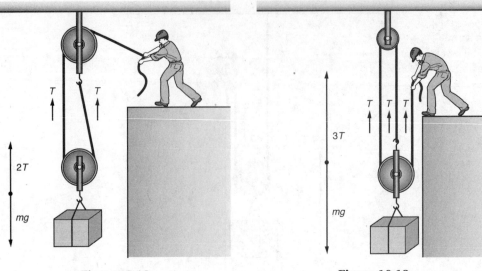

Figure 10.12.　　　　　　　　**Figure 10.13.**

Effort distance is load distance times the number of supporting strands; effort is larger than load divided by the number of strands.

THE WORK PRINCIPLE

While pulleys are useful, they don't really give you something for nothing. Ignoring the problem of friction, the input and output forces are in inverse ratio to the respective distances:

$$\frac{\text{effort}}{\text{load}} = \frac{\text{load distance}}{\text{effort distance}}$$

Or, to put it another way,

$$(\text{effort})(\text{effort distance}) = (\text{load})(\text{load distance})$$

A frictionless pulley, then, does not alter the product of force and distance; it is the same for the mover who pulls on the rope as it is for the piano. This product occurs repeatedly in physical situations, so it is given a special name. Force times distance is called *work*.

Work is done whenever a force moves something through a distance. If you stand still holding a boulder over your head, you might get tired, but—in the physical sense—you are doing no work.

There is another limitation on the definition of work. Only the force in the direction of motion counts. For example, look at Figure 10.14—a child on a sled. The tension in the rope is pulling the sled, but it is also lifting the sled. Only the component of the force that is acting in the direction the sled is going is doing work on the sled. Since the sled is moving horizontally, the horizontal component of the tension is the only part that is doing the work of moving the sled.

Figure 10.14.

The effort times the effort distance is called the *work input*, and the load times the load distance is the *work output*. While there are no real frictionless pulleys, we can use the ideal of a frictionless, weightless pulley in doing useful calculations. With such an ideal pulley, the work output is exactly the same as the work input. If you use this idea to calculate how hard you will have to pull on the rope, the best you can do, when you have finished the calculation, is to say that the effort will be *at least* the amount you figure. How much more it will be depends on the friction and on the weight of the wheels.

With a real pulley, you always have to pull a little harder than the calculated value. The work input is therefore always more than the work output. The ratio between the work output and the work input is called the efficiency of the machine:

$$\text{efficiency} = \frac{W_{out}}{W_{in}}$$

Efficiency is usually expressed as a percent. It tells you what fraction of the work that you put into a machine comes out as useful work at the other end. Or, in other words, *efficiency* is the fraction of the work input that emerges as useful work output.

LEVERS

Another type of simple machine is a *lever*. A lever consists of a rigid bar pivoted at some point. An effort force applied to the bar at some point produces a different force on a load at some other position on the bar. The crowbar in Figure 10.15 is typical. The load is the weight of the rock being lifted. The effort is the force exerted by the person who is trying to move the rock.

Figure 10.15.

Usually, the purpose of a machine is to make it possible to exert a large load force with a smaller effort. The machine magnifies force. The amount of this magnification, the ratio of load to effort, is called the *mechanical advantage* of the machine. It can be defined algebraically as the ratio of the two forces:

$$MA = \frac{F_L}{F_E}$$

In a pulley, the mechanical advantage is equal to the number of strands of rope supporting the load. For a lever, it can be found by considering the torques acting on the bar. The torque around the pivot that is exerted by the worker is $F_E r_E$ where r_E (the *effort arm*) is the distance from the point where the effort is applied to the pivot. Similarly, the torque produced by the weight of the rock is $F_L r_L$, where r_L is the load arm. If the system is rotating in equilibrium, these two torques must have the same magnitude, so

$$F_E r_E = F_L r_L$$

from which we find that the mechanical advantage, F_L / F_E, is given by

$$MA_{Lever} = \frac{r_E}{r_L}$$

Or, in other words, in a lever the mechanical advantage is equal to the ratio of the effort arm to the load arm.

For many kinds of levers, friction at the pivot is very small, so efficiencies approach 100% and the arm ratio is very near the force ratio. Usually, no correction is needed.

Levers are classified according to the relative positions of the pivot, load, and effort. The three classes are represented by the tools shown in Figure 10.16. In the pliers (first class) the pivot is between the effort and the load. In the nutcracker (second class) it is the load that is between the other two. And in the sugar tongs (third class), the effort is in the middle.

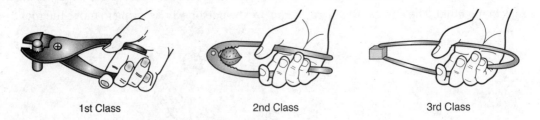

1st Class   2nd Class   3rd Class

Figure 10.16. Levers.

Note that in the third-class lever (the sugar tongs), the load arm is longer than the effort arm, so the mechanical advantage is less than 1. This lever magnifies distance at the expense of force.

Mechanical advantage is the ratio of load to effort; in a lever, it is equal to the ratio of the effort arm to the load arm.

HYDRAULIC JACK

Liquids are almost incompressible, i.e., they cannot be "squeezed" to take up less space. This property makes them suitable as a means of transforming work.

A *hydraulic jack* is a device in which force is applied to the oil in a small cylinder. As shown in Figure 10.17, this force causes some of the oil to be transferred to a larger cylinder. This forces the piston in the larger cylinder to rise, lifting a load.

Figure 10.17. Hydraulic jack.

This device takes advantage of the fact that oil, being nearly incompressible, transmits whatever pressure is applied to it. The pressure applied in the small cylinder appears unchanged in the big one, pushing up its piston.

Ideal mechanical advantage is the ratio between effort distance and load distance; for a hydraulic jack, it is equal to the ratio of the area of the load piston to that of the effort piston.

Hydraulic machinery is used in construction equipment, aircraft, and heavy industry. Hydraulics use the same mechanical principles as levers, pulleys, and gears: using a small force over a longer distance or a large force over a shorter distance. Hydraulics use a liquid or a gas to transmit forces from one surface to another. A force acting on a surface is called pressure, which is calculated by this formula:

$$\text{Pressure} = \text{Force/Area}$$

In hydraulic systems, the pressure is the same throughout the fluid. Therefore, you can control the forces by changing the size of the surface area.

Hydrostatic Pressure

Pressure in liquids that are not moving (flowing somewhere) is called *hydrostatic pressure* and is caused by gravity. Pressure increases proportionately as you go deeper in the liquid—for instance, doubling depth doubles pressure. To calculate total pressure at any depth in a fluid, add the hydrostatic pressure to the atmospheric pressure.

LOADING RAMP

A *ramp* is a device commonly used to aid in lifting. To raise a heavy load a few feet onto a platform, it is common practice to place it on a dolly and wheel it up an inclined plane.

The work output of an inclined plane is the work that would have to be done to lift the load directly: the weight of the load times the vertical distance it goes. The work input is the actual force exerted in pushing the dolly up the ramp times the length of the ramp.

The ideal mechanical advantage of an inclined plane is equal to its length divided by its height.

VISE

The vise in Figure 10.18 is a complex machine in which the handle acts as a lever operating a new kind of machine: a screw. How can we calculate the constants of this gadget?

It would be very difficult to calculate the ratio of the force the jaws apply to the force on the handle. The best we can do is work with the distances.

A *screw* consists of a single continuous spiral wrapped around a cylinder. The distance between ridges is known as the *pitch* of the thread, as shown in Figure 10.19. Every time the screw makes one complete turn, it advances a distance equal to the pitch. In a vise, one complete turn is made when the end of the handle travels in a circle whose radius is the length of the handle (l). Therefore, when the effort moves a distance $2\pi l$, the load moves a distance equal to the pitch of the thread. Therefore, for a screw,

$$\text{ideal MA} = \frac{2\pi(\text{length of handle})}{\text{pitch of thread}}$$

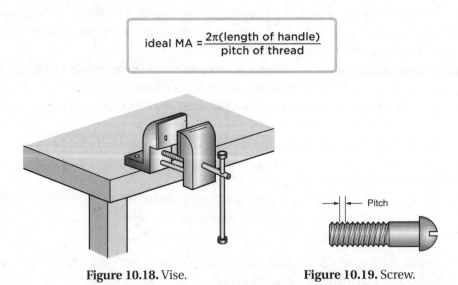

Figure 10.18. Vise.   **Figure 10.19.** Screw.

However, if you use this expression to calculate the forces, you will get it all wrong. A vise is a high-friction device. It has to be because it is the friction that keeps it from opening when you tighten it. A vise is a self-locking machine because its efficiency is considerably less than 50 percent.

MACHINES THAT SPIN

What is the mechanical advantage of a winch, such as that shown in Figure 10.20? The principle is not much different from that of a lever. Since the crank and the shaft turn together, the torque exerted by the effort (the force on the handle) must be equal to the torque exerted by the load (the tension in the rope). The mechanical advantage is then the ratio of the radius of the crank to the radius of the shaft.

Figure 10.20. Winch.　　　　　　　**Figure 10.21.** Gears.

In mechanical devices, gears are commonly used to change torque. Consider the gears in Figure 10.21, for example. We assume that both gears are mounted on shafts of equal diameter and that the small gear is driving the large one. What is the mechanical advantage of this combination?

First of all, the teeth must have the same size and spacing on both gears in order for them to mesh properly. With 12 teeth in the large gear and only 4 in the small one, the small gear has to make three complete revolutions to make the big one turn once. The large, load gear moves only one-third as far as the smaller, effort gear. And the ratio of the two distances is the same as the ratio of the number of teeth in the two gears. Then we can say that the ideal mechanical advantage of a gear is the ratio of the number of teeth in the load gear to the number of teeth in the effort gear.

POWER

When a piano mover rigs his tackle, he has to consider many factors. For one, the more pulleys he puts in, the longer it will take him to get the job done. If he has to pull more rope—using less force, though—he will have to keep pulling for a longer time.

There is a definite limit to the amount of work the mover can do in a given amount of time. The rate at which he does work is called the power. *Power* is work done per unit time.

The English unit of power is the foot-pound per second, and it takes 550 of these units to make 1 horsepower. The SI unit is the joule per second, or *watt* (W). A horsepower is 746 watts. The watt is a very small unit, and the kilowatt (1,000 W) is commonly used.

In all the machines we have discussed so far, work comes out the load end as it goes in at the effort end. Thus, the power output of any machine is equal to the power input. Machines do not increase your power. A pulley or a windlass will spread the work out over a longer period of time, so that you can do it with the power available in your muscles and without straining for a force larger than convenient.

PRACTICE QUESTIONS

1. A bicycle sprocket is most similar to which of these simple mechanical devices?

   (A) A pulley
   (B) A lever
   (C) A spring
   (D) A gear

2. For two gears to mesh properly, they must

   (A) rotate in the same direction.
   (B) have the same number of teeth.
   (C) have the same size teeth.
   (D) rotate at the same speed.

3. Gear A has 25 teeth and is meshed with gear B, which has 5 teeth. When gear B makes 5 revolutions, how many revolutions does gear A make in the same time?

   (A) $\frac{1}{5}$
   (B) 1
   (C) 5
   (D) 25

4. If the lever system below balances as shown, what is the mechanical advantage demonstrated?

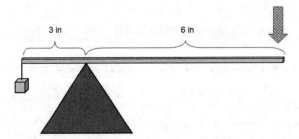

   (A) 2
   (B) 3
   (C) 4
   (D) 8

5. A screw having 16 threads per inch has _____ than a screw with 12 threads per inch.

   (A) more length
   (B) less length
   (C) less mechanical advantage
   (D) more mechanical advantage

6. Using the diagram below (which is not drawn to scale), what mechanical advantage would allow 50 pounds of downward effort to raise the 300-pound weight on the other end of the lever arm?

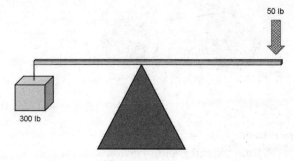

    (A) 6
    (B) 3
    (C) 12
    (D) 60

7. If a bicycle rider changes to a larger gear on the bike's rear wheel but still wants to go the same speed, the rider

    (A) should apply more force on the pedals.
    (B) should apply less force on the pedals.
    (C) should apply the same force on the pedals.
    (D) It depends on whether the bike is going uphill or downhill.

8. A bolt has 12 threads per inch. How far does it move when you tighten the bolt seven turns and then loosen it five turns?

    (A) $\frac{1}{6}$ inch

    (B) $\frac{1}{8}$ inch

    (C) $\frac{5}{12}$ inch

    (D) $\frac{7}{12}$ inch

9. What is the easiest way to find the mechanical advantage in a pulley system?

    (A) Count the pulleys.
    (B) Measure the load and the effort.
    (C) Count the supporting strands of rope.
    (D) Count all the strands of rope involved in the system.

10. Which of the following is a type of lever?

    (A) Tongs
    (B) Vise
    (C) Screw
    (D) Pulley

11. If pulley D is the driver and turns in direction 2, in what direction does pulley A turn?

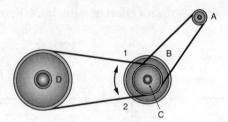

(A) Direction 1
(B) Direction 2
(C) Pulley A spins freely.
(D) You cannot tell from the information given.

12. If arm H is held stationary as gear A turns in direction 1,

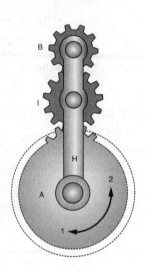

(A) gear I must turn in direction 1.
(B) gear B must turn in direction 1.
(C) gear B must turn in direction 2.
(D) gear I will spin freely.

13. The SI unit used to measure power is the

(A) horsepower.
(B) foot-pound per second.
(C) joule per second.
(D) kilowatt.

14. In mechanical devices, gears are commonly used to

(A) change torque.
(B) change the direction of work output.
(C) increase power in the system.
(D) transmit power over long distances.

15. If gear B makes 15 revolutions, gear A will make

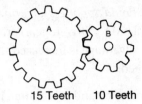

15 Teeth   10 Teeth

(A) 5 revolutions.

(B) 10 revolutions.

(C) 15 revolutions.

(D) 25 revolutions

16. Cranks are used to

(A) transmit power over relatively long distances.

(B) change straight-line motion into rotary motion.

(C) change the direction of power transmitted.

(D) conserve power until it is needed.

Answers Explained

1. **(D)** A bicycle sprocket is most similar to *a gear,* which is defined as a toothed cylinder or wheel that meshes with a chain or with another toothed element to transfer motion or energy.

2. **(C)** For two gears to mesh properly, they must *have the same size teeth.* The two gears can have a different number of teeth and rotate at different speeds. They will, however, rotate in opposite directions if they are meshed.

3. **(B)** When gear B makes 5 revolutions, gear A makes *1* revolution in the same time. Gear A has a ratio relative to gear B of 1:5. In other words, for every revolution that gear B makes, gear A makes $\frac{1}{5}$ of a revolution. Therefore, if gear B turns 5 times, gear A makes 1 complete revolution.

4. **(A)** If the lever system balances as shown, the mechanical advantage demonstrated is *2.* In this case, the formula for mechanical advantage is MA = effort distance/load distance. Since the system balances, we divide $\frac{6}{3}$, which results in a mechanical advantage of 2.

5. **(D)** A screw having 16 threads per inch has *more mechanical advantage* than a screw with 12 threads per inch. Each turn of the screw with 16 threads per inch will move the load a shorter distance than the other screw. So the screw with 16 threads per inch has a greater mechanical advantage. Based on the information given in this problem, determining the length of either screw is not possible.

6. **(A)** A mechanical advantage of *6* would allow 50 pounds of downward effort to raise the 300-pound weight on the other end of the lever arm. Use the formula MA = load/effort.

$$MA = \frac{300 \text{ pounds}}{50 \text{ pounds}}$$

$$MA = 6$$

7. **(B)** If a bicycle rider changes to a larger gear on the bike's rear wheel but still wants to go the same speed, the rider *should apply less force on the pedals*. Mechanical advantage is calculated with the formula MA = driven gear/drive gear. If the rider changes to a larger sprocket, mechanical advantage is increased. Therefore, less force is needed on the pedals to go the same speed.

8. **(A)** If a bolt has 12 threads per inch and you tighten it seven turns and then loosen it five times, the bolt moves $\frac{1}{6}$ *inch*. Moving the screw seven turns tighter and then five turns looser is a net of two turns tighter. At $\frac{1}{12}$ inch per turn, the screw moves $\frac{2}{12}$ inch, which simplifies to $\frac{1}{6}$ inch.

9. **(C)** The easiest way to find the mechanical advantage in a pulley system is to *count the supporting strands of rope*.

10. **(A)** *Tongs* are a type of lever. In fact, they are a class 3 level. The screw is a type of inclined plane. The vise and pulley are each examples of a wheel and axle.

11. **(B)** Pulley A turns in *direction 2* if pulley D is the driver and turns in direction 2. As pulley D turns in direction 2, pulley assembly BC turns in direction 1 and pulley A turns in direction 2.

12. **(B)** If arm H is held stationary as gear A turns in direction 1, *gear B must turn in direction 1*. As gear A turns in direction 1, gear I turns in the opposite direction (direction 2) and gear B turns in direction 1.

13. **(C)** The SI unit used to measure power is the *joule per second*. This SI unit of power is also known as the watt. The English measurement system uses foot-pounds per second to measure power.

14. **(A)** In mechanical devices, gears are commonly used to *change torque*.

15. **(B)** If gear B makes 15 revolutions, gear A will make *10 revolutions*. To calculate the revolutions made by gear A, use the formula $r = \frac{(D \times R)}{d}$, where

    D = number of teeth on gear B (the known gear)
    R = number of revolutions of gear B
    d = number of teeth on gear A (the partially unknown gear)
    r = number of revolutions of gear A

    $$r = \frac{(D \times R)}{d}$$
    $$r = \frac{(10 \times 15)}{15}$$
    $$r = \frac{(150)}{15}$$
    $$r = 10 \text{ revolutions}$$

16. **(B)** Cranks are used to *change straight-line motion into rotary motion*. They can also do the opposite and change rotary motion into straight-line motion.

Assembling Objects

11

OVERVIEW

The Assembling Objects (AO) subtest measures *spatial apperception,* also known as *visualizing spatial relationships*—your ability to visualize how an object will look when its parts are put together, or how different objects will look when connected.

As of this writing, only the Navy uses the AO score to specifically qualify service members for a particular specialty (operational and some mechanical jobs), but that could and probably will change. And, if you are thinking about trying to become a pilot or getting into some other aircraft-related specialty later on, you will definitely need to develop your ability to visualize spatial relationships. All the services test their prospective pilots in this area—for more information and examples, see *Barron's Military Flight Aptitude Tests.*

You might initially think that spatial apperception skills are just intuitive—you either have them or you don't. However, if you study the tips and techniques in this chapter—and, most importantly, *practice* them—you will find that there is no magic or voodoo to solving these problems.

The Assembling Objects subtest has two types of problems. In both types, you will be shown five drawings. The first drawing will contain some unconnected shapes, and the remaining four drawings will each try to persuade you that they are the final result of correctly assembling the shapes.

We're going to call the first type of problem jigsaw puzzle-piece assembly. The ASVAB doesn't call them by that name—it just presents you both types of problems in the AO subtest and expects you to answer them correctly. For our ease of reference and your analysis, though, we'll call them jigsaw puzzle-piece assembly.

And, for that same ease of reference, we're going to call the second type of problem line-connector assembly problems.

Let's examine how to solve the jigsaw puzzle-piece assembly problems.

JIGSAW PUZZLE-PIECE ASSEMBLY PROBLEMS

Which figure best shows how the objects in the group on the left will appear if they are fitted together?

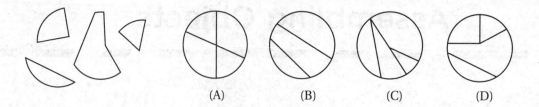

(A) (B) (C) (D)

In this example, the correct answer is "D."

Here are some tips to help you solve this type of problem:

1. **DON'T TRY TO ASSEMBLE THE PIECES IN YOUR HEAD—LET THE TEST DO IT FOR YOU.** There is more than one way to assemble the pieces the test shows you, but only one of the choices is one of those ways—only one choice is correct. Therefore, what you have to do is disqualify three out of the four choices and then confirm that the remaining choice is, in fact, one way to assemble the parts you started out with.

2. **SEE WHICH OF THE CHOICES HAS THE RIGHT AMOUNT OF AREA OR MASS.** Potential choices that are much bigger or smaller than the pieces given to you to assemble are usually pretty easy to identify. This doesn't help you in the first example problem above, because all the choices have about the same overall size or volume—but it can and does happen on other problems.

3. **DISQUALIFY THE CHOICES THAT HAVE A SHAPE, EXTERNAL CURVE, OR ANGLE THAT IS NOT IN THE PIECES GIVEN TO YOU TO ASSEMBLE.** In the example above, Choice A has two very wide "pie slice" shapes, and two more pie slices that are more "medium" size. The pieces you have to work with include only one wide and one small pie slice—so Choice A is out.

4. **DISQUALIFY THE CHOICES THAT DON'T HAVE AN UNUSUAL OR DISTINCT CURVE OR ANGLE REPRESENTED IN THE PIECES GIVEN TO YOU TO ASSEMBLE.** In the example above, the pieces given to you to assemble include one fairly distinctive shape:

Look for this shape in Choices B, C, and D (you've already discarded Choice A). It's not there in Choices B or C, but there it is in the middle of Choice D. So, there's your answer.

5. **EXPECT THAT SOME OR ALL OF THE PIECES YOU ARE SUPPOSED TO ASSEMBLE ARE ROTATED TO SOME DEGREE.** In the example above, two of the four pieces in the initial group have to be rotated to fit together with the other shapes. Imagine those shapes as jigsaw pieces, lying flat on a table—but *don't mentally flip any of the shapes over.* Leave them flat on the imaginary table.

6. **WATCH OUT FOR MIRROR IMAGES.** Shapes that are reversed—mirror images—will never be able to be rotated into place, no matter how smart you are. Whether it's a unique-looking shape or a fairly plain one, don't get in so much of a hurry that you get fooled by this trick on your eyes.

LINE-CONNECTOR ASSEMBLY PROBLEMS

In the second (line-connector assembly) type of problem, you will be shown two shapes and a connector line. One point on each of the shapes will be labeled with a letter (for instance, "A" on the first shape and "B" on the second shape). The ends of the connector line will be labeled with the same letters—in this case, one end with "A" and the other end with the letter "B." You will be asked which of the four figures best shows how the two shapes and a connector line in the first group will touch if the letters for each object are matched, as in the example below.

Which figure best shows how the objects in the group of objects on the left will touch if the letters for each object are matched?

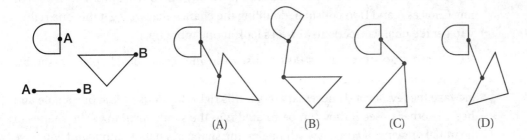

In this example, the correct answer is "C."

Again, here are some general principles that will help you with this kind of problem.

1. **CHECK THE PLACEMENT OF THE POINTS.** In the example above, there are two shapes: a kind of half-oval and a rotated right triangle. Point A is midway along the flat side of the half-oval, and Point B is at one of the non-right-angle corners of the triangle. Look at the placement of the dot on first one shape and then the other to see if you can eliminate any choices. (Proper placement may be as simple to see as it is in this problem, or it may involve determining its relationship to a landmark on an irregular shape. Either way, this principle will help you figure it out.) By doing this in the example above, you can quickly eliminate Choice B from the running because the dot (Point A) on the half-oval is on the corner instead of in the middle of the flat side. Likewise, in this example, if you check the choices for the proper placement of Point B, you can eliminate Choices A and D because the dot on the triangle is in the middle of a side instead of at an angle. The only remaining choice is Choice C.

Hey, wait, we just solved the whole problem! See how checking the placement of the points on both shapes eliminated all the incorrect choices? Just like Sherlock Holmes said: "When you have eliminated the impossible, whatever remains, no matter how improbable, must be the truth."

Not all of this type of problem will be this easy, though. Here's another example that's not as easy.

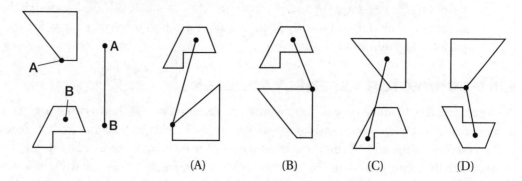

(A)   (B)   (C)   (D)

Here, we will look at a point or points inside the shape instead of on the edge. If we use the same principle we used before and look at the shape with Point A, we can eliminate Choice B because it has what is supposed to be Point A on the wrong side of the shape (the longer side instead of the shortest side). We can also eliminate Choice C because it has the point placed incorrectly on both shapes. This leaves us only Choices A and D to consider, doubling the chance that we'll get this one right.

To get the final (correct) answer, let's look at one more tip.

2. **WATCH OUT FOR MIRRORED SHAPES.** Just as in the jigsaw puzzle-piece assembly problem, this can be tricky, but you can figure it out if you take a systematic approach and take the few seconds necessary to get this right. Just look at first one shape and then the other to see if they can be rotated into the same position as the shapes in the initial drawing. If you have to, imagine the shape is a paper cutout and you have just stuck a straight pin through the middle of the shape into the cork bulletin board behind it. This leaves the shape free to spin around its axis (the pin). By doing this, you can see that the shapes in Choice A are OK—one of them is already in the same position as the shape in the initial drawing. The shapes in Choice D, though, are a different matter—by mentally spinning them around that straight pin through their middles, you can see that both these shapes are mirror images—just tricksters and very much not correct. That leaves only Choice A as the correct choice.

The exact format of the Assembling Objects subtest is still evolving, so the types of shapes and illustrations you see here may change, but these suggestions will still help you. None of the ASVAB subtests, however, exist to give you a free ride—you will have to put some effort into deducing the correct answer to each question. This means that more than one of the choices may be plausible at first glance. However, if you follow these steps—and especially if you use them to practice this skill of assembling objects in each of the practice tests in this book—you should do well on the actual ASVAB.

PRACTICE QUESTIONS

1.

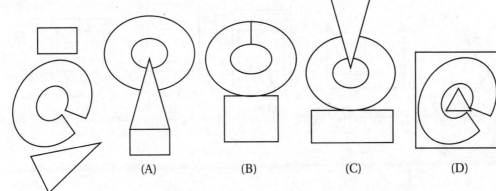

(A) (B) (C) (D)

2.

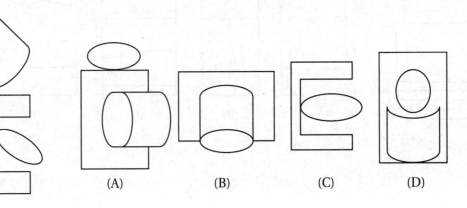

(A) (B) (C) (D)

3.

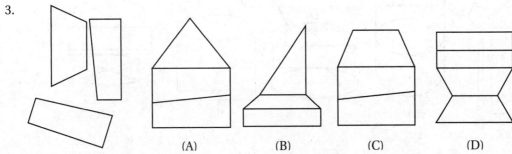

(A) (B) (C) (D)

4.

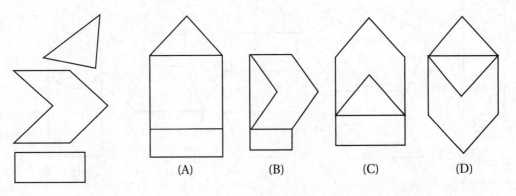

(A) (B) (C) (D)

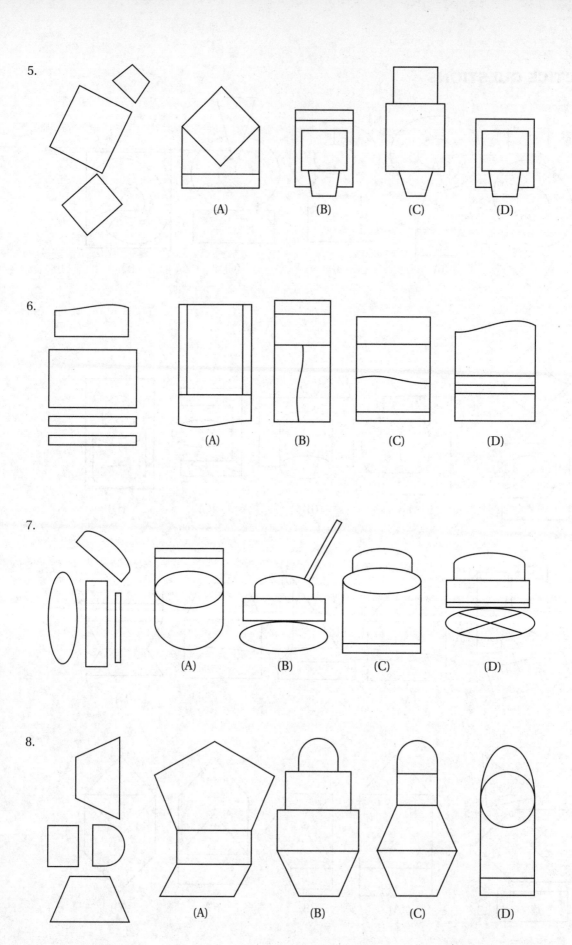

5.

(A) (B) (C) (D)

6.

(A) (B) (C) (D)

7.

(A) (B) (C) (D)

8.

(A) (B) (C) (D)

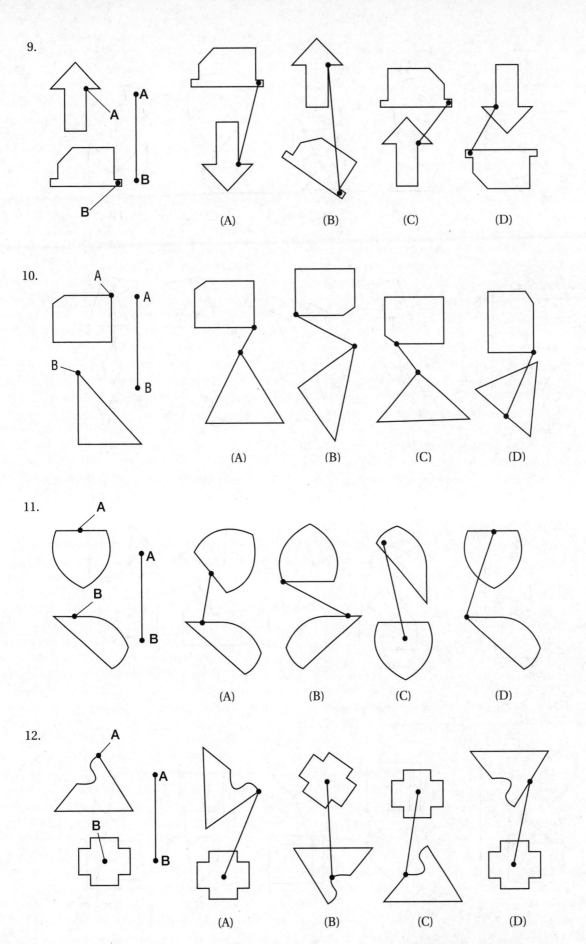

9.

(A) (B) (C) (D)

10.

(A) (B) (C) (D)

11.

(A) (B) (C) (D)

12.

(A) (B) (C) (D)

13.

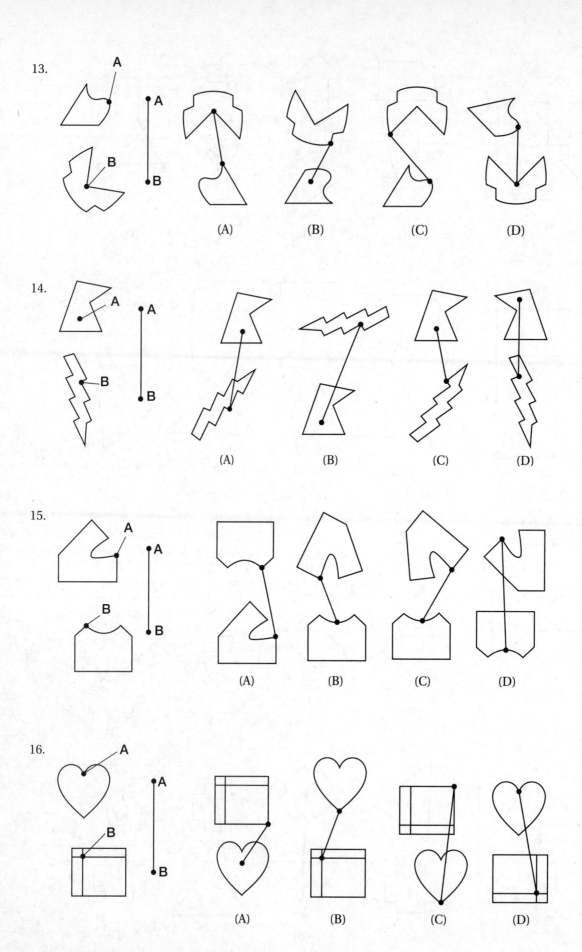

14.

15.

16.

Answer Key

1. **A**	5. **C**	9. **B**	13. **D**
2. **B**	6. **A**	10. **B**	14. **B**
3. **C**	7. **B**	11. **A**	15. **A**
4. **C**	8. **C**	12. **A**	16. **D**

ANSWER SHEET
Practice Exam One

General Science—Subtest 1

1. Ⓐ Ⓑ Ⓒ Ⓓ   6. Ⓐ Ⓑ Ⓒ Ⓓ   11. Ⓐ Ⓑ Ⓒ Ⓓ   16. Ⓐ Ⓑ Ⓒ Ⓓ   21. Ⓐ Ⓑ Ⓒ Ⓓ
2. Ⓐ Ⓑ Ⓒ Ⓓ   7. Ⓐ Ⓑ Ⓒ Ⓓ   12. Ⓐ Ⓑ Ⓒ Ⓓ   17. Ⓐ Ⓑ Ⓒ Ⓓ   22. Ⓐ Ⓑ Ⓒ Ⓓ
3. Ⓐ Ⓑ Ⓒ Ⓓ   8. Ⓐ Ⓑ Ⓒ Ⓓ   13. Ⓐ Ⓑ Ⓒ Ⓓ   18. Ⓐ Ⓑ Ⓒ Ⓓ   23. Ⓐ Ⓑ Ⓒ Ⓓ
4. Ⓐ Ⓑ Ⓒ Ⓓ   9. Ⓐ Ⓑ Ⓒ Ⓓ   14. Ⓐ Ⓑ Ⓒ Ⓓ   19. Ⓐ Ⓑ Ⓒ Ⓓ   24. Ⓐ Ⓑ Ⓒ Ⓓ
5. Ⓐ Ⓑ Ⓒ Ⓓ   10. Ⓐ Ⓑ Ⓒ Ⓓ   15. Ⓐ Ⓑ Ⓒ Ⓓ   20. Ⓐ Ⓑ Ⓒ Ⓓ   25. Ⓐ Ⓑ Ⓒ Ⓓ

Arithmetic Reasoning—Subtest 2

1. Ⓐ Ⓑ Ⓒ Ⓓ   7. Ⓐ Ⓑ Ⓒ Ⓓ   13. Ⓐ Ⓑ Ⓒ Ⓓ   19. Ⓐ Ⓑ Ⓒ Ⓓ   25. Ⓐ Ⓑ Ⓒ Ⓓ
2. Ⓐ Ⓑ Ⓒ Ⓓ   8. Ⓐ Ⓑ Ⓒ Ⓓ   14. Ⓐ Ⓑ Ⓒ Ⓓ   20. Ⓐ Ⓑ Ⓒ Ⓓ   26. Ⓐ Ⓑ Ⓒ Ⓓ
3. Ⓐ Ⓑ Ⓒ Ⓓ   9. Ⓐ Ⓑ Ⓒ Ⓓ   15. Ⓐ Ⓑ Ⓒ Ⓓ   21. Ⓐ Ⓑ Ⓒ Ⓓ   27. Ⓐ Ⓑ Ⓒ Ⓓ
4. Ⓐ Ⓑ Ⓒ Ⓓ   10. Ⓐ Ⓑ Ⓒ Ⓓ   16. Ⓐ Ⓑ Ⓒ Ⓓ   22. Ⓐ Ⓑ Ⓒ Ⓓ   28. Ⓐ Ⓑ Ⓒ Ⓓ
5. Ⓐ Ⓑ Ⓒ Ⓓ   11. Ⓐ Ⓑ Ⓒ Ⓓ   17. Ⓐ Ⓑ Ⓒ Ⓓ   23. Ⓐ Ⓑ Ⓒ Ⓓ   29. Ⓐ Ⓑ Ⓒ Ⓓ
6. Ⓐ Ⓑ Ⓒ Ⓓ   12. Ⓐ Ⓑ Ⓒ Ⓓ   18. Ⓐ Ⓑ Ⓒ Ⓓ   24. Ⓐ Ⓑ Ⓒ Ⓓ   30. Ⓐ Ⓑ Ⓒ Ⓓ

Word Knowledge—Subtest 3

1. Ⓐ Ⓑ Ⓒ Ⓓ   8. Ⓐ Ⓑ Ⓒ Ⓓ   15. Ⓐ Ⓑ Ⓒ Ⓓ   22. Ⓐ Ⓑ Ⓒ Ⓓ   29. Ⓐ Ⓑ Ⓒ Ⓓ
2. Ⓐ Ⓑ Ⓒ Ⓓ   9. Ⓐ Ⓑ Ⓒ Ⓓ   16. Ⓐ Ⓑ Ⓒ Ⓓ   23. Ⓐ Ⓑ Ⓒ Ⓓ   30. Ⓐ Ⓑ Ⓒ Ⓓ
3. Ⓐ Ⓑ Ⓒ Ⓓ   10. Ⓐ Ⓑ Ⓒ Ⓓ   17. Ⓐ Ⓑ Ⓒ Ⓓ   24. Ⓐ Ⓑ Ⓒ Ⓓ   31. Ⓐ Ⓑ Ⓒ Ⓓ
4. Ⓐ Ⓑ Ⓒ Ⓓ   11. Ⓐ Ⓑ Ⓒ Ⓓ   18. Ⓐ Ⓑ Ⓒ Ⓓ   25. Ⓐ Ⓑ Ⓒ Ⓓ   32. Ⓐ Ⓑ Ⓒ Ⓓ
5. Ⓐ Ⓑ Ⓒ Ⓓ   12. Ⓐ Ⓑ Ⓒ Ⓓ   19. Ⓐ Ⓑ Ⓒ Ⓓ   26. Ⓐ Ⓑ Ⓒ Ⓓ   33. Ⓐ Ⓑ Ⓒ Ⓓ
6. Ⓐ Ⓑ Ⓒ Ⓓ   13. Ⓐ Ⓑ Ⓒ Ⓓ   20. Ⓐ Ⓑ Ⓒ Ⓓ   27. Ⓐ Ⓑ Ⓒ Ⓓ   34. Ⓐ Ⓑ Ⓒ Ⓓ
7. Ⓐ Ⓑ Ⓒ Ⓓ   14. Ⓐ Ⓑ Ⓒ Ⓓ   21. Ⓐ Ⓑ Ⓒ Ⓓ   28. Ⓐ Ⓑ Ⓒ Ⓓ   35. Ⓐ Ⓑ Ⓒ Ⓓ

Paragraph Comprehension—Subtest 4

1. Ⓐ Ⓑ Ⓒ Ⓓ   4. Ⓐ Ⓑ Ⓒ Ⓓ   7. Ⓐ Ⓑ Ⓒ Ⓓ   10. Ⓐ Ⓑ Ⓒ Ⓓ   13. Ⓐ Ⓑ Ⓒ Ⓓ
2. Ⓐ Ⓑ Ⓒ Ⓓ   5. Ⓐ Ⓑ Ⓒ Ⓓ   8. Ⓐ Ⓑ Ⓒ Ⓓ   11. Ⓐ Ⓑ Ⓒ Ⓓ   14. Ⓐ Ⓑ Ⓒ Ⓓ
3. Ⓐ Ⓑ Ⓒ Ⓓ   6. Ⓐ Ⓑ Ⓒ Ⓓ   9. Ⓐ Ⓑ Ⓒ Ⓓ   12. Ⓐ Ⓑ Ⓒ Ⓓ   15. Ⓐ Ⓑ Ⓒ Ⓓ

Mathematics Knowledge—Subtest 5

1. Ⓐ Ⓑ Ⓒ Ⓓ   6. Ⓐ Ⓑ Ⓒ Ⓓ   11. Ⓐ Ⓑ Ⓒ Ⓓ   16. Ⓐ Ⓑ Ⓒ Ⓓ   21. Ⓐ Ⓑ Ⓒ Ⓓ
2. Ⓐ Ⓑ Ⓒ Ⓓ   7. Ⓐ Ⓑ Ⓒ Ⓓ   12. Ⓐ Ⓑ Ⓒ Ⓓ   17. Ⓐ Ⓑ Ⓒ Ⓓ   22. Ⓐ Ⓑ Ⓒ Ⓓ
3. Ⓐ Ⓑ Ⓒ Ⓓ   8. Ⓐ Ⓑ Ⓒ Ⓓ   13. Ⓐ Ⓑ Ⓒ Ⓓ   18. Ⓐ Ⓑ Ⓒ Ⓓ   23. Ⓐ Ⓑ Ⓒ Ⓓ
4. Ⓐ Ⓑ Ⓒ Ⓓ   9. Ⓐ Ⓑ Ⓒ Ⓓ   14. Ⓐ Ⓑ Ⓒ Ⓓ   19. Ⓐ Ⓑ Ⓒ Ⓓ   24. Ⓐ Ⓑ Ⓒ Ⓓ
5. Ⓐ Ⓑ Ⓒ Ⓓ   10. Ⓐ Ⓑ Ⓒ Ⓓ   15. Ⓐ Ⓑ Ⓒ Ⓓ   20. Ⓐ Ⓑ Ⓒ Ⓓ   25. Ⓐ Ⓑ Ⓒ Ⓓ

Electronics Information—Subtest 6

1. Ⓐ Ⓑ Ⓒ Ⓓ   5. Ⓐ Ⓑ Ⓒ Ⓓ   9. Ⓐ Ⓑ Ⓒ Ⓓ   13. Ⓐ Ⓑ Ⓒ Ⓓ   17. Ⓐ Ⓑ Ⓒ Ⓓ
2. Ⓐ Ⓑ Ⓒ Ⓓ   6. Ⓐ Ⓑ Ⓒ Ⓓ   10. Ⓐ Ⓑ Ⓒ Ⓓ   14. Ⓐ Ⓑ Ⓒ Ⓓ   18. Ⓐ Ⓑ Ⓒ Ⓓ
3. Ⓐ Ⓑ Ⓒ Ⓓ   7. Ⓐ Ⓑ Ⓒ Ⓓ   11. Ⓐ Ⓑ Ⓒ Ⓓ   15. Ⓐ Ⓑ Ⓒ Ⓓ   19. Ⓐ Ⓑ Ⓒ Ⓓ
4. Ⓐ Ⓑ Ⓒ Ⓓ   8. Ⓐ Ⓑ Ⓒ Ⓓ   12. Ⓐ Ⓑ Ⓒ Ⓓ   16. Ⓐ Ⓑ Ⓒ Ⓓ   20. Ⓐ Ⓑ Ⓒ Ⓓ

Automotive & Shop Information—Subtest 7

1. Ⓐ Ⓑ Ⓒ Ⓓ   6. Ⓐ Ⓑ Ⓒ Ⓓ   11. Ⓐ Ⓑ Ⓒ Ⓓ   16. Ⓐ Ⓑ Ⓒ Ⓓ   21. Ⓐ Ⓑ Ⓒ Ⓓ
2. Ⓐ Ⓑ Ⓒ Ⓓ   7. Ⓐ Ⓑ Ⓒ Ⓓ   12. Ⓐ Ⓑ Ⓒ Ⓓ   17. Ⓐ Ⓑ Ⓒ Ⓓ   22. Ⓐ Ⓑ Ⓒ Ⓓ
3. Ⓐ Ⓑ Ⓒ Ⓓ   8. Ⓐ Ⓑ Ⓒ Ⓓ   13. Ⓐ Ⓑ Ⓒ Ⓓ   18. Ⓐ Ⓑ Ⓒ Ⓓ   23. Ⓐ Ⓑ Ⓒ Ⓓ
4. Ⓐ Ⓑ Ⓒ Ⓓ   9. Ⓐ Ⓑ Ⓒ Ⓓ   14. Ⓐ Ⓑ Ⓒ Ⓓ   19. Ⓐ Ⓑ Ⓒ Ⓓ   24. Ⓐ Ⓑ Ⓒ Ⓓ
5. Ⓐ Ⓑ Ⓒ Ⓓ   10. Ⓐ Ⓑ Ⓒ Ⓓ   15. Ⓐ Ⓑ Ⓒ Ⓓ   20. Ⓐ Ⓑ Ⓒ Ⓓ   25. Ⓐ Ⓑ Ⓒ Ⓓ

Mechanical Comprehension—Subtest 8

1. Ⓐ Ⓑ Ⓒ Ⓓ   6. Ⓐ Ⓑ Ⓒ Ⓓ   11. Ⓐ Ⓑ Ⓒ Ⓓ   16. Ⓐ Ⓑ Ⓒ Ⓓ   21. Ⓐ Ⓑ Ⓒ Ⓓ
2. Ⓐ Ⓑ Ⓒ Ⓓ   7. Ⓐ Ⓑ Ⓒ Ⓓ   12. Ⓐ Ⓑ Ⓒ Ⓓ   17. Ⓐ Ⓑ Ⓒ Ⓓ   22. Ⓐ Ⓑ Ⓒ Ⓓ
3. Ⓐ Ⓑ Ⓒ Ⓓ   8. Ⓐ Ⓑ Ⓒ Ⓓ   13. Ⓐ Ⓑ Ⓒ Ⓓ   18. Ⓐ Ⓑ Ⓒ Ⓓ   23. Ⓐ Ⓑ Ⓒ Ⓓ
4. Ⓐ Ⓑ Ⓒ Ⓓ   9. Ⓐ Ⓑ Ⓒ Ⓓ   14. Ⓐ Ⓑ Ⓒ Ⓓ   19. Ⓐ Ⓑ Ⓒ Ⓓ   24. Ⓐ Ⓑ Ⓒ Ⓓ
5. Ⓐ Ⓑ Ⓒ Ⓓ   10. Ⓐ Ⓑ Ⓒ Ⓓ   15. Ⓐ Ⓑ Ⓒ Ⓓ   20. Ⓐ Ⓑ Ⓒ Ⓓ   25. Ⓐ Ⓑ Ⓒ Ⓓ

Assembling Objects—Subtest 9

1. Ⓐ Ⓑ Ⓒ Ⓓ   5. Ⓐ Ⓑ Ⓒ Ⓓ   9. Ⓐ Ⓑ Ⓒ Ⓓ   13. Ⓐ Ⓑ Ⓒ Ⓓ
2. Ⓐ Ⓑ Ⓒ Ⓓ   6. Ⓐ Ⓑ Ⓒ Ⓓ   10. Ⓐ Ⓑ Ⓒ Ⓓ   14. Ⓐ Ⓑ Ⓒ Ⓓ
3. Ⓐ Ⓑ Ⓒ Ⓓ   7. Ⓐ Ⓑ Ⓒ Ⓓ   11. Ⓐ Ⓑ Ⓒ Ⓓ   15. Ⓐ Ⓑ Ⓒ Ⓓ
4. Ⓐ Ⓑ Ⓒ Ⓓ   8. Ⓐ Ⓑ Ⓒ Ⓓ   12. Ⓐ Ⓑ Ⓒ Ⓓ   16. Ⓐ Ⓑ Ⓒ Ⓓ

Practice Exam One

GENERAL SCIENCE—SUBTEST 1

TIME: 11 MINUTES
25 QUESTIONS

> **Directions:** This test has questions about science. Pick the best answer for each question, then blacken the space on your separate answer form that has the same number and letter as your choice.
>
> Here is a sample question.
>
> 1. The planet nearest to the sun is
>
>   (A) Venus.
>   (B) Mars.
>   (C) Earth.
>   (D) Mercury.
>
> Mercury is the correct answer, so you would blacken the space for D on your answer form.
>
> Your score on this subtest will be based on the number of questions you answer correctly. You should try to answer every question. Do not spend too much time on any one question.
>
> When you begin, be sure to start with question number 1 in Part 1, and number 1 in Part 1 on your answer form.
>
> THE ACTUAL TEST WILL SAY:
>
> **Do not turn this page until told to do so.**

1. Sound travels fastest through

    (A) air.
    (B) steel.
    (C) water.
    (D) a vacuum.

2. In order to use seawater onboard ship for boilers, the water must first be

    (A) distilled.
    (B) aerated.
    (C) chlorinated.
    (D) refined.

3. The most abundant metal in a free state in the earth's crust is

    (A) nitrogen.
    (B) aluminum.
    (C) copper.
    (D) iron.

4. An object will most effectively absorb the sun's rays if it is

    (A) polished, and dark in color.
    (B) polished, and light in color.
    (C) rough, and light in color.
    (D) rough, and dark in color.

5. The most effective farming method for returning minerals to the soil is

(A) crop rotation.
(B) strip farming.
(C) contour plowing.
(D) furrowing.

6. An example of a lever is

(A) a wedge.
(B) a crowbar.
(C) a saw.
(D) an escalator.

7. A lunar eclipse occurs when the

(A) earth casts its shadow on the sun.
(B) sun casts its shadow on the moon.
(C) earth casts its shadow on the moon.
(D) moon casts its shadow on the earth.

8. The part of the body that would suffer most from a diet deficient in calcium is the

(A) pancreas.
(B) stomach.
(C) skeleton.
(D) skin.

9. Which of the following is found in greatest quantities in automobile exhaust gases?

(A) sulfur dioxide
(B) sulfur trioxide
(C) carbon monoxide
(D) water

10. Which common electrical device contains an electric magnet?

(A) flatiron
(B) lamp
(C) telephone
(D) toaster

11. In a vacuum, radio waves and visible light waves must have the same

(A) intensity.
(B) frequency.
(C) wavelength.
(D) speed.

12. The most accurate description of the earth's atmosphere is that it consists

(A) mostly of oxygen, argon, carbon dioxide, and water vapor.
(B) entirely of ozone, nitrogen, and water vapor.
(C) of a mixture of gases, liquid droplets, and minute solid particles.
(D) of gases that cannot be compressed.

13. Object A with a mass of two kilograms and object B with a mass of four kilograms are dropped simultaneously from rest near the surface of the earth. Neglecting air resistance, at the end of three seconds, what is the ratio of the speed of object A to the speed of object B?

(A) 1:4
(B) 1:2
(C) 1:1
(D) 2:1

14. In June, a weather station in a Virginia city reports a falling barometer and southeast winds. The best weather forecast is probably

(A) fair and warmer.
(B) fair and colder.
(C) rain and warmer.
(D) rain and colder.

15. Which substance can be removed from water by filtration?

(A) sand
(B) ink
(C) alcohol
(D) sugar

16. As a balloon rises, the gas within it

    (A) solidifies.
    (B) freezes.
    (C) condenses.
    (D) expands.

17. The best estimate of the age of the earth comes from the study of

    (A) the salt content of the oceans.
    (B) the thickness of sedimentary rock.
    (C) radioactive material.
    (D) the rate of erosion of the land.

18. The presence of coal deposits in Alaska shows that, at one time, Alaska

    (A) was covered with ice.
    (B) was connected to Asia.
    (C) was connected to Europe.
    (D) had a tropical climate.

19. When an airplane is in flight, the air pressure on the top surface of the wing is

    (A) less than on the bottom surface.
    (B) the same as on the bottom surface.
    (C) slightly more than on the bottom surface.
    (D) more or less than on the bottom surface, depending on the shape of the wing.

20. In the human eye, which structure is like the film in a camera?

    (A) pupil
    (B) retina
    (C) lens
    (D) cornea

21. When a water molecule is "taken apart" by electricity, what two substances are formed?

    (A) carbon and oxygen
    (B) hydrogen and oxygen
    (C) oxygen and nitrogen
    (D) hydrogen and nitrogen

22. Which of the following statements is true for the right side of this equation?

$$Fe + H_2SO_4 \rightarrow FeSO_4 + H_2$$

    (A) There are two elements on the right side.
    (B) There are two compounds on the right side.
    (C) There is an element and a gas on the right side.
    (D) There is a compound and an element on the right side.

23. The three elements found most commonly in commercial fertilizers are

    (A) calcium, phosphorus, iron.
    (B) phosphorus, nitrogen, sulfur.
    (C) nitrogen, phosphorus, potassium.
    (D) magnesium, iron, calcium.

24. Two nonporous rocks seem to lose the same weight when a string is attached to each and they are submerged in water. These two rocks must have the same

    (A) weight in air.
    (B) weight in water.
    (C) volume.
    (D) chemical and physical properties.

25. The thermos bottle is most similar in principle to

    (A) storm windows.
    (B) the freezing unit in an electric refrigerator.
    (C) solar heating systems.
    (D) radiant heaters.

ARITHMETIC REASONING—SUBTEST 2

> **Directions:** This test has questions about arithmetic. Each question is followed by four possible answers. Decide which answer is correct. Then, on your answer form, blacken the space that has the same number and letter as your choice. Use scratch paper for any figuring you wish to do.
> Here is a sample question.
>
> 1. If 10 pounds of sugar cost $2.00, what is the cost of 1 pound?
>
> (A) 90 cents
> (B) 80 cents
> (C) 50 cents
> (D) 20 cents
>
> The cost of 1 pound is 20 cents; therefore, the answer D is correct.
> Your score on this test will be based on the number of questions you answer correctly. You should try to answer every question. Do not spend too much time on any one question.
> Notice that Part 2 begins with question number 1. When you begin, be sure to mark your first answer next to number 1 on your answer form.
>
> THE ACTUAL TEST WILL SAY:
>
> **Do not turn this page until told to do so.**

1. You need 8 barrels of water to sprinkle $\frac{1}{2}$ mile of roadway. How many barrels of water do you need to sprinkle $3\frac{1}{2}$ miles of roadway?

   (A) 7
   (B) 15
   (C) 50
   (D) 56

2. A snapshot 8 inches long and 6 inches wide is to be enlarged so that its length will be 12 inches. How many inches wide will the enlarged snapshot be?

   (A) 8 inches
   (B) 6 inches
   (C) 9 inches
   (D) 10 inches

3. Travis Lee has an ordinary life insurance policy with a face value of $10,000. At his age, the annual premium is $24.00 per $1,000. What is the total premium paid for this policy every 6 months?

   (A) $100
   (B) $120
   (C) $240
   (D) $400

4. If 2 lbs. of cottage cheese cost $3.20, what is the cost of a 3-ounce portion of cottage cheese?

   (A) $0.30
   (B) $0.20
   (C) $0.25
   (D) $0.15

5. Mr. Green drove for 12 hours at a speed of 55 miles per hour. If his car covered 22 miles for each gallon of gas used, how many gallons of gas did he use?

   (A) 32 gallons
   (B) 34 gallons
   (C) 36 gallons
   (D) 30 gallons

6. Max earns $7.50 per hour. If he works from 8:45 A.M. until 5:15 P.M., with one hour off for lunch, how much does he earn in one day?

   (A) $58.50
   (B) $56.25
   (C) $55.00
   (D) $53.75

7. If 5 shirts and 3 ties cost $52 and each tie costs $4, what is the cost of a shirt?

   (A) $6
   (B) $8
   (C) $10
   (D) $7.50

8. What is the fifth term in the series:
   5; 2; 9; 6; ____?

   (A) 16
   (B) 15
   (C) 14
   (D) 13

9. In a theater audience of 500 people, 80 percent were adults. How many children were in the audience?

   (A) 20
   (B) 50
   (C) 100
   (D) 125

10. A table usually sells for $240, but because it is slightly damaged, the store manager lets it go for $210. What is the percentage of reduction?

    (A) $12\frac{1}{2}\%$

    (B) $14\frac{2}{7}\%$

    (C) $16\frac{2}{3}\%$

    (D) $18\frac{3}{4}\%$

11. Mr. and Mrs. Clifton bought a home for $55,000. It was assessed at 80 percent of the purchase price. If the real estate tax was $4.74 per $100, how much realty tax did the Cliftons pay?

    (A) $2,085.60
    (B) $1,985.60
    (C) $2,607.00
    (D) $285.60

12. A scale on a map is 1 inch to 50 miles. On the map, two cities are $2\frac{1}{2}$ inches apart. What is the actual distance between the two cities?

    (A) 75 miles
    (B) 100 miles
    (C) 225 miles
    (D) 125 miles

13. A shipment of 2,200 pounds of fertilizer is packed in 40-ounce bags. How many bags are needed for the shipment?

    (A) 800
    (B) 880
    (C) 780
    (D) 640

14. A television priced at $400 was reduced 25 percent during a weekend sale. In addition, there was a 10 percent discount for paying cash. What was the cash price of the set during the sale?

    (A) $130
    (B) $260
    (C) $270
    (D) $320

15. In a store four clerks each receive $255.00 per week, while two part-timers each earn $120.00. What is the average weekly salary paid these six workers?

    (A) $200.00
    (B) $210.00
    (C) $187.50
    (D) $190.00

16. The perimeter of a rectangle is 40 feet. If the length is 15 feet, 6 inches, what is the width of the rectangle?

    (A) 4 feet, 6 inches
    (B) 9 feet, 6 inches
    (C) 5 feet, 6 inches
    (D) 5 feet

17. What is the result of dividing 0.675 by 0.9?

    (A) 7.5
    (B) 0.075
    (C) 75
    (D) 0.75

18. Two planes leave the same airport traveling in opposite directions. One is flying at the rate of 340 miles per hour, the other at 260 miles per hour. In how many hours will the two planes be 3,000 miles apart?

    (A) 5 hours
    (B) 4 hours
    (C) 6 hours
    (D) 10 hours

19. What is the cost of 5 feet, 3 inches of plastic material that sells for $8.00 per foot?

    (A) $14.00
    (B) $42.00
    (C) $23.00
    (D) $21.12

20. If one gallon of milk costs $3.84, what is the cost of three pints?

    (A) $1.44
    (B) $2.82
    (C) $2.04
    (D) $1.96

21. A man left $72,000 to his wife and son. The ratio of the wife's share to the son's share was 5:3. How much did his wife receive?

    (A) $27,000
    (B) $14,000
    (C) $45,000
    (D) $54,000

22. A recipe calls for $2\frac{1}{2}$ ounces of chocolate and $\frac{1}{2}$ cup of corn syrup. If only 2 ounces of chocolate are available, how much corn syrup should be used?

    (A) $\frac{1}{2}$ cup

    (B) $\frac{1}{3}$ cup

    (C) $\frac{2}{5}$ cup

    (D) $\frac{3}{10}$ cup

23. A ship sails x miles the first day, y miles the second day, and z miles the third day. What was the average distance covered per day?

(A) $\dfrac{xyz}{3}$

(B) $\dfrac{x+y+z}{3}$

(C) $3xyz$

(D) none of these

24. A man invests $6,000 at 5 percent annual interest. How much more must he invest at 6 percent annual interest so that his annual income from both investments is $900?

(A) $3,000
(B) $5,000
(C) $8,000
(D) $10,000

25. Which of these is an example of similar figures?

(A) a plane and a scale model of that plane
(B) a pen and a pencil
(C) a motorcycle and a car
(D) an equilateral triangle and a right triangle

26. Find the numerical value of $5a^2b - 3ab^2$ if $a = 7$ and $b = 4$.

(A) 846
(B) 644
(C) 488
(D) 224

27. If the circumference of a circle is divided by the length of its diameter, what is the result?

(A) 2
(B) 27
(C) π
(D) 7

28. A businesswoman spends $\dfrac{1}{5}$ of her income for office rent, and $\dfrac{3}{8}$ of the remainder of her income for salaries. What part of her income does she spend for salaries?

(A) $\dfrac{23}{40}$

(B) $\dfrac{3}{10}$

(C) $\dfrac{1}{2}$

(D) $\dfrac{3}{4}$

29. Using the following formula, find the value of C when $F = 50$.

$$C = \frac{5}{9}(F - 32)$$

(A) 10
(B) 18
(C) 90
(D) 40

30. What is the average of these temperature readings, taken on a cold day last winter?

6:00 A.M.	-12 degrees
7:00 A.M.	-7 degrees
8:00 A.M.	-2 degrees
9:00 A.M.	0 degrees
10:00 A.M.	+6 degrees

(A) 0 degrees
(B) 2 degrees
(C) -1 degree
(D) -3 degrees

WORD KNOWLEDGE—SUBTEST 3

TIME: 11 MINUTES

35 QUESTIONS

Directions: This test has questions about the meanings of words. Each question has an **underlined boldface word**. You are to decide which one of the four words in the choices most nearly means the same as the underlined boldface word; then mark the space on your answer form that has the same number and letter as your choice.

Now look at the sample question below.

1. It was a **small** table.

   (A) sturdy
   (B) round
   (C) cheap
   (D) little

The question asks which of the four words means the same as the boldface word, **small**.

"Little" means the same as **small**. Answer D is the best one.

Your score on this test will be based on the number of questions you answer correctly. You should try to answer every question. Do not spend too much time on any one question.

When you begin, be sure to start with question number 1 in Part 3 of your test booklet and number 1 in Part 3 on your answer form.

THE ACTUAL TEST WILL SAY:

Do not turn this page until told to do so.

---

1. **Opulence** most nearly means

   (A) affluence.
   (B) generosity.
   (C) poverty.
   (D) luxury.

2. **Mimesis** most nearly means

   (A) impersonation.
   (B) pretense.
   (C) cartoon.
   (D) imitation.

3. Her **languid** appearance was revealing.

   (A) sad
   (B) energetic
   (C) healthy
   (D) listless

4. **Inherent** most nearly means

   (A) essential.
   (B) intrinsic.
   (C) accidental.
   (D) necessity.

5. **Anomie** most nearly means

   (A) essential.
   (B) vacuum.
   (C) control.
   (D) anonym.

6. **Tenuous** most nearly means

   (A) tensile.
   (B) tentative.
   (C) ethereal.
   (D) substantial.

7. Most letters require a **salutation**.

   (A) offering
   (B) greeting
   (C) discussion
   (D) appeasement

8. **Mesmerize** most nearly means

   (A) hypnotize.
   (B) hypostatize.
   (C) metabolize.
   (D) change.

9. A **panoply** of flowers covered the shelf.

   (A) pansophy
   (B) display
   (C) resistance
   (D) parry

10. **Syntactic** most nearly means

    (A) morphological.
    (B) grammatical.
    (C) standard.
    (D) inflexional.

11. **Umbrage** most nearly means

    (A) resentment.
    (B) umbo.
    (C) impertinence.
    (D) pleasure.

12. **Raucous** most nearly means

    (A) ravenous.
    (B) harsh.
    (C) pleasing.
    (D) rankling.

13. **Prosecution** most nearly means

    (A) protection.
    (B) imprisonment.
    (C) trial.
    (D) punishment.

14. The **miasma** of modern cities causes discomfort.

    (A) pollution
    (B) fumes
    (C) exhalations
    (D) stench

15. **Paragon** most nearly means

    (A) paradox.
    (B) model.
    (C) prototype.
    (D) ideal.

16. She has **innate** talent.

    (A) eternal
    (B) well-developed
    (C) temporary
    (D) native

17. **Urbanity** most nearly means

    (A) loyalty.
    (B) refinement.
    (C) weakness.
    (D) barbarism.

18. We all **encounter** difficulties.

    (A) recall
    (B) overcome
    (C) retreat from
    (D) meet

19. **Banal** most nearly means

    (A) commonplace.
    (B) forceful.
    (C) tranquil.
    (D) indifferent.

20. **Small** most nearly means

    (A) sturdy.
    (B) round.
    (C) cheap.
    (D) little.

21. The accountant **discovered** an error.

    (A) searched
    (B) found
    (C) enlarged
    (D) entered

22. You must **inform** us.

    (A) ask
    (B) turn
    (C) tell
    (D) ignore

23. The wind is **variable** today.

    (A) shifting
    (B) chilling
    (C) steady
    (D) mild

24. **Cease** most nearly means

    (A) start.
    (B) change.
    (C) continue.
    (D) stop.

25. Drinking can **impair** your judgment.

    (A) direct
    (B) improve
    (C) weaken
    (D) stimulate

26. We knew the **rudiments** of the program.

    (A) basic methods and procedures
    (B) politics
    (C) promotion opportunities
    (D) minute details

27. **Imprudent** most nearly means

    (A) reckless.
    (B) unexcitable.
    (C) poor.
    (D) domineering.

28. **Dissension** stimulated the discussion.

    (A) friction
    (B) analysis
    (C) injury
    (D) slyness

29. **Disconnect** most nearly means

    (A) separate.
    (B) cripple.
    (C) lesson.
    (D) dismiss.

30. **Rudimentary** most nearly means

    (A) discourteous.
    (B) brutal.
    (C) displeasing.
    (D) elementary.

31. The commission made **autonomous** decisions.

    (A) self-improvement
    (B) self-educated
    (C) self-explanatory
    (D) self-governing

32. **Meander** most nearly means

    (A) grumble.
    (B) wander aimlessly.
    (C) come between.
    (D) weigh carefully.

33. **Destitution** most nearly means

    (A) fate.
    (B) lack of practice.
    (C) extreme poverty.
    (D) recovery.

34. Do not **malign** his name.

    (A) slander
    (B) prophesy
    (C) entreat
    (D) praise

35. **Impotent** most nearly means

    (A) unwise.
    (B) lacking strength.
    (C) free of sin.
    (D) commanding.

PARAGRAPH COMPREHENSION—SUBTEST 4

TIME: 13 MINUTES
15 QUESTIONS

Directions: This test is a test of your ability to understand what you read. In this section you will find one or more paragraphs of reading material followed by incomplete statements or questions.

You are to read the paragraph and select which of the four lettered choices best completes the statement or answers the question. When you have selected your answer, blacken the correct numbered letter on your answer sheet.

Now look at the sample question below.

In certain areas water is so scarce that every attempt is made to conserve it. For instance, on one oasis in the Sahara Desert the amount of water necessary for each date palm tree has been carefully determined.

1. How much water is each tree given?

   (A) no water at all
   (B) exactly the amount required
   (C) water only if it is healthy
   (D) water on alternate days

The amount of water each tree required has been carefully determined, so answer B is correct.

Your score on this subtest will be based on the number of questions you answer correctly. You should try to answer every question. Do not spend too much time on any one question.

When you begin, be sure to start with question number 1 in Part 4 of your test booklet and number 1 in Part 4 on your answer form.

THE ACTUAL TEST WILL SAY:

Do not turn this page until told to do so.

1. The duty of a lighthouse keeper is to keep the light burning no matter what happens, so that ships will be warned of the presence of dangerous rocks. If a shipwreck should occur near the lighthouse, even though he would like to aid in the rescue of its crew and passengers, the lighthouse keeper must

   (A) stay at his light.
   (B) rush to their aid.
   (C) turn out the light.
   (D) quickly sound the siren.

2. In certain areas water is so scarce that every attempt is made to conserve it. For instance, for one oasis in the Sahara Desert the amount of water necessary for each date palm tree has been carefully determined.

   How much water is each tree given?

   (A) no water at all
   (B) exactly the amount required
   (C) water only if it is healthy
   (D) water on alternate days

3. Plants should be gradually "hardened" or toughened for two weeks before being moved outdoors. This is done by withholding water and lowering the temperature. Hardening slows down the plants' rate of growth to prepare them to withstand such conditions as chilling, drying winds, or high temperatures.

You toughen a seedling

(A) by putting it in a cooler environment.
(B) by putting it in a 6-inch pot.
(C) by watering it thoroughly.
(D) by using ready-made peat pellets.

4. At depths of several miles inside the earth, the weight of rocks causes great pressure. This rock pressure, as well as other forces, sometimes causes rocks to break and slip. Faults (great cracks) form. When slippage occurs, shock waves are felt and can be detected with seismographs thousands of miles away.

The most frequent cause of major earthquakes is

(A) faulting.
(B) folding.
(C) landslides.
(D) submarine currents.

5. A leaf can catch sunlight and turn this energy into food which is stored in a tree or plant. To run this factory the leaf must have air, water, and sunlight. By a chemical process called *photosynthesis*, the leaf combines the air and water with the energy of the sun.

The process of *photosynthesis*

(A) combines air, water, and sun to make food.
(B) makes leaves grow in fancy shapes.
(C) causes water to form in clouds.
(D) is a physical process.

6. Most telephone sales are made by reputable persons who try to sell in an honest manner. These persons use the telephone as an aid to business, and they know success depends on being fair and reasonable. The opposite of reputable salesmen are overaggressive talkers who try to force you to make up your mind quickly.

The word *reputable* is closest in meaning to

(A) reasonable.
(B) trusted.
(C) friendly.
(D) aggressive.

7. When someone in your family suffers a minor burn, reach for an ice cube fast. Place it directly over the burn until the sting is gone when the cube is removed. Ice is great first aid for burns and kills the pain. Afterward you'll be amazed to discover there is very little swelling, blisters probably won't appear, and healing will be much faster.

The topic sentence or key idea in this paragraph is that

(A) ice prevents burn blisters.
(B) ice cubes remove the pain.
(C) ice is great first aid for burns.
(D) ice reduces swelling.

8. A stranger meets you and shows you some cash he has just "found." He wants to divide it with you. He says that you must show your "good faith" and put up some of your own money. When you agree to give him your money, the stranger finds some reason to leave for a while. Do you see him again? Not likely; you have just been swindled.

The main theme of this passage is

(A) do not speak to strangers.
(B) be careful of "get-rich-quick" plans.
(C) how to make money.
(D) do not believe strangers.

9. Statistically, by far the most common types of home accidents are falls. Each year over 15,000 Americans meet death in this way, within the four walls of their homes or in yards around their houses. Nine out of 10 of the victims are over 65, but people of all ages experience serious injuries as a result of home falls.

Falls most frequently result in death for

(A) children.
(B) adults under 35.
(C) all age groups.
(D) adults older than 65.

10. "Gray water" is slightly used water—the water you have collected at the bottom of the tub after you have showered or the rinse water from the washing machine. It is still useful, and we cannot afford to let it go down the drain.

Which of the following is an example of gray water?

(A) carbonated water
(B) rainwater
(C) soapy water
(D) tap water

11. Glaciers are frozen masses of snow and ice. As the weight of the snow increases each year, the lower layers become hard-packed like ice. The weight also causes the glacier to move slowly downhill. Speeds of glaciers are usually figured in inches per day rather than miles per hour.

A glacier moves as a result of its

(A) speed.
(B) weight.
(C) temperature.
(D) layers.

12. It is time to get this country moving again. No American wants to stand by and see this country go the other way. The men who have been elected are no longer in touch. A fresh point of view, new ideas, and more action are needed. The voters should finally wake up and give power to those who will make changes.

This passage tries to make you believe that

(A) changes are needed.
(B) no changes are needed.
(C) changes will never happen.
(D) no action is needed.

13. Up until a few years ago most parents, teachers, baby doctors, and coaches felt that right was right. There was even an old wives' tale that left-handed people did not learn as well. But, I'm happy to report, this right-thinking is gone. Today parents and teachers understand left-handedness, and our number is rising.

The main idea of this passage is that the feelings about left-handedness

(A) have not changed at all.
(B) have completely changed.
(C) have partly changed.
(D) will not change.

14. According to Newton's Third Law, for each action there is an equal and opposite reaction. You can illustrate the principle by blowing up a rubber balloon and then allowing the air to escape. Notice that the balloon moves forward as the air escapes in the opposite direction.

Which of the following describes Newton's Third Law?

(A) an object at rest
(B) gravitational force
(C) falling bodies
(D) action equals reaction

15. Water is a good conductor of sound waves. If you were swimming underwater while someone struck two rocks together underwater 10 feet away, you would be surprised at how loud the sound was. The U.S. Navy makes use of this knowledge in detecting enemy submarines.

Of the following, which is the best restatement of the main idea?

(A) Fish cannot hear ordinary sounds.
(B) Sound waves become compressed in very deep water.
(C) Water is a good conductor of sound waves.
(D) Submarines cannot detect sound waves.

MATHEMATICS KNOWLEDGE—SUBTEST 5

TIME: 24 MINUTES
25 QUESTIONS

Directions: This is a test of your ability to solve general mathematical problems. Each problem is followed by four answer choices. Select the correct response from the choices given, then mark the space on your answer form that has the same number and letter as your choice. Use scratch paper to do any figuring that you wish.

Now look at this sample problem.

1. If $x + 8 = 9$, then x is equal to

(A) 0.

(B) 1.

(C) 3.

(D) $\frac{9}{8}$.

The correct answer is 1, so B is the correct response.

Your score on this test will be based on the number of questions you answer correctly. You should try to answer every question. Do not spend too much time on any one question.

Start with question number 1 in Part 5. Mark your answer for this question next to number 1, Part 5, on your answer form.

THE ACTUAL TEST WILL SAY:

Do not turn this page until told to do so.

---

1. If $a - 4 = 8$, then a is equal to

(A) 12.

(B) 4.

(C) 22.

(D) 13.

2. If $x > y$ and $y > z$, which of the following statements is true?

(A) $x = z$

(B) $x < z$

(C) $x > z$

(D) $y + z = x$

3. The town of Yeehaw has a public pool in the shape of a hexagon. If the town parks manager wants to put a lifeguard on each side of the pool, how many lifeguards will he need to hire?

(A) four

(B) five

(C) six

(D) eight

4. The paint that Amanda is using to paint Maddalyn's room comes in two sizes, small (16 ounces) and large (one gallon/64 ounces). The only size paint can left at the hardware store is the small size. If she used up an entire large can painting $\frac{3}{4}$ of Maddalyn's room, how many small cans does she need to buy to finish painting?

(A) one
(B) two
(C) three
(D) four

5. Solve the following equation for x: $4x + 2 = -14$.

(A) $x = -6$
(B) $x = -4$
(C) $x = 4$
(D) $x = -12$

6. A writer has gotten five of his short stories published so far. These five stories are 20 percent of all the stories he has written. How many total stories has he written?

(A) 15
(B) 22
(C) 25
(D) 40

7. One of the equal angles of an isosceles triangle is 50 degrees. What is the angle opposite the unequal side?

(A) 50 degrees
(B) 80 degrees
(C) 130 degrees
(D) 140 degrees

8. 40 percent of 20 is 20 percent of what number?

(A) 10
(B) 20
(C) 40
(D) 80

9. Which of the following is a cone?

(A) The Great Pyramid of Cheops
(B) The Washington Monument
(C) a dunce cap
(D) an entire pencil

10. 10 percent of 25 percent of 750 is

(A) 3.00
(B) 18.75
(C) 187.5
(D) 300.0

11. An equilateral triangle has the same perimeter as a square whose sides each measure 15 inches. What is the length of one side of the triangle?

(A) 9 inches
(B) 12 inches
(C) 20 inches
(D) 30 inches

12. Which of the following is not a prime number?

(A) 3
(B) 17
(C) 37
(D) 39

13. A round armored vehicle hatch is 18 inches in diameter. It has connected to it a circular hatch cover that measures 20 inches across at the middle. How much greater is the area of the hatch cover than the area of the hatch?

(A) 19π square inches
(B) 20π square inches
(C) 40π square inches
(D) 100π square inches

14. If the area of a triangle is 45 square inches and its base is 9 inches, what is the length of the altitude to that base?

(A) 5 inches
(B) 10 inches
(C) 18 inches
(D) 22.5 inches

15. What is the value of $(3)(-7)(2)(-4)$?

   (A) 16
   (B) −46
   (C) −84
   (D) 168

16. If $x = -7$, then $2x^2 - 3x + 10 =$

   (A) 3
   (B) −67
   (C) 106
   (D) 129

17. $(x^3)^4 =$

   (A) x^7
   (B) x^{12}
   (C) x^1
   (D) x^{-1}

18. What is the reciprocal of $\frac{7}{4}$?

   (A) $\frac{4}{7}$

   (B) $1\frac{3}{4}$

   (C) $4\frac{1}{7}$

   (D) 28

19. What is the fraction $\frac{12}{18}$ when it is changed to a percentage?

   (A) 60.67%
   (B) 66.67%
   (C) 75.00%
   (D) 80.00%

20. What is the value of $(-15)^2$?

   (A) −30
   (B) −225
   (C) 225
   (D) 2,250

21. What is the perimeter of the square shown below?

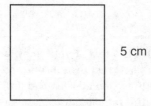

5 cm

   (A) 10 centimeters
   (B) 20 inches
   (C) 25 centimeters
   (D) 20 centimeters

22. In the right triangle shown below, what is the length of side AC?

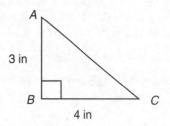

   (A) 4 inches
   (B) 5 inches
   (C) 6 inches
   (D) 7 inches

23. Factor the expression $a^2 - 81$.

   (A) $(a + 9)(a + 9)$
   (B) $(a - 9)(a - 9)$
   (C) $(a + 9)(a - 9)$
   (D) $2a(81)$

24. Round off 3,191.785 to the nearest hundredth.

   (A) 3,200
   (B) 3,191.8
   (C) 3,191.79
   (D) 3,191.78

25. Solve the following inequality.
   $x + 3 > 5$

   (A) $x = 2$
   (B) $x > 2$
   (C) $x - 5 > 3$
   (D) $x - 3 > 8$

ELECTRONICS INFORMATION—SUBTEST 6

TIME: 9 MINUTES
20 QUESTIONS

Directions: This is a test of your knowledge of electrical, radio, and electronics information. You are to select the correct response from the choices given. Then mark the space on your answer form that has the same number and letter as your choice.

Now look at the sample question below.

1. What does the abbreviation AC stand for?

   (A) additional charge
   (B) alternating coil
   (C) alternating current
   (D) ampere current

The correct answer is "alternating current," so C is the correct response.

Your score on this test will be based on the number of questions you answer correctly. You should try to answer every question. Do not spend too much time on any one question.

When you are told to begin, be sure to start with question number 1 in Part 6 of your test booklet and number 1 in Part 6 of your answer form.

THE ACTUAL TEST WILL SAY:

Do not turn this page until told to do so.

---

1. A 9-volt transistor contains how many cells?

   (A) one
   (B) four
   (C) six
   (D) nine

2. Compared to a number 12 wire, a number 22 wire is

   (A) longer.
   (B) shorter.
   (C) larger in diameter.
   (D) smaller in diameter.

3. A resistor marked "1.5 K Ω" has a value of

   (A) 1.5 ohms.
   (B) 105 ohms.
   (C) 1,500 ohms.
   (D) 1,500 watts.

4. An equivalent term for electromotive force is

   (A) voltage.
   (B) current.
   (C) resistance.
   (D) reactance.

5. The property of a circuit that opposes any change in voltage is

   (A) conductance.
   (B) capacitance.
   (C) resistance.
   (D) inductance.

6. The composition of $\frac{60}{40}$ rosin core solder is

   (A) 60% lead, 40% tin.
   (B) 60% tin, 40% lead.
   (C) 60% silver, 40% rosin.
   (D) 60% lead, 40% silver.

7. A hair dryer is rated at 1,200 watts. Assuming it is operated at 120 volts, how much current will this appliance draw?

    (A) 10 amps
    (B) 100 amps
    (C) 1,000 amps
    (D) 144,000 amps

8. Another term for cycles per second is

    (A) hertz.
    (B) henry.
    (C) kilo.
    (D) mega.

9. A crystal microphone is an example of what electrical phenomenon?

    (A) thermoionic emission
    (B) piezoelectric effect
    (C) inductance
    (D) hysteresis

10. The process of transmitting voice by varying the height of a carrier wave is known as

    (A) frequency modulation.
    (B) amplitude modulation.
    (C) demodulation.
    (D) detection.

11. The primary of a transformer is connected to 120 volts. The voltage across the secondary is 40 volts. This transformer has a turns ratio of

    (A) 1:1.
    (B) 1:4.
    (C) 1:3.
    (D) 3:1.

12. A carbon resistor marked with the color bands of red, red, red, gold is of what value and tolerance?

    (A) 2,000 ohms ± 5%
    (B) 222 ohms ± 5%
    (C) 2,200 ohms ± 5%
    (D) 6 ohms ± 5%

13. Which is the correct schematic symbol of a tetrode tube?

    (A)

    (B)

    (C)

    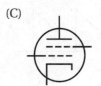

    (D)

14. What is the total resistance in this circuit if all resistors are 500 ohms?

    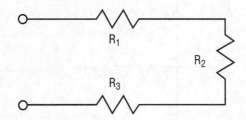

    (A) 1,500 watts
    (B) 1,500 ohms
    (C) 1.5 ohms
    (D) 500 ohms

15.

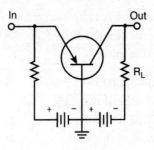

The above schematic represents which transistor configuration?

(A) common gate
(B) common collector
(C) common base
(D) common emitter

16. Which choice correctly identifies the waveform pictured?

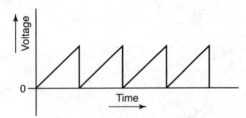

(A) sine wave
(B) square wave
(C) sawtooth wave
(D) pure DC

17. Of the choices illustrated, which is the correct schematic symbol for a potentiometer?

(A)

(B)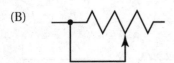

(C)

(D)

18. A component on a parts list has the following specifications, "1μF, 50 wvdc." The component specified is a

(A) potentiometer.
(B) coil.
(C) transistor.
(D) capacitor.

19.

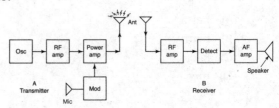

This illustration is a block diagram of a transmitter and receiver. What is the purpose of the oscillator?

(A) to generate a radio frequency
(B) to produce a carrier wave
(C) to produce a high-frequency current
(D) all of the above

20. Referring to the schematic in question 19, what is the purpose of the detector stage?

(A) to amplify the audio signal
(B) to tune in the carrier wave
(C) to separate the audio from the radio wave
(D) to amplify the radio frequency

AUTOMOTIVE & SHOP INFORMATION—SUBTEST 7

TIME: 11 MINUTES
25 QUESTIONS

Directions: This test has questions about automobiles, as well as tools and common shop terminology and practices. Pick the best answer for each question, then blacken the space on your separate answer form that has the same number and letter as your choice.
  Here is a sample question.

1. The most commonly used fuel for operating automobile engines is

   (A) kerosene.
   (B) benzene.
   (C) crude oil.
   (D) gasoline.

   Gasoline is the most commonly used fuel, so D is the correct answer.
   Your score on this test will be based on the number of questions you answer correctly. You should try to answer every question. Do not spend too much time on any one question.
   When you are told to begin, be sure to start with question number 1 in Part 7 of your test booklet and number 1 in Part 7 on your separate answer form.

THE ACTUAL TEST WILL SAY:

Do not turn this page until told to do so.

---

1. Which is the right side of an engine?

   (A) the right side when you stand in front of the car and look toward the engine
   (B) the side that the distributor is on
   (C) depends on the manufacturer
   (D) the right side when you sit in the driver's seat and look forward

2. A brake spoon is used to

   (A) adjust drum brakes.
   (B) adjust disc brakes.
   (C) remove cotter pins.
   (D) clean the backing plate.

3. Ring and pinion backlash is checked with

   (A) a micrometer.
   (B) a round feeler gauge.
   (C) Prussian blue.
   (D) a dial indicator.

4. The clutch aligning arbor is used to align the clutch disc to the

   (A) transmission.
   (B) pilot bearing.
   (C) pressure plate.
   (D) main drive gear.

5. An oscilloscope is used to diagnose problems in which automotive system?

   (A) charging
   (B) starting
   (C) fuel
   (D) ignition

6. Reciprocating motion is changed into rotary motion by which one of the following engine parts?

(A) camshaft
(B) connecting rod bearings
(C) pistons
(D) crankshaft

7. L or L_0 on an automatic transmission gear indicator is the same as

(A) first gear on a manual transmission.
(B) second gear on a manual transmission.
(C) third gear on a manual transmission.
(D) fourth gear on a manual transmission.

8. The "Park" (P) position on an automatic transmission indicator means the transmission

(A) is in idle and can be towed.
(B) is in a locked position that prevents the car from moving.
(C) is in its highest speed position.
(D) is ready for pulling heavy loads through a park at slow speeds.

9. The internal combustion engine can be best described as

(A) a high-torque engine even at low speeds.
(B) a low-torque engine even at low speeds.
(C) a low-speed engine.
(D) a high-speed engine.

10. In a small gasoline engine's fuel tank, the ball drops when suction stops. This prevents

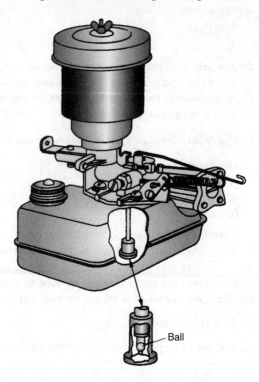

Ball

(A) the engine from running any more.
(B) the gasoline from running back into the tank.
(C) backfiring.
(D) the engine from exploding.

11. The units shown below are used on small gasoline engines as

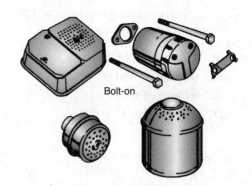

Bolt-on

(A) carburetors.
(B) filters.
(C) magnetos.
(D) mufflers.

12. The outboard engine shown is water-cooled and gets its cooling water from

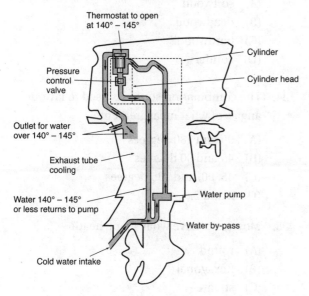

Thermostat to open at 140° – 145°

Pressure control valve

Cylinder

Cylinder head

Outlet for water over 140° – 145°

Exhaust tube cooling

Water 140° – 145° or less returns to pump

Water pump

Water by-pass

Cold water intake

(A) its radiator.
(B) its oil cooler.
(C) the lake or river.
(D) its water holding tank.

13. The thickness gauge shown in the figure is used most often in

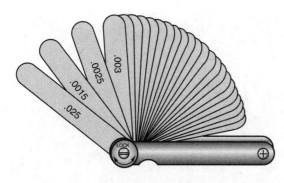

(A) plastics manufacturing.
(B) automotive work.
(C) woodworking shops.
(D) sheet metal refinishing.

14. A coping saw blade is placed in the saw

(A) with the teeth pointing upward.
(B) with the teeth pointing toward the handle.
(C) so it cuts with the wood grain.
(D) so it cuts across the wood grain.

15. Carpenters use

(A) ball-peen hammers.
(B) chisel point hammers.
(C) claw hammers.
(D) planishing hammers.

16. The term *penny* is used

(A) to designate the cost of a nail.
(B) to designate the size of a nail.
(C) to indicate a rosin-coated nail.
(D) to indicate a galvanized nail.

17. A tool used to cut sheet metal is a

(A) bar folder.
(B) box and pan brake.
(C) slip roll.
(D) squaring shear.

18. One of the most common ways to fasten sheet metal today is to

(A) solder it.
(B) braze it.
(C) spot-weld it.
(D) glue it.

19. A welding torch can also be used as a

(A) light source.
(B) burning tool.
(C) cutting torch.
(D) pipe wrench.

20. Tubing cutters are smaller versions of

    (A) pipe cutters.
    (B) ring cutters.
    (C) hole cutters.
    (D) glass cutters.

21. If you "overwork" concrete, it will cause

    (A) loss of a smooth surface.
    (B) separation and create a less durable surface.
    (C) loss of strength throughout the slab.
    (D) puddles in the middle of the slab.

22. Concrete reaches 98 percent of its strength in

    (A) 3 days.
    (B) 50 days.
    (C) 28 days.
    (D) 10 days.

23. Deciduous trees produce

    (A) softwood.
    (B) deadwood.
    (C) hardwood.
    (D) conifers.

24. The combination square is used to lay out angles of what measurement?

    (A) 90 and 180 degrees
    (B) 45 and 90 degrees
    (C) 45, 90, and 135 degrees
    (D) π and 2π

25. Most bolts have what shape head?

    (A) round
    (B) hexagonal
    (C) square
    (D) octagonal

MECHANICAL COMPREHENSION—SUBTEST 8

TIME: 19 MINUTES
25 QUESTIONS

Directions: This test has questions about general mechanical and physical principles. Pick the best answer for each question, then blacken the space on your separate answer form that has the same number and letter as your choice.

Here is a sample question.

1. The follower is at its highest position between points

(A) Q and R.
(B) R and S.
(C) S and T.
(D) T and Q.

The correct answer is "between Q and R," so you would blacken the space for A on your answer form.

Your score on this test will be based on the number of questions you answer correctly. You should try to answer every question. Do not spend too much time on any one question.

When you are told to begin, be sure to start with question number 1 in Part 8 of your test booklet and number 1 in Part 8 of your answer form.

THE ACTUAL TEST WILL SAY:

Do not turn this page until told to do so.

1. The follower is at its lowest point between points

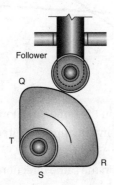

(A) Q and R.
(B) R and S.
(C) S and T.
(D) T and Q.

2. If pulley A is the driver and turns in direction 1, which pulley will turn the slowest?

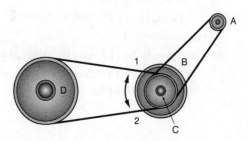

(A) A
(B) B
(C) C
(D) D

3. Two 30-pound signs are attached to a rafter using cords, as shown below. Which one of the following statements is true?

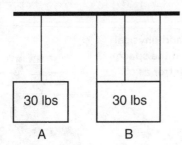

(A) The cord holding sign A is under $\frac{1}{3}$ the tension of the cords holding sign B.

(B) The cords holding sign B are each under $\frac{1}{3}$ the tension of the cord holding sign A.

(C) The cords holding sign B are under $\frac{1}{6}$ the tension of the cords holding sign A.

(D) All cords are under the same tension because gravity acts on them equally.

4. What is the difference between mass and weight?

(A) Weight remains constant, but mass depends on velocity.

(B) Mass remains constant, but weight depends on altitude.

(C) Weight can be changed by buoyancy, but mass is relative based on gravity.

(D) Mass and weight are equivalent.

5. In the drawing below, if the fulcrum is moved closer to the weight on the resistance arm, the result will be that

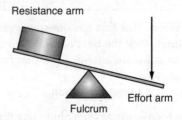

(A) the weight will be easier to lift and will travel higher.

(B) the weight will be easier to lift and will not travel as high.

(C) the weight will require more effort to lift and will travel higher.

(D) the weight will require more effort to lift and will not travel as high.

6. In the drawing below, if pulley A is rotating in the direction shown, then pulley B will

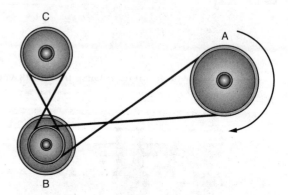

(A) rotate in the same direction as pulley A.

(B) rotate in the opposite direction as pulley A.

(C) rotate in the same direction as pulley C.

(D) rotate in the same direction as pulleys A and C.

7. In the pulley system in question 6, which pulley will rotate the slowest?

(A) pulley A
(B) pulley B
(C) pulley C
(D) they will all rotate at the same speed.

8. Water flows out of a water tower at a rate of 3 gallons per minute and flows in at a rate of 180 gallons per hour. What will happen to the level of the water in the tower over 2 hours?

(A) It will rise.
(B) It will lower.
(C) It will stay the same.
(D) It will rise initially, then lower.

9. If arm H is held stationary while gear B turns in direction 1, gear

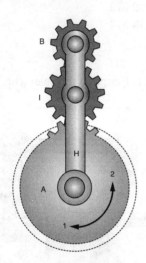

(A) A will turn in direction 1.
(B) A will turn in direction 2.
(C) I will turn in direction 1.
(D) I will spin freely.

10. When two or more forces act in such a way that their combined result has a net effect of zero, this is called

(A) similarity.
(B) congruence.
(C) stasis.
(D) equilibrium.

11. As the shaft in the illustration below spins in a clockwise direction and increases its speed, balls A and B will

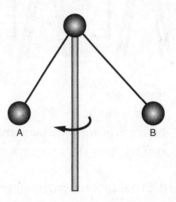

(A) stay at the same level since the rotation direction is the same.
(B) move inward and downward due to the coriolis force.
(C) move outward and upward due to centrifugal force.
(D) move outward due to centripedal force.

12. The town of Dry Gulch has two water towers as shown below. If both water towers A and B are full, the same size, and the same height above the ground, which water tower will be able to provide more water to the thirsty townspeople below?

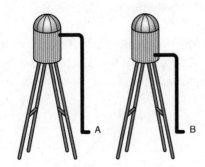

(A) water tower A
(B) water tower B
(C) both will provide the same amount
(D) neither, since Dry Gulch is a ghost town

13. Jonathan the airborne paratrooper has just performed a proper exit from a C-130H aircraft and his T-11 ATPS parachute has deployed properly. His descent to the ground is primarily affected by what forces?

(A) lift and drag
(B) gravity and drag
(C) gravity and temperature
(D) initial velocity and gravity

14. Moisture forming on the inner surface of a windshield on a cold day is an example of

(A) vaporization.
(B) evaporation.
(C) distillation.
(D) condensation.

15. Which of the following statements concerning the poles of a magnet is correct?

(A) South repels north.
(B) Like poles attract.
(C) North attracts north.
(D) Unlike poles attract.

16. Torque means

(A) number of cylinders.
(B) turning effort.
(C) ratio of driveshaft to rear axle.
(D) driveshaft.

17. Water in an automobile engine may cause damage in cold weather because

(A) ice is a poor conductor of heat.
(B) water expands as it freezes.
(C) cold water is compressible.
(D) ice is denser than water.

18. What is the rear axle ratio in a standard differential with 11 teeth on the pinion gear and 43 teeth on the ring gear?

(A) 4.10 to 1
(B) 3.90 to 1
(C) 3.73 to 1
(D) 3.54 to 1

19. Gear B is intended to mesh with

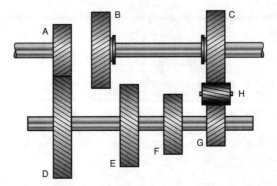

(A) gear A only.
(B) gear D only.
(C) gear E only.
(D) all of the above gears.

20. As cam A makes one complete turn, the setscrew hits the contact point

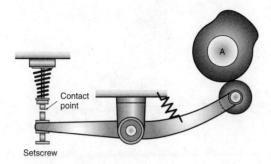

Contact point

Setscrew

(A) once.
(B) twice.
(C) three times.
(D) not at all.

21. If gear A makes 14 revolutions, gear B will make

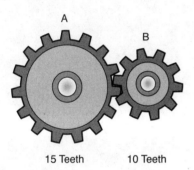

A

B

15 Teeth   10 Teeth

(A) 21.
(B) 17.
(C) 14.
(D) 9.

22. Which of the other gears is moving in the same direction as gear 2?

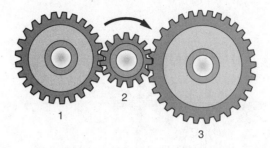

1   2   3

(A) gear 1
(B) gear 3
(C) neither of the other gears
(D) both of the other gears

23. Floats X and Y are measuring the specific gravity of two different liquids. Which float indicates the liquid with the highest specific gravity?

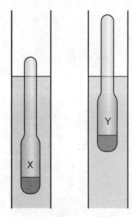

X

Y

(A) Y
(B) X
(C) neither X nor Y
(D) Both X and Y are the same.

24. Which vacuum gauge will indicate the highest vacuum as air passes through the carburetor bore?

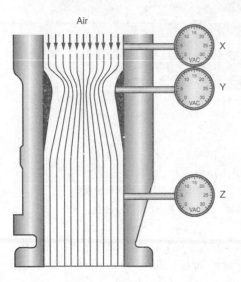

(A) X
(B) Y
(C) Z
(D) X and Z

25. The wheelbarrow is an example of a

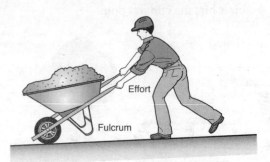

(A) first-class lever.
(B) second-class lever.
(C) third-class lever.
(D) first- and third-class lever.

ASSEMBLING OBJECTS—SUBTEST 9

TIME: 9 MINUTES
16 QUESTIONS

Directions: This test measures your ability to picture how an object will look when its parts are mentally put together or connected. There are two types of problems. In the first type of problem, each question will show you several separate shapes, from which you will then pick the choice that best represents how the shapes would look if they were all fitted together correctly, as in the example below. There is only one best answer for each shape. Pick the best answer for each question, then blacken the space on the answer form that has the same number and letter as your choice.

Here is a sample question.

1. Which figure best shows how the objects in the group on the left will appear if they are fitted together?

 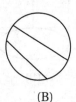  

                 (A)   (B)   (C)   (D)

In this example, the correct answer is "D."

In the second type of problem, you will be shown two shapes and a connector line. One point on each of the shapes will be labeled with a letter (for instance, "A" on the first shape and "B" on the second shape). The ends of the connector line will be labeled with the same letters—in this case, one end with "A" and the other end with the letter "B." You will be asked which of the four figures best shows how the two shapes and a connector line in the first group will touch if the letters for each object are matched, as in the example below. There is only one best answer for each shape. Pick the best answer for each question, then blacken the space on the answer form that has the same number and letter as your choice.

Here is a sample question.

2. Which figure best shows how the objects in the group of objects on the left will touch if the letters for each object are matched?

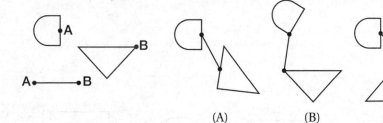

                           (A)   (B)   (C)   (D)

In this example, the correct answer is "C."

Your score on this test will be based on the number of questions you answer correctly. You should try to answer every question. Do not spend too much time on any one question.

When you are told to begin, be sure to start with question number 1 in Part 9 of your test booklet and number 1 in Part 9 on your separate answer form.

THE ACTUAL TEST WILL SAY:

Do not turn this page until told to do so.

1.

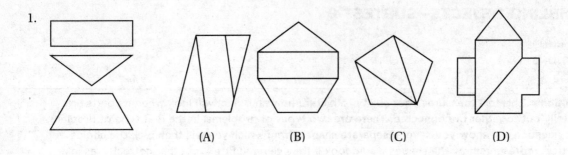

(A) (B) (C) (D)

2.

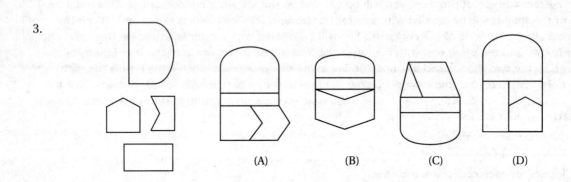

(A) (B) (C) (D)

3.

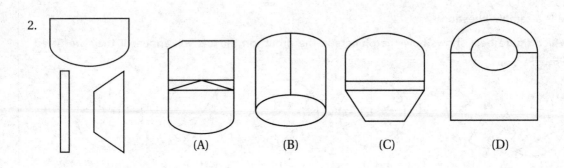

(A) (B) (C) (D)

4.

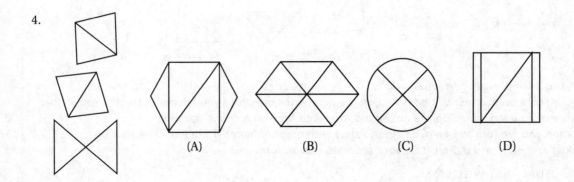

(A) (B) (C) (D)

5.

6.

7.

8.

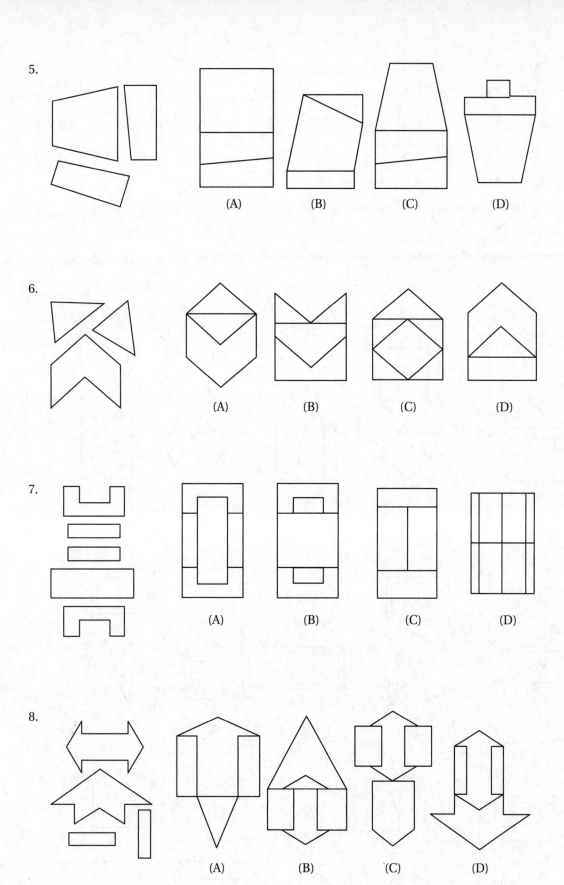

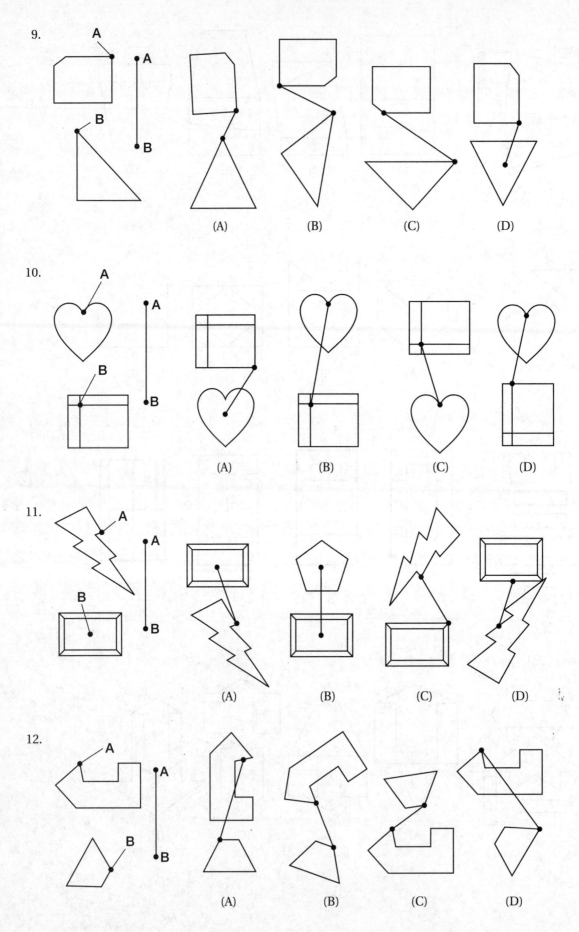

9.

(A) (B) (C) (D)

10.

(A) (B) (C) (D)

11.

(A) (B) (C) (D)

12.

(A) (B) (C) (D)

13.

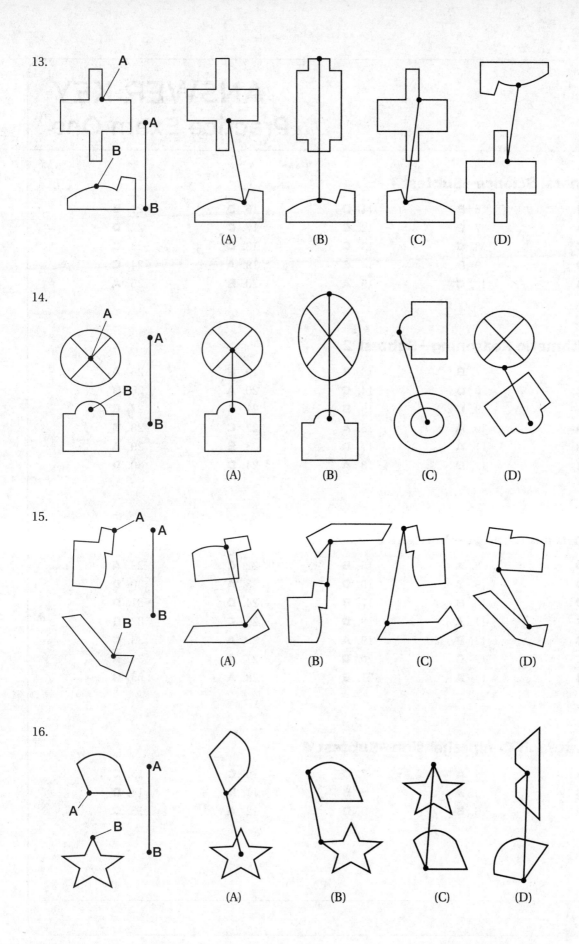

(A) (B) (C) (D)

14.

(A) (B) (C) (D)

15.

(A) (B) (C) (D)

16.

(A) (B) (C) (D)

ANSWER KEY
Practice Exam One

General Science—Subtest 1

1. **B**	6. **B**	11. **D**	16. **D**	21. **B**
2. **A**	7. **C**	12. **C**	17. **C**	22. **D**
3. **C**	8. **C**	13. **C**	18. **D**	23. **C**
4. **D**	9. **D**	14. **C**	19. **A**	24. **C**
5. **A**	10. **C**	15. **A**	20. **B**	25. **A**

Arithmetic Reasoning—Subtest 2

1. **D**	7. **B**	13. **B**	19. **B**	25. **A**
2. **C**	8. **D**	14. **C**	20. **A**	26. **B**
3. **B**	9. **C**	15. **B**	21. **C**	27. **C**
4. **A**	10. **A**	16. **A**	22. **C**	28. **B**
5. **D**	11. **A**	17. **D**	23. **B**	29. **A**
6. **B**	12. **D**	18. **A**	24. **D**	30. **D**

Word Knowledge—Subtest 3

1. **D**	8. **A**	15. **B**	22. **C**	29. **A**
2. **D**	9. **B**	16. **D**	23. **A**	30. **D**
3. **D**	10. **B**	17. **B**	24. **D**	31. **D**
4. **B**	11. **A**	18. **D**	25. **C**	32. **B**
5. **B**	12. **B**	19. **A**	26. **A**	33. **C**
6. **C**	13. **C**	20. **D**	27. **A**	34. **A**
7. **B**	14. **A**	21. **B**	28. **A**	35. **B**

Paragraph Comprehension—Subtest 4

1. **A**	4. **A**	7. **C**	10. **C**	13. **C**
2. **B**	5. **A**	8. **B**	11. **B**	14. **D**
3. **A**	6. **B**	9. **D**	12. **A**	15. **C**

Mathematics Knowledge—Subtest 5

1. **A**	6. **C**	11. **C**	16. **D**	21. **D**
2. **C**	7. **B**	12. **D**	17. **B**	22. **B**
3. **C**	8. **C**	13. **A**	18. **A**	23. **C**
4. **B**	9. **C**	14. **B**	19. **B**	24. **C**
5. **B**	10. **B**	15. **D**	20. **C**	25. **B**

Electronics Information—Subtest 6

1. **C**	5. **B**	9. **B**	13. **C**	17. **B**
2. **D**	6. **B**	10. **B**	14. **B**	18. **D**
3. **C**	7. **A**	11. **D**	15. **C**	19. **D**
4. **A**	8. **A**	12. **C**	16. **C**	20. **C**

Automotive & Shop Information—Subtest 7

1. **D**	6. **D**	11. **D**	16. **B**	21. **B**
2. **A**	7. **A**	12. **C**	17. **D**	22. **C**
3. **D**	8. **B**	13. **B**	18. **C**	23. **C**
4. **B**	9. **D**	14. **B**	19. **C**	24. **B**
5. **D**	10. **B**	15. **C**	20. **A**	25. **B**

Mechanical Comprehension—Subtest 8

1. **C**	6. **B**	11. **C**	16. **B**	21. **A**
2. **D**	7. **A**	12. **B**	17. **B**	22. **C**
3. **B**	8. **C**	13. **B**	18. **B**	23. **A**
4. **B**	9. **A**	14. **D**	19. **C**	24. **B**
5. **B**	10. **D**	15. **D**	20. **A**	25. **B**

Assembling Objects—Subtest 9

1. **B**	5. **C**	9. **B**	13. **D**
2. **C**	6. **A**	10. **B**	14. **A**
3. **D**	7. **A**	11. **A**	15. **B**
4. **B**	8. **D**	12. **C**	16. **C**

GENERAL SCIENCE—SUBTEST 1

1. **(B)** Sound travels fastest in the densest, or heaviest, materials. The molecules in heavy materials are closer together and transmit sound vibrations more rapidly than the molecules in light materials. Sound does not travel through a vacuum.

2. **(A)** In the process of distillation, a liquid is evaporated by heat and then condensed by cooling. When seawater is distilled, the salt remains behind as a residue, and the distilled water is very pure. Seawater is distilled before it is used in a ship's boilers in order to get rid of the salt, which would form a scale and ruin the boilers.

3. **(C)** Copper is found in combination with other elements and also in a free state. Nitrogen is a gas. Iron is seldom found in a free state, and aluminum occurs in combination with other elements in the earth's crust.

4. **(D)** When the sun's rays strike a surface that is smooth, shiny, or light in color, the rays are reflected. When the sun's rays strike a surface that is rough and dark, more of the rays are absorbed.

5. **(A)** In crop rotation, plants such as legumes are planted periodically to add nitrogen to the soil after other crops have exhausted it. None of the other methods returns minerals to the soil.

6. **(B)** A crowbar is a form of lever. By placing a crowbar over a support, you can exert pressure on one end and overcome resistance at the other. A crowbar can be placed on the surface of a rock as a fulcrum, for example, with one end under the edge of another rock, and then presed hard to dislodge the other rock.

7. **(C)** The lunar surface is darkened when the earth comes between the sun and the moon. This is caused by the fact that the shadow of the earth falls on the moon's surface.

8. **(C)** Calcium is a very important component of bones. Without it, the bones in our skeleton become brittle.

9. **(D)** The oxidation of the gasoline, which contains hydrogen, produces moisture. There is also an oxidation of the carbon in gasoline, which produces carbon dioxide (not mentioned in the question) and traces of carbon monoxide. These traces can be dangerous when the engine of a car is running in a confined, poorly ventilated place.

10. **(C)** The telephone receiver has an electromagnet with a metal diaphragm mounted close to it. The metal diaphragm vibrates (moves back and forth) and reproduces the sounds spoken into the transmitter. The sound waves produced by the speaker's voice cause the transmitter to make the current in the wires weaker and stronger. These changes occur thousands of times per second. These changes in current affect the electromagnet in the receiver at the other end of the phone call. The receiving electromagnet affects its diaphragm strongly or weakly as the current changes. This in turn reproduces the sound waves made originally by the speaker's voice.

11. **(D)** Radio and light waves are two forms of electromagnetic radiation. In a vacuum, all electromagnetic waves have the same speed—that is, the speed of light.

12.	**(C)** The earth's atmosphere consists of a mixture of nitrogen (about 78 percent by volume); oxygen (about 21 percent); carbon dioxide (about 0.03 percent); small amounts of rare gases such as neon, xenon, krypton, and helium; and some water vapor and dust particles.

13.	**(C)** All freely falling objects, regardless of their masses near the earth, fall toward the earth with equal acceleration. Any two objects at rest that begin to fall at the same instant will have equal velocities at the end of three seconds, or at any other time interval. Thus the ratio of their speeds will be 1:1.

14.	**(C)** A falling barometer indicates the approach of low pressure and rising air. The rising of warm, moist air usually results in precipitation. We have reason to assume that the air is warm since we know that southeast winds come from lower latitudes where the air was warmed, picking up moisture when it passed over the Atlantic Ocean.

15.	**(A)** Sand particles are visible and comparatively large. They can be caught in the small holes of a filter. Sugar, alcohol, and most inks form true solutions in which the particles are of molecular size, which will pass through filters.

16.	**(D)** Barometric pressure decreases 1 inch for every 900 feet of altitude. The gas in the balloon expands because it enters regions of lower and lower pressure. Balloons being prepared for ascent are only partially filled with helium. The balloonist knows that the gas will expand and fill the balloon completely at higher altitudes.

17.	**(C)** The analysis of radioactive material has given scientists an accurate estimate of the age of the earth.

18.	**(D)** Coal deposits were formed when layers of giant ferns as well as other vegetation were compressed into layers of coal by the earth's movement. Its coal deposits tell us that Alaska must have had a tropical climate.

19.	**(A)** The curve in the top of an airplane wing forces the air to flow faster over the top of the wing than below it. This faster flowing air results in less pressure above the wing. The principle behind this was first described by Bernoulli. In any flowing liquid, the pressure becomes less as the speed of the flowing liquid becomes greater.

20.	**(B)** The lens focuses the light on the retina, which "records the image," sending impulses along the optic nerve to the brain. The cornea is the transparent tissue covering the eyeball. The pupil is the opening through which light enters the eye.

21.	**(B)** When a water molecule is decomposed by electrolysis, it breaks up into hydrogen and oxygen; the ratio is two molecules of hydrogen to one of oxygen.

$$2H_2O \rightarrow 2H_2\uparrow + O_2\uparrow$$

22.	**(D)** $FeSO_4$ is a compound of three different elements—iron (Fe), sulfur (S), and oxygen (O). Hydrogen (H) is a separate element.

23.	**(C)** Nitrogen is needed most by plants. They also have some need for phosphorus and potassium. Only traces of the other elements are needed by plants; they are not a major concern for companies that produce fertilizers.

24.	**(C)** When an object is placed in water, it loses the exact same weight as the weight of the water it displaces. If two objects that are placed in water appear to lose the same weight, then they must have both displaced the same amount of water. That means that they are equal in size, or volume.

25. **(A)** A thermos is made with a vacuum between its double walls. In this vacuum, there are no molecules to receive the transfer of heat energy from the wall near the contents of the thermos. Thus, the vacuum prevents the loss of heat. Even though a storm window allows some air between it and the "year-round" window, it is the closest match to a thermos among the choices given.

ARITHMETIC REASONING—SUBTEST 2

1. **(D)** You need 8 barrels of water to sprinkle $\frac{1}{2}$ mile. You need 16 barrels of water to sprinkle 1 mile. You need 3 × 16 (or 48) barrels to sprinkle 3 miles.

   You need 48 + 8 (or 56) barrels to sprinkle $3\frac{1}{2}$ miles.

2. **(C)** Since the picture and its enlargement are similar, the lengths have the same ratio as the widths.

$$\frac{\text{length of picture}}{\text{length of enlargement}} = \frac{\text{width of picture}}{\text{width of enlargement}}$$

$$\frac{8}{12} = \frac{6}{\text{width of enlargement } (x)}$$

   To solve this, cross-multiply the measurements, using x for the one you don't know.

$$8 \times x = 12 \times 6 = 72$$

$$x = \frac{72}{8} = 9 \text{ inches (width)}$$

3. **(B)** There are 10 units of $1,000 in $10,000. Thus, Travis Lee pays 10 × $24 (or $240) each year in premiums. That means that every 6 months,

   Travis Lee pays $\frac{1}{2}$ of $240, or $120.

4. **(A)** There are 16 ounces in 1 pound. Therefore, if 2 pounds of cottage cheese costs $3.20, then 1 pound of cottage cheese costs $1.60. 1 ounce costs $1.60 ÷ 16 (or $0.10). 3 ounces cost 3 × $0.10 (or $0.30).

5. **(D)** To find the distance Mr. Green drove, multiply the hours by the miles per hour. Thus,

$$12 \times 55 = 660 \text{ (distance covered)}$$

   To find the number of gallons he used, divide the distance by the miles per gallon. Thus,

$$660 \div 22 = 30 \text{ (gallons used)}$$

6. **(B)** From 8:45 A.M. to 4:45 P.M. is 8 hours. From 4:45 P.M. to 5:15 P.M. is $\frac{1}{2}$ hour.

   Subtract Max's lunch hour.

$$8\frac{1}{2} - 1 = 7\frac{1}{2} \text{ (or 7.5 hours)}$$

Multiply his work hours by his hourly rate.

$$7.5 \times \$7.50 = \$56.25 \text{ (day's salary)}$$

7. **(B)** Find the cost of 3 ties: $3 \times \$4 = \$12$. Find the cost of the shirts alone:

$$\$52 - \$12 = \$40$$

Find the cost of 1 shirt:

$$\$40 \div 5 = \$8$$

8. **(D)** Find the relationship between each pair of numbers in the series. Thus,

$$(5; 2)\ 5 - 3 = 2$$
$$(2; 9)\ 2 + 7 = 9$$
$$(9; 6)\ 9 - 3 = 6$$

The pattern so far is $-3, +7, -3$. To continue the series, add 7 to the fourth number in the series:

$$6 + 7 = 13$$

9. **(C)** If 80 percent of the audience were adults, then the percentage of children was

$$100\% - 80\% = 20\% \ (0.2)$$

To find the number of children, multiply

$$500 \times 0.2 = 100.0 = 100 \text{ children}$$

10. **(A)** Find the amount of reduction by subtracting.

$$\$240 - \$210 = \$30$$

To find the percentage of reduction, divide it by the original price.

$$\frac{\text{(reduction) } \$30}{\text{(original price) } \$240} = \frac{1}{8} = 12\frac{1}{2}\%$$

11. **(A)** Multiply the cost of the home by the assessment rate.

$$\$55,000 \times 80\% =$$
$$\$55,000 \times 0.8 = \$44,000$$

The realty tax is $4.74 for each $100 in $44,000.

$$\$44,000 \div 100 = 440 \text{ (hundreds)}$$
$$\$4.74 \times 440 = \$2,085.60 \text{ (tax)}$$

12. **(D)** If 1 inch equals 50 miles, then $2\frac{1}{2}$ inches equal $2\frac{1}{2}$ times 50.

$$\frac{50}{1} \times \frac{5}{2} = 125 \text{ (miles)}$$

13. **(B)** One pound equals 16 ounces. Find the number of ounces in 2,200 pounds by multiplying.

$$2,200 \times 16 = 35,200 \text{ (ounces)}$$

Find the number of 40-ounce bags needed to pack 35,200 ounces by dividing.

$$35,200 \div 40 = 880 \text{ (bags)}$$

14. **(C)** Find the first reduction and the weekend sale price. $\left(25\% = \dfrac{1}{4}\right)$

$$\$400 \times \frac{1}{4} = \$100 \text{ (first reduction)}$$

$$\$400 - \$100 = \$300 \text{ (weekend sale price)}$$

Use this weekend sale price to find the reduction for paying cash and the final price. (10% = 0.1)

$$\$300 \times 0.1 = \$30 \text{ (second reduction)}$$
$$\$300 - \$30 = \$270 \text{ (cash price)}$$

15. **(B)** Find the combined salaries of the four clerks.

$$\$255 \times 4 = \$1,020$$

Find the combined salaries of the part-timers.

$$\$120 \times 2 = \$240$$

Add both totals and divide by 6 for the average.

$$\$1,020 + \$240 = \$1,260$$
$$\$1,260 \div 6 = \$210 \text{ (average salary)}$$

16. **(A)** The perimeter of a rectangle is equal to the sum of two lengths and two widths. If 15 feet, 6 inches $\left(15\dfrac{1}{2} \text{ feet}\right)$ equal 1 length, then

$$2 \times 15\frac{1}{2} = 31 \text{ feet (2 lengths)}$$

$$40 - 31 = 9 \text{ feet (both widths)}$$

$$9 \div 2 = 4\frac{1}{2} \text{ feet (1 width)}$$

17. **(D)** Before dividing by a decimal, clear the decimal point in both the divisor and the dividend.

$$\frac{0.675}{0.9} = \frac{6.75}{9} = 0.75$$

18. **(A)** In the first hour, the two planes will be a combined distance of 340 miles plus 260 miles apart. Thus,

$$340 + 260 = 600 \text{ miles apart in 1 hour}$$

Find how many hours it will take them to be 3,000 miles apart by dividing.

$$3,000 \div 600 = 5 \text{ (hours)}$$

19. **(B)** Multiply the cost per foot by the length of the material.

12 inches equal 1 foot.

3 inches equal $\frac{1}{4}$ foot.

5 feet, 3 inches equal $5\frac{1}{4}$ feet (or 5.25 feet)

$$\$8 \times 5.25 = \$42$$

20. **(A)** Find the cost of 1 pint. (There are 8 pints in 1 gallon.)

$$\$3.84 \div 8 = \$0.48$$

Find the cost of 3 pints.

$$\$0.48 \times 3 = \$1.44$$

21. **(C)** Begin by letting x equal 1 share of the inheritance. According to the ratio, the widow received 5 shares ($5x$), and the son received 3 shares ($3x$). Together, they inherited \$72,000. This can be written as an equation:

$$5x + 3x = \$72,000$$

Solve for x by combining similar terms.

$$8x = \$72,000$$
$$x = \$9,000 \text{ (one share)}$$

Multiply the value of 1 share by the number of shares the mother received.

$$5x = \$45,000 \text{ (mother's share)}$$

22. **(C)** Begin by setting up a statement of proportion.

$$\frac{\text{chocolate}}{\text{chocolate}} = \frac{\text{corn syrup (recipe)}}{\text{corn syrup (amount available)}}$$

$$\frac{2\frac{1}{2}}{2} = \frac{\frac{1}{2}}{x} \text{ (or) } \frac{\frac{5}{2}}{2} = \frac{\frac{1}{2}}{x}$$

Simplify each side of the proportion.

$$\text{(a) } \frac{5}{2} \div \frac{2}{1} = \frac{5}{2} \times \frac{1}{2} = \frac{5}{4}$$

$$\text{(b) } \frac{1}{2} \div \frac{x}{1} = \frac{1}{2} \times \frac{1}{x} = \frac{1}{2x}$$

Then solve the proportion by cross-multiplying.

$$\frac{5}{4} = \frac{1}{2x} \text{ (or) } 10x = 4$$

Divide each side of the equation by 10 to find the value of x.

$$10x = 4$$
$$x = \frac{4}{10}$$
$$= \frac{2}{5} \text{ cup of corn syrup}$$

23. **(B)** To find the average of three numbers, divide their sum by 3.

$x + y + z$ (sum of three numbers)

$$\frac{x + y + z}{3}$$ (sum of numbers divided by 3)

24. **(D)** First find the income he gets on the $6,000 at 5 percent annual interest.

$$\$6,000 \times 0.05 = \$300.00 \text{ (income)}$$

Next find how much more interest he wants to earn in a year.

$$\$900 - \$300 = \$600 \text{ (additional interest)}$$

This $600 will equal 6 percent of the amount (x) he has to invest. Write this as an equation.

$$\$600 = 0.06 \text{ times } x$$
$$\$600 = 0.06\,x$$

To solve for x, divide each side of the equation by 0.06. (Clear the decimal in the divisor.)

$$\frac{\$600.00}{0.06} = \left(\frac{0.06}{0.06}\right)x$$
$$\$10,000 = x$$

(new amount needed) $x = \$10,000$

25. **(A)** Two figures are similar if they have the same shape. They may or may not have the same size. A plane and a scale model of that plane have the same shape and are therefore similar.

26. **(B)** Solve by substituting number values for letters and then doing the arithmetic operations.

$5a^2b - 3ab^2$
$= (5 \times a^2 \times b) - (3 \times a \times b^2)$
$= (5 \times 7^2 \times 4) - (3 \times 7 \times 4^2)$
$= (5 \times 49 \times 4) - (3 \times 7 \times 16)$
$= 980 - 336 = 644$

27. **(C)** The formula for the circumference (C) of a circle can be written in terms of its radius (R) or its diameter (D).

$$C = 2 \times R \times \pi \text{ (or) } C = D \times \pi$$

Thus, if you divide the circumference of a circle by its diameter, you are left with π.

$$\frac{C}{D} = \frac{D \times \pi}{D}$$
$$\frac{C}{D} = \pi$$

28. **(B)** If the businesswoman spends $\frac{1}{5}$ of her income for office rent, she has $\frac{4}{5}$ of her income left.

$$\frac{5}{5} - \frac{1}{5} = \frac{4}{5} \text{ (remainder)}$$

She then spends $\frac{3}{8}$ of the remainder on salaries.

$$\frac{4}{5} \times \frac{3}{8} = \frac{12}{40} = \frac{3}{10} \text{ (salaries)}$$

29. **(A)** Solve by substituting the number value for F and then doing the arithmetic operations.

$$C = \frac{5}{9}(F - 32)$$
$$C = \frac{5}{9}(50 - 32)$$
$$C = \frac{5}{9} \times (18)$$
$$C = 10$$

30. **(D)** To obtain the average, add the five temperatures and divide the total by 5.

Add: $\quad -12 + (-7) + (-2) + 0 + 6$
$\quad\quad = -21 + 6$
$\quad\quad = -15$
Divide: $-15 \div 5 = -3$

WORD KNOWLEDGE—SUBTEST 3

1. **(D)** *Luxury*, like **opulence** (from the Latin for "rich, wealthy"), is conducive to sumptuous living.

2. **(D)** **Mimesis** (from the Greek for "imitation") means reproduction of the supposed words of another, usually in order to represent his or her character.

3. **(D)** **Languid** means weak, indifferent, weary, or exhausted, implying a *listless* person.

4. **(B)** **Inherence** (from the Latin for "sticking in or to") means the state of existing in something as a permanent and inseparable element, quality, or attribute, and thus, like *intrinsic*, implies belonging to the nature of a thing itself.

5. **(B)** **Anomie** (from the Greek for "lawlessness") describes a social condition marked by the absence of social norms or values, and therefore, like *vacuum*, implies the absence of components from an area.

6. **(C)** *Ethereal* describes something that is light and airy and thus may be unsubstantial, as implied by **tenuous** (from the Latin for "thin").

7. **(B)** Like **salutation**, *greeting* means to address with some expression of pleasure.

8. **(A)** *Hypnotize*, like **mesmerize**, means to put in a condition or state allied to sleep.

9. **(B)** *Display*, similar to **panoply**, means an impressive array of assembled persons or things.

10. **(B)** Like **syntactic** (from the Greek for "arrangement"), which pertains to patterns of formation of sentences and phrases in a particular language, *grammatical* pertains to the sound, formation, and arrangement of words.

11. **(A)** *Resentment*, like **umbrage**, describes a feeling of indignation at something regarded as an injury or insult.

12. **(B)** *Harsh* means rough to any of the senses, while **raucous** denotes hoarseness or harshness of voice or sound.

13. **(C)** *Trial*, like **prosecution**, means determining a person's guilt or innocence by due process of law.

14. **(A)** *Pollution*, which means defiling, making foul, unclean, or dirty, is closely related to **miasma** (from the Greek for "pollution").

15. **(B)** *Model*, like **paragon**, is a pattern of excellence for exact imitation.

16. **(D)** **Innate**, like *native*, means belonging by birth.

17. **(B)** **Urbanity** indicates elegant courtesy or politeness, and hence *refinement*.

18. **(D)** To **encounter** means to come upon, hence to *meet*.

19. **(A)** **Banal**, like *commonplace*, characterizes as lifeless and uninteresting.

20. **(D)** **Little**, like *small*, means not much in comparison to other things.

21. **(B)** *Found*, like **discover**, means to unearth something hidden or lost.

22. **(C)** *Tell*, like **inform**, means to communicate knowledge or give information.

23. **(A)** *Shifting*, like **variable**, means subject to change.

24. **(D)** *Stop*, like **cease**, means to end.

25. **(C)** *Weaken*, like **impair**, means to worsen or to damage.

26. **(A)** **Rudiments** are fundamental skills or basic principles, like *basic methods and procedures*.

27. **(A)** *Reckless*, like **imprudent**, means lacking discretion.

28. **(A)** *Friction*, like **dissension**, refers to quarreling.

29. **(A)** *Separate*, like **disconnect**, means to become detached.

30. **(D)** *Elementary*, like **rudimentary**, refers to something fundamental or imperfectly developed.

31. **(D)** *Self-governing*, like **autonomous**, means governing without control.

32. **(B)** *Wander aimlessly*, like **meander**, means to follow a winding course without a definite destination.

33. **(C)** *Extreme poverty*, like **destitution**, characterizes the state of lacking resources and possessions.

34. **(A)** *Slander*, like **malign**, means to speak misleading or false reports about someone.

35. **(B)** *Lacking strength*, like **impotent**, means lacking power or vigor.

PARAGRAPH COMPREHENSION—SUBTEST 4

1. **(A)** The first sentence states that the duty of the lighthouse keeper is to keep the light burning no matter what happens.

2. **(B)** The second sentence mentions that the exact amount of water needed has been carefully determined.

3. **(A)** "Hardening" or toughening seedlings is accomplished by reducing the water the seedlings get and lowering the temperature.

4. **(A)** Earthquakes occur when rock layers break and slip, forming cracks or faults.

5. **(A)** Photosynthesis combines air, water, and energy from the sun to make food.

6. **(B)** In this selection *reputable* means honest or trusted.

7. **(C)** The main idea of the selection is that ice can relieve many of the effects of a burn and is therefore great first aid.

8. **(B)** The main idea of the selection is to warn you to be careful of "get-rich-quick" plans.

9. **(D)** The third sentence mentions that nine out of 10 victims of fatal falls are older than 65.

10. **(C)** "Gray water" is defined as slightly used water. The only choice that represents "used" water is soapy water.

11. **(B)** The third sentence specifies that a glacier moves because of its weight.

12. **(A)** Every sentence of the selection expresses disapproval of the present state of things and implies that changes are needed.

13. **(C)** The selection states that some categories of people have changed, but the fact that the "number is rising" implies that not everyone has changed.

14. **(D)** According to the first sentence, Newton's Third Law is that to each action there is an equal and opposite reaction, or action equals reaction.

15. **(C)** The first sentence, and main idea of the paragraph, states that water is a good conductor of sound waves.

MATHEMATICS KNOWLEDGE—SUBTEST 5

1. **(A)** This equation means "some number, when decreased by 4, is equal to 8."

$$a - 4 = 8$$

To arrive at a true statement for *a*, we want to eliminate the –4 on the left side of the equation. We do this by adding 4. (This is, essentially, undoing the subtraction.) We then add 4 to the other side so that the statement remains an equation—i.e., the two sides remain equal, even when they are restated.

$$(a - 4) + 4 = 8 + 4$$

By simplifying both sides, we isolate a and thus find the solution.

$$a = 12$$

2. **(C)** This is practically right out of the math textbook. The Transitive Property of Inequality—a *postulate* or assumption we use as a basis for how math works—says that if $a > b$ and $b > c$, then $a > c$.

3. **(C)** Since a hexagon is a six-sided figure, the town will need six lifeguards.

4. **(B)** There are several ways to approach this problem. Let's set the small size can as x, and the amount of paint needed to complete painting the room as y. We know that the large can of paint that Amanda already used up is equal to four of the smaller cans, and we know that she finished $\frac{3}{4}$ of the room. So, to put what we know into an equation looks like this:

$$4x = \frac{3}{4} y$$

From here, we need to find out how much paint (i.e., how many small 16-ounce cans) it will take to finish painting the room. Stated differently, we need to find out what it takes to get to $1y$, which is $\frac{1}{4} y$. Since the quantity on the right side of the equation that we've already set up is three times the amount that we want to find, we'll divide both sides by 3 to get

$$\frac{4}{3} x = y$$

Therefore, Amanda needs to buy two more of the small paint cans, since it will take $\frac{4}{3}$ or $1 \frac{1}{3}$ cans.

5. **(B)** First, subtract 2 from each side of the equation in order to eliminate the "+2" from the left side. This will get you closer to finding what x is.

$$4x + 2 - 2 = -14 - 2$$
$$4x = -16$$

Now divide each side by 4 to find x. (You are undoing the multiplication.)

$$\frac{4x}{4} = -\frac{16}{4}$$

$$x = -4$$

6. **(C)** The five stories that the writer has gotten published are 20 percent of the total stories that he's written. The total stories that he's written—the number we're looking for—is 100 percent, so first we need to figure out what it will take to get from 20 to 100. To do that, divide 100 by 20:

$$\frac{100}{20} = 5$$

So we can see that doing the opposite of this operation—multiplying 20 times 5—will give us the 100 percent we are seeking.

Now, multiply the writer's five published stories (20 percent) likewise by 5 to see what that 100 percent consists of:

$$5 \times 5 = 25$$

The total number of stories that the writer has completed is 25.

7. **(B)** In an isosceles triangle, two of the sides are equal, which means that the angles opposite them are equal, too. If one is 50 degrees, then so is the other one. To find the angle opposite the unequal side, begin by adding the equal angles.

$$50 + 50 = 100 \text{ degrees}$$

To find the third angle, subtract this amount from 180 (the total number of degrees in the angles of any triangle):

$$180 - 100 = 80 \text{ degrees (third angle)}$$

8. **(C)** You could transform the word problem into a mathematical equation like this:

$$0.40 \times 20 = 0.20x$$
$$\frac{0.40 \times 20}{0.20} = x$$
$$40 = x$$

However, you don't have to go through all that work if you pay attention to the numerical relationships in the problem: a certain percentage of a number will be half that percentage of twice that number.

9. **(C)** A cone is a solid (i.e., three-dimensional) object that has a circular base and one vertex. A dunce cap, once used to make fun of someone because they didn't know the answer to a school question, here serves as the answer itself. You might consider the writing end of a pencil as a cone, but here it specifies the entire pencil.

10. **(B)** First, find 25 percent of 750 by multiplying $0.25 \times 750 = 187.50$. Next, multiply 0.1 by 187.50, which equals 18.75.

11. **(C)** The perimeter of a square is four times the length of an individual side. Therefore, the perimeter of this square is 4×15 inches or 60 inches. The equilateral triangle has the same perimeter as the square. Since the three sides of an equilateral triangle are equal, divide by 3 to find the length of one side of the triangle.

$$60 \text{ inches} \div 3 = 20 \text{ inches}$$

12. **(D)** A prime number is one which can only be divided by itself and 1. The number 39 can be divided by both 3 and 13, as well as 1 and itself.

13. **(A)** First, find the area of the hatch cover. Since its diameter is 20 inches, its radius is 10 inches and therefore its area is $\pi(10)^2 = 100\pi$ square inches. The diameter of the hatch itself (i.e., the hole) is 18 inches, so its radius is 9 inches and its area is $\pi(9)^2 = 81\pi$ square inches. Therefore, the area of the hatch cover is $100\pi - 81\pi = 19\pi$ square inches larger than that of the hatch itself.

14. **(B)** The altitude to the base of the triangle is just another way of saying the height of a triangle. The formula to find the area of a triangle is $\frac{1}{2}bh$, or one-half the triangle's base multiplied by its height. So, if the triangle's area is 45 square inches and its base is 9 inches, we can find the height like this:

$$45 = \frac{1}{2}(9)h$$

$$\frac{45}{9} = \frac{1}{2}h$$

$$5 \text{ inches} = \frac{1}{2}h$$

$$2(5) = 2\left(\frac{1}{2}h\right)$$

$$10 \text{ inches} = h$$

15. **(D)** To find the product of more than two numbers, work with only two numbers at a time. If both of these numbers are positive, their product is positive. If both numbers are negative, their product is positive, but if only one is negative, the product is negative.

$$(3)(-7)(2)(-4)$$
$$= (-21)\,(2)\,(-4)$$
$$= (-42)\,(-4)$$
$$= 168$$

16. **(D)** Since we are given the value of x, all that's necessary is to "plug and chug" (but watch your order of operations and positive and negative signs!):

$$2x^2 - 3x + 10$$
$$= 2(-7)^2 - 3(-7) + 10$$
$$= 2(-7)(-7) - 3(-7) + 10$$
$$= 2(49) - 3(-7) + 10$$
$$= 98 + 21 + 10$$
$$= 129$$

17. **(B)** Exponents that are combined in this way should be multiplied.

18. **(A)** The reciprocal of a fraction is obtained by transposing the numerator and the denominator, i.e., by inverting the fraction.

19. **(B)** With a fraction that has double-digit numerators and denominators, the first thing to do is try to simplify the fraction to make it easier to work with. In this case, we can quickly see that both 12 and 18 are divisible by 2, 3, and 6. If we divide both by the largest number by which they are divisible, we'll get the simplest form of the fraction—so dividing both by 6 gives us the simplest form of the fraction, $\frac{2}{3}$. Now, to make it a percentage, multiply the numerator only by 100 and then do the division implied by the fraction—in other words, divide 200 by 3. The result we get is a repeating decimal, $66.\overline{66}$ or, to round off, 66.67 percent.

20. **(C)** This is very simple, but you still have to pay attention or the sign will trip you up. Square (multiply by itself) -15 and you are calculating $-15 \times -15 = 225$. The simple (but sometimes overlooked) thing here is to remember that a negative number multiplied by another negative number is a positive number.

21. **(D)** The formula for the perimeter of a square is $4l$, where l is the length of one side: $4 \times 5 = 20$. The thing to watch out for here is the unit of measurement, which is in centimeters.

22. **(B)** Solve this problem using the Pythagorean Theorem, which states that, for a right triangle, the square of the hypotenuse is equal to the sum of the squares of the other two sides. Here, we have the length of sides AB (3 in) and BC (4 in). Squaring them gives us 9 and 16, respectively, and adding those together gives us 25, the square root of which is 5.

23. **(C)** There are three big things you need to pay attention to in doing this problem. First, a multiplied by a equals a^2. Next, notice that you have an easily found square root of 81: 9. And last, notice that there is a minus or negative sign in the expression—this means that the term in one factor will be a plus sign and the other a minus sign. Taking all these into account gives you the factors $(a + 9)(a - 9)$.

24. **(C)** The "nearest hundredth" means having two digits to the right of the decimal point. Since the thousandths number is 5, the rule is that we round up, so the correct answer is 3,191.79.

25. **(B)** The expression $(x + 3 > 5)$ is a statement of inequality, meaning that x plus 3 is greater than 5, not equal to it. To solve this inequality, subtract 3 from both sides of the statement.

$$x + 3 > 5$$
$$x + 3 - 3 > 5 - 3$$
$$x > 2$$

Therefore, the statement of inequality is true for any value of x that is greater than 2. Try it with 4, for example.

$$4 + 3 > 5$$
$$7 > 5, \text{ a true statement}$$

ELECTRONICS INFORMATION—SUBTEST 6

1. **(C)** A cell has a voltage of approximately 1.5 volts. A 9-volt battery therefore contains 6 cells, because 1.5 volts $\times$ 6 = 9 volts.

2. **(D)** The higher the gauge number of a wire, the smaller its diameter.

3. **(C)** The symbol K represents "kilo" or 1,000. A 1.5 K-ohm resistor therefore has a value of 1.5 $\times$ 1,000 or 1,500 ohms. Choice D is incorrect because the unit of measurement for resistance is ohm. Watts is a unit of measurement for power.

4. **(A)** The interchangeable terms for *voltage* are electrical pressure, electromotive force, potential difference, difference of potential, and electrical force. The other choices are incorrect because they represent other circuit properties that cannot be substituted for the property of voltage.

5. **(B)** Capacitance can be defined as the circuit property that opposes any change in voltage. Inductance is the circuit property that opposes any change in current. Resistance is the circuit property that opposes the flow of electrons, and reactance is the opposition to the flow of an alternating current as a result of inductance or capacitance present in a circuit.

6. **(B)** Choice A has the quantities reversed, and choices C and D are incorrect because the amount of silver present in solder is minute, and rosin is a substance in the center of solder added to aid in the soldering process.

7. **(A)** To calculate the current requirement of an appliance, the power law can be applied.

$$\text{power} = \text{current} \times \text{voltage}$$
$$P = I \times E$$
$$1.200\,\text{W} = I \times 120\,\text{V}$$
$$I = 10\,\text{amps}$$

8. **(A)** Hertz is another term used for cycles per second. (B) The "henry" is the unit of measurement for inductance. (C) Kilo represents a quantity of 1,000 and (D) mega represents a quantity of 1 million.

9. **(B)** The *piezoelectric effect* is the property of certain crystalline substances to change shape when a voltage is impressed upon them, as in the crystal microphone. *Thermoionic emission* is the escape of electrons from a surface because of the presence of heat. *Inductance* is the circuit property that opposes any change in current, and *hysteresis* is the property of a magnetic substance that causes magnetization to lag behind the force that produces it.

10. **(B)** The height of a wave is known as the wave's *amplitude*. Varying the height of a carrier wave is known as AM or amplitude modulation. Frequency modulation transmits *information* by varying the frequency of the carrier wave. Demodulation is the process of separating the intelligence from the carrier wave. Another term for this process is detection.

11. **(D)** The primary of this transformer has three times the voltage of its secondary. Therefore, the primary must have three times as many turns of wire as the secondary, or a turns ratio of 3:1. If its turns ratio was 1:1, the primary and secondary would have the same voltage. In choice B, a turns ratio of 1:4 would result in an output voltage of 480 volts. In choice C a turns ratio of 1:3 would result in a secondary voltage of 360 volts.

12. **(C)** Reading the resistor color code, the first two bands indicate numbers; the third band is the multiplier or the number of zeros to write after the first two numbers. The fourth band indicates the tolerance of the resistor. Following the color code, the value of this resistor is 2,200 ohms $\pm$ 5 percent. Red, representing a number value of 2 and a multiplier value of 100 (or two zeros to write after the first two numbers) would indicate a resistor coded as follows:

$\dfrac{2}{\text{Band 1 – red}}$	$\dfrac{2}{\text{Band 2 – red}}$
$\dfrac{00}{\text{Band 3 – red}}$	$\dfrac{\pm 5\%}{\text{Band 4 – red}}$

The tolerance of a fixed carbon resistor is a $\pm$ value. Gold represents 5 percent tolerance.

13. **(C)** Choice A = diode; choice B = triode; choice D = pentode.

14. **(B)** In a series circuit, the total resistance is equal to the sum of the individual resistors, or $R_T = R_1 + R_2 + R_3 + \ldots + R_n$. As all resistors have a value of 500 ohms, the total resistance in this circuit is equal to

$$
\begin{aligned}
R_T &= R_1 + R_2 + R_3 \\
&= 500 + 500 + 500 \\
&= 1{,}500 \text{ ohms}
\end{aligned}
$$

Choice A is incorrect because a watt is a unit of power, not a unit of resistance.

15. **(C)** The base element is common or shared by both circuits. Choice A is not a transistor circuit configuration, since there is no gate element in a transistor.

16. **(C)** The waveforms corresponding to the other choices are given in the review section on waveforms.

17. **(B)** A potentiometer is a variable resistor. Choice A is the symbol for a fixed resistor, and choice B is the symbol for a variable resistor; note the arrow connected to the fixed symbol. Choice C is a fixed capacitor, and choice D is the symbol for a variable capacitor.

18. **(D)** The unit of measurement for capacitance is the farad, abbreviated F. A potentiometer would be specified in ohms, a coil in henrys, and a transistor by its type or generic number.

19. **(D)** The purpose of the local oscillator is to generate a high frequency, also known as a radio or carrier wave.

20. **(C)** A detector demodulates a signal. This is the process of separating the audio or intelligence from the radio wave. An AF amp is used to amplify the audio signal, and the RF amp is used to amplify the radio frequency. A tuner is used to tune in a frequency, making choices A, B, and D incorrect.

AUTOMOTIVE & SHOP INFORMATION—SUBTEST 7

1. **(D)** When viewed from the driver's seat looking forward, the side to your right is the right side of the engine. This method is used by all manufacturers.

2. **(A)** The brake spoon is used to turn the star wheel adjuster of a drum-type brake system. Turning the adjuster with the spoon decreases the clearance between the brake shoes and the drum. Disc-type brakes are not adjustable.

3. **(D)** The dial indicator uses a gauge to register movement. It is used to measure variations in dimensions and backlash (clearance) between two meshed gears.

4. **(B)** A pilot bearing is pressed into a hole at the end of the engine crankshaft. The purpose of the bearing is to support the tip of the transmission input (clutch) shaft. During the installation of a new clutch assembly, it is necessary to line up the clutch disc with the pilot bearing. If these parts are not aligned, the transmission will not slide into place on the engine.

5. **(D)** The oscilloscope is a special type of voltmeter that displays traces and oscillations on a TV-type picture tube. The scope has the capability of showing the rapid changes in

voltage that occur in the *ignition* system. This is helpful in diagnosing problems in the circuit.

6. **(D)** The crankshaft changes the reciprocating (up and down) motion of the piston to rotary motion.

7. **(A)** L or L_0 on older automatic transmissions was the same as first gear in manual transmissions. In modern cars, the L has been replaced by a 1 to indicate first gear and 2 to represent second gear instead of D1, S, or L2.

8. **(B)** The "Park" (P) position on the automatic transmission gear selector indicator represents the position that locks up the transmission and prevents the wheels from rolling.

9. **(D)** The internal combustion engine is best described as a high-speed engine. An internal combustion engine cannot run at slow speed and get enough torque to get the vehicle moving. A higher speed engine is needed to produce the torque. That is where the transmission plays an important role in allowing the engine to speed up and still not have a very fast moving drive shaft connected to the wheels. The transmission's gear ratio plays a role in producing the torque needed to get the car moving from a stopped position.

10. **(B)** The drop of the ball prevents all the gasoline from draining from the carburetor so that it can be easily started again if the need arises quickly after the loss of suction or a few days later.

11. **(D)** The units shown in the diagram are some of the different types of devices used to muffle the noise made by small gasoline engines.

12. **(C)** Outboard engines use water from the lake, river, or other body of water that the boat is in to get cooling water. The water pump pulls the water into the engine and circulates it to the areas that need cooling.

13. **(B)** The thickness gauge shown is most often used in automotive work to check valve clearance, set points, and check other tolerances.

14. **(B)** A coping saw blade is placed in the saw with the teeth of the blade facing the handle. That means that you cut with a coping saw on the downward stroke. It also calls for a special type of vise to hold whatever it is you are cutting.

15. **(C)** Carpenters use claw hammers so they can remove nails if they don't go where they belong or are bent on the way into the wood. Machinists use ball-peen hammers. Planishing hammers are used by people trying to flatten or shape sheet metal. There is no such thing as a chisel point hammer.

16. **(B)** The term *penny* is an old English way to designate the size of a nail. It has no definite relation to today's measuring units. You can, however, keep in mind that the larger the number, the larger the nail.

17. **(D)** A squaring shear is used to shear or cut sheet metal.

18. **(C)** One of the most common ways to fasten sheet metal is by spot-welding it. This is done with the bodies of automobiles to make them sturdier.

19. **(C)** A welding torch can be used as a cutting torch when the proper amount of oxygen is used.

20. **(A)** A tubing cutter is nothing more than a smaller version of a pipe cutter.

21. **(B)** If you overwork concrete, it brings up all the water to the surface and the cement comes to the surface also. The heavier particles settle farther down into the slab, and you wind up with separation and create a less durable surface when it is dry.

22. **(C)** Concrete reaches 98 percent of its strength in 28 days.

23. **(C)** Deciduous trees are those that produce leaves that drop off in the fall. The wood produced by this type of tree is usually hard when properly dried.

24. **(B)** A combination square is used to lay out 45- and 90-degree angles of measurement.

25. **(B)** Most bolts have a hexagonal head.

MECHANICAL COMPREHENSION—SUBTEST 8

1. **(C)** The lowest point that the follower will reach is between S and T, which is the shaft of the pivot.

2. **(D)** When a series of pulleys is connected by drive belts, the pulley with the largest diameter rotates at the slowest speed.

3. **(B)** Because there are three cords holding sign B, they are under $\frac{1}{3}$ the tension of the single cord holding sign A.

4. **(B)** Mass remains constant no matter where an object is, but the weight of an object will vary based on its distance from the gravitational pull of Earth.

5. **(B)** The closer the fulcrum is to the weight on the resistance arm, the less the amount of force or effort that is required to lift the weight, but the resistance arm will not be able to rise as high above the surface on which the fulcrum rests.

6. **(B)** Pulley B will rotate in the opposite direction from pulley A.

7. **(A)** Pulley A will rotate the slowest because it is the largest pulley in the system.

8. **(C)** Water is flowing out of the water tower at a rate of three gallons per minute. To convert that to gallons per hour, multiply by 60 minutes per hour: $3 \times 60 = 180$ gallons per hour. Since that is the same rate as the inflow to the tower, the level will remain the same over two hours (or any number of hours).

9. **(A)** Two meshed gears will turn in opposite directions. When an idler gear (gear I) is placed between the two, both A and B turn in the same direction.

10. **(D)** When two or more forces act in such a way that their combined result has a net impact or effect of zero, this is called equilibrium.

11. **(C)** Centrifugal force from the spin (regardless of which direction) will cause the balls to move outward, and the tension on the strings holding them will result in them also moving upward.

12. **(B)** Water tower B will be able to provide the most water because its outlet pipe is near the bottom of the cistern and can let all or almost all of its contents out. The outlet pipe on water tower A is near the top of the cistern and will stop providing water as soon as A's water level drops below where the pipe leaves the cistern. Engineering such as water tower A is probably the reason that Dry Gulch is a ghost town.

13. **(B)** The descent of Jonathan the airborne paratrooper (or anyone else descending to the ground via parachute) is *primarily* affected by gravity and the drag (air resistance) of his parachute.

14. **(D)** Condensation takes place when a gas or vapor changes to a liquid. Moisture on the windshield is the result of water vapor in the air changing back to liquid.

15. **(D)** Unlike (opposite) poles attract; like poles repel.

16. **(B)** The differential on an automobile, which connects the driveshaft to the rear axle, increases engine torque through gear reduction. Engine torque is increased because the driveshaft turns faster than the rear axles.

17. **(B)** Water expands as it freezes. Water is not compressible.

18. **(B)** To calculate the gear ratio of a rear axle assembly, divide the number of teeth on the pinion gear into the number of teeth on the ring gear: 43 divided by 11 = 3.90.

19. **(C)** A and D are in constant mesh and F is too small.

20. **(A)** When the lobe (high spot) on cam A makes contact with the follower (roller) on the contact arm, the contacts will close. Since cam A has only one lobe, the contacts will close one time per revolution.

21. **(A)** To calculate the revolutions of gear B, use this formula: $r = (D \times R)$ divided by d.

   D = number of teeth on gear A;
   R = revolutions of gear A;
   d = number of teeth on gear B;
   r = revolutions of gear B;
   $r = (D \times R)$ divided by d.

$$r = \frac{15 \times 14}{10}$$

$$r = \frac{210}{10}$$

$$r = 21$$

22. **(C)** Gears that are meshed turn in opposite directions. Gear 2 is turning clockwise; gears 1 and 3 are turning counterclockwise.

23. **(A)** Hydrometers use floats to measure specific gravity. Specific gravity is the weight of a liquid compared to the weight of water. The liquid with the highest specific gravity will cause the float to rise higher in the glass tube.

24. **(B)** Vacuum is greatest at the narrow or restricted area of an air passage. The narrow area is called a venturi. Gauge Z will also indicate a vacuum, but it will be less of a vacuum than Y.

25. **(B)** On a second-class lever, the fulcrum is at one end, the effort is at the other end, and the load is between.

ANSWER SHEET
Practice Exam Two

General Science—Subtest 1

1. Ⓐ Ⓑ Ⓒ Ⓓ	6. Ⓐ Ⓑ Ⓒ Ⓓ	11. Ⓐ Ⓑ Ⓒ Ⓓ	16. Ⓐ Ⓑ Ⓒ Ⓓ	21. Ⓐ Ⓑ Ⓒ Ⓓ
2. Ⓐ Ⓑ Ⓒ Ⓓ	7. Ⓐ Ⓑ Ⓒ Ⓓ	12. Ⓐ Ⓑ Ⓒ Ⓓ	17. Ⓐ Ⓑ Ⓒ Ⓓ	22. Ⓐ Ⓑ Ⓒ Ⓓ
3. Ⓐ Ⓑ Ⓒ Ⓓ	8. Ⓐ Ⓑ Ⓒ Ⓓ	13. Ⓐ Ⓑ Ⓒ Ⓓ	18. Ⓐ Ⓑ Ⓒ Ⓓ	23. Ⓐ Ⓑ Ⓒ Ⓓ
4. Ⓐ Ⓑ Ⓒ Ⓓ	9. Ⓐ Ⓑ Ⓒ Ⓓ	14. Ⓐ Ⓑ Ⓒ Ⓓ	19. Ⓐ Ⓑ Ⓒ Ⓓ	24. Ⓐ Ⓑ Ⓒ Ⓓ
5. Ⓐ Ⓑ Ⓒ Ⓓ	10. Ⓐ Ⓑ Ⓒ Ⓓ	15. Ⓐ Ⓑ Ⓒ Ⓓ	20. Ⓐ Ⓑ Ⓒ Ⓓ	25. Ⓐ Ⓑ Ⓒ Ⓓ

Arithmetic Reasoning—Subtest 2

1. Ⓐ Ⓑ Ⓒ Ⓓ	7. Ⓐ Ⓑ Ⓒ Ⓓ	13. Ⓐ Ⓑ Ⓒ Ⓓ	19. Ⓐ Ⓑ Ⓒ Ⓓ	25. Ⓐ Ⓑ Ⓒ Ⓓ
2. Ⓐ Ⓑ Ⓒ Ⓓ	8. Ⓐ Ⓑ Ⓒ Ⓓ	14. Ⓐ Ⓑ Ⓒ Ⓓ	20. Ⓐ Ⓑ Ⓒ Ⓓ	26. Ⓐ Ⓑ Ⓒ Ⓓ
3. Ⓐ Ⓑ Ⓒ Ⓓ	9. Ⓐ Ⓑ Ⓒ Ⓓ	15. Ⓐ Ⓑ Ⓒ Ⓓ	21. Ⓐ Ⓑ Ⓒ Ⓓ	27. Ⓐ Ⓑ Ⓒ Ⓓ
4. Ⓐ Ⓑ Ⓒ Ⓓ	10. Ⓐ Ⓑ Ⓒ Ⓓ	16. Ⓐ Ⓑ Ⓒ Ⓓ	22. Ⓐ Ⓑ Ⓒ Ⓓ	28. Ⓐ Ⓑ Ⓒ Ⓓ
5. Ⓐ Ⓑ Ⓒ Ⓓ	11. Ⓐ Ⓑ Ⓒ Ⓓ	17. Ⓐ Ⓑ Ⓒ Ⓓ	23. Ⓐ Ⓑ Ⓒ Ⓓ	29. Ⓐ Ⓑ Ⓒ Ⓓ
6. Ⓐ Ⓑ Ⓒ Ⓓ	12. Ⓐ Ⓑ Ⓒ Ⓓ	18. Ⓐ Ⓑ Ⓒ Ⓓ	24. Ⓐ Ⓑ Ⓒ Ⓓ	30. Ⓐ Ⓑ Ⓒ Ⓓ

Word Knowledge—Subtest 3

1. Ⓐ Ⓑ Ⓒ Ⓓ	8. Ⓐ Ⓑ Ⓒ Ⓓ	15. Ⓐ Ⓑ Ⓒ Ⓓ	22. Ⓐ Ⓑ Ⓒ Ⓓ	29. Ⓐ Ⓑ Ⓒ Ⓓ
2. Ⓐ Ⓑ Ⓒ Ⓓ	9. Ⓐ Ⓑ Ⓒ Ⓓ	16. Ⓐ Ⓑ Ⓒ Ⓓ	23. Ⓐ Ⓑ Ⓒ Ⓓ	30. Ⓐ Ⓑ Ⓒ Ⓓ
3. Ⓐ Ⓑ Ⓒ Ⓓ	10. Ⓐ Ⓑ Ⓒ Ⓓ	17. Ⓐ Ⓑ Ⓒ Ⓓ	24. Ⓐ Ⓑ Ⓒ Ⓓ	31. Ⓐ Ⓑ Ⓒ Ⓓ
4. Ⓐ Ⓑ Ⓒ Ⓓ	11. Ⓐ Ⓑ Ⓒ Ⓓ	18. Ⓐ Ⓑ Ⓒ Ⓓ	25. Ⓐ Ⓑ Ⓒ Ⓓ	32. Ⓐ Ⓑ Ⓒ Ⓓ
5. Ⓐ Ⓑ Ⓒ Ⓓ	12. Ⓐ Ⓑ Ⓒ Ⓓ	19. Ⓐ Ⓑ Ⓒ Ⓓ	26. Ⓐ Ⓑ Ⓒ Ⓓ	33. Ⓐ Ⓑ Ⓒ Ⓓ
6. Ⓐ Ⓑ Ⓒ Ⓓ	13. Ⓐ Ⓑ Ⓒ Ⓓ	20. Ⓐ Ⓑ Ⓒ Ⓓ	27. Ⓐ Ⓑ Ⓒ Ⓓ	34. Ⓐ Ⓑ Ⓒ Ⓓ
7. Ⓐ Ⓑ Ⓒ Ⓓ	14. Ⓐ Ⓑ Ⓒ Ⓓ	21. Ⓐ Ⓑ Ⓒ Ⓓ	28. Ⓐ Ⓑ Ⓒ Ⓓ	35. Ⓐ Ⓑ Ⓒ Ⓓ

Paragraph Comprehension—Subtest 4

1. Ⓐ Ⓑ Ⓒ Ⓓ	4. Ⓐ Ⓑ Ⓒ Ⓓ	7. Ⓐ Ⓑ Ⓒ Ⓓ	10. Ⓐ Ⓑ Ⓒ Ⓓ	13. Ⓐ Ⓑ Ⓒ Ⓓ
2. Ⓐ Ⓑ Ⓒ Ⓓ	5. Ⓐ Ⓑ Ⓒ Ⓓ	8. Ⓐ Ⓑ Ⓒ Ⓓ	11. Ⓐ Ⓑ Ⓒ Ⓓ	14. Ⓐ Ⓑ Ⓒ Ⓓ
3. Ⓐ Ⓑ Ⓒ Ⓓ	6. Ⓐ Ⓑ Ⓒ Ⓓ	9. Ⓐ Ⓑ Ⓒ Ⓓ	12. Ⓐ Ⓑ Ⓒ Ⓓ	15. Ⓐ Ⓑ Ⓒ Ⓓ

Mathematics Knowledge—Subtest 5

1. Ⓐ Ⓑ Ⓒ Ⓓ   6. Ⓐ Ⓑ Ⓒ Ⓓ   11. Ⓐ Ⓑ Ⓒ Ⓓ   16. Ⓐ Ⓑ Ⓒ Ⓓ   21. Ⓐ Ⓑ Ⓒ Ⓓ
2. Ⓐ Ⓑ Ⓒ Ⓓ   7. Ⓐ Ⓑ Ⓒ Ⓓ   12. Ⓐ Ⓑ Ⓒ Ⓓ   17. Ⓐ Ⓑ Ⓒ Ⓓ   22. Ⓐ Ⓑ Ⓒ Ⓓ
3. Ⓐ Ⓑ Ⓒ Ⓓ   8. Ⓐ Ⓑ Ⓒ Ⓓ   13. Ⓐ Ⓑ Ⓒ Ⓓ   18. Ⓐ Ⓑ Ⓒ Ⓓ   23. Ⓐ Ⓑ Ⓒ Ⓓ
4. Ⓐ Ⓑ Ⓒ Ⓓ   9. Ⓐ Ⓑ Ⓒ Ⓓ   14. Ⓐ Ⓑ Ⓒ Ⓓ   19. Ⓐ Ⓑ Ⓒ Ⓓ   24. Ⓐ Ⓑ Ⓒ Ⓓ
5. Ⓐ Ⓑ Ⓒ Ⓓ   10. Ⓐ Ⓑ Ⓒ Ⓓ   15. Ⓐ Ⓑ Ⓒ Ⓓ   20. Ⓐ Ⓑ Ⓒ Ⓓ   25. Ⓐ Ⓑ Ⓒ Ⓓ

Electronics Information—Subtest 6

1. Ⓐ Ⓑ Ⓒ Ⓓ   5. Ⓐ Ⓑ Ⓒ Ⓓ   9. Ⓐ Ⓑ Ⓒ Ⓓ   13. Ⓐ Ⓑ Ⓒ Ⓓ   17. Ⓐ Ⓑ Ⓒ Ⓓ
2. Ⓐ Ⓑ Ⓒ Ⓓ   6. Ⓐ Ⓑ Ⓒ Ⓓ   10. Ⓐ Ⓑ Ⓒ Ⓓ   14. Ⓐ Ⓑ Ⓒ Ⓓ   18. Ⓐ Ⓑ Ⓒ Ⓓ
3. Ⓐ Ⓑ Ⓒ Ⓓ   7. Ⓐ Ⓑ Ⓒ Ⓓ   11. Ⓐ Ⓑ Ⓒ Ⓓ   15. Ⓐ Ⓑ Ⓒ Ⓓ   19. Ⓐ Ⓑ Ⓒ Ⓓ
4. Ⓐ Ⓑ Ⓒ Ⓓ   8. Ⓐ Ⓑ Ⓒ Ⓓ   12. Ⓐ Ⓑ Ⓒ Ⓓ   16. Ⓐ Ⓑ Ⓒ Ⓓ   20. Ⓐ Ⓑ Ⓒ Ⓓ

Automotive & Shop Information—Subtest 7

1. Ⓐ Ⓑ Ⓒ Ⓓ   6. Ⓐ Ⓑ Ⓒ Ⓓ   11. Ⓐ Ⓑ Ⓒ Ⓓ   16. Ⓐ Ⓑ Ⓒ Ⓓ   21. Ⓐ Ⓑ Ⓒ Ⓓ
2. Ⓐ Ⓑ Ⓒ Ⓓ   7. Ⓐ Ⓑ Ⓒ Ⓓ   12. Ⓐ Ⓑ Ⓒ Ⓓ   17. Ⓐ Ⓑ Ⓒ Ⓓ   22. Ⓐ Ⓑ Ⓒ Ⓓ
3. Ⓐ Ⓑ Ⓒ Ⓓ   8. Ⓐ Ⓑ Ⓒ Ⓓ   13. Ⓐ Ⓑ Ⓒ Ⓓ   18. Ⓐ Ⓑ Ⓒ Ⓓ   23. Ⓐ Ⓑ Ⓒ Ⓓ
4. Ⓐ Ⓑ Ⓒ Ⓓ   9. Ⓐ Ⓑ Ⓒ Ⓓ   14. Ⓐ Ⓑ Ⓒ Ⓓ   19. Ⓐ Ⓑ Ⓒ Ⓓ   24. Ⓐ Ⓑ Ⓒ Ⓓ
5. Ⓐ Ⓑ Ⓒ Ⓓ   10. Ⓐ Ⓑ Ⓒ Ⓓ   15. Ⓐ Ⓑ Ⓒ Ⓓ   20. Ⓐ Ⓑ Ⓒ Ⓓ   25. Ⓐ Ⓑ Ⓒ Ⓓ

Mechanical Comprehension—Subtest 8

1. Ⓐ Ⓑ Ⓒ Ⓓ   6. Ⓐ Ⓑ Ⓒ Ⓓ   11. Ⓐ Ⓑ Ⓒ Ⓓ   16. Ⓐ Ⓑ Ⓒ Ⓓ   21. Ⓐ Ⓑ Ⓒ Ⓓ
2. Ⓐ Ⓑ Ⓒ Ⓓ   7. Ⓐ Ⓑ Ⓒ Ⓓ   12. Ⓐ Ⓑ Ⓒ Ⓓ   17. Ⓐ Ⓑ Ⓒ Ⓓ   22. Ⓐ Ⓑ Ⓒ Ⓓ
3. Ⓐ Ⓑ Ⓒ Ⓓ   8. Ⓐ Ⓑ Ⓒ Ⓓ   13. Ⓐ Ⓑ Ⓒ Ⓓ   18. Ⓐ Ⓑ Ⓒ Ⓓ   23. Ⓐ Ⓑ Ⓒ Ⓓ
4. Ⓐ Ⓑ Ⓒ Ⓓ   9. Ⓐ Ⓑ Ⓒ Ⓓ   14. Ⓐ Ⓑ Ⓒ Ⓓ   19. Ⓐ Ⓑ Ⓒ Ⓓ   24. Ⓐ Ⓑ Ⓒ Ⓓ
5. Ⓐ Ⓑ Ⓒ Ⓓ   10. Ⓐ Ⓑ Ⓒ Ⓓ   15. Ⓐ Ⓑ Ⓒ Ⓓ   20. Ⓐ Ⓑ Ⓒ Ⓓ   25. Ⓐ Ⓑ Ⓒ Ⓓ

Assembling Objects—Subtest 9

1. Ⓐ Ⓑ Ⓒ Ⓓ   5. Ⓐ Ⓑ Ⓒ Ⓓ   9. Ⓐ Ⓑ Ⓒ Ⓓ   13. Ⓐ Ⓑ Ⓒ Ⓓ
2. Ⓐ Ⓑ Ⓒ Ⓓ   6. Ⓐ Ⓑ Ⓒ Ⓓ   10. Ⓐ Ⓑ Ⓒ Ⓓ   14. Ⓐ Ⓑ Ⓒ Ⓓ
3. Ⓐ Ⓑ Ⓒ Ⓓ   7. Ⓐ Ⓑ Ⓒ Ⓓ   11. Ⓐ Ⓑ Ⓒ Ⓓ   15. Ⓐ Ⓑ Ⓒ Ⓓ
4. Ⓐ Ⓑ Ⓒ Ⓓ   8. Ⓐ Ⓑ Ⓒ Ⓓ   12. Ⓐ Ⓑ Ⓒ Ⓓ   16. Ⓐ Ⓑ Ⓒ Ⓓ

Practice Exam Two

GENERAL SCIENCE—SUBTEST 1

TIME: 11 MINUTES
25 QUESTIONS

Directions: This test has questions about science. Pick the best answer for each question, then blacken the space on your separate answer form that has the same number and letter as your choice.

Here is a sample question.

1. An example of a chemical change is

   (A) melting ice.
   (B) breaking glass.
   (C) rusting metal.
   (D) making sawdust from wood.

The correct answer is "rusting metal," so you would fill in the space for C on your answer form.

Your score on this subtest will be based on the number of questions you answer correctly. You should try to answer every question. Do not spend too much time on any one question.

When you begin, be sure to start with question number 1 in Part 1, and number 1 in Part 1 on your answer form.

THE ACTUAL TEST WILL SAY:

Do not turn this page until told to do so.

1. Which of the following determines the sex of a human offspring?

   (A) egg cell
   (B) polar body
   (C) egg nucleus
   (D) sperm

2. Rocks are frequently split apart by

   (A) running water.
   (B) wind.
   (C) sudden changes in temperature.
   (D) meteorites.

3. Sand is made up of colorless crystals of

   (A) iron.
   (B) mica.
   (C) shale.
   (D) quartz.

4. Which material is an acid?

   (A) ammonia water
   (B) baking soda
   (C) vinegar
   (D) rainwater

5. Isotopes of the same element have the same number of

(A) protons only.
(B) electrons and protons only.
(C) neutrons only.
(D) neutrons and protons only.

6. As heat is applied to boiling water, the temperature remains the same. The best explanation for this is that

(A) convection increases at the boiling point of water.
(B) radiation increases at the boiling point of water.
(C) escaping vapor is taking away energy.
(D) the applied heat is absorbed quickly by the surroundings.

7. Which of the following is outside the solar system?

(A) Mars
(B) nebulae
(C) moons
(D) asteroids

8. Solar energy is transmitted through space by

(A) convection.
(B) radiation.
(C) reflection.
(D) absorption.

9. Which is an example of a sex-linked trait?

(A) eye color
(B) anemia
(C) height
(D) hemophilia

10. A fact that supports the position that viruses are living is that viruses

(A) are made of common chemicals.
(B) cause disease.
(C) duplicate themselves.
(D) are protein molecules.

11. A thermometer that indicates the freezing point of water at 0 degrees and the boiling point of water at 100 degrees is called a

(A) Centigrade thermometer.
(B) Fahrenheit thermometer.
(C) Kelvin thermometer.
(D) Reaumur thermometer.

12. Vegetation should be kept on slopes because

(A) plants aid weathering.
(B) runoff increases.
(C) plant roots hold the soil.
(D) plants enrich the soil.

13. A 25-pound force has two components at right angles to each other. If one component is 15 pounds, the other component is

(A) 10 pounds.
(B) 20 pounds.
(C) 40 pounds.
(D) 25 pounds.

14. What device is used to test the solution in a storage battery?

(A) voltmeter
(B) hydrometer
(C) ammeter
(D) anemometer

15. Fluorides are added to drinking water in order to

(A) improve taste.
(B) increase metabolism.
(C) prevent caries.
(D) prevent typhoid fever.

16. Blinking in response to bright light is an example of a(n)

(A) phototropism.
(B) habit.
(C) reflex.
(D) instinct.

17. The Rh factor is important in the study of

   (A) fingerprinting.
   (B) the blood.
   (C) the acidity of a solution.
   (D) the determination of sex.

18. What mineral element is part of hemoglobin?

   (A) calcium
   (B) fluorine
   (C) carbon
   (D) iron

19. In the winter the coldest areas are usually

   (A) island coasts.
   (B) continental interiors.
   (C) oceans.
   (D) hilltops.

20. If the mass of an object were doubled, its acceleration due to gravity would be

   (A) halved.
   (B) doubled.
   (C) unchanged.
   (D) quadrupled.

21. Respiration in plants takes place

   (A) only during the day.
   (B) only in the presence of carbon dioxide.
   (C) both day and night.
   (D) only at night.

22. Wind is mainly the result of

   (A) clouds.
   (B) storms.
   (C) high humidity.
   (D) unequal heating of air.

23. Which appeared most recently on the earth?

   (A) reptiles
   (B) mammals
   (C) amphibians
   (D) insects

24. When all the colors of the spectrum are mixed, the light is

   (A) yellow.
   (B) black.
   (C) white.
   (D) blue.

25. A solution that has a high ratio of solute to solvent is said to be

   (A) unsaturated.
   (B) saturated.
   (C) dilute.
   (D) concentrated.

ARITHMETIC REASONING—SUBTEST 2

TIME: 36 MINUTES
30 QUESTIONS

Directions: This test has questions about arithmetic. Each question is followed by four possible answers. Decide which answer is correct. Then, on your answer form, blacken the space that has the same number and letter as your choice. Use scratch paper for any figuring you wish to do.
  Here is a sample question.

1. If 1 quart of milk costs $0.80, what is the cost of 2 quarts?

  (A) $2.00
  (B) $1.60
  (C) $1.20
  (D) $1.00

  The cost of 2 quarts is $1.60; therefore, answer B is correct.
  Your score on this test will be based on the number of questions you answer correctly. You should try to answer every question. Do not spend too much time on any one question.
  Notice that Part 2 begins with question number 1. When you begin, be sure to mark your first answer next to number 1 on your answer form.

THE ACTUAL TEST WILL SAY:

Do not turn this page until told to do so.

---

1. Mr. Winter bought a $500 TV that was marked at a 15 percent discount. He made a down payment of $65 and agreed to pay the balance in 12 equal monthly installments. How much was each installment?

  (A) $25.00
  (B) $30.00
  (C) $42.50
  (D) $360.00

2. A farmer uses two gallons of insecticide concentrate to spray each $\frac{1}{4}$ acre of his land. How many gallons of the concentrate will he need to spray $10\frac{1}{2}$ acres?

  (A) 80
  (B) $80\frac{1}{4}$
  (C) 82
  (D) 84

3. An engineering drawing on a sheet of paper that measures 12 inches wide by 18 inches long is to be enlarged so that the length is 45 inches. How many inches wide will the enlarged drawing be?

  (A) 30 inches
  (B) 39 inches
  (C) 66 inches
  (D) 33 inches

4. In a quality control test at a factory, of 280 products inspected at random, 266 were found to be acceptable. What percentage of the items inspected were found acceptable?

  (A) 66%
  (B) 95%
  (C) 5%
  (D) 86%

5. A candy store sells 3 lbs. of a candy mix for $4.80. What is the price of a 5-oz. bag of this mix?

   (A) $1.00
   (B) $2.40
   (C) $0.25
   (D) $0.50

6. The perimeter of a square is 13 feet, 8 inches. What is the length of one side of the square?

   (A) 3 feet, 2 inches
   (B) 3 feet, 5 inches
   (C) 3 feet, 3 inches
   (D) 3 feet, 6 inches

7. A military unit has 360 members, and 20 percent are officers. How many members of the unit are enlisted personnel?

   (A) 90
   (B) 270
   (C) 72
   (D) 288

8. Kate earns $8.50 per hour with time and a half paid for overtime in excess of 8 hours on any one day. One day she worked 10 hours. How much did she earn on that day?

   (A) $85.00
   (B) $117.50
   (C) $97.75
   (D) $93.50

9. What is the next term in the series: $2\frac{1}{4}, 3\frac{3}{4},$ $3\frac{1}{4}, 4\frac{3}{4},$ ___?

   (A) $4\frac{1}{4}$

   (B) $6\frac{1}{4}$

   (C) $5\frac{1}{4}$

   (D) $3\frac{1}{4}$

10. Tickets for movie admission for adults are $4.00 each, but half-price is charged for children. If 265 adult tickets were sold and the box office collected $1,200, how many children's tickets were sold?

    (A) 70
    (B) 35
    (C) 280
    (D) 140

11. A woman budgets her income so that she spends $\frac{1}{4}$ of it for rent and $\frac{2}{5}$ of the remainder for food. What part of the total income does she budget for food?

    (A) $\frac{1}{10}$

    (B) $\frac{1}{5}$

    (C) $\frac{3}{20}$

    (D) $\frac{3}{10}$

12. A survey of a small group of people found that 3 of them each watched 2 hours of TV per day. Two of them watched 1 hour per day, and 1 watched 4 hours per day. What is the average number of hours of TV watched by members of this group?

    (A) $1\frac{1}{3}$ hours

    (B) $2\frac{2}{3}$ hours

    (C) 2 hours
    (D) 3 hours

13. What is the cost of 3 yards, 2 feet of an upholstery edging material that costs $9 per yard?

    (A) $30
    (B) $36
    (C) $29
    (D) $33

14. A partnership agreement calls for the two partners to share the profits of their business in the ratio 4:5. If the profit for the year is $63,000, what is the share paid to the partner who gets the smaller portion?

(A) $28,000
(B) $7,000
(C) $35,000
(D) $15,750

15. A courier leaves an office driving at an average rate of 30 miles per hour but forgets part of the material he was supposed to take with him. An hour later, a second courier is dispatched with the missing material and is instructed to overtake the first courier in 2 hours more. How fast must the second courier travel?

(A) 90 miles per hour
(B) 60 miles per hour
(C) 45 miles per hour
(D) 40 miles per hour

16. A merchant buys radios listed wholesale for $60 a piece at a 25 percent discount. He sells these radios at a 20 percent markup above the original wholesale price. What is his profit on each radio?

(A) $9.00
(B) $27.00
(C) $12.00
(D) $18.00

17. An airplane travels a distance of x miles in y hours. What is its average rate of speed in miles per hour?

(A) $\dfrac{xy}{y}$

(B) $\dfrac{x}{y}$

(C) $\dfrac{y}{x}$

(D) $\dfrac{x+y}{2}$

18. The cost of sending a telegram is $1.50 for the first 10 words and $0.05 for each additional word. How many words can be sent by telegram for $4.00?

(A) 50
(B) 60
(C) 81
(D) 90

19. A mapmaker is told to prepare a map with a scale of 1 inch to 40 miles. If the actual distance between two points is 110 miles, how far apart should the mapmaker show them on the map?

(A) 7 inches

(B) $3\dfrac{1}{2}$ inches

(C) $2\dfrac{1}{2}$ inches

(D) $2\dfrac{3}{4}$ inches

20. In the town of Hampshire, houses are assessed at 75 percent of the purchase price. If Mr. Johnson buys a house in Hampshire for $80,000 and real estate taxes are $4.83 per $100 of assessed valuation, how much realty tax must he pay?

(A) $2,898
(B) $3,864
(C) $600
(D) $604.83

21. The ingredients in a cake recipe include $4\dfrac{1}{2}$ cups of flour and $\dfrac{3}{4}$ cup of sugar. It is desired to make a cake that will require only $\dfrac{1}{4}$ cup of sugar. How much flour should be used?

(A) $1\dfrac{1}{4}$ cups

(B) 1 cups

(C) 4 cups

(D) $1\dfrac{3}{4}$ cups

22. When the tolls on a bridge were increased, the traffic declined from 1,200 cars crossing per day to 1,044. What was the percentage of the decline in traffic?

   (A) 87%
   (B) 156%
   (C) 13%
   (D) 15%

23. If a two-gallon bucket of liquid floor polish costs $19.20, how much should a one-quart can cost?

   (A) $4.80
   (B) $2.40
   (C) $1.20
   (D) $0.60

24. A man takes a trip in which he first drives for 3 hours at 50 miles per hour. He then drives for 2 hours more at 55 miles per hour. If his car gets 20 miles per gallon, how many gallons of gas did he use for the trip?

   (A) 10 gallons
   (B) 9.5 gallons
   (C) 26 gallons
   (D) 13 gallons

25. A woman has $5,000 invested at 8 percent annual interest. At what rate must she invest an additional $10,000 so that her annual income from both investments is equivalent to 9 percent of her total investment?

   (A) 10%
   (B) 10.5%
   (C) 9%
   (D) 9.5%

26. The fuel tank of a gasoline generator contains sufficient capacity to operate the generator for 1 hour and 20 minutes. How many times must the fuel tank be filled to run the generator from 9:15 A.M. to 3:55 P.M.?

   (A) 5
   (B) 6
   (C) $4\frac{1}{2}$
   (D) 4

27. A nursery employee mixes 10 pounds of hardy grass seed worth $1.20 per pound with 8 pounds of premium grass seed worth $3.00 per pound. At what price per pound should she sell the mixture?

   (A) $2.10
   (B) $2.00
   (C) $1.90
   (D) $2.50

28. What is the value of $\frac{0.02 \times 3}{0.001}$?

   (A) 60
   (B) 6
   (C) 0.6
   (D) 0.06

29. Find the numerical value of $1 + 5xy^2 - 3x^2y$ if $x = 3$ and $y = 2$.

   (A) 25
   (B) 18
   (C) 739
   (D) 7

30. Using the formula $I = \sqrt{\frac{P}{R}}$, find the value of I when $P = 48$ and $R = 3$.

   (A) 12
   (B) 8
   (C) 4
   (D) $\frac{4}{3}$

WORD KNOWLEDGE—SUBTEST 3

TIME: 11 MINUTES
35 QUESTIONS

Directions: This test has questions about the meanings of words. Each question has an **underlined boldface word**. You are to decide which one of the four words in the choices most nearly means the same as the underlined boldface word; then mark the space on your answer form that has the same number and letter as your choice.

Now look at the sample question below.

1. It was a **small** table.

    (A) sturdy
    (B) round
    (C) cheap
    (D) little

The question asks which of the four words means the same as the boldface word, **small**.

"Little" means the same as **small**. Answer D is the best one.

Your score on this test will be based on the number of questions you answer correctly. You should try to answer every question. Do not spend too much time on any one question.

When you begin, be sure to start with question number 1 in Part 3 of your test booklet and number 1 in Part 3 on your answer form.

THE ACTUAL TEST WILL SAY:

Do not turn this page until told to do so.

1. **Inform** most nearly means

    (A) ask.
    (B) heed.
    (C) tell.
    (D) ignore.

2. The dress was **crimson**.

    (A) crisp
    (B) neatly pressed
    (C) reddish
    (D) colorful

3. **Caution** most nearly means

    (A) signals.
    (B) care.
    (C) traffic.
    (D) haste.

4. Rain fell **intermittently**.

    (A) constantly
    (B) annually
    (C) using intermediaries (to stay)
    (D) at irregular intervals

5. **Occurrence** most nearly means

    (A) event.
    (B) place.
    (C) occupation.
    (D) opinion.

6. The disguise was a clever **deception**.

    (A) secret
    (B) fraud
    (C) mistrust
    (D) hatred

7. **Cease** most nearly means

   (A) start.
   (B) change.
   (C) continue.
   (D) stop.

8. **Acclaim** most nearly means

   (A) amazement.
   (B) laughter.
   (C) booing.
   (D) applause.

9. The city plans to **erect** a civic center.

   (A) paint
   (B) design
   (C) destroy
   (D) construct

10. **Relish** most nearly means

    (A) care.
    (B) speed.
    (C) amusement.
    (D) enjoy.

11. **Sufficient** most nearly means

    (A) durable.
    (B) substitution.
    (C) expendable.
    (D) appropriate.

12. **Fortnight** most nearly means

    (A) two weeks.
    (B) one week.
    (C) two months.
    (D) one month.

13. That action was a **blemish** on his record.

    (A) defect
    (B) mixture
    (C) accusation
    (D) decoration

14. Rules **impose** order on the group.

    (A) disguise
    (B) escape
    (C) require
    (D) purchase

15. **Jeer** most nearly means

    (A) peek.
    (B) scoff.
    (C) turn.
    (D) judge.

16. **Alias** most nearly means

    (A) enemy.
    (B) sidekick.
    (C) hero.
    (D) assumed name.

17. **Impair** most nearly means

    (A) direct.
    (B) improve.
    (C) weaken.
    (D) stimulate.

18. **Itinerant** most nearly means

    (A) traveling.
    (B) shrewd.
    (C) insurance.
    (D) aggressive.

19. I don't often **abandon** a good idea.

    (A) relinquish
    (B) encompass
    (C) infiltrate
    (D) quarantine

20. The association met to **resolve** the issue.

    (A) end
    (B) understand
    (C) recall
    (D) forget

21. **Ample** most nearly means

    (A) plentiful.
    (B) enthusiastic.
    (C) well-shaped.
    (D) fat.

22. The chemical spill left a **stench**.

    (A) puddle of slimy water
    (B) pile of debris
    (C) foul odor
    (D) dead animal

23. **Sullen** most nearly means

    (A) grayish-yellow.
    (B) soaking wet.
    (C) very dirty.
    (D) angrily silent.

24. **Rudiments** most nearly means

    (A) basic methods and procedures.
    (B) politics.
    (C) promotion opportunities.
    (D) minute details.

25. **Clash** most nearly means

    (A) applaud.
    (B) fasten.
    (C) conflict.
    (D) punish.

26. **Camaraderie** most nearly means

    (A) interest in photography.
    (B) close friendship.
    (C) petty jealousies.
    (D) arts and crafts projects.

27. The report was **superficial**.

    (A) excellent
    (B) official
    (C) profound
    (D) cursory

28. **Tapestry** most nearly means

    (A) fabric of woven designs.
    (B) tent.
    (C) piece of elaborate jewelry.
    (D) exquisite painting.

29. The response was **terse**.

    (A) pointed
    (B) trivial
    (C) oral
    (D) lengthy

30. We had never seen such a **concoction**.

    (A) combination of ingredients
    (B) appetizer
    (C) drink made of wine and spices
    (D) relish tray

31. **Brevity** most nearly means

    (A) boldness.
    (B) shortness.
    (C) nearness.
    (D) length.

32. **Clemency** most nearly means

    (A) justice.
    (B) punishment.
    (C) mercy.
    (D) dismissal.

33. That was an act of **insubordination**.

    (A) humiliation
    (B) rejection
    (C) disobedience
    (D) carelessness

34. She advised against **preferential** treatment.

    (A) weekly
    (B) constant
    (C) unlimited
    (D) special

35. **Doldrums** most nearly means

    (A) fearful.
    (B) diseased.
    (C) low spirits.
    (D) embarrassment.

PARAGRAPH COMPREHENSION—SUBTEST 4

TIME: 13 MINUTES
15 QUESTIONS

Directions: This test is a test of your ability to understand what you read. In this section you will find one or more paragraphs of reading material followed by incomplete statements or questions.

You are to read the paragraph and select which of the four lettered choices best completes the statement or answers the question. When you have selected your answer, blacken the correct numbered letter on your answer sheet.

Now look at the sample question below.

In certain areas water is so scarce that every attempt is made to conserve it. For instance, on one oasis in the Sahara Desert the amount of water necessary for each date palm tree has been carefully determined.

1. How much water is each tree given?

    (A) no water at all
    (B) exactly the amount required
    (C) water only if it is healthy
    (D) water on alternate days

The amount of water each tree required has been carefully determined, so answer B is correct.

Your score on this subtest will be based on the number of questions you answer correctly. You should try to answer every question. Do not spend too much time on any one question.

When you begin, be sure to start with question number 1 in Part 4 of your test booklet and number 1 in Part 4 on your answer form.

THE ACTUAL TEST WILL SAY:

Do not turn this page until told to do so.

---

1. Professional drivers, people who drive trucks and buses for a living, have a low opinion of the average motorist. They complain that the average driver does not maintain proper speed, changes lanes without signaling, and stops without warning.

   The topic sentence or key idea in this paragraph is that

   (A) professional drivers do not think much of the average driver.
   (B) people who drive trucks are professional drivers.
   (C) the average driver is not a good driver.
   (D) the average driver does not like professional drivers.

2. The trees stood quietly under the dark gray clouds. Their bare branches shuddered as the cold wind slipped around them. Sailing along on the wind a few birds flew to shelter. No other animals were to be seen.

   In this paragraph the word *shuddered* means:

   (A) fell.
   (B) shook.
   (C) cracked.
   (D) remained still.

3. Many think of the log cabin as a New England invention. Others feel it was first made by the pioneers who crossed the Appalachian Mountains. According to one authority, the log cabin was introduced to America by the Swedes. The area around the Delaware River was settled by Swedes and Finns. These two European peoples were first to use the log cabin.

According to this passage, the log cabin was introduced to this country by

(A) New England colonists.
(B) Swedes and Finns.
(C) Appalachian Mountain pioneers.
(D) the English.

4. Down the gently drifting stream, the boat glided softly. Soft breezes and warm sun bathed him. The fishing pole lay unused. The floppy hat shaded his half-closed eyes and much of his face. Only his lower features, framed in a pleasant smile, could be seen.

This passage describes a man who is

(A) sad.
(B) active.
(C) contented.
(D) exhilarated.

5. Would you like to be good at a trade? Would you like to know a skill that pays well? One sure way to skill, good pay, and regular work is to train on the job. This is called apprentice training. While it is not the only way to learn, apprentice training has good points. You can earn while you learn, can learn the skill "from the ground up," and can advance on the job.

Apprentice training is described in this paragraph by

(A) discussing both sides.
(B) discussing only the good side.
(C) discussing only the bad side.
(D) comparing it to other types of training.

6. Move into a house with six closets and all of them will be jammed in a short time. Move into a house with 15 closets and the same thing will happen. In short, we never have enough closets, no matter how many closets we have. But there's one thing we can do: we can make better use of the space within a closet.

The author of this paragraph suggests that we

(A) should build more closets in houses.
(B) never have enough things to fill the closets.
(C) usually fill every closet in the house.
(D) make the best use of space within a closet.

7. There is a big difference between a classical and a reactionary. The person who favors new ideas, tries to change, and looks for new ways is more free or liberated. On the other hand, a person may look back or want to return to the way things used to be. This person does not like progress and resents change.

The word *reactionary* can be used to describe a person who

(A) looks ahead to the future.
(B) looks back to the past.
(C) favors new ideas.
(D) likes change.

8. This forest must be preserved. These trees have stood against natural forces for over a hundred years. Within the area wildlife flourishes and the streams are clear and sparkling. Thousands of people can find pleasure through camping or walking in a spot of unspoiled nature. The beauty and peace of this forest can renew the spirit of many a person.

This passage was probably written by a

(A) lumber company spokesperson.
(B) religious society.
(C) house-building company.
(D) conservation group.

9. There has been enough talk. The problem has been studied from every viewpoint. The figures add up to the need for the bridge. When the bonds are approved their cost will be met by future tolls. All groups favor this and no property owners will be hurt by it. The time for action has come.

According to this paragraph, the next logical step would be to

(A) build the bridge
(B) pass a law to raise the money
(C) decide how to collect the tolls
(D) have a meeting of property owners

10. Lightning is a gigantic spark, a tremendous release of energy between earth and cloud. The shorter the gap between earth and cloud, the greater the chances of discharge. Thus, lightning tends to favor objects that thrust above the surrounding terrain. This might mean you sitting in a boat or the lone tree on the golf course.

Lightning is described as

(A) man-made energy.
(B) a bolt from heaven.
(C) a release of electrical energy.
(D) a poorly understood phenomenon.

11. Every large city has problems of traffic and people trying to use transportation. The problem is at its worst in the two hours before 9 A.M. and the two hours after 4 P.M. So many businesses, stores, and companies start work and end work at the same time. This becomes a very great problem in the downtown business centers with their many-storied skyscrapers and their thousands of workers.

The morning transportation rush starts at

(A) 9 A.M.
(B) 7 A.M.
(C) 8 A.M.
(D) 6 A.M.

12. A vision care technician assists the patient in frame selection and fitting and provides instruction in the use of contact lenses. Such a technician works with children in visual training programs and assists with testing for corneal curvature, visual acuity, and eye pressure.

The word *acuity* means

(A) cuteness.
(B) strength.
(C) sharpness.
(D) pressure.

13. An agricultural research scientist wishes to test the germination power of a particular strain of wheat. That is, he wants to know what proportion of the seeds will grow to maturity. He picks one seed at random from a bunch of wheat and that particular grain of wheat produces a strong and healthy stalk of wheat.

We can conclude from this experiment that

(A) the rest of the seeds are the same.
(B) this seed is the only healthy one.
(C) more seeds must be tested.
(D) it was an accident that this seed was good.

14. Most breads and cereals are well-liked, fit easily into meal plan, and cost little per serving. These foods, with whole-grain or enriched bread as examples, provide good food value. Mostly they give food energy, but they also supply vitamins and minerals. According to a recent survey, bread and cereal products provided 40 percent of the thiamine (a B vitamin) and 30 percent of the iron needed daily by a person.

What percent of the daily needs of a B vitamin come from bread and cereals?

(A) 30 percent
(B) more than half
(C) 40 percent
(D) 70 percent

15. In the many years before 1800 there was a great fear of plague and other illnesses. Most of the problem came from poor medical knowledge and no scientific way to fight the diseases. People knew the results of plague would be suffering and death. Naturally they tried to stay away from infection or they tried to keep the danger away from them.

The main reason for the fear of plague before 1800 was

(A) crowded cities and seaports.
(B) little medical or scientific knowledge.
(C) long time needed for quarantine.
(D) difficulty in avoiding infection.

MATHEMATICS KNOWLEDGE—SUBTEST 5

TIME: 24 MINUTES
25 QUESTIONS

Directions: This is a test of your ability to solve general mathematical problems. Each problem is followed by four answer choices. Select the correct response from the choices given, then mark the space on your answer form that has the same number and letter as your choice. Use scratch paper to do any figuring that you wish.

Now look at this sample problem.

1. If $x + 8 = 9$, then x is equal to

(A) 0.

(B) 1.

(C) 3.

(D) $\frac{9}{8}$.

The correct answer is 1, so B is the correct response.

Your score on this test will be based on the number of questions you answer correctly. You should try to answer every question. Do not spend too much time on any one question.

Start with question number 1 in Part 5. Mark your answer for this question next to number 1, Part 5, on your answer form.

THE ACTUAL TEST WILL SAY:

Do not turn this page until told to do so.

---

1. Solve for x: $2x + 6 = 12 - x$.

(A) 6
(B) 9
(C) 2
(D) 3

2. From $8x^2 - 7x$ subtract $2x - 3x^2$.

(A) $11x^2 - 9x$
(B) $5x^2 - 5x$
(C) $6x^2 - 4x$
(D) $10x^2 - 10x$

3. What is the product of $2x^3y$ and $(3x^2y - 4)$?

(A) $6x^5y^2 - 4$
(B) $6x^5y^2 - 8x^3y$
(C) $6x^6y^2 - 8x^3y$
(D) $6x^6y - 8x^3y$

4. A worker can do $\frac{1}{3}$ of a job by herself in one day, and her helper can do $\frac{1}{5}$ of the job by himself in one day. What portion of the job can they do if they work together for one day?

(A) $\frac{1}{4}$

(B) $\frac{8}{15}$

(C) $\frac{1}{8}$

(D) $\frac{2}{15}$

5. A length of chain is 5 feet, 3 inches long. If a piece 3 feet, 9 inches in length is cut from the chain, what is the length of the remaining piece?

(A) 2 feet, 6 inches
(B) 1 foot, 1 inch
(C) 1 foot, 4 inches
(D) 1 foot, 6 inches

6. In a regular hexagon, all the angles are equal and one of them is 120 degrees. What is the sum of all the angles of the regular hexagon?

(A) 240 degrees
(B) 480 degrees
(C) 720 degrees
(D) 360 degrees

7. What is the product of $(3a - 2)$ and $(a + 3)$?

(A) $4a + 1$
(B) $3a^2 - 6$
(C) $3a^2 - 2a - 6$
(D) $3a^2 + 7a - 6$

8. If $x = 3$, what is the value of $|x - 7|$?

(A) 4
(B) -4
(C) 10
(D) -10

9. Solve the following system of equations for

$x : 3x + y = 13$
$\quad x - 2y = 2$

(A) 18
(B) 4
(C) 3
(D) 6

10. How many feet are there in a length of y yards and i inches?

(A) $3y + i$
(B) $3y + 12i$
(C) $\dfrac{y+12i}{3}$
(D) $\dfrac{36y+i}{12}$

11. Solve the following formula for

$F: C = \dfrac{5}{9}(F - 32)$.

(A) $F = \dfrac{9}{5}C + 32$

(B) $F = \dfrac{5}{9}C + 32$

(C) $F = \dfrac{9C+32}{5}$

(D) $F = \dfrac{9}{5}C + 288$

12. A woman travels 3 miles directly east and then travels 4 miles directly north. How many miles is she from her starting point?

(A) 7 miles
(B) 5 miles
(C) 25 miles
(D) $3\dfrac{1}{2}$ miles

13. A line is drawn perpendicular to the base of an equilateral triangle at one of the vertices of a triangle. Find the number of degrees in the angle made by the perpendicular and the other side of the triangle that contains this vertex.

(A) 30 degrees
(B) 45 degrees
(C) 60 degrees
(D) 90 degrees

14. Solve the following inequality: $x - 6 \leq 5$

   (A) $x \leq 1$
   (B) $x \leq 11$
   (C) $x \geq 11$
   (D) $x < 11$

15. A fence that had been installed around a rectangular field 40 feet long and 36 feet wide is torn down. The entire fence is then reused to completely enclose a square field. What is the length in feet of a side of the square field?

   (A) 76 feet
   (B) 19 feet
   (C) 42 feet
   (D) 38 feet

16. A cereal manufacturer packages breakfast cereal in individual-sized boxes measuring 2 inches by 3 inches by 4 inches. The same product is also packaged in large family-sized boxes measuring 3 inches by 8 inches by 12 inches. The contents of how many of the individual-sized boxes would be required to fill one family-sized box?

   (A) 6
   (B) 12
   (C) 10
   (D) 8

17. A wheel has a diameter of 14 inches. How many inches will the wheel roll along the ground during one rotation? (Use $\frac{22}{7}$ as the value of π.)

   (A) 44 inches
   (B) 22 inches
   (C) 14 inches
   (D) 28 inches

18. In a right triangle whose hypotenuse has a length of 21 feet, the sine of one of the angles is $\frac{3}{7}$. What is the length in feet of the side opposite this angle?

   (A) 6 feet
   (B) 14 feet
   (C) 9 feet
   (D) 10 feet

19. Find the value of $-x^4$ if $x = -0.1$.

   (A) −0.1
   (B) 0.0001
   (C) −0.0001
   (D) −0.4

20. Under the terms of a federal subsidy, a real estate developer is required to rent at least 30 percent of the apartments she builds to low-income families. If she plans on having 108 low-income apartments, what is the maximum number of apartments of all types that she can build?

   (A) 360
   (B) 252
   (C) 324
   (D) 396

21. A student has grades of 60 on each of two tests and a grade of 70 on a third test. What grade must he get on a fourth test to raise his average to 75?

   (A) 95
   (B) 85
   (C) 100
   (D) He cannot achieve a 75 average.

22. A motorist travels for 3 hours at 40 miles per hour and then travels for 2 more hours at 50 miles per hour. What is her average rate of speed in miles per hour for the entire trip?

(A) 45 miles per hour
(B) 44 miles per hour
(C) 43 miles per hour
(D) 90 miles per hour

23. A radar device is capable of detecting objects within the area around it up to a radius of 10 miles. If it is used to cover a 36 degree angular portion of this area, how many square miles of area will it cover?
(Use 3.14 as the value of π.)

(A) 360 square miles
(B) 6.28 square miles
(C) 31.4 square miles
(D) 3.6 square miles

24. Solve for x: $x^2 + 2x = 15$.

(A) $x = 3, x = 5$
(B) $x = -3, x = 5$
(C) $x = -5, x = 3$
(D) $x = -15, x = 1$

25. 12 quarts of a radiator coolant contains 25 percent antifreeze and 75 percent water. How many quarts of water must be added to change the mixture to one containing 20 percent antifreeze?

(A) 1 quart
(B) 2 quarts
(C) 3 quarts
(D) 4 quarts

TIME: 9 MINUTES
20 QUESTIONS

Directions: This is a test of your knowledge of electrical, radio, and electronics information. You are to select the correct response from the choices given. Then mark the space on your answer form that has the same number and letter as your choice.

Now look at the sample question below.

1. What does the abbreviation AC stand for?

    (A) additional charge
    (B) alternating coil
    (C) alternating current
    (D) ampere current

The correct answer is "alternating current," so C is the correct response.

Your score on this test will be based on the number of questions you answer correctly. You should try to answer every question. Do not spend too much time on any one question.

When you are told to begin, be sure to start with question number 1 in Part 6 of your test booklet and number 1 in Part 6 of your answer form.

THE ACTUAL TEST WILL SAY:

Do not turn this page until told to do so.

---

1. Which of the following causes the inductance of a coil to decrease?

    (A) a copper core
    (B) an iron core
    (C) more turns of wire
    (D) shortening the length of the coil

2. Permeability is

    (A) a unit of measurement of magnetism.
    (B) a force field intensity measurement.
    (C) the ease with which magnetic lines of force distribute themselves throughout a material.
    (D) a property of a permanent magnet.

3. Which of the following is not a factor in determining capacitance of a capacitor?

    (A) area of the plates
    (B) distance between the plates
    (C) material used as a dielectric
    (D) voltage applied to the plates

4. Capacitors placed in series produce

    (A) less capacitance.
    (B) a lower WVDC rating.
    (C) more capacitance.
    (D) higher reliability.

5. XC is equal to

    (A) $\left(\frac{1}{2}\right)\pi \times FC$
    (B) $\left(\frac{1}{2}\right)\pi \times FL$
    (C) $2\pi \times FL$
    (D) $2\pi \times FC$

6. Capacitors connected in parallel

    (A) produce more capacitance.
    (B) produce less capacitance.
    (C) produce a higher WVDC rating.
    (D) handle more voltage.

7. Parallel resonance occurs in a circuit when

    (A) $Z = X_L$
    (B) $Z = X_C$
    (C) $X = 2\pi \times FC$
    (D) $X_L = X_C$

8. Impedance (Z) of a series RL circuit can be found by using

    (A) $Z = \sqrt{R^2 + X_C^2}$

    (B) $Z = \sqrt{R^2 + X_L^2}$

    (C) $Z = \sqrt{R + X_L}$

    (D) $Z = \sqrt{R + X_L^2}$

9. A filter is used in a power supply to

    (A) change AC to DC.
    (B) change DC to AC.
    (C) smooth out voltage variations.
    (D) smooth out power surges.

10. Another name for a transistor is

    (A) diode.
    (B) semiconductor.
    (C) crystal amplifier.
    (D) integrated circuit.

11. Radio frequency amplifiers are used in

    (A) audio amplifiers.
    (B) differential amplifiers.
    (C) operational amplifiers.
    (D) receivers and transmitters.

12. A crystal microphone uses

    (A) the piezoelectric effect.
    (B) the pressure pack effect.
    (C) magnetic waves to operate.
    (D) a permanent magnet to operate.

13. The voice coil of a speaker has an impedance that is

    (A) high.
    (B) low.
    (C) made of ceramic materials.
    (D) made of ferrite materials.

14. A crossover network is used to

    (A) direct the proper frequency range to the right speaker.
    (B) eliminate noise.
    (C) filter out high frequencies.
    (D) filter out low frequencies.

15. The klystron is used in

    (A) low-frequency transmitters.
    (B) radar units.
    (C) audio frequency amplifiers.
    (D) frequency detectors.

16. There are two basic types of oscillators used for microwave generation. They are the magnetron and the

    (A) klystron.
    (B) op amp.
    (C) Clapp oscillator.
    (D) multivibrator.

17. There are two types of diodes used in electronics work. They are the semiconductor diode and the

    (A) vacuum tube diode.
    (B) full-wave diode.
    (C) half-wave diode.
    (D) zener diode.

18. Color television relies on three colors to produce the full color range needed for a good picture. These colors are red, blue, and

(A) gray.
(B) orange.
(C) yellow.
(D) green.

19. The folded dipole antenna has an impedance of

(A) 72 ohms.
(B) 300 ohms.
(C) 600 ohms.
(D) 75 ohms.

20. Television sets in the United States use a horizontal frequency of

(A) 525 hertz.
(B) 60 hertz.
(C) 15,750 hertz.
(D) 15,625 hertz.

AUTOMOTIVE & SHOP INFORMATION—SUBTEST 7

TIME: 11 MINUTES
25 QUESTIONS

Directions: This test has questions about automobiles, as well as tools and common shop terminology and practices. Pick the best answer for each question, then blacken the space on your separate answer form that has the same number and letter as your choice.

Here is a sample question.

1. The most commonly used fuel for operating automobile engines is

(A) kerosene.
(B) benzene.
(C) crude oil.
(D) gasoline.

Gasoline is the most commonly used fuel, so D is the correct answer.

Your score on this test will be based on the number of questions you answer correctly. You should try to answer every question. Do not spend too much time on any one question.

When you are told to begin, be sure to start with question number 1 in Part 7 of your test booklet and number 1 in Part 7 on your separate answer form.

THE ACTUAL TEST WILL SAY:

Do not turn this page until told to do so.

---

1. The universal joint is needed to

   (A) allow the driveshaft to flex.
   (B) hold the driveshaft rigid.
   (C) make the transmission shift.
   (D) make the differential turn corners.

2. Three major pollutants emitted by a gasoline engine are

   (A) carbon dioxide, carbon monoxide, and oxygen.
   (B) hydrocarbons, nitric acid, and nitrogen.
   (C) hydrocarbons, carbon monoxide, and oxides of nitrogen.
   (D) nitrogen, oxygen, and carbon monixide.

3. The catalytic converter

   (A) converts gasoline to the air/fuel ratio needed.
   (B) reduces the input pressure of exhaust gases to the muffler.
   (C) converts intake manifold pressure to a lower value.
   (D) converts exhaust gases to better-quality emissions.

4. The differential

   (A) is located in the transmission.
   (B) is located in the clutch housing.
   (C) consists of three small bevel gears on the ends of the axle shafts.
   (D) consists of two small bevel gears on the ends of the axle shafts.

5. PCV is the abbreviation for

(A) pollution control valve.
(B) pollution valve control.
(C) positive crankcase ventilation.
(D) pollution control ventilator.

6. The formation of NO_x in an engine is minimized by

(A) diluting the fuel/air mixture entering the combustion chamber.
(B) burning more fuel.
(C) using an alcohol-enriched fuel.
(D) not using a muffler.

7. With any two meshed gears, the gear with the greater number of teeth will

(A) turn slower than the smaller gear and produce less torque.
(B) always turn slower and produce greater torque.
(C) never produce much torque.
(D) always turn faster and produces less torque.

8. The clutch is used to

(A) change compression ratios.
(B) stop the car.
(C) make it possible to change gears.
(D) drive the transmission.

9. First gear in a car is used

(A) at high speeds.
(B) in starting the car from a standstill.
(C) when the car is moving faster than 35 miles per hour.
(D) at speeds above 55 miles per hour.

10. The torque converter is found in

(A) the differential housing.
(B) the manual transmission housing.
(C) the engine compartment.
(D) in an automatic transmission.

11. Disc brakes are made with

(A) two pads and a rotating drum.
(B) two pads and a rotating disc.
(C) two brake shoes that slide along the inside drum mounted on the rear wheels.
(D) all-steel pads to stop the car quickly.

12. In a front-wheel-drive car the transmission

(A) is located in the rear of the car.
(B) is located in the engine compartment.
(C) has a long propeller shaft.
(D) has a short propeller shaft.

13. Which of these tools breaks easily when twisted?

(A) folding rule
(B) ruler
(C) yardstick
(D) handsaw

14. Which type of saw is mounted in a mitre box?

(A) ripsaw
(B) hacksaw
(C) cross-cut saw
(D) backsaw

15. In order to shape concrete it is placed in a

(A) lake.
(B) form.
(C) hole.
(D) large, round object.

16. In concrete work a "darby" is a

(A) metal pole.
(B) metal trowel.
(C) type of wooden float.
(D) stake to hold a form.

17. Nail sets are used for

    (A) driving tacks.
    (B) setting nails below the surface of the wood.
    (C) setting nails above the surface of the wood.
    (D) setting carpet tacks.

18. A tool used for marking wood is called a

    (A) saw.
    (B) plane.
    (C) screwdriver.
    (D) scratch awl.

19. In selecting the proper grinding wheel it is important to

    (A) choose the proper grain size for the job to be done.
    (B) choose the proper manufacturer.
    (C) choose the properly priced wheel.
    (D) choose the proper concrete binder.

20. Which of these metals can be made thinner than a coat of paint?

    (A) copper
    (B) aluminum
    (C) gold
    (D) silver

21. When making a hole in sheet metal, it is safer to

    (A) drill it.
    (B) punch it.
    (C) cut it.
    (D) burn it.

22. Rapid, uncontrolled drying of wood causes

    (A) checking and cracking.
    (B) warping.
    (C) no harmful effects.
    (D) discoloration only.

23. A bumping hammer is used to

    (A) perform final alignment on newly forged metal components.
    (B) indent or compress metal.
    (C) smooth out dents.
    (D) hammer out and form sheet metal elements.

24. Steel is an alloy of iron that

    (A) is made with carbon and magnesium.
    (B) does not rust.
    (C) has added strength.
    (D) all of the above.

25. Bolting and riveting provide

    (A) a permanent connection between two metals.
    (B) a temporary or semipermanent connection.
    (C) fused joints.
    (D) a soldered connection.

MECHANICAL COMPREHENSION—SUBTEST 8

TIME: 19 MINUTES
25 QUESTIONS

Directions: This test has questions about general mechanical and physical principles. Pick the best answer for each question, then blacken the space on your separate answer form that has the same number and letter as your choice.

Here is a sample question.

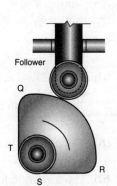

Follower

Q

T

S

R

1. The follower is at its highest position between points

(A) Q and R.
(B) R and S.
(C) S and T.
(D) T and Q.

The correct answer is "between Q and R," so you would blacken the space for A on your answer form.

Your score on this test will be based on the number of questions you answer correctly. You should try to answer every question. Do not spend too much time on any one question.

When you are told to begin, be sure to start with question number 1 in Part 8 of your test booklet and number 1 in Part 8 of your answer form.

THE ACTUAL TEST WILL SAY:

Do not turn this page until told to do so.

---

1. Most of the lift on an aircraft's wings is because of

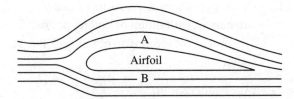

A
Airfoil
B

(A) a decrease in pressure on the upper side, A.
(B) a decrease in pressure on the bottom side, B.
(C) a vacuum created under the wing at point A.
(D) none of the above.

2. It is well known that oil rises in lamp wicks, melted wax rises in the wick of a candle, and water rises in a narrow tube. This phenomenon is called

(A) wicking.
(B) erosion.
(C) capillary action.
(D) osmosis.

3. Two strips of metal, one iron and one brass, are welded or riveted together to form a

(A) heating element.
(B) thermal bridge.
(C) heat switch.
(D) thermostat.

4. Which of the following metals expands the most when heated?

(A) steel
(B) aluminum
(C) iron
(D) tungsten

5. Clocks with pendulums tend to run faster when cold. This is caused by

(A) the pendulum becoming longer when cold.
(B) the pendulum becoming shorter when cold.
(C) the air expanding and slowing the pendulum.
(D) the air contracting and speeding up the pendulum.

6. Heat is a form of

(A) energy.
(B) motion.
(C) thermal.
(D) calories.

7. Which of the metals listed below is the best conductor of heat?

(A) aluminum
(B) copper
(C) iron
(D) silver

8. Heat is transferred from one place to another by conduction, convection, and

(A) condensation.
(B) evaporation.
(C) radiation.
(D) cooling.

9. When a salt is dissolved in water, it causes

(A) an increase in the freezing point of the solution.
(B) a decrease in the freezing point of the solution.
(C) little or no difference in the freezing point.
(D) the water to freeze and leave the salt.

10. When a liquid is changed to vapor, the process is called

(A) evaporation.
(B) dehydration.
(C) pressurization.
(D) condensation.

11. When water is heated and confined to a closed container so the steam cannot escape, the pressure inside increases and the temperature of the boiling water

(A) becomes lower.
(B) becomes higher.
(C) stays the same.
(D) does none of the above.

12. Crude petroleum is a mixture of many substances with different boiling points. The process of refining to obtain gasoline is called

(A) condensation.
(B) pressurization.
(C) dehydration.
(D) fractional distillation.

13. The speed of sound at 0 degrees has been found to be

(A) 1,492 meters per second.
(B) 3,500 meters per second.
(C) 1,086 feet per second.
(D) 186,000 miles per second.

14. The meter used to measure extremely high resistances is called a(n)

(A) ohmmeter.
(B) megger.
(C) resistance meter.
(D) ammeter.

15. In the figure below a hole is being drilled in 1. What is taking place in 2?

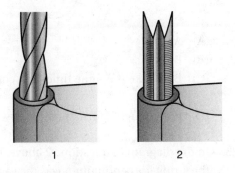

1   2

(A) The hole is being reamed.
(B) The hole is being drilled.
(C) The hole is being tapped.
(D) The hole is being plugged.

16. Two cylinders (A and B) contain hydraulic fluid and are connected by a hydraulic line as shown in the drawing below. If the diameter of cylinder A is 3 inches and the diameter of cylinder B is 6 inches, and the piston in cylinder B presses down 1 inch, what will happen to the piston in cylinder A?

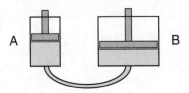

(A) It will rise 1 inch.
(B) It will rise 2 inches.
(C) It will drop 2 inches.
(D) It will remain stationary.

17. Water is flowing through the 3-inch-diameter pipe A into a 1-inch-diameter pipe B as shown below. Which one of the following statements is true?

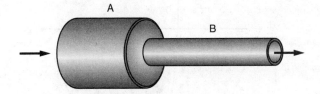

(A) The water is flowing faster in pipe A than in pipe B.
(B) Water pressure is greater in pipe A.
(C) Water pressure is greater in pipe B.
(D) Water pressure is equal in both pipes, since the water is coming from the same source.

18. Which one of the following would feel hottest to the touch if one end was placed in a pot of boiling water?

(A) a plastic fork
(B) a wooden spoon
(C) a metal knife
(D) ceramic chopsticks

19. What is the formula to calculate a lever's mechanical advantage?

(A) load × effort
(B) load/effort
(C) effort distance × load distance
(D) load distance/θ

20. In the drawing below, when the plug in the tube is removed, water will flow

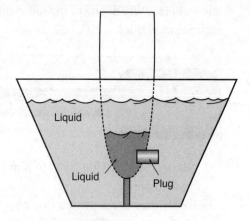

(A) out of the tube.
(B) into the tube.
(C) in neither direction.
(D) not enough information to answer.

21. In the water pipe and valve system below, assume that the main tank starts empty and that all valves are closed to start off with. Which valves would have to be open for the tank to fill about halfway and maintain that level?

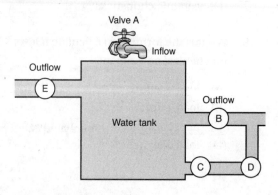

(A) valves A, B, and C
(B) valves A, B, and D
(C) valves A, B, and E
(D) valves B, C, and D

22. Which pendulum takes more time to make one complete swing?

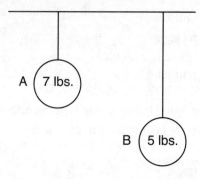

(A) A
(B) B
(C) Both take the same time for a complete swing.
(D) not enough information to answer

23. In the diagram in question 22 above, if the string for pendulum A was the same length as the string for pendulum B, which pendulum would take more time to make one complete swing?

(A) A
(B) B
(C) Both would take the same amount of time.
(D) not enough information to answer

24. Condensation on cold water pipes can be prevented by

   (A) insuring that long sections of the pipe are vertical.
   (B) keeping the cold water near 32°F.
   (C) insulating the pipes.
   (D) not allowing air into the cold water pipes.

25. If gear A makes 10 revolutions, how many revolutions will gear B make?

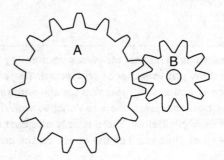

   (A) 5
   (B) 10
   (C) 15
   (D) 20

TIME: 9 MINUTES
16 QUESTIONS

Directions: This test measures your ability to picture how an object will look when its parts are mentally put together or connected. There are two types of problems. In the first type of problem, each question will show you several separate shapes, from which you will then pick the choice that best represents how the shapes would look if they were all fitted together correctly, as in the example below. There is only one best answer for each shape. Pick the best answer for each question, then blacken the space on the answer form that has the same number and letter as your choice.

Here is a sample question.

1. Which figure best shows how the objects in the group on the left will appear if they are fitted together?

                                             (A)   (B)   (C)   (D)

In this example, the correct answer is "D."

In the second type of problem, you will be shown two shapes and a connector line. One point on each of the shapes will be labeled with a letter (for instance, "A" on the first shape and "B" on the second shape). The ends of the connector line will be labeled with the same letters—in this case, one end with "A" and the other end with the letter "B." You will be asked which of the four figures best shows how the two shapes and a connector line in the first group will touch if the letters for each object are matched, as in the example below. There is only one best answer for each shape. Pick the best answer for each question, then blacken the space on the answer form that has the same number and letter as your choice.

Here is a sample question.

2. Which figure best shows how the objects in the group of objects on the left will touch if the letters for each object are matched?

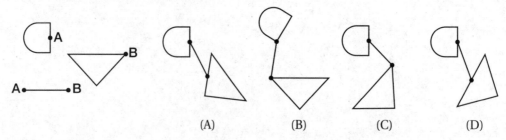

                                       (A)   (B)   (C)   (D)

In this example, the correct answer is "C."

Your score on this test will be based on the number of questions you answer correctly. You should try to answer every question. Do not spend too much time on any one question.

When you are told to begin, be sure to start with question number 1 in Part 9 of your test booklet and number 1 in Part 9 on your separate answer form.

THE ACTUAL TEST WILL SAY:

Do not turn this page until told to do so.

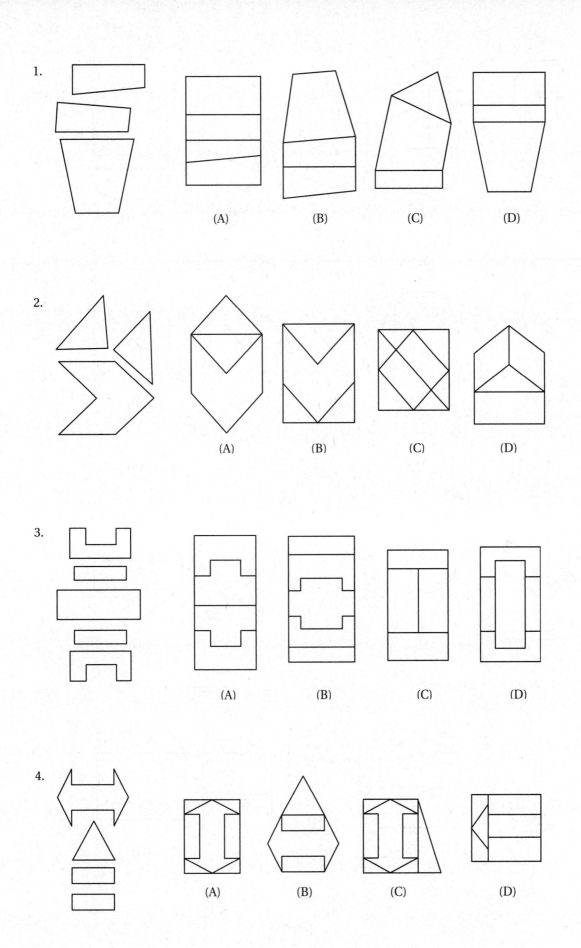

1.

(A)   (B)   (C)   (D)

2.

(A)   (B)   (C)   (D)

3.

(A)   (B)   (C)   (D)

4.

(A)   (B)   (C)   (D)

5.

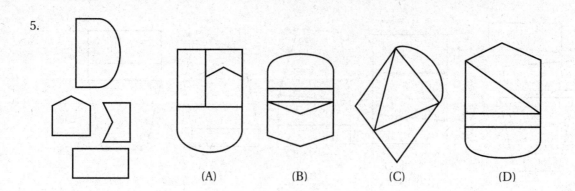

(A) (B) (C) (D)

6.

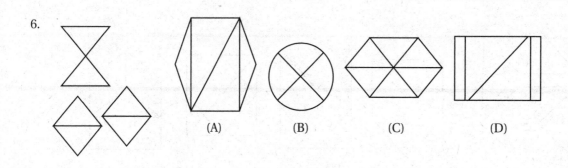

(A) (B) (C) (D)

7.

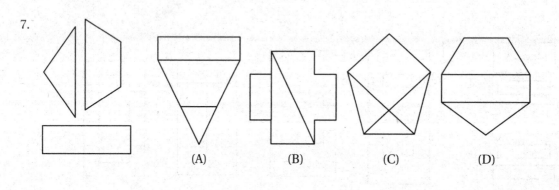

(A) (B) (C) (D)

8.

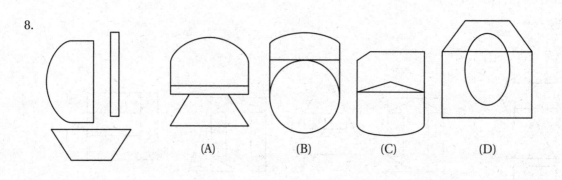

(A) (B) (C) (D)

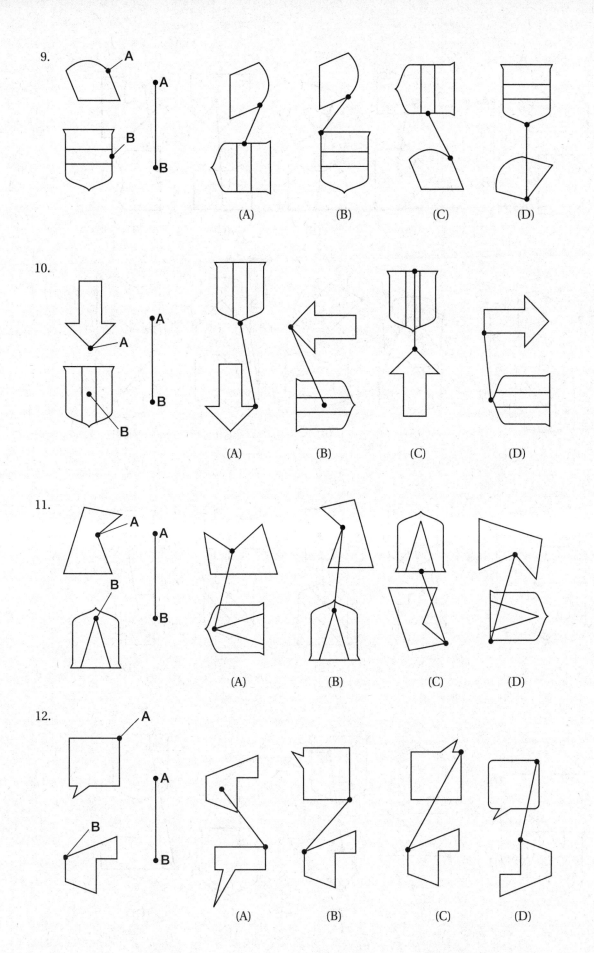

9.

(A) (B) (C) (D)

10.

(A) (B) (C) (D)

11.

(A) (B) (C) (D)

12.

(A) (B) (C) (D)

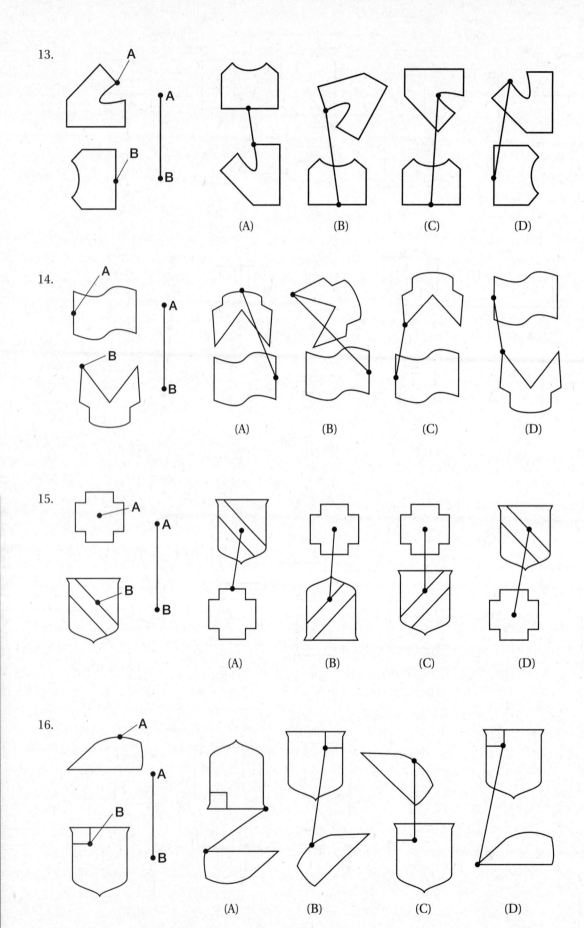

13.

(A) (B) (C) (D)

14.

(A) (B) (C) (D)

15.

(A) (B) (C) (D)

16.

(A) (B) (C) (D)

ANSWER KEY
Practice Exam Two

General Science—Subtest 1

1. **D**	6. **C**	11. **A**	16. **C**	21. **C**
2. **C**	7. **B**	12. **C**	17. **B**	22. **D**
3. **D**	8. **B**	13. **B**	18. **D**	23. **B**
4. **C**	9. **D**	14. **B**	19. **B**	24. **C**
5. **B**	10. **C**	15. **C**	20. **C**	25. **D**

Arithmetic Reasoning—Subtest 2

1. **B**	7. **D**	13. **D**	19. **D**	25. **D**
2. **D**	8. **D**	14. **A**	20. **A**	26. **A**
3. **A**	9. **A**	15. **C**	21. **B**	27. **B**
4. **B**	10. **A**	16. **B**	22. **C**	28. **A**
5. **D**	11. **D**	17. **D**	23. **B**	29. **D**
6. **B**	12. **C**	18. **B**	24. **D**	30. **C**

Word Knowledge—Subtest 3

1. **C**	8. **D**	15. **B**	22. **C**	29. **A**
2. **C**	9. **D**	16. **D**	23. **D**	30. **A**
3. **B**	10. **D**	17. **C**	24. **A**	31. **B**
4. **D**	11. **D**	18. **A**	25. **C**	32. **C**
5. **A**	12. **A**	19. **A**	26. **B**	33. **C**
6. **B**	13. **A**	20. **A**	27. **D**	34. **D**
7. **D**	14. **C**	21. **A**	28. **A**	35. **C**

Paragraph Comprehension—Subtest 4

1. **A**	4. **C**	7. **B**	10. **C**	13. **C**
2. **B**	5. **B**	8. **D**	11. **B**	14. **C**
3. **B**	6. **C**	9. **B**	12. **C**	15. **B**

Mathematics Knowledge—Subtest 5

1. **C**	6. **C**	11. **A**	16. **B**	21. **D**
2. **A**	7. **D**	12. **B**	17. **A**	22. **B**
3. **B**	8. **A**	13. **A**	18. **C**	23. **C**
4. **B**	9. **B**	14. **B**	19. **C**	24. **C**
5. **D**	10. **D**	15. **D**	20. **A**	25. **C**

Electronics Information—Subtest 6

1. **A**	5. **A**	9. **C**	13. **B**	17. **A**
2. **C**	6. **A**	10. **C**	14. **A**	18. **D**
3. **D**	7. **D**	11. **D**	15. **B**	19. **B**
4. **A**	8. **B**	12. **A**	16. **A**	20. **C**

Automotive & Shop Information—Subtest 7

1. **A**	6. **A**	11. **B**	16. **C**	21. **B**
2. **C**	7. **B**	12. **B**	17. **B**	22. **A**
3. **D**	8. **C**	13. **A**	18. **D**	23. **C**
4. **D**	9. **B**	14. **D**	19. **A**	24. **D**
5. **C**	10. **D**	15. **B**	20. **C**	25. **B**

Mechanical Comprehension—Subtest 8

1. **A**	6. **A**	11. **B**	16. **B**	21. **B**
2. **C**	7. **D**	12. **D**	17. **B**	22. **B**
3. **D**	8. **C**	13. **C**	18. **C**	23. **C**
4. **B**	9. **B**	14. **B**	19. **B**	24. **C**
5. **B**	10. **A**	15. **C**	20. **B**	25. **C**

Assembling Objects—Subtest 9

1. **B**	5. **A**	9. **C**	13. **D**
2. **A**	6. **C**	10. **B**	14. **D**
3. **D**	7. **D**	11. **A**	15. **D**
4. **B**	8. **A**	12. **B**	16. **C**

GENERAL SCIENCE—SUBTEST 1

1. **(D)** The sperm carries an X or Y chromosome, while all eggs normally have one X chromosome. An XX union results in a female, while the union of an X chromosome with a Y chromosome results in a male.

2. **(C)** Rocks do not conduct heat very quickly. If a rock becomes cold during the night but is rapidly heated during the day, the expansion and contraction may cause the outer layer to peel off. If water gets into a crack in the rock, freezing and thawing may cause the rock to split.

3. **(D)** Sand results from the weathering of igneous rock containing quartz crystals. Because of the relative hardness and insolubility of quartz, the crystals of quartz remain after other portions of the eroded rock have been dissolved or carried away.

4. **(C)** Vinegar contains acetic acid.

5. **(B)** All atoms of the same element have the same number of protons. In a neutral atom the number of electrons is the same as the number of protons. (Protons are inside the nucleus of an atom; electrons are outside it.) Atoms of the same element (isotopes) may differ in the number of neutrons.

6. **(C)** When heat is applied to a liquid at its boiling point, the added energy is used to separate the molecules from their neighbors, but no increase in the temperature of the liquid occurs. The molecules of vapor that leave the surface of the liquid possess increased potential energy because of the work done to overcome the forces acting on them.

7. **(B)** Nebulae are large clouds of gas and dust located between the stars. Our solar system is made up of the sun, the planets and their moons, and asteroids.

8. **(B)** Space is a nearly perfect vacuum. The process by which solar energy (in the form of ultraviolet rays) is transmitted through space is called *radiation.*

9. **(D)** The gene for hemophilia lies on the X chromosome; this condition is therefore inherited as a sex-linked disorder.

10. **(C)** Only living things can duplicate themselves.

11. **(A)** The thermometer that indicates the freezing point of water at 0 degrees and the boiling point of water at 100 degrees is known as the centigrade, or Celsius, thermometer.

12. **(C)** A steep surface will increase runoff since the water will flow rapidly, giving it little time to be absorbed by the soil. Vegetation will make the surface more porous, decreasing the runoff and thereby decreasing erosion of the soil.

13. **(B)** The 25-pound force is the resultant of two forces acting at right angles to each other. The resultant can be represented as the hypotenuse of a right triangle, with one side representing the 15-pound force and the other side the unknown (x) force. Then, applying the Pythagorean Theorem,

$$
\begin{aligned}
(\text{hypotenuse})^2 &= (\text{side})^2 + (\text{side})^2 \\
(25)^2 &= (15)^2 + x^2 \\
625 &= 225 + x^2 \\
400 &= x^2 \\
20 &= x
\end{aligned}
$$

14. **(B)** A hydrometer is used to test the specific gravity of the acid in a storage battery. The specific gravity is an index of the extent of charge of the battery.

15. **(C)** Fluorides are added to drinking water to reduce the occurrence of dental caries (cavities).

16. **(C)** A reflex is a simple inborn response. An instinct involves a series of reflexes. A habit is an acquired trait. Phototropism is a response that occurs in plants.

17. **(B)** The Rh factor is an inherited characteristic of the blood.

18. **(D)** Iron is part of hemoglobin, the pigment of red blood cells.

19. **(B)** Land heats up rapidly in summer and cools off rapidly in winter. The result is the climate found in continental interiors where the winters are extremely cold and the summers extremely hot.

20. **(C)** All freely falling objects, regardless of their masses near the earth, fall toward the earth with equal acceleration. Any two objects at rest that begin to fall at the same instant will have equal velocities at the end of three seconds or any other time interval.

21. **(C)** Living things carry on respiration at all times. Respiration in plants goes on independently of photosynthesis, which occurs only in the presence of sunlight.

22. **(D)** Where a place is heated, the warm air rises on overflows, far above the earth, toward a colder region. Meanwhile other unheated air flows in to take its place. This causes a horizontal air current which, when close to the earth's surface, is called wind.

23. **(B)** Mammals appeared most recently on earth.

24. **(C)** White light is a mixture of all of the colors of the spectrum. With the aid of a prism it can be separated into the individual colors.

25. **(D)** A solution has a high ratio of solute to solvent if there is a large amount of solute dissolved in a small amount of solvent. Such a solution, by definition, is a concentrated solution.

ARITHMETIC REASONING—SUBTEST 2

1. **(B)** This discount is 15 percent (or 0.15) of the marked price.

$$\$500 \times 0.15 = \$75$$

The cost is $500 − $75 = $425. Subtract the down payment to find the balance due.

$$\$425 - \$65 = \$360$$

Each installment is $\frac{1}{2}$ of $360.

$$\frac{\$360}{12} = \$30$$

2. **(D)** 2 gallons will cover $\frac{1}{4}$ acre.

4×2 gallons, or 8 gallons, will cover 1 acre.
10×8 gallons, or 80 gallons, will cover 10 acres.

Since 2 gallons cover $\frac{1}{4}$ acre, 2×2 gallons, or 4 gallons, cover $\frac{1}{2}$ acre.

80 gallons + 4 gallons, or 84 gallons, will cover $10\frac{1}{2}$ acres.

3. **(A)** The drawing and its enlargement will be similar. Therefore the lengths and widths will be in proportion.

$$\frac{\text{length of original}}{\text{length of enlargement}} = \frac{\text{width of original}}{\text{width of enlargement}}$$
$$\frac{18}{45} = \frac{12}{\text{width of enlargement } (x)}$$

Reduce $\frac{18}{45}$ by dividing the numerator and denominator by 9.

$$\frac{2}{5} = \frac{12}{x}$$

To solve, cross-multiply the measurements.

$$2 \times x = 5 \times 12 = 60$$
$$x = \frac{60}{2}$$
$$x = 3$$

4. **(B)** Divide the number of acceptable products by the total number inspected. Then change your answer to a percentage.

$$\frac{266}{280} = \frac{133}{140} = \frac{19}{20}$$
$$\frac{19}{20} = \frac{95}{100} = 0.95 = 95\%$$

5. **(D)** If 3 lbs. of candy cost $4.80, then 1 lb. costs $4.80 ÷ 3, or $1.60.
There are 16 oz. in 1 lb.

1 oz. of the mix costs $\dfrac{\$1.60}{16}$ = $0.10

5 oz. cost 5 × $0.10 = $0.50

6. **(B)** The perimeter of a square is the sum of the lengths of all four sides. But the four sides of a square are all equal in length.
The length of one side = 13 feet, 8 inches ÷ 4.
Change 1 foot to 12 inches so that 13 feet, 8 inches becomes 12 feet, 20 inches.
12 feet, 20 inches ÷ 4 = 3 feet, 5 inches

7. **(D)** If 20 percent of the unit are officers, then the percent of enlisted men is

$$100\% - 20\% = 80\%$$

To find the number of enlisted men, multiply the total number by 80 percent.

$$360 \times 0.80 = 288.00 = 288 \text{ enlisted men}$$

8. **(D)** Her overtime is 10 hours − 8 hours regular work = 2 hours.

2 hours at "time and a half" is paid as

$2 \times 1\frac{1}{2}$ hours, or $2 \times \frac{3}{2}$ hours, or $\frac{6}{2}$ hours, or 3 hours.

8 hours + 3 hours = 11 hours of pay.

$11 \times \$8.50 = \$93.50$

9. **(A)** Find the relationship between each pair of numbers in the series. Thus,

$$2\frac{1}{4}; \; 3\frac{3}{4} \quad 2\frac{1}{4} + 1\frac{1}{2} = 3\frac{3}{4}$$

$$3\frac{3}{4}; \; 3\frac{1}{4} \quad 3\frac{3}{4} - 2\frac{1}{2} = 3\frac{1}{4}$$

$$3\frac{1}{4}; \; 4\frac{3}{4} \quad 3\frac{1}{4} + 1\frac{1}{2} = 4\frac{3}{4}$$

The pattern so far is

$$+1\frac{1}{2}, \; -1\frac{1}{2}, \; +1\frac{1}{2}$$

To continue the series, subtract $\frac{1}{2}$ from the fourth member of the series.

$$4\frac{3}{4} - \frac{1}{2} = 4\frac{1}{4}$$

10. **(A)** Find the amount collected for adult tickets.

$$265 \times \$4 = \$1,060$$

Out of the $1,200 in receipts, the remainder came from the sale of children's tickets.

$$\$140 \div \$2 = 70 \text{ tickets}$$

11. **(D)** If she budgets $\frac{1}{4}$ of her income for rent, she has $\frac{3}{4}$ of her income left.

$$\frac{5}{4} - \frac{1}{5} = \frac{3}{4} \text{ (remainder)}$$

She then budgets $\frac{2}{5}$ of this remainder for food.

$$\frac{2}{5} \times \frac{3}{4} = \frac{6}{20} = \frac{3}{10} \text{ (food)}$$

12. **(C)** The three people who watched two hours each watched a total of 3×2 hours, or 6 hours. The 2 who watched 1 hour each watched a total of 2×1 hours, or 2 hours; 1 watched for 4 hours.
Add the numbers of hours watched.
6 + 2 + 4 = 12 hours (total time spent).
Add the number of people.
3 + 2 + 1 = 6 persons were in the group. Divide the total time spent by the number of persons in the group to find the average number of hours one person watches.
12 hours ÷ 6 persons = 2 hours per person average.

13. **(D)** Multiply the cost per yard by the length of the material in yards.

3 feet = 1 yard, so 2 feet = $\frac{2}{3}$ yard.

3 yards, 2 feet = $3\frac{2}{3}$ yards.

$$\$9 \times 3\frac{2}{3} = \frac{9}{1} = \frac{11}{3} = \$33$$

14. **(A)** Let x represent one of the 9 shares in which the profit must be divided. According to the ratio agreed on, the smaller partner's share is $4x$ and the larger partner's share is $5x$. Together the shares must add up to the $63,000 profit. This can be written as an equation.

$$4x + 5x = 63,000$$

Solve by combining similar terms.

$$9x = 63,000$$
$$x = 7,000 \text{ (one share)}$$

Multiply the value of 1 share by the number of shares the smaller partner is to get

$$4x = 4 \times 7,000 = \$28,000$$

15. **(C)** The first courier will travel for 1 hour + 2 hours, or a total of 3 hours, before he is overtaken. Traveling 30 miles per hour for 3 hours will take the first courier 30×3 or 90 miles away.

The second courier must travel the 90 miles in 2 hours. Therefore, he must travel at a rate of $90 \div 2$ or 45 miles per hour.

16. **(B)** Find the discounted price paid by the merchant.

$60 \times 25\% = \$60 \times 0.25 = \$15$ (discount)

$60 - \$15 = \$45$ (price paid by the merchant)

Next find the merchant's selling price, based on an increase of 20 percent over the original wholesale price.

$60 \times 20\% = \$60 \times 0.20$ or

$\$60 \times \frac{1}{5} = \$12$ (increase over wholesale price)

$\$60 + \$12 = \$72$ (merchant's selling price)

Finally, find the merchant's profit.

$$\$72 - \$45 = \$27$$

17. **(B)** To find the rate of speed when the distance and the time are known, divide the distance, x, by the time, y.

x divided by y is expressed as $\frac{x}{y}$

18. **(B)** Since the first 10 words cost $1.50, the balance is left for the cost of the remaining words.

$$\$4.00 - \$1.50 = \$2.50$$

To find the number of words $2.50 will pay for at $0.05 per word, divide $2.50 by $0.05.

$2.50 \div \$0.05 = 250 \div 5$ (clearing decimals)

$250 \div 5 = 50$ words

50 words added to the first 10 words makes a total of 60 words.

19. **(D)** Since 1 inch represents 40 miles, divide 110 miles by 40 miles to find the number of inches required to represent it.

$$110 \div 40 = \frac{110}{40} = \frac{11}{4} = 2\frac{3}{4} \text{ inches}$$

20. **(A)** Multiply the purchase price of the home by the assessment rate to find the assessed value.

$$\$80{,}000 \times 75\% = \$80{,}000 \times \frac{3}{4} =$$

$$\frac{80{,}000}{1} \times \frac{3}{4} = \frac{20{,}000}{1} \times \frac{3}{1} =$$

$$\$60{,}000 \text{ (assessed value)}$$

$$\$60{,}000 \text{ (assessed value)}$$

Find the number of hundreds in the assessed value.

$$60{,}000 \div 100 = 600 \text{ (hundreds)}$$

Multiply the number of hundreds by the tax rate.

$$600 \times \$4.83 = \$2{,}898.00 \text{ (tax)}$$

21. **(B)** Set up a proportion.

$$\frac{\text{recipe sugar}}{\text{sugar actually used}} = \frac{\text{recipe flour}}{\text{flour actually used}}$$

$$\frac{\frac{3}{4}\text{cup}}{\frac{1}{4}\text{cup}} = \frac{4\frac{1}{2}\text{cups}}{x \text{ cups}} \text{ or } \frac{\frac{3}{4}}{\frac{1}{4}} = \frac{\frac{9}{2}}{x}$$

Simplify each side of the proportion.

$$\frac{3}{4} \div \frac{1}{4} = \frac{3}{4} \times \frac{4}{1} = \frac{3}{1}$$

$$\frac{9}{2} \div \frac{x}{1} = \frac{9}{2} \times \frac{1}{x} = \frac{9}{2x}$$

Solve the proportion by cross-multiplying.

$$6x = 9$$

Divide each side of the equation by 6 to find the value of x.

$$x = \frac{9}{6} = 1\frac{1}{2} \text{ cups of flour}$$

22. **(C)** Find the amount of the decline by subtracting.

$$1{,}200 - 1{,}044 = 156$$

To find the percent of decline, divide the amount of the decline by the original number of cars crossing the bridge.

$$156 \div 1{,}200 = \frac{156}{1{,}200} = \frac{13}{100} = 13\%$$

23. **(B)** First find the cost of 1 gallon. If 2 gallons cost $19.20, 1 gallon will cost $19.20 ÷ 2 or $9.60.

There are 4 quarts in 1 gallon. Divide the cost of 1 gallon by 4 to find the cost of 1 quart.

$$\$9.60 \div 4 = \$2.40$$

24. **(D)** Find the distance he drove on each leg of the trip by multiplying the rate in miles per hour by the time in hours.

$$50 \times 3 = 150 \text{ miles}$$
$$55 \times 2 = 110 \text{ miles}$$

Add the two distances to get the total distance he traveled.

$$150 + 110 \text{ miles} = 260 \text{ miles}$$

Divide the total distance traveled by the number of miles per gallon of gas to get the amount of gas used.

$$260 \div 20 = 13 \text{ gallons}$$

25. **(D)** First find the income from the $5,000 invested at 8 percent.

$$\$5,000 \times 0.08 = \$400.00$$

Next find the income desired from the total investment of $15,000.

$$\$15,000 \times 0.09 = \$1,350.00$$

Subtract the income from the first investment to find out how much income she must get from the second.

$$\$1,350 - \$400 = \$950$$

Divide the income, $950, by the investment, $10,000, to find the rate of interest.

$$\$950 \div \$10,000 = \frac{950}{10,000} = \frac{95}{1,000} = 0.095 \text{ or } 9.5 \text{ percent}$$

26. **(A)** Find the number of hours the generator operates.
From 9:15 A.M. to 3:15 P.M. is 6 hours.

From 3:15 P.M. to 3:55 P.M. is 40 minutes (or $\frac{2}{3}$ of an hour).

6 hours + 40 minutes = $6\frac{2}{3}$ hours.

Divide the total time run by the time provided by one fuel tank filling

(1 hour, 20 minutes, or $1\frac{1}{3}$ hours).

$$6\frac{2}{3} \div 1\frac{1}{3} = \frac{20}{3} \times \frac{3}{4} = 5 \text{ fillings}$$

27. **(B)** Find the total value of each kind of seed in the mixture.
10 pounds at $1.20 per pound is worth 10 × $1.20, or $12.00.
8 pounds at $3.00 per pound is worth 8 × $3.00, or $24.00.
Add the values of each kind to get the total value of the mixture.

$$\$12.00 + \$24.00 = \$36.00$$

Divide the total value of the mixture by the total number of pounds, 18, to get price per pound.

$$\$36.00 \div 18 = \$2.00 \text{ per pound}$$

28. **(A)** First multiply out the numerator.

$$\frac{0.02 \times 3}{0.001} = \frac{0.06}{0.001}$$

Clear the decimal in the divider by moving the decimal point in both numerator and denominator three places to the right.

$$\frac{0.06}{0.001} = \frac{60}{1} = 60$$

29. **(D)** Substitute the number values for the letters and then do the arithmetic operations.

$$1 + 5xy^2 - 3x^2y =$$
$$1 + (5 \times x \times y^2) - (3 \times x^2 \times y) =$$
$$1 + (5 \times 3 \times 2^2) - (3 \times 3^2 \times 2) =$$
$$1 + (5 \times 3 \times 3 \times 4) - (3 \times 9 \times 2) =$$
$$1 + 60 - 54 = 7$$

30. **(C)** Substitute the number values for P and R.

$$I = \sqrt{\frac{P}{R}}$$
$$I = \sqrt{\frac{48}{3}}$$
$$I = \sqrt{16}$$

The square root of 16 is the number that when multiplied by itself is 16; therefore $\sqrt{16} = 4$

$$I = 4$$

WORD KNOWLEDGE—SUBTEST 3

1. **(C)** *Tell*, like **inform**, means to communicate knowledge or give information.

2. **(C)** **Crimson** is a vivid reddish color.

3. **(B)** **Caution** means forethought to avoid danger or harm; carefulness.

4. **(D)** **Intermittently** means starting and stopping, as in rain starting and stopping at irregular intervals.

5. **(A)** *Event*, like **occurrence**, means a happening or incident.

6. **(B)** *Fraud*, like **deception**, means the use of deceit.

7. **(D)** *Stop*, like **cease**, means to end.

8. **(D)** *Applause*, like **acclaim**, means enthusiastic approval.

9. **(D)** *Construct*, like **erect**, means to raise upright, as to erect or construct a building.

10. **(D)** *Enjoy*, like **relish**, means to take pleasure in.

11. **(D)** **Sufficient** means enough, adequate. Of the words given, *sufficient* most nearly means appropriate, as in a sufficient or appropriate amount.

12. **(A)** **Fortnight** means two weeks.

13. **(A)** A *defect*, like a **blemish**, is an imperfection or fault.

14. **(C)** To **impose** or *require* means to make compulsory.

15. **(B)** *Scoff*, like **jeer**, means to mock or poke fun at.

16. **(D)** An *assumed name* is an **alias**.

17. **(C)** *Weaken*, like **impair**, means to worsen or to damage.

18. **(A)** **Itinerant** means *traveling*, as in an itinerant salesperson.

19. **(A)** **Relinquish**, like *abandon*, means to give up possession.

20. **(A)** **Resolve** means to bring to a conclusion or *end*.

21. **(A)** *Plentiful*, like **ample**, means existing in great quantity.

22. **(C)** A **stench** is a *foul odor*, a stink.

23. **(D)** *Angrily silent*, means about the same as **sullen**.

24. **(A)** **Rudiments** are basic methods and procedures.

25. **(C)** To *conflict*, or **clash**, means to disagree or to be in opposition.

26. **(B)** **Camaraderie** means goodwill and rapport among friends.

27. **(D)** *Cursory*, like **superficial**, means hasty, not thorough.

28. **(A)** A **tapestry** is a fabric with multicolored woven designs.

29. **(A)** **Terse**, or *pointed*, as in a terse or pointed comment, means brief but expressing a great deal.

30. **(A)** A *combination of ingredients*, as in cooking, is a **concoction**.

31. **(B)** *Shortness*, or **brevity**, means briefness of duration.

32. **(C)** *Mercy*, like **clemency**, means leniency, especially toward an offender or enemy.

33. **(C)** *Disobedience*, like **insubordination**, means failure to recognize or accept authority.

34. **(D)** **Preferential** means having or obtaining an advantage, as in receiving *special* treatment.

35. **(C)** *Low spirits*, like **doldrums**, are marked by listlessness, inactivity, or depression.

PARAGRAPH COMPREHENSION—SUBTEST 4

1. **(A)** The main idea of this paragraph is given in the first sentence, which states that professional drivers have a low opinion of the average motorist.

2. **(B)** In this selection the word *shuddered* means shook.

3. **(B)** The paragraph clearly states that the Swedes and Finns "these two European peoples" were the first to use log cabins.

4. **(C)** The tone or mood of this passage is one of contentment. The man is described as at rest with a smile on his face.

5. **(B)** This paragraph points out the favorable or good points about apprentice training. It does not discuss any negative or bad points, and it does not compare it to any other type of training.

6. **(C)** The paragraph states, "We never have enough closets no matter how many closets we have."

7. **(B)** A reactionary person looks to the past. The paragraph describes a classical, using the key words *liberated* and *free*. The words *on the other hand* tell you that the description is about to shift from one way to another.

8. **(D)** You can infer from the passage that a conservation group wrote it. A lumber company or house-building company would more likely want to cut down the forest to use the lumber in its businesses. There is no reason to think that a religious group wrote the paragraph.

9. **(B)** The "time for action" phrase suggests that the bridge should be built, but the paragraph makes it clear that official action—approval of bonds—must be taken first.

10. **(C)** The paragraph describes lightning as a "spark" and as a "release of energy."

11. **(B)** The paragraph clearly states that the morning rush hour starts two hours before 9 A.M.

12. **(C)** Acuity means sharpness. If you do not know the meaning of the word, you can figure it out from the context. You can immediately eliminate choice A; you can eliminate D because pressure is referred to in the phrase "eye pressure." You must then choose between strength and sharpness, and in terms of the subject of this passage—vision—sharpness is more accurate.

13. **(C)** More than one seed of wheat has to be tested to form a conclusion.

14. **(C)** The last sentence states that bread and cereal provide 40 percent of the daily need for thiamine, one of the B vitamins.

15. **(B)** The second sentence states that most problems came from poor medical knowledge and lack of ways to fight disease.

MATHEMATICS KNOWLEDGE—SUBTEST 5

1. **(C)** First isolate all terms containing x on one side of the equation and all terms not containing x on the other side. To do this, add x to both sides of the equation and also subtract 6 from both sides of the equation. Remember to change the sign of any term when it is moved from one side of the equation to the other.

$$2x + x + 6 - 6 = 12 - 6 - x + x$$
$$3x = 6$$

Divide each side of the equation by 3 to undo the multiplication of 3 by x.

$$\frac{3x}{3} = \frac{6}{3}$$
$$x = 2$$

2. **(A)** Write the binomial to be subtracted underneath the binomial from which it is to be subtracted, placing similar terms in the same columns.

$$\text{From} \qquad 8x^2 - 7x$$
$$\text{Subtract} \quad -3x^2 + 2x$$

Change the signs of the terms in the bottom row (the subtrahend) and combine the similar terms in each column.

$$8x^2 - 7x$$
$$\underline{3x^2 - 2x}$$
$$11x^2 - 9x$$

3. **(B)** Multiply $3x^2y$ by $2x^3y$ and also multiply -4 by $2x^3y$. To multiply $3x^2y$ by $2x^3y$, first multiply their numerical factors.

$$3 \times 2 = 6$$

To multiply powers of the same letter, add the exponents.
Remember that y stands for y^1.
Thus, $x^2 \times x^3 = x^5$ and $y \times y = y^2$.
$2x^3y \times (3x^2y - 4) = 6x^5y^2 - 8x^3y$

4. **(B)** Add the portions that each one does.

$$\frac{1}{3} + \frac{1}{5}$$

To add fractions, they must have a common denominator. The least common denominator for 3 and 5 is 15, the smallest number into which they both divide evenly.

Change $\frac{1}{3}$ and $\frac{1}{5}$ to equivalent fractions having 15 as their denominator. Fractions

with the same denominator may be added by adding their numerators.

$$\frac{5}{15} + \frac{3}{15} = \frac{8}{15}$$

5. **(D)** Subtract the length of the piece to be cut off.

5 feet, 3 inches
−3 feet, 9 inches

Since we cannot subtract 9 inches from 3 inches, we borrow 1 foot from the 5 feet and convert it to 12 inches; thus 5 feet, 3 inches becomes 4 feet, 15 inches.

4 feet, 15 inches
−3 feet, 9 inches
1 foot, 6 inches

6. **(C)** A hexagon is a polygon having 6 sides. If it has 6 sides, it must also have 6 angles.

The sum of the 6 equal angles is 6 times the size of one of them.

$$6 \times 120° = 720°$$

7. **(D)** Set up the product like a multiplication example in arithmetic. Multiply each term of $(3a - 2)$ by a and write the results as the first line of partial products. Remember that the product of a positive number and a negative number is negative. Next multiply

each term of $(3a - 2)$ by $+ 3$ and write the results as the second line of partial products. Add the partial products as you do in arithmetic to get the final answer.

$$
\begin{array}{r}
3a - 2 \\
a + 3 \\
\hline
3a^2 - 2a \\
+\, 9a - 6 \\
\hline
3a^2 + 7a - 6
\end{array}
$$

8. **(A)** Substitute 3 for x in the given expression.

$$|x - 7|\ \text{becomes}\ |3 - 7|\ \text{or}\ |-4|$$

$|-4|$ stands for the absolute value of -4. The absolute value of a number is its value without regard to sign. Thus, $|+4|$ equals 4, and $|-4|$ also equals 4.

9. **(B)** To solve these equations for x, we must eliminate y. First multiply both sides of the first equation by 2.

$$2 \times (3x + y) = 2 \times 13$$
$$6x + 2y = 26$$

Adding the original second equation to the new form of the first equation will eliminate y.

$$
\begin{array}{r}
6x + 2y = 26 \\
x - 2y = 2 \\
\hline
7x \phantom{{}+ 2y} = 28
\end{array}
$$

Divide both sides of the equation by 7 to undo the multiplication of x by 7.

$$\frac{7x}{7} = \frac{28}{7}$$
$$x = 4$$

10. **(D)** Convert all units of measure to inches.
    In 1 yard, there are 36 inches, so in y yards there are y times as many, or $36y$. The total length of y yards and i inches, expressed in inches, is $36y + i$ inches.
    There are 12 inches in 1 foot. To find the number of feet in $36y + i$ inches, divide $36y + i$ by 12.
    The goal is to find an equation with

$$(36y + i) \div 12 = \frac{36y + i}{12}$$

11. **(A)** F alone on one side and all other letters and numbers on the other side.
    Begin by multiplying both sides of the formula by 9 to get rid of the fraction.

$$9 \times C = 9 \times \frac{5}{9}(F - 32)$$
$$9C = 5(F - 32)$$

Next remove the parentheses by multiplying each term inside them by 5.

$$9C = 5 \times F - 5 \times 32$$
$$9C = 5F - 160$$

To isolate the term containing *F* on one side of the equation, add 160 to both sides of the equation.

$$9C + 160 = 5F - 160 + 160$$
$$9C + 160 = 5F$$

To get an expression for *F* alone, divide both sides of the equation by 5.

$$\frac{9C + 160}{5} = \frac{5F}{5}$$
$$\frac{9}{5}C + 32 = F$$

The equation may be transposed to read

$$F = \frac{9}{5}C + 32$$

12. **(B)** The path directly east forms a right angle with the path directly north. The distance from the starting point is measured on the third side (or hypotenuse) of the right triangle, which contains the paths to the east and to the north.

    The Pythagorean Theorem states that in any right triangle, the square of the hypotenuse (c^2) equals the sum of the square of the other two sides, $a^2 + b^2$.

    $$\text{Thus, } c^2 = a^2 + b^2$$
    $$c^2 = 3^2 + 4^2$$

    Perform the arithmetic operations.

    $$c^2 = 9 + 16$$
    $$c^2 = 25$$

    To find *c*, take the square root of both sides of the equation. The square root of a number is another number which, when multiplied by itself, equals the original number. Thus, the square root of 25 is 5, and the square root of c^2 is *c*.

    $$c = 5$$

13. **(A)** The line perpendicular to the base of the triangle makes a right angle with the base; a right angle contains 90 degrees.
    An equilateral triangle has 3 equal sides and 3 equal angles. Since the sum of all three angles of any triangle is 180 degrees, each angle of an equilateral triangle is $\frac{180°}{3}$ or 60 degrees.

    The 60-degree angle must be subtracted from the 90-degree angle to find the angle formed by the perpendicular and the other side of the triangle.

    $$90° - 60° = 30°$$

14. **(B)** The inequality, $x - 5 \leq 5$, is a statement that *x* minus 6 is less than or equal to 5. To solve this inequality, isolate *x* on one side of it by adding 6 to both sides.

    $$x - 6 + 6 \leq 5 + 6$$
    $$x \leq 11$$

The solution states that the inequality is true if x has any value less than or equal to 11. For example, suppose $x = 9$. Substitute 9 for x in the original inequality:

$$9 - 6 \le 5 + 6$$
$$x \le 11 \text{ (this is the answer)}$$

Now, let's test the solution, which states that the inequality is true if x has any value less than or equal to 11. For example, suppose $x = 9$. Substitute 9 for x in the original inequality:

$$9 - 6 \le 5$$
$$3 \le 5, \text{ which is a true statement}$$

15. **(D)** If the same fence fits around the rectangle and the square field, then their perimeters are equal. The perimeter of a rectangle is the sum of the lengths of its four sides.

$$P = 40 + 36 + 40 + 36 = 152 \text{ feet}$$

The perimeter of a square is the sum of its four equal sides. Therefore, the length of one side is the perimeter divided by 4.

$$152 \div 4 = 38 \text{ feet}$$

16. **(B)** The volume of a rectangular box is equal to the length times the width times the height.

The volume of one individual-sized box = $3 \times 2 \times 4 = 24$ cubic inches.

The volume of one family-sized box = $8 \times 3 \times 12 = 8 \times 36 = 288$ cubic inches.

Divide the volume of the larger box by the volume of the smaller box.

$$288 \div 24 = 12$$

17. **(A)** Rotation of a wheel as it rolls on the ground has the effect of "laying out" its circumference along the ground. One rotation will move the wheel along by a distance equal to the circumference. The circumference, C, of a circle is given by the formula $C = 2 \times \pi \times R$, where R is the radius, or by the formula $C = \pi \times D$, where D is the diameter. If the first formula is used, R can be computed since the radius is one-half the diameter. However, it is easier in this case to use the second formula since we are given the diameter.

$$C = \frac{22}{7} \times 14 = \frac{22}{7} \times \frac{14}{1} = \frac{22}{1} \times \frac{2}{1} = 44 \text{ inches}$$

18. **(C)** The sine of an angle in a right triangle is the ratio of the length of the side opposite the angle to the length of the hypotenuse. If the unknown length is x, the ratio of x to the length of the hypotenuse must be the same as the ratio $\frac{3}{7}$.

$$\frac{x}{21} = \frac{3}{7}$$

To solve for x in this proportion, cross-multiply.

$$7 \times x = 3 \times 21$$
$$7x = 63$$

To undo the multiplication of 7 by x, divide both sides of the equation by 7.

$$\frac{7x}{7} = \frac{63}{7} = 9$$

19. **(C)** $-x^4$ means $-(x)(x)(x)(x)$.

Substitute 0.1 for x.

$$-x^4 = -(0.1)(0.1)(0.1)(0.1)$$

To multiply $(0.1)(0.1)(0.1)(0.1)$, remember that the number of decimal places in the product is the total of the number of decimal places in the numbers being multiplied together.

$$-x^4 = -0.0001$$

20. **(A)** Change 30 percent to a decimal and let x represent the total number of apartments; 30 percent of x is 108.

$$0.30x = 108 \text{ or } 0.3x = 108$$

Clear the decimals by multiplying both sides of the equation by 10.

$$10 \times 0.3x = 10 \times 108$$
$$3x = 1{,}080$$

Undo the multiplication of 3 by x by dividing both sides of the equation by 3.

$$\frac{3x}{3} = \frac{1{,}080}{3}$$
$$x = 360$$

21. **(D)** Let x equal the grade on the fourth test. The average is obtained by dividing the sum of the four grades by 4.

$$\frac{60+60+70+x}{4} = 75$$

To remove the fraction, multiply both sides of the equation by 4.

$$4 \times \frac{60+60+70+x}{4} = 4 \times 75$$
$$60+60+70+x = 300$$
$$190+x = 300$$

To isolate x on one side, subtract 190 from both sides of the equation.

$$190 - 190 + x = 300 - 190$$
$$x = 110$$

He would need a grade of 110 on the fourth test, which is impossible.

22. **(B)** First find the distance traveled.

Distance traveled is found by multiplying rate of speed by time.

3 hours $\times$ 40 miles per hour = 120 miles

2 hours $\times$ 50 miles per hour = 100 miles

The entire trip was 120 miles + 100 miles, or 220 miles.

The total time was 3 hours + 2 hours, or 5 hours.

The average rate of speed is obtained by dividing the total distance by the total time.

220 miles $\div$ 5 hours = 44 miles per hour

23. **(C)** The radar is capable of covering a complete circle whose radius is 10 miles.

First find the area of this circle, using the formula $A = \pi \times R^2$, where R is the radius.

$A = 3.14 \times 10^2 = 3.14 \times 100 = 314$ square miles.

There are 360 degrees of rotation in the complete circle. If the radar is used to cover a portion of this, it covers $\frac{36}{360}$ or $\frac{1}{10}$ of the complete circle.

$$\frac{1}{10} \times 314 = 31.4 \text{ square miles}$$

24. **(C)** To solve a quadratic equation like $x^2 + 2x = 15$, first move all terms to the same side of the equation so that they equal 0 on the other side.

$$x^2 + 2x - 15 = 0$$

Find the two binomial factors that would multiply to produce the polynomial on the left side. The factors of the first term, x^2, are x and x. Use them as the first term in each of the binomial factors.

$$(x \quad)(x \quad) = 0$$

Now find the two numbers that would multiply together to give 15. They could be 15 and 1 or 5 and 3. Remember that when multiplying the two binomials together, $+2x$ must result for the middle term. This suggests that $+5x$ and $-3x$ were added to give $+2x$. Therefore, $+5$ and -3 are the factors to choose for -15.

$$(x + 5)(x - 3) = 0$$

The equation is now in a form in which the product of two factors equals 0. This is possible if either one or both of the factors equals 0.

$$x + 5 = 0 \qquad\qquad x - 3 = 0$$
$$x = -5 \qquad\qquad x = 3$$

These results may be checked by substituting them in the original equation.

$$
\begin{array}{ll}
x^2 + 2x = 15 & x^2 + 2x = 15 \\
(-5)^2 + 2(-5) = 15 & (3)^2 + 2(3) = 15 \\
25 - 10 = 15 & 9 + 6 = 15 \\
15 = 15 & 15 = 15
\end{array}
$$

25. **(C)** First find the number of quarts of antifreeze in the original mixture.

0.25×12 or $\frac{1}{4} \times 12 = 3$ quarts of antifreeze

Let x equal the number of quarts of water to be added. The total mixture will now be $12 + x$ quarts; 20 percent of the new total mixture will be the 3 quarts of antifreeze still present in the mixture.

$$0.20(12 + x) = 3 \text{ or } 0.2(12 + x) = 3$$

Remove the parentheses by multiplying each term inside by .2.

$$2.4 + 0.2x = 3$$

Clear decimals by multiplying each term in the equation by 10.

$$10 \times 2.4 + 10 \times 0.2x = 10 \times 3$$
$$24 + 2x = 30$$

Isolate the term containing x by subtracting 24 from both sides of the equation.

$$24 - 24 + 2x = 30 - 24$$
$$2x = 6$$

Undo the multiplication of 2 by x by dividing both sides of the equation by 2.

$$\frac{2x}{x} = \frac{6}{2}$$
$$x = 3$$

ELECTRONICS INFORMATION—SUBTEST 6

1. **(A)** Inserting copper inside a coil makes the inductance decrease.

2. **(C)** Permeability is the ease with which magnetic lines of force distribute themselves throughout a material.

3. **(D)** The area of the plates, the distance between the plates, and the material of the dielectric all have a direct relationship on the capacitance of a capacitor. The voltage on the capacitor does not have an effect on its capacitance.

4. **(A)** When capacitors are placed in series, it is the same as placing the plates farther apart. This causes a *decrease* in the amount of capacitance for the series combination.

5. **(A)** Capacitive reactance is equal to the reciprocal of the product of $2\pi \times FC$.

6. **(A)** Capacitors connected in parallel effectively *increase* the plate area, allowing for more storage of electrons and more capacity or capacitance.

7. **(D)** Resonance occurs in any circuit when the inductive reactance and the capacitive reactance are equal.

8. **(B)** The impedance of a series *RL* circuit can be found by taking the square root of the sum of the squares of the resistance and the inductance. The inductance is in henrys and the resistance is in ohms.

9. **(C)** A filter is placed in the power supply to *smooth out the voltage variations*. In some cases a choke is used in the filter to smooth out the current variations.

10. **(C)** Another name for the transistor is the *crystal amplifier*. It has also been called the *transfer resistor*, from which it takes its common name, *transistor*.

11. **(D)** Radio frequency amplifiers are used in *receivers and transmitters* to amplify frequencies above the human hearing range.

12. **(A)** A crystal microphone relies on the *piezoelectric effect*, where a pressure on a crystal produces an electric current.

13. **(B)** The voice coil of a speaker usually has a very low impedance. Some specially made speakers have higher impedances to match the system.

14. **(A)** A crossover network is designed to make sure that the right frequencies get to a speaker so it can reproduce them better.

15. **(B)** The klystron is used as a frequency source in microwave units—whether it be a microwave range for the kitchen or a radar unit for an aircraft.

16. **(A)** The two basic types of oscillators used in microwave installations are the *klystron* and the magnetron.

17. **(A)** The two general types of diodes are the semiconductor and the *vacuum tube diode*. Both types have particular applications and advantages.

18. **(D)** Color television uses red, blue, and green "guns" to direct electron streams toward the phosphors in the front of the picture tube. They produce the full-color spectrum when combined properly.

19. **(B)** The folded dipole antenna has an impedance of 300 ohms. It is the one most commonly used for home television reception. The dipole has an impedance of 72 ohms.

20. **(C)** Television sets in the United States use a horizontal frequency of 15,750 Hz, while those in Europe use 15,625 Hz. There are 525 lines that make up the television picture in the United States but 625 in Europe. The vertical oscillator frequency is 60 Hz in the United States but 50 in Europe.

AUTOMOTIVE & SHOP INFORMATION—SUBTEST 7

1. **(A)** The universal joint allows the drive shaft to flex up and down as the road surface changes. At least one, and in most instances two, are needed for rear-wheel-drive cars and trucks.

2. **(C)** Lots of attention has been given to the pollutants emitted from internal combustion engines. Nitrous oxides (NO_x) are of particular concern, and the air pump and the catalytic converter are designed to reduce these emissions. Hydrocarbons, carbon monoxide, and the oxides of nitrogen are concerns since they can contaminate the air and kill trees, plants, and small animals, as well as damage the lungs of humans.

3. **(D)** The catalytic converter eliminates some pollutants and reduces other pollutants. It reaches high temperatures and needs to be shielded from the body of the car by a heat deflector. An air pump is used on most cars to add to the combustion that takes place inside the converter and helps to reduce the amount of NO_x emitted from the exhaust pipe.

4. **(D)** The differential is located in the rear of the car when it is a rear-wheel-drive vehicle. It is located in front of the car on a front-wheel-drive vehicle. It consists of *two small bevel gears on the ends of the axle shafts* that are mounted in the differential frame. These bevel gears mesh with others to allow one wheel to turn faster than the other whenever the car makes a turn.

5. **(C)** The PCV valve is used to recirculate the fumes that would normally be exhausted to the atmosphere from the crankcase. By recirculating these fumes it is possible to cut down on the hydrocarbon contents of auto exhaust. This valve provides *positive crankcase ventilation* from the valve cover through the carburetor for recirculation.

6. **(A)** One of the ways to reduce the NO_x produced by the combustion of the internal combustion engine is to *dilute the air/fuel mixture as it enters the combustion chamber.*

7. **(B)** The number of teeth in a gear determines its speed when meshed with a second gear with similar teeth. The number of teeth in one gear is compared to the number of teeth in the one it meshes with. The number of teeth in the first gear as compared to the second is the gear ratio. If, for instance, one gear has 16 teeth and the one it meshes with has only 8, the gear ratio is 2:1 or 2 to 1. *The gear with the greater number*

of teeth always turns slower and produces greater torque than the gear with the smaller number of teeth.

8. **(C)** The clutch is used to disconnect the engine from the wheels while the car is in neutral or when gears are being shifted.

9. **(B)** The first gear is used because of its ability to produce the starting torque needed to get the car moving from a standstill.

10. **(D)** The torque converter is located in the *automatic transmission.* It produces the torque needed to get the car started and to change speeds. Most torque converter transmissions also provide an intermediate and low gear range that can aid in braking the car when coming down steep hills and in hard pulling.

11. **(B)** Disc brakes use two pads to grasp the rotor that is attached to the wheel. The pads press against the rotor (disc) from both sides to make a faster and surer stop with little fading on hot days and with heavy braking.

12. **(B)** The "transmission" on front-wheel cars is located in the engine compartment. It must be small enough to fit into the space allowed for the engine and the accessories.

13. **(A)** The folding rule is well known for breaking easily when it is twisted even a little bit.

14. **(D)** The mitre box uses the back saw—the one with the metal band across the top of it—to cut angles as needed or provided by the type of mitre box being used.

15. **(B)** In order to shape concrete it is placed in a *form.*

16. **(C)** In concrete work the "darby" is made of wood and is used to float the concrete after it has set for the proper length of time.

17. **(B)** Nail sets are used to *set nails just below the surface of the wood.* Then a filler is added before painting or finishing so that there is a smooth surface.

18. **(D)** A scratch awl is used to do many things, one of which is to mark wood where you want to cut it. A saw is used to cut wood. A plane is used to smooth wood. A screwdriver is used to drive screws.

19. **(A)** In selecting the proper grinding wheel there are a number of things to be considered, one of the most important being the *proper grain size* for the job to be done.

20. **(C)** Gold can be hammered into leaves so thin that it takes a fine camel hair brush to pick them up. This is usually the way gold is placed on the domes of state capitol buildings. Once placed on the surface, it is burnished or rubbed with a piece of smooth metal to make the extremely thin foil stick to the surface being coated.

21. **(B)** When making a hole in sheet metal, it is safer for the person performing the work to *punch* the hole rather than drill it. If the piece of sheet metal is not properly secured, the drill bit will catch and cause it to be whirled, possibly cutting the operator who may not be quick enough to get out of the way of the spinning object.

22. **(A)** Rapid, uncontrolled drying of wood causes checking and cracking, which is why new lumber is sometimes submerged in water until it is ready to be cut.

23. **(C)** A bumping hammer is used by auto body repair workers to *smooth out dents.* A peen or machinist's hammer is used for riveting or to indent or compress metal.

24. **(D)** Steel is an alloy of iron made with carbon and magnesium that does not rust and that has added strength; therefore, the answer is "all of the above."

25. **(B)** Bolting and riveting provide *a temporary or semipermanent connection*. Welding produces a permanent connection between two metals.

MECHANICAL COMPREHENSION—SUBTEST 8

1. **(A)** When oncoming air meets the leading edge of the wing, part flows over the top and part flows underneath. The air flowing over the top of the wing has to go farther in the same amount of time because it must meet the air underneath the wing at the far side—physical laws act together to prevent or minimize vacuums in most cases. Because the air flowing over the top must go faster than that underneath, the pressure on the top of the wing is decreased, whereas the pressure underneath the wing remains relatively unchanged. Therefore, most of the lift on an aircraft's wing is because of a decrease in pressure on the wing's upper side.

2. **(C)** *Capillary action* is responsible for the wax creeping up the wick and the water remaining on the sides of the small tube once the major portion of the water is back in a lower level. *Osmosis* is the gradual penetration of a shell or membrane. *Erosion* is the wearing away by wind or water or some gradual process.

3. **(D)** Two dissimilar metals put together expand at different rates, so they can be used to form a *thermostat*—to move a switch and turn a furnace or other object on or off as the temperature makes the metals expand or contract.

4. **(B)** *Aluminum* is the metal that expands the most of those listed. Tungsten expands very little even at high temperatures and is used for incandescent lamp filaments.

5. **(B)** As the cold causes the pendulum to contract, it is *shortened*. This shortened pendulum causes the clock to run faster since it moves back and forth more quickly.

6. **(A)** Heat is a form of *energy*. The calorie is one unit of measurement of heat. Thermals are usually upward movements of columns of air caused by heat rising.

7. **(D)** The best conductor of heat of the metals listed is silver. Aluminum expands rapidly, but it does not conduct heat as readily as silver because its atoms are not as closely packed as silver.

8. **(C)** There are three ways of transferring heat from one place to another: conduction, convection, and *radiation*.

9. **(B)** Putting salt into water increases the specific gravity of the solution and *lowers its freezing point*.

10. **(A)** Changing a liquid to a gas or vapor is called *evaporation*. Boiling is one method of accomplishing the process.

11. **(B)** Adding heat to a container of boiling water that is totally enclosed increases the pressure of the steam inside the compartment or container and *increases the temperature* of the water. This can be very dangerous if the container is not capable of handling the pressure.

12. **(D)** *Fractional distillation* is the process used to produce gasoline, kerosene, tar, and heating oil, as well as other products from petroleum.

13. **(C)** Sound travels at *1,086 feet per second* at 0°C. It travels at 1,492 meters per second in seawater and at 3,500 meters per second in copper. The speed of light is 186,000 miles per second.

14. **(B)** The meter used to measure extremely high resistances is called a *megger* since the units of measurement will be in the millions, or megs.

15. **(C)** The hole is being *tapped* with a tap. This tool is used to make threads in the drilled hole.

16. **(B)** The piston in cylinder A will rise 2 inches. The mechanical advantage formula in this kind of problem is

$$\frac{a_2}{a_1} = \frac{d_1}{d_2}$$

where a_1 is the area of the smaller cylinder, a_2 is the area of the larger cylinder, d_1 is the vertical distance moved by the piston in the smaller cylinder, and d_2 is the vertical distance moved by the piston in the larger cylinder. In this case, the smaller cylinder's diameter is 3 inches and the larger cylinder's diameter is 6 inches. Therefore, the mechanical advantage is $\frac{6}{3}$ = 2. This means that we take the 1 inch moved by the piston in the larger cylinder and multiply it by the mechanical advantage to see that the piston in cylinder A will be forced upward 2 inches.

17. **(B)** Because water cannot be compressed, the same amount of water must be flowing through all parts of the pipe system. Since the same amount of water is flowing through all parts of the system, the water will be flowing faster in the smaller-diameter pipe, decreasing pressure in pipe B relative to pipe A (Bernoulli's Principle), which means the water pressure is greater in pipe A.

18. **(C)** Since metal is a better conductor of heat than plastic, wood, or ceramics, the *metal knife* would feel hottest to the touch.

19. **(B)** To calculate mechanical advantage, use the formula *load /effort*. You can also use the formula effort distance/load distance.

20. **(B)** When the plug is removed, liquid will flow *into the central tube* to equalize the level of the liquid both inside and outside the tube.

21. **(B)** Valves A, B, and D have to be open for the tank to fill halfway and maintain that level. Water comes in through valve A, so any choice not including choice A is automatically incorrect. Water then flows out through valve B when the tank is half full—and, for that water to go anywhere, valve D must be open, too.

22. **(B)** The length of time for a swing depends entirely on the length of the string, not the weight.

23. **(C)** Both would take the same amount of time to make one complete swing. The time taken for one swing depends on the string's length, not the weight at the end of it.

24. **(C)** When cold water pipes are *insulated*, it keeps warm moisture-rich air from contacting the cold water pipe, preventing condensation.

25. **(C)** Gear A has 15 teeth and gear B has 10 teeth, so the gear ratio is 3:2. This means that for every two turns that the larger gear (A) makes, the smaller gear (B) makes three. Therefore, if gear A makes 10 turns (the "2" part of the gear ratio), divide that by two and then multiply by three. $\frac{1}{2}$ times 10 5 5; 5 3 3 5 15.

ANSWER SHEET
AFQT Focus Exam

Arithmetic Reasoning

1. Ⓐ Ⓑ Ⓒ Ⓓ	7. Ⓐ Ⓑ Ⓒ Ⓓ	13. Ⓐ Ⓑ Ⓒ Ⓓ	19. Ⓐ Ⓑ Ⓒ Ⓓ	25. Ⓐ Ⓑ Ⓒ Ⓓ
2. Ⓐ Ⓑ Ⓒ Ⓓ	8. Ⓐ Ⓑ Ⓒ Ⓓ	14. Ⓐ Ⓑ Ⓒ Ⓓ	20. Ⓐ Ⓑ Ⓒ Ⓓ	26. Ⓐ Ⓑ Ⓒ Ⓓ
3. Ⓐ Ⓑ Ⓒ Ⓓ	9. Ⓐ Ⓑ Ⓒ Ⓓ	15. Ⓐ Ⓑ Ⓒ Ⓓ	21. Ⓐ Ⓑ Ⓒ Ⓓ	27. Ⓐ Ⓑ Ⓒ Ⓓ
4. Ⓐ Ⓑ Ⓒ Ⓓ	10. Ⓐ Ⓑ Ⓒ Ⓓ	16. Ⓐ Ⓑ Ⓒ Ⓓ	22. Ⓐ Ⓑ Ⓒ Ⓓ	28. Ⓐ Ⓑ Ⓒ Ⓓ
5. Ⓐ Ⓑ Ⓒ Ⓓ	11. Ⓐ Ⓑ Ⓒ Ⓓ	17. Ⓐ Ⓑ Ⓒ Ⓓ	23. Ⓐ Ⓑ Ⓒ Ⓓ	29. Ⓐ Ⓑ Ⓒ Ⓓ
6. Ⓐ Ⓑ Ⓒ Ⓓ	12. Ⓐ Ⓑ Ⓒ Ⓓ	18. Ⓐ Ⓑ Ⓒ Ⓓ	24. Ⓐ Ⓑ Ⓒ Ⓓ	30. Ⓐ Ⓑ Ⓒ Ⓓ

Word Knowledge

1. Ⓐ Ⓑ Ⓒ Ⓓ	8. Ⓐ Ⓑ Ⓒ Ⓓ	15. Ⓐ Ⓑ Ⓒ Ⓓ	22. Ⓐ Ⓑ Ⓒ Ⓓ	29. Ⓐ Ⓑ Ⓒ Ⓓ
2. Ⓐ Ⓑ Ⓒ Ⓓ	9. Ⓐ Ⓑ Ⓒ Ⓓ	16. Ⓐ Ⓑ Ⓒ Ⓓ	23. Ⓐ Ⓑ Ⓒ Ⓓ	30. Ⓐ Ⓑ Ⓒ Ⓓ
3. Ⓐ Ⓑ Ⓒ Ⓓ	10. Ⓐ Ⓑ Ⓒ Ⓓ	17. Ⓐ Ⓑ Ⓒ Ⓓ	24. Ⓐ Ⓑ Ⓒ Ⓓ	31. Ⓐ Ⓑ Ⓒ Ⓓ
4. Ⓐ Ⓑ Ⓒ Ⓓ	11. Ⓐ Ⓑ Ⓒ Ⓓ	18. Ⓐ Ⓑ Ⓒ Ⓓ	25. Ⓐ Ⓑ Ⓒ Ⓓ	32. Ⓐ Ⓑ Ⓒ Ⓓ
5. Ⓐ Ⓑ Ⓒ Ⓓ	12. Ⓐ Ⓑ Ⓒ Ⓓ	19. Ⓐ Ⓑ Ⓒ Ⓓ	26. Ⓐ Ⓑ Ⓒ Ⓓ	33. Ⓐ Ⓑ Ⓒ Ⓓ
6. Ⓐ Ⓑ Ⓒ Ⓓ	13. Ⓐ Ⓑ Ⓒ Ⓓ	20. Ⓐ Ⓑ Ⓒ Ⓓ	27. Ⓐ Ⓑ Ⓒ Ⓓ	34. Ⓐ Ⓑ Ⓒ Ⓓ
7. Ⓐ Ⓑ Ⓒ Ⓓ	14. Ⓐ Ⓑ Ⓒ Ⓓ	21. Ⓐ Ⓑ Ⓒ Ⓓ	28. Ⓐ Ⓑ Ⓒ Ⓓ	35. Ⓐ Ⓑ Ⓒ Ⓓ

Paragraph Comprehension

1. Ⓐ Ⓑ Ⓒ Ⓓ	4. Ⓐ Ⓑ Ⓒ Ⓓ	7. Ⓐ Ⓑ Ⓒ Ⓓ	10. Ⓐ Ⓑ Ⓒ Ⓓ	13. Ⓐ Ⓑ Ⓒ Ⓓ
2. Ⓐ Ⓑ Ⓒ Ⓓ	5. Ⓐ Ⓑ Ⓒ Ⓓ	8. Ⓐ Ⓑ Ⓒ Ⓓ	11. Ⓐ Ⓑ Ⓒ Ⓓ	14. Ⓐ Ⓑ Ⓒ Ⓓ
3. Ⓐ Ⓑ Ⓒ Ⓓ	6. Ⓐ Ⓑ Ⓒ Ⓓ	9. Ⓐ Ⓑ Ⓒ Ⓓ	12. Ⓐ Ⓑ Ⓒ Ⓓ	15. Ⓐ Ⓑ Ⓒ Ⓓ

Mathematics Knowledge

1. Ⓐ Ⓑ Ⓒ Ⓓ	6. Ⓐ Ⓑ Ⓒ Ⓓ	11. Ⓐ Ⓑ Ⓒ Ⓓ	16. Ⓐ Ⓑ Ⓒ Ⓓ	21. Ⓐ Ⓑ Ⓒ Ⓓ
2. Ⓐ Ⓑ Ⓒ Ⓓ	7. Ⓐ Ⓑ Ⓒ Ⓓ	12. Ⓐ Ⓑ Ⓒ Ⓓ	17. Ⓐ Ⓑ Ⓒ Ⓓ	22. Ⓐ Ⓑ Ⓒ Ⓓ
3. Ⓐ Ⓑ Ⓒ Ⓓ	8. Ⓐ Ⓑ Ⓒ Ⓓ	13. Ⓐ Ⓑ Ⓒ Ⓓ	18. Ⓐ Ⓑ Ⓒ Ⓓ	23. Ⓐ Ⓑ Ⓒ Ⓓ
4. Ⓐ Ⓑ Ⓒ Ⓓ	9. Ⓐ Ⓑ Ⓒ Ⓓ	14. Ⓐ Ⓑ Ⓒ Ⓓ	19. Ⓐ Ⓑ Ⓒ Ⓓ	24. Ⓐ Ⓑ Ⓒ Ⓓ
5. Ⓐ Ⓑ Ⓒ Ⓓ	10. Ⓐ Ⓑ Ⓒ Ⓓ	15. Ⓐ Ⓑ Ⓒ Ⓓ	20. Ⓐ Ⓑ Ⓒ Ⓓ	25. Ⓐ Ⓑ Ⓒ Ⓓ

AFQT Focus Exam

ARITHMETIC REASONING

TIME: 36 MINUTES
30 QUESTIONS

Directions: This test has questions about arithmetic. Each question is followed by four possible answers. Decide which answer is correct. Then, on your answer form, blacken the space that has the same number and letter as your choice. Use scratch paper for any figuring you wish to do. Here is a sample question.

1. If 10 pounds of sugar cost $2.00, what is the cost of 1 pound?

(A) 90 cents
(B) 80 cents
(C) 50 cents
(D) 20 cents

The cost of 1 pound is 20 cents; therefore answer D is correct.

Your score on this test will be based on the number of questions you answer correctly. You should try to answer every question. Do not spend too much time on any one question.

Notice that Part 2 begins with question number 1. When you begin, be sure to mark your first answer next to number 1 on your answer form.

THE ACTUAL TEST WILL SAY:

Do not turn this page until told to do so.

1. At Chez Marie, one-fifth of the patrons are male and one-fourth of the patrons are from out of town. What proportion would you expect to be both male and from out of town?

(A) $\frac{1}{4}$

(B) $\frac{1}{9}$

(C) $\frac{1}{20}$

(D) $\frac{1}{25}$

2. There are 124 certified nursing assistants and 36 registered nurses working at a hospital. What percentage of the workforce are registered nurses?

(A) 18.7%
(B) 22.5%
(C) 36.0%
(D) 41.3%

3. Of a thousand dogs at a dog show, 54 percent were male. Among these males, 4 out of 5 were over the age of 3. How many of the dogs were males 3 years old or older?

(A) 216
(B) 332
(C) 432
(D) 540

4. A mail carrier can deliver mail to 800 addresses in one day. In the city of Woodway, there are 36,800 residents. How many mail carriers must be hired to deliver mail to all of the Woodway citizens each day?

(A) 36
(B) 46
(C) 92
(D) 138

5. A heart attack victim can be saved 90 percent of the time if a defibrillator is used within 5 minutes of the heart attack's onset. Of the people who have heart attacks, defibrillators are nearby 40 percent of the time, but they are only used 60 percent of the time even when they are available. How many people who suffer a heart attack are saved because of the use of a defibrillator?

(A) 20%
(B) 22%
(C) 42%
(D) 30%

6. A college student scored 74, 97, 88, 83, and 86 on his physics tests during the course of the semester. His professor will drop the lowest test grade to compute each student's average for the semester. What is the student's final average in the class?

(A) 82.0%
(B) 85.6%
(C) 86.0%
(D) 88.5%

7. The manufacturer's suggested retail price of the new Guzzler 300 SEV (Sport Everything Vehicle) went from $22,399 last year to $23,999 for this year's model. About what percentage increase was this?

(A) 2.07%
(B) 7.1%
(C) 9.3%
(D) 11.4%

8. The Midway Panthers high school football quarterback attempted 82 passes and completed 57 of them while the team ran up a 8-1 record. What was his completion percentage?

(A) 30.4%
(B) 69.5%
(C) 43.8%
(D) 81.7%

9. Mackenzie has a 20-year term life insurance policy for $100,000. The annual premium is $12.00 per thousand. What is the total premium paid for this policy every 6 months?

(A) $600
(B) $1,200
(C) $100
(D) $2,400

10. The deli in the local super grocery store sells 2 pounds of smoked deli turkey breast for $13.98. What would the cost be of a 5-ounce portion?

(A) $0.44
(B) $0.87
(C) $1.40
(D) $2.20

11. Jonathan gets a bonus check and goes to the haberdasher's outlet. He finds that five shirts and four ties cost $173 and each tie costs $12. What is the cost of one shirt?

(A) $15.00
(B) $22.60
(C) $19.22
(D) $25.00

12. A regional waste disposal expediter company wants to calculate a price to charge for their new Super-Duper Dumpster. In order to do that, the operations manager needs to calculate the volume of the new container. What is the volume of the container if it is 23 feet long, 15 feet wide, and 11 feet high?

(A) 2,530 square feet
(B) 3,450 cubic feet
(C) 3,795 square feet
(D) 3,795 cubic feet

13. A college football player's parents spent $119 on tickets for family and friends to attend a conference playoff game. If the general admission tickets were $7 and $10, and they bought an equal number of both kinds of tickets, how many $7 tickets did they buy?

(A) 4
(B) 5
(C) 7
(D) 11

14. While working her way through college, Amanda earns an average of $22 an hour in tips as a supervising waitress at the best steak restaurant in town. If her hourly wage is $2.50 and she has to pay a 10 percent tip share to the hostesses and busboys, how much does she take home at the end of a day where she worked from 10:30 A.M. to 5:30 P.M.?

(A) $32.90
(B) $121.11
(C) $138.60
(D) $156.10

15. The local performing arts troupe saw, before the curtain went up, that 76 percent of a 500-seat theater was occupied, and that three-quarters of those attending were adults. How many children were seated in the theater?

(A) 95
(B) 100
(C) 76
(D) 285

16. While home one weekend from college, Jonathan spent 4 hours studying, 1 hour playing with the dogs, 30 minutes doing his laundry, and 2 hours watching TV. What percentage of his time was spent studying?

(A) 46.6%
(B) 50.0%
(C) 53.3%
(D) 57.1%

17. Mrs. D. found a chandelier for the dining room for $1,400. However, since the model had been discontinued and the display had no factory packaging material, the store manager discounted the price to $1,150. What was the percentage of the reduction?

(A) 1.78%
(B) 13.0%
(C) 15.0%
(D) 17.9%

18. To complete the decoration of her new home, Kate bought a rectangular Persian rug that measured 45 feet around its outer edge. If the long sides measure 15 feet each, how long is each short side of the rug?

(A) 7.5 feet
(B) 10 feet
(C) 12.5 feet
(D) 15 feet

19. While working in the Floors 'R' Us suburban store, four customer service representatives each receive $320 a week, while two sales managers each earn $12 per hour plus an average $100 per day commission. What is the total weekly compensation paid to these six employees for a 5-day, 40-hour work week?

    (A) $2,420
    (B) $3,240
    (C) $2,260
    (D) $4,520

20. The USS *Texas* (SSN 775) sails x miles the first day, y miles the second day, and z miles the third day. What is the formula for the average number of miles sailed per day?

    (A) $3xyz$
    (B) $3 \cdot (x + y + z)$
    (C) $(x + y + z) \div 3$
    (D) $(x + y + z)$

21. If a train can travel 500 miles in 5 hours, how far can it travel in 15 minutes?

    (A) 25 miles
    (B) 30 miles
    (C) 57 miles
    (D) 125 miles

22. Which one of these pairs of objects is an example of similar figures, mathematically speaking?

    (A) a right triangle and an isosceles triangle
    (B) a motorcycle and a sidecar
    (C) a bicycle and a motorcycle
    (D) an airplane and a scale model of that airplane

23. Upon his death, a man's life insurance policies paid $750,000 to his wife and three children. The policies were set up to pay the wife and children in the ratio of 5:1:1:1. How much did the children receive altogether?

    (A) $150,000
    (B) $200,000
    (C) $250,000
    (D) $281,250

24. Although the table of organization and equipment specifies that an infantry rifle company has a total 131 soldiers authorized, B Company (Bulldogs), 3rd Battalion, 144th Infantry Regiment has only 125 total soldiers assigned, of whom 4 percent are officers. How many enlisted soldiers are assigned to the company?

    (A) 114
    (B) 123
    (C) 120
    (D) 121

25. James, the high-tech electronics store owner, makes a deal to buy 20 DVD players for the listed wholesale price of $80 apiece, but receives a 25 percent discount because he is a frequent customer of the wholesale dealer. Being a shrewd entrepreneur, he then sells these DVD players at a 20 percent markup above the original wholesale price. What is his profit on each DVD player?

    (A) $16
    (B) $720
    (C) $20
    (D) $36

26. A mapmaker is told to prepare a map with a scale of 1 inch = 50 miles. If the actual ground distance between two points is 120 miles, how far apart should the mapmaker show them on the map?

    (A) 0.4 inch
    (B) 2.4 inches
    (C) 1.2 inches
    (D) 4.8 inches

27. In the city of Hewitt, houses are assessed for tax purposes at 80 percent of the purchase price. If Mr. Thomas buys a house in Hewitt for $120,000 and real estate taxes are $4.75 per $100 of assessed valuation, how much property tax must he pay per year?

    (A) $3,648
    (B) $5,472
    (C) $4,560
    (D) $4,845

28. Travis' hunting lodge does not have electrical lines run to it, but it does have a gasoline generator that powers the lights, heater, and stove. The fuel tank of the generator holds enough to run the generator for 75 minutes. About how many times must the fuel tank be filled to run the generator from 6:15 P.M. to 7:00 A.M.?

    (A) 9.4
    (B) 10.2
    (C) 10.8
    (D) 11.5

29. When a stretch of Loop 1 was converted from non-paid to a toll road, the traffic declined from 11,200 cars per day to 10,044. What was the percent of the decline in traffic?

    (A) 10.3%
    (B) 11.5%
    (C) 10.1%
    (D) 8.9%

30. Mr. Lee is a high-tech cutlery salesman. On a sales trip, he first drives for two hours at 70 miles per hour. He then drives for another one and a half hours at 65 miles per hour. If his car gets 25 miles per gallon on the highway in this speed range, how many gallons of gas did he use for the trip?

    (A) 5.4 gallons
    (B) 8.2 gallons
    (C) 8.4 gallons
    (D) 9.5 gallons

WORD KNOWLEDGE

TIME: 11 MINUTES
35 QUESTIONS

1. The retired first sergeant moved with surprising **alacrity** to pick up the child's fallen tricycle.

   (A) slow, painful progress
   (B) brisk willingness
   (C) indecision
   (D) clumsiness

2. **Infraction** most nearly means

   (A) protection from external dangers.
   (B) the bending of light through a lens.
   (C) violation of a rule or law.
   (D) quiet, uninterrupted thought.

3. **Beseech** most nearly means

   (A) to beg or plead.
   (B) insult or degrade.
   (C) give to upon one's death.
   (D) underneath something else.

4. He was **articulate** and well-mannered.

   (A) able to express one's self clearly
   (B) bending at the joints
   (C) austere, self-denying
   (D) having to do with beauty

5. **Imperative** most nearly means

   (A) curious.
   (B) having to do with a vital requirement.
   (C) rudely bold.
   (D) accidental.

6. **Shear** most nearly means

   (A) see-through.
   (B) to cut with a sharp instrument such as scissors.
   (C) unmitigated.
   (D) to reinforce or prop up.

7. "The change of **milieu**," he said to his sick daughter, "will do you good."

   (A) context
   (B) orientation
   (C) despairing sickness
   (D) surroundings

8. **Curtail** most nearly means

   (A) work with someone else.
   (B) to cause to curl (e.g., hair).
   (C) cut short or reduce.
   (D) travel quickly.

9. **Deride** most nearly means

   (A) to ridicule contemptuously.
   (B) to transform into something else.
   (C) to keep something from someone else.
   (D) to simplify.

10. **Intimidate** most nearly means

    (A) to frighten by being threatening.
    (B) having an extremely close relationship.
    (C) to imply a hidden meaning.
    (D) to make more complicated.

11. **Deportment** most nearly means

    (A) category.
    (B) behavior.
    (C) location.
    (D) punctuality.

12. The message will be **conveyed** by an ambassador at large.

    (A) punctuated
    (B) translated
    (C) spoken
    (D) carried

13. The commander gave his **tacit** approval.

    (A) silent
    (B) lethargic
    (C) absolute
    (D) effusive

14. "What do the omens **portend**?" the oracle was asked.

    (A) feign
    (B) give warning beforehand
    (C) develop pores or holes
    (D) assume a pose

15. **Itinerary** most nearly means

    (A) migrant.
    (B) not permanent.
    (C) invention.
    (D) schedule.

16. The new student was **vexatious**.

    (A) annoying
    (B) contagious
    (C) at a high volume
    (D) insatiably hungry

17. **Equivalent** most nearly means

    (A) complicated.
    (B) inferior.
    (C) evident.
    (D) equal.

18. **Criterion** most nearly means

    (A) standard.
    (B) disaster.
    (C) environment.
    (D) excerpt.

19. **Mercurial** most nearly means

    (A) having compassion.
    (B) specious.
    (C) unpredictably changeable.
    (D) metallic.

20. This is a **critical** task.

    (A) conversational
    (B) influencing
    (C) less worthy
    (D) highly important

21. **Telemetry** most nearly means

    (A) mental communication.
    (B) rashness, audacity.
    (C) transmission of measurements by
        automatic instruments.
    (D) study of climactic variations.

22. His **antagonist** caught up with him.

    (A) ally
    (B) main character
    (C) soothing to the stomach
    (D) adversary

23. **Diagnose** most nearly means

    (A) predict the outcome.
    (B) cut in two.
    (C) identify a situation.
    (D) speak about.

24. There is usually a **kinetic** solution to any problem.

    (A) relating to the motion of material bodies
    (B) referring to motion pictures
    (C) moving at a high speed
    (D) referring to a relative

25. **Rectify** most nearly means

    (A) dealing with the digestive system.
    (B) cause trouble or havoc.
    (C) correct.
    (D) give new life to.

26. He tried to **camouflage** himself and his equipment.

    (A) substitute
    (B) conceal
    (C) redeem
    (D) divide

27. **Equivocal** most nearly means

    (A) equal.
    (B) poised.
    (C) open to question.
    (D) removed.

28. In such a situation, **centripetal** force must be taken into account.

    (A) away from a center or axis
    (B) relating to the feet
    (C) having more than 100 petals
    (D) toward a center or axis

29. **Disconsolate** most nearly means

    (A) hopelessly sad.
    (B) cease using.
    (C) rearrange sloppily.
    (D) recognize mentally.

30. His outlandish outfit was somewhat **anachronistic**.

(A) seemingly from a different time
(B) cursed
(C) dealing with organism structure
(D) attributing conscious thought to inanimate objects or animals

31. **Modulate** most nearly means

(A) speak.
(B) decay.
(C) dry out.
(D) adjust.

32. The student waited an hour just to ask one **picayune** question.

(A) unnoticed
(B) insignificant
(C) intense
(D) hot

33. **Tenacious** most nearly means

(A) annoying.
(B) persistent.
(C) religious.
(D) hot-tempered.

34. **Entente** most nearly means

(A) relaxation of tensions.
(B) volition.
(C) agreement providing for joint action.
(D) freedom of entry or access.

35. "Don't be **redundant**," he told his protégé.

(A) brilliant
(B) held back
(C) repetitive
(D) unruly

PARAGRAPH COMPREHENSION

TIME: 13 MINUTES
15 QUESTIONS

Directions: This test is a test of your ability to understand what you read. In this section you will find one or more paragraphs of reading material followed by incomplete statements or questions.

You are to read the paragraph and select which of the four lettered choices best completes the statement or answers the question. When you have selected your answer, blacken the correct numbered letter on your answer sheet.

Now look at the sample question below.

In certain areas water is so scarce that every attempt is made to conserve it. For instance, on one oasis in the Sahara Desert the amount of water necessary for each date palm tree has been carefully determined.

1. How much water is each tree given?

(A) no water at all
(B) exactly the amount required
(C) water only if it is healthy
(D) water on alternate days

The amount of water each tree required has been carefully determined, so answer B is correct.

Your score on this subtest will be based on the number of questions you answer correctly. You should try to answer every question. Do not spend too much time on any one question.

When you begin, be sure to start with question number 1 in Part 4 of your test booklet and number 1 in Part 4 on your answer form.

THE ACTUAL TEST WILL SAY:

Do not turn this page until told to do so.

1. The first American Army Ranger unit of World War II was formed in North Ireland in the spring of 1942. Over 2,000 soldiers volunteered from the recently arrived 1st Armored and 34th Infantry divisions. Stringent medical examinations, long foot marches, strenuous physical conditioning, and other tests eliminated many volunteers. Those who remained were interviewed by First Ranger Battalion commander Major William O. Darby; volunteers were seldom sure they were answering his questions correctly. By June 19, 1942, the 500 or so volunteers who remained were the initial nucleus of what would become one of America's most elite and legendary fighting forces.

According to this passage, what eliminated many volunteers from the Rangers?

(A) Major Darby's questioning
(B) medical exams, short road marches, and parachutist training
(C) strenuous physical conditioning, foot marches, and medical exams
(D) the battalion commander's interviews, medical exams, and map reading

2. According to the passage in question 1, where did the volunteers come from?

(A) North Ireland
(B) the 1st and 34th Infantry Divisions
(C) the 1st Armored Division and 34th Infantry Division
(D) the First Ranger Battalion

3. The Greek mythological deities most often found in art are all ultimately the offspring of Earth (*Gaia* in Greek, *Ge* in Latin) and heaven (*Ouranos/Uranus*). They produced 12 Titans, including Ocean (*Okeanos/Oceanus*) and his youngest brother *Kronos* (*Saturn* for the Latin-speaking Romans). Kronos castrated his father so he could rule in his place, married his sister *Rhea*, and then swallowed all his children right after their birth so that none of them could overthrow him. When *Zeus* (*Jupiter*) was born, Rhea fed Kronos a stone wrapped in clothes instead of the baby. When Zeus was grown, he forced Kronos to vomit up his siblings, and together they overthrew their father and the other Titans, ruling the world from Greece's highest peak, Mount Olympus. The later 12 Olympian gods and goddesses appear far more often in Greek art than do Gaia, Ouranos, and the Titans—and not only in Greek, Etruscan, and Roman times, but also in the Middle Ages, the Renaissance, and even up to the present.

Which Greek mythological deities are found most often in art?

(A) Gaia and Kronos
(B) Zeus and his siblings
(C) Rhea and her children
(D) the 12 Titans who ruled from Mount Olympus

4. In the passage from question 3, who swallowed Zeus to avoid being overthrown?

(A) Rhea
(B) Kronos
(C) Saturn
(D) no one

5. The infantry is the main land combat force and core fighting strength of the Army. Junior infantry officers are expected to be proficient in leadership and small unit tactics; technically competent with weapons and a variety of high-tech equipment; physically fit; and most of all, have the integrity and character to perform under physical and mental pressure. A leader must exhibit self-discipline, initiative, confidence, and intelligence to be able to confidently lead soldiers while earning loyalty and trust. Leaders must often make decisions quickly, focusing on completing the mission successfully while still taking care of their soldiers. Leaders of all ranks and specialties are judged by their ability to make decisions on their own and bear ultimate moral responsibility for those decisions.

What qualities must a leader have in order to earn loyalty and trust?

(A) self-discipline, technical competence, and creativity
(B) intelligence, confidence, caring, and proficiency
(C) initiative, self-discipline, intelligence, and confidence
(D) decision-making ability, technical confidence, and responsibility

6. Church design during the Middle Ages set the stage for ecclesiastical architecture from the Renaissance to the present. The typical western European Christian church had a "basilican" plan, an evolution from the Roman columnar hall or *basilica*. One of the earliest and most famous of the churches was the original St. Peter's in Rome, Italy, begun about 320 A.D. Typical of early Christian church design, it was rectangular, had a simple timber roof, a wide central area called a *nave*, two *aisles* on each side parallel to the nave and marked off by columns, and ending on the far end from the doors in a semicircular area called an *apse*. St. Peter's also had an area perpendicular to the nave called a *transept*. The intersection of the nave and transept is called the *crossing*. The basilican church design went through many changes in the thousand years after the construction of Old St. Peter's (which was completely rebuilt starting in the 15th century), but the basics remained the same.

How did Christian church design change from the fourth to the 15th century?

(A) added additional aisles
(B) added a transept
(C) was completely rebuilt
(D) remained essentially the same

7. In the passage from question 6, what is a transept?

(A) the intersection of the nave and the crossing
(B) an area at right angles to the nave
(C) an area perpendicular to the apse
(D) an area parallel to the aisles

8. All nations must confront the central economic questions of what to produce, how to produce, and for whom to produce it. However, the nations of the world approach these central issues with vastly different production possibilities. The United States, Canada, Brazil, and China each has more than three million acres of land, which gives those countries far more production possibilities than Dominica, Tonga, Malta, or Liechtenstein, which all have less than 500 acres of land apiece. Populations vary widely—China, with well over 1.3 billion people, has four and a half times the population of the United States and almost 38 thousand times that of Liechtenstein. Decision-making mechanisms also run the gamut, from highly centralized (North Korea, Cuba, Iran, Burma) to mostly free-market (Ireland, New Zealand, Singapore, the United States, and even Liechtenstein). Everyone has their own approach, based on these factors, their heritage and culture, and other factors.

What factors affecting national production does the passage mention?

(A) amount of land, size of population, planning approach, and culture
(B) size of the country, type of population, decision-making structure
(C) geography, population, market forces, and national security
(D) size of the country and its population, decision-making approach, and culture

9. In the passage from question 8, what are the central economic issues that all countries have to face?

(A) land, population, planning approach, and culture
(B) what to produce, how to produce it, and for whom to produce it
(C) centralized vs. decentralized decision making
(D) production possibilities, land, and population

10. There are several different varieties of quarks. First, there are six "flavors" (that have been discovered so far, anyway), which we call *up, down, strange, charmed, bottom,* and *top.* Each flavor comes in three "colors," red, green, and blue. (It's important to note that these terms are just arbitrary labels: quarks are much smaller than the wavelength of visible light and so do not have any color in the normal sense. It's just that modern physicists no longer restrict themselves to Greek or Latin in order to name things.) A proton or neutron is made up of three quarks, one of each color. A proton contains two "up" quarks and one "down" quark; a neutron has two "down" and one "up."

According to the passage, how many different "flavors" of quarks are there?

(A) 2
(B) 4
(C) 6
(D) 12

11. The War of 1812 was in some ways one of the most unfortunate events in American history. For one thing, it was needless—the British Orders in Council that had caused the worst irritation on the part of the still-young United States were being unconditionally repealed just as Congress declared war. For another, the United States suffered from internal divisions of the most serious type. While the South and West favored war, New York and New England were generally against it; toward the end of the relatively and mercifully brief conflict, important New England groups went to the very edge of disloyalty. Third, the war was far from glorious for the United States in a military sense. The American army was in terrible shape to fight.

Why does the author of the passage believe that the War of 1812 was an unfortunate event?

(A) It lasted too long and the American army and navy were not ready to fight.
(B) It was unnecessary, Americans were divided in their support, and their army was unready.
(C) The British declared war before the American army was ready to fight, and the war lasted too long.
(D) British descendants in New England were against it, and the army was in bad shape.

12. During the Battle of the Bulge, the French town of Bastogne was occupied by the American 101st Airborne Division to control the vital crossroads there. The division was surrounded by the German Army as it tried to sweep to the port of Antwerp. After several days of determined resistance by the Americans holding the crossroads town, four Germans under a flag of truce approached the lines of the 327th Infantry Regiment on the outskirts of the town. The message they carried demanded the surrender of the encircled town within two hours. The surrender demand was soon delivered to acting division commander Brig. Gen. Anthony C. McAuliffe as he was about to leave his headquarters to congratulate the defenders of a roadblock who had driven off a heavy attack. He dropped the message on the floor, said "Nuts," and left. When he returned, his staff reminded him of the message, which he at first had not taken seriously. McAuliffe asked his staff what they thought the reply should be. One officer said, "That first remark of yours would be hard to beat." So the message delivered to the Germans read, "To the German Commander: Nuts! The American Commander." The confused German major asked if this was affirmative or negative. He was told by the regimental commander that it was "decidedly not affirmative."

Why was the 101st Airborne Division holding out at Bastogne?

(A) to protect the vital nut and berry agricultural center at Bastogne
(B) to set up a roadblock
(C) to deny the Germans an important crossroads
(D) to keep the Germans from reaching the crossroads at Antwerp

13. In the passage from question 12, what news did the German major have to take back to his commander?

(A) The Americans would surrender within two hours.
(B) The Americans would surrender, but not within two hours.
(C) The Americans would not surrender.
(D) The passage is not clear.

14. The "zero tolerance on fighting" policy some of our schools have instituted sounds wonderful at first, but it's actually a smokescreen that lets school and district leaders avoid tough decisions while teaching kids the wrong lessons. The biggest problem happens when the student who is attacked gets the same punishment as the one who started the fight—unless he doesn't fight back and lets himself get pummeled. It is morally wrong to teach our kids that the attacked person is as much in the wrong as the attacker. The correct solution, instead, is balanced judgment by administrators, backed up by a determination to tell parents the truth. Parents also have the obligation to recognize that their little angel may not be perfect, and not to sue the school because a teacher or principal told them an unpleasant truth.

The author of this passage believes that

(A) "zero tolerance on fighting" policies sound wonderful.
(B) zero tolerance policies call for sound judgment by school administrators.
(C) parents should sue school personnel who tell them something they don't want to hear.
(D) the student who defends himself should be viewed differently than the attacker.

15. It is either exceptionally naïve or depressingly cynical to equate an analysis of incomplete facts—even an analysis that turns out to be completely wrong—with knowing untruths (otherwise known as "lies"). Military, political, and economic intelligence—information about a known or potential adversary or competitor—is especially open to gaps, misinterpretation, and other confusion. Perfect information seldom if ever exists even in non-adversarial situations, much less when an adversary is actively trying to deny you the facts—or sell you the wrong ones. The quest for perfectly complete and accurate information results in *analysis paralysis*: the inability to make a decision until you have all the information, which is never going to happen.

According to this passage, the reader can infer that the author

(A) likes to make decisions based on 100 percent accurate information.
(B) knows that complete information will usually be available eventually.
(C) believes that acting on incomplete information is often necessary.
(D) supports a search for a non-adversarial interpretation.

MATHEMATICS KNOWLEDGE

TIME: 24 MINUTES

25 QUESTIONS

Directions: This is a test of your ability to solve general mathematical problems. Each problem is followed by four answer choices. Select the correct response from the choices given, then mark the space on your answer form that has the same number and letter as your choice. Use scratch paper to do any figuring that you wish.

Now look at this sample problem.

1. If $x + 8 = 9$, then x is equal to

   (A) 0.

   (B) 1.

   (C) 3.

   (D) $\frac{9}{8}$.

The correct answer is 1, so B is the correct response.

Your score on this test will be based on the number of questions you answer correctly. You should try to answer every question. Do not spend too much time on any one question.

Start with question number 1 in Part 5. Mark your answer for this question next to number 1, Part 5, on your answer form.

THE ACTUAL TEST WILL SAY:

Do not turn this page until told to do so.

---

1. The expression "4 factorial" or "4!" means

   (A) 16.

   (B) $\frac{1}{24}$.

   (C) 256.

   (D) 24.

2. An F/A-18E Super Hornet is flying a circular or "racetrack" orbit around a 4,000-meter-high mountaintop. Assuming that the pilot flies a perfectly circular course and that it is 40 kilometers from the mountaintop to the outer edge of his racetrack, what is the distance in kilometers he travels during each orbit? (use $\pi = \frac{22}{7}$)

   (A) 13 kilometers

   (B) 25 kilometers

   (C) 126 kilometers

   (D) 251 kilometers

3. The reciprocal of 7 to the nearest thousandth is

   (A) 0.143.

   (B) 1.428.

   (C) 14.

   (D) 21.

4. The second digit of the square of 525 is

   (A) 2.

   (B) 5.

   (C) 6.

   (D) 7.

5. The area of a square with an outside perimeter measurement of 40 yards is

   (A) 100 square feet.

   (B) 180 square yards.

   (C) 300 square feet.

   (D) 300 square yards.

6. Solve the following equations for x.

$$5x + 4y = 27$$
$$x - 2y = 11$$

(A) $x = \dfrac{5}{3}$

(B) $x = 4.5$

(C) $x = 9$

(D) $x = 7$

7. Find the square root of 85 correct to the nearest tenth.

(A) 9.1

(B) 9.2

(C) 9.3

(D) 9.4

8. Solve for x: $8x - 2 - 5x = 8$

(A) $x = 1.3$

(B) $x = 3\dfrac{1}{3}$

(C) $x = 2\dfrac{1}{2}$

(D) $x = 7.0$

9. $2(a - b) + 4(a + 3b) =$

(A) $6a - 10b$

(B) $6a + 2b$

(C) $8a^2 + 2b^2$

(D) $6a + 10b$

10. Which of the following is the smallest prime number greater than 200?

(A) 201

(B) 205

(C) 211

(D) 214

11. If a is a negative number, and ab is a positive number, then which of the following must be true?

(A) b is greater than a.

(B) a is greater than b.

(C) b is negative.

(D) b is positive.

12. What is the product of $(a + 2)(a - 5)(a + 3)$?

(A) $a^3 + 2a^2 + 15a - 30$

(B) $a^3 + 6a^2 - 49$

(C) $a^3 - 19a - 30$

(D) $a^3 + 2a^2 - 15a + 30$

13. Solve for z: $3z - 5 + 2z = 25 - 5z$

(A) $z = 1$

(B) $z = 3$

(C) $z = -3$

(D) $z = 0$

14. An architect has won a contract to place a memorial sculpture at each of the corners of the Pentagon in Washington, D.C. How many sculptures will there be?

(A) 4

(B) 5

(C) 6

(D) 8

15. If one of the angles of a right triangle is 30 degrees, what are the measurements of the other two angles?

(A) 30 degrees, 120 degrees

(B) 60 degrees, 45 degrees

(C) 60 degrees, 90 degrees

(D) 45 degrees, 90 degrees

16. Factor $x^2 - 11x + 30$.

(A) $(x - 6), (x - 5)$

(B) $(x + 6), (x - 5)$

(C) $(x - 10), (x - 1)$

(D) $(x - 3), (x + 10)$

17. Solve $\dfrac{15a^3b^2c}{5abc}$

(A) $10abc$

(B) $3abc$

(C) $5a^2b^2$

(D) $3a^2b$

18. Two circles have the same center. If their radii are 7 centimeters and 10 centimeters, find the area that is part of the larger circle but not part of the smaller one.

(A) 3 square centimeters
(B) 17 square centimeters
(C) 51 (π) square centimeters
(D) 71 (π) square centimeters

19. Amanda took five midterm tests for five different college classes; her average for all five tests was 88. That night at home, she could remember only her first four scores: 78, 86, 94, and 96. What was her score on the fifth test?

(A) 82
(B) 86
(C) 84
(D) 88

20. How many cubic yards of concrete are needed to make a cement floor that measures $9' \times 12' \times 6''$?

(A) 2 cubic yards
(B) 18 cubic yards
(C) 54 cubic yards
(D) 210 cubic yards

21. A new wildlife preserve is laid out in a perfect circle with a radius of 14 kilometers. The lion habitat is shaped like a wedge and has an 8-foot-high razor wire fence around it. Two inner sides of the fence meet at a 90-degree angle in the center of the base. How much ground space (area) does the lion habitat have?

(A) 140 square kilometers
(B) 3.5 square kilometers
(C) 210 square kilometers
(D) 154 square kilometers

22. Factor $6x^2 + 3xy$.

(A) $2x(3x - y)$
(B) $x^2 + 3y$
(C) $x + 3y$
(D) $3x(2x + y)$

23. A cylindrical container has a radius of 7″ and a height of 15″. How many gallons of hydraulic fluid can it hold? (There are 231 cubic inches in a gallon.)

(A) 15 gallons
(B) 14 gallons
(C) 140 gallons
(D) 10 gallons

24. A 10-foot-high ladder is resting against an 8-foot-high wall around a recreation area. If the top of the ladder is exactly even with the top of the wall, how far is the base of the ladder from the wall?

(A) 18 feet
(B) 6 feet
(C) 12 feet
(D) 9 feet

25. A cook is mixing fruit juice from concentrate for a catered event. Ten ounces of liquid contain 20 percent fruit juice and 80 percent water. He then further dilutes the mixture by adding 40 additional ounces of water. What is the percent of fruit juice in the new solution?

(A) 4%
(B) 10%
(C) 14%
(D) 18%

ANSWER KEY
AFQT Focus Exam

Arithmetic Reasoning

1. **C**	7. **B**	13. **C**	19. **B**	25. **D**
2. **B**	8. **B**	14. **D**	20. **C**	26. **B**
3. **C**	9. **A**	15. **A**	21. **A**	27. **C**
4. **B**	10. **D**	16. **C**	22. **D**	28. **B**
5. **B**	11. **D**	17. **D**	23. **D**	29. **A**
6. **D**	12. **D**	18. **A**	24. **C**	30. **D**

Word Knowledge

1. **B**	8. **C**	15. **D**	22. **D**	29. **A**
2. **C**	9. **A**	16. **A**	23. **C**	30. **A**
3. **A**	10. **A**	17. **D**	24. **A**	31. **D**
4. **A**	11. **B**	18. **A**	25. **C**	32. **B**
5. **B**	12. **D**	19. **C**	26. **B**	33. **B**
6. **B**	13. **A**	20. **D**	27. **C**	34. **C**
7. **D**	14. **B**	21. **C**	28. **D**	35. **C**

Paragraph Comprehension

1. **C**	4. **D**	7. **B**	10. **C**	13. **C**
2. **C**	5. **C**	8. **D**	11. **B**	14. **D**
3. **B**	6. **D**	9. **B**	12. **C**	15. **C**

Mathematics Knowledge

1. **D**	6. **D**	11. **C**	16. **A**	21. **D**
2. **D**	7. **B**	12. **C**	17. **D**	22. **D**
3. **A**	8. **B**	13. **B**	18. **C**	23. **D**
4. **D**	9. **D**	14. **B**	19. **B**	24. **B**
5. **C**	10. **C**	15. **C**	20. **A**	25. **A**

ARITHMETIC REASONING

1. **(C)** If one-fifth of all patrons are male, then you could reasonably expect one-fifth of the out-of-town patrons to be male. One-fifth of one-fourth is $\frac{1}{20}$ $\left(\frac{1}{5} \times \frac{1}{4} = \frac{1}{20}\right)$.

2. **(B)** First, find the total number of people in the workforce by adding both groups together: $124 + 36 = 160$. Then, because a percentage is the proportion of 100, multiply the number of RNs by 100 ($36 \times 100 = 3,600$)—this will set you up to get the actual percentage after the next step. Now, divide 3,600 by the total number of people in the population: $\frac{3,600}{160} = 22.5$.

   The percentage of RNs in the workforce is 22.5 percent.

3. **(C)** If 54 percent of a thousand dogs were male, then we are talking about 540 male dogs to start with ($1,000 \times 0.54 = 540$). Among those males, we are told, 4 out of 5 are over age three. If we convert that to a percentage so that we can work with it more easily, that means the denominator must be 100. Multiplying anything by one (or any of its forms) is still the number that we started with, so $\frac{4}{5} \times \frac{20}{20} = \frac{80}{100}$ ($\frac{20}{20}$ is a restated form of 1, so the amount we are talking about is the same, just stated in a different form). Simplifying $\frac{80}{100}$ gives us $\frac{8}{10}$ or 0.8. Multiplying $540 \times 0.8 = 432$, so we now know that there were 432 male dogs over the age of 3 at the dog show.

4. **(B)** To find the number of required mail carriers, divide 36,800 by 800 to get 46. The city needs 46 mail carriers.

5. **(B)** If a defibrillator is used, we know that the patient will have a 90 percent survival rate; however, only 40 percent of heart attack victims have this option available. Therefore we multiply 0.9×0.4 and conclude that only 0.36 or 36 percent of the people have this opportunity.

   However, we also know that of the 36 percent survivors, a defibrillator is only used 60 percent of the time. Therefore, we must further multiply 0.6×0.36 to find out how many patients are saved by the use of a defibrillator. This results in 0.216 or (rounded off, especially since you can't have partial people) 22 percent of patients are saved by the use of a defibrillator.

6. **(D)** First, drop the lowest grade (74), leaving you to add the remaining scores ($97 + 88 + 83 + 86 = 354$) and then divide that total by the total number of scores (which is now four, not five) ($\frac{354}{4} = 88.5$ percent), resulting in a final average of 88.5% for the semester.

7. **(B)** First, find the amount of the price increase.

$$\$23,999 - \$22,399 = \$1,600$$

Multiply the amount of the increase ($1,600) by 100 (this sets you up for your final answer to be the percentage that you need, without having to convert it in some way), then divide by last year's price:

$$1,600 \times 100 = 160,000$$
$$160,000 \div 22,399 = 7.1$$

The price increase was about 7.1 percent.

8. **(B)** Multiply the number of completed passes by 100, then divide it by the number of attempted passes. The result will be the percentage.

$$57 \times 100 = 5,700$$

$$\frac{5,700}{82} = 69.5 = 69.5\%$$

9. **(A)** There are 100 units of $1,000 in $100,000. Thus, Mackenzie pays $100 \times \$12$ (or $1,200) every year in premiums, or $100 every month. Therefore, every 6 months, Mackenzie pays $\frac{1}{2}$ of $1,200 (or six times $100), which equals $600.

10. **(D)** There are 16 ounces in 1 pound. Therefore, if 2 pounds of smoked deli turkey breast cost $13.98, then 1 pound costs $6.99.

$$1 \text{ ounce costs } \$6.99 \div 16 = \$0.44$$
$$5 \text{ ounces cost } \$0.44 \times 5 = \$2.20$$

11. **(D)** Find the cost of four ties:

$$4 \times \$12 = \$48$$

Find the cost of the shirts alone:

$$\$173 - \$48 = \$125$$

Find the cost of one shirt:

$$\$125 \div 5 = \$25.00$$

12. **(D)** The formula for the volume of an object with parallel sides and right-angle corners is

$$\text{Length } l \times \text{width } w \times \text{height } h \text{ or}$$
$$l \times w \times h$$
$$23 \text{ ft} \times 15 \text{ ft} \times 11 \text{ ft} = 3,795 \text{ cu ft}$$
$$(\text{"cubic feet"})$$

13. **(C)** Let x be the number of tickets bought at each price (remember, the sister bought the same number of both kinds of tickets). So,

$$7x + 10x = 119$$

Now combine the terms and continue solving the equation for x.

$$17x = 119$$
$$\frac{17x}{17} = \frac{119}{17}$$
$$x = \frac{119}{17}$$
$$x = 7$$

14. **(D)** First, calculate the amount of Amanda's hourly wages for a shift of 10:30 A.M. to 5:30 P.M., which is 7 hours.

$$7 \times \$2.50 = \$17.50$$

Next, calculate the amount of Amanda's tips for her 7-hour shift.

$$7 \times \$22 = \$154$$

Now, calculate the amount of her tips she has to share with the busboys and hostesses.

$$\$154 \times 0.10 = \$15.40$$

Now add everything up.

Wages	$17.50
Tips	+$154.00
Tip share	− $15.40
Net pay	$156.10

15. **(A)** First, calculate the number of total attendees by multiplying the total seats available by the percentage.

$$500 \times 0.76 = 380$$

Since "three-quarters" (75 percent) of those attending were adults, that means that one-quarter or 25 percent were children (which is the final result we are trying to find). Therefore, multiply the number of total attendees by the percentage of children to find out how many children saw the performance.

$$380 \times 0.25 = 95 \text{ children}$$

16. **(C)** Add all the blocks of time together.

$$4 + 1 + 0.5 + 2 = 7.5 \text{ hours total}$$

Now multiply the time spent studying (4 hours) by 100 and divide it by the total time.

$$4 \times 100 = 400$$
$$400 \div 7.5 = 53.3\%$$

17. **(D)** Subtract the discounted price from the original price.

$$\$1,400 - \$1,150 = \$250$$

Now multiply the amount of the discount by 100 and divide it by the original price.

$$\$250 \times 100 = 25,000$$
$$25,000 \div 1,400 = 17.857142 = 17.9\%$$

18. **(A)** The formula for the perimeter of a rectangle is

$$P = 2l \times 2w$$

If the long sides of the rug measure 15 feet each, then both long sides together equal 30 feet. Subtract the length of both long sides from the total perimeter measurement.

$$45 - (2 \times 15) = 45 - 30 = 15 \text{ feet}$$

Now we have the part of the perimeter made up by the short sides, but we need to divide it by 2 to get the length of each short side.

$$15 \text{ ft} \div 2 = 7.5 \text{ feet}$$

19. **(B)** First add up the wages made by the four customer service reps.

$$\$320 \times 4 = \$1,280$$

Now calculate how much the two sales reps make each week.

2 sales reps $\times$ [($12 per hour $\times$ 40 hr) + (5 days per week $\times$ $100)]
= 2 sales reps $\times$ ($480 + $500)
= 2 sales reps $\times$ $980 = $1,960 per week

Now add the pay for the four customer service reps to the pay for the two sales managers.

$$\$1,280 + \$1,960 = \$3,240$$

20. **(C)** To find an average, add the values for each day together and then divide by the total number of days: $(x + y + z) \div 3$.

21. **(A)** First find the number of miles per hour the train travels.

$$500 \text{ miles} \div 5 \text{ hours} = 100 \text{ miles per hour (mph)}$$

Now calculate how many miles the train travels in 1 minute.

$$100 \text{ mph} \div 60 \text{ minutes} = 1.67 \text{ miles per minute}$$

Now multiply the train's speed in miles per minute by the number of minutes in question.

$$1.67 \text{ miles per minute} \times 15 \text{ minutes} = 25 \text{ miles}$$

22. **(D)** Two figures are similar in the mathematical sense if they have the same shape; they may or may not have the same size. An airplane and a scale model of that plane have the same shape and are therefore similar.

23. **(D)** Start by letting x equal one share of the insurance money. According to the ratio, the wife received five shares ($5x$) and the children received one share (x) apiece for a total of eight shares. Divide the total amount by the total number of shares.

$$\$750,000 \div 8 = \$93,750 \text{ per share}$$

Now multiply the amount of each share by the total number of shares received by the children.

$$\$93,750 \times 3 = \$281,250$$

24. **(C)** If 4 percent of the unit are officers, then the percent of enlisted men is

$$100\% - 4\% = 96\%$$

To find the number of enlisted men, multiply the total number by 96 percent or 0.96.

$$125 \text{ total soldiers} \times 0.96 = 120 \text{ enlisted soldiers}$$

25. **(D)** First find the discount received from the wholesale dealer for each DVD player by multiplying the listed price by the discount percentage.

$$\$80 \times 0.25 = \$20$$

Now find the final price per DVD player paid to the wholesale dealer.

$$\$80 - \$20 = \$60$$

Now find the retail markup by multiplying the markup percentage by the original wholesale price.

$$\$80 \times 0.20 = \$16$$

Now find the retail price for which the electronics store owner sells the DVD players to his customers by adding the markup amount to the listed wholesale amount.

$$\$80 + \$16 = \$96$$

To find the profit, subtract the retail price from the actual price paid to the wholesale dealer.

$$\$96 - \$60 = \$36 \text{ profit per DVD player}$$

26. **(B)** Since 1 inch represents 50 miles, divide the ground distance (120 miles) by the scale (50 miles to the inch) to find the number of inches required to represent 120 miles.

$$\frac{120}{50} = 2.4 \text{ inches}$$

27. **(C)** Multiply the purchase price of the home by the assessment rate to find the assessed value.

$$120,000 \times 0.80 = \$96,000 \text{ (assessed value)}$$

Find the number of hundreds in the assessed value.

$$\$96,000 \div 100 = 960 \text{ (hundreds)}$$

Multiply the number of hundreds by the tax rate.

$$960 \times \$4.75 = \$4,560 \text{ (property tax)}$$

28. **(B)** First find the total time needed to run the generator = 12 hours and 45 minutes or 12.75 hours. Now divide the total time needed to run the generator by the amount of time each tank of fuel will last.

$$12.75 \div 1.25 = 10.2 \text{ tanks of fuel}$$

29. **(A)** First find the amount of the decline in traffic.

$$11,200 \text{ cars} - 10,044 = 1,156 \text{ fewer cars per day}$$

Now multiply the amount of traffic decrease by 100 and then divide it by the amount of original traffic. This will yield the percentage decrease without further calculation.

$$1,156 \times 100 = 115,600$$
$$115,600 \div 11,200 = 10.3\% \text{ decrease}$$

30. **(D)** First calculate the distances driven during the two legs of the trip.

$$\text{Leg 1: 2 hours} \times 70 \text{ mph } = 140 \text{ miles}$$
$$\text{Leg 2: 1.5 hours} \times 65 \text{ mph } = 97.5 \text{ miles}$$
$$140 \text{ miles} + 97.5 \text{ miles } = 237.5 \text{ miles}$$

Now divide the total distance traveled by the car's gas mileage rate.

$$237.5 \text{ miles} \div 25 \text{ mpg} = 9.5 \text{ gallons}$$

WORD KNOWLEDGE

1. **(B)** <u>Alacrity</u> means *brisk willingness*.

2. **(C)** <u>Infraction</u> most nearly means *violation of a rule or law*.

3. **(A)** <u>Beseech</u> most nearly means *to beg or plead*.

4. **(A)** <u>Articulate</u> most nearly means *able to express one's self clearly*.

5. **(B)** <u>Imperative</u> most nearly means *having to do with a vital requirement*.

6. **(B)** <u>Shear</u> most nearly means *to cut with a sharp instrument such as scissors*.

7. **(D)** <u>Milieu</u> most nearly means *surroundings*.

8. **(C)** <u>Curtail</u> most nearly means *to cut short or reduce*.

9. **(A)** <u>Deride</u> most nearly means *to ridicule contemptuously*.

10. **(A)** <u>Intimidate</u> most nearly means *to frighten by being threatening*.

11. **(B)** <u>Deportment</u> most nearly means *behavior*.

12. **(D)** <u>Conveyed</u> most nearly means *carried*.

13. **(A)** <u>Tacit</u> most nearly means *silent*.

14. **(B)** <u>Portend</u> most nearly means *give warning beforehand*.

15. **(D)** <u>Itinerary</u> most nearly means *schedule*.

16. **(A)** <u>Vexatious</u> most nearly means *annoying*.

17. **(D)** <u>Equivalent</u> most nearly means *equal*.

18. **(A)** <u>Criterion</u> most nearly means a *standard* against which something is judged.

19. **(C)** <u>Mercurial</u> most nearly means *unpredictably changeable*.

20. **(D)** <u>Critical</u> most nearly means *highly important*.

21. **(C)** <u>Telemetry</u> most nearly means *transmission of measurements by automatic instruments*.

22. **(D)** <u>Antagonist</u> most nearly means *adversary*.

23. **(C)** <u>Diagnose</u> most nearly means *identify a situation*.

24. **(A)** <u>Kinetic</u> most nearly means *relating to the motion of material bodies*.

25. **(C)** <u>Rectify</u> most nearly means to *correct*.

26. **(B)** <u>Camouflage</u> most nearly means *conceal*.

27. **(C)** <u>Equivocal</u> most nearly means *open to question*.

28. **(D)** <u>Centripetal</u> most nearly means *toward a center or axis*.

29. **(A)** <u>Disconsolate</u> most nearly means *hopelessly sad*.

30. **(A)** <u>Anachronistic</u> most nearly means *seemingly from a different time*.

31. **(D)** <u>Modulate</u> most nearly means *adjust*.

32. **(B)** <u>Picayune</u> most nearly means *insignificant*.

33. **(B)** <u>Tenacious</u> most nearly means *persistent.*

34. **(C)** <u>Entente</u> most nearly means an *agreement providing for joint action.*

35. **(C)** <u>Redundant</u> most nearly means *repetitive.*

PARAGRAPH COMPREHENSION

1. **(C)** The passage states that "stringent medical examinations, long foot marches, strenuous physical conditioning, and other tests eliminated many volunteers." It also implies that Major Darby's interview questions possibly eliminated even more volunteers, but it does not say so. The passage says nothing about parachutist training or map reading.

2. **(C)** The passage states that the volunteers came from the "recently arrived 1st Armored and 34th Infantry Divisions."

3. **(B)** The Greek mythological deities found most often in art through the ages were *Zeus and his siblings.*

4. **(D)** No one swallowed Zeus—Rhea, his mother, tricked Kronos by feeding him a stone wrapped in clothes instead of the infant Zeus.

5. **(C)** The passage states, "A leader must exhibit self-discipline, initiative, confidence, and intelligence to be able to confidently lead soldiers while earning loyalty and trust."

6. **(D)** Even though the basilican church design went through many changes in the thousand years after the construction of Old St. Peter's, the basics remained the same.

7. **(B)** The transept was an area perpendicular to the nave.

8. **(D)** The passage mentions the size of the country, the size of its population, its decision-making approach, and its culture. It also mentions that there are other factors, but does not say what they are.

9. **(B)** All nations must confront the central economic questions of what to produce, how to produce it, and for whom to produce it.

10. **(C)** The passage states that there are six different "flavors" of quarks.

11. **(B)** The passage lists three reasons why the War of 1812 was an unfortunate event. First, the British acts that contributed to friction between the two countries were being repealed just as the American Congress declared war; second, the United States was seriously divided about supporting the war; and third, the American army was unprepared for the war.

12. **(C)** The 101st Airborne Division was holding out at Bastogne to deny the Germans an important crossroads.

13. **(C)** The German major who approached the American lines with the German surrender demand had to tell his commander that *the Americans would not surrender.* The passage states that the American slang reply was clarified for the German officer as "decidedly not affirmative."

14. **(D)** The author of this passage believes that the student who defends himself should be viewed differently than the attacker. The passage states, "The biggest problem

happens when the student who is attacked gets the same punishment as the one who started the fight," and "it is morally wrong to teach our kids that the attacked person is as much in the wrong as the attacker."

15. **(C)** According to this passage, the reader can infer that the author believes that acting on incomplete information is often necessary. The passage states that "the quest for perfectly complete . . . information results in . . . the inability to make a decision until you have all the information, *which is never going to happen* [emphasis added]." Therefore, we can conclude that the author believes the opposite, giving us our answer.

MATHEMATICS KNOWLEDGE

1. **(D)** A factorial is the product of all the positive integers from 1 to a given number. The expression "4 factorial" or 4! means $1 \times 2 \times 3 \times 4 = 24$.

2. **(D)** The formula for the circumference of a circle is:

$$d \text{ (diameter)} \times \pi = \text{circumference}$$

   The pilot flies in a circle with a radius of 40 km and therefore a diameter of 80 kilometers.

$$80 \text{ km} \times \frac{22}{7} = \text{circumference}$$

$$\frac{80 \times 22}{7} = \text{circumference}$$

$$\frac{1,760}{7} = \text{circumference}$$

$$251 \text{ km} = \text{circumference}$$

3. **(A)** The reciprocal of any number is 1 over that number. The reciprocal of 7 to the nearest thousandth is $\frac{1}{7} = 0.143$.

4. **(D)** The square of any number is that number times itself. The square of 525 is

$$\begin{array}{r} 525 \\ \times\ 525 \\ \hline 27,625 \end{array}$$

   Therefore the second digit of the square of 525 is 7.

5. **(C)** The area of a square with four sides of length s is $s \times s$ or s^2. A square with a perimeter of 40 yards has four sides where length = 10 yards. This means that the area of this square is 10 yd $\times$ 10 yd = 100 square yards. Since this is not one of the choices, let's convert it to square feet:

$$\frac{100 \text{ ft}^2}{1} \times \frac{3 \text{ ft}}{1 \text{ yd}} = 300 \text{ ft}^2$$

6. **(D)** To solve these equations for x, start by finding a way to get rid of y: multiply both sides of the second equation by 2.

$$2(x - 2y) = 2 \times 11$$
$$x - 4y = 22$$

Then add the new form of the second equation to the first equation and solve for x.

$$5x + 4y = 27$$
$$\underline{2x - 4y = 22} \text{ (+4 cancels out –4)}$$
$$7x \quad\;\; = 49$$
$$x = 7$$

7. **(B)** One way to solve this is to square each of the possible answers to see which one is closest to 85.

9.1	9.2	9.3	9.4	9.5
× 9.1	× 9.2	× 9.3	× 9.4	× 9.5
91	184	279	376	475
819	828	837	846	855
82.81	84.64	86.49	88.36	90.25

The squares of 9.2 and 9.3 are closer to 85 than the squares of 9.1, 9.4, or 9.5. Now find the difference between the square of each of the closest numbers and 85.

$$\begin{array}{cc} (9.2) & 85.00 \\ & \underline{-\,84.64} \\ & 0.36 \end{array} \qquad \begin{array}{cc} (9.3) & 86.49 \\ & \underline{-\,85.00} \\ & 1.49 \end{array}$$

The square of 9.2 is closer to 85 than the square of 9.3. Therefore, the square root of 85 to the nearest tenth is 9.2.

8. **(B)** To solve for x, combine all similar terms and set the equation equal to 0.

$$(8x - 5x) + (-2 - 8) = 0$$

Do the operations inside the parentheses first.

$$(3x) + (-10) = 0 \;\; \text{or}$$
$$3x - 10 = 0$$

Next, add 10 to each side to undo the subtraction.

$$3x - 10 + 10 = 0 + 10$$
$$3x = 10$$

Finally, divide each side by 3 to find the value of x. You are undoing the multiplication to find the value of a single x.

$$\frac{3x}{3} = \frac{10}{3}$$
$$x = 3\frac{1}{3}$$

9. **(D)** Clear the parentheses by multiplying $(a - b)$ by 2 and $(a + 3b)$ by 4. Line up similar terms and add.

$$2(a - b) + 4(a + 3b) =$$
$$2a - 2b$$
$$\underline{+\, 4a + 12b}$$
$$6a + 10b$$

10. **(C)** A prime number is a number larger than 1 that has only itself and 1 as factors—i.e., it can be evenly divided only by itself and 1. 201 is divisible by 3. 205 is divisible by 5. 211, however, is a prime number.

11. **(C)** The product of a negative number and a positive number is always negative. The result of multiplying (product) two negative numbers is always a positive number. Since ab is positive and a is negative, b must be negative, too.

12. **(C)** Set this up as a two-stage multiplication problem. Remember that when you multiply terms with opposite signs, the product is negative (i.e., it has a minus sign).

$$
\begin{array}{r}
a + 2 \\
\times\ a - 5 \\
\hline
-5a - 10 \\
a^2 + 2a \\
\hline
a^2 - 3a - 10
\end{array}
$$

$$
\begin{array}{r}
a^2 + 3a - 10 \\
\times\ a - \ \ 3 \\
\hline
3a^2 - 9a - 30 \\
a^3 - 3a^2 - 10a \\
\hline
a^3 - 19a - 30
\end{array}
$$

13. **(B)** Begin by combining like terms.

$$3z - 5 + 2z = 25 - 5z$$
$$5z - 5 = 25 - 5z$$

Next, add $5z$ to each side, to eliminate the $-5z$ from the right side.

$$5z - 5 + 5z = 25 - 5z + 5z$$
$$10z - 5 = 25$$

Now, add 5 to each side to cancel out the remaining subtraction.

$$10z - 5 + 5 = 25 + 5$$
$$10z = 30$$
$$z = 3$$

14. **(B)** A pentagon is a five-sided figure, which therefore has five corners. If the architect places a sculpture at each corner, there will be five sculptures.

15. **(C)** Every right triangle contains an angle of 90 degrees. This particular right triangle also has an angle of 30 degrees. To find the third angle, subtract the sum of these two angles from 180 degrees.

$$180 - (30 + 90) =$$
$$180 - 120 = 60 \text{ degrees in third angle}$$

The other two angles are 60 and 90 degrees.

16. **(A)** Find the factors of the first term in the trinomial—the factors of x^2 are x and x.

$$(x\ \ )(x\ \ )$$

Then, look at the last factor in the trinomial—in this case, it has a plus sign. This means that both factors of the trinomial are either positive or negative. Which one, though? Since we see that the middle term ($-11x$) has a minus sign, both factors must have minus signs.

$$(x -\ \ )(x -\ \ )$$

The next step is to find the factors of 30. There are several numbers you can multiply to get 30—30 × 1, 10 × 3, 15 × 2, etc. However, the two multipliers that you use have to also combine somehow to give you the middle term, which is 11. When 5 and 6 are multiplied, they give you 30; when they're added, they give you 11. We know the factors have minus signs, so the factors of 30 are actually −6 and −5.

$$(x - 6)(x - 5)$$

17. **(D)** Divide only similar terms. First divide numbers, then letters. When dividing powers of a letter (variable), just subtract the exponents.

$$\frac{15a^3b^2c}{5abc} = \frac{15}{5} \times \frac{a^3}{a} \times \frac{b^2}{b} \times \frac{c}{c} = 3a^2b$$

18. **(C)** The formula for the area of a circle is $\pi \times r^2$. Find the area of the larger circle first.

$$\pi \times 10^2 = 100(\pi) \text{ square inches}$$

Then find the area of the smaller circle.

$$\pi \times 7^2 = 49(\pi) \text{ square inches}$$

To find the part of the larger circle that the smaller one doesn't touch, subtract the smaller area from the larger one.

$$100 - 49 = 51(\pi) \text{ square inches}$$

19. **(B)** The simplest way to solve this is to form an equation with x as the unknown grade.

$$\frac{78 + 86 + 96 + 94 + x}{5} = 88$$

$$\frac{354 + x}{5} = 88$$

Multiply both sides by 5. This will cancel out the division so you will no longer have a fraction to deal with, but instead whole numbers.

$$5 \times \frac{354 + x}{5} = 88 \times 5$$

Simplify both sides of the equation.

$$354 + x = 440$$
$$x = 440 - 354$$
$$x = 86 \text{ (missing grade)}$$

20. **(A)** First, change all measurements to yards.

$$9' = 3 \text{ yards} \qquad 12' = 4 \text{ yards} \qquad 6'' = \frac{1}{6} \text{ yards}$$

To find the volume of the concrete (the volume of a rectangle), multiply the length times the width times the height.

$$3 \times 4 \times \frac{1}{6} =$$

$$12 \times \frac{1}{6} = 2 \text{ cubic yards}$$

21. **(D)** First, find the area of the entire new wildlife preserve. Since the preserve is in the shape of a circle, use the formula for the area of a circle (area = π times the square of the radius or $A = \pi \times r^2$).

$$A = \pi \times r^2$$
$$A = \frac{22}{7} \times (14)^2 = \frac{22}{7} \times 196$$
$$= 616 \text{ square kilometers}$$

The lion habitat area is a wedge formed by a 90-degree angle at the center of the circle.

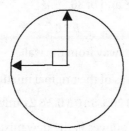

Since a circle has 360 degrees, we can find the part of the preserve that belongs to the lion habitat.

$$\frac{90}{360} = \frac{1}{4}$$

(reduce the fraction to simplest terms)

Next find what this fraction of the whole equals in square kilometers.

$$\frac{1}{4} \times 616 = 154 \text{ square kilometers}$$

22. **(D)** Find the highest common factor that will divide into the numerical coefficients, 6 and 3, which is 3. Then find the highest literal factor that will divide into x^2 and xy, which is x (note that y is not contained in the first term at all). The next step is to divide the highest common factor, $3x$, into $6x^2 + 3xy$ to find the remaining factor. Thereby we see that the factors are $3x(2x + y)$.

23. **(D)** To find the volume (V) of a cylinder, multiply π times the square of the radius (r) times the height (h).

$$V = \pi \times r^2 \times h$$
$$V = \frac{22}{7} \times \left(\frac{7}{1} \times \frac{7}{1} \right) \times \frac{15}{1}$$
$$V = 154 \times 15$$
$$V = 2{,}310 \text{ cubic inches (volume)}$$

To find the number of gallons this cylinder will hold, divide its volume by 231.

$$2{,}310 \div 231 = 10 \text{ gallons}$$

24. **(B)** The wall, the ladder, and the ground in the recreation area form a right triangle. The ladder is on a slant and is opposite the right angle formed by the wall and the ground. In this position, the ladder is the "hypotenuse" of the right triangle. In geometry, the Pythagorean Theorem states that the square of the hypotenuse (c^2)

of a right triangle equals the sum of the squares of the other two sides ($a^2 + b^2$). Thus, $a^2 + b^2 = c^2$.

$$8^2 + b^2 = 10^2$$

Solve by doing the arithmetic operations and by clearing one side of the equation for b^2.

$$64 + b^2 = 100$$
$$b^2 = 100 - 64$$
$$b^2 = 36$$

Then find the square root of b^2 and of 36.

$$b = 6$$

The base of the ladder is 6 feet away from the wall.

25. **(A)** First find how many ounces of the original mixture were fruit juice.

$$10 \times 20\% = 10 \times 0.2 = 2 \text{ ounces}$$

Next, find the total number of ounces in the new mixture.

$$10 + 40 = 50 \text{ ounces}$$

Then find what part of the new mixture is fruit juice and convert that to a percentage.

$$\frac{2}{50} = \frac{4}{100} = 4\%$$

Abbreviations and Acronyms

ACES	ASVAB Career Exploration System
AFQT	Armed Forces Qualification Test
AFSC	Air Force Specialty Code
AO	Assembling Objects (ASVAB subtest or score)
AS	Automotive & Shop Information (ASVAB subtest or score)
AR	Arithmetic Reasoning (ASVAB subtest or score)
ASVAB	Armed Services Vocational Aptitude Battery
CAT-ASVAB	Computer-Administered Test version of the ASVAB
CEP	Career Exploration Program
DoD	Department of Defense
EI	Electronics Information (ASVAB subtest or score)
GED	General Equivalency Diploma
GS	General Science (ASVAB subtest or score)
IQ	intelligence quotient
IUPAC	International Union of Pure and Applied Chemistry
MC	Mechanical Comprehension (ASVAB subtest or score)
MEPS	Military Entrance Processing Station
MET	Military Entrance Test
MK	Mathematics Knowledge (ASVAB subtest or score)
MOS	Military Occupational Specialty
MPFI	multi-point fuel injection
NPS	Non-prior Service
PC	Paragraph Comprehension (ASVAB subtest or score)
PiCAT	Pre-screening, Internet-delivered Computer Administered Test
SFI	sequential fuel injection
SI	International System of Units (French: *Système International* (*d'Unités*))
TBI	throttle body injection
USA	United States Army; also United States of America
USAF	United States Air Force
USCG	United States Coast Guard
USMC	United States Marine Corps
USN	United States Navy
VE	Verbal Expression (ASVAB subtest or score)
WK	Word Knowledge (ASVAB subtest or score)

Bibliography

American Heritage Dictionary of the English Language, 5th Edition. Houghton Mifflin Harcourt Trade and Reference Publishers, Boston, MA, 2011.

Andersen, Hanne and Hepburn, Brian. "Scientific Method," *The Stanford Encyclopedia of Philosophy* (Summer 2016 Edition), Edward N. Zalta (ed.), Accessed September 2017 at *https://plato.stanford.edu/archives/sum2016/entries/scientific-method/.*

Anderson, John D., Jr. *Introduction to Flight.* McGraw-Hill, Inc., New York, 1978.

"ASVAB Online: Available Online, Anytime, Anywhere." *Recruiter Journal,* November–December 2013.

Bartlett, John, author; Beck, Emily Morison (editor). *Familiar Quotations, 14th Edition,* Little, Brown and Company, Boston, 1968.

Cain, A.J. "Taxonomy," *Encyclopædia Britannica* (online), Encyclopædia Britannica, Inc. Accessed September 2017 at *https://www.britannica.com/science/taxonomy.*

Dalrymple, G. Brent. *The Age of the Earth,* Stanford University Press, 1991.

Department of the Navy. *Manual of Navy Enlisted Manpower and Personnel Classifications and Occupational Standards, Vol. I.* NAVPERS 18068F, June 2012.

Duran, Terry L. *Barron's Military Flight Aptitude Tests, 3rd Edition.* Barron's Educational Series, Inc., Hauppauge, NY, 2014.

Edwards, Gabrielle I. *E-Z Biology, 4th Edition.* Barron's Educational Series, Inc., Hauppauge, NY, 2009.

Gilroy, Curtis L. "Defending the All-Volunteer Force," *Armed Forces Journal,* April 2010.

Goldberg, Deborah T. *Barron's AP Biology, 6th Edition.* Barron's Educational Series, Inc., Hauppauge, NY, 2017.

Hawking, Stephen W. *A Brief History of Time.* Bantam Books, New York, 1988.

Headquarters, Department of the Army. *Field Manual 6-22: Army Leadership.* Department of the Army, Washington, D.C., 2006.

Headquarters, Department of the Army. *Field Manual 7-0: Training for Full Spectrum Operations.* Department of the Army, Washington, D.C., 2008.

Hibbeler, R.C. *Statics and Dynamics, 12th Edition.* Pearson Prentice Hall, Upper Saddle River, NJ, 2010.

http://www.101science.com/

https://www.britannica.com/science/chemical-reaction (accessed October 2017)

http://chemed.chem.purdue.edu/genchem/topicreview/bp/ch12/trans.php (accessed October 2017)

http://www.chemicalelements.com/groups/transition.html (accessed October 2017)

https://www.cnpp.usda.gov/sites/default/files/usda_food_patterns/ EstimatedCalorieNeedsPerDayTable.pdf (accessed August 2017)

http://www.dynamicearth.co.uk/media/1514/geological-timeline-pack.pdf (accessed September 2017)

http://www.enchantedlearning.com/subjects/Geologictime.html (accessed September 2017)

http://energy.gov/eere/water/history-hydropower

http://www.familycar.com/

http://grammar.about.com/od/words/a/wordroots.htm

https://www.grc.nasa.gov/www/k-12/airplane/newton.html (accessed August 2017)

http://www.af.mil/News/ArticleDisplay/tabid/223/Article/466900/new-asvab-pretest-available- for-applicants.aspx

http://www.hsph.harvard.edu/nutritionsource/pyramid-full-story/

https://iupac.org/what-we-do/periodic-table-of-elements/ (accessed August 2017)

https://www.livescience.com/27585-human-body-system-circulation-infographic.html (accessed August 2017)

https://www.livescience.com/29436-clouds.html (accessed August 2017)

https://www.nasa.gov/mission_pages/sunearth/science/atmosphere-layers2.html (accessed August 2017)

https://www.navycs.com/asvab-test.html

https://nssdc.gsfc.nasa.gov/planetary/factsheet/ (accessed September 2017)

http://www.official-asvab.com/

https://phys.org/news/2014-04-planets-sun.html (accessed September 2017)

http://www.physics.about.com/

https://pubs.usgs.gov/gip/geotime/age.html (accessed August 2017)

http.//www.sciencedaily.com/

https://www.space.com/16105-asteroid-belt.html (accessed September 2017)

https://www.space.com/17777-what-is-earth-made-of.html (accessed September 2017)

http://www.srh.noaa.gov/jetstream/clouds/cloudwise/types.html (accessed September 2017)

http://www.ssa.gov/policy/docs/ssb/v50n3/v50n3p25.pdf

https://www.thoughtco.com/types-of-chemical-reactions-604038 (accessed October 2017)

http://www.uscg.mil/hr/cgpc/epm/AO/Non-Rate/Rate%20Requirements.asp

Keegan, John. *A History of Warfare.* Alfred A. Knopf, Inc., New York, 1993.

Kleiner, Fred S., and Mamiya, Christin J. *Gardner's Art Through the Ages: The Western Perspectives, Volume II, 12th Edition*, Thomson/Wadsworth, Mason, OH, 2006.

Lehrman, Robert L. *E-Z Physics, 4th Edition.* Barron's Educational Series, Inc., Hauppauge, NY, 2009.

Manwell, J.F., McGowan, J.G., and Rogers, A.L. *Wind Energy Explained: Theory, Design, and Application, 2nd Ed.* John Wiley & Sons Ltd., Chichester, England, 2009.

Matloff, Maurice (editor). *American Military History, Vol. 1: 1775–1902.* Combined Books, Conshohocken, PA, 1996.

Merriam-Webster Dictionary, The. Merriam-Webster, Inc., New York, 2004.

Miller, Rex. *Electronics the Easy Way, 4th Edition.* Barron's Educational Series, Inc., Hauppauge, NY, 2002.

Nevins, Allan, and Commager, Henry Steele, with Morris, Jeffrey. *A Pocket History of the United States, 9th Revised Edition.* Simon & Schuster, New York, 1992.

The New York Public Library Desk Reference. Simon & Schuster, New York, 1989.

Nickels, William G., McHugh, James M., and McHugh, Susan M. *Understanding Business, 7th Edition.* McGraw-Hill, Inc., New York, 2005.

Powers, Rod. *Barron's Officer Candidate School Tests.* Barron's Educational Series, Inc., Hauppauge, NY, 2006.

Rocklin, Sara G., and Mattson, David R. "The Employment Opportunities for Disabled Americans Act: Legislative History and Summary of Provisions." *Social Security Bulletin, March 1987.*

"Scientific Method." *Encyclopædia Britannica* (online), Encyclopædia Britannica, Inc. Accessed September 2017 at *https://www.britannica.com/science/scientific-method.*

Stonemetz, Hillary, Staff Sgt. "New ASVAB Pretest Available for Applicants." Air Force Recruiting Service, August 20, 2013.

U.S. Military Entrance Processing Command. *ASVAB Counselor Manual.* North Chicago, IL, 2005.

Young, Hugh D.; Freedman, Roger A.; and Ford, A. Lewis. *University Physics, 12th Edition.* Pearson Addison-Wesley, San Francisco, 2008.

Wikander, Örjan. *Handbook of Ancient Water Technology.* Brill Academic Publishers, Leiden, The Netherlands, 1999.

Williams, Mary H. *The U.S. Army in World War II: Chronology 1941–1945.* Center of Military History, Washington, D.C., 1958.

Index

Automobile(s) 295
    axles and wheels 307–308
    braking system 308–309
    carburetor(s) 300
    drive train 311–320
    electronic control unit 302
    engine(s) 295–305
    fuel injection 300
    fuel pump 300, 301–302
    lights 321
    shaft and universal joint
        309–311
Axial tilt 117
Axis (of the earth) 117

B

Battery 162, 163, 164, 282–287
Becquerel, Antoine Henri 110
Bernoulli's Principle 155
Bernstein, Al 209
Binomial nomenclature 100
Biology 93, 95, 105
Bipedalism 101
Bird(s) 100
Blood 99
Botany 93
Bromine 116, 144

C

Calcium 97, 102
Calorie(s) 102, 103, 104
Camera 160
Candela 133
Capacitance 273
Capacitive reactance 273
Capacitor(s) 272
Carbohydrate 98, 99, 102, 103
Carbon 97, 145
Carbon-14 dating 111
Carbon dioxide 95, 96, 99, 145
Carnivore(s) 100
Cat(s) 100
Catalyst, organic 98
Cell, biological 96, 97, 98
    cell wall 97
    fertilization 98
    specialization 99
Cellulose 97
Chemical bonding 138

Chemical change 128
Chemical compound 97
    inorganic 97, 102
    organic 97, 98, 102
Chemical precipitate 128
Chemical reactions 142, 143
Chemistry 93, 97, 105, 125
    equations 128
    organic 145
    symbols 128
Chlorine 97, 144
Chlorophyll 97, 99
Chloroplast 97
Chromosomes 96, 105
Cilia 97
Circulation 95
Circulatory system 95, 100
Class (in taxonomy) 100
Climate 121
Cloning 98–99
Cloud(s) 123–124
Coal 158
Coast Guard, United States 3, 7,
        8, 14, 21, 22
    Coast Guard rate 14, 21
    Coast Guard rating 14, 21
    Coast Guard Reserve 7
Coulomb (measurement of
        electrical charge) 246
Coulomb's Law 163
Comet(s) 119
Compound(s) 125
Concrete 340–342
Conductance, electrical 163,
        255
Conduction 156
Conductor, electric 243, 248
Convection 123, 156
Copper 145, 156
Current, electric 133
Cyber 8
Cytoplasm 96, 97

D

da Vinci, Leonardo 23
Democritus 137
Density 125, 154
Department of Agriculture,
        United States 103

Department of Defense (DoD),
        United States 3, 22
Design and layout 349–350
Digestion 95
Diode(s)
    point contact 279
    semiconductor 278
    silicon-controlled rectifier
        280
    tunnel 279
Disease(s) 104
DNA (deoxyribonucleic acid) 95,
        98, 102, 105
Dog(s) 100
Domain (in taxonomy) 100

E

Earth 117–119
Earth science 93, 110
Echinoderm 100
Eclipse 118, 119
Ecology 72, 105
Ecosystem 105, 106
Edison, Thomas 1, 23
Effort 151, 152
Einstein, Albert 151
Einstein's theory of relativity
        151
Electric/electrical current 162,
        245, 246, 248
    alternating current (AC) 162,
        163, 245, 267–268, 273, 277
    conventional current flow 245,
        246
    direct current (DC) 162, 245,
        273, 277
    frequency 163
Electric meter(s) 288
Electric motor(s) 287
Electrical charge 243, 244
Electrical circuit 245, 259–262
Electrical energy 163, 244
Electrical field(s) 159, 162
Electricity 147, 162, 243
Electrode(s) 163, 164
Electromagnet(s) 245
Electron(s) 128, 137, 156, 162,
        163, 243, 244–246
    valence electrons 137

Life functions 95
Light 72, 93, 147, 159, 160, 161
  infrared 160
  spectrum 160
  ultraviolet 160
  visible 160
Light wavelengths 159
Light-year 72
Linnaeus, Carl 100
Lipid 98
Liquid(s) 125, 138, 140, 154
Lithium 128
Lithosphere 113
Lombardi, Vince 1
Lysosome 97

M

Machines, complex
  vise 370
Machines, simple 151, 364
  levers 367–368
  pulley principle 364–366
  ramp 370
  work principle 366–367
Macronutrients 102
Magnesium 97, 102, 116,
  145
Magnet 163
Magnetic field 159, 245
Magnetic pole(s) 163, 245
Magnetism 93, 147, 245
Mammal(s) 100
  hooved 100
Manganese 116
Mantle, Earth's 113
Marine Corps, United States 3, 7,
  19, 22
  Marine Corps ASVAB
    composite scores 19
  Marine Corps Reserve
    7, 22
  Military Occupational
    Specialty (MOS) 19–20
Marine zones 115
Mars 118, 119
Mass 125, 133
Mathematics
  addition 167
  algebra 181

calculating interest 180
cancellation 172
composite numbers 169
decimals 175–179
decimal fractions 175, 176
equations 182
exponents 169
factor(s) 169
factorial(s) 169
fractions 170, 171, 173
mixed numbers 171, 172
multiplication 167, 168, 170
order of operations 168
parentheses, use of 168
percentage(s) 178–180
prime numbers 169
quotient 168
reciprocal(s) 169
remainder 168
rounding 168, 178
sequences 170
series 170
square root(s) 181
subtraction 168
whole numbers 167
Matter 125, 126
  chemical change 126
  physical change 126
  properties 126
Meiosis 98
Melting point 142
Mendel, Gregor 105
Mendeleyev, Dmitry I. 128
Mercury 116, 119
Mesosphere 121, 122
Metabolism 95
Metal(s) 144, 156
  alloys 144
  brass 144
  bronze 144
Metalworking 344–347
Meteor(s) 119
Meteorite(s) 119
Meteorology 93, 121
Meter 133
Metric system 133, 134
Michelangelo 23
Micronutrients 102
Microscope 160

Military Entrance Processing
  Command 22
Military Entrance Processing
  Station (MEPS) 3, 5, 22, 30,
  31
Military Entrance Test (MET) 3,
  4, 5
Mineral(s) 102
Mirror
  concave 160
  convex 160
  plane 160
Mitochondrion 97
Mitosis 96, 98
Mixture 125
Mnemonic 94
Mole (SI measurement) 133
Molecule(s) 126, 137, 138, 156
Mollusk 100
Motion 93
Multimeter(s) 289
Multiple-choice questions
  26–28

N

Natural gas 116
Navy, United States 3, 7, 14, 22
  Navy Reserve 7, 22
  occupational fields 15–17
  rate 14
  rating 14
Neptune 119
Neutron(s) 137, 162, 243, 244
Newton (unit of force) 147,
  252
Newton, Sir Isaac 147
Newton's Law of Universal
  Gravitation 150
Newton's Laws of Motion
  149–150
Nitrogen 97, 144
Nobel Prize 110
Noun(s) 215–223
Nucleic acid(s) 98
Nucleus (of an atom) 137, 162,
  243
Nucleus (of a cell) 96, 97
Nutrients 95, 104
Nutrition 95, 102